Fighting for Mine

Thomas Allred Jr.

Maple Leaf Publishing Inc. Alberta Canada

Fighting For Mine

MAPLE LEAF PUBLISHING INC.

3rd Floor 4915 54 St Red Deer, Alberta T4N 2G7 Canada

General Inquiries & Customer Service

Phone: +1 (403) 356-0255

Toll Free: 1-(888)-498-9380

ISBN Hardback: 978-1-77419-052-4

Paperback: 978-1-77419-053-1

Email: info@mapleleafpublishinginc.com

TABLE OF CONTENTS

CHAPTER 1

I'm the last superhero call me Mr.. Monopoly I'm playing with you Eden look here you see how professional I am one movie Eden and I'm a make you rich beyond comparison I am a got damn leader Mr.. Monopoly go over there and sit down me and Reign think you would be a professional if we gave you some of our shared of our company Eden I'm a say it like this and then I'm a go take time out for the little things just because you never know when love is fend to come your way. The Hustle is Eden Reid and Thomas Allred Jr one more question and I mean it I'm thinking about moving to California will you move with me Eden after the three movies and the books are done just making sure that we're on the same page because this feels like a movie we got to give Reign his chance to speak go head and speak Reign thanks Thomas I'm just telling all that

The Hustle is Eden Reid and it should be a movie all in favor girl say I we done pa**ed everybody Eden by just speaking on the telephone be professional Eden I can't call you but Eden call me Monday like you promised me I'm getting ready to get me a drink look Thomas just gone and tell her yep I found my soulmate that a boy Eden we have got something's to discuss Mr.. Monopoly what Superman what if she it's involved with someone Thomas send the got damn message to her time your time speak to her yes Reign mined your mother f*cking business than who The Hustler is you got me who The Hustler is Eden that's Thomas Allred Jr and who the other Hustler is Thomas I pick Superman Eden Reid and Superman shall work on our books we have got to give her some time to adjust to every one of us Mr.. Monopoly sine you lost your damn woman I feel like Eden Reid she could be a heavyweight listen to me and listen to me well I made plans to run my company and that's exactly what I'm a do with or without Eden Reid she doesn't scare me.

Thomas well we're fighting all kinds of people just make sure that you know how you love Superman Eden listen to me I have to go to the restroom I need you to think about the things that were said in this message but who are you I'm Superman girl and I need your help with these books and my life Eden I'm a tell my next book report that you and I took on a heavyweight Eden girl and won The Hustler Eden I'm to professional you have got to call me just so I can talk to you about business Mr.. Monopoly and Superman and Reign and Thomas we all say that Eden is our

Queen I love you so much baby Superman call me Mr. Monopoly damn it.

Without farther ado introduce to you Mr.. Ebony. Buy It Mr.. Buy it only talked when there's money involved but Superman can handle my business now for me Ebony Buy It I thought that you was retired I'm eighty something years old I got one more chance to win the title out here working with Eden Reid I know that I can Thomas you better appreciate me tell Superman that it's people everywhere that's wanting to hear his story put Ebony Buy It on his chair thank you Reign I am King and if Eden Reid choose to be I'm a have a new princess give Eden Reid the throne Eden do you except the terMs. and conditions of our contract? It's a movie coming out about struggle and sacrifice I the this movie make sure my damn money straight no Eden I'm not talking to you it's just the critics that's watching look to the hills where cometh your help if Eden and Thomas is going to work together than we all can speak at once be silent young gra**hopper.

Reign you lucky dog you getting Eden to help with writing the books was a stroke of genius under pressure we rise to the occasion I'm a put my time and patience together with my intuition and ask Eden Reid what she doing for the next couple centuries or two give Eden Reid a contract Thomas tell Ebony Buy It to sit down for a minute give Eden Reid her contract do you hear him Superman yes I hear him officer Reign where is Mr.. Monopoly I'm doing everything that I can do Ebony Buy It if you want Eden Reid we going to put in work for her Thomas tell Eden that I appreciate her for giving a man like me a chance he said Thomas I heard what he said Reign don't get no attitude with me here my words I am a police officer please officer Reign remain calm all I'm saying is that Eden Reid got Ebony Buy It on her side we about to make some money for the kids who are sick and in bed at St Jude's Children's Hospital Thomas put Ebony Buy It on the phone Mr.. Monopoly this is Ebony Buy It speaking give Eden Reid her contract first thing Monday morning yes Mr.. Monopoly is there anything else sir talk to Ebony Buy It Eden just when you need help with your story because it goes like this weather or not the story gets told isn't the point the point is that you Eden Reid are really and angel for helping my write the books up I'm saying Thomas Allred Jr is completely indebted to you Ms.. Eden Reid everything that we do is going to be professional Eden Reid talk like she has the time to finish our seven books and three movies watch her this girl is a work of art tell her I'm through with you Ebony Buy It.

Thomas tell Superman that we have got and another adventure that's about to be coming tell the police officer Reign talking about starting his own line of books called the fantastic seven my girl I hope that she can read between the lines I'm giving you a contract Eden Reid just as soon as I get my money back Ebony Buy It all help her to understand that I'm a Trillion lire with a book writer down in me where are you going with this Thomas Allred Jr I want Eden to be my partner in life be professional I'll give you $1700 million dollars Eden as soon as I get my check if you would take care of yourself and be my life partner Ebony Buy It said stop

Thomas Allred Jr I need her put that b*tch on a jet me Ebony Buy It she's going to have to get use to us that's where the story begins Mr. Monopoly I'm saying well done Eden Reid you're not going anywhere Thomas look officer Reign Eden is my soulmate do you want her to be your life companion yes I do officer Reign than talk to her Thomas Allred Jr see Eden know matter who I may be I'm still a story writer I'm putting my heart on hold for you Eden until we get finished with working on the seven books and the three movies I know what you're thinking if she is lucky than why are we apart this is a movie Eden Reid and King and Queen always have some difficulties at the start of any relationship so without any farther ado look girl and your penthouse I'm telling you girl that I know what I'm doing after you read this Eden Reid write your name and number down in a piece of paper and burn it in the kitchen sink that representing your new life with Ebony Buy It teaching you that every winner deserves a King and Queen short story or not Eden I need you I love you to Eden so I do I Eden and I love you too get to the point Ebony Buy It I'm a let Mr. Monopoly do this Eden I am the richest man this country has ever seen and I'm speaking in money put your a** up on the screen you got my heart and that's Mr. Monopoly I have got to catch him who Mr.. Monopoly that boy done stole my game off of me Eden after his a** here Eden my number to my cellphone is don't worry about it.

Thomas you need to tell a short story Once a pun a time there was a King and a Queen I could have sworn that Eden was my princess here Thomas we are running out of time tell Superman that I Thomas Allred Jr except his contract for Eden and myself to prosper what is the contract Eden don't say a Superman contract it's a Superman contract that I am giving to my queen if Eden excepts now let it be known that Ebony Buy It agrees that Thomas Allred Jr and Ms.. Eden Reid should be one Eden do you agree sweetheart because I'm wasting my time just talking you the most professional thing that's out here and Eden I would like for you to say you'll be my wife and soulmate Thomas you haven't got your money back yet from your ideas and music Thomas okay Mr.. Monopoly I just don't want to waste no time the game is over and I've heard enough of that sh*t my boss Frank Y why can't I have her you can Thomas you just have to go slow and write your books and movies Frank -Y let Kristen know that I love her okay Thomas Allred Jr you just focus on Eden Reid right now you better stop this story oh sh*t what is it Thomas Eden I had a bad dream go on back to sleep Superman I can f*ck with you that's a Superman for you take my words seriously Eden Reid from I am Superman and I am Ebony Buy It and I am officer Reign and I am Mr. Monopoly but most of all I am Thomas Allred Jr and this is a short story called Imperial designs will you come rule this company with me Eden give her a contract for being who she is and who is that people Eden that contract makes you our Queen and also if you except the contract Eden you will become my wife Eden put Ms.. Eden Reid on a plane besides me if you wanted the fast life Eden you finally aboard the Enterprise your contract is real

Eden $1700 million dollars for you to take over the position as queen in my house you can see that I don't play games with anybody so I'm telling you to think before you speak I get my money back sometime this month will you handle my business for me Eden don't play with this Superman Ebony Buy It give Superman his contract Eden give Superman his contract Ebony Buy It Thomas. To be continued.

CHAPTER 2

Thomas on the big screen Eden Reid give me my contract I'm asking you to see what you stand for just gave me and swear when you talk to me Ebony Buy It and Mr.. Monopoly can rule the world with Eden Reid beside of them and there goes my story of how I took a professional and made her my Queen Thomas tell Eden you really love her let's see Eden I miss you it's been two whole days and I can't stop thinking about you what I'm doing is getting my frustrations out on this phone in order to write you a bestseller and a movie that will shake the nation I believe that this belongs to you what is it it's another short story called talk to that girl Thomas I'm a say this one more time you guys have got to stop playing let's put Eden Reid on a flight with Mr.. Monopoly Eden I can't do nothing with or without you and I'm ending this by saying there's only one was out of the Hustle Eden and that's to marry a prince charming girl now love you Eden all make a good team

Ebony Buy It had to say that love is the foundation of our people's existence and with that Eden I want to tell you something girl remember me as humble as it is I truly love you Superman and Eden that is our short story who a man with everything because and Prince and then a King because of girl named Eden Reid sacrifice your heart for love is the name of the short story in which I've given you can use it if you think that I'm that good for publication pick your game up Thomas Allred Jr sacrifice your heart in needing that Eden Reid across my chest of matrimony and Bliss Eden there just one more thing I needed you off in my heart when there was no one sacrifice my heart I have to go to a book store giant near you let me get Control of myself and that was my story of how Eden Reid And Thomas Allred Jr Slade the evil King of rescued the public for all time with a kiss on each other's faces our kiss

Eden is going to be called thanks giving Eden time to listen I know girl that you are the reason that this opportunity has come my way you got to slay the King in order for us to have our kingdom back girl reach inside of you and bring out your power of listening power I am not never seen nothing like this it is a circle of some kind we going to call it a ring put it on your finger Ms.. Eden Reid I have one also I'll do the same as you pick your game up Ms.. Eden Reid because I'm telling you and you are a wizard and I am your Superman dream Ms. coach to be continued Thomas.

Eden Reid this is Thomas Allred Jr again and girl I'm just going over messages look I appreciate what it is that you do and I want to let you all know that I would like to be a**ociate girl you took the time out to send me the information I needed to make and informative decision what I'm saying is that I have made my decision Which is Ebony Buy it stop that excuse me Eden there's someone I need to talk to get your a** over here and sit down Ebony Buy it what's wrong what's wrong Thomas is that that girl has got to know that you're the best my best game is going down Ebony Buy it you simple fool and you own two companies your self do you see what I'm getting at Superman your almost making yourself clear I need you to talk to me they are going to be recording you on the phone tomorrow so the books have got to be straight one other thing.

Thomas don't say Ebony Buy it say Mr.. Monopoly I just want to date Eden Reid give that girl a break say nothing about dating until after all your work is completed Mr.. Monopoly does she know that I'm a Superman named Superman yeah she knows it how do you think that Canada got your address and your phone number we are the government Thomas like I said realize and tell Eden Reid your story on the phone at two o clock tomorrow precisely oh yeah I don't gamble if there isn't a beautiful woman on the line what you saying is that Eden Reid is my publisher.

Thomas listen to me if Eden Reid is your publisher than what do that make you and Arthur and the best story teller in the world Eden are you reading this we'll help you to get out that position I swear help me God if Eden and me don't get together I don't give a f*ck officer Reign will you calm Me Ebony Buy it down cause this boy is and up and coming artist we going to put Ebony Buy it of a sound track all get your hand out your a** Thomas and do a hundred push-ups we have got to pick him up I heard that Thomas took a bullet over some body Ebony Buy it I need to talk to you in private yes Superman Thomas has got to grow a long inside of Eden Reid your success and our success is depending on you Ebony Buy it Thomas yes officer Reign to much won't mean Happiness I know but I want to live by my own rules so be it than you say that you want a compound with all of your woman there write the vision Eden I love you professional I'm making one last book so Eden Reid can take home her business I call this book that I'm going to be writing It called Superman And His Allies by Eden Reid and by Thomas Allred Jr what do you Eden Reid Eden Reid is professional Thomas I'm wrapping the story up around you Eden Reid because of you Eden I could have never found my way through the dark what are you saying Superman and Batman must square off again just for the world to see on a movie screen we have the best government agents in the world squaring up to take over the entertainment industry my girls and in Superman my money and I'm Batman.

Mr. Monopoly got everything thing under control in this movie where going to write we are going to fight for the love of a girl who is she Mr.. Monopoly the girl on TV with us is none other than Eden Reid that's your cue Thomas Eden I am Superman and I'm the best story teller in the world will you work with me and listen to me girl as I say to love that I love you Eden Reid Thomas ask that girl to join you in holy matrimony well Eden will you it join me in holy matrimony Eden just look at my book and we haven't begun yet to write Thomas yes Eden Reid you had me at hello say Superman Thomas Superman Eden you and me got damn are going places Eden nice work in recruiting a superhero before I go Eden I want to ask you one simple question Which end of the bed do you like to sleep on the top or the bottom put my stories that I have texted you together compiled them and watch Eden I'm listening to you use my work Eden because you know that I can walk in darkness listen Thomas yes Batman you and Eden are one Thomas dose Eden feel the same way as me Batman I live in darkness continue writing your story this is my music Thomas tell the world what your wanting to do superman is here Ebony Buy it it's about got damn time Batman but I'm leaving Batman you don't have to be ashamed of what you are Eden Reid I respect you for taking good care of Thomas that woman is on the Justice League we call Ms.. Eden Reid our Wonder Woman Wonder Woman has a crush on Thomas and Superman has his Lois Lane working with him but Ebony Buy it who do I have listen Dark Knight you want the city.

As I position myself to head in to darkest I remember that Eden Reid isn't my friend she is my publisher Batman I like superman yes sir Mr.. Ebony Buy it I'm telling you let's see what they say about this piece of manuscript right here Batman we got superman right here take a hold of my dream Mr.. Ebony Buy it what you saying is that you want a woman Thomas if Mr.. Ebony Buy it speaks for me than I believe that I can get a woman terrible Mr.. Monopoly how did you get in here I used my key it has powers would you help me to explain the reason that I got a contract is because I am none other than the incredible hulk come on Batman you need that girl Thomas so don't hold no punches incredible hulk I just don't believe that she is paying any attention to me I'm with you stay still yes Wonder Woman call my name Thomas Ms.. Eden Reid I'm writing a book for my life I've been through all these different kinds of people before but Eden Reid I am Superman and I have chosen you to be the wife and soulmate of Thomas Allred Jr there's only one thing missing where is that joker he's after me Mr.. Monopoly got his attention this is for the hand in marriage of Ms.. Eden Reid we are going to fight over this sh*t so be it joker superman you have nothing to do with this this is around here we got our stuff together so joker Batman let him be Superman Mr.. Ebony Buy it said that Thomas and Reign could stand up for they selves we programmed you to see the best side of life and worse side of life Ms.. Eden Reid I think Superman is read for his contract now what are you saying Mr.. Ebony Buy it I'm eighty something years old and you don't play no games I'm giving to you our entire industry if you want it Thomas Mr.. Monopoly what can I say I believe yes is in order yes Mr.. Ebony Buy it put Eden Reid on a jet next to me come along Thomas we have got a lot to talk about didn't I tell you that joker would be mad now I'm just wondering how many women do you want Thomas Mr.. Monopoly I want them all get the incredible hulk over here hulk we need a contract if you need a contract go after Emily Thomas and Inger and Vivien because see here Thomas those women depend on you to be yourself and how am I The Dark Knight.

Ms. Eden Reid this is a story yours and mines called Superman And His Allies I want you to try and piece together all of the messages that I sent you to try to make since out of your movie what I'm doing is alerting you to the fact Eden that this is an industry take over Eden and in our best goals we have tried to be fair Thomas what are you doing in there I'm coming Iron Man you very professional Eden and I love you Superman now that we're done playing I'm a tell you now that Superman has a crush on someone other than Ms.. Lois Lane Invisible Man stop your lying stop communicating with one another yes Mr.. Ebony Buy it you know that you have less than a couple of weeks to get into shape to see Thomas whispering Batman what is wrong with you well I have known life there is only Darkness of here in the streets I'm taking you to see a mother f*cking therapist Thomas don't laugh there's nothing funny what you say Thomas is Eden Reid worth your movie deal?

We going to get to find out come on why where are we going to see your girlfriend Superman your girl is Ms. Kristen Beam it's it well nothing has been made official I'm doing the work for Ms. Eden Reid my other love interests Thomas you here that I sure did Superman has to love interests don't play with Superman Thomas don't play no games Batman what's is wrong with you the night is about to come and with Thomas's new invention I can see more clearly now than I have ever seen before I'm saying that we a bunch of superheroes but who gave that joker a key to the palace Mad sit your a** down who else is in here Thomas you can handle that I'm going to finish writing mines and Ms. Eden Reid's story I story am not nothing Batman that is where your wrong get my grappling hook Superman stop Thomas tell him that we know how he is hurting my feelings go out to him what just happened Batman almost busted into the future girl using a device Thomas new invention that means our situation is going to change huh look at it this way Princess She-Ra if He Man and Man At ArMs. can hold back the Legion Of Doom long enough than our books we'll be finished and we can rest in peace without looking for a way out of our movie screen Thomas can you do this I'm writing the story as we speak She-Ra

I'm nasty with my hand writing I just got to get this through text over the Ms. Eden Reid in our planet put Mr.. Ebony Buy it in to the conversation got damn Thomas you done went and created another invention again what do you call this one The Superhero Machine what does it do hurry Thomas because The Legion Of Doom is breaking our wall defense's you see how we are talking now I flip this thing on and the conversation goes elsewhere where conversation where dose to conversation go I don't know exactly you don't know exactly Thomas your supposed to be a superhero listen here the conversation is back listen all I found another dimension that will allow us to take and give our Superpowers to our people and still be the same how do we get there girl through a portal She-Ra we have nothing to lose I believe in you Thomas but what are you doing I'm making out our last Wills And Testaments listen to me Thomas are you coming with me Superman anything I do is going to have a bang to it so when do we leave He Man what kind of sword are you willing By The Power Of Gray skull I'm willing Thomas it depends on Mr.. Monopoly and Eden Reid to make the call Me Ebony Buy it.

The Whole entire industry is your Thomas Allred Jr and Kristen Beam we need to get the f*ck out of here before it gets to late it's already too late Inspector Gadget anybody that turns his back on his department is Doomed for destruction Thomas just have Ms.. Eden Reid to type up the book because this story stinks of Injustice Thomas get Superman Thomas now go and write our story you see Eden it starts like this all of the women thought that you were a King Thomas people want to see you but I had a dream of my own and that dream is to be the biggest entrepreneur and actor in this whole wide world dreaMs. come true Thomas if you believe they do movie professional gave me respect Thomas get me the f*ck out of the screen yes incredible hulk what where you just doing Superman I was daydreaming where is officer Reign he went into the restroom Thomas Mr.. Monopoly has made a decision that you could use your Superhero Machine to transport everybody to safety I'm a say a little prayer get to Eden Reid now come on every last go you about to be crazy Batman come on I'm not going Superman but why Batman wants to go home he wants Gotham City Eden Reid Superman

Ms.. Eden Reid I sent for you a dozen roses of flowers for you I'm Mr.. Monopoly Ms.. Eden Reid and our movie is going great take my information that I give to you over the phone so you can put together this book called Superman And His Allies we heard this before Mr.. Monopoly you did than come with me to a place where my people should be living the place is called Gotham City slow down Batman hell no I said that I want to go home Superman get him Thomas what do we do they are going to fight officer Reign fail up the police department yes Mr.. Monopoly Mr.. Ebony Buy it you're not going to be starting know sh*t in here today Mr.. Monopoly I'm with you tell Ms.. Eden Reid to begin making arrangements for Thomas Allred Jr and his family to walk out of their neighborhood for some place better with a view now can you do that for me Ms.. Eden Reid yes Mr.. Monopoly okay now Thomas can you please tell me again how many females that you want to have for yourself I want them all Mr.. Monopoly Thomas say that again just so that we all can here you on this movie screen Mr.. Monopoly I said I want all of the f*cking ladies to be mine why Thomas because I risk my life for them on the daily me and the New York police department and also the NSA and FBI damn it less give that man what he's after Ms.. Eden Reid can you help us to acquire a place that is fitting for over 40000 women I should be able to now Superman He Man where have you been Thomas I'm doing my best to walk through Gotham City without Batman but He Man you know that Gotham City belongs to the joker the joker is no longer here I sent him through another time continuum what are you saying that time moves on He Man I'm saying Man At ArMs. and Battle Cat are fighting the good fight for you now officer Reign what is that that I wanted to say that you are doing a great job at the writing the script yes but that's not it Thomas is I love you Emily make sure that Emily and Inger and Vivien and Kristen gets there credits in the books alright Mr.. Monopoly.

Thomas tell me just how you feel yes She-Ra I feel like everything is just pa**ing me by some talk to me Thomas you need to come outside its beautiful here She-Ra because you're a woman that man is a Superstar MS. Eden Reid hurry up and not this down the movie is about to start your better hold on to your hats what do you think he means hit me Mr.. Ebony Buy it I see your 12 Trillion dollars and I rise you up to a hundred Trillion dollars Thomas what we going to do Mr.. Ebony Buy it I want the females and I'm willing to die for them I see what you're doing Thomas has Ms.. Eden Reid and have Superman to draw up a contract saying this Thomas that you are now the owner of all kinds of women I didn't say that I wanted all kinds of women I said Mr. Ebony Buy it that I want them all checkmate and I'll die over my sh*t get Kristen Beam and Emily in here all better do as he says he's Superman MS. Eden Reid your apart of his life but I love you Mr.. Ebony Buy it get professional the industry is yours and Superman it's not a dream my genie is going to miss you but Thomas has broken me with that move right there Ms.. Eden Reid I do believe that you are mine Superman your my hero Man At ArMs. and Battle Cat get all clothes ready we are about to move in to a palace with Emily and Kristen and Inger And Vivien along with Ms.. Eden Reid.

Thomas be professional I'm trying to be professional dude this is a movie and Superman has done captured your queen put that on the big screen Communicate with me Ms.. Eden Reid girl I need you to hold down your position because in the economy it is us that holds all of the cheese the cheddar the moolah we own our own businesses Ms.. Eden Reid so I'm a capture your dreaMs. for you and hand them to you because I love you checkmate you and Thomas are a King and Queen all through history Thomas has been a good role model save our kids Ms.. Eden Reid and we will talk later about this subject well who are you I'm still Batman Superman

This message is to whom that it may concern so far I've taken over my position as King Of The World my a**istant is under me her name is Elizabeth I've located Samantha and Evelyn and Kathy and Nada alongside of Porsche and Heather and Maya and Kay may I dream about these women what kind of movie is this Thomas it's a fantasy movie to where everybody that's in this film gets paid where's my evil sister Kesha evil sister can you run me some place no Thomas Mr.. Ebony Buy it said that you were a star along with Ms.. Eden Reid oh yeah that reminds me Emily good save honey can you please hand me my notebook yes Mr.. Ebony Buy it what's in it Mr.. Ebony Buy it all have got to listen to me Nada come in here with me Mr.. Ebony Buy it I'm getting close to giving up not as long as we're together slow and you'll be able to see that as chairman of the League we can do anything we want damn where Inger and Vivien at Maya all I know is that out to get you some kind of present for your upcoming birthday Mr.. Ebony Buy it say Monopoly here your dream Ms. coming true Thomas I want Ms.. Eden Reid I want her to Superman but you have got to put in the work to get that woman Thomas damn it incredible hulk get She-Ra back in this place this instance yes Mr.. Ebony Buy it give him a contract you have up on a contract to damn easy watch it I'm a give up before I have to hurt anybody listen you here that bell what is it Mr. Monopoly.

I put a crown off on you Ms.. Eden Reid and I also put a crown around the necklace that I am giving you be smart Ms.. Eden Reid now tell me who is your man is it your buster that you have been seeing or is it Thomas Allred Jr we call him Superman he works nights so the movie is a box office smash watch it you have got no idea of what this movie is going to pay girl help that boy out of his situation like this keep listening Ms.. Eden Reid because Heather would like to speak to you Heather speak to the cameras I'm just saying that Mr.. Ebony Buy it is the sh*t and you should trust Thomas Allred Jr girlfriend that enough of that I believe that this is a movie and it isn't going to write it self-Thomas I see where you are headed Frank Y I'm glad that I met you Thomas as of now I'm pulling up rank on the industry listen to me Thomas sometimes things just don't work out you have got to stay on top Frank Y is this what you have to tell me that I can work but I have to be alone all of my life because all of the women are taking that's some bullsh*t ladies we come from nothing absolutely nothing together and now that we finally make something for ourselves all want to leave me girl it hurts Frank Y a man we sacrificing you Thomas get Aladdin over here Thomas make your wish hurry before the phone runs out of charge Aladdin I wish for the genie to grant every woman that's in the United States and surrounding areas one hundred million dollars apiece granted.

Thomas now what's next we finish the book I mean the movie shoot again Emily I love you are the shadows to my heart honey you have got to be patient I'm a make your dreaMs. come true to come true you are going to need a lamp do you believe in magic Thomas Allred Jr ask Superman in managing getting up early and going to sleep late Ms.. Eden Reid I welcome you to Superman And His Allies charter two I through that this was a movie it is a movie give Aladdin back his damn lamp Batman I want this Aladdin Superman don't let him take the lamp I'm escaping to another dimension Ms.. Eden Reid stop him I'm a stop him you can't stop me close that damn book I can't it's a damn movie what is it called Superman And His Allies Thomas now get the lamp I got it Mr.. Ebony Buy it make a wish I give Thomas Allred Jr and I give Ms.. Eden Reid everything is my wish Ms.. Eden Reid Thomas Allred Jr we finally meeting at last thanks Mr.. Ebony Buy it I got something to say about that Aladdin the lamp belongs to me Mr.. Monopoly because I rule this office the box office I'm saying Thomas know I out bid you Mr.. Monopoly how can it be Thomas when I wrote the book but you see Mr.. Monopoly this is a movie screen and I am the King Of The World along with Ms.. Eden Reid the story is our to share so give back his damn lamp now yes Thomas Allred Jr and Ms.. Eden Reid we are the new rulers of the world what kind of movie is this called heartbreak I'm just saying that if my women listen we could have a good life to be continued on a bigger screen that man is professional that is what I'm trying to tell Ms.. Eden Reid girl be with me I got your so called man in checkmate marry me Ms.. Eden Reid I'm Superman.

CHAPTER 3

This is the beginning of something Ms.. Eden Reid I just don't know what it is well Thomas Allred Jr I see things like this either we sell the movie as partners and as best friends or we can make love and just call it a day so tell me Superman how do you feel Ms.. Eden Reid I haven't been with anybody since my wife got murdered over fifteen years ago I want you to know that I could make love to you it's just that I don't think that I know how to make love to you are you serious Superman Ms. Eden Reid I just came out of a very long relationship with a joker and you and me are coming into a lot of money with writing this movie say Superman I told you Ms.. Eden Reid that I was going to give you half of everything I have all because I have to leave to world to someone you Superman Thomas yes I'm Superman I can see it now Ms. Eden Reid will you be my wife and soulmate not in the movies but in real life yeah Superman but how do we get out of the book it's a movie.

Thomas the same way we do anything else we go to sleep you mean together Ms.. Eden Reid that is exactly what I mean Superman will you respect me in the morning it depends on how much time that we spend just working on our business I can hear the people Thomas remember I'm Superman okay Lex Luther pay me the rest of my f*cking money I got Superman to write his story down make Ms.. Eden Reid a bad guy who are you talking to Lex he knows exactly who I'm talking to who the one writing the story on the computer screen I done shot you once so called Superman now your starting to feel me Lex Luther is back and I'm the King of Happily Ever After this is my dream Superman stop his a** the Invisible Man locate Lex Luther before sunrise gets here why sunrise Lex You see Ms.. Eden Reid Superman has been shot before and he has got to talk medicine day and night for and emotional problem he's been by his self for going on twenty two years saving people for an outfit called The Justice League Superman knows me because I killed his wife with a gunshot to the heart I got you where I want you Lex Luther Thomas I see you auntie Back up and placed your d*ck on the table well I had to have something to f*ck Lex Luther enough with the games Thomas you killed my wife you bastard I just gave the orders it's doesn't matter to me she's gone you got damn piece of sh*t but your our there and I'm in here controlling your computer screen so how the f*ck are you going to get me Superman see Lex I always knew that it was you who shot me Superman slow down Ms.. Eden Reid I'm a kill you Lex Luther what in another story Thomas I'm killing you in real life look at your wife the me how is she you want to be Superman but I put you in the hospital and you almost died do you get what I'm saying to you Thomas you are going to respect me or you can die again

Superman Thomas shut the f*ck b*tch Lex don't do anything to hurt another woman it's hurt that I'm after Batman wry must finish the job and kill Superman so his wife won't be lonely you son of a b*tch watch that Superman remember you got y sunrise to figure I this story just for your publisher Ms.. Eden Reid yes the clock is ticking so whatever happens Superman you're going down Lex I never give up on anybody that's great because I'm a kill your a** Thomas Allred Jr or should I say Mr.. Ebony Buy it or is it Mr. Monopoly or officer Reign come on Thomas I need you to work with me who are you tell that girl that I'm leaving the incredible hulk and The Dark Knight that's some bullsh*t Thomas I got the game here what is it you bow down to me or you die I have already take every woman you loved from you get Control of yourself.

Thomas before you leave just this about this I shot you and I killed your wife in the rap game well sh*t Lex you are a p**sy mother f*ck and that's why I work with the government I'm a f*cking cop b*tch and I don't care how long it takes me I'm going to be there to kill you now you talk a good game Lex Luther but for twenty years the Justice League and I have saved every one that you tried to kill you didn't save one Thomas Allred Jr a duel has been set there's no way Thomas that you're getting out of here alive there's people watching I see you Lex Superman kick his a** yes Ms.. Eden Reid see all week I been doing push-ups Lex so after this here is over Ms.. Eden Reid is going to be my new wife talk about her boyfriend Superman you don't understand be Lex Luther I'm Superman I respect all of the women what are you saying Superman Mr.. Ebony Buy it explain it to him we got you surrounded and this is game over squad kill Lex Luther damn it Superman by Lex Luther okay Ms.. Eden Reid our movie stops here for a brief interlude are you going to be my wife and soulmate Lex Is gone forever you're the King superman where is my beautiful wife Emily and Inger and Thomas I mean Superman Mr.. Ebony Buy it please send off the message oh sh*t Thomas now where is Batman with the lamp Aladdin you got to understand that Superman is a normal creature and Ms.. Eden Reid I got you in my eyesight's checkmate Ms.. Eden Reid I bet you boyfriend to the punch sweetheart put I love you so much down and send the message Thomas Allred Jr okay Batman Mr.. Bruce Wayne sh*t what I tell you about playing with Thomas he's on fire thank God for you and Superman Ms.. Eden Reid

When you think about it Ms.. Eden Reid there's only two things that will be able to stop us from capturing our dreaMs. and that's you and me Ms.. Eden Reid we are both under contracts I just thought that you should know that I'm working day and night on the books and the movies there is a sequel coming out after this tell

Mr.. Ebony Buy it that I said hello Mr.. Monopoly yes but what I'm trying to put through your head is that you and I Ms.. Eden Reid are actors they playing a got damn roll look Ms.. Eden Reid the movie script is the first thing and then there is an endorsement and later on we turn it into movies did all catch my drift I been looking for a wife who knows how to handle her business what does this got to do with Superman Thomas take your time this is entertainment Ms.. Eden Reid pardon me Thomas he knows what I'm doing I'm saying you lovely thang you come get me out of my situation after we finish the movie Thomas but Ms.. Eden Reid I need Chelsea on this Chelsea you and Elizabeth get back in that office until I tell you to come out yes Thomas Allred a man has got to do what he got to do look at this Porsche go get Nada these are my wishes you got the lamp shut the f*ck up before.

Aladdin finds out kiss the moon I'm going to have to stop forgetting your name these are just a sample of all the women that I want to love why are you telling me this Thomas or should I say speaking of Batman who is Bruce Wayne anyway well Chelsea it is me I am Superman didn't Batman kill you that Vivian is in the movies now Ms.. Eden Reid our movie has Batman in it the one that crucified Jesus we want you to star in it look Thomas I do like your offer it's just that I am with somebody right at the moment I'll get you anything that you want Ms.. Eden Reid Thomas just read my story all of the way through and then decide if Superman isn't right for you it's called Superman and His Allies I wish you would come on I'm a business man Chelsea I have to do business where ever it is Evelyn now Kay it's someone that I would like you to meet officer Reign tell Mr.. Ebony Buy it to come and introduce me I am Superman Mr. Ebony Buy it how much is it going to cost me Ms.. Eden Reid a house a brand new car I'm a take all this money and give to her Thomas Allred Jr Ms.. Eden Reid that man is not playing no games with you take over business with me Ms.. Eden Reid

Thomas I can't do it because I you what our movie has just started all I want you to do is trust me you trust me don't you Ms.. Eden Reid where is Kathy at she's at work at the dollar general store go see her Thomas who is Kathy anyway one of my wives you see Ms.. Eden Reid I just have my money and my words now that's it Inger said that you was in some kind of trouble Thomas call me Superman I think that Superman is in trouble where is Batman he is with Emily Superman loves you Batman he LL never understand what I'm pregnant and the baby is he's we'll tell him Emily thanks Batman just call me Bruce Wayne Superman Emily is pregnant is about time he got to Emily baby I'll treat you good come on over here and sit down that's all I got to say Thomas I just need your permission to go ahead and stop the story Mr. Monopoly it's your choice not before I can hear it Thomas I love you Thomas the people they watching you Thomas give me a calculator now Mr.. Ebony Buy it I want to buy all that land that you have over there I don't think that you can pay for it that's a Shame because Inger says that you're a nice gentleman who needs a wish Aladdin yeah Mr.. Ebony Buy it I am also Aladdin but the genie has got away from me once before Mr.. Ebony Buy it the damn Genie is me Superman Thomas Allred Jr Batman Bruce Wayne Mr.. Monopoly and Reign officer Reign that is you all are the genie together we are so who am I speaking with now Ms.. Eden Reid you are talking to us to Mr.. Ebony Buy it are the genie how did I do officer Reign put Reign in the story well Ms.. Eden Reid here I go you have got to read the whole story before you can judge me asks me for anything Ms.. Eden Reid and you will get it Thomas Allred Jr but I'm scared of people might make fun of me see there Ms.. Eden Reid I am a genie and your wish is my command I love you to Superman all that that girl needs is a kiss we going to get Aladdin to give that girl her first real kiss Ms.. Eden Reid close your eyes in your heart you have your dreaMs. Aladdin kids her now my girlfriend say something to the Justice League I am here to stay that's Wonder Woman for you put your name across the movie screen Ms.. Eden Reid and Mr.. Thomas Allred Jr at last together in the movies see all you got to do.

Ms.. Eden Reid is keep watching I'm working on our future to my businesses called Imperial designs LLC and Stratosphere in putting my best feet forward Thomas look at here what Inger it's all five in the morning and you got to get see rest not before I finish this book your movie is complete Thomas not yet Thomas Ms.. Eden Reid tell me more about Superman here he comes I love you girl Ms.. Eden Reid Batman is a figment of my imagination the hell if he is I love you Thomas for getting me this far you just read the story Ms.. Eden Reid okay Superman go to work on a house for my superheroes that is Frank Y and the girly that in the FBI your really are Superman' aren't you I'm Batman Ms.. Eden Superman is just a figment of my imagination tell her that you love her Superman I love you girl please say you'll be my wife and soulmate Ms. Eden Reid your finger deserves my wedding ring Superman stand back why Ms. Eden Reid is and all powerful Genie what your name than Genie just call me Guinevere don't push a genie Thomas write your book I mean movie it's a true story about finances and pulling together in love with one another Superman yes Ms.. Eden Reid man call me Guinevere Superman.

This is Superman Ms.. Eden Reid just let me tell you about me Superman the human that I am see Ms.. Eden Reid my name is Thomas Allred Jr but you can call me Superman I received a call from you the other week day about four or five weeks ago but to make a long story short Ms.. Eden Reid I won the game what do you mean that you won the game is it Superman or is it Thomas Mr.. Monopoly she is very perceptive now what is it Mr.. Monopoly or is it Mr.. Ebony Buy it got damn this woman is good I've been listening to you officer Reign now what is it that you want Aladdin or am I getting close Batman or shall I call you Mr.. Bruce Wayne of Gotham City but what really gets me all is nobody has seen or heard from the Joker in our story that's because I am the Joker Ms.. Eden Reid so what are you telling me that I have a multiplex disorder and I have to take medicine for it all I need to know is that you're alright what ever happened to Lex Luther Thomas he went swimming that's all that I know that's all that I'm going to admit to you a Justice League champion Thomas people want you from all across the world Thomas are you sure that you need me as your wife Ms.. Eden Reid I'm sure than stick out your head I'm And all powerful genie I take over your company's and work it for you Guinevere lady I also have a wish what is your wish to make love to you Ms.. Eden Reid your wish had been granted Superman you see I mean Ms. Eden Reid I'm asking you to sell apart of us put it down Thomas Guinevere I got you in a dream capsule so my superheroes can know that we did this honestly say West side Ms. Eden Reid Westside Superman I have got to go I'll see you around time for dinner I got to tell my momma something alright baby girl I just want to see you will.

Thomas after I get back from at my mother's house Guinevere I love you now talk to your mother about me that's what I'm doing on the phone I'm supposed to be your partner Guinevere Ms.. Eden Reid hold up I want to tell you something what is it now this is our level three two more levels and we have beating all of the games that the state has put for us are you Thomas Allred Jr or are you Officer Reign right now because Superman I have to tell you something I have already beat the game and I am your guide to the future of your book or shall I say movie so your saying that we are going to make love if we want to yes Batman see this clock I need one hour to do what I have got to do okay I'm a be patient for one hour Superman I love you yes Ms.. Eden Reid I mean Ms.. Guinevere now don't say nothing after I leave you I'm saying nothing I got Superman in my house sleeping on my couch tell that other man to get the hell out of my house why sweetheart because he's Superman momma get me and autograph Eden momma I'll get you and autograph but get that fellow the hell out of my house I'm listening to you what dose Superman looks like momma he has a personality disorder is he going to stay with you momma I hope so he's doing a movie I'll tell you the rest when I get there Superman yes my dear my mother said can she please have your autograph certainly my dear about money now how are we splitting this movie Ms.. Eden Reid you get 21% and I get 21% the rest a go to the Federal government for us being together but how can I explain this Ms.. Eden Reid honey take your time think about this Superman what if your movie goes that's around the world Thomas.

Lois Lane don't say that I'm not Superman I love this man but Thomas if this movie goes viral you and imperial designs LLC we be able to a Ford a new bedroom suite I want you to come and live with me say Superman there watching who is watching our people and who are our people the audience Ms.. Eden Reid if you don't believe me just look for yourself Thomas your scaring me see Ms.. Eden Reid I can see through my mind the movie good to be a success I'm a take you out to get something to eat Ms.. Eden Reid slow down Superman you just said that the movie is going to be a success but how do you know this Superman I worked all night to make it so Ms.. Eden Reid I am your man wait Thomas Allred Jr you're getting ahead of yourself how much money do you have I don't have none and your Superman because of who because of you Ms.. Eden Reid I've come back in time to save you from a terrible mistake and to give you a chance at a new life Thomas Allred Jr quit playing I'm serious Ms.. Eden Reid you have known clue at how much that I want you I can smell your perfume right now but I'm not wearing any you see what I'm saying there is two things a good thing and a bad thing in this world what is the bad thing Superman you have got to take my advice and me my wife Ms.. Eden Reid and what is the good thing Thomas our times is running short you're a pretty girl you better not lose my contract Ms.. Eden Reid because I'm from the future and I know your situation checkmate Superman had just made Ms.. Eden Reid man eat a** for a living Ms.. Eden Reid it's not me I'm your new man just call me Superman Batman no Superman no there is Batman where in my dreaMs. you are the guys from the future yes Guinevere I understand Superman just read my book and my movie alright Thomas your kind of hustling really hard here it's called work Ms.. Eden Reid call me Guinevere and all powerful genie so what I'm a get a genie for myself watch and see what I do Superman send me the message alright Guinevere or shall I say my wife I'm a send the message to you right now this is out movie cut the music off Guinevere put all of these messages together why Superman we are racing against time I love you Thomas Allred Jr and I love you too Ms.. Eden Reid read the book that I wrote you cover to cover see it's a movie inside call me Superman Ms.. Eden Reid talk to Mr.. Ebony Buy it that man does not play any games no he don't he is Superman

Look in my eyes Ms.. Eden Reid and tell me what you see wait on me Superman I'll be worth your while I'm trying to see how I can say this I a gentle way you Superman tell me straight up we'll Ms.. Eden Reid we are making progress on the book and movie what is it called again Thomas Allred Jr go and write your movie the name of the movie is called Superman And His Allies take three what do you mean take three this is our movie Ms.. Eden Reid and I'm staring in it by talking to you Thomas Allred Jr why do you always say my last name when you are talking to me that's so I and know who I'm dealing with cause people got emotional probleMs. where is He Man and Man At ArMs. at Thomas it's a movie they do exist but Emily no Thomas Allred Jr I'm Ms.. Eden Reid this is about your contract I know but keep on going I didn't take my medicine last night probably because your Superman that's not it than what is it Thomas Allred Jr I just want a compound with nothing but women and myself there listen to me you can have your dream Thomas you just have got to believe in miracles Ms.. Eden Reid I'm too old to believe in miracles I don't even believe in God anymore since they shot me and killed my wife all I'm saying is that whatever you want Thomas Allred Jr you can have. Incorporation Superman let me talk some sense into you yes Ms.. Eden Reid Thomas Allred Jr you and me are both Stars our book and movie prove it I'm a give you a chance to go after my love but Superman you better be good okay Thomas Allred Jr okay Ms.. Eden Reid what is your company's name again Superman there called Imperial designs LLC and stratosphere this is a movie Superman I'm a get you a house for the time being what about my family they need two houses than let it be said that Ms.. Eden Reid and Mr.. Thomas Allred Jr have and agreement all Eden yes mother is that Superman standing right there yes momma will you give him a hug and a kiss for me I'm a do more than that I heard what you said Thomas you need to talk to me Ms.. Eden Reid I don't know what to say I've been alone by myself for the last fifteen years I've I through all kinds of superhero stuff why did you murder Lex Luther he gave the order to kill my wife that is why I dropped his a** off of a bridge where is Lex Luther body Superman in my secret place now police are listening Superman come clean and be of your sins I'd rather be roasting in hell with Jesus pouring me water than to answer any more of your questions Superman one last quick question what is it does my a** look fat in those jeans hell no it don't look fat you have a beautiful a** and a beautiful face checkmate you are my wife Ms.. Eden Reid.

Superman come and get your a** with my pleasure there goes Superman what are you talking about call the police momma I have got to throw a man outside of my house they talking about you Superman I don't believe that she is who are you by the way I'm soon to be Ms.. Eden Reid husband my name is well that's ok Superman see you after the movie premier girls take your places have you seen the movie Thomas Allred Jr no Batman you see I wrote it I was a screen play but now it's a motion Cinema movie thanks to Ms.. Eden Reid Thomas answer your phone not when I have business to do so you think that it's going to be a smash only time will tell Batman I was just thinking that if you and Ms.. Eden Reid hadn't met each other where would we all a be now in our future Bruce Wayne so you see Superman shut the hell up and watch the movie Batman either way it goes we did our best to make all fill welcome Superman can we come and sit with you know I have to pa** cause this spot is reserved Emily come and sit down before the movie starts Superman be getting on my nerves hang on my phone is ringing Ms.. Eden Reid I know what you did last summer Thomas is the Inspector gadget he wants you think that your slic* Superman you got everyone fooled your movie is a cover up and I got you on film with Lex Luther I am a King your right King Superman but guess what Lex Is not dead enjoy your night King Superman stop the movie why Superman my name isn't Superman its officer Reign of the new York police department Thomas what wrong there's a madman somewhere lose in the building I need you to slowly walk to your cars checkmate I told you Ms.. Eden Reid that I was going to get in Superman's a** listen you don't have to do this here Lex Luther well yes I do King Superman that is take these people out of here the people will stay and watch your movie Lex Luther shut that b*tch up before I blow the whole place up stop talking Elizabeth did you think that you would be able to live and I wouldn't find you Superman you owe me this moment for throwing me in jail or prison a maximum-security dungeon how does it feel Thomas Allred Jr you're going to die right in front of the people that you love Ms.. Eden Reid roll the footage checkmate I love you

Ms.. Eden Reid Superman don't give up Superman won't but you will Ms.. Eden Reid he's got a gun pow Ms.. Eden Reid is down Superman damn it that's my baby not anymore she isn't Thomas Allred Jr.

Keep it going and then what happened next Superman well I had the gun that Lex Luther had dropped after shooting Ms.. Eden Reid hold up now who did you say Lex Shot Ms.. Eden Reid I hate to tell you this Superman but you have been in a coma for the last twenty nine years what are you saying that Ms.. Eden Reid never did get shot and there wasn't any movie premier in fact Superman you never even wrote an album or a book we going based on your story that you had the weapon of choice here me Superman Ms.. Eden Reid is alive and well and you do got a problem because she arrested you for capital murder of Lex Luther I don't remember slow down Superman and you'll be able to remember everything as we get ready to take you to death row Superman may God be with your soul who you think I am huh this is Superman it's been twenty five years we have been watching you be professional now tell us what you did with Lex Luther's head cause we have his body in our migratory.

Superman stand up for capital murder how do you plead not guilty I'm challenging you Thomas Allred Jr to think long and hard about this you need to stop I'm looking for the fingerprints that a match your fingers to the scene of the crime oh my God where is Emily at you mean your girlfriend it seeMs. that you shot her also did Emily survive no I don't know what I have to tell you Superman you were at one time a decorated officer with all said and done how do you feel Superman the women are all over the place I just need to speak to Ms.. Eden Reid the only people that you are going to speak to is that *ssh*le that's in your cell with you and Superman you can sign anything you want but you belongs to me man on the state MS. Eden Reid Warden Eden Reid that is didn't I tell you she got a book coming out and a movie called Superman cry tears Superman one other thing listen if this is a movie like you say it is get your a** out of this cause if not you'll be stuck here for the rest of your natural Born life so what is going to be I need me a lamp Thomas there is a lamp in your cell but it is unbreakable Thomas Allred Jr oh and another thing Thomas Allred Jr take your medicine Hollywood is starting to here is Aladdin yes Superman I need my last wish of course Thomas tell the keep going Aladdin genie what is it this time I want to take myself back almost third years your wish is granite I'm still in this prison cell on the contrary look around checkmate you're watching TV at Emily's house now do you remember I remember everything stop Emily from killing Lex Luther Thomas you are a time cop damn it that is right I'm a cop name officer Reign of the new York police department all need to help me to remember things how that girl get that gun Thomas Allred Jr Lex Is coming by here like in four minutes take Emily upstairs my career is on the line Ms.. Eden Reid I'm giving you this call to let you know exactly what I'm doing I'm typing up this book right now I mean movie called Superman And His Allies what I am trying to do is answer your question that a** is fat in those jeans let me call you back someone is at the door it's Lex Superman so we meet again Superman checkmate where's Emily in her room studying we need to talk Superman go outside on the porch I'll meet you there Lex Luther oh sh*t Thomas Emily had got a gun Lex Luther you raped me thank you Superman for what Lex Luther for putting me in your story call Ms.. Eden Reid and she'll fill your a** in Ms.. Eden Reid yes Superman I'm reading your movie as we speak I'm a call you again at two a clock Eastern standard Time and Superman loosen up Thomas Allred Jr I do want you but you just got to prove yourself I'll talk to you real soon by Ms.. Eden Reid Superman

In the beginning there was equal justice for everyone but as we can tell that Ms.. Eden Reid and Superman try to get and opportunity in the big leagues I help them to discover a part of theMs.elves that only a few have dared to know I'm Superman brother and best friend now I want you Ms.. Eden Reid to look inside of yourself and realize that you and Superman have both been up working desperately all night long see Ms.. Eden Reid I want to tell you that I truly hope that you and Superman are compatible because without you Ms.. Eden Reid Thomas Allred Jr would be nothing more than a pencil pusher listen to us we know what we are doing this is the Justice League Ms.. Eden Reid and you and Superman our in the Justice League movie we call that movie Superman And His Allies cry tears Thomas Allred Jr yes Ms.. Eden Reid call me Guinevere okay Eden Reid we going to help you just give us a day or two Superman tell Superman to be professional hey what the hell are you doing Guinevere if you open up your heart I said I'll do anything is this a movie or what Mr.. Monopoly you damn right it is back to the plan hell no Mr.. Monopoly I done flown with you before Mr.. Ebony Buy it get your a** in the plan I am not got nothing to lose I'm eighty something years old tell me Mr.. Monopoly tell you what Mr.. Ebony Buy it did we do a good job fixing them both up I'm a make sure that they find happiness Mr.. Ebony Buy it yes Superman officer Reign came to speak.

I want you to f*ck the hell out of Ms.. Eden Reid Thomas will do and lic* her toes would you for me Thomas Allred Jr I don't even know if our plan will work take over the industry professional Which is Superman stand right here I want a picture of you before and after photo why officer Reign because when you and Ms.. Eden Reid have your kid it's money in the bank I'm having a kid by Ms.. Eden Reid lower it down your fend to wake up Mr.. gadget Thomas I hear something take your pictures now that your a** Ms.. Eden Reid I'm saying this with all sincerity in my heart Yes Thomas will you be my wife and soulmate Thomas is getting married to Ms.. Eden Reid so what will it be finish the book and movie Thomas first and then we agree to talk alright than the Justice League is you and I and the rest of the FBI agents don't ever do anything wrong to me I'll whoop his a** if he does you any kind of hurt full way Mr.. Monopoly where are we going we taking you home my boy we are taking you home Mr.. Ebony Buy it I'm eighty something years old I don't care where it is that we are going to Ms.. Eden Reid do you understand that I love you yes Thomas Allred Jr right now we are going to Paradise

I'm the story and you are the research Ms.. Eden Reid what Mr.. Ebony Buy it say I'm answering your questions all of them Ms.. Eden Reid okay Mr.. Ebony Buy it see I want a mansion sitting on a hill can Superman help me to reach that goal and how? Give me the microphone all Superman she asked Mr.. Ebony Buy it what you think Mr.. Ebony Buy it it's Superman for Christ sakes you want to let him talk well then so be it Mr.. Ebony Buy it I can hear you that's Superman there for you now when I came in this world I always loved women I never had a reason to dis one listen Thomas will Mr.. Ebony Buy it please come up here and sit down okay Superman but I got your a** Mr.. Ebony Buy it appears to be a hundred years old don't you Mr.. Ebony Buy it what would you say if I told you that I could reverse what time did to you Mr.. Ebony Buy it I'd give you anything please Superman help and old man out of his troubles Aladdin bring the lamp that am not no fair you're in cahoots with Aladdin Mr.. Ebony Buy it say that you want to be a genie I want to be a genie Aladdin your wish had been granted now you look like Mr.. Ebony Buy it but how do you feel on the inside magnificent alright a done saved the genie of the lamp Superman as long as no one touches me your powers will be fine pick your damn game up Thomas we got Ms.. Eden Reid on the line I can't lose Ms.. Eden Reid Superman am I rich enough am I handsome enough is our movie off the chain no it's is going to be on the big screen right next to you Superman wear are my allies at on top of you we got you covered Thomas Allred Jr we going to need a director Because action the movie is over oh sh*t this can't be the end of the film all sit down and watch that movie we got Superman in it Ms.. Eden Reid you can join me in history of you want Superman you already have a girl let a broad no when your single again look who is that it's Ms.. Kristen Beam well done Superman the only thing that's missing now is a steak dinner you know that I never forgot about you Lois Lane don't you forget it either wait a minute honey I want all of my superheroes to stand up we are the Justice League and most of us have afflicted I'm here to tell you that Mr.. Ebony Buy it is your genie got damn it Superman say bring cash and that's what you get or receive Thomas yes Ms.. Kristen Beam what you remember Thomas that I'm a police officer and what is your name officer Reign of the New York police department and I'm a**ociated with the government and the NSA you missing one thing what take your time Thomas what am I missing you missing the ending to our story Kristen it goes like this Superman of her want the last laugh Mr.. Monopoly see Superman I'm a get you your compound where you can have all of the women that you asked for why Mr.. Monopoly cause I too am a time cop Mr.. Monopoly the movie is over not yet it isn't Ms.. Eden Reid Thomas Allred Jr is crazy about you look at how professional he is Thomas he's working to impress all of you Thomas is a King that needs a good woman pick your damn game up Thomas

Superman let me talk if it where up to me I would date Mr.. Ebony Buy it all know who Lois Lane is Ms.. Kristen Beam and you want that it is my destiny to be King over all of the women Ms.. Eden Reid don't forget about Emily and Nada either Kay Thomas Kathy yes Thomas the movie is about to end the first name you need to say is Samantha you got two minutes ladies I'm very sorry if I hurt you Thomas the compound is already for you to go well everybody this is good by for now Mr.. Monopoly who is going with me on the compound boy every woman that you see and then some I hope that you use a condom leave it the next Superman am not going to cry there's I believe that Superman And His Allies take one represent that's the end Mr.. Monopoly do you think we should shoot another movie that seeMs. like a plan get Ms.. Eden Reid on the phone I'm right here Mr.. Monopoly to keep Mr.. Ebony Buy it safe and warm I am eighty something years old my d*ck gets hard Mr.. Ebony Buy it stop doing that take me with you Mr.. Ebony Buy it Kristen all know where we are headed to right Las Vegas because what's done in Vegas stays in Vegas that a boy Thomas this boy tough me something what he teach you Mr.. Monopoly to reason with myself before I give a speech except this book I'm mean except this movie me and Ms.. Eden Reid a be movie starts you are already movie starts welcome to the entertainment industry Thomas and Kristen Beam this was all set up for the both of you mean Ms.. Kristen Beam belongs to you Thomas to do whatever you want to with see Thomas won't slow down Superman and takes to end of our movie Superman And His Allies are the Justice League action

Eden Reid welcome to the new story we will call Getting It In I'm warning you Eden Reid as the story goes you may tend to get hot lite your fuse no longer waiting if Ebony Buy it was here go on in Thomas Superman wake your a** up it was the night before Christmas and all through the house not a creator was stirring not even a Ebony Buy it Ms.. Eden Reid doesn't believe in the spirit of Christmas anymore and none do the families Ebony Buy it tell us a story it was the night before Christmas and an angel appeared look at Mr.. Ebony Buy it continue with the story this story has money and crooked power all up in it give Ebony Buy it another contract can you please tell me what Ms.. Eden Reid is doing right now well she is reading the story that I gave her why would she read your story Mr.. Ebony Buy it because I'm a Christmas Angel no wonder Ebony Buy it you're a fraud watch and see Ms.. Eden Reid this hope is for you and Kristen Beam tell the story Mr.. Ebony Buy it there I was just sitting at the fire place about to return the presence when before I knew it the chimney had smoke in it now I'm a Christmas Angel I can't interfere with domestic stuff but when I see Kristen Beam it made me give up my powers Kristen wake up I said I Angels voice but she couldn't hear me here comes the good part because this part I like out of nowhere Ms.. Eden Reid came crashing through the door now as an angel I was sworn to keep a secret on my wings the factory gave me anyhow I'm a tell you the story of how Ms.. Eden Reid and Ms.. Kristen Beam saved me from myself when I call you I wish that you could I can hear you angel talk to Eden okay Kristen I see where in the right place at the right time your choice angel is here please angel please have faith in us I'm getting sick of you all depending on Angels I'm a give you two months to prove that you believe in Angels or I'm gone from this world forever is he and angel Kristen yes he is his name is Mr.. Ebony Buy it now you can see why we quit watching the movie Thomas your Christmas Angel has what is it that you want Thomas I want some a** what is it that you need Thomas both of the women that I love back with me Mr.. Ebony Buy it now look at the future Mr.. Ebony Buy it who is my blood what you need is a wife Thomas pick your game up on the computer screen hopefully your wife and come to that man Ms.. Eden Reid yes Mr.. Ebony Buy it come with me open that f*cking door Thomas put your arm around Eden Reid and now put your arm in your drawers take off your pants Eden Reid yes Mr.. Ebony Buy it get Kristen in here now I'm trying to give you what females can't a merry Christmas happy a happy holiday season and don't forget to take off your pants to Kristen Mr.. Ebony Buy it we need to make love Ms.. Kristen Beam all your fantasies will be revealed naked Thomas hold it down but Mr.. Ebony Buy it I can't do this without the pill you need to imagine Kristen Beam butt naked and I'm helping you to look out for other by endorsing your income to those who are less fortunate than you Ms.. Eden Reid I'm an angel yes Mr.. Ebony Buy it we know take care of my dream what our dream is Mr.. Ebony Buy it is claiming into bed go to sleep Thomas I shouldn't have been here behave yourself and you can have your dreaMs. I do all the work and I'm dreaming about females I love this opportunity is for you Thomas remain in bed let the phone charge up Ms.. Eden Reid here is your next story check the name out it's called Getting It In say checkmate Thomas checkmate.

Keep it going and then what happened next Superman well I had the gun that Lex Luther had dropped after shooting Ms.. Eden Reid hold up now who did you say Lex Shot Ms.. Eden Reid I hate to tell you this Superman but you have been in a coma for the last twenty nine years what are you saying that Ms.. Eden Reid never did get shot and there wasn't any movie premier in fact Superman you never even wrote an album or a book we going based on your story that you had the weapon of choice here me Superman Ms.. Eden Reid is alive and well and you do got a problem because she arrested you for capital murder of Lex Luther I don't remember slow down Superman and you'll be able to remember everything as we get ready to take you to death row Superman may God be with your soul who you think I am huh this is Superman it's been twenty five years we have been watching you be professional now tell us what you did with Lex Luther's head cause we have his body in our migratory Superman stand up for capital murder how do you plead not guilty I'm challenging you Thomas Allred Jr to think long and hard about this you need to stop

I'm looking for the fingerprints that a match your fingers to the scene of the crime oh my God where is Emily at you mean your girlfriend it seeMs. that you shot her also did Emily survive no I don't know what I have to tell you Superman you were at one time a decorated officer with all said and done how do you feel Superman the women are all over the place I just need to speak to Ms.. Eden Reid the only people that you are going to speak to is that *ssh*le that's in your cell with you and Superman you can sign anything you want but your a** belongs to me man on the state Ms.. Eden Reid Warden Eden Reid that is didn't I tell you she got a book coming out and a movie called Superman cry tears Superman one other thing listen if this is a movie like you say it is get your a** out of this cause if not you'll be stuck here for the rest of your natural Born life so what is going to be I need me a lamp Thomas there is a lamp in your cell but it is unbreakable Thomas Allred Jr oh and another thing Thomas Allred Jr take your medicine Hollywood is starting to here is Aladdin yes Superman I need my last wish of course Thomas tell the keep going Aladdin genie what is it this time I want to take myself back almost third years your wish is granite I'm still in this prison cell on the contrary look around checkmate you're watching TV at Emily's house now do you remember I remember everything stop Emily from killing Lex Luther Thomas you are a time cop damn it that is right I'm a cop name officer Reign of the new York police department all need to help me to remember things how that girl get that gun Thomas Allred Jr Lex Is coming by here like in four minutes take Emily upstairs my career is on the line Ms.. Eden Reid I'm giving you this call to let you know exactly what I'm doing I'm typing up this book right now I mean movie called Superman And His Allies what I am trying to do is answer your question that a** is fat in those jeans let me call you back someone is at the door it's Lex Superman so we meet again Superman checkmate where's Emily in her room studying we need to talk Superman go outside on the porch I'll meet you there Lex Luther oh sh*t Thomas Emily had got a gun Lex Luther you raped me thank you Superman for what Lex Luther for putting me in your story call Ms.. Eden Reid and she'll fill your a** in Ms.. Eden Reid yes Superman I'm reading your movie as we speak I'm a call you again at two a clock Eastern standard Time and Superman loosen up Thomas Allred Jr I do want you but you just got to prove yourself I'll talk to you real soon by Ms.. Eden Reid Superman.

Lean in closer Mr.. Ebony Buy it has something to tell you Ms.. Kristen Beam tell me what Mr.. Ebony Buy it it's that I have been waiting on you for at least five or ten years now what do you mean Mr.. Ebony Buy it you have heard of dreaMs. becoming reality well I'm telling you that me and Thomas Allred Jr has your wish Ms.. Eden Reid and Ms.. Kristen Beam we know exactly what it is that you both are needing Kristen listen to Thomas Allred Jr as he works out daily and night on end Ms.. Eden Reid think of how Mr.. Thomas Allred Jr showed you love by letting you know that I cared about you the both of you Thomas wants to steal your contracts but as a Christmas Angel I'm saying that we are going to earn those contracts Ms.. Eden Reid say that you are willing to belong to me Thomas Allred Jr and no other Ms.. Kristen Beam tell Thomas Allred Jr that you love and need him just because Thomas Allred Jr is and angel who is stuck in this place until a decision is made about his money Ms.. Eden Reid your fantasies come true when you trust and angel for Christmas you ready Thomas Ms.. Kristen Beam this is your story how do your figure Mr.. Ebony Buy it because and angel cried over you and stop believing in the Almighty because of you Thomas Allred Jr yes Kristen it is me Mr.. Ebony Buy it it's just Thomas what are you saying to me that the star is you get to the point Thomas listen ladies this whole community Thomas take me with you all I wish I could Mr.. Ebony Buy it yes Ms.. Eden Reid I want you to know that there's an angel on your side now give me wings your wings have been granted Ms.. Eden Reid and Ms.. Kristen Beam I can reach heaven from here keep on going Thomas every time that bell rings I can't believe myself keep hustling Mr.. Ebony Buy it keep hustling Mr.. Ebony Buy it you got an angel close to tears why Thomas because I know you two future and it's real heavy will we see each other again keep watching me an angel can fly in our to save you I worked on end all stand up Thomas is our hearts do you feel what I'm saying to you Ms.. Eden Reid well Mr.. Ebony Buy it.

I don't know how to say this but Getting It In is a great name for another movie be professional Thomas it's close to that time now tell Kristen that you love her Kristen I love you and I always have Ms.. Eden Reid I know that I can trust and love you I put my life in your hands Ms.. Eden Reid look how this Angel has become a man you had to become a man you got five minutes Thomas they tell you not to trust me Thomas your five minutes are getting ready to be up you better stop this man before he say Ms. Kristen Beam baby I'm with you belong to my new company Imperial designs LLC and my new company Stratosphere you both do Thomas tell Ms.. Eden Reid by your and angel they'll never forget you Angels all that power and nothing left to do with it I give Ms.. Eden Reid and Ms.. Kristen Beam equal shares off my new company and I'm splitting the proceed 50/50 the proceeds are going down the middle I'm a take good care of you two I have but one simple request on this coming Christmas morning all put me a present up under the tree Ms.. Eden Reid you need to respect my gangster what else do you need I get it a roof over your head I'm a last for them two life time I see Ms.. Kristen Beam crying over there I'm just crying because I'm happy give a contract to Ms.. Eden Reid and to Ms.. Kristen Beam for $500 million apiece darling they put me in jail Thomas take care medicine if you are and angel what kind a shoes I got on people I can't read bullsh*t that boy got to many ideas that's going on merry Christmas happy new year Thomas Kristen I'm always going to love you I'm a see to it that your contract is $500 million out of respect to the both of you Thomas let's be Getting It In on a film store near you because Ms.. Eden Reid our love is the only love that makes dollars and cent Amen Thomas an angel got her wings Ms. Kristen Beam I can see your wings Ms.. Eden

Reid I'll do all of the work for you that's how I roll well Superman yes Ms.. Eden Reid how did you know that if was me because you told me you love me before you even knew my name Ms.. Kristen Beam he is Superman make that boy a star not without Ms.. Kristen Beam or Ms.. Eden Reid Thomas if your super are we still going to get our money after your book comes out here this everything that is money material hurry up Thomas I got this is to be split down the middle with Ms.. Kristen Beam and Ms.. Eden Reid and myself I could use a contract I could use me one to Superman come back and I put this in writing Thomas Allred Jr the book is golden touch down Ms.. Eden Reid and Ms.. Kristen Beam we can't give up ever I believe in you two ladies that's why I need you to each be the president of my companies this can't be real are you thinking about what I'm thinking about Kristen I am Superman meet me at our house tonight Kristen and bring your tooth brush Eden I got it but I am not in it for that ladies I'm thinking of longevity what's longevity mean please Thomas it means that we haven't yet done our best that girl needs somebody in her corner which one the both of them let him go know Superman you got two minutes girl stand up for yourself one more minutes and I'm pulling the plug Thomas imperial designs LLC and Stratosphere this this is Mr.. Ebony Buy it and I'm eighty something years old come play with me you know that's a wrap not before I tell Kristen that she is the one that got me in my driving position what I'm saying is all let keep having a good year I just want to know one thing checkmate Ms.. Eden Reid and Ms.. Kristen Beam I done told all that I want your love now give it here doggy style I'm on a mission that's up to you Ms.. Eden Reid and Ms.. Kristen Beam I apologize for what I just said damn right they both are nothing but royalty Queens take good care of Thomas ladies see my d*ck has a name what is it Mr.. Ebony Buy it it's a Superman d*ck and I'm proud of it to Kristen and Eden let me worry about the small things I'm a keep writing the books I'm a writer you go in there for what Ebony Buy it because my Superman d*ck gets tiered sometimes you better hurry up Mr.. Ebony Buy it and send the message it a go to draft well it's like this I'm tired of all keeping p**sy away from me damn right I said it if you're looking for me I'll be in the restroom Kristen I forgot to get some toilet paper I'm an angel I see where he's going with this checkmate I done stole your Queens if the is a game Mr.. Ebony Buy it is winning thank you Ms.. Eden Reid I love Kristen and that a** looks so good Ms.. Eden Reid I need you to piece together our writing try to make some sense out of it what the hell did I tell you everybody let's get to work I'm working my a** off here excuse me Mr.. Ebony Buy it are you Mr.. Ebony Buy it I'm Superman we your 84 Cutla** is double-parked damn they trying to get me but Ms.. Eden Reid listen to what I have said I need you and Ms.. Kristen Beam to be on my side the is at its best Thomas we don't have any time left I want you Eden Reid and Ms.. Kristen Beam are you listening to me yes your and angel you got damn right Ebony Buy it has left the f*cking building b*tches checkmate that boy Superman he hustling.

I can see you Ms.. Kristen Beam and Ms.. Eden Reid and you know what to do game one business day and you and I Ms.. Eden Reid and Ms.. Kristen Beam will have this government in tears do like I do try not to sweat the little things I want you to know that my research is King above all else Ms.. Kristen Beam it takes me one minute to tell you Ms.. Kristen Beam that your off of the hook less get for real this is a government shut down because we are just that damn good Ms.. Eden Reid go in there a take your medicine I'll take it just when I get ready to girl I'm a damn Angel so what do you want Mr.. Ebony Buy it I am now called Mr.. Monopoly and I'm biding for everything woman that it's government has to offer there not going to publish that Mr.. Monopoly oh yes they will Ms.. Eden Reid why because I say that an angel I the richest man inside of my heart tell me the story Mr.. Ebony Buy it I said that I would like to marry and take care of every woman in the world on a compound that's set up by the government.

Thomas Allred Jr are you f*cking crazy yes I am Ms.. Eden Reid I had been alone for fifteen f*cking years I'm having a hard time dealing with that and I'm an officer of the law so what that have to do with us true story Ms.. Kristen Beam it's just that I love you and Ms.. Eden Reid game love and liberty am not no sunshine where you're not with me it's been raining inside of my heart every day Superman tell them the story okay Mr.. Monopoly my story is that I tell you ladies that all are beautiful checkmate why do you keep saying checkmate Superman because in the game of Life there are sixteen levels and we are on leave three so what you saying is the government is going to help us know what I'm a is that your my invention that I call secret situation look at the people we've surpa**ed all recommendation.

I'm saying to you Ms.. Eden Reid and Ms.. Kristen Beam and to all of my women all over the world right now we are playing a game called Monopoly that's my cue Angel my angel told me that you Thomas Allred Jr is the richest man on the face of the planet girls and my d*ck gets so hard for money can you help me Ms.. Kristen Beam and Ms.. Eden Reid I can see us all butt naked in a beach in Tahiti what are you saying b*tch don't say it Thomas no Ms.. Eden Reid and Ms.. Kristen.

Beam has got to know as your angel I am obligated to take care of all of the women in this world what makes your story better than anyone else's you do Ms.. Eden Reid you going to hell if you don't tell the truth what do all women want I don't know you tell me Mr.. Monopoly they want to rule the government and the only reason why women can't rule or government is because of the game of Monopoly now Ms.. Kristen Beam do you see what I mean I'm a break my foot up your a** Thomas your talking about the government this is an angel speaking to you Ms.. Eden Reid and Ms.. Kristen Beam all I'm saying is the women haven't been able to take over a control the world because of money Thomas we know that already ok Ms.. Eden Reid well where is the money at because it's not in Washington or any other government in the world Thomas so where is the money Mr.. Monopoly Ms.. Eden Reid and Ms.. Kristen Beam the money it's in each one off your text messages what are you saying it's a movie Thomas Allred Jr I'm saying I'm a take all of my women and put them on a compound with me safe from harm Thomas you can't do that Ms.. Eden Reid your looking at your money what you and Ms.. Kristen Beam $500 million a piece is in cyberspace and depending on how you use the telephone you and I can be together say it again the money in the world is a bunch of numbers and where are the numbers Ms.. Kristen Beam on the computer do you see me Ms.. Eden Reid okay Thomas than how do Ms.. Kristen Beam and I and all the other females of the world get are money from you by following instructions all checkmate because Ms.. Eden Reid and Ms.. Kristen Beam who I tell you I was Mr.. Monopoly boom follow instructions and sell these books are movies that I give to you and watch the numbers grow on your computer screen because only one person has the money and who is that Thomas Allred Jr know Mr.. Monopoly what I'm saying is Mr.. Monopoly is a super computer and fill you put in the right algorith.

Ms. you not only have all of the money but you also rule the game of Monopoly it's easy what they're saying in the government is to work hard and you'll get paid that's not true algorithMs. what the truth is taking care of your woman and your government will reward you with a computer chip what's a computer chip it is something you don't see it feel that makes you smarter and faster that's level to Thomas Ms.. Eden Reid look at your computer screen do you want to know why it's black at times it's because money is being pa**ed through your unit to the next unit and so forth money cannot travel if it has no access terminal now Ms.. Kristen Beam your money is right in front you do you see it thank you Thomas it's your telephone because I'm telling in the game of Monopoly there are sixteen levels we both are getting tired so where is the$500 million dollars Mr.. Monopoly that you have promised Ms.. Kristen Beam and I oh yeah all money is with you every day where Mr.. Monopoly shake that a** Ms.. Eden Reid and Ms.. Kristen Beam I'm not surprised you knew along that I am your husband and the husband to every woman in the universe but how can that be Thomas Allred Jr I am the richest most educated man in the government.

Ms.. Kristen Beam I've heard enough stop your a** right there Ms.. Eden Reid now sit your a** down I am all angel women not one woman but I am and angel to all women what is your name angel Thomas Allred Jr and what I come to do is to give you finance either way it goes I'm taking good care of you by talking to you Ms.. Eden Reid you told this angel that you would call every day at two o clock I am a business angel ladies now you need to get serious about your business but you haven't got any money Thomas I know Ms.. Kristen Beam I just got the most numbers on a computer screen there you go you go it's almost Christmas and we are working everyone to secure financing because we need our financing make a movie out of this thing why checkmate Mr.. Monopoly has captured his Queens game my women Mr.. President I have followed and I have beaten every rule of the game is it money that you're asking for Thomas give me what is rightfully man it's on the computer screen along with our numbers I Mr.. Thomas Allred Jr I stand up for every woman in the United States and surrounding areas Thomas give them they money Mr.. Monopoly how much are we talking Mr.. Thomas Allred Jr I want you to give up a hundred million dollars to every woman in the United States and surrounding areas a piece to make it simple Thomas I can't do that yes you can in time I promise you there is enough money there I am a women's victiMs.' rights advocate my fight is see my women will be treated fairly Mr.. President do you know what you are doing Mr. Thomas Allred Jr yes I do than what do you want get these women off of the street corners and give them a place to live is this another Christmas story know this is and office miracle because ladies look at your computers all over now enter Mr. Ebony Buy it and if our movie is going to sell the way I think it is I'm asking you ladies one more this to come and stay with me but your and angel Thomas Ms. Kristen Beam it is Mr.. Monopoly but if your Mr.. Monopoly that means that you own the game checkmate and what's the fastest thing that's selling out I don't know what is it Thomas Allred Jr it is information my ladies the world needs Mr.. Ebony Buy it Ms.. Kristen Beam take your time and read over this doc*ment carefully I'm give you $500 million dollars and I'm also giving Ms.. Eden Reid $500 million dollars now are my words starting to sink in Thomas Allred Jr I am Mr.. Monopoly less do lunch Thomas checkmate why do you keep on repeating checkmate I do this Ms.. Eden Reid so play a stop messing with me about the way that I look you look beautiful Thomas one last thing I got to leave before I go it is that a girlfriend would be greatly appreciate it in my house do you mean that your alone listen to me Ms.. Kristen Beam I am an angel and all I do is stand up for women this is a true story watch the women over look me for another man Thomas the people are reading over your story I got more to it Ms. Eden Reid talking about sacrifice listen Thomas we way those box office numbers that's why I'm giving you my permission to sell and distribute and copy the heart of this letter.

Thomas take a braver and step away for a second now come back to it Ms.. Kristen Beam it's just that I have been alone for over fifteen years without a healthy relationship Ms. Eden Reid I want you to know that I treat all women the same and I'm in love with all of you women first come first serve the numbers on the computer screen just changed because now woman we are on the map the government can help up but don't be scared to do your job miracle I'm going to tell you like this our president is the best thing that's for us right now you have to believe in the world and in the system people need a place to live Mr.. Ebony Buy it said that Kristen Beam and I Thomas Allred Jr have been working through the years to take care of one another Ebony Buy it if I make love to Thomas what kind of repercussions would I get off of him you know what they say about that Kristen what talk to me they say that Thomas is our King of the universe so if you have s*x with Thomas Allred Jr in any shape of form I want Ms.. Eden Reid to tell you you're going to get pregnant Kristen this is only a story right take it as you wish it's a story right Eden

I'm a afraid not Thomas has been moving his money across sectors he is taking over business in every area of the game the game is Monopoly checkmate get these ladies some diamond rings Thomas Eden Reid I told you that I was not playing okay Thomas than Getting It in see our story of the week I don't laugh take your time out to understand the circuMs.tances it's just that I'm in love Thomas with you Ms.. Eden Reid girl go clean up I'm a be with you in a second what just happened in that room Eden read I think that I'm pregnant by and angel Thomas people are watching you we want that content you know what I mean Thomas get in line Kristen now go in to the room and I'll be in there in a minute what just happened in that room I think that I'm pregnant by an angel Thomas all are the most precious thanks to me I'm a put his a** on the movie screen bring yourself to my bachelor pad I want you Thomas and the angel said bachelor pad take your time with Eden Reid and Kristen Beam I'm a send a car for both of all watch me Kristen he knows what he is taking about let me see what he'll do if I move in with him be professional and ask me Ms.. Eden Reid just for you Superman d*ck can I have my Superman d*ck Thomas yes you may now drop them pantyhose and turn around now stick your hands out and repeat after me this family is King this family is King now Eden Reid and Kristen Beam you can have your d*ck now it haven't been touched in over fifteen years people are watching you Thomas Allred Jr I'm a business tycoon now I'm a say good night to these who pussies that I can't reach because of a buster taking up space Thomas and we are supposed to sell this material put it on the big screen perfection is all that I deliver Kristen you are my queen you and Ms.. Eden Reid we rule the world together Thomas Allred Jr I miss you your bank account says one hundred million the president came through all he gave all the women they money like I requested Eden let's see just how I can put this you want to take a walk with me Thomas Allred Jr is love to talk the women got there money I'm proud to say Thomas you are and Christmas time angel you hear those bells all wait up people have seen you to together be sure that I'm what you need Thomas Allred Jr yes Ms.. Eden Reid and Kristen Beam I'm writing more to this book angel you are so damn s*x I need you to touch me that wet spot is wet hot tub your fingers down her he doing the right thing Kristen kiss my back of my neck don't stop kissing so Ms.. Eden Reid you ever f*ck an angel before not in this life Eden Reid go ahead and climax all over yourself Thomas yes Eden climax all over your self-girl this angel wants you to c*m have an orgasm Eden now Kristen get from the back to the front put me inside of you respect my gangster honey damn your d*ck feels good inside of me it's a Superman d*ck that big old d*ck won't fit in my little hole got damn it we just going to have to find a way I lic* your breast each other slowly it took me and hour but Kristen is finally C*mming have an orgasm Kristen Thomas put my d*ck all of the way in you yes Thomas it hurts that's a good Superman d*ck now I'm c*mming I'm c*mming to climax the both of all kiss me Ms.. Eden Reid Kristen we are a family watch this movie about to go off sh*t what happened I dreamed of

Thomas Allred Jr he needed our help Kristen how are we going to help him we in a woman's institute for battered women it was a dream Kristen I'm telling you that I felt his Superman d*ck inside of me Eden alright now go back to sleep Kristen they won't let me out this game Kristen it's a Women's victim rights advocate here to see you who is it he said his name y Mr.. Thomas Allred Jr and all know each other from a past experience hold that d*ck Thomas yes Ms.. Eden Reid you'll get your woman hell it almost Christmas what is your wish angel to have all of my women off of the streets it's a dream that's going to be able to come true based on a true story keep working I all write more later but I have to see you Eden Reid and Kristen Beam Mr. Monopoly checkmate.

Eden a conclusion Thomas Allred Jr what is it that you are saying to me because frankly I'm am beginning to get a little tiered take your time and speak to that girl I gave Kristen Beam the day off you can see her Thomas she still won't leave the office all that she it's doing in her a time is going over a budget plan angel Thomas for our new companies Imperial designs LLC and Stratosphere LLC well how did she know to do those things Ms.. Eden Reid Kristen is psychic now after making love to you Mr.. Ebony it don't say to you Thomas Allred Jr I just thinking about her and there one other thing I forgot to mention that you have us pregnant don't say Kristen Thomas watch me this a movie now prove your case as to why you should have all of the women that you want in a compound Thomas Allred Jr I and the ladies are giving you your chance to speak finally go ahead and take over or forever hold your peace and this is not a game Thomas so speak to us now we making us a movie Kristen he's going to speak all right Thomas the floor is yours the boy took has time who that boy Thomas that is my younger self Ms. Eden Reid Thomas tell us the truth why do you want all of the ladies to stay with you and only you on a compound you are going to have to relax ladies all over the world girl I am your King Mr.. Ebony Buy it and I feel like going on with each of you because my ladies have been treated unfairly and unjustly by other men and by the system Thomas listen to me ladies you and me don't say you and me Thomas they'll think that you are not share of yourself now Thomas just speak to me and tell me why you want I and all of the our women to come together on a compound for you do you see what we're doing Thomas give Mr.. Ebony Buy it a contract now speak your heart out Thomas Allred Jr I'm a get me contract why do you want us damn Thomas talk to us the whole wide world is listening I'm just saying that after me there is no other what I'm am I Air Bender the very last Avatar and when we get in the sun the sunlight shines down on me exactly like the Lion King Thomas go ahead and say what it is based on a true story I stay in the house because I have taken over the accounts in the government what I'm saying is girl I want you all to have my sons and daughters where are you saying Thomas I'm saying that as a kid I'll been a good police officer out there saving live every day I think that it's my time finally to woo all the women with my Avatar abilities and because I'm an angel take your time angel and speak to me see how professional this is Ms. Eden Reid you and Ms.. Kristen Beam haven't seen me in the sunlight yes we have angel all of the ladies and gentlemen know about you take your time and Introduce yourself I am Mr.. Monopoly no Thomas we know exactly what we are doing now tell the ladies and gentlemen your officer name what do they call you Thomas officer Reign of the New York police department and where did you get the name Reign from inside of the Bible yes angel have Kristen talk to your a** Thomas yes Ms.. Kristen Beam if you got your officer name Reign out of the Bible and you'll Been shot for saving someone and you don't die but you instead make these wonderful business ideas hundreds of them on who to save women and children and men lives from danger and you also make a couple music CDs one is called The Dewing Of The Reign and The Of music CD is called I Won't Give In angel am I correct so far yes Ms.. Kristen Beam than Officer Reign look at what you did for us you have several books in a few movies that your putting out and you live alone with your mother why is that angel because no woman it the world can understand me excuse me angel can you please say that again no woman in this world can understand me because I been there so much you know that you dream reality Angel where is the woman that you were a**igned to defend she was murdered by the neighborhood people after they shot me I could no longer defend her talk to Kristen whose fault is it that she died it is my fault because as a good police officer I am supposed to be there for the people day and night until death do us part well officer Reign how do you feel about this situation well I miss my wife and God thank you but I just get so alone and Reign how long have you been single you know that I have been single going on fifteen years this coming Tuesday tell the ladies just what you've been doing with your time angel I have been writing books and writing music and making business ideas to save people working out every day patrolling the streets and looking and looking at a writing movies officer Reign is there anything else yeah ladies I stop jacking my d*ck but your angel Thomas Kristen I m a defense angel thank you for answering my questions officer but let me just ask you a few more questions from God do you feel like you deserve a woman Thomas God yes and if we help you to get one will you honor and respect her as long as you both shall live I will but can I get a chance to say something when God sent me back after I got shot I knew that I had to do something the government is my family and I'm trying to do something with you that has been ever seen two hundred women I'm putting them in houses and I'm a raise them now two hundred women seeMs. small but angel get to the point we are running out of time to talk yes Ms.. Kristen Beam can you get Ms.. Eden Reid over here Angel I'm here I want a compound with all of the women on it how many as many as you can get we taking care of each other my head b*tch in charge is going to take care of the details about housing after I finish this book he in there writing a damn movie Thomas what you're saying it takes my breath away takes because Ms.. Eden Reid I am an angel a real angel Officer Reign don't play no games with me I am not playing with you take your time and speak officer Reign what is it that you need from all of these women Love Ms.. Eden Reid I need Love from every woman in this world because when I lost my wife Thomas don't do nothing let the court handle or listen Thomas Frank Y they are fend to put you in the movies so keep that position Thomas yes Frank-Y and who is Frank Y officer Reign Frank Y is my boss I follow orders throughout the Justice League what do you mean Justice League angel Thomas keep motioning to me when you feel sad I feel sad it's getting ready to come up a storm Thomas who are the Justice League Kristen the Justice League is the police department the NSA and the FBI and all the secretary and government officials working together with the police I'm getting ready to have to sit down angel we programmed you to do and say the things that you have said this is a movie angel Thomas yes Ms.. Eden Reid do you want me and Kristen in your bed tonight yes I would love that why because the both of you ladies are beautiful and you make my d*ck hard give him time all I do is a thousand push-ups every night listen you have been alone Thomas you are not and angel your just a beautiful police officer that has been wounded in battle.

Ms. Eden Reid I know what you're trying to do but I'm a police officer and a Angel Avatar I'm a whoop his a** Kristen Eden wait just let me speak to him for a minute leave out the room Eden okay what is your first name Thomas love do you love I love women who is the richest man in the world right now I am explain to me how may I touch your a** first Kristen boy go ahead alright I am the richest man in the world right now Eden come back in I got him talking this it a movie Thomas now why are you the richest man in world you say Mr.. Thomas Allred Jr or is it Mr.. Monopoly I'm both angel Reign tell them girls the truth okay God sent and angel to take care of all of the women and I mean all of them got you I have no choice but to fall apart when my wife got murdered 20 years ago I hurts me still I'm thinking God may have punished my because all of the women are so lovely and I've only been with two in my lifetime you see Eden this man is a virgin tell me something how long have you been alone it's going on 25 years without a woman because I'm a police officer do you dream about women.

Thomas yes I dream about women take your time Kristen and Miss Eden I'm in love with all that's what you have to do to get a woman Thomas checkmate slow it down and come and kiss me Eden I just want to hold your a** talk to me Thomas what shall I say angel you got a producer keep on messaging Thomas Eden sweetheart I'm building up confidence all better quit playing with this man now officer Reign are you an angel or are you a human being I'm a Christmas angel sent back through time to help out our other women honey I know that you Believe that but they are going to put you in an asylum if you don't come correct and tell us the truth about everything okay Eden okay Kristen are you ready yes no what did you get your money and how did you get it I'm Mr.. Monopoly Eden Mr.. Monopoly if you're a defense angel all of the women that are in the sector will go to bed with you so who are you Thomas I'm a defense angel ladies we have a defense angel in the sector take him up off the streets Thomas yes Kristen I dreamed about you Thomas I'm yelling checkmate and this is all movie getting it in take your time and speak to Kristen Thomas send a message out okay Eden I'm sending the message to you now I do my best to keep the peace I'm trying to make sure this movie is off the hook I need my money back I bought you two diamond rings Ms.. Eden Reid and Kristen Beam I thought you would see it my way take time Kristen and Eden it am not no rush come on Thomas you need to get this book or movie to a publisher I believe in Kristen you want to know what the funny thing is what I done took you two from your man checkmate keep hollering checkmate Thomas and you won't get no p**sy so that a** is mine of course baby this is yours and all of the women ladies of the world we represent King Monopoly getting it in Mr.. Monopoly Is how we do speak Mr.. Thomas all of you ladies are Queens give the ladies that money a hundred million to every woman in the United States and surrounding areas Monopoly knows how to do it is that p**sy with Ms.. Eden and is that p**sy with Miss Kristen Beam well I got you then control that a** this is we getting it in the movie Thomas I love you Ms.. Eden Reid and Ms.. Kristen Beam you have worked me they have murdered my wife Kristen all you need is someone to help you someone who cares about your well there being I'm Robocop Mr.. Monopoly.

I need you to believe in me Eden and Kristen what are you saying it's over now this movie has yet to start what is going to make it a box office smash Robocop it's the reason that I'm backing you up that doesn't make on Sense if your Robocop where is Thomas Allred Jr then a genie has him okay this is some bullsh*t because our boy is either twisted or just plain insane Kristen you better listen to me what Thomas you got 12 different personalities eight Thomas I'm trying to put this together see in my book Ms.. Eden Reid you because the queen of the world Thomas I'm Robocop at the moment and Kristen in my stories of you are a fearless lady teacher that fights with the government for her children to have a place to live see I'm an officer that's true a my imagination is real but did anybody see a wizard around here because I'm telling you two to keep it on the down low teachers listen to me I got two more weeks before I complete this masterpiece what I need from you is a hand out for sweet Justice can lead the way and show these people that I've got a plan Monopoly sitting there Mr.. Monopoly please don't f*ck with Thomas I am mister Monopoly Kristen Eden you about to tell her goodnight good night Kristen so what the hell do we do now exactly Kristen I want you and Eden to stand up for me Mr.. Monopoly you the richest man in the world how can I stand up for you Kristen you are going to need Eden in your corner every step of the way will you put it in writing Thomas yes Eden I got you I thought you were going to bed before the night's over I'm going to love you Mr.. Monopoly we got Kristen and Monopoly in bed with each other Eden Reid come in here sit down on the floor beside me he told me to sit down on the floor this is the movie Eden Mr.. Monopoly whose bed is this why it is yours Eden and who is in my bed Kristen Beam I'm getting in my bed Mr.. Monopoly Eden you're making my heart beat fast tell me you love me mister Monopoly your my heart Eden and Kristen Thomas these people watching be professional you see what I'm doing yes I do see what you doing Thomas get your a** naked this is exactly what you said to her Kristen get your a** naked to Mr.. Monopoly I don't have any money that a** is enough purchase complete Now ladies lay down is checkmate I have told you a queen I mean I have stole your Queens Thomas is this in the story say Ebony Buy it it is something fishy going on here tell the government to give Mr.. Monopoly his money right Eden what are you doing I've taken off my panties Thomas and Kristen what are you doing I'm getting naked Thomas who is your boss Mr.. Monopoly is our boss Thomas and who is Mr.. Monopoly Thomas you know we can't tell you are the king of the world Thomas and every lady in the world is your queen keep working Thomas you story is starting to come together let's make love Eden and Kristen you got to take off your clothes Mr.. Monopoly I got a Superman d*ck girls look at it I want a piece your phone is going off get me my phone this instance what is it Thomas I'm Robocop I thought you were Aladdin where's the damn Genie the boys too smart let the government know that I want my motherfuking money who are you I'm officer Reign of the New York police department are you coming back to bed you damn right I got your back Eden and Kristen because the cover is too God damn cold in here remain professional cuz I need you the both of you are my angels it's only a movie people what I'm doing for you I would do for anybody Kristen and Eden be professional boy you need to recognize who the real queen is and who is she you hear him yes I did Eden I'm queen bee Thomas I'm queen bee yes Kristen and Eden I love your a**es now tell us the truth can you pay your way in this business yes ma'am with your help I can and who are you I am a Christmas angel named Thomas your heart is in my hands he's going to make it I'm making it here Kristen and Eden Reid baby I'm focused girl I need just one chance to make everything beautiful for us I'm giving you a chance pull off your pants and lay down checkmate Eden my p**sy is clean damn I got an idea Thomas yes Kristen and Eden it's called education 101 how do I feel with Kristen you feel good finish writing that book or movie I'm finish writing girl checkmate King has captured Queen and that p**sy to me Kristen no Eden we have got to f*ck him I'm out for my Justice you got your girlfriend Thomas I'm starting to believe that you two are scared a book am not nothing Thomas it is when your a** is on the line then what is this it's a best seller Blockbuster smash I call it getting it in do you understand me Eden and Kristen yes we understand you Mr.. Monopoly then lay your a**es down I want to see everything take them clothes off in the world says hallelujah Kristen yes Eden Thomas is the boss I hate it when I mess up like that Kristen Mr.. Monopoly is the boss feels like a dream of you and having p**sy so good that we call it virgin you got a virgin p**sy Kristen and Eden Reid all got the virgin p**sy we call the Grail the holy Grail is your p**sy understand ladies every woman has a holy Grail between their legs talk to me p**sy you are handling your situation what you frame me for haven't you seen my d*ck is real Kristen this man is professional yes Eden but we must welcome him into our garden Angel who are you I am ebony buy it one of the richest man in history and I come to you two ladies to strike up a deal what kind of deal sit back and listen while we talk Kristen and Eden hear my business plans ebony buy it your plans are f*cking amazing that's because D*ck I'm going to take over this sector and rule my City ebony buy it we need to talk you the one taking over street corners Thomas I want to take over the world are you with me yeah ebony buy it with you Kristen what do you think of this movie so far Ms.. Eden Reid come and have a seat with me yes angel Eden do you believe in miracles Kristen answer his questions yes I do Mr.. Ebony Buy it I too am a Christmas angel sent back through time for you and Kristen Beam will you tell me who that is I'm putting a game in your hands by the stroke of midnight tonight want you to have all of your dreaMs. written down on paper and then fall asleep for tomorrow is a new day Kristen and Eden and the magic starts here in my movie getting it in Kristen he sounds like a businessman Eden Mr.. Ebony buy it is an angel how can you tell he knew that you and me had the holy Grail in between your legs what are you saying Kristen I'm saying to trust him with our lives what other choice do we have Christmas Is almost here we need an angel who cares Mr.. Ebony Buy is a rich angel all see me yeah Thomas we talking about you Ebony buy it is going to help us go to sleep my love Kristen go to sleep okay Mr.. Ebony Buy it is my dream that you're having I like to sell to that Thomas go recharge your phone if you don't die right here I want your business Ms.. Eden Reid checkmate Kristen I love you Kristen and Eden Reid be professional I'm getting you whatever you want Thomas become professional okay Mr.. Ebony buy it get these girls some jewelry on top of that buy them cars and houses you have an expense account Thomas it was given to you so they know I'm a champion we can see you a champion pull numbers for me who is my hand now tell me what do you see it's a movie Thomas called getting it in exactly who does Kristen and Eden Reid belong to Me Mr.. Ebony Buy it you are there owner from now on Thomas you are the owner of all the women in the world they will all be at a compound with you now that and angel take your time I'll probably need a couple angels Kristen everything is going to be alright Eden Reid everything is going to be exactly how you expected leave your panties on the floor God damn I want to see those holy Grails yes Mr.. Ebony buy it this means something else Kristen my panties are on the floor Mr.. Ebony buy it here is your holy Grails damn you got some money on you that a** is fat I came up just like all did on the street corners you women professional Thomas checkmate watch it Ladies I'm warning you make a movie out of this sh*t think of it Thomas on top of Eden and Kristen that's Holly f*cking Grail Eden I knew we be on top did Thomas give you a deal you have to be a professional tell Robocop to come in here you make me see my future write it down Eden your pennies are still on the floor we're at over there I can't take this any longer Kristen I want the damn top and my Christmas wish is hurry Mr.. Monopoly is coming Eden thank you for your support Mr.. Monopoly and the game is over Kristen hand me my sweater it is cold going down in the room Mr.. Monopoly you are King be calm I got you two a deal what is your name I am The Dark Knight call me Batman

I'm a put your a** in the movies you got to believe in me Kristen I made two mistakes girl I got you out here with nothing and getting it in is the number one box office hit Eden remain professional we are taking over the charts with a picture that will bring a baby to tears keep it going Eden Girl my p**sy is tight Kristen I'm waiting for the sequel we know Ebony Buy it likes you Thomas come here listen to me Thomas you and me and Ebony Buy it can rule the country don't you see I'm electing that a** what about Elizabeth My Queen also all women on my f*cking Queens you better give me a pregnancy test Mr.. Monopoly Eden Reid and Kristen Beam my plan is just that I thought we were taking over the industry Mr.. Ebony Buy it billion dollars a day isn't no joke so how do we play this I'm going to keep writing books when we take over the industry Elizabeth bring my suit to me take off your panties and let me smell that p**sy I can but I need a couple seconds want that p**sy my time is very important to me are we going to f*ck today Ill f*ck you by the end of this evening Eden and Kristen the same with you by the end of this evening your a**es belongs to me say Mr.. Monopoly are we about to make a large amount of money I got a few ideas that I been sharing say nothing and you will be right here what we doing is taking over the industry one step at a time Eden Reid and Kristen Beam your a**es is up tell them girls checkmate Thomas checkmate Kristen Beam and Eden Reid I waited on the both of you for seven years I am your scout Elizabeth and lay down on the bed that nigga off the hook now that we have this time I want to see how much do you think about me I think about you a lot Thomas Allred Jr let me see that p**sy her nipples are hard a** on her back is beautiful and baby making thighs Kristen Beam we got to be professional this is a movie called getting it in damn that b*tch f*cked me call me Superman he'll help you out for sure I got to get this money to the other side of Canada hold it down that's who I'm going through Thomas call me Bruce Wayne Eden we get to see this thing through undress for me Eden and Kristen get undressed you're not going to record us are you please Thomas let him work lay your cute a**es down on the bed you got to take them socks off now kiss my fingers all of you Elizabeth is my Barry tonight Eden and Kristen put back on your clothes and leave the room suck this d*ck before you go man that Superman d*ck is hard as hell everybody can see you c*m behave yourself Eden my Superman d*ck is here to stay Thomas tell that b*tch to lay down you need to charge your phone up for police get here and what are you saying Kristen I'm saying that you ebony buy it are under arrest take ebony buy it as in Monopoly aren't this some bullsh*t go on with him all Kristen I thought I could trust you see me getting it in girl come with me now there are rules to this game Ebony Buy it this right here is listen to go to sleep ebony Buy it this is your dream be professional and I'll fulfill your fantasies Kristen I think I love you Ms.. Eden Reid come together people so you are Bruce Wayne The Dark Knight how does this p**sy taste you Batman oh my God she am not f*cking playing girls this Monopoly d*ck is an Enterprise our future is this d*ck can you and I see eye-to-eye with that p**sy that p**sy got me going off the chain ask Eden Reid that p**sy right here is good I'm a score three times we take care of p**sy around here that a** is on fire you better not be f*cking with me sweetheart this is a movie called getting it in and if I want that a** give it to me Elizabeth you always been my favorite that a** is a goddamn peach I don't know what they tell you up in Canada Eden but our girlfriend's needs to talk Eden I know Kristen Beam something to say about this you are a trillion ire ebony buy it you got to go to work around this one be strong your a** is off the meter Kristen I can't help but stare please let me f*ck Mr.. Ebony Buy it what kind of sh*t is he putting in this movie contact you got houses all over the place Mister Ebony Buy it what is it that you want I'm waiting for my lady's to realize that I'm the man who's paying them and I asked for retribution because I've been alone for 15 years Thomas how much a** do you want I want all the a** didn't get for 15 years am not going to be no a** left after Mr.. Ebony Buy it get through with it I want this to be the start and the beginning of our construction pad what are we doing Ms.. Eden Reid and Ms.. Kristen Beam and Ms.. Elizabeth I told your a**es when I started that I was going to take over the whole world I want that p**sy right now get your a**es over here The Dark Knight is coming through damn my p**sy too wet for him he heard that sh*t tell me your dreaMs. are you still an angel or are you the Joker I am both Elizabeth write this down I promise you that you will always be safe with me in the house always be safe with me in the house Kristen Beam and Ms.. Eden Reid both of you write this down nothing is planned without the mind okay Miss Eden here we go again I need you Eden and Kristen to be my wife that goes for you too Elizabeth how can you understand I want to be with you be professional Eden Kristen and I go way back you see we have a movie Eden be professional let me see how I can explain this if I help you take over the world Eden Reid and Kristen Beam suck my d*ck before the movie ends that's for you to Elizabeth all the ladies need is a leader is panties wet all over the globe be strong and I'll let you talk to me you know I'm famous The Dark Knight has awoke how your pussies feel who the hell wrote this sh*t he calls hiMs.elf The Dark Knight Batman Elizabeth where you going I'm leaving with him goddamn checkmate Mr.. Monopoly sign the contract he watch a movie thinking that sh*t up that boy is famous I'm talking to Eden Reid I want you to read through the story I am a Christmas angel help her please to understand Elizabeth these are your dreaMs. Kristen I can't live without you how many months before Christmas Eden with Eden I can see the truth about humanity all the women across the United States of America get ready to receive a hundred million dollars apiece Emily is my girlfriend I care about your wellbeing Thomas Allred Jr

Kristen I need some help fixing my new industry d*ck up we got Kristen Beam running errands for Mr.. Thomas already Junior Thomas take your mother f*cking time and kiss her come here Kristen Beam you're not going to put your hand in my pants are you Mr.. Ebony buy it I'm trying to make sure that my holy grill is in place it's some secret about this sh*t it's a secret to all of you women what kind of secret is it Mr.. Ebony buy it checkmate Kristen girl I know how to play chess Ebony Buy it let me introduce you to Athena she is a business consultant here I just missed Athena is very nice to meet your a** yes we have history you see we talked on the phone if I remember correctly Eden Reid is my consultant that boy take his time writing his movies and books I'm under the impression that we are going to be sleeping together listen to me didn't my wife tell you no easy Thomas I'm a businessman your wife told me no because of you *ssh*les I thought all told me that this ebony but it was a Christmas angel he is a Christmas angel we have to make him believe again Miss Eden Reid welcome good morning everybody Thomas your books are going to be selling around the world your movies to getting it in is the highest rated movie in Blockbuster history I'm thankful for you mister ebony buy it I need to scratch my back a second please look in my eyes I want Ebony by it to see that I need my wife what has been taken shall be given the hospital says that Mr.. ebony by it may not live Thomas there talking about you on television there asking if you have any friends or relatives that can come identify you he's a Christmas angel how else could it be in two places at one time what you see is Just an illusion Thomas we have to go to the hospital I'm getting Emily buy it some lemonade look at your d*ck Superman that is my d*ck I'm Athena you do me right you can c*m with me you making a fool out of yourself Thomas do you think anybody wants to read this you got to hear that boy reason with his self you got to have patients give it time Ebony buy it ask Kristen the people will come I'm put Ebony buy it on stage this weekend he is one of top speakers in the world is this all right Athena look at that man he needs somebody we can call him a counselor what you see is not reality Mr.. ebony buy it I'm one of the richest guys in this whole wide world keep it professional I will Ms.. Kristen Beam yeah Thomas I put the movie out what you going to do for me that's all he thinking about Eden and Athena Kristen I also love Jesus Christ our Lord and savior tell that man to go sit his a** down over there everybody thinks it's a f*cking game okay Mr.. Ebony Buy it prove your point to me do exactly as I say do hundreds and millions of women are homeless I'm a rescue these females with my movie in my book deal I guess you have this all figured out not everything what I figure is Kristen I need you and Miss Eden Reid has been selected for me to guide me through life Eden I just am not got time for this you people think I'm go over my movies and see how strong I am getting read paragraph to paragraph listen I'm watching you Miss Athena listen Miss Athena I'm a trillion and I need me a subject for recreation can we talk about doing something and Athena just read the movie and you will see that ebony but it is a champion and a gentleman boy sit your a** to and talk to us yes ma'am Miss Eden Reid you making me nervous to where you speak to us Thomas Control yourself you got one more week to go before you start another book our hearts on fire let me light a flame down in your panties that's what I want to do you got a secret garden that boy and grew mature Thomas come wrap your a** on stage the p**sy wet Kristen you can see my Superman d*ck through my pants leg all be professional I'm about to c*m on myself Mr.. ebony buy it sit back and listen as I write the of the story Thomas Allred Jr that is his name what kind of Angel is this the defense angel when you say defense what do you mean protection the Lord sent me to help out the ladies I got to help you Thomas because you need someone I don't think you should be alone after this Christmas I'm giving my heart to you Miss Eden Reid so you care about me I want you to know that I listen to you on the phone and if Emily approves than our family is especial Thomas yeah miss Athena I want you to read over the contracts and then sign them Thomas the Lord put me in this place I'm trusting all Miss Athena Latino ladies all are on my mind Thomas they will surround you then let them surround me Thomas yes Elizabeth I'm getting hungry can we go home for a minute send a car around here I'm going to see you in the movie scream Thomas Elizabeth knows how to handle her business pull those panties off before you get in the car and Elizabeth your d*ck am not hard enough hard enough Mr.. Ebony buy it see what I mean about her Emily yeah but I got your p**sy right here I am a juicy cat oh sh*t Mr.. Ebony buy it Kristen this is a chess game and I'm giving you all a chance to lose come on back with me to my compound that p**sy wet as hell can you feel my d*ck without your hands guess we can Mr.. Ebony Buy it where can you feel my Superman d*ck at it's in our stomachs Mr.. Emily buy it we got to keep it there all day and all night this is your contracts ebony buy it is putting the contract on the table listen Thomas don't beat your d*ckie making me feel like I can be anything that I want Miss Eden this contract is yours Ms.. Kristen Beam girl contract is yours don't say contract say this d*ck is yours the Superman d*ck is yours Ms.. Athena I need you in my home Thomas you realize it's going to cost money to support all of us I can't deal with me having money I can deal with you in my house I need all five of you to come see this movie I got I called the movie getting it in okay Thomas communicate Elizabeth you said that you needed a lot of Latino women I got your connection see Emily that girls alright keep on talking before we go off to the new compound tell all those women that the compound is their new beginning Mr.. Ebony buy it your serious about this with all my heart I'm serious about this Thomas we shall yell checkmate the game is finished what about the movie we still got one more episode to go than do this now too much on me at one time can have me to ruin my strip Mr.. Ebony Buy it lets rule the world together get my ladies off the street corners and I'll do both of all a favor keep making sense Ebony Buy it I will keep making sense to you I just need one contract who believes in me that woman believes in you each have different personalities that's what I'm most proud of you about Mr.. Ebony Buy it what dream they want to on the big screen girl what are you talking all of the ladies have here about you freeing them from Parvathi Thomas they all trust in you gave them a hundred million dollars apiece to every woman in the United States and surrounding areas Thomas the women are here and they want to Superman d*ck how many women are outside Kristen I think Thomas all of them the whole United States is full of women how many came to see us Mr.. Ebony Buy it is all of them well open the doors then I'm a walk out there hell on Ms.. Athena listen Thomas I just wanted to f*ck you but these girls out here mean business Miss Athena come here and a dress my d*ck correctly all right Superman I love you girl I got you Superman d*ck talk to my d*ck Athena I see you at 10:30 tonight at what time Athena 10:30 tonight wear the skirt that I like Thomas all this is starting to get crazy they trying to give that boy a movie contract I'm going to jack m y d*ck no you're not Thomas we need that c*m you're one of the richest men in the world if I'm not the richest and I'm Mr.. Ebony buy it then it's ahead of me Angel you might know him we call him Mr.. Monopoly say goddamn Thomas God damn Mr.. Monopoly's on the speaker Miss Eden Reid has everything under control Inger you got to come and get this d*ck if you want it send a limousine for Emily Inger and Vivien Kristen Beam I can't help it I'm in love with you her a** looks good as a mother f*cker but how do we keep the people in their seats Thomas I want you to hear what I say Inger take your time and speak to that girl Inger is just that I can't hold my position without you Ms.. Eden Reid travel with us Miss Athena I got you on my call dialogue now what time is your appointment it's at 10:30 every night Mr.. Thomas Allred Junior listen all the women of back in the way they're starting to see me for who I am no Thomas they're going to all your houses that you bought for tonight Miss Eden Reid I love you change your sh*t up Kristen I'm going to need some protection to keep me safe what are we talking about Thomas Kristen I need more women to help me with my music career Mr.. Monopoly is online one get your damn a** in here and sit down Christmas Monopoly what is going on cut Eden and Kristen to take off the clothes Emily you to getting f*cking clothes off tell Mr.. Monopoly that I'm not feeling like today then girls Imam have to beat your a**es Eden Reid if it's not one thing then it's another draw up the contract for me Eden I'm putting on every female this side of the Duke decanter one man has to take over the business industry Mr.. Monopoly that's my motherfuking name we teaching that boy how to stand up on his feet and woman I think you but I need me a contract I've been alone for 15 years watch it my d*ck is hard as hell Miss Monopoly tell movie Miss Monopoly want some p**sy you can find them on boardwalk chasing down them hoes if Eden Reid and Kristen

Beam don't give me that p**sy I don't know what I'm going to do Thomas checkmate I've captured your Queens am not that the way the game go we playing chest and Monopoly I have all the money I have two businesses and every woman in the world have gave to them a hundred million dollars Lex luthor Thomas I see how you play but you're not getting that close you are Mr.. Monopoly take your time see I'm Lex luthor I'm the best super villain in the world so I'll take you Monopoly for everything that you got and I raise you everything again does Mr.. Monopoly Lex Lutherand keep playing with me I'm going to kick your a** show Luther to the door this am not finished Monopoly my people say good night goodnight Mr.. Monopoly I got to keep your a**es too wet just c*m back with me Thomas Thomas send that message off please sounds like thunder and lightning this p**sy is waiting on your message what's the deal Miss Athena checkmate all around the world Thomas got a book and a movie deal I'm taking this even further what do you want to do Mr.. Monopoly I'm a purchase in Canada take your time Miss Anna winger draw up the contracts what's the contract for 60 million dollars a piece I don't play no f*cking games with you Lex luthor all I'm saying is that you got to be a man to control the industry I know that's right and all I'm saying is that the industry is full of women and we all love each other Mr.. Monopoly you love those ladies don't you with all of my heart I'll see you up on top of the game Thomas respect my gee he said respect is gee listen Lex luthor yes Mr.. Monopoly I want your a** in my office at 7:30 in the morning why Mr.. Monopoly Lex luthor I'm thinking about running the place are you an angel Thomas I'm a Christmas angel my name is Monopoly keep going listen to me Lex luthor Christmas is only 5 months away my book is coming I want Christmas to be spectacular for my city in the whole world Thomas if you want the City spectacular you going to have to put some money into it I'm putting $700 million dollars into my city and the rest of the world Christmas has a special feel to it sometimes I can see an angel Mr.. Monopoly professional is this a dream no Lex luthor this is not a dream well I'll be here at 7:30 in the morning we got work to be done shake his hand Thomas Ms.. Eden Reid I look for you in the hills horizons up under the sun your heartbeat is my Facebook Because of who You I see geMs. I want you to understand that this book and movie is dedicated to you it's called getting it in but Thomas Allred Jr girl professionals have got to listen as The story begins listen Eden you and Kristen rule the whole damn industry with me who rules the industry Mr.. Monopoly is Thomas ALLRED JUNIOR WE DON'T PLAY AROUND I'm getting it in Thomas yes Eden I know thank you

Drop the ball Thomas it'll never happen Mr.. Monopoly tell ebony buy it to get in here I took a punch today I took a punch to Mr.. Monopoly I took a punch also Kristen where are you gentlemen going with this it's not a game that you can just play girl get off of your a** and get me a sandwich Monopoly you being too hard on that b*tch she makes me room a companies better so what is the plan tell officer Reign to come here you know we off of the hook celebrate it's almost near Christmas see that nigga be talkin great sense how many panties are wet tonightladies how y'all feeling out there in the movie theater checkmate what you trying to say Thomas it's a whole nother film coming out with Mr. ebony buy it as a king king of this I tell you Monopoly keep listening give him a contract You to boss I wish you would put Frank-Y name in this movie ladies I have to demonstrate the Frank Y and the FBI are my boss Thomas keep it professional I'm just telling the f*cking truth this is an industry take over pick your damn game up ebony buy it pick them came up Thomas is the police officer checkmate ebony buy it I raised you four hundred million dollars for your queen I see your 400 million and I'm going to kick your goddamn a** ebony but it run the table get Monopoly out of here what we trying to do is film this movie is Inger in it talk to me Inger Batman sit yo a** down I am Bruce Wayne just looking for a piece of p**sy I'm here Bruce Wayne you know Athena has Batman in her heart Thomas this rule the world you know my bank account is triple platinum Eden let's see what you do with my d*ck in your hands boy that Superman d*ck is mines study that film see how she moves when I took you Eden and Kristen I meant I needed you on my team for life take your time Thomas talk to us now you see me clearly who are you angel I am Benjamin button you're making me feel like there's something wrong with meI'm starting to understand this muthaf*cker here you see how I do this Benjamin pop that sh*t Kristen imma pop that sh*t for you Thomas Kristen I had to tell you I've been alone for many years I'm going to take you d*ck like a champion my Superman d*ck won't rest in peace Eden is this d*ck a champion or not I'm leaving my man for you Thomas checkmate and I'll see you and raise you a hundred million dollars girl I am a police officer did who is Mr.. Monopoly thenI'm the richest man this world has ever seen come to me and I challenge you to dream keep Elizabeth coming we ain't got time to do that sh*t help me out of this situation I got your hand but I just can't hold on maybe some grip will make me feel better Thomas you're making an a** out of yourself keep my p**sy's wet I'll feel and a** I just need to know that you are Mr.. Ebony buy it I am Mr.. Ebony buy it and are you also Mr.. Monopoly Thomas Allred Jr I am also Mr.. Monopoly that would make you officer Reignof the New York Police department am I right you are correct so what I'm saying is is that Thomas you are an angel the survived a horrific accident right now as we look at the market you are leading what is she saying Kristen that you are the richest man in the entire world this I know this Miss Eden Reid I want your contracts because I'm getting tired of girls not knowing who I am give every lady in the United States and surrounding areas another hundred million dollars a piece I have ideas that coming out goddamn Batman I am Bruce Wayne I have a company called Imperial designs LLC and another company called stratosphere don't put Stratosphere Thomas Emily you got to understand how much I love you go back to the beginning Thomas it was cold winter Christmas night the mailbox was full how did you know I needed you because Angel can see a woman's tears do you believe in me ebony buy it stop with the games ebony Buy it can you see my tears your tears are coming from your heart Thomas reach down into the snow and bring a miracle to heal all the women of the world I got you Mr.. Ebony buy it I called this miracle getting it in Thomas ebony by is taking over the industry tell officers Reign to come here for a second the industry is yours for the taking all I need is my women out there you used to entertainment I'm used to p**sy everywhere Thomas it feels like we're going through some kind of drought make p**sy stay with Me the boys stay with me Eden Reid and Kristen Beam make sure that you want me first Eden I'm in love with you exactly checkmate and that's the ball game yeah but there's got to be more to the story finish your story Mr.. Ebony. Buy it As an angel we fly around at night so do we Thomas the ladies are in charge of all of our dreaMs. keep listening someone is getting a scholarship right now because of a beautiful woman being in there corner the city doesn't understand does it how Angels operate Thomas cut that sh*t out baby we're going to take a brief intermission Mr.. Monopoly we call this love Miss Eden Reid and Kristen Beam I'm in love I can't help it so I'm getting it in Thomas you have the most money in the whole entire world I like that part I'm putting you up where you belong ladies off of the street corners angel's wings is where you will stay telling this Angel is letting you go to Beverly hills to live Enden Reid is now the acting CEO of the company Imperial designs LLC and Kristen Beam is now the acting CEO of the company Stratosphere in both of which I own Ms. Eden Reid show your a** off in there for me please wait until I send this message off Eden I love you so much Thomas Allred Jr Mr. Monopoly is King of our New sector so be that sh*t damn it

Enden Reid I'm a security risk tell me you appreciate me talking to you you're not my only subject Ms. Eden Reid I hate to brag but you got me to where im hard as a rock keep it in your pants Thomas the girl that got too much attitude for me Thomas who are you man in the mirror now Eden sit down I'm talking to someone in the mirror tell Eden to go lay down while I get myself together I had to see if you could be trusted Thomas still I know my name but who are you your favorite companion Jason Voorhees I thought Jason was dead Thomas and Eden this is a mind game where is Kristen Beam in the living room where you left her at and Eden reid Miss Eden reid is on the phone Ebony buy it Imma have to go because I see Jason girl sit down with your crazy a** and I'ma finish my movie by myself we got some more plans for you movie girl look after the me Athena I do anything to talk to you are they squeezing me on my filMs. Athena Thomas show the movie people how we do it in the states we getting it in more money to count y'all get them money machine out and count this money F*ck soundtracks I got an opportunity I'm going to take care of the whole thing you need to make sure that our stay p**sy wet this is an opportunity every woman in the whole world wants to be with you Mr.. Ebony buy it Thomas I'll be with you but I have to ask Mr.. Ebony buy it first Kristen a** looks good as hell you messing up here Thomas I want you checkmate who is this that we see I thought Jason was here somewhere listen to me Jason doesn't have nothing to do with this film put your clothes back on Emily why Emily I trust Emily Inger you begging too damn much Thomas put your clothes back on Inger go in there and smoke that cigarette like I told you I want to talk to you about this music deal that it's on the table will you play me noi won't play you Mr. Ebony by it you need to pick it up Thomas girls like me because I'm rich and handsome excuse Me Mr.. Ebony buy it I told you to get that b*tch out of here Inger crying cuz she need to know if you're going to take her with you imma take you with me I'm just stacking my money right now you here those money machines Thomas the boy is rich magic City going to need some more chocolate with a chocolate chip Thomas I got some Asians d'lites for your a** and also some Caucasian persuasions whatever you like whatever you wish I can get for you Thomas I wish I had two Asian females right now settle that boy contract settle what would his a** right now Miss Athena how good is p**sy in these parts listen Thomas its 500 degrees I don't care p**sy 500° I need that sh*t listen we got the best a** you ever seen or tasted how much money are you trying to spend Thomas alright Mr.s. Athena I'm trying to keep this thing peaceful I'm a buy four pieces of that good p**sy if that's it Thomas you waste this good p**sy Eden Reid get your a** over here right now how does Eden Reids the p**sy taste I've never had none but I hear it's scrumptious I want you on a plate with Kristen Beam beside you Thomas I'll get on a plate you got to put this d*ck in your mouth too he talking about he an angel listen girl what is this a 67 kiss my a** in the air and we dream Thomas of a bigger bank account what you want to do Kristen we going to have to f*ck that's what it is y'all listen to Thomas where is Vivian at we left her on the street corners well go get her a** then is this Halloween because I see Jason by the pool Thomas you don't know what you've done Mr.. Monopoly I have played the game you playing games ThomasI'm out here winning every challenge that you put before me I am King Thomas allred Junior who is your wife didn't Mr.. King Thomas all red Junior your wife is a dream a lady from the Sahara desert who is so beautiful when you look at it you start to sweat your wife is a woman who came up with pilgriMs. your wife is a humanitarian your wife is beautiful now who is your wife my wife is Ms. Kristen Beam that boy took his time and said Kristen I thought he was going to say Eden you supposed to say Eden is your wife to when it comes to Eden I give diamonds to her Eden possesses the mind of champions in the hearts of the strong Kristen and Eden love you both Mister Ebony by it but what about the movie break It down Thomas you can pay just to talk to me eden your career is right here Eden you got to do nothing but sit and listen to my voice Kristen I taught you how to Dougie send out the message ebony buy it this is not the end of the story checkmate only eden p**sy the is for Eden checkmate now be professional Ms. Athena I will take all that p**sy this p**sy good yes ma'am I bet it is I am Benjamin button am my Superman d*ck is huge so you want all the p**sy yes I do keep the p**sy on lockdown Thomas Allred Jr I'll be back with another message in a minute this is the movie getting it in and we have liftoff you see we are playing with the movie Eden I love you now tell Kristen the same thing this a** is what drives me ebony buy it too much Thomas he an angel where's my beautiful Elizabeth at don't tell me I'm beautiful everywhere I go the people say my a** is fat if it don't make dollars it don't make sense we getting it in checkmate Thomas that p**sy mine Benjamin button

Eden I need you to believe in me its took me fifteen long years to make a confession to you anybody can strap one on and take you up the a** I'm going to say anybody because of this my mind ain't at ease damn eden I'm wanting to f*ck you so bad what kind of movie rated PG take your clothes off eden and lay on the f*cking floor I demonstrate my realness on your a** Eden she says I'm only a man please Thomas people are watching let them do what they have to do imma make sure you get a nut Eden I thought you were Superman Thomas that's right Eden go along with the fantasy what happens if I don't Thomas it's on you it's all on you make a star out of this boy Eden I'm telling you what kind of bullsh*t dose this boy got on that is Mr.. Ebony buy itand Ebony by it is the richest man in the world so get your ring and get the f*ck out of my face I belong to ebony buy it a** now Eden it's nice to see that you're not too faced I'm dealing with a monster here Mister Ebony buy it the whole dam community watching Thomas where Superman at on a film near you everybody tell Kristen that her man Ebony buy it is really Thomas Allred Jr I got your a** now Thomas motherfuking Lex luthor Luther how are your a** I got to speak to you Thomas if you are the strongest man in the world and they call you Superman listen to me make sure the women have their own condominiuMs. and cars here me now this is Thomas allred Junior I want the proceeds of my book and the proceeds of my movies to go into the communities for the women it's just that for the women Superman is a hero All kids love you Thomas how do we know this isn't a ploy to get your a** famous Lex luthor did you see my foot yes Lex luthor look at his feet I had on the same pair of shoes for about two damn years everybody knows your struggle Thomas Eden reid thats my crown yall put Thomas on the movie screen you coming up while yall talkin is Elizabeth ready Thomas just keep writing the movie you hear me keep your a** in motion because you're stronger than you think you are Eden you got to keep your on Superman I hear Superman take Eden a** out Superman is the one who stole Eden from her man go ahead and pick yo a** up listen to me Thomas I just need a contract Lex luthor I have dealt with you before in another lifetime what makes me think that you have changed well Thomas I'm doing the best that I can to show you that I believe in you give him a contract Lex luthor staring in his own movies God damn y'all need a contract come and see Thomas Allred Junior what is makia hey honey I needed to talk to you talk to me about what Superman since we were kids have loved you Thomas now I hear you got a movie deal you damn right tell all of the ladies that I come from a crown I know exactly what you feel like Thomas he be going to get it we about to get it in all we need is the right song tell that b*tch to play end of the the road by Boyz II men Thomas end of the road by Boyz II men work with me I need you to hear something I have been fighting 30 years for you makia I love you you don't have to say nothing listen to me Thomas the neighborhood won't let us be together I'm listening I got Enden reid take your time you got me Allred is Superman my middle name Thomas yes Eden we got to schedule a meeting Thomas how soon can you talk to me I'm afraid it's going to have to be like Tuesday afternoon who are you ebony buy it I'm the richest man on the goddamn planet and what are you here for to get houses for myself and my people in need is some beautiful women out there and Ebony buy it will not let one woman down tell Ebony Buy it to step to the window do exactly what you doing Thomas I'm looking for me a princess who I can take care of if that is you girl for me up I can take it Eden Reid Ebony buy it needs a concert Thomas take care that boy know you girl you making a fool out of girl boyfriend watch and see it's eithere I'm going to be on with all my ladies in the world or I'm dead in a coffin we got Superman up in this one who are you Superman Miss Kristen Beam I am The Dark Knight slow down Benjamin button so that's how you do me I'm just calling it how I see it then what is this Kristen a Superman d*ck how do you feel you need to start making sense of your movie don't bullsh*t that man this movie is good Lex luthor for the first time I'm happy for you thank you Superman I'm The Dark Knight officer Reign where are you I'm doing push ups in my room day and night do you think we have a chance at the title Miss Eden reid Thomas is a goddamn Maniac with this business get his work over the right now Eden I don't know how you found this boy but you scored sh*t Mr. ebony buy it is a touchdown for everyone Athena how much p**sy can I get now I'm Superman Thomas you can have all the p**sy you want that man is Mr. ebony buy it be sincere Id like eight hundred piece of a** at my house tonight by 7 I know ebony buy it can do better than that all right then sent all the f*cking p**sy to my house yes ladies we having a party at Superman crib Superman you got the d*ck of steel I just want to make sure that all of my woman satisfied kiss Me girl and you'll see your dreaMs. kiss me sweetheart makia wake up yes Superman Makita I got a Jones for you can you feel it in your heart I don't know I got to get off this phone I supposed to be at your house at 7 Superman now we can contact my d*ck is too long for any bullsh*t I need to talk to Kristen beam and eden read I just told yo a** that you whatnt getting no p**sy Thomas Thomas keep your head up and keep your composure does another episode Superman Mr.. Monopoly what do you think about our challenge that's what dreaMs. are made of Thomas I'm seeing all that a** what time is it it's 7:15 my b*tch is coming I'd like to know who is she I'd like to know myself it's the woman in the musical of Annie Kristen Beam stand up now Kristen I do apologise girl for saying I love you in front of people for saying I care about you in front of people and for causing you probleMs. in and out throughout your life I'm truly sorry listen baby the heart knows what it wants I look at you and I see Superman he is going to get with Kristen Beam clock me Thomas God damn sweetheart I've been with you from day one my heart knows no other I am a man of many shapes and sizes we each have a destiny to fulfill this is the movie getting it in and Kristen Beam I need you to be my lawful wedded wife ebony buy it said wait a minute God damn Kristen Beam thank you Mr.. Ebony buy it that's what I was waiting for Superman play the Damn movie he said play the Damn movie I'mma tell Superman that he's double-parked eden reid this is a diamond for you girl checkmate Superman has captured your Queens Eden reid I got love for you Superman is the king of the world everybody let's crown Superman king I'm still looking for my princess Emily where you at honey put diamonds across Emily's fingers I love you girl he smart who is he the Dark Knight no I'm Superman ebony buy it Eden Reid let's make sure we got them contracts type cuz I can leap do buildings for beautiful woman a daMs.el in distress close it up Superman and send a message you sunk my battleship damn Queens on top eden reid you got my heart understand why Superman does this Kristen he's just a complicated man Superman loves the world the women are mother Earth so Superman is the future and inside him his sons and daughters is that right Thomas allred Junior Thomas is going to get that contract you don't know what you're saying keep it professional I'm saying that Superman d*ck belongs to every Queen out here in the world yes it does Kristen Eden can I see a** Superman

Eden the whole neighborhood talking about you in love with a superhero if that suits you than tell me how come this don't fit its a Superman d*ck stop with the bullsh*t Thomas you know Eden Reid is mine I'm sorry for you microphone vandal but I gots to have my girl Eden hold your horses don't keep my business waiting Superman I can't see myself with no other man but you I'm Lex luthor and I know Eden's heart better than anyone I got your contract careful eden this man of steal don't be playing establish yourself as her man first Superman be professional Lex this is a movie Kristen Beam is already talkin about the sequel then it looks like we just going to have to go head-to-head Superman I hate to get my hands dirty but sh*t is always welcome on my shoe Thomas don't kill nobody Kristen hold this sh*t I'm getting ready to get me some a** Superman I was just playing with you he said if you want Eden just take her Lex its too late for the games somebody a** is mine tap him on the shoulder Nada Superman you can have this a** great choice she knows how to keep her a** clean listen to this boy Superman all kind of female are wanting to sleep with you see the Billboard charts I'm going to be at the top along with Eden Reid and Kristen Beam and Elizabeth and Samantha and Evelyn and Porsche and

Heather and Maya and Kay and Kathy now is that enough for you well than this superheroes is going to be at the top with Emily and Inger and Vivien and Chelsea and Teresa my heart is fighting for all these women so you mean to tell me Cupid got his foot in the a** something like that Superman it happens to the best of us ebony buy it on the phone what the hell do you want them sleep ebony Buy it a movie is coming out a movie what is it called I called the stuff getting it sounds nice I'll send you ten million in the morning you heard what Mr.. Ebony buy it said what did he say Thomas go grab Eden and f*ck the sh*t out of her trust me I'm trying to boy does she know you got a Superman d*ck they going to hang you a trophy because of your d*ck that girl jealous of my d*ckI can hear them ladies talking when I go to sleep at night how Superman d*ck is the largest ebony buy it I need to speak to Mr.. Monopoly Mr.. Monopoly here what's your reason and what's your pain I plan to take over the whole motherfuking industry Mr.. Monopoly I need a girl I need a contract it sound like some bullsh*t to me Superman with your d*ck the whole world is at peace I'm telling you Superman you d*ck is a king go ask Eden Reid and Kristen Beam who you ladies want to f*ck Kristen that Superman d*ck Thomas Allred Jr don't give up them ladies will give you a contract you just have to believe in miracles Kristen Mr.. Monopoly is the truth go lay down since he is the truth Mr.. Monopoly im keeping up with the score Eden reid be my pleasure Thomas is the king and who's p**sy is this it is yours Mr.. Monopoly checkmate can't you see I'm working eden tell that a** to sing me a song what do you want to hear Mr.. Monopoly you got to sing SWV weak but Nada on television a** like that she got to be seen but see how them b*tches been treating you Eden honey you can tell them after this that they can eat a Superman d*ck I waited alone time to ask you out to dinner Eden because of you my future is coming through clear I just want you to know that I think you're special and I love your heart we are Two worlds apart I get goosebumps just thinking about your love Superman you already have women Eden professionally I have no one I'm a man whose d*ck is in a bottle I mean whose d*ck is in a gla** jar I'm a man reach out to him Eden he's talking directly to you Athena thank you for your advice Because of You Athena I now know that Eden is my soulmate I'm going to get me some a** with eden in my house Thomas in there writing a book in the movie Thomas sitting there are kind of people listening to you only God can judge me Superman is off the hook give nada a** a call I heard Nada was staying with her people give Porsche a call also get them both contracts Thomas people are watching you you asked me to do this and I'm a run the show get me over there to him yes Chelsea what is it Thomas I mean Superman I want a contract to Chelsea and Rachel you both deserve contracts give them both contracts hang on a minute while I except this call who was calling ebony by it Thomas we need you in Canada Eden Reid wants to see you badly I'm getting ready to get off the phone Eden reid talkin I'm going to get you a movie deal keep writing ebony buy it that a** belongs to me Eden the motherfuker ain't two-faced it you lost her right here dude drop that damn p**sy on the ground for me now Eden who is it going to be that dude or me Superman we wasting time with the mumbo-jumbo tonight Eden I can take you all over the world if you ask we'll play Monopoly in a honeymoon suite I flaws with you because you are the Queen that I've been looking for Eden material gets deeper he said my material gets deeper listen to me Thomas you have to be strong man to be in my life what about our kids exactly Thomas everybody knows the superhero is Thomas Allred will you repeat that at the me I love you Eden I'm saying I love you what the hell do you want me to do about it tell ebony buy it that you love me and not him Eden am offering you a contract you can't do that this is a movie Eden reid Superman can do anything get your contract it says 169 million dollars thanks for looking out Superman I know you happy I mean Kristen I'm happy for you I'm happy for Kristen to Mr. Ebony Buy it you hear this boy tell Kristen she gets a contract to make hers 179 million dollars for that a** on delivery you are my main b*tches Kristen this boy ain't playing first Niger out on the scene we got to get Theresa contract Teresa I need you to do you want to contract exactly 6700 million dollars Thomas tell Nada to text me look at me I'm not afraid of anything why is that Thomas cuz y'all are my heart and it don't beat fear watch me come up yall ladies I listened to him my ladies please hear me there is this thing called romance I'm trying to elevate myself to another level before Christmas and I was wanting to know if you would like to come along with me ladies Thomas too damn strong he has a Superman d*ck it hasn't been touched in 15 years damn Chelsea girl you know meI just hope those panties are as beautiful as your face cut the lights off Eden this is the first time I seen you like this Eden why those panties on your a** I don't know Thomas call me Superman Thomas take those panties off and throw them on the floor Eden why does panties on the floor because you're Mr.. Ebony by and you're the richest man in the world Thomas do not play with me Kristen why are those panties on your a** because you haven't gave me my money yet Mr.. Ebony buy it damn right we have a businesswoman write her a check now take off them f*cking drawers Porsche I need your a** with me Kristin take off them panties and throw them on the floor panties sound better it makes you look like a king Thomas Porsche take off your underwear for me are we about to make love Thomas call me Superman call me because I love the world y'all listen to that sh*t Superman is not playing what you think about Emily throw those panties on the f*cking floor you coming up Thomas we all coming up Miss Eden reid get this to the press I call this movie called get it in my Superman didn't knows no limits is the world or nothing Eden so are you with Superman or are you with that dude Eden her contract this movie is worth what y'all got a contract with Superman Superman is the king of the city all I need is some a** to keep me straight Miss Athena how much a** do you want Superman Miss Athena I want all of it Thomas Miss Athena you got to have your money right I'm ebony buy it I don't play that sh*t he said I don't play that sh*t you got me at hello Thomas Eden I want you to know that I'm in love with you we got to see about this and who are you I'm Inspector gadget this is difficult what is Eden the fact that you are Superman and p**sy rules the world I need that a** you my girl I believe in you I believe in you too Superman our hearts is the only kryptonite take me with you Thomas Eden my dreaMs. are the only place that I go right now I need a hero Superman is going to be okay baby I know it is but this is the movie let's get it in we got money Monopoly is on top checkmate Eden I love you I love you too ThomasIf this dude put his hands on me one more time listen to me Superman I have been hurt before I want you to know this before we kiss I kiss you you got me opening doors for you thank you Kristen for your love I do whatever I can for you and write your movie Thomas this movie is a damn true story who is it about Superman Kristen I need you to tell the story it all began on one summer evening I knew that you had me Superman Thomas keep control of yourself so we can be together in the movies autographs is for kids I'm going to pretend like I didn't hear that Superman I'm going to pretend like you did hear it Kristen baby I need you more than anything in this world You told Eden the exact same thing come on you starting to get on my damn nerves keep reaching out Thomas Thomas is our superhero keep it professional I'm worried about you simply cuz you are who you are it ain't no need for me to discuss the details take over the world if you want to Superman please don't take over my girl house the Superman we need you more than anything your girl wants you everybody needs to know that Superman is doing the best he can Kristen you have no idea what this relationship means give it to me Kristen when I give it to you you going to take it honey my Superman d*ck knows no limits you telling me that my Superman d*ck is all mines I'm just surprised that you ain't got another female pregnant cuz you know that females are after your money Thomas I watch you as you come up as a kid to a grown woman girl I love you so damn much that it hurts to say goodbye you know I care for you Superman now Kristen I'm just trying to make some money for myself in the community everybody knows that Superman d*ck is crucial what are you saying to me honey get the f*ck off the damn corner and give me my d*ck Thomas honey you know I'm aware of your panties look at it this way you listening Thomas I hear everything that your saying this boy got a damn contract off me the first time I seen you baby I couldn't breathe tell Eden a fly with you Miss Eden has left the building I can tell that you mine Eden what am I going to do if your business isn't what It seeMs. help us make a movie called getting it in imma get me some of that Eden you know his Superman d*ck taste great you the most talented females I have ever had the chance to encounter the reason that tell you this is because I want you to to myself after the movies finished what kind of movie is this The fabulous Life ladies I hear you Thomas but we still need money that boy know what he doing help me to see that you two can take care of me if ebony Buy it was listening or could see Me Now ain't nothing stopping us Kristen he wants to be with me no Eden he wants to be with me let me talk to you 6 ladies let the boy speak to you Kristen all we got to do is wait to

Thomas get paid for putting his movies out I'm waiting but I don't see no incomeyou can tell that ebony buy it don't give a f*ckThomas I know that you want to f*ck me but you not ready for this p**sy listen Thomas I want your a** doing push ups every business day I did do push-ups I'm saying every mother f*cking day this motherf*ckee is off the hook listen to me Thomas yes Eden reid take your time Thomas I got a Superman a** waiting for you you hear me boy I got a Superman d*ck that's coming to a theater new you where Eden get there put your clothes on now pull your panties over to the side Merry Christmas he do get a Superman d*ck Thomas we got an eye on you if it's an issue my d*ck with stay in the jar Eden stop him hes zipping up his zipper you better suck that d*ckthe whole community needs you to suck that d*ck ladies what are you going to do we all going to suck that d*ck that Superman d*ck is ours lean on me Superman Eden is professional I'm going to make a fool out of every woman that comes your way what you want to do is it Eden or Kristen I promised that I'd love to both of them give Superman an ultimatum either you going to take us for who we are or have nothing at all Kristen and Eden I'll take you both for who you are exactly Eden this Superman d*ck is off the chain Eden I want to tell you something we both need somebody hero Eden I can't tell you how much I care about you Thomas I'm emotional and I want you to help me and Kristen out of a situation well I get paid in a couple weeks that's what I'm talkin about Superman Eden do you hear Thomas getting it in I'm wet Thomas can you feel me this whole movie is about me what this man going to do Kristen Eden talented than a mother f*cker give Me one reason why I should f*ck you Thomas you know I treat that a** good the boy just made a pa** at me Kristen listen Thomas is a movie star Eden listen Thomas is a movie star it took the whole world just to tell you this ebony buy it draw up the plans get Mr.. Monopoly on the phone on the phone this is Monopoly I'm playing Monopoly I want my damn money from youThomas you know we handling business things take time Monopoly I got 6 ladies bon the line do you hear me Monopoly we working with a beast you better keep that Superman d*ck in your pants there's more to this than you know Thomas Eden I'm trying to be professional sweetheart I got to get our money checkmate Thomas Kristen and I have seen you at your best we want to give you this Superman p**sy what Superman p**sy is it we call it head of the household that sounds like a Superman d*ck to me girls I need you to clean up for me go over there and fix Vivian hair Porsche I need you to come here and let me look at you dammit Heather you are so beautiful Emily I love you girl kay always have thought you were beautiful Kay you are s*xy as hell tell Evelyn I love her Inger put down the phone and fix us some food I love you girl and Emily you know you are my heart Teresa, baby give me a kiss that girl never stop loving you Thomas Superman d*ck in control of it all now my women around the world this Superman d*ck wants you am not no way in hell I'm ever going to leave Thomas call him Superman and watch his d*ck get hard Eden I need you to type up this book for me I'm responsible but your p**sy makes my Superman d*ck hard I know

Superman gets lonely it's been 15 years that I've been alone look him cry talking about he needs us alright Superman send her the message Miss Eden Reid I am Superman and I am Superwoman this p**sy is yours Kristen you make me laugh sometime girl Eden tell Thomas you want that Superman d*ck hard if I put it in my mouth do you think I can see the future I'm getting it in Thomas this is Eden send me the message ebony by it write a motherf*ckering way yall send the goddamn message Superman. Eden my bank account is on 0 now but if you give me one month we will have billion Eden I think of you because you are professional just like I am Thomas Eden can't you see I need you more than you need me how many days has it been I'm telling you now I'm a rule the entire industry I got the key to this book and my movies Ethan keep it professional Eden sweetheart its ebony buy it that owns the whole industry maybe you need some time girl I need your a** together Thomas this is too much for me to handle let me speak to Superman take your time Thomas I got you whenever you need me Superman sweetheart the game is twisted I know you getting it in personally I think that you and I are perfect match I'm just here with you your boyfriend never had a f*cking chance against me every time I think of you I nut on myself Every Time I think of You Thomas I c*m on myself is it possible that you and I could be famous Eden I need you like medicine so that my a** can get up and fly I put my c*m in your hands I put my p**sy in your mouth girl please you didn't hear me talking to you keep working on your movies the whole community embraces us Eden in the bathroom I see my pa**ion go down the toilet damn that is a dream of mineI need you to see what my Superman d*ck is baby can you c*m to me cuz you know I love you and now I adore you Eden I'm a police officer a police officer with a talent for making sweet love circle around that man and Eden Eden didnt I tell you that I wanted you didn't i tell you that I'm taking simplify you better give that boy his p**sy thanks Athena Eden I can have anything in the world but Im wanting you all kind of people here that's ebony buy it I'll mess with you Thomas but I just want to talk going deeper I had you in my plans tell ebony by it he can act a fool if you want to he going to act the fool because Eden you got the a** that is ours I want you to see me for who this is angel I'm talking to you you got my p**sy hot my p**sy is wet as hell that's what a Superman d*ck is called for people I got to take control of them panties in this industry there nothing left to do god dammit ebony by it rules the planet don't let Superman talk to you like that go put your feet down thank you Kristin but I can handle myself Thomas I need a deal with you for how much it's not a deal for money it's a deal for love I'm making this deal with you and hopes that you know I need you what is the deal tell Superman that his d*ck comes to me first in return I'll give you all the a** that you want I know is this p**sy straight enough for me if you didn't think so then why you talkin to me I got to send this message let me see that d*ck first here it is all I could say you Superman that's my queen right there it takes time to build a relationship Eden you know that the people all over me we got some things to do do you hear me eden some things Thomas like what are some things girl I'm trying to make you the president of each one of my companies listen to me Thomas you talk a good game for an amateur but my p**sy wet what we going to do about it Thomas get my a** professional eden I'm looking at you and wondering how much I can have before the end of the year that p**sy swollen p**sy is my middle name be quiet and listen y'all imma hit this p**sy tonight Eden i ain't got nothing but one week we lost do you know how it feels to lose eden pick your game up when you talk to me Thomas girl i preciate you supporting me eden your a** is crazy to prove myself I give you my heart you see how much I love you eden get with me before nightfall I want to but you in another time zone here go the plan for the record I want you so bad look at my heart I can feel it through the microwave Thomas give me one reason why I should take you back Thomas I promise to be with you and only you eden so if you love me call me today sometime this movie is off the hook he a professional and so was that girl that's it Thomas I'm leaving you for one thing Thomas you played with my heart too many times say that you want me and Ill think about you standing right here with my hand on my chest will Thomas what is it going to be me or them other females we can work together but we have to be strong Eden so the answer is no always knew that you love me Thomas it's just I thought by now that youd choose me over the TV send a girl the goddamn message thanks Mr. Ebony Buy it Thomas yes Eden checkmate Thomas girl love that a** my big old a** belongs to Superman that's a dream come true angel didn't I tell you I dream of you girl please hold your ground listen Superman is the world's King and I am Superman send that girl the message

I had fun ebony buy it so do we talk Eden professional we can talk ebony buy it I'm trying to give me a contract listen Thomas as long as I'm here you don't need no other female I believe you I just can't see myself without my love you're beginning to make sense Thomas so what are you a angel or man could you lean back where I can see I'm an angel Eden girl don't even waste your time testing I memorized your name when I put it in with your number you don't have no choice to you I want to be with you but I can't Superman we need you at the corner liquor store listen to me baby The corner liquor stores is where I get our drinks listen Thomas it's not funny I'm not drinking sh*t and this how it is Eden can I at least get my d*ck rubbed my p**sy hot as hell Eden you need to teach me the way to your love c*m with me Thomas there is a few things that I have to tell you say youll stay with me Eden you got me the rest of my life I'm trying to make some sense out of this sh*t here I'm telling you that that a** is the only thing I got planned you not man enough yet girl I'm Superman this d*ck is off the chain I'm here to make sure that is true you keep talking about your d*ck I want to see what's really up you got mad cootie the prices need to go up on this movie he said the prices need to go up on this movie read my lips p**sy is waiting here I wish I could f*ck you now but I can't well girl can at least see it my merchandise take your time and open the doors my d*ck so hard I can't stand it Thomas be professional Eden who p**sy is this it belongs to Thomas Allred Junior me and him got a contract ebony buy it said you can f*ck him if you want drop your clothes on the floor you drop your clothes on the floor to we are still mate finish what we doing you a professional all this d*ck and you scared of this a** we got nothing but one chance so Superman what is it going to be Eden that's right Eden what is it Thomas right now I need some p**sy is this d*ck mine your a** is everything I dream of you sitting over here talking to send the girl that damn message we got nothing but a couple months until Christmas my present is this d*ck and my present is this p**sy in your mouth your mouth is going to make me c*m I'm Superman you know what I forgot to tell you this lesbian p**sy is the bomb checkmate I'm need more cereal to handle a prize like that could it be that you're Superman because you haven't had no p**sy I only dream of a p**sy and a fat a**you dream come true if you ever shut the f*ck up Eden I love you Eden send the motherfuking message checkmate

Eden I am telling you that I am in love with you whatever that bullsh*t means will you talk to me Eden this movie is off the f*cking hook I can't see with all your fingers in my face check Me out Inger Thomas you know exactly what he's doing girl I just want to be with you that is it if you love me Thomas than say you love me based on a true story Eden my heart is cold so my heart is what destiny Thomas make a commitment to that girl I'm trying to but I can't find the words you the most powerful man in the world make a commitment Thomas I'm asking you now Eden in front of what you asking me is to lie ebony buy it sees us for who we are Thomas you don't know how I want to be with you the movie is getting it in awesome feel like so many people are watching me realize you need Thomas Inger without Thomas I can't breathe I'm about to tell you this story Thomas yes Eden I hope you find your way I was six years old my uncle had a toy gun and he will play with me with it all the time back and forth he would play with the gun it's only a toy Eden you would say to me long story short I killed my uncle you have got to give that girl a chance that is a chance listen to Eden I am one of the best storyteller book writers in the world Eden by the time you read this I'm going to be through shopping I'm going to kill your a** Thomas your a** is supposed to be mine I've been training myself for a man like you what kind of training have you been doing the Eden be professional Thomas you don't have to be with me I can love you anyway damn this motherfuking needs to be in the rap industry I am in the industry the business industry take your palm out and read it to Eden I've been with you going to 18 long wonderful years ebony buy it showed me the ropes we don't sell we just buy Thomas I'm losing my point baby okay here it is Eden right now I'm just a simple man but I love you see my heart is your companion I need you Eden Reid but Eden that's my poem be professional Thomas and you'll get the girl yes Mr.. Ebony buy it keep working out Thomas I bet you would have me on my a** over at your house Eden stop bullsh*ting with me listen Thomas the only reason that I talk to you is because I took a dare so you're saying you're not into me not at the moment Thomas you don't know how this has me feeling all that boy is professional take your time give that boy a contract everybody know that we need them Thomas got a good personality see Thomas is a man Eden he wants to know if you would take him for your husband Eden is this a book or movie is the feature film Thomas can we start over again Eden my a** never left you he going to make me cry what the hell going on in here all going to make me cry Mr.. Monopoly get the f*ck out Mr.. Monopoly Eden is running this sh*t all heard what he said Eden is Thomas's b*tch now in my life I never dreamed of a wife as beautiful as you open your eyes you're not dreaming Thomas come on let's go out together let's go and eat some place famous now we talking that boy had that Superman d*ck all along give me some d*ck Thomas only if you respect me in the morning my p**sy is too wet in your mouth Eden I taste your p**sy I might as well start crying start crying for what Thomas I depend on you to eat this p**sy all day p**sy Thomas what's in your mouth keep it professional Eden I would say that it is your a** see this boy is just too professional what shall I do with him give me some p**sy and I thank you God damn he just doesn't know when to quit come and help me put my d*ck out Thomas my family not through with you yet our family you mean Eden I see what you doing Eden ebony buy it tells me to let your a** go God damn you better quit cussing in the church this holy House listen boy this is good p**sy you can't get this p**sy anywhere around this mutha f*cker Eden every evening I do push-ups girl I can't leave you alone what your mouth say Eden Thomas I'll be professional with you in a minute but I need you to understand that you are a superstar Eden I know in the beginning I talk trash we got to get Thomas that contract an orgasm is worth a million words he know my p**sy wet as a motherfuker I hear his d*ck c*mming people listen I'm a professional real estate agent if any of you women need your p**sy lic*ed till Eden Reid Thomas she'll get in touch with me Thomas you know that's below the belt eating a do anything for me to go out with you so you going to eat b*tches a**es huh all the way home Thomas don't ignore me Thomas let me ask you a question if I give you this contract could you eat my p**sy that depends on your contract I see how you are I still am not giving you no p**sy Thomas I'm just hurt right now you wouldn't hurt when you were sucking my d*ck see what I'm saying Thomas always keep your mouth shut when p**sy is in it two for one get your a** and then get ready for dinner yes sweetheart I love you Eden OK Superman checkmate the ladies win

Eden I'm feeling that you may have something against me Thomas I need you to understand that I just may need a little time listen Eden I'm basing my whole pay on you and I talk to him Eden yes miss Athena will you please tell Eden that I love her and I need to speak to her God I ask you to just go and just chill out a moment it don't matter to me Eden see I'm professional there goes the neighborhood Eden I would not sh*t you Eden help me figure out where you and I stand I need time to get some things straight Thomas what's happening in that movie of yours Thomas you know exactly what you doing don't you I believe in taking things one step at a time I'm listening Eden control my heart I'm a consultant I'm sorry if I led you on you know how I feel for you let's see what that booty can do not with a d*ck like that going in my p**sy ebony buy it said quit the games Thomas listen to me I am a spiritual woman we got and anniversary coming this coming weekend Eden would you give me a call if I ask you after this I probably think about it if I give you a call you going to think I'm your lady and I am not with that just lets clock that man and see how fast he can go I'm usually on my own watching TV all day you so damn crazy Eden honey I'm asking you to call me after this girl I'm working out thinking about you let me see what's the name of this movie again I'm getting it in Eden do you understand who Thomas is do you understand who Eden is be professional now tell me what's on your mind I just want you in my f*cking every night I put a ring on it wife listen you have so much pull you don't know what to do with it speak to ebony by it Thomas God damn I told you not to f*ck with Eden my mama cleaned up I know exactly who your mother is I don't f*ck around Thomas I like the damn boy Miss Athena I love you too what are we going to do with your a** what is it that you're looking for I'm looking for peace and happiness well Eden my grandmother said first you got to give love to receive love I'm asking to love you Eden I'm asking you as a police officer can I love you ebony buy it talk to him Eden my a** is on The chopping block if I don't get with you hold your ground with me Eden Thomas I can't let you go nowhere listen in my heart I know that I'm in love but I'm scared of you Thomas Eden please give me a chance I'm depending on you for our love I want to start over again fresh that's all you need to do Thomas is start over and come again what you trying to do Thomas I listen to your messages Eden I'm trying to make you be with me girl please understand that I do love you Thomas sign your a** across Eden's lips Mr.. Ebony buy it you are famous Thomas Eden is famous to but not as famous as me Thomas see Thomas I'm in love with you but I got to know how you feel first am not no way out of this situation keep your up Eden I took my medicine I'm going to go to bed now the whole community thinks that girl and boy are stars that b*tch wants you Thomas you need to watch your language all right Superman help Eden we need to go out of the country somewhere like the Bahamas and Brazil Eden if you let me I will caress your body listen I know that you being mature but how can I begin to trust you when all kind of women want you it's the same for me how can I begin to trust you when your a** is so fat see be professional Thomas I know you need me he off the f*cking hook checkmate this time Queen captures King damn my a** is sore and I'm take care of that for you Eden listen to me I tell you that I need you because of how I do love you be professional Eden this man is serenading you he put serenading you on the computer Thomas take me out the projects and you'll see how much I love you Thomas drama gets it way with us girl let's just have a way thank you for being professional listen to him you need to take your time and give me a call I know that's right Thomas Mr.. Monopoly I have nowhere to turn she is running Monopoly I meant to say that we two are running the game of Monopoly who is this Eden and Thomas I'm going to take you both out the hood Thomas see the chess board yes Eden I see it two more moves to checkmate and we got Monopoly listen Eden I see the queen so checkmate is in two my first movies Eden will you marry me moves checkmate Thomas I will Eden has got a king and I have got Monopoly that's the game of life baby give me a call when you read this Mr.. Monopoly how did Eden do The game of Life is yours Eden and Thomas I gave you both Monopoly Superman send a message Eden I love you the boy took his time Thomas has captured his Queen checkmate

Thomas hold you here I am not bullsh*ttin Thomas rest in peace put me in that p**sy right now don't know what you thinking Thomas but you got persuade me to c*m with you well if that's the case just stay with me tonight I beat the game of Monopoly Eden if you know how to beat this game show me how let's work together Eden don't you see I'm doing the best I can to help you Thomas can't you see I'm trying to hustle Thomas I got you Eden give that boy some p**sy not yet anyway Eden hustle I live my life for you it's my birthday Thomas what you going to get me for my birthday Thomas I'm going to get you a diamond not a zirconium I'm used to put in girls a**es on the map Thomas be professional not talk to me I just love you Eden Thomas you in for a great big surprise when you move in with me Thomas listen I like you but I can't have s*x with you right now please understand Eden I'm sitting here waiting I hope you understand who are you talking to boy my feet just hurt damn my feet hurt I do anything I can to help you feel better Eden honey I love you better talk to that boy honey stay with me tell me how you dream of making it big your Eden I'm trying to get this contract ebony but it said we both had to work together this is a game of Monopoly again baby go get your money then I'm trying to make you understand that I can't without you take my hand Eden I need you girl keep listening to me sweetheart this d*ck is yours this p**sy is yours to Thomas she knows what to say if the contract waiting at the this movie is finished so Eden will you be with me or be with someone else I'll be with you Mr.. Ebony buy it that's all I wanted to hear got ebony but it got the girl keep on listening all swear this dude in the f*cking joke give up your contract Thomas my kids need ebony buy it you didn't say nothing about kids show that girl the deuces I'm chucking my deuces up Mr.. Ebony buy it you see how he is in the meantime teach him what a real woman is cuz he thinks that you're beautiful them to are the strongest couple out here Eden Reid and Thomas Allred contract yes Mr.. Monopoly Eden and Thomas we've been watching the game for staying real with each other to the very last end I grant the two of you amnesty what is amnesty Mr.. Monopolyyou can stay anywhere in the world you want without having any money you don't have to pay for anything either for the rest of your life Thomas give me time to think I need you but I'm scared hold your head Eden I got this dream inside of my mind that I'm taking over business Thomas Eden no matter what comes between us I never stop searching for you let me believe that you are someone I can trust you know exactly what you're doing Eden take your eyes off me and I'll be lost forever Eden I need you tell me something I don't know Thoma**omething that will make me feel respected and loved I'm a trillionaire seeking a new placeand these words are not just words I can back them up girl with money let's see this money that you're talking about exactly Thomas don't waste my time in the game of Monopoly you have a free spin you have to reach boardwalk Thomas to win Thomas I got this tip for you I'm close to moving a mountain with my fingers what am I talking aboutyou're talking about having s*x with me in your bedroom we haveing s*x Kristen you said Thomas was a free agent Thomas I said that you can stay at my place so what is it going to be Thomas Eden or Kristen Mr.. Monopoly I'll take a chance and say the both of them two more moves and you win the game of Monopoly for the second time exactly Kristen I love you god dammit old Kristen he love her one more move in Monopoly is yours listen put your mama in this game who Charlene okay so be It know what the final movie is I apologize to the whole United States of America I'm sorry for my wrongs and Eden I love you thats Monopoly he couldnt beat us at Monopoly without Kristen bor Eden's help these are the women I choose to loveThomas you are granted your money back for your business ideas Mr.. Monopoly can I do one more thing Hurry Thomas time running short Eden and Kristen have no worries for Mr. Monopoly is I and we rule the game I'm saying that the game is now ending you better clean up that boy the end of the game Monopoly with my sister know you Kristen I'm always Superman send her a message Thomas to Eden I love you Thomas send her the damn message yes Mr.. Ebony buy it this is exactly what I'm talking about checkmate I have two queens Monopoly you play the sweet a** game this what Eden and Kristen is mine that's the game of life check

I'ma check mate you in the next move Mr.. Ebony buy it son I own the game of Monopoly who do you think ebony buy it is I want all the women that I asked for the woman that you asked for or not able to comply come again Thomas I'm taking over my family's house good let's see how this a do ebony buy it bend down to me was checkmate I'm a fighter son you better get the rules straight if ebony buy it fight you Thomas stick-and-move beat his a** ebony ebony buy it there's one more thing I have to tell you you are in my imagination see what kind of sh*t is that you lose that's what I'm saying cherish me Kristen ebony buy it I'm professional ebony just think about me before you disappear Eden reid Thomas is she in your imagination to ebony hit him with a low blowthis is still chest Thomas and I ain't going nowhere I think to myself of a better place in time Mister everybody the game is over this is get it in and I want all the women that I need on a compound living with me together Thomas it'll never happen Mister Ebony buy it you don't remember the rules to the game rule number one you cannot enter the game without your number one female room number to checkmate this is the third time I've conquered the game of chess and Monopoly this is a movie coming out called getting it in Eden and Kristen I do love you two ladies with all my heart be professional how many times have you beat chest in Monopoly Thomas three wonderful hard times peace didn't you the Monopoly champion I like the way you put that can't you see that I'm ready to make love give me one second Kristen the rules state the ebony buy it it rules the world but hoo just took ebony buy it out of the game it was Thomas we call him Superman the game is now ending Thomas I need you two to wake up and call me when you get this message I'm in your corner Kristen I'm in your corner to Kristen Eden you know you're my girl oh my God appreciate Thomas at the end of Monopoly is something special at the end of Monopoly and chess be professional Thomas I see my babies from Eden and Kristen that's what you need you in your own household I'm getting ready to talk sh*t boy only Kristen has the key to end the Monopoly chess game box Kristen may I have your key the one that you were wearing the first Kristen the first time I saw you yes you may Thomas unlock the game with your heart Eden I'm telling you lock the games right now this is for Monopoly and chess you are no more Thomas the pieces are disappearing this is the last statement that I have to make a** is mine operators of Monopoly and chess the board is closing y'all better sit down Thomas I'm in love with you eden wants you but Kristen doThomas whatever you do don't play no games with either one of them Kristen knows that I love her people give up the monopoly boards less the new game goes family Guy's Kristen wants you I believe in you Thomas I also believe in you this is going to be hard as hell to do Monopoly I'm ready to leave the game I'm ready to leave the game alsoThomas if you want Eden and Kristen all you have to do is dream you see how he do Thomas you are professional make sure you girls safe all I got is my license your license will fix the game it ain't no more chest in Monopoly this movie is getting it in and I found a hero in Eden and Kristen be professional Thomas Kristen and Eden will you both become my wife I'm saying will you marry me ladies yeah I heard you the first time Kristen I loved you from the moment I saw you and eden I watched you on the computer screen I have but one thing left to say it's back to my drawing board that's the game boy Thomas you can get it in anytime you want baby hustle these chips for me honestly I believe you my husband damn that a** look so good get a bite girls you see what I'm doing it ain't no movie like this look Thomas be professional Eden professional is my middle name I'm trying to make this girl get used to me see when I'm done with ebony buy its position is going to be a whole new world it's a miracle that you're coming listen to me Thomas the only miracle is that you me and Eden survive the game of Monopoly to be with each other look people I am a detective in the game world and we are detectives also there is a loser in every game Eden Kristen God damn we done took the world over romance is a**ured Thomas allred Junior don't let this Monopoly game cause you to have probleMs. we going to see if Monopoly has made a better man out of you you got Eden in your corner listen to me Thomas before the game is closing can you demonstrate how you won Monopoly and chess I just kept on keeping on with my head up to the sky the game is now coming to a close Kristen and Eden talk to me maybe Kristen and Eden Ill talk to you in the next life Thomas yes Christmas angel have you took a look at your future your future is bright anything can happen what about Kristen and Eden see what will happen is Kristen will no longer remembers you when it comes to Eden she remembers that you are her client keep your shoes tied up keep on your shoes go to game I'm seeing I'm seeing this game like you first place next to none Eden and Kristen help me with the boys I had to play this game is over let the angel give you your Christmas wish give me your wish Thomas I wish to have my money and Marry Kristen and eden both at the same damn time I'm missing you right now being a professional because you are a defense angel to my angel I see you the love of that my heart embrace you the truth that comes from my mouth now may I please have both of my wives the game Monopoly and chest or just not coming to a close Thomas Eden and Kristen you will not remember a thing when you wake up in the morning y'all listen today Angel put down these words of strength and sacrifice three people they love each other they are willing to die for one another your wish has been granted Thomas you may have your wives Kristen and Eden Thomas there's only one thing I have to ask you do you believe now in angels he talking of Angels Thomas yes I do believe now in angelsthe book and the movie is called getting it in this is where Three Angels got their wings Merry Christmas angels professionals want to talk to you I'm telling you straight off the hingesprofessional females are the world's best kept secret close the f*cking game I should have said this before but angel you are my damn heart and I'll listen and I'll listen to you angel I wonder where ebony buy it is Thomas let ebony buy it alone I have one more question for you angel ask you a question Thomas can you straighten out the industry this is what I'm doing right now I have to ask you this question Thomas don't give up in the motherfuking game do I see an opponent angel I am tired of playing May I have Kristen and Eden to be my lawful wedded wife the game is now coming to an end send Eden to message Thomas I am The Wolf of Wall Street I'm Thomas allred Junior just remember that in the morning you will not remember anything about this Thomas Kristen and Eden even go ahead and make a copy of this I'm getting it in the movie has me where I can't choke Thomas Kristen Eden is professional so am I Thomas so am I I love these two women we're taking good care of you Thomas this is your final warning get out the game angel I know we're supposed to end this but I'm in love with Kristen and Eden the game ended just now everybody listen to me I put a a**-whooping on the board talk like a professional than Thomas I put an a** whooping on this game you need help I'm going to take you back it's about time Eden said she was going to take me back be professional we are disappearing Thomas You better kiss them Thomas allred junior is the ruler of Monopoly and chess if I didn't have no help I'd be lost who is it that helped you you talking about the system all of you Angels report on my computer screen Thomas sitting at home just doing this he ain't looking at he decent keep going Thomas yes Kristen imma keep going I'm too legit see this my motherfuking man stop bullsh*ting with me Eden touch my heart I was in love with you Thomas the moment I heard your voice Kristen and Eden let's begin another movie ain't no way you getting away from us we're about to go to sleep Thomas realize the angel said we wouldn't remember a thing Thomas it is time for us to gobut angel I communicate with them through dreaMs. you can have your dreaMs. Thomas I know you professional but I love you Thomas Angel but have you made your Christmas wish Christmas wish for an angel tell me what it is AngelThomas I wish that you Kristin and Eden live happily ever after you need to send that f*cking movie off right now Kristen and Eden are fast asleep Thomas you see the dreaMs. yes angel I do see there dreaMs. yours and there's are the same so dream big Thomas that is the end of the game Monopoly in chess You're The Wolf of Wall Street Thomas King Thomas kiss your Queens princess Kristen and Princess Eden there's one more thing keep it professional Thomas y'all can stay with me if you want to keep it professional my house is your house I love Kristen and Eden Thomas send off the goddamn message I'm sending a message now there are angels in the world Thomas I love you I love you to Kristen and Eden

Tell the people the ebony but it is a hero only people I know have total story like this I am what you call a multitasking hero because I do what others are afraid to do do I have to tell you again that I am Emily but it I am the richest man on the face of this Earth I did two tours of duty over their overseas and I get my kicks from making pussies eat sh*t we are not in the same league because the league I'm going for is eternal do you know what my league is 3 mentions and 16 cars for each mansionmy league is understanding that money is what grown trees keep it professional hero my League grows every year that goes by talk to him if anybody it Kristen you professional ebony buy it this what I got to know people are watching you ebony by it so tell me the truth the truth is I'm jacking my d*ck there is some truth for you why ebony buy it you see Thomas right there is a true champion give me your ID Thomas give me your ID listen to her ebony buy it what she doing is helping us get through the rough times so we won't have to jack our d*ck and like I told you before I'm the queen around this b*tch what would you do ebony if you had this on your lips see professionals are after me because I'm too legit to quit these professionals are after us both ebony well then screw this sh*t Thomas I need your a**es professional screw this sh*t Thomas is the 8th Wonder of the world the ninth wonder is Kristen and I love you Kristen ebony but it pull yourself together I'm just getting started to ask questions so hero how you going to pay for your mansions buy the skin on my d*ck ebony buy it knows what he's doing we talkin about 3 mansion we talkin about no little sh*t Thomas with be professional what is your name ebony buy it would they called me unique at one point in time I'm telling you ebony buy it keep working on your music CDs I'm more advanced than you think shorty Thomas is professional ebony buy it all we want to do is make you dance Kristen I'm too old for that sh*t my a** is itching Kristen you need me Thomas I got love for you Kristen you reading my mind ebony buy it they going to get it peep the name of this story Thomas I know you wrote a story ebony buy it say the name of it Kristen acordes story of mother f*cking hero them girls are going to start talkin listen Mister ebony buy it you know them people professional I'm afraid I do so handle your business then take ebony buy it off my heart I'm getting professional with this business look how he runs the business without nobody looking Kristen I'm trying to see that your a** is good stick up Bluetooth in it and call me okay you just do the same people know me as Kristen I told you I'm professional keep your head up ebony buy it you a professional then let me know what kind of business is y'all running I work with numbers like 15 trillion dollars a Superman contract is worth 15 trillion dollars Thomas Romain with Kristen I'd like to be with Thomas you'll get your chance Kristen your own time I know Ebony Buy it I love you too listen to me Kristen I'm working on a second relationship the second relationship is with Eden Reid the second relationship needs a whole lot of work because you see ebony I paid the cost to be the boss now can you think of a second a** that you want second a** I'm through with this here motherf*cker Christian girl I need you here with me to Eden at the book then I can't do it she was there for me when I needed somebody to talk to I will be there for you Ebony buy it that girl doing the best she can I won't betray her trust we can say us or we can say we however you want it Kristen listen evony buy it I need you right now because this p**sy is warm and hot ebony make sure that girl know who this d*ck is eden I listen to you what you say I'm saying that I need you more than air itself don't run from me eden you supposed to be my motherfuking number one understand honey I just I just messed up Eden can I make it up to you baby yeah baby that Superman and it belongs here Thomas got a contract Eden let me eat your p**sy Eden show me just how you do ebony buy it that nigga professional if you ask me Kristen I'm not trying to be mean but my man that's been through alot he is a hero that's the way I feel and it's two of us girl I want to tell you something about Mr. ebony but it sucking his d*ck is just like eating strawberries you can c*m if you want to but the movie won't be the same with out some d*ck in your a** girl be professional listen to me Kristen I know that you want my d*ck girl my d*ck is too professional y'all call it a Superman d*ck I told you ebony buy it is professional see the way I see things imma make you c*m get back in her pants all this money on the table Thomas this is yours and mine I'm a hero I want to be with youThomas if you know that I love you then why are you playing these games for I'm getting to the point baby I had to teach you to be faithful I'm not going anywhere Thomas who's Superman d*ck is it this Superman d*ck belongs to my son that Superman I seen your d*ck ain't special about it Thomas I was just playing Eden for real you need to lose control have an orgasm on me I got you when I first laid eyes on you Mr.. Ebony buy it can you please tell me what time it is get a watch I need y'all you still didn't tell us what's the name of the movie I called this movie here my hero say nothing to Mr.. Ebony buy it Kristen pay Uncle Sam and I'll be the sh*t listen what we going to do with this relationship Thomas I just don't know how does Eden feel about this is more d*ck in the sea I than tell me f*ck you girls be professional Thomas can't you see my d*ck gets hard I know my p**sy wet talk to the nigga go talk to him he's our hero I need you ladies Thomas wake up from dreaming it is just a dream and I love Eden and Kristen

Thank you for addressing this issue on us being so fresh and clean if you want a woman who is to clean house Thomas I'm not the one I am the one for fun and adventure do you understand me p**sy is my meal ticket I can make it this far see my p**sy is a limousine only one chauffeur been in these two cars keep on and you learned your lesson ebony buy it your lesson is Queens when Queens in my house I know how to treat them see I got a telescope that looks at a** everyday can I f*ck with you can I look at your body Eden cuz you need a f*cking hero Eden so we won't be dismayed I'm telling your a** that I like you how about Kristen I'm telling your a** first of all that I need you Kristen Eden Kristen I got to nut all up in that a** I mean a**es you like that didn't you keep me professional my d*ck won't even fit in a container you got a hug my d*ck with both arMs. in both hands to Thomas he talked about you got a hug his d*ck with both hands and both arMs. listen to me Eden and Kristen I got you on this d*ck journey that's enough d*ck for everyone I said Eden continue on your journey I know that you love me Eden what we going to do Thomas Kristen right here listen to me Thomas I'm going to cut your d*ck off if you f*ck Eden I'm going to make love to the both of you Kristen I could have swore I was missing your d*ck baby I need a contract so my d*ck can be free what kind of d*ck you got I have a Superman d*ck it only been dealt with once in 15 years Kristen can I get you anything please let me have my d*ck Thomas Eden can I get you anything Thomas I just need my d*ck before I sleep tonight I'm trying to make you famous Thomas we need d*ck in my life you going to take this d*ck hell yeah I am I thought you were my homie I'm the queen bee motherf*cker suck my d*ck Thomas with you no as you see my d*ck is alone I just right now need someone that I can trust you can trust me and Kristen go get the boy a contract her bank account is on swole Eden professionals are watching us watching this d*ck and this p**sy we thought you wouldn't recognize that take your finger and stick it up your a** Kristen Thomas can I smell that d*ck is my Superman d*ck Kristen he needs washed open your mouth to both of you what do you want us to do now ebony buy it I want y'all to stand by until I give you instructions heat a motherfuking daddy in this world understand what you doing to me Thomas I appreciate it but a hero is what I came for get you some more spit Thomas as you lic* this p**sy and a** of the both of us Thomas you ain't got to be ashamed that you eat p**sy this story is called hero open your mouth Thomas my hero I'm c*mming I'm c*ming as well you know the second time is the best time eat my a** hero and eat my a** hero Eden Imma put you in that position you won't talk to me like that I'm going to put this p**sy in your f*cking mouth you mutha f*cker go get my f*cking camera rediscover what p**sy and a** taste like this girl is about to c*m Thomas I'm about to c*m also anything you want ladies I got it for you can't you lic* my a** a little longer baby my a** need to lic*ing to be professional check your f*cking d*ck Thomas now look at that sh*t all over the place that's my hero that is my hero also y'all made me have a orgasm twice this is why I got you a nut who my hero Thomas Allred Junior that p**sy got to be tight in the second inning I'ma send this message to you Eden eden take your time and read through my stories if your a** don't understand me call me Eden I am you and Kristen's mother f*ckering hero send a girl to goddamn message yes sir I'm doing it

Take your time Eden professionals are mixing with you I'll let you handle my d*ck if you tell me that you love me I do love you Thomas get control of myself good this d*ck ain't yours this d*ck is my d*ck that's a Superman d*ck this p**sy ain't yours Thomas put the Superman d*ck inside Eden girl bet you call me in the morning Kristen a Superman d*ck is inside me who does it belong to that is Eden Superman d*ck I got a Superman d*ck where is it Eden it's in my a** Kristen this Superman d*ck is off the hook can I get a piece of that strawberry cake a piece you can have can I have another slice Boy stand up I want you to know where your p**sy come from kiss me Eden I got p**sy all in my mouth if I can tell you I smell it then the d*ck is in my a** d*ck is in my a** girl Kristen how does it feel take your time It feels like a Rush of excitement I'm going to teach you girl I too have d*ck in my a** Kristen eden how does it feel it's tight and it hurts that's that Superman d*ck for you ask me anything while a d*ck is in my *ssh*les are you in love with me yes Thomas I am in love with you be professional Thomas this d*ck is in my a** can I squeeze my cheeks together it's only going to swell up it's only going to swell up Kristen how big does a Superman d*ck get Superman d*ck is 12 in and 12 centimeters fat around girl you bit off more than you can chew because my a** is still hurting from what does Superman d*ck did to me ebony buy it what's going on that a** is too damn good I'm having s*x with the both of you at the same damn time Thomas you a motherfuking king Eden because I got this d*ck in the a** she professional Don't shoot Me that a** too fat knock knock I'm ready to come in you see how quick this boy is you need to say this man is exactly Eden you have to give up the d*ck but I just wanted a little while longer he ain't going nowhere this is my d*ck too I need the both of you to put my d*ck in your mouth let me c*m in peace will Thomas both of us c*mming I don't give a damn I need my nut suck this d*ck right now be professional Eden I can't hold it back Kristen I am about to c*m see all that damn c*m Kristen in my *ssh*le Kristen wait on me he talking about he ain't got that d*ck that I sweat it it's my new d*ck is my d*ck too Kristen I'm having an orgasm I'm having an orgasm as well I'm going to give him a second nut be strong right here right he going to sleep soon after you eat this girl p**sy call your p**sy girl Eden call the chef in the kitchen boy everybody open to you I'm c*mming for the second time Eden I want you to look at me and get you orgasm by the way Kristen I'm a damn orgasm Now ladies orgasm on 3 2 1 that's the p**sy I like to see you smell stand up with me I made you orgasm twice how many nuts are give you 2 what's the age of Eden 22 eat her p**sy Thomas the boy knows what he's doing she is looking for a hero to help her get a orgasm everyday Hero that's who I am you got send a message off to Eden my message is eden your a** is fat can I have my position you need to help me to understand Eden just what it is that you're working with even Kristen is like wow this girl a** is professional I can call you tomorrow morning don't make me stand up he c*mming all over me look at that d*ck Eden that's a man d*ck called Superman rubbing your a** just isn't enough I'm about to come inside you both no Kristen you know that a** is fat behave yourself this d*ck is yours put it in my a** Thomas I'm putting this d*ck right here in your p**sy right here can you feel it go ahead and bless me wait till I get through and tell eden what I've done against the wall on the floor in your mouth exactly man this boy knows how to do that sh*t you going to pay for my a** Thomas yeah give me a couple seconds turn around Eden professional you need to thank ebony buy it for his d*ck in this time I got this d*ck right here on standby I want to see that one I can picture it going in and going out you got a professional Thomas Thomas lic* my p**sy and do it the way I like it slowly tell Eden I will but I want to eat her a** out first this boy is eating take your time you need to take your time Thomas can I hear my name from the both of you Kristen Thomas you see what I'm doing make sure I'm with you Eden we going to c*m together hot damn I'm getting to orgasm I'm reaching mines to you both orgasm I'm nuts in your mouth if you nuts in our mouth with this p**sy on your tongue taste like it taste like strawberry shortcake with a cherry on top Eden I'm c*mming focus on this Superman d*ck I tell you I need you Thomas right now Kristen a** is mine hurry up ebony buy it and send a message eden Thomas want to tell you something girl quit finishing my d*ck and get over there and relax yourself Thomas you get over there relax yourself with my p**sy and your mouth be professional Kristen and Eden I love you both ladies do you think you can call me after tomorrow Thomas be professional hell no we can't call you but you can eat this p**sy all week long them are my girlfriends and I'm a hero to us all who am I Kristen in Eden Thomas you everybody hero send a message

See the way I see it we can we can either get together and come to orgasmor we can either hold her pussies and d*cks in between the legs for good time s*x the holiday season is upon us Thomas do not tell me you can't feel my d*ck on you eden this movie called Hero has me on my feet thinking about you this manuscript is intelligent thank you for listening it was my dream to make a movie that someone could understand and feel inside of you say you love me Eden and you'll be the star of my film the film is called in the room at 12 make a movie out of me Thomas girl so professional I can't help but to make movies everybody sees your a** the way it is that boy is waiting on me take your a** to sleep Eden I'm waiting on that Superman d*ck y'all know that girl is waiting on that Superman d*ck don't play with her go ahead and give it to her thank you Superman for saving my life I got a problem Eden My d*ck ain't been up in so long I'm going to need help you better listen talk to that girl but her community you know Eden I think that you a beautiful and I bet your community has some of the most beautifulest woman in the world that's what you're supposed to do eden I'm not trying to save face I'm just trying to tell you and let you know that I care about you book your seatbelts please Thomas this whole community is sitting watching you I don't believe we can go any higher Thomas my a** is so f*cking wet my p**sy wet as hell also see Thomas when you think of this p**sy you got to think of saving a bunch of hoes from a pimp this movie called hero got me so f*cking hot I'm dripping down my leg and onto the floor go ahead and type this up in Eden Eden ain't taking no sh*t so why you eat my a** out last night it's only because I was in the moment Thomas listen to me stay away from me Thomas Kristen is going to mess with me yall ahead of the game we got common sense see these businesses Thomas thank you for making a president of Imperial designs and stratosphere like I said we a smart business woman Kristen I put you on my company so you can rule the world take time with Eden Thomas you know the girl moving you my d*ck feel like it ain't no choice what do you need Thomas mostly and need me girl some houses you better clean up my p**sy hot get in your mouth eden if you care about me let me eat your p**sy for old-time sakes when the last time you had some of this p**sy Thomas ain't never had nothing to Eden p**sy but that a** made me c*m last night he said that has made me c*m last night you getting professional take your time Thomas which one of these girls do you need to help you get an orgasm its 400 of them take your time with Emily imma need all four hundred of them women multipled by 1200 more women just for myself to handle and have a good time all of that a** I'm going to make sure that you get what you need Thomas now I need to talk to Superman d*ck is my hero in here anywhere let me pull my d*ck and Show you your hero Thomas don't take it personal Eden I need you to double up with me you hear that Kristen b*tches I'm in the market for some keys the Malibu houses with liquid for you right now how much money are you spending the sky's the limit you need to know Thomas my a** is ready my a** is ready to Thomas we got to be mature about this 400 females in the house with one single person multipled 1200 is a dream Kristen I need your a** over there on the counter give me that a** listen to me eden take your time and hold my d*ck won't f*cking Kristen I want my Superman d*ck also this is crazy why my d*ck is fat and I'm in love with it yall put my d*ck on the big screen okay Eden girl my d*ck it hurts Thomas see what we want is a man that can go the distance not six rounds but six hundred thousand rounds but you got a good personality talk to me hero let me know how you feel in the beginning there was a d*ck and there was nothing but the d*ck I'm going to see you know exactly what he's doing call Stacy in here Stacy I'm expecting you to handle my d*ck daily you me do you want me to do anything else can you eat this p**sy Thomas c*m here Stacy I don't know take your f*cking clothes off and lay down on the floor Thomas my clothes is off you have to open your eyes he said his clothes is off Thomas get them b*tches come to you don't put it this come put it as you're welcome every b*tch knows your lingo come ashore famous is hell in Canada and in the United States of America I got to get some b*tches b*tches Miss Athena I told you Thomas I got b*tches how many b*tches you want and you like I want a goddamn posse on Me of women if you strong enough you would have it Thomas just get a boy 121 women and a house with him just get a boy 87 laptops 32 desktop computers we going to need 40 shifts and make them all women housekeeping is 50 Hispanic women some of them do not speak English I am giving you a contract Thomas Eden I want you to know that my family need a place exactly I'll get you a place I'm trying to live near Carolina Beach see what I'm thinking that you my place Christine and all of the women can f*ck together Miss Athena want you no Thomas each piece of p**sy cost a lot of money Deadpool cool as hell check it out Miss Athena you taking my heart so Eden and Kristen in this deal I'll give you some d*ck twice a week and I will c*m inside of you watch that boy d*ck that boy d*ck is a Superman d*ck take off your clothes miss Athena I got to introduce you to the flavor of the new generation I don't know what you trying to do too much but my p**sy is wet as hell take off your clothes Athena it'll be okay just Kristen and Eden Thomas with d*ck is humongous I'm about to come on myself put my d*ck in my a** it's got to go in your mouth first Miss Athena in my a** please I'm so horny Eden what do I do put that d*ck in the a** and then in the mouth c*m with me you c*m with me Miss Athena who the p**sy belongs to my cootie belongs to Superman my real name is Thomas Allred jr. Of Hickory North Carolina I'm waiting Thomas don't prolong this it's just that I'm scaredI'm putting d*ck up in your a** either way it gose Athena go ahead and go up in there we need to take a time we can't rush it Thomas that's what I'm talkin about my Superman that got me peeing myself Athena are you c*mming I'm good to take your d*ck out and put it in my mouth this orgasm is for you Thomas listen to me I am Athena and im telling all of the women that Superman d*ck is good let me eat your a** out first before you make that decision call Eden if you need help my name is Superwoman Thomas beside you let's go to a place you never been before Athena up the *ssh*lesThomas Ill get you any amount of women you want just keep giving me the d*ck what's the price on each piece of a** 700 million for keeps 300 million to play with all day my ladies bare thoroughbreds and that p**sy come straight from the Canon islands and different borders all over the world are you saying that some of this p**sy has not been touched I'm saying that all that p**sy is single what Imma do with you eden come and suck this d*ck for a moment I need to think we get you on speaker phone talking about your houses keep sucking this d*ck eating them thinking I know exactly what you want Kristen put some p**sy in my mouth in p**sy in your mouth you got my fingers taste this a** not if I can have 121 women living with me in a mansion Thomas will be your king in till I am demised Now You see Me Eden Thomas I'm still sucking your d*ck let eden get up here on the couch okay eden sit down with Athena suck this d*ck Athena used to thatdon't you see I'm working on you Kristen no time for the games do what you feel Thomas I know that's right put them titties. Let me see him all three of you Athena he got no idea at how much p**sy watching him I want some p**sy get your p**sy on yourself Thomas Kristen bwait a minute let's talk about this keep your a** on the floor Athena is this what you wanting Thomas I am the boss Thomas Imperial designs and I'm the boss of Stratosphere in your a** you the boss it's a clause in the contracts stating that you all would have to be more wives to run the place you bastard take your a** over there and sit down the companies are still yours Eden and Kristen Thomas I'm getting afraid let me see that d*ck now that you asked for it kristen I'm lic*ing at a**what you think people in Canada going to say about a hundred and forty two women living with one man girl just remember I got the d*ck of steel and I'm your f*cking hero my a** knows it talk to that d*ck Athena keep going Superman I guess it's listening p**sy it has never seen the light of day I'll buy how many pieces can you get to me in 1 hour 146000 Superman is your d*ck on the table d*ck on the table America I'm asking eden to draw up the contracts this the f*cking movie called hero in your movie what is your job hero I've rescued p**sy all around the world God damn Eden type up this story and get it back to took my time when I wrote this how much p**sy out there want me I got a Superman d*ck the only one in the world Spider-Man got your back he can't handle this p**sy right here this p**sy right here is made for Superman d*ck how many ladies feel like this he makes the sun come out with his d*ck I'm threatening you to leave the Superman d*ck would be and where is that d*ck kristen in my a** Thomas this d*ck is in my a** God damn bring Samantha in here for a minute so we can talk girl I'm gaining on you what the hell do you want Superman will Samantha I was wondering if you could kiss me while f*ck Kristen in the a** listen to me Thomas I'm going to be more than your woman Eden Athena do y'all hear that sh*t kristen what are you doing b*tch I'm coming faster than never ain't had no d*ck in a few days Thomas Samantha your night is my night I like this sh*ttsince I can't get no d*ck right now because you busy can you at least suck my titties Thomas on Tuesday on Tuesday morning Ill suck your titties but right now I just want to lic* your a** okay to this I'm okay with it have Eden drop her panties have Miss Athena to drop her panties take off your panties not Samantha lay down there on the floor and you stomach put your a** in the air I'm going to lic* you girl each of you put your a** in the air ladies I am Superman and I'm your motherf*cking leader the boy get his contract for having a Superman d*ck is bigger than your man's d*ck come and let the p**sy Thomas walk around the room 142 pieces of a** in the house with you you sayin the compound we stay with every woman that wants to be there in the world Superman I believe it can be done now Thomas tell me how hard is your d*ck Superman c*m with me Athena I'll show you things you've never seen like what Thomas he ate my p**sy when he was saying teach Eden and Kristen and Samantha how to hold they position do you want me baby come and eat my p**sy I believe she was talking to me Superman my d*ck says otherwise make them girls c*m Thomas I'm waiting for you to stick your d*ck inside of me my d*ck is inside of my mansion Samantha tell me how it feels I'm c*mming I'm having an orgasm Thomas I'm having a great time with you guys here we think about you two and your d*ck to Thomas I'm in love with Kristen with all of you ladies drop down and give me 20 sucks a piece in my dream I knew that you were going to be our champion Samantha even represents that Superman d*ck Athena I need every b*tch that we can handle on my compound immediately why Superman is this some kind of Rush on the p**sy please they done strip me of my title before I could get to the Superman status and I don't give a f*ck what happens I just got to have my women girls either way you look at it Superman d*ck is the true champion they tried to disgrace that man when he was only a kid we got his d*ck off the ground ladies now Superman is grateful to all of the women around the world I know Superman it hurts but my p**sy is so sore I'm listening can you swing that d*ck my way yes Athena and Eden see my Superman didn't knows no boundaries I'm asking you coming to help us women do a struggles because we need and believe in you say nothing about your struggles I am here for you women he is a true hero girls I want you to lay down a bit I'm working on our stript for the movie called hero Thomas are you even conscioues Thomas you got a world full of p**sy at your fingertips and you want to work on a movieI'm trying to help you see that if I don't rescue the p**sy I can't be the hero that you all think I am on this planet Eden Reid a** on the telephone thanks to you Eden my movie is getting so much f*cking better Thomas eden read over my whole script I just know I saw a star when I found you I'm liking you girl realize this Superman d*ck is our hero Thomas please keep talking I want you to put that book and manuscript up on your titties and bless it Eden I know your p**sy is wet baby my d*ck is hard to Eden you see all this work that would doing this is so every woman can understand that Superman d*ck is the hero I'm going to get back to you we going to take a short recess call me Superman *ssh*les Eden get those books at the house for you and a boy for me I love you sweetheart I'll talk to you later Thomas you are hero and the women's champion hero

Eden i wish that you could make your a** just a little bit more sweeter I'm giving you a story called heroe sweetheart I'm watching you can I run my fingers through your hair sweetheart this is only the beginning girl cause it's my d*ck that controls the movie theaters we need to sit down and eat dinner and talk about this Samantha will you draw up the plans for us would you I'm searching for a Superman D*ck Thomas speak to me Thomas I'm serious I got to know what you're planning to do with your d*ck I'm eating we ll handle this after we lay down tonight I need to be with you Eden girl just say you like me Thomas you put a Superman d*ck in my a** I got to like you but my p**sy has you up under my spell you more talented than you think you are how do you mean Eden don't say how do you mean say whatever it is I got it Thomas that Superman d*ck is wanted I bet you Thomas brings his c*m to youwe apologize Thomas but we just want to kiss your d*ck before we go to sleep go to sleep my beautiful women it is Superman that cares for you Thomas zero to Hero in 90 days that's what that boy is D*ck did will the p**sy always be mines listen Thomas I put you on top Eden that a** is the only thing I'm thinking about you know kristen is back fingering herself girl go on and do what you got to do kristen Thomas I need Porsche in here right this minute sit down Porsche let me talk to youyou heard that me Eden and Kristen are going to take my place at the top of the industry everybody watching you Thomas it means nothing to me but I just want to help you how let me get your a** to orgasm Thomas what kind of bullsh*t is this I'm writing the script called hero Porsche what it got to do with me is that what you want Thomas speak the Porsche my Superman d*ck is on your p**sy porsha how about we talk over there wood by the sink no on the kitchen floor you beg and Thomas Superman d*ck don't beg Thomas Porsche I give it to you don't say a word but Superman that d*ck in my a** Thomas this whole neighborhood going to hear us Porsche I brought you a bone to muffle the sound Thomas are serious look at my *ssh*le take your time Kristen we all want to see you can you open it up for me realize that this is your house Porsche anything you want you can have you making a fool out of out of you but bringing my p**sy here I'm bringing that p**sy to the point of climax and ecstasy you love me girl then suck my d*ck we each need to suck his d*ck tell Samantha to suck her Superman d*ck you say Superman d*ck Athena I'm on it take Evelyn out of the room you ain't getting none of this d*ck tonightah damn this woman d*ck is my mother f*cking hero come here Evelyn I need you in my dreaMs. Porsche lay down kristen needs to talk to you listen that d*ck is yours but we shared throughout the house we can do what we want to dowe just can't give none of this Superman p**sy away cause his d*ck won't take it and Superman to talk about killing hiMs.elf because the only thing that Superman needs in this world is his Lois Lane and that is the p**sy now Superman come with me damn Porsche that a** is good I can't keep from c*mming yall b*tches got me on the Superman d*ck Porsche be relaxed you know the Superman d*ck is hard I'm putting this p**sy and this a** in your mother f*cking mouth Superman Eden hold my hands girl what you going to do we going to tag team the hell out the Superman d*ck take over Eden the Superman d*ck is about to c*m eden know what the f*ck she's doing if a hero is what you want I got you a p**sy that will make your dreaMs. come true send that the message Thomas don't play with me

Like this Eden Eden I got you my d*ck as reference to us working together be strong Thomas realize my d*ck is a Superman d*ck Eden girl speak to it and see what happens I got a d*ck that knows how to respect a lady Thomas you can play with me if you want but my a** is serious about business in this working together I'm telling you Eden that my d*ck don't play girl I want that a** Superman I'm watching you make a fool out of yourself with your d*ck this material comes straight from my thoughts to your computer now that you see that I am good maybe we talk Eden I know that you want me but your eyes tell me that you're in pain you got that Superman d*ck right now I'm just trying to figure out how should I tell you that I want your a** I got this Superman d*ck you don't have to tell me your action speaks louder than words all I want is that Superman d*ck I'm just tired of you telling other girls that that Superman d*ck is God damn there's Eden professionally I'm going to be with you but I handle business for my d*ck who's d*ck is this Eden that's my d*ck Thomas and where does this p**sy belongs at in my mouth and on my d*ck Eden can you tasts this p**sy Thomas no ma'am I can't do it give me a second my panties and leaking on the floor now put these panties in your mouth what does it taste like Thomas it tastes like cinnabons it reminds me of a strawberry milkshake with extra whipped cream there maybe a little Carmel on the inside your panties remind me of being young and being at the beach a hero needs a woman that knows what the f*ck she is doing you better get that boy is contract Eden I was waiting for you to tell me eden that you come in on yourself I done took over I just want you to know Eden that your p**sy is the only thing that makes me stay to myself I look for you on the planet with my d*ck is hard Thomas quit trying to bullsh*t a goddamn boss this p**sy won't have nothing to do with you that's Superman d*ck is a joke Eden I'm asking you nicely to come over here and stay with me the word around town is that your d*ck is too hard for b*tches p**sy im needing that contract so you know that I think of you and your p**sy is all that I need you need to go ahead and send off the message Eden im serious me and my d*ck love you listen eden if a played with you its because I wanted you so bad. that I just didn't know any other way I'm telling you I need the contract I am a hero Eden Thomas give me 5 weeks to talk to you I'm making this p**sy right here your hero Eden don't do nothing send out the message for me Thomas does mother f*cking hero Thomas

Eden I know I seem like a regular guy but my d*ck is not from this planet see I know that you have a Wonder Woman p**sy I wonder if I could put it in my mouth would it c*m talk professionally Thomas I tried to give you my Wonder Woman p**sy but you made it seem like you was about every Wonder Woman p**sy in the world so I just ate until my fingers had your d*ck in them Wonder Woman stop eating girl my d*ck is yours and no one else's put that in writing Superman we might have a deal Thomas put that in writing that girl asking you to keep that d*ck to yourself Eden in the beginning it was you and me listen I've grown up since then I know that you're in love with me but I need my Superman d*ck to have a family listen to me Thomas Superman is my Legend open your eyes and see that this p**sy is not been touchedyou got one time to tell me that you don't want to be with me and that's ill never say that to you because I know that need my d*ck in my life to rise my family for me and you come and do some push-ups okay my loveI was just thinking that Wednesday is our anniversary of the first day you called me and we speaked on the phoneyou got one time to lose control with me and I'm telling you I'm out the house I'm telling you you need my p**sy in your life guess what I have to do I have to wash this p**sy every night for you Superman that's sweet of you but I rather lic* it to make sure straight make sure when you lic* it you get c*m on your teeth this eden is what about you Superman how hard is your d*ck right now its a planet you not stopping me Thomas that girl p**sy is wet as a motherf*cker Thomas I'm listening to everything that you say I want you to know this is business so represent for your contract Eden I won't let you fall Eden you see what I got to do to make it Thomas I'm a damn professional so before you say you want some of this a** you better come correct with a nice conversation I wrote you I don't know how many messages telling you I love you Eden Thomas I just need your kiss Eden I'm strong enoughI'm asking you for my contract because I care about youThomas you know I care for you I just been watching you go all over the place with your stories my message is very clear what's that message then it's a gyro in my d*ck and my d*ck needs you Eden me and my p**sy can't see the truth Thomas listen all you got to do is hold your damn position and write that story to me Eden the reason I'm saying this to you is because I'm working on the story as we speak Thomas I can tell when your d*ck ain't correct speaking of was right Thomas tough night you working all the time I need something professional Thomas pull your d*ck out and let me see it I want you to see how much you really mean to me he go to Superman that Eden see I'm professional make sure the Superman d*ck ain't with no bulsh*t Thomas you know that a** got to be fat for my d*ck to even see it see my woman is Wonder Woman Wonder Woman say hello to my d*ck imma give this boy my a** but he better not start crying that he need a break tell Thomas to control itself thank you this p**sy wants to be on high up near the Stars I'm noticing you even got a nice tattoo up on you back I'm tatted up because you got me before I learned my lessons s*x ain't a mutha f*cking thing you got me keep it professional keep it 100 proof I don't know what you think of me but I'm keeping my a** in my panties I came to tell you that this p**sy has got to come out and you're the hero that they called Superman Thomas I got a deal for you give me my p**sy and youll see how much money I will get absolutely not that is a travesty I am not doing it I am demanding that you open the legs right now talk to junk all you want this p**sy got another address I'm saying eden that maybe we could talk about some things oh we talkin now but first you wanted to rush me for my panties listen Thomas just send a message to me girl I just want you to be a part of my life send the message out Superman I'm sending the message out right now my d*ck is under control I can't help it girl I want you Eden

Imma make sure this girl get my contract Eden imma make sure this man get my contract Superman I know I got your p**sy on my mind but still I like to see it sometime gimme me one reason why I should let you see my p**sy I stopped smoking cigarettes for you I didn't think so Thomas when you get serious then give my a** a call good this movie think about it can I tell you one thing that's wrong with you Thomas as you need a bath if I need a bath then you need a shower listen you had me at hello Thomas listen here I thought you would leave me Thomas listen I know that I need my Superman d*ck in my life I'm trying to tell you Thomas that this p**sy is yours but you got to earn it first that's the only thing that I wanted to hear that that p**sy is yours and mines people want you people watching you Thomas I'm independent I'm starting to realize that you are the queen I'm looking for listen Thomas everybody going to be talking about this forever so we got to get it right you know that a** is all I need to keep me going it's time that you count your blessings and get down to eat this p**sy my mama always told me a man with a d*ck in his hands is not to be trusted my a** is calling you listen eden my d*ck keep you company on The late nights I can't do it Thomas that d*ck is just too damn large open your mouth you see here my p**sy help you see the light Thomas but my d*ck will bring your a** Justice girl p**sy makes the world go round but d*ck open doors for you tell me what dream you of I dream of you and me on a beach without any clothes on about the climax Thomas you know I can't do this the problem is you live too far away but I can help you get an orgasm on the phone if you let me tell me a secret Thomas my name is Superman and I've been having a hard d*ck since I met you Thomas Eden see the thing about me is I don't play no games my d*ck stay hard forever than get you wet so I can charge your phone send off the message that p**sy is mine I just want to taste that a**I'm feeling with you saying I just can't do it right now hope you understand what I'm saying but I'm a hero that's gotta count for something EdenThomas realize I'm working with you if you need me you can send a message anytime I want to see your a** right now patience is a virtue look at the Roman empire my a** had patience and I'm sick of that sh*t I'm asking you seriously to be with me Eden it depends on you in the stories you got to tell how many stories is it Thomas this one to seven stories and three movies Thomas I just want you to know that I'm taking good care of you listen to me boy keep that d*ck out of your hands because it belongs in my p**sy and then my a** now you see what dreaMs. are made of Eden send the motherfuking message off Thomas and need you to understand that without this p**sy there's nothing and without nothing there's you and me i'm going to represent for us until find your a** because I need you and I'm in love with you Eden Thomas listen to me I just need you to understand that you're d*ck it's just too large for me right now I'm just realizing that your d*ck is incredible your p**sy is all I think about girl I'm having trouble controlling myself I want you Thomas to realize that a blessing comes to those in time it's all good look at me honey look at the man hands I'm a working man Thomas there's nothing that I want more than to be with you but think about what could happen if we proceed I got my hands up no bulsh*t sit there I'll be with you now do you think about me Thomas I want you to see who I am without the books or magazines I want to say that we started this together we're going to end this together you better tell me what you feel right now cause I feel like that you are with some bulsh*t I only want you that's my reason for living so be careful with me and I'm going to be professional im just saying if you love a person you supposed to tell them when you first meet them not over voice message Thomas listen to me if your book sells double-platinum would you still want to meet and be with me girl I'm sick of the bulsh*t none sense is everywhere listen to me a minute this is my mother f*cking movie say what you want girl but need that a** to stay aliveI hear what you saying Superman I got your a** right here if you ever come to get it girl look I got on time I keep you walking in the latest girl give me some p**sy please Thomas you doubt yourself when you say please I think you need a few more weeks to think about it I'm being professional but eden I doubt myself because your a** is so fat that me and myself can't get along together think about what he saying I'm only being a police officer Eden but you tell me that you're the one for me how am I supposed to know that you're not just going to up and leave me like the wind cause in the ground I made roots and my heart see through your window Thomas I'm right here thinking me daily while you do push-ups Eden I keep thinking about you when you by yourself keep a finger in a special place for me watch and see. This movie take off Eden see I'm working on you to see how you act soon Eden we both famous because there's no one not that I can handle us overhears your dreaMs. keep reaching Thomas I just marry people when the dreaMs. are where I can see you said that you marry people Thomas I got dreaMs. everyday put your hand in my hand I have you seen I do eden what do you think of that girl attitude Thomas Thomas give that a damn compliment you need to love me because I know exactly that I need you Thomas that's the sh*tt I was looking for girl I think that you are professional on the stand point of a boss a both needs a good supervisor you a good supervisor Thomas I'm the damn best supervisor send me my message I see how you working it ain't nothing to it the reason why I didn't tell you I love you is because there's too much work on my hands and eden I need you I love you be professional when you get your prize Thomas I'm working night and day I dream about you eden as you can see my a** get up for you your a** a get up when I let you know you have to when I let you know this d*ck is in need I will be there for you it's a movie you better get the p**sy I'm not trying to see your a** anymore you shouldn't have said that come on a** that's go girl im playing with you one more second here go my ring Eden professionally you've been the best thing that ever happened to me Thomas say what you want to but my a** is leaving Eden I'm putting my best foot forward kiss my a** for talking sh*t to me Thomas already Eden if that's the way you want it then pull down your pants my pants are down show improve it's magic ain't it you kiss my a** in public I'm thinking about kissing your a** tonight to after we make love Thomas tell me what is mine that a** is mine for the taking Eden send a message to me right now

I think about you Thomas Superman I can't help it if I'm in love with you Eden you need a hero to respect you and I can't Thomas I've been in love with you all my life and not do anything for you you need to take me with you cause I can't see myself doing without You Thomas everybody is going to kiss you when they read your book about the stories of a hero Thomas I got you in my heart and in my a** I'm waiting for you to kiss meyou don't have to wait any longer cuz then professional I got a movie deal off my d*ck in your a** I'm just reading Thomas I can't see myself making another mistake cause this a** is to fat to just give away keep a professional Eden I put you on this d*ck one of these days Thomas you hear me you would not to be so f*cking large that a d*ck would have to be huge in the area Eden my d*ck somehow knows how your a** thinks I'm moving with every motion is your p**sy wet for me be professional Thomas my p**sy don't get wet my p**sy gets ocean cant you see you are f*cking with a champion my book report eden is the most important thing to me in this Earth but your a** come before that so you want to a** keep it professional Thomas I'm going to get you paid with this a** I am keeping it professional my d*ck won't let me stand still cause your a** keep calling it how long has it been with me talking to you Thomas it's been about three weeks and I miss you and that a** more than ever Eden Eden can I put my business in your mouth that is it thomas can't you see them titties here they come home with loan liner generation you can't tell me sh*t about no Superman d*ck even though I didn't mean to offend you I thought your mouth and your a** was open let me see how much is it to get rid of a d*ck damn girl professionals looking at us I'm a hero and every one of them movies I'm the movies Thomas but I'm not no daMs.el in distress eat my p**sy Thomas you making me feel like you don't need me hush Thomas I see my p**sy trying to get to you Eden if you ever give me that one chance Ill make sure you have everything you need because my d*ck out here is strong enough to take over the world you going to get your chance you professional Mandingo Thomas if your d*ck is small I can't deal with it I need my d*ck huge just like my man is Eden the only thing professional about you is that fat a** and them titties and that beautiful face I'm trying to tell you girl my d*ck is huge I'm professional get up and me Thomas cause im open to you bulsh*t no longer Thomas I believe you you owe me a f*cking manion Thomas say you trying I might can work with you but if you bulsh*t on me I'm taking your a** outside and I'm going to kick it Thomas get your a** and then go right that movie right now I got a Superman in my life listen he knows what he's doing I done took him out the hood for contract like this come with come yourself you didn't need some push-ups can't you see I'm working on p**sy right now Eden Thomas professional see that your d*ck is not to be f*ck with my d*ck is not to be f*ck with because its lethal to Eden all kind of b*tches know your d*ck coming after me we help me get him off of me I like this I was almost ready to c*m but you made me stop it listen Thomas if you think that you are strong enough to be my man you going to have to do a whole lot of more push-ups to get to this a** Eden I'm trying to do more push-ups but my d*ck keep getting in the way I need you to hold it for me and come tie it down that d*ck must be huge it is what it is I can't complain I've learned to work with what I got so the p**sy is always satisfied everyone understands you told me you *ssh*les clean Eden I like it when you talk sh*t that's the only way I can kiss your a**es when you happy what I'm doing is trying to put more material into that a** Eden i want you to have everything Eden right now I'm almost satisfied thomas to win with me you have to be a strong individual you have to be business-minded with a strong hard d*ck and confident Eden I am confident and I'm open to new suggestions on how to put my d*ck in New horizons my New horizons got you working night and day Thomas keep up the good work and you can have this a** in your dreaMs. I'm making sure that my dreaMs. eden have you in them because you and I are a couple if we a couple stop eating p**sy Thomas imma eat your a** out and then I'm through with it eden I'm going to kick it cold turkey Thomas you sure that's what you want turkey cause turkey looks good on Thanksgiving I'm just saying to you you didn't don't make me have to c*m with you you don't understand Thomas everyday you trying to get you some a** and my p**sy is just too important to give away to any private d*ck on the street here my hero learn to control yourself this thing is bigger than you think I'm professional so I only want to work with you Eden you got a picture of your d*ck yeah I got a picture of it Thomas but it's kind of foggy you got to let me hold your d*ck for a second so I can take this photo you snap a picture of this d*ck and all kind of b*tches a be jumping on you eden yall see what my d*ck is half a man and half a billionair lets recalibrate this whole situation Thomas before we start moving too fast we were going to start f*cking for what I'm recalibrating Eden give me one chance and I'll prove myself to you this Superman d*ck is it's amazing you need to know me if you want me to know you come to me like a man is supposed to stop with all that talking sh*t okay Eden my name is Thomas and I like your a** my a** is strong enough to help you what kind of business are you in mutual funds eden I need your help raising them up girl I can't see myself handling business in this game here without you there to tell me the score that is exactly why I'm sitting up here reading these messages instead of calling you because I got to know that you have the ball to finish the job first see if I told you I was rich and successful you wouldn't believe me so I just do the work to show you girl that I got a Superman d*ck I'm working around the clock see I'm working around the clock to Thomas and keep it professional what we going to do is stack up ourbmoney and then talk to each other I like your d*ck attitude because it's real simple to see that you and your d*ck work well together girl I've been through so much bulsh*t that I'm hoping to find a new life I'm hoping that your a** is that for me in time I'll be there for you but you have to prove yourself worthy of a p**sy and a a** like this because I'm going to tell you something Thomas my a** is special I know you special that's why I keep trying to eat your p**sy because that's the only way I can get through to you about this business that we got on the table Eden boy if p**sy is all that you want why didnt you say so Eden don't say nothing about this eden but I've been thinking about you since the first moment we spoke on the telephone stop talking sh*t baby that a** is serious you want some p**sy if you want a wife you let me know okay eden I'm a hero and I'm doing my best to do my job to better the situation for my d*ck and your p**sy and a** and titties all over the place just think about what you just said to me talk to me again with lawyer present your d*ck ain't hard it a super it's just work Eden I see what is happening you don't trust in this d*ck but we can't let one mistake ruin a nation I'mma beat your a** Superman Eden girl if you need me just call my number cause I'm thinking about you while I'm writing these books right now you know how we do Thomas I promise you I'll call you but you got to wait for that p**sy to c*m there you go talking sh*t again you know my d*ck can't handle it that situation too tight for mesend me the message so I can think about it and think about how your d*ck might feel in my a** and p**sy Thomas this is some p**sy is Superman sh*t how long is your d*ck Thomas my d*ck is super huge Eden it stretches all over the globe that's why I need your a** to hold me down im going to let you eat this a** out but before I do say it with me

Thomas this a** is the only thing I came for this a** is the only thing I came for Thomas you got some sh*t with you I'm help you clean that sh*t up here eat my p**sy get strong and get back up on your feet I'm just talkin about having you suck my d*ck to make me feel better for the mistakes that I made eden I want you to know that in my heart you always Wonder Woman you need to know that I love you Eden always see Thomas I'm being professional that's why I'm not sucking your d*ck but when I do suck your d*ck its guarantee that you're going to come all over yourself so eden this d*ck all this d*ck is good in your a** hell know Thomas this a** is tight you better stop playing with yourself before you bust a nut in the place Thomas I got you c*mming by your damn self so why I want to give my good a** and p**sy to you see eden you looking at a d*ck that's done been through some stuff i'm a hero because I raised the p**sy up I don't tear down a woman you got to see who I am Thomas and then we can talk about your d*ck going up in my a** and my p**sy you Superman and im Wonder Woman we got this game on lock your a f*cking hero ain't you I'm sending the message to you right now EdenEden just think about me because I'm working all night and day and doing push-ups all night and day also just waiting for your call Thomas I do what I can but ain't no promise on these a** and titsI want to tell you Thomas that you're important to me and my p**sy feels everything that you said my d*ck is so professional that he knows when to act up and when not to Eden Thomas just send me the message and move out of the f*cking way I got this I'm professional so you think you want to be a boss Thomas look at me eden sh*ting on me with her a** on my lips that damn boy if you make me c*m boy I'll never write you this d*ck is with you Eden so turn in your work so let me see what I can do with this d*ck Thomas here go the message Eden I love you

Edem yo got damn panties missing today that's because you were chewing on them Thomas last night before you fall asleep in my bedroom Thomas you telling a goddamn lie that p**sy is what I chewed on you saying this a** didn't get none of you when you went to work Thomas Eden its just funny to me you had me over I went to sleep and now I got a p**sy smell against my face and a** i like you so I put my p**sy somewhere where you can rest good that's in your mouth and against your a** i like you eden but I don't want to be a birden so imma take my d*ck out of your a** and put it and send it home and you put it where it belongs get your a** in here and eat my p**sy like a f*cking told you girl can't you see I'm working Ill eat that p**sy all day at the next semester Thomas don't mess with me because my p**sy is mad at you for getting your d*ck in some sh*t my a** belongs to you Eden my d*ck is another story sweetheart I heard Thomas d*ck is king but a queen like this deserves a fat d*ck to keep her a** in Check sweetheart I'm listening to everything you got to say Eden and I'm going to tell you a big old d*ck like this deserves a queen like you to f*ck me thomas you need to tell your *ssh*le to come get me because my p**sy in my a** together they talking and you know what they saying that you dookie take your clothes off you see that print you in danger of a goddamn blow job eden it's Got damn blow job is raining right now I'm a send this message and I want you to get it to the press because your a** is working with me and I want you to know that I need you girl all you got to do is just send me the damn message I can handle my sh*t my a** is tight Eden I know you pissed off at me about what I said to you but that p**sy and a** girl has me worried about tomorrow you must remember that I'm a professional working woman with a degree on that a** so get your a** over there and send a message to Thomas eating you my f*cking hero baby that smart hero now send the f*cking message hero

Eden all these messages that I've been sending you are parts of my story hero don't you say you want me Thomas and your story not make it Thomas cause I believe in your a** more than you know l'mma tell you this be a professional you can have anything you want if you believe in me and you Thomas look and see if I don't hold you down there's only one thing that I want Thomas that's to see your d*ck come in first place you making me feel like there's a chance for me and you my p**sy aint able to handle the situation but my a** can deal with everything you got to give Thomas do you worship my a** and titties and p**sy Thomas I do worship you but what I'm saying is I'm getting my d*ck off the ground and it's hard to get noticed out here in the world especially by you Eden so you telling me that no matter what happens with your books and movies that you and I got a place in history I'm telling you that this a** it's always biding on your d*ck day and night Thomaslisten to me eden I got a choke this sh*t I can't be running around hurting all day and I need your a** to put me to sleep listen to me and I want you to get this f*cking clear if you put one hand on that d*ck without my motherf*cking permission by a** is going to sh*t all over you Thomas Eden this isn't my idea of a movie its just coming to me as I go I hope you understand that my d*ck is too hard to be working these nights alone I'm scared of yo D*ck Thomas that's the only reason I talk to you because I want you to calm down before you hurt my a** Eden you see that we can't do without each other we going to be in Hollywood if that a** and this d*ck come correct with each othercome with us if my p**sy is the bomb and you d*ck is professional count Your Blessing because we both might be some Stars off in Hollywood cause yo d*ck is the bomb with this p**sy Thomas oh sh*t you want to help me raise up my game take your panties off and throw them over here against the wall Thomas you can see on spanking you if I try to let your d*ck down you ain't going to do nothing but f*ck me in my a** Eden I can control myself my d*ck is a legend it belongs to the Greek gods of Justice as you look into my eyes your d*ck gets hard from speaking up to me Thomas I need you Eden Here go a movie called hero it's about your p**sy and my d*ck taking over the planet taking over this p**sy would sound better on the title Thomas Thomas I'm not knocking what you do but you need to take time to come together and handle this a** and p**sy because this a** and p**sy came together and they told me that your d*ck can't be touched Eden you got too much game woman for me you know that this d*ck enjoys that p**sy and that a** you can see my p**sy is throbbing Because of You Thomas you better tell me something quick cause I'm about to c*m all over the place you can see that d*ck is professional Eden I can't watch TV girl too much guns and violence all I wanted is and a** to make me feel safe so I can rest good at night I got yo too much you can handle this p**sy you can handle this a** in your mouth straighten up your game we trying to make it off in Hollywoody yeah Thomas one more thing if my a** wasn't that good I'll let you know but my a** is professional so you just sweat a b*tch you hear me Eden I'm doing my best to show you that I'm professional just like you are but if Holly wood wants to see this d*ck and that p**sy we can go do number rise to the occasion baby you my f*cking star checkmate it takes time for me to have a orgasm Thomas your checkmate was too immature i'mma tell you one thing say what you want to say about eden but she know how to handle a f*cking business man and that's the ballgame imma send a message but right now it's just my p**sy it wants you thomas so I'm saying send the message so I can handle myself eden you handle yourself I'm a put my d*ck up your a** we don't handle sh*t until we see what's up with these books and these movies you got me girl thomas send of the message Ill read it and c*m on myself manually that's what the game is about we heroes listen Thomas I want to be with you and you make my p**sy hurt too bad I need some time to think I love you eden you my hero we need a touchdown even so tell your a** to see me before I go any further with this book or these movies because I need to see you girl I love you my p**sy is not going to wait for person who's not have his game on capital I don't know what to tell you Thomas you need to raise your game up a little bit I'm a capitalize Eden on everything that I say to you my game is on smash I just need your panties to prove it get my d*ck across the dresser and send me my goddamn message Hero Thomas imma give you the last word because that p**sy deserves a chance to speak it's going down in history with this d*ck girl we heroesb you seem professional some of that you taste it says but don't tell nobody because this nookie ain't yours is mines send off the goddamn message Thomas my hero yes baby I'm going to send it to you but my d*ck is hard I can't think what am I supposed to do without you go ahead and send the f*cking message Thomas girl you my hero

Eden I'm trying to communicate with you on the professional tip I'm going out of my way to show you that I care about you and my movies are going to take me and you on top gorilla. This movie is just a single picture film and this a** is yours in need you girl Eden I got professional are you talkin to me Thomas yes I am eden but I do realize that your a head of the game baby we ain't no mutha f*cking joke eden look professionals are looking out for me how can I show you that I love you without money involved be careful Thomas people are talking about us I need you to do your work and I'm a hold my a** together professionally communicate with me Eden because I know that you want this d*ck in your life I just want you to know that you set me off with your words hello I will be with you Thomas if I could baby every time I try to do something right its always all kind of f*cking bulsh*t in the way I just can't understand it I love you Eden God I love you so much Thomas we working on a deal emotionally I'm sitting my a** on the chair until you c*m with me let me know if I'm holding my position long enough eden to make you scream your a** off I can't handle this sh*t a Thomas I'm putting my p**sy on the line to make you see that I'm a woman that would do anything to satisfy her man I need you honey step your game up say what you want to about this game eden I own to f*cking companies I made 200 business ideas and I'm waiting on money for them and I wrote 7 books and 3 movies I don't know about this but tell me what your game like my game is like this I get up every day and go to work and sit down and handle my mother f*cking business I look at the computer and work on the computer and answer the phones all day and then when I get tired and can't take it no more I go back home to sit down and take me a shower get me something to eat and I think about all the work that I had to do that day and I start the next day over again that's what my game is like Thomas Eden I didn't mean to offend you I just thought you might want to use my conversation to help you I'm professional Thomas tell me that you love me and I'll be okay you can contact me if you need me eden right now I'm at home just sitting back going through my phone thinking about you Thomas is you capable of handling a relationship and business at the same time because I need your d*ck strong to the finish yeah I'm capable of handling a relationship I just want you to know that when I get my money back I'm moving in with you everybody no that Thomas is getting money back but we want to see how you act with your d*ck in new shoes and new clothes Thomas Eden I'm going to tell you right now I don't give a f*ck about new clothes and new shoes all I care about is my woman and taking care of financial issues Thomas them girls on you what you think I'm going to do when the d*ck is mine this is a movie called hero that I'm making I'm sending it to you Eden for your approval I hope I didn't put yourself in a difficult situation cause my d*ck couldn't handle that Eden be straight with me Thomas are we famous or are you famous because my a** and p**sy need to know thats a movie right there eden I want you to know girl that people talk about us like we Stars and I appreciate that a** and that p**sy all the same I love you girl watch dude wake up Eden im taking over my p**sy Thomas if you want this p**sy you going to have to go out there four it I'm going to see if my d*ck has a time cause you professional wait on me Thomas can't you see eden that I'm waiting on you indefinitely see Thomas my p**sy gets tired of motherf*ckers lying to me talking about they going to be there for me my a** knows the truth Eden this is a movie that I'm writing called Hero please understand I understand how much you need me Ill hit you up as soon as I can please get back in touch with me if you want me you can call me listen Thomas I've been doing my thing ever since I was a little freshman in high school my a** know the rules so don't you ever question me about being professional my a** is beautiful and you like that I got to send this message to you eden I'm just trying to think of everything that I need to say it's just that you beautiful my p**sy beautiful and I just want to be with you Thomas we professional and we can have anything that we want just take your time and keep sending me my goddamn messages I love you Eden I know you love this d*ck I'm trying to get you to look out for me because I'm trying my best to be there for your a** in mine Eden I have to send you my message Thomas whatever you do don't hold back with this movie because I need you so much that d*ck got me going crazy be professional Thomas this p**sy you can depend on eden im telling you this d*ck is hard and when I c*m its going to be with you and you only you should see my p**sy Thomas imma play with it for you just to see you smile we trying to operate on a professional level take that p**sy over there and sit down Eden when I sit down Thomas it's going to be on your face cause a** don't go on the chair I'm asking you to send the message Thomas professionally your a** is the bomb Eden I'm going to send a message out right now cause my d*ck is hard I got you in my a** wet Hero that's my mother f*cking girl I love it you sweetheart Eden you are my hero Thomas

I know exactly what I'm doing for you Thomas damn eden every time I think of you you appear with that same dress on your a** my dress Thomas is representing my p**sy and a** as well get with the program Thomas there is a movie called hero coming as soon I see d*ck in your future Eden I got you get up on this p**sy if my dialog is professional then you giving me some a** as soon as I finish my manuscript Eden I wish you help me make up my mind about what it's going to be Thomas this p**sy or his *ssh*le be professional Thomas cause we both got to eat eden you can tell I'm blanking on this manuscript what I'm saying is my d*ck is the future and you're the queen long as I keep my composure and my p**sy ain't bothering you your d*ck ain't going to bother me I got dreaMs. of you give me the a** making me feel like a man is supposed to call this a dream Eden it is a manuscript and I love you girl see im sitting back thinking about all of the ways that I can hold that d*ck down stand up for your p**sy Thomas go all out if you have to make that manuscript real eden you know you on my mind so much that I can't even get my manuscript together the right way because my d*ck is so hard I know I'm thinking of you that's the truth im telling you right now Thomas if you cheat on me you'll never hear from this p**sy or a** again that's some truth for your a** eden raise up all kind of people looking at that a** listen to me Thomas stick your d*ck up inside you y'all got a professional on the loose listen eden my manuscript can't see your a** cause you wear that sh*t to tight that's a mutha f*cker realize what you doing Thomas I'm just sitting there doing my work and you got your d*ck all in my a** and face what are you doing Thomas first of all eden I'm just standing here in my position and my d*ck is here to stay I'm just saying that you are beautiful and I need a woman like you to step in and to show me the ropes Thomas if you serious about what you talkin about putting it on the dotted line people eden your a** is some kind of amazing maniac show me what you got for me and stuff for Christmas I'm producing your a** Thomas so you better be polite Christmas is here in this a** I guess that cookie don't want to be Eaten huh Eden listen to what you said to me my cookie love to be eat especially with some whipped cream and a plum to go up my a** i'm jacking my d*ck too much I need and opportunity to make a man out of me eden that a** look good Eden don't holler this the d*ck been looking for go head and show me the D*ck Thomas I'm taking my a** home you want to c*m with me girl I got to tell you this p**sy is everything that I could imagine it makes me dream of gum drops and peppermint scotch and berries I'm going to make you dream all kind of sh*t Thomas when your heart beating fast and your d*ck is in my hand what you going to do Eden I'm at a loss for words all I know is my d*ck is ready for another ten rounds I'm a established you as the man in my community but don't play with my p**sy Thomas you better to f*ck the sh*t out of me every night you hear that you better not be f*cking with me you want this d*ck Eden well I want you so let's make it happen on the manuscript take your a** in there and send off my message I got your a** with this d*ck on top eat my p**sy and you'll see who's on top Thomas listen to this Thomas Ill finish your book before you get a chance eat the p**sy I'm still working on the p**sy but yo a** already belongs to me eden didn't I tell you not to count your chickens before they hatch in your mouth what I tell you eden the first time I spoke to you I knew that a** was humongous if you want some eggs just say so don't be playing no games cause I'm a stay with you Thomas send a message off you didn't get to see much ill send a message off eden this movie is called hero that's you and me eden professionals are watching us but my d*ck is still hard Eden and you priceless that's it cause girl I need you I'm a see you your a** is on my mind I need you to handle your business Thomas I'm your hero Eden my manuscript starts with hero and the ends with money on that a** why don't you do what you supposed to do because I need you EdenThomas these are the days that my p**sy is all grown up so don't tell me what the f*ck I'm supposed to damn do Thomas unless you want some a** in your face hold up Thomas I just got one last thing to say I need you to understand that p**sy is more than dripping it's a waterfall over here listen and see you a professional f*ck this sh*t listen eden let's get married right f*cking now I'm your hero see now p**sy is on a shift that is if you looking for me you can email me anytime my a** can read that's all good and dandy but see now my d*ck keeps coming up with these amazing manuscripts that's if your a** care to listening listen Thomas that manuscript is a soldier I put my p**sy on it anytime day or night if you need your d*ck to work

I'm telling you eden you can look in my eyes and see that I want that a** and that p**sy and see I got an ego that helps me stand up you need to stand up for this p**sy and worry about that manuscript some other time cause tonight my p**sy all on you you ain't gotta go nowhere eden I'm taking my time to express it myself through the letters and manuscripts I hope that you see that I'm a nice guy I'm a business man make sure that yo d*ck can handle any situation because I no that your strong but my p**sy needs a champion and my a** needs a hero I'm a champion all of my life what you want to do with me Eden I'm going to work my a** off for you so they can't be no discussion about who the p**sy belongs to Eden f*ck that damn sh*t I want to eat that p**sy and go to bed girl I don't do no damn playing see my plan is listen my pedigree cuMs. second and your panties cuMs. first and then my work cuMs. imma send you the message listen to me Thomas if you want this p**sy you will continue to be professional all day and all night hold your d*ck I know it hurts but this p**sy is waiting for you girl you thinking what I'm thinking Thomas are you thinking what I'm thinking this manuscript is off the motherf*cking hook eden and you my mother f*cking hero a** up in yo face you my goddamn hero Thomas girl I'm telling you go ahead and marry me Eden if she call me girl that's your a** eden what my face and your p**sy is a perfect match for that a** Eden send f*cking message out Thomas before I put my a** in that mouth of yours I'm here baby

IEden this is going to be my last entry on my triple surprise story called hero Thomas listen to me this a** belongs to Me myself and I only Eden I was hoping you have sense enough to at least let me feel your a** once before the story ends some stories worked itself out without you making sweet delicious love you hear me Thomas right now I got stories and movies business ideas and companies that's a triple threat eden your a** ain't going nowhere what is it that you want from me Thomas my a** is looking good but it seeMs. like that's the only thing you want so I got to turn you down Eden after this story im a let you see the real side of Thomas in the bedroom can you handle my grip baby listen to me I want you but you have to make know noises in our bedroom cause this a** get frightened easy all I need is you to get past my fears and to stand up like the man that I am supposed to be in this world Eden well i also need things Thomas put my p**sy up on a pedel stool where no one can get it take me out of my community to a place where I can relax and listen to me when I tell you my a** is over my other contracts Thomas because that d*ck is the only thing that's waiting on me in my a** do you hear me thomas Thomas I know you have ambition Thomas I saw you dream last night and when you talk to me I'm a put you up on a pedal stool because with you Thomas my p**sy is waiting on you I need my trust in you to be King keep thinking Thomas these stories that you have are just a vision of our future if you work hard enough my a** to come to you Eden you know me girl I can't do nothing without my p**sy in my a** with me I've been watching you Thomas and you got to stand up for me and yourself I put in a couple hundred hours on your a** think of all the work that I'm doing listening to your stories ain't no a** that you going to find that's going to be there for you like mine Thomas my a** is the hero to you and your story eden operate on the level of complete splendidcy because when I finished with this that a** is going to be mushy listen to me Thomas take me out of this community my a** is tired of the stand still and to repay you my a** will let you eat your sandwich Enden I thank you the sandwich means the world to me I just need a couple pieces of lettuce to go on those tomato slices let me get my money is straight and I'll check you out before the end of the story if we're playing a game then I'm going for mine I know that you're a trillionaire Thomas that I'm making my a** available for eden promise me that you will wait for me until all of the stuff gets worked out because that a** is just too amazing for me to go without Eden that boy writing you is a trillionaire to the stars eden every time he writes you you look at me miss Athena ilI put my a** on the line for that boy eden your a** ain't the only thing that's going to be in trouble Thomas d*ck you read about in magazines Eden listen to me Thomas d*ck has rescued people Thomas is a police officer and a businessman tycoon you think he'll want me Miss Athena after seeing me listen to me Athena I'm going to give Thomas what he deserves a a** that believes in him and that will listen to him eden why don't you take a picture of your a** so I can see you eden yall give that boy contract you know me Thomas I just can't give away my a** for free that just wouldn't be in the rule book for princesses Eden I hear what you saying I've been a hero all my life and I'm going to save your a** call me Prince charming your hero watch yourself Prince charming I got people coming after me now that my a** is so fat you got no clue at what I'm doing with this d*ck in my hands cause the movie is the only way I can see your a** hero eden I'm going to ask you one last time to be my wife before the story ends I'm a Neel down on one knee with my sword in my hands I need you Eden please say youll be my wife I'm asking you Thomas to please be patient until I can make my decision because your manuscript is together but it's missing a little something eden what the manuscript missing or what the manuscript is missing is your hand in this dookie I call life right now eden take you f*cking a** to sleep exactly what I'm saying Thomas you don't respect me a Eden I'm just tired I've been working for a week day and night on this manuscript I apologize if I disrespected you I'm sorry if a hero saves me that would be nice but I'm always need you Thomas Eden you got to hear me I am Superman and this is your dream imma give you diamonds after the story is over you realize your dream is my dream are you playing to win it or are you playing a game Superman or Thomas I want to know Eden or Wonder Woman I'm playing to win this whole industry and I need my Queen beside me I can't be without your a** girl I'm Superman I am your Wonder Woman Superman but I am Eden too I want you to know what you dream of I dream of the d*ck is mine don't play no games with me Superman Superman can you hear me you are a trillionaire that needs a contract Thomas a look here the story doesn't end until I say so so if you're talkin to me say right now how you feel about this d*ck Eden Thomas come and get me as soon as the story end because I need you more than you realize just take your time eden Thomas will be right here I get a tingling in my drawers that must mean my cootie must be in danger call Superman Thomas your a professional music musician write a story that means something to people and Eden will be with you you got to trust yourself believe me I do the job that no one wants to do I see my dreaMs. so clear and right now see my dreaMs. on the computer screen Eden sit down for second girl all my dreaMs. are with you Superman i listen to you Superman and you make all my dreaMs. come true but I'm worlds apart from you that's why I listen to your stories so you can melt my heart and save the world Wonder Woman I listen to you with every single moment that pa**es girl enden I need my a** Eden I just have to be straight up because I'm Superman Thomas you need to take a break off that bulsh*t because somehow I Eden and Wonder Woman have found thereselves listen to me Thomas I'm making you head of household because you have demonstrated respect for all kinds of people your book is called hero and you need a contract to save Superman never once did you ask that you need a contract to save Thomas an injustice has been done what you think of Thomas is what we think ofwe are the Justice League and we need *ssh*les like you so straighten that your manuscript Thomas tell kristen beam that you love her she depending on you Thomas to wake your a** up you are famous in the community you got to f*cking CDs out two companies and 200 business ideas without having any children the back you down be professional Thomas you want Eden reid keep on telling me you want her because Superman we're depending on you we got to stand up ground people Eden reid is Wonder Woman I like kristen beam as Wonder Woman kristen beam is Lois Lane you know what that a** is mine Thomas you can talk to people but I care for you so much that it brings tears to my eyes listen Thomas keep sitting there writing that movie I'm watching you them White people listening and watching you realize that I can do nothing that you Dana Thomas speak to our people let them know what you are doing I'm putting together this movie called hero And I need Queen to help me deliver this content intact I just need my queen listen to me Thomas who are you after what queen are you at the Thomas I'm fighting for the love of Miss Eden reid and Miss kristen Bean that boy needs a major contract as Superman I can't be in two places at one time Thomas I'm asking kristen and Eden for there help because I've been alone for 15 years and my heart doesn't know what to do with all this money that I have I just think to myself how beautiful kristen is and how special eden is to me Thomas I need your help with something yes eden right now I'm working on this book and movies but you can count on me for anything that you need i need my contract Thomas to show my family that I am the Wonder Woman that you talked about in the book kristen what do I do you know what to do Thomas okay as Superman I give every woman in the United States a hundred million dollars a piece and in Canada a hundred million dollars a piece Every Woman goes to each and Every Woman I am Superman kristen will you tell Thomas that the contract is his d*ck in his britches me and kristen can't stop thinking about your d*ck Thomas I know that you both thinking about my d*ck but I can't because I'm a superhero thats put here to feed families and save these communities you making a fool out of yourself you need to put this a** in your mouth and just go to sleep somewhere Thomas see I put his a** in check because he keep calling me you damn right listen to me Thomas our movie is coming to a close take a bath and get you something to eat and think about the last portion of this film if the movie is good enough Eden reid will probably give me a call no matter where I go no matter where I be I will always remember that Lois Lane is kristen beam and Wonder Woman is eden reid and we are the Justice League heroes listen to my heartbeatI just realized that the Justice League is full of women fighting for what's right I see you girl talk to that girl Thomas cause she needs some guidance from a hero Superman The flash doesn't possess the abilities that I do he dosent possess the powers I am one with nature I am one with your a** when its in a jam keep on listening people challenging megirl I need to see you on the movie screen with me don't say nothing I know that a** is okay Wonder Woman talk to me it's that I need your a** Eden you got to talk to me to kristen let it be known the court system is not playing not even with heroes pick yourself up Reign our Justice League is full of heroes women and men we just wanted you to realize who you are Eden and Thomas before the story ended Eden reid is now called Wonder Woman for the rest of the term of her life and Kristen beam is Lois Lane of the daily planet for the rest of the term of her life Thomas this movie is based on true events you got to admit Thomas that you are Supermanjust make sure that the women in the US and in Canada all get $100 million dollars a piece and I'm Superman for anybody every day what about these other superheroes kristen I mean Lois Lane what do you want me to do Superman I want you to give evenly shares of your money to everybody all over the Justice League Wonder Woman is also how you feel yes it is Superman listen as this day I want this to go in the record and set the past that all the 900 trillion or whatever it is is set for all the people in the Justice League men and women will split the momey evenly in the Justice League Eden Wonder Woman is there anything else that I'm forgetting you need to contact kristen Beam and have her to understand that you're working on a movie called Superman And His Allies hero that's the movie Thomas girls if you need me I'm sitting at home just waiting on a response from eden reid and Kristen Beam take your time and talk to me Thomas you Superman listen to me Thomas you ain't gotta prove no point to nobody just closed out the movie like you supposed to we love you you ain't strong enough i'm making sure the women get there Money in the US and Canada $100 million dollars a piece and I put this on doc*ment for the courts to hear I'm Thomas allred Junior and I am Superman and this is our movie called hero based on a true story I did exactly what I'm supposed to do eden my manuscript is on your desk read it and don't judge me I'm doing the best I can I'm just a hero I need my a** realize that your more than a hero you're my motherfuking man Thomas now I got to businesses that have got to be straight before the end of the movie realize I need you if kristen needs you she going have to see you on the big screenEden I know you proud of your position but as Wonder Woman you have to be aware that that a** is all mine I'm Lois Lane and putting a bid in for his d*ck Thomas I do what I have to do because they program me to you know I love you and inside of my heart you know its real when I tried to contact you kristen all kinds of people went crazy I'm Superman I need to speak to you Miss Lois Lane I wish you would make love to that woman Superman you know how long I've been working on this contract maybe 6 or 7 years I'm coaching you back to your feet to where you would stay with my a** on your side I'm asking for you to give me a chance Thomas this is Kristen Beam my alias Louis Lane I've never seen no one so beautiful after looking at the two of you ladies kristen I want you in my life and eden I need you Lois Lane, you are my Wonder Woman and Wonder Woman you are my Lois Lane I need the both of you to be my wives cause ladies look how far we've come in just a few weeks I got my manuscript or our manuscript is ready for the press and two ladies that love me and love each other Thomas Superman the movie is called hero who's heart are you going to break when your check come to you see as Superman when I'm saving my people I feel like a hero but when it comes to you and all the ladies Lois Lane my heart gets broke and I feel defeated Kristen who's accusing you of breaking hearts Superman me or Eden Lois Lane and Wonder Woman I love you both I just need to stand up for myselfI see the movie for what it is and you are and *ssh*les to think you can take advantage of people SupermanI'm walking to my neighborhood Superman and I'll see you as the criminal that you are a heartbreaker Wonder Woman we've already established ourself as a good woman and a good man kristen I need you to go to the daily planet and tell them our dream even Lois Lane was smart enough to come back to Superman so why don't all you ladies of the world do the same and come to Supermancan you hear me Thomas keep it straight and Wonder Woman a be right there with you my a** and everything Eden you look like you're about ready to go to sleep so I'm going to dream about you all night and all day long until your dreaMs. come true Wonder Woman superman I had you at my house last night you just couldn't make my a** understand either your side of the story that's why on my desk is your manuscript I keep it near my a** do you want it Superman kristen beam and Eden reid our story is finished and here's the manuscript our forever ever after starts Now what just happened kristen Eden I don't know about you but I think that Superman just ended the storyto prove that Superman is the true king take this story to the y'all can see who Superman is when that book and movie get published and come out thats Lois Lane speaking to the crowd I know that kristen has your back Superman that was nice of you to say Eden it appears that you are a super hero after all Wonder Woman realizes the truthit's Superman is my man Thomas focus on my a** this a** is special so what we going to do Superman kristen you helped me through a hard time and I love you but I need Eden because she's beautiful and her a** stays on my mind realize Thomas that you can help millions of people and your sitting here thinking about a** and p**sy what kind of hero are youI have to stop for a minute I just now woke up to Eden and kristen both that I'm in love with them it started out as a story for fun I love you Eden and Kristen and I'm just now recognizing that people all over the planet need my help and I am Superman I'm going to give money to where needs to belong to and as Superman I'm going to make it to where every woman has the right to have any job she want to in this world as long as money provides it takes time to understand that people are dying and need help from me or super policelisten to me I am Superman and my money will go to sit and homeless children all over the globe when I think about it my heart goes out to those stranded they can't get to the family members all over the globe I'm standing here myself needing the family to help me go on Thomas I'm with you on this endeavor that we call the Justice League and my name is Superman I am Wonder Woman and I am Lois Lane don't pretend Thomas this is not a movie yes it is it's called hero I love you Kristen Beam and Eden reid we do have us a new champion Thomas allred Junior we crown you Superman of the new rim all we need Thomas is your signature that all the women get that hundred million dollars a piece that you promised them all over the world Superman those women out there Thomas helped you to become Superman everybody still waiting for the movie that's called hero I'm just thinking that you can do a little something for a children cause you know that we need your help Superman listen to me Superman I'm just trying to make you see that the girls in the world are there for you just listen to there voices I got you your contract because you have proving to be a hero that somebody can trust whoever be mean to you Thomas take your pencil and write that down the women know that Superman is the true king listen to me Thomas as Superman if you pick Kristen and Eden they are both true queens of the world Thomas you got to think it Eden Wonder Woman stood by you this is a true Queen and Kristen made you fall in love when you needed someone the most that's a true Queen also we got four more minutes in the show is about to be ended Superman I will take on every challenge head first in our communitycongratulations Superman you now are the king of this universe you may kiss your wives I noticed that you look baffled as somewhat Superman do you want this p**sy Thomas than send me my message Thomas you need this contract than act right and get your money together Eden and Kristen I know I dreamed of you ladies as superheroes but need your a**es right now so I can go to sleep the end and they all went to sleep heroes get a boy contract Eden my manuscript is on your desk let the community know that I am Superman and I am a hero of here and the first chapter take all my work and put it together to make a movie of the century Eden eden be kind to yourself because that a** is all I can think about Eden mix and match all of my work until you have a story focus Clean and clear where you can see my queen Thomas don't tell Eden how to do a job I don't know you eden but your a** is cool with me I do respect you for your kind words kristen you hold it down we got Superman this manuscript isout of control Thomas talk to me about you saving the world how you plan to do it if you Superman I plan to make inventions that will help and heal the sick people's lives are in danger so imma do the best I can to be there for them everyday with everything that I know how I want to ask you one last question Thomas okay go ahead now that you're famous would you speak to the people and tell him how you feel about me you got 30 seconds Eden kristen I love both of you with all my heart I'm crying and my feelings and my emotions feel like they're going to explode I want to be with you both and a true man is with you I'm praying that you understand me be my wive and understand the love that inside of my heart that is why they call me Superman I guess you automatically know that kristen and I Eden want to be with you Thomas you are a true Superman and the hero of our world you are a hero forever Superman Wonder Woman and Lois Lane and Superman are King and Queens we heroes Thomas eden and Kristen yeah Superman

I'm the last f*cking hero eden your bank account won't be full until this book and these movies is complete the thing about your bank account is that you need my bank account to go along with it so I can help you see how a hero is supposed go into your bank account my zurek numbers 7771 I'm a police officer Eden I play this game for real but our community thinks that you're going to leave them high and dry Thomas Eden ain't done nothing but keep my word all of my nlife eden I love you can I have a shot Thomas I care about you for the man that you are I hope you realize that this is your dreaMs. and I don't want you to play with my a** Thomas I look at you and your dreaMs. as a man that knows exactly what he wants if you're Superman tell me how It feels to have my a** in your hands it feels so amazing we finally looking at stardom kristen I can't ignore you now you know me for who I am Catwoman I'm telling you right now this d*ck belongs to Wonder Woman and Lois Lane Catwoman we got to talk about this both of you back away from me and let Superman talk game because I'm his true woman in this whole city knows it Thomas we done been down this road before Superman you need to talk to me Catwoman I want to be with you but you need to take off your mask so I can see you cause my heart beat faster when I'm looking at you you know who I am Superman that is enough for now Catwoman made a mistake to come into our life at this point Catwoman is no other than Elizabeth Elizabeth the real estate investor Superman its gotta make sense she comes and she goes and you don't even see her maybe you a superwoman Elizabeth I'm a cat woman and I will have my revenge on Superman for leaving me Thomas Lois Lane knows exactly what I've been going through I need kristen near me all the time second time Superman around have you figured out which woman you want Wonder Woman Eden when I think about you I think about Catwoman and Lois Lane all three of you are on my mind I need you to stay Wonder Woman Thomas you chose listen to me I can help you Thomas your a** is Superman listen to me Thomas all we got to do is write down our story in our phone and send it off to Eden Wonder Woman is a future every time I see you I'm thinking of f*cking you up ThomasCatwoman this d*ck is confidential so you can not scratch your way into it Elizabeth you know what I do for you Thomas I've been trying to teach you that you are a man of steel and not no joke Elizabeth I wanted you since the moment I saw you but business is calling me elsewhere I just have to think about this for a moment to myself while you think about this kristen beam is all over the news she telling people that you gave all your ideas to her Superman is it true Superman Wonder Woman our hero has fallen Wonder Woman I gave my ideas to Kristen because I knew she would do more good than I would Lois Lane is a true champion Eden all three of you ladies have good instincts and good potential so Elizabeth your three are beautiful so will you marry me alone with Kristen and Eden Catwoman you are Superman and you deserve your pleasure I will marry you and take my place on the throne Thomas there's only one condition you need to write down everything you thinking because Catwoman has a lot of cats to feed Eden the rest of the world thinks that you and Superman are just friends Tell Me Wonder Woman if you love me I said I love you Thomas but Superman is famous Superman I will marry Superman and take my place on the throne Eden Lois Lane what are you going to doI will marry my Superman I've been in your life longer than anybody else try to treat me with respect and I'll be there for you Superman you need to show the community how to act with or without you because this p**sy is coming to you and you going to have to be there to receive it Superman Lois Lane Catwoman has been here by your side through everything you went through Thomas Elizabeth I want you to know that me and you are more than just friends girl you my wife and I need you Elizabeth Zena warrior Princess is battling for your contract Thomas look Thomas I'm here for you and I've been here for you ever since my conception on this Earth I need Thomas and Superman to know that Superman contract is worth everything to Zena warrior Princess if Zena battles for my contract Louis Lane is open for suggestions about Zena warrior Princess Zena you can't have his contract because it's mine and I am kristen beam a police officer well my name is Evelyn and I believe the Superman has a thing for me and my a** Eden I know you wonder woman what I'm saying to you is I have a Superman contract that I'm given to all the women of the world if they can prove yourself to me im with you on that Superman contract Thomas you just got to stop and think for a second what my a** is worth to you because of me Thomas your books and movies will be read in front of millions across the globe my girl is eden my girl is Kristen Beam my girl is Elizabeth my girls Evelyn I'm Superman I and these movies are selling off the shelf there's only one thing left that you got to do Superman get the world to understand that you love us for I'm calling now for the help from all the superheroes and super women in the United States and surrounding areas this is Superman and I come to you with the humblest respect asking you to please help me marry my superwomen I got to see what you are to help you in this world that we call Gotham City just stick around for a minute and I'll prove myself to you as Superman Thomas allred Juniortransfer my money into my account and I'll do things for you that you can't even imagine listen if you don't respect me then who will respect me this is Superman the last hero asking everybody not to give up our pay day will come my ladies are watching this game as we play it Superman to my friends I'm called Thomas allred Junior I got to get this contract over to the ladies Superman is still going to be a hero no matter what goes wrong with his money I need a contract you'll get over it Superman say you prayers Thomas give me what I asked you for I'm the boss of Imperial designs LLC and Stratosphere I made over 200 business ideas that save people's lives if I'm not Superman the new is the people have come to a decision Superman sit down and write and your movie I need protection for my women and for the women all over the world here superman I done seen you take on tremendous competition you are ready to receive your contracts as the ruler of the world kingdoMs. we Grant Superman the access to every Superwoman in this world furthermore if there's another superhero out there who believes hiMs.elf to be better than Superman he must go through seven challenges first before pursuing his bride its the queen that sets the challenges for each superhero and Thomas you past yours all seven times woman called Thomas our Superman every last woman in the United States will help you out with your contract Superman if we live dude respects you for being able to fight against evil and stand up and save a child and saved the world Thomas you are Superman beginning Thomas just listen to this verse there's not one person in this world that could have done the things that you've done imma make sure that you have everything that you need to help you along the way in this journey that we call life people are watching you act responsible and my people don't waste time in crowning a super hero that's if you want to be crowded Thomas I do want to be crowned be professionalI could have sworn Thomas with Superman because he loved the cartoon but as I looked at him he seemed like a man of great statue this man is coming back from a gunshot wound will you saved a man life and testified on the stand without even making a mistake then you work at these companies into your heart give out and you couldnt stand anymore you didn't say one word when your girlfriend left you all you did was let her leave and then cry we call you Superman Thomas allred Junior because no matter what it is you go through your attitude remains the superhero in the companies that you have it's a good thing because we have a plan for you and your family of superheroes what is itit is another level that you will be on that's why if you finish that book I can help you to concur your fears and help you be with all the women in the world that you want that exactly the Superman you deserve to be being with all of the women is your destiny and your calling can I say something the second time I was around I thought women liked to see me in pain and in agony no Superman we wanted to help you because we knew that the challenges were evenly matched can't you see that I've been through all kind of things they murdered my wife at a young age Superman we fought for you everyday in the business sector the things you dream of all reality in the world today looking at my dreaMs. yall will find a way to be a people again with or without the games this is Superman we love you and we did a kid our lives to helping you succeed the how many of you women feel that wayevery last one of us Superman we're here Thomas we're here for you so how many professional wives do you have Thomas I don't know could you please explain them to me you have a wife for every challenge that you've been through I've been to so many the 17 beautiful women is waiting to talk to you besides your four challenges is hard to count 17 and 4 is 21 you have twenty one wives that's waiting for you to approve there contract that haven't been touched did we major Thomas Superman yes ma'am you did what do I have to do to have my family take your a** to sleep and send that message off look Thomas you seem like a really nice person and a hero just realize that your getting a chance that no one else in the world gets now I got 21 wives to companies i have 200 business ideas two music CDs and books and no kids why in the world have you blessed me because of you we can see our visions clearer with the sunlight in your path our reasons are clear okay will you tell every last one of my wife every last one of my wives all over the world that I love them and I need them people love you Thomaswe are granting you access to every woman in the whole wide world Thomasall you had to say is that you are Superman the champion and you will get a queen be strong and look on the bright side you were down for so many years but you pa**ed every single challenge we gave to you I just want for my woman and my family to be okay Thomas thomas I'm a ask you if you could start over again what's the one thing that you would want in this world to see all of the beautiful women smile this what I would want Thomas you know you pa**ed your final test to get you a woman think about that sh*t Thomas I want you to listen to my heart I need you to Thomas now that the sh*t go as for me my contract is heavy I need you to know that being the champion of the world means that you must step to all the women exactly like a Superman you are today you see how we programmed you Thomas they watching you everywhere you go who are watching me the secret service and the FBI so you finally see that you are the champion that everybody talks about all over the country Mr. Buy it listen to me you don't have to do nothing but send me the text message I am Superman I'm the champion of the world I'm a champion your a** if you don't send me that message one more thing Thomas

Superman was a hero and always will be ladies Superman a champion hero Miss Eden Reid my book is coming to a close ain't mean to say that I meant to say movie there are other stuff that I want to deliver through email to you and I hope that you enjoyed your read of this movie that I called hero Eden I'm begging you to ride with me through this life hills and valleys there's only one thing that's missing from this movie script Eden I want you to know I love you King Superman Eden I want you to be my wife all entries are complete enough walking through fire I seen a shadow and it was my angel saying believe in me and I got trust in you Eden cause you're the angel that I've been dreaming of my whole life long Superman hero to you and the rest of the world girl give me my contract see my contract is your love Eden that's the angel I'm dreaming about girl you an angel and my hero listen to me thomas we need that contract for self Kristen I realize that you and Evely need my contract but I'm trying to tell you that all the people are waiting so lets start the book over Elizabeth you telling the truth Thomas in there movie called heroremember Superman that your contract is professional I got you 21 women thats waiting on you so send your booking one mistake hero and your life with your girls and your movies and books are finish go ahead and cool off superhero we doing all the work Thomas I thank all of the professionals for helping me through when I didn't have no one to talk to me and to Chris and Keisha I give my deepest regards and love to my brother and sister Mama I'm trying to take you places that we never been before I'm happy that you working truly yours Thomas allred Junior Superman this is the conclusion of the movie Hero manuscript Eden i got a plan for my movie if I can just get you to talk to me on the phone I trust you Superman and Eden taking over the country with Catwoman and Lois Lane Kristen Evelyn and Elizabeth these are the super Women that saved my life from kryptonite baby I get you now I'm going to send the message zena warrior Princess and Wonder Woman Superman's wives of the century this is the conclusion of this movie walk out the theater in here to your cars I'm just messing with you making myself look good Eden boy be professional I know you want this a** in your mouth hell yeah I do because I'm the hero Superman it's one thing left to do Superman

I want to be with you because is our next door eden because when I look at you I can see myself in the captain's position making sure the world's okay I'm just a coward without you Eden I know my position is behind my woman Eden you are a star in my dreaMs. and horizons I remember you emailing me the first time we talked on the phone and you have no idea how much I think about you and hope that your my soulmate I want to be with you because every day has been different since you and I spoke on the phone I just want to be with you because you're the best thing in my life right now Eden a know you need a professional in your life and I'm here for you you got to see me eating I'm doing push-ups every weekend and working on the weekdays I want to be with you because there's no one else that deserves this contract you have proven to me that your worthy of the crown eden you got the whole world screaming your name because of this book I guess to be with you or to see you I'm a have to contact your agent we got b*tchitis be professional Eden I want to be with you because I knew if I be with her when life will change for the better I'm waiting for you to tell me that your number is my number so I can stop playing with you in this book and we can both go home if you stroke my pencil make me want you more and more eden when I look in your eyes I see my future you know me eden I never give up this book is dedicated to you and our love is forever eternal I got to prove myself to you Eden excuse me our love is calling I'm working daily just trying to make some sense out of why your not calling me you can tell Thomas anything Eden I want to be with you I know you feel like you owe me Eden but you don't I'm Superman and I care for you you see what happens when a person works too hard all they heart comes out on paper I'm training myself to make this right a hundred million goes out to my beloved lady eden she is my queen of the world girl I can be with you right now I'm just too congested with thoughts I won't give in until you have second thoughts about you and I because I need you so much baby I want to be with you because it's a long hard road back to where I started from and your the only one that can pull me through it I'm writing so much dialogue that my hands are so damn tired of from thinking about you if you want Thomas to let me know this is Superman I'm going into the contract eating and I hope you deal with me at the finish line Superman I believe in myself because eden you have helped me through everything Thomas any more food left I'm hungry and I need to eat something Thomas listen to me Thomas take over the world if you want to but you still can't have eden because that girl is to fine and she mine Superman Superman if you don't mind that a grown man handle this Thomas I might not be from this world Thomas but my strength is real and even knows the truth Superman I'm giving you one chance to go home pack up your sh*t cause eden is with a superhero named Thomas already Junior see Thomas I heard that you can handle your business so I guess you handle your business with me some other time because my girl ain't feeling you Superman Superman and Thomas y'all need to cut that sh*t out even belongs to me give me my muthaf*cking paper b*tches Mr. ebony buy it there's only one thing I got to say you messed up when you lost eating Thomas Supermansee I know this sh*t aint motherf*cking happening tell the both of them to get in the room I'm going to whoop they a** Mr. Ebony Buy it and you have Monopoly because I gave it to you Superman just like ebony buy it to start sh*t and can't finish it my wife can handle that light work Superman I've conquered every challenge thats been sent my way ever since I was a motherf*cking kids Superman Thomas I'm too professional for you ebony buy it and Thomas Eden's heart belongs to me Superman I guess we can call it a draw cause your a** is mine ebony buy it I'm the champion of my ring and that's why eden takes after me Thomas see the attitude you portray Thomas Thomas tell the people I really bad you are without your woman Superman talking to you b*tches is like going in my room with no clothes on it's cold as hell eden help me out going to fix me a sandwich ebony buy it i see now you know what the funny thing about this is I know that Eden is mine because I sent her my manuscript and she read my book Thomas Allred Jrain't going to deal with you Thomas cause that book you write in his mouth book Superman officer Reign want to speak to Eden your messing up with your conversations with other people I'm here to keep you safe officer Reignof the rain be sincere with your approach to eden I got a 12 bedroom mansion ebony buy it I know exactly what you looking for Rein y'all this girls had to please so imma give her my whole f*cking world Superman lady I keep thinking that how come we never spoke on the phone until now I come to the conclusion that you are an angel and I need my wings from you Thomas Allred Jr Eden I know it's too late to stop me here's the book that I wrote I love you Superman a girl what we doing here is debating on who loves you more and I'm telling you girl I'm a mother f*cker to knock them all-out ebony buy it eden what's going on here I don't want to lose you so I'm giving you my word that you in heaven in my arMs. Thomas allred Junior you ain't got a clue about what you up against the girls love me I'm Superman king of the world and I got eden on my arm Thomas Superman how many Pampers both y'all need to clean up all that sh*t you talkin ebony buy it you can talk all that sh*t you want to but love is a three-letter word I do Thomas Allred Jrthe boy to professional the operating on bulsh*t Eden come on Ill take you someone where we can get something to eat your record is up for grabs Superman I'm coming from my woman you and Ebony buy it can kiss a** motherf*ckers Thomas Allred Junior I don't listen *ssh*leslisten Thomas keep on telling her you love her because my girlfriend only need one push to break your heart forever Superman does some cold as sh*t ebony buy it officer Reign of the New York Police department says no matter who she chooses I'm still going to take care of her my girl officer Reign you might as well give up officer Reign cause I didn't come to this world for no bulsh*t eden is my queen of the century Superman im saying the sh*t might be hard to y'all but to me it's a piece of cake the book going to sell out the damn market with me on the cover Eden come with me it's a piece of cake ebony buy it I hope you ensured yourself ebony buy it I've been working on bulsh*t all motherf*cking day officer Reign I don't need no backup I'm just upset that y'all want to talk to my girl when we supposed to be cool Superman I know that your helping me superman but the truth is I'm in love with Eden and I just want you to be happy for us Thomas allred Juniorand I feel the same way he does Superman I'm in love with eden she makes me laugh and smile please respect our relationship ebony buy it you ain't got coming since they have relationship everybody Supermanimma just sit back and let a grown man get the best of another grown man before I kick both their a**es over Eden office Reign y'all listen to me there's only one way to solve this lets ask Eden who she want Thomas allred Junior who wrote the book Thomas Allred jr. And who wrote my movies for me Thomas alreadyJunior eden you know that this ain't no joke with me send you all this material I hope you respect the fact that I want to here from you so already telling you so you're in for a treat with the story I'm writing right here so get ready get to a seat cause I'll be back in like two minutes with more of I want you because.

Eden I know this may seem a little complicated but I find you attractive and I would like to know if I could possibly become your husband I want you to cause I got to know Thomas Allred Junior this is my world Thomas and eden is going to share with me Superman I done lost the game but my a** runner up in the next enning ebony buy it I'll be with you guys but your a** has to stop fighting over me my a** can't take all this fighting Eden Reid you know what they say kristen if anybody Thomas and Superman you can lead a horse to water but you can't make him drink you motherf*ckers I'm a baseball rookie office Reign excuse me for a second can I talk to Eden sweetheart I bought you a diamond 10 carat solitaire ring for your birthday I just want to know where you live so I can give it to you Thomas Allred Jr Ebony says you're not getting no ring you going to get my foot up your a** if you don't get on the phone and talk to me Ebony buy it my heart just meditate on your love just lays my heart between your legs and hold it there I kiss on you all the time you need to know that I care about you and my love is here for you always and forever Superman it's just like this Eden that my love to drop drops in your head give up a room in your house and let me come roommate with you I'm almost finished with this book Eden I want to see you because girl you been running through my mind all week this is my interlude here eden be professional but when I see you you will be butt naked Eden are we okay Eden I told you this book will be off the meter so you will believe in me I work day and night for two weeks Eden this opportunity that you gave me means the world to me I hope that we have the opportunity to speak and share warm conversation over some lunch you can speak to her all you want love a boy but I'm getting them panties ebony buy it you ought to see how he got you eden calling me cause he won't leave you alone officer Reign and Mr.. Monopoly says eden I see that you having a problem with my boys I tell you what I'll give you a free spin and you can take a trip around boardwalk with me Mr.. Monopoly Superman mad as a motherf*cker okay Eden and Mr.. Monopoly since you want her so bad I might as well leave the planet alone because without eden I'm not a superhero anyway Superman Matt Dillon coming for Eden see Eden I done rescue some cutie pies in my days but you had to come and break my heart Matt Dillon The Lion King I am Simba and I need you eden to the stop messing around you can have my baby if you want to The Lion King Batman look at you eden crying for nothing I own the whole entire industry eden wipe your eyes and come with me

Batman Batman already told you don't mess with my girlfriend I'm getting ready to talk to a woman named Kristen Beam I called her Lois Lane Superman ebony buy it the only one that got some sense both of you can kiss my *ssh*le Ebony buy it look at all this bulsh*t right here all this d*ck and ain't none of us got no p**sy eden just read the manuscript and get back to me officer Reign if Thomas aint going to serenade you correctly I get down on my knee and give you a ring officer Reign Eden I'm not thinking about all the bulsh*t that they all be talking I been waiting for the moment Eden that you and I could start talking I need you and my manuscript dose to Thomas Allred Jr I'm am Simba the Lion King and eden I'll treat you like a Queen in my jungle Eden did I catch a smile it's all good Eden that's what I'm here for I need time to get to you to be continued later on this evening The Lion King Thomas Allred Jr listen Thomas I like you but I have work that I have to do check my messages eden okay Thomas I'm a get to you Superman Ebony buy it is here also darling we're threw Thomas I need some rest Thomas just let me get one hours worth of sleep okay eden but I just want to tell you this that I need you to work on this manuscript for me thank you for understanding Thomas you need me you can call me what I think about you cutie pie I love you Thomas Eden Reid gimme one hour to fix myself up Superman one hour Eden Reid because your very special to me Thomas Allred Jr Superman.

I want to be with you because you won my heart of a phone conversation I want to be with you because you true to your words happy anniversary I want to be with you because you care about me Eden Simba the Lion King wants to be with you eden because your heart is the heart of the jungle Superman wants to be with you eden because it's you that guides his strength ebony buy it wants to be with you eden because he says it's the right thing for you to do ebony buy it batman The Dark Knight wants you eden eden I put myself in your position try to be with me if you can Batman the dark Knight listen to Eden you professional Superman wants to be with you Eden it's just that I know I'm too good for this planet but I'm here for you eden and you only girl I love you talk to me Superman Eden listen this is Officer Reign of the New York Police department eden Superman is good Ebony buy it is good Simba of The Lion King is good but a** is what I want if you looking for a contract get in touch with me officer Reign excuse me Thomas ebony buy it want to use your cell phone do you think he can hell no Eden I'm offering you a contract ebony buy it Superman Batman The Dark Knight and Simba a contract we don't get to do that much talking Eden but my love for you is worldly Thomas allred Junior you know me Thomas I'm disrespectful to people that don't use the letter or my steps eden Reid Eden i told you I want my own place and your place is as good as mine so I might as well move in with you a move over that a** is mine ebony buy it I'm Superman and eden this planet is yours for one kiss of your lips I'm Superman think about me I'm The Dark Knight and I've been held back too long for my satisfaction I can bust through walls because I need you so much talk tonme eden I'm The Dark Knight Batman eden going to tell you what to do after you suck her foot for about ten minutes in some hot and cold water Miss Athena I knew the girl before any one of you and yall trying to take my woman be professional ebony buy it if isnt one thing it's another that's why it manuscript is blazing like the sun eden Superman that man is going to get that girl you wait and see Simba the lion king take a break on that sh*t eden I care for you Batman The Dark Knight all I hear is game eden Superman the world King Batman and Superman cannot be together Eden Reid Ebony Buy it said if they want the damn girl they got to come and fight me for her hand in marriage Ebony buy i already gave you a contract ebony buy it Superman and Batman don't make me pull your coats tells Thomas Allred Junior your new identity remains suspect until we finish this manuscript get get off your a** I love you eden I'm a cop you should come and get with me office Reign officer Reign who expected you to want a piece of a** you muthaf*cker ebony buy it Simba from The Lion King needs to speak to you Eden I will protect you eden I will protect us eden we all one under the sun Simba the lion king rest in peace to those corny a** lyrics of y'all y'all need bank on me save that sh*tt you offering you know that sh*t ain't going to fly with me you think Id give up on that a** no way I need eden like I need air to breathe I'm officer Reign hold up did you say you need a** like you need air to breathe a little dude I'll let you kiss my a** all day long if you Eden say I can Matt Dillon I don't know what to do if eden won't let me get with her I'm taking My chances and multiplying the situation what's the worst case scenario I'm alone for another fifteen years Eden i need You Batman The Dark Knight I don't know what to do its just that they all seem so good to me it's just officer Reign face to me keeps sticking out let me talk to him and see what's up reigns face eden reid made this comment see Thomas what am I going to do with you what am I going to do with myself sitting at home feeling sorry for yourself everyday get up and make yourself a business person that's not what a business person about eden Reid Eden there one thing that I forgot to tell you Eden I'm the richest man in the United States of America that's why I'm sending you these books and movies because I can't be there in person to tell you that I love you Thomas Allred Junior eden I love you the Lord put me here to protect you and keep you safe just give me one f*cking chance to prove myself eden I love you so much Ill take good care of you officer Reign I got to take my time and tell you the world is yours if you could only look at it through my eyes eden Batman The Dark Knight eden before you say no to me this is Thomas Allred and I'm in love with you come and hear me out edenI speak to you eden because I don't have anybody else in my life that I can talk to I'm doing the best job I can on my books and my movie manuscripts I want you to realize that I do anything for you to come back to me I'm going through hell eden because you don't know what it felt like you felt like I an angel talking to me girl I want you because I need you in my life to make me stronger and tougher and wiser you going to have to admit that I keep trying until I get an answer on that a** Eden sweetheart I'm going to put my heart go down as payment for a night with you Eden I'm doing everything I can to help you understand that I'm a businessman and a tycoon if you don't believe in me just call me and we'll work it out and work the manuscript together put your game on Thomas my motherf*cking a** is beautiful Eden Reid your whole city eden want Thomas you got a nerve asking me for a my a** Thomas prove yourself and then we can talk eden Reid there's simply know clue at how much I love you Thomas i've been waiting on this Thomas since I was a little bitty kid tell me that you get your manuscript finished Eden Reid my eyes has been set on you since we talked eden girl I'm a professional your eyes is the key to my ambition let's talk and see if you and me can make a kids together Thomas I'm doing everything I can to help you with your manuscript talk to me with some respect or leave my a** alone Eden Reid that meant more to me than all the work I've done eden you got to appreciate me I'm being real with you to you got to respect I need you so much Thomas Allred jr.can't you look at me until I'm just not to be f*cked with Thomas Allred Jr Eden Reid Eden my business has me working sometimes days and nights but I do push ups every night until I'm tired and then I lay down and think of you and go to sleep Thomas Allred jr.Thomas if you had any sense at all you'll be sending me more of the manuscript I enjoy the Read its funny and fresh Eden Reid imma give up my secret identity for you eden my name is Thomas already Junior I have a secret identity also Thomas my name is kiss my a** and have a nice day Eden Reid just so we can be clear I can kiss your a** anytime I want to Eden Reid watch your face Thomas it feels like I got to go take a sh*t eden you waisting time telling me that sh*t let it run down your leg I get you Ebony buy itit feel like it's running down my leg Thomas can I use your tongue to go ahead and end this mess real quick Eden Reid Eden the only reason to talk to you this way is cause your a** tell me to Thomas Allred Jr you going to put me on top Eden ebony buy it don't put him on top Eden let me have his place instead The Dark Knight Batman I'm just so over this Eden this is The Lion King Simba I know exactly what you're missing the wide open space so you can lay back in just enjoy the sun and how beautiful the world is Eden The Lion King Simba ebony buy it got his hand in the p**sy it ain't no way from getting away from their finger I want that a** eden Ebony Buy it Eden see I'm two different people actually a me and them that nigga that you love Thomas Allred Junior become Eden I got your back this Police department f*cking rich officer Reign I've been listening and these people trust you eden that's what I need in a superwoman Superman girl I'm just sure of myself with you I'm just holding the title but you can hit me with the belt if you want to The Dark Knight Batman I need a couple moments to myself to think this over so you guys talk amongst yourself and just get everything straight Eden Reid sh*t she said talk amongst yourself if you want to hell but Ill give everybody a hundred million dollars a piece to drop the ball and go home Thomas Allred Jr Bruce Wayne going to end up kicking your a** Superman I heard that sh*t eden Reid it's been twenty years I've been single and searching for a wife I don't want to look no longer eden Thomas allred Junior it's a lot of women thats hearing what you're saying Thomas be sure to strap your seatbelts ebony buy it it's amazing I'm this close to falling in love again but you *ssh*les are in my way Thomas already Junior Eden you know me I run this joint office Reign The Dark Knight tell me eden picture you laying on my chest with no clothes on what thoughts run through your mind Batman The Dark Knight in coming call for Eden I want some a** and I'm not playing girl don't you hang up on me don't you hang up the phone Ebony Buy it I'm watching you and the rest of you make a fool out of yourself but the damn manuscript is hot Eden Reidas soon as I get my a** out of bed you come and tell me that you don't want to be with me because of these dumba**es officer Reign officer Reign is out of position because im bidding on eden one move at a time Mr.. Monopoly that boy sound just like my a** I keep it clean for you eden Supermanyou guys put a hundred percent in everything that you doing I don't know yet which one I'm going to choose just keep on doing your thing and I'll get back to you Eden Reid I'm officer Reign eden and I just want to tell you that Superman kisses a** and ebony buy it does to officer Reign Superman if you have something to say then say it i didn't come to this world for violence I just want my baby mama and the rest of y'all can go in peace come with me Eden I'll catch you Superman y'all been keeping my a** woke for three business days with this manuscript I'll let y'all know something in a couple more days Eden Reid I guess I'm glad I'm the one thats lasts in this b*tch I think all y'all zeros if you want something to get the job done Eden you need to come and talk to me Ebony Buy it romance is not overrated because I knew I loved you when I first laid eyes on you Eden Thomas allred Junior you can use that against me if you want but I'm still cool with Eden this is Officer Reign you doing the same sh*t Thomas just let me read my manuscript in peace and I'll get back to you Eden Reid you need to get back to me Eden Reid if you don't you get tired of me Thomas Allred Junior Thomas send me the manuscript message Eden Reid.

I wish I could tell you Eden Reid that you mean the world to me I'm a multimillionaire Eden Reid Thats waiting on his first settlement to come my book is based on a true story Eden Reid we got too many Eden Reids in this if I need your help discovering who my woman is can I call you Eden Reid I'm going to be professional I'm a businessman with a police officer at heart realize your heart that's the resting place for my words and my thoughts Eden Reid Eden be sure my permission is on your a** before you breaking any rules I'm going to make this story the hottest thing ever Eden Reid I just need one chance to prove that I really love you you know you remember me Eden Reid our conversation had you dripping like a faucet don't you mess up I'm trying to hold it together without nobody in my life I'm telling you Eden Reid this is your one chance for stardom so let's go all the way one chance for stardom I forgot to see if you can see it I'm famous you the one famous Eden Reid if you got candy let me taste it if you got milk let me have some it's a worldwide Discovery than panties know my d*ck come help me out this rain coat girl it took me a long time to rescue you from a triple threat Eden Reid all kind of people want me to finish this book but you in it I can't close it and hurt our feelings I see that dude for what he is a s*x artist professional I had you twisting and turning in your sleep why don't you do the same for me Eden Reid Eden Reid on top call me after your done reading the manuscript because I can take it you'll do anything for me and Ill do anything for you that's why I'm in love with you Eden Reid you need me just let me know I'm there for you anytime you want Eden Reid see Ebony Buy it stole my flavor on his manuscript Superman Eden Reid Superman is telling God damn lie Eden Reid ebony buy it as of today you are I can not be no longer just friends Eden Reid the manuscript proves that were partners for Life you think you got a superman but that dude don't know that Ebony buy it is in the houseI hear you talkin Eden Reid Christmas is coming soon I just want you wrapped up under my tree when I wake up Christmas morning Eden Reid I'm telling you we own our contracts we can get a new home all we got to do Eden Reid is cling to each other I got bulsh*t on my radar that bulsh*t will get you farther than you think you keep working with me Eden Reid they took me out the hood to show you that there's magic in this holiday season Eden Reid you have done your work be a professional get on the phone and call me Eden Reid the price of tea is going up now I need two manuscripts to afford you Eden Reid thats why professions is laughing cause they know this conversation is worth more than a hundred million dollars for you Eden Reid I came to see you Eden with my words on this paper all cause i think about you before I sleep at night don't quit Eden Reid you're my wifey Eden I let my ambitious go for your love I need your contract being professional Thomas allred Junior Eden Reid he wants a contract from Eden Reid if he wants it then he's going to stand up for it representative either way it goes I can't win at y'all rules so I make my own rules Eden Reid you and I are getting married soon as I get my money Thomas allred Junior she said she hear what you saying just get your manuscript to her Thomas I hear what you saying just stay focused and get your manuscript to me to send my manuscript off early will be a travesty but Imm a trust you Eden Reid here it is your manuscript I was supposed to give you okay so I'm going to take your manuscript and read it I'm Eden Reid send me your manuscript Thomas Allred jr. Yes ma'am Eden This is my oath to be there for you to provide for you and to protect you I Eden Reid i listen to your thoughts from far away Eden Reid we are changing history with this man uscript we'll get money togetherbbb bbut I need you to understand that this is a grown man's game.

Eden sweetheart I wrote it down every little thought that I had in order for you to help yourself for the upcoming movies and book manuscripts I see myself with you Eden out there standing from the White House and also going looking at the statue of liberty the United States of America and Canada combined forces on a manuscript so many people are lost and now giving up Eden so many people live in the lives now without having anything to eat Eden I put this on me and you to do the best that we possibly can Eden a book like This hold the title to the Future Eden either way it goes Eden we knew each other for a second so life is just what it is a beautiful rainbow girl look at my future it seeMs. so bright and your future seem so fabulous Eden take a little time Thomas Eden I see you and i in a mansion cleaning up our house Eden you know that I complete my sentences Every one of you should be ashamed of yourself because Eden is the queen and you know it I communicate on this level to what I'm stopping the bulsh*t from happening I'm a women's victiMs. rights advocate and my name is Thomas Allred Junior of the New York Police department and NSA we also affiliated with the FBI girl what planet are you on if you think that I shouldn't speak to you I know my business is Eden so Thomas Allred why all these amazing stories because when I needed someone I depending on you to talk me through a bad situation Eden being professional Eden I know my limits I wish I could touch and kiss on you so what are you Thomas or Ebony Buy it officer Reign the police officer you have to give me a second to come myself down Thomas he'll know Eden I'm getting ready to do some major with the police station helping me what is it that you plan to do officer Reign well I've made these inventions like 200 of them that save lives that's all I know is this a joke or game cause I'm going home Thomas no this is another step in our plan to free the women from captivity Eden Eden a told you I was thinking about turning our police station into a mansion fortress I mansion fortress that we can all be proud of listen to me Thomas it's about time you communicate how you feeling Eden officer Reign what makes you think that you can just publish your book like this without the government following your steps I have to tell you Eden I believe in myself throughout the circuMs.tances i done so much work for the government that I think we hustle together are you a mercenary officer Reign I'm a police officer and government agent Eden you got to keep saving up money cause everybody's not going to like the fact that your a government agent Thomas baby listen to me take me to a place where only you know the secret Eden what the hell are you saying Thomas I'm saying Eden that we have money we just got to wait for the government to let me break the seal on our deposit quit playing musical chairs Thomas and tell me what's going on Thomas quit making fun of them people these people were with me when I had nothing at all all of us in the streets of Canada and around the world have gotten to know each other as being people and friends and family my community hustles to come up just like you do Thomas now you see that I'm not just a person that you can replace that I'm a person who cares for my brothers and sisters Eden you need not worry about me I was not making fun of the people it's just that I'll go to my grave to help somebody and I believe in the people see anyone officer Reign the whole community is listening Eden I'm afraid for your well-being out here on the streets in Canada let me come to you too much circuMs.tances has put my book on the stand still continue to write your book Thomas I see what your manuscript looks like once you turn it into me before the deadline the deadline is two weeks from today Eden you are my publisher and my business consultant I'm going to need more time than that than that to the issues too much time will make you lose your train of thought I'm listening to your stories there funny and educated well how about me and you get together on the romantic boat when we get together in the states Eden do y'all see Ebony buy it anywhere yeah b*tch I'm right here Thomas your personalities are helping you write the book but they're not getting you any closer to me I hope you understand that I'm your publisher and consultant and that's it Eden West we changing the Superman that was smart Eden I want to talk to you please girl just give me another chance Thomas I'm giving you another chance not Superman not ebony buy it not the Dark Knight Batman not office Reign not The Lion King Simba Thomas if you're serious about writing and movies and books than show me who you are without those other memories I want to see you Thomas look and listen Eden people respect me for being all of these different people no they don't Thomas all these females respect you for being the person that you are I'm just getting tired of you thinking life's a game and everything's funny we work hard and take life seriously work Thomas do you have any clue that you had me running around my place all day with your messages my father gave me this medallion when I was 7 years old I want you to have it even there's a diamond in it and it goes around your neck you got to see what that boy just gave me what did he give you Eden he gave me a number one best-selling book Charlie well get off this phone and get back to him we got a quote this man Eden the whole police station wants you to be Ebony buy it Thomas thats all we need in our community Eden a billionair that wants to have it all with you I think yo a** is special Thomas Eden listen I want to talk I'm just a police officer the do the best job we can the people now I've waisted my time writing a book before you said that you wanted to see me this is me hang on for a second I got to get this tape player working Eden ask me any three questions you like and Ill answer them but Ill never answer any more questions pertaining to me and my lifeis Superman the Man of steel or Superman a part of you Thomas I'm the Man of Steel Eden and Superman is my code name given to me by the NSA and FBI how did you become a government agent Thomas my whole life ive been a government agent I didn't know until I grew older that my calling was being a police officer Thomas the money that you made and raised from your ideas from saving all those people what are your plans to do with it and why did you save all those people Eden me and the government worked together and came up with all those ideas to save the people see what issue is with making sure that women and children all over the world have what they need because the government or the governments can't stainless self without them where does the money go Thomas Eden I have no idea this is the government Eden I really like to talk to you but this is our time that man is interesting to me sleep with him if you have to but just get them to talk Eden you go to hell Eden yes Charlie I'm get them to talk Thomas listen to me you you a goddamn trillionaire I'm with a personality complex that you don't like okay who am I speaking to now Thomas this is Mr.. Monopoly Eden and we going to rule the world Thomas Mr.. Monopoly got shut down in the other games well this is Batman The Dark Knight Eden Superman fougth you Batman and one what does ebony buy it richest man in the world your 87 years old ebony buy it there ain't nothing you can do with this p**sy Thomaswith getting short on time so who are you it's going to rainI am officer Reign of the New York Police department no your sitting there with a phone your hand writing books and writing movies you're not officer Reign Eden girl who I am is a man that loves you I am Superman I believe you Thomas I've been just waiting on you to come clean with everything you are not The Lion King Simba Thomas Eden its hard to be me or myself because I have so many different responsibilitiesso Superman are you a police officer that works for the NSA and the New York Police department and the FBI I'm trying to tell you Eden Thomas allred junior is and Eden we beat this whole entire government in finances you are my lady and im right now to be my wife Eden thanks for you help me figure out my other personalities The Texas chainsaw ma**acre Eden I put the Texas chainsaw ma**acre on there to let you know that even through a sadistic crime I'm still a good man this is a baby the story why I want you I want you reason with yourself Eden how much money do you think this is worth Eden I'm smarter than you think I am Eden see I know that you need this manuscript and these pages I'm becoming the right person for the job of being there for you Eden and girl I know that you need my attention so I work night and day to perform a duty that is untouchable along side of you what I'm saying is Eden you know we ain't got nothing but a few weeks to prove ourselves imma let you know who I am Eden I am yours truly count Dracula.

Listen Thomas you are unbelievable the first time I laid eyes on you I knew that you were someone that I just couldn't believe exists in my existence please explain more to me about your story and how you came to be Dracula first of all too many stories in the together this is why I want you because Eden I've been traveling all over the world from the sick people and saving them I became a police officer in my early days as Thomas allred Junior these are the stories are amazing Thomas I just hope that you realize just who it is that you talkin to because seeing Eden now that you know that I'm Dracula I must fight for you until sunlight takes me into my palace enough of the games Thomas talk to me straight up why aren't you on the big screen somewhere pick your game up I listen to you Eden talking about the big screen books and movies I wrote this manuscript because women have been treated unjustlyband I care about them so I fight Eden I'm a police officer what is your police officer's name officer Reign Eden so you telling me your name officer Reign is your personality and every last one of your name's is your personality I'm telling you that I programmed myself to have strength in each personality that I that is me that's needed Eden Thomas you become a police officer because your the most talented individual on this Earth listen to me police officer this is government agent Eden Reid of the LA Police department I knew there was something about you Eden I just knew there was something about you stay professional on this book and movie the whole damn city is watching you Thomas have you come up with a new idea to help out the people in the community yes officer Eden Reid of the government and the LA Police department secret agent.

I've come up with an idea called mega system this book is too much for me to handle I need you to stop worrying about the book and tell me that I did that you have for the people in the country and others well Eden its starts like this and may God save us all it is a system carrier system that's what we figured out so far Reign we figured out that you want to employ every woman in the world on the network computer system to work it the only thing we haven't figured out is what makes the computer system work Reign Eden the network systeMs. computer system works by the sound of a person's heartbeat and their breathing patterns all over the world yes but how do you get that system to work Reign exactly you create a pules system that is amplified by people's breathing and there heart rate and then it is electronically shifted from one person to another.

Eden break it down to me Reign the heart rate has a certain rhythm to it and so does your breathing pattern process see the medical system of mines remembers that process of your breathing and your heart rate and ask the internet to it along with your thought waves to create world domination in healthcare peace and information because the mega system scans a person's body in the mind delivering the thought process all around the world even next door do text messages and phone conversations Eden yes, so I understand what you're saying but tell me how does it work the mega system is a multi anti computer it works with your heartbeat in your breathing and your brain patternsif your heartbeat and your breathing and your brain patterns Thomas it will move on to the next person to survive because the mega system is an artificial being that will one day ensure life on this planet can survive Thomas so what does it do it uses your energy your knowledge and your thought waves to counter product a thought wave of a song Eden imagine everyone's in the world thought waves coming together as one and onebThought we have a unique Bean I like to call him and her Adam and Eve Mega System put Adam and Eden your Brain Eden Thomas that's all you got to do is help communicate your ideas to someone the Adam and Eve Mega System will take care of you but how Thomas through your feelings and through your mind Eden what you saying is the Adam and Eve Mega System can go into my head Thomas that's exactly what I'm saying to youthe Adam and Eve Mega System can relay messages to you from across the world through your mind Thomas get your a** and take you sleeping medicine right now a listen Eden the Adam and Eve Mega System communicates people with each other by taking a person's thought process and teleporting it to another person and it's through voice messages inside your brain that are being delivered to you from one another Eden I see you working on my books and my movies but I'm an inventor named Thomas allred Jr listen to me Thomas.

I'm a special agent with the FBI my code name is Wonder Woman I'm Eden Reid you have no idea what you just did with that I did that you just put in this book Thomas book and movie Thomas Eden I just want to make sure that all the women have something before I leave this world see Thomas a nudity in love with the women this is the beginning of your life you don't have to be scared Thomas we're going to take good care of you Eden I want you because you're beautiful listen Thomas given up your ideas for the people in the government is an angel doing that take my idea out this book and let the world see the Adam and Eve Mega System it works all kind of females would like to talk to you Thomas picture yourself in the place where there's no worries just all women I seen such a place Eden and it's in my heart is called love oh my God he nasting and everything fix your game.

Thomasbthe reason why I sit to myself all the time Eden is because I'm a federal agent for the government waiting on this book to pay mehold you position Thomas I'm just thinking of how you can be secret service agent and all the things that you've done without you looking for me before now Eden we found each other would I tell you I'm count Dracula Eden and I am Wonder Woman Thomas I need your help Thomas to get out the situation that I'm in anything Wonder Woman just asked me Eden will you give me six hundred million when the book and movie gets finished Dracula Thomas Eden theres no way I'm giving you 600 million but Dracula will you can have the money sweetheart I love you Wonder Woman Eden I'm just being professional your services are no longer needed Thomas what you saying Eden I am part of the NSAand Thomas you're being reprimanded for the thieft of these ideas take the boy out of here look Eden the Adam and Eve Mega System will work it's my idea along with the government we all work together Thomas yall take good care of him it's something about that boy that I just can't put my finger on but I like it what you want to do Eden let's go over all these ideas you need to go over the payment price I get Thomas back in here I just seen something just now yes Eden Thomas how come none of these ideas work without your code because I told you even I invented them so how do I work them Thomas watch me communicate ebony buy it code 610-954-3281 and what is this what code is this you're saying Eden just type this into your computer sh*t Eden I new I was going to meet you I put this security code in so you would always be taken care of it's showing me the Federal Reserve Thomas there you have it Eden girl i put in a code to protect you and show you exactly where all our money is located you need to tell me the truth count Dracula Eden I have more than count Dracula yall make sure Thomas gets the help he deserves Eden I'm serious you don't understand that I'm a Time cop timecop where you from 1976 Eden I heard of you my grandmother used to talk to me about you what is your mission Thomas Allred JuniorI'm here to grant all the girls Financial freedom in the World as we know It and how do you plan on doing this Thomas with a corrupt justice system Eden i really don't know about our justice system but I made up these ideas through time to save people lives how you going to ensure that those women receive the money Thomas you know what my secret is Eden I know I cant ensure that all those women receive there money Eden but I can use the help of every woman in the world to ensure that things are taking care of the right way as a time cop my job is to ensure that these women have a better chance at a new life Eden your book is going to be a best seller think of it Thomas you going to be able to do whatever you want to Eden I'm serious about my book and my movies it's just that I really am a Time cop I'm Eden Reid of the federal government Thomas they watching you don't say anything else to me Eden I'm saying just what I want to this is a case we have to solve what's the matter with you the federal government doesn't put fear into your heart Eden I'm just here to make sure that all the women have the finances that they need and I can't be happy until I do now you see why we got you in a room by yourself writing these books and movies Eden I'm broke but I got everything meaning what did Thomas I'm sitting here looking at a picture of the federal reserve's Eden the federal reserve's is talking about shutting down because of me Thomas so why did you show me this picture Dracula of the federal reserve's they got you confused Eden confused the federal reserve's is not what you looking at on that picture okay Dracula Thomas or whoever you are what am I looking at you looking at a blank computer screen Thomas your starting to scare me this computer screen has a picture of the federal reserve's no it doesn't even the computer screen is black with numbers all over it so we what are you saying to me are you trying to make me believe that there's no picture there and it's only numbers this'll make you believe move out the way Eden I put a code into my invention devices for when download into the computer the thing about it is I didn't know I was installing the code when I was making ideas but I did Thomas you need to make your ideas where everybody can see bet you are timecop Eden I promise you after this youll understand exactly who I am I love you girl now as it is when I was making ideas I knew that people would be jealous and they would cause people not to want to talk to me so I installed a security protocol security protocol what's that it's a device system that frees your mind from people trying to trap you there making device systeMs. Thomas yes Eden that's what a computer is right now your computer is sending out a single all over the country my computer a single all over the country tell me what you're saying Thomas Eden I'm saying that even though you standing and doing what you want to there is a person controlling your every move this person heads up the Federal Reserve in every government in the world if you knew all this why don't you do something about it then Thomas because Eden I'm trying to make sure the women have all the money financially that they need but you you make me where I want to make sure that the body and your mind and your spirit is free totally you're saying there will be a controlled by someone Thomas I'm saying that you know you're being controlledand as a timecop I am here to stop that sh*t what are the words to stop it then Thomas God put me here to help women out of the situation you need to stop and think clearly Thomas what are the words to the man that is controlling everyone I am with timecop in the women and men want to be free this is Thomas Allred Junior police code 76920702 I want you to release a woman and men from the mental telepathy they computers have over them I offer up to you my life as a token and a gesture now free my woman in men I'm saying as a police officer amen Eden listen to me this is a case that I'm working on go back to sleep eating and in the morning everything will be fine your mind will be clear and you will be able to think better Thomas people depending on you the mental telepathy comes through the telephone wires say i question you Thomas okay Eden Reid FBI agent what is it that you want to know about me you don't know what people are thinking there is a way of handling this the Federal Reserve doesn't have any money anyway Eden Eden theres money in the state but not in the Federal Reserve then what is the military for if you really are timecop to protect the city from defeating each other in case of a government shutdown listen to me Thomas you need to say that's your opinion Eden I already told you that I love you you can't love me if you're making up ideas like this it's going in my books and then my movies that I want the women to have a hundred million dollars a piece all over the worldout of the money that I've raised through my movies my books and my business ideas and working Ms. Eden Reid of the FBI people want you to be mature Thomas listen Thomas I mean listen Eden my thing is I'm just waiting for my money to come from the ideas that I've given to the government ideas can you tell us who you really are I am count Dracula and this is my book manuscript you make me sick Thomas I'm ebony buy it the richest man in the universe I am officer Reign the New York Police department I am Matt Dillon and I'm used to Dodge City I am mister Monopoly and I want boardwalk and Park place back I am Bruce Wayne the richest man in the world you can call me The Lion King Batman The Dark Knight Clark Kent Superman Simba ebony buy it officer Reign Matt Dillon RoboCop Beetlejuice Eddie Monster slimer from the Ghostbusters Thomas as your queen I need you to tell me who you are I'm your husband Eden and King The scorpion King I'm listening to you Thomas And I know who You are your Rumpelstiltskin aren't you listen to me Eden Rumpelstiltskin is my real name why you here with me Rumpelstiltskin because happily ever after starts at the beginning of this manuscript manuscript what are you saying this book is a movie feature film and Eden you are staring in it right now as my queen welcome to happily ever after look Thomas it's alright to be about us but I don't know about movies and filMs. I don't know that's why make believe has become a dream and you are a princess in my own mind in this manuscript Eden it is a kiss that seals the dream I need yo Eden for the rest of my life here is the end of the story I want you because I love you manuscript Eden ebony buy it says he loves you Eden I'm sending you the message now Thomas.

CHAPTER 4

This the movie called Heartbeat Eden I'm working night and day on these books and manuscripts for movies the next movie that I'm writing is Heartbeat didn't I tell you that you have to be above average for your books and movies to make it Thomas I'm not trying to let you down it's just that I want you to raise your game up to a level to people comparable to people see right there you can think what you want but I'm making you work for what you want you got to believe me it's just one thing that I want and you got to believe me what it's to carry Heartbeat into these theaters Eden Thomas if you can throw yourself say nothing in this world that you can't have a do with your ability just look at it this way I believe in myself and I want people to believe in me Thomas Eden you talk a good game but I've been coming up through major situations I almost died out there Eden Thomas keep focus on your books and movies people see you imma keep trying to Eden but I don't know where this road is going to lead me what's the meaning of your movie Heartbeat Thomas a heartbeat is and motion you all that brings that tears from your eyes it's like spoken words between one another or lovers and friends is the emotion in between the conversation II of complete awareness of love that's what Heartbeat is how did you come up with this idea Thomas I said meditated in my room for hours get the sh*t right.

Thomas realize you ain't got to prove yourself to nobody but you Thomas where's the story coming from it's coming from the streets that I grew up in Eden I'm listening to him speak to me Eden I realize that I don't have nothing but what I'm saying is if you believe in me I can make you wealthy all I need Your Love to straighten me out I need to ask you if you could be my wife I said I need to ask you if you could come live with me because Thomas is working don't mean that Eden have to listen Thomas you need to talk about the movie where you going with the story I realize that this movie is the only thing that can save all of us from destruction so I'm taking it to a new level I'm going after the gato Eden the gato is a legend in a film Thomas tell me you're not for real what do you want from me I want my chance to have a family and riches that I can't believe with you in my life Eden I can't record you like this I should have known Thomas that all you were going to talk about it that you want me talk to me when you start to make sense this is exactly what I'm saying Eden this already makes sense because the movie is already begun this is my Heartbeat and I want the gato you telling me that the filming us right at this moment I'm seeing the Godo is your love Eden if the Godo is my love and what is the Holy Grail Thomas the holy Grail is spiritual Eden then what is it Thomas the Holy Grail is your a** I love you so much didn't gato is my p**sy am I making any sense honey Eden if you give me a chance with you I will show you all kind of riches the world has to offer rich is like what Thomas Eden up in the mountains theres a spring the run warm water through it it's supposed to be a healing spring people have fought and died over this water because it believe it give me energy Legend has it Eden that me and you are the ones that are supposed to retrieve this water and bring it back to our civilization a civilization cant survive without the heat from the spring water and another thing Eden soon as I bust onto the movie scene I just realized that you are my agent and my best friend what are you going to do for me Thomas girl I put you on TV if you'd like me toThomas I know you got your act together but I can't get to you the way I want to would you wait for me there's no need in waiting a position has been claimed Eden you have the title title what about the gato we just have to figure that out a little bit later on the whole community thinks that I'm going to leave them Eden I need to talk to you you starting to act not very professional give up you loved me Thomas Ill make you very happy what you want me to do lay down the strip off my clothes right here Eden thats is exactly what I want you to do Thomas wake up Thomas you've been sleeping you trust me just yes Eden I trust you here the first installment check for you books and movies nice job with those books and movies Thomas do you feel this Eden feel what this Heartbeat between us patience is my virtue the whole community is waiting on this check Thomas pay your rent first what are you saying Eden I don't have no rent I live with my mother I just bought you a three-story 47 room mansion complete with cooks and chefs know who's your agent Thomas Allred Junior my agent is Eden Reid give the boy credit Union he a damn book and movie professional yes Miss Athena how much p**sy can I get Miss Athena it depends Thomas the p**sy as went straight through the roof since your books and movies came out Miss Athena my books and my movies red tape North Carolina it's got to be some p**sy out there for me somewhere I see you got your p**sy on layaway I'm trying to help you tell me if they trying to pull you down listen to me Thomas to get your p**sy out of layaway you get me four more movies to get you straight Miss Athena I can't afford to get my p**sy out of layaway right now can I put something on it no Thomas the p**sy is too good you must buy top dollar top dollar filled these heartbeat Miss Athena im saying Miss Athena for every piece of p**sy in North Carolina and in the United States and surrounding areas I will make you a movie that will make your f*cking mama cry for every piece of p**sy I would do this Miss Athena would you lower the pricelet's see now this p**sy over here is called roughneck p**sy it depends on your a** to find out what the price let see this cootie over here is a businessman cootie it has a bow tie on it select the p**sy you desire for the price you deserve do you have any other p**sy Miss Athena I like to look at something decent you know I got the penthouse p**sy the belonging sheets no I'm looking for something more wholesome down the earth Miss Athena could you be more specific what kind of p**sy are you looking for then Thomas I'm looking for the tight p**sy that would help you out when you have nothing at all they will be in their a** for you I will help you with this purchase is there a master or Visa card right now I'm just looking at the merchandise I'll be ready to buy in like a couple days Mr.s. Athena you better hurry your a** up cause this p**sy hot as hell Eden you need to talk to that dude the boy got sense enough to ask me for some hot as hell p**sy I'm going to check his a** out to see if his d*ck really real or not I'm glad I caught you miss Athena is there any way a motherf*cking work they self up to some p**sy no a motherf*cker gets no p**sy but each man go through a seven-level test before p**sy is granted to him I'm going to pa** the seven level test Miss Athenayou need to pa** a d*ck test and then you can pa** the seven level test what d*ck test you talkin about Miss Athena come here and let me show you Ebony Buy it you need to be serious Ebony Buy it now pull out your d*ck Thomas place your d*ck under my bosoMs. I feel that Thomas that's a big old Mandingo d*ck big old Mandingo d*ck you think Eden is going to like this d*ck Miss Athena Eden going to like this d*ck Thomas it's some strength in your d*ck Thomas that I never felt before Miss Athena I've been opening cans with my d*ck for fifteen years now what are the cans you you talking about Mr.. Ebony buy it talk low Thomas I got kids around here absolutely not the p**sy I want Miss Athena you made your purchase there are no refunds you felt my bris you pay me ebony buy it me find you no p**sy I give you two days you bring my motherf*cking money Mr.. Ebony buy it how can everyone be so cold to me all I want is a decent piece of p**sy to talk to see how easy it is to lose your d*ck in here Thomas Eden I've been looking for you all over the place I know Ms.. Athena told me her breasts hurt because of your d*ck Thomas those are rumors I ain't touch her breast and she never seen my d*ck well she got you on videotape saying that you robbed her and she's going to taking warrant out on you this evening Thomas what was I going to do with her can't go back Athena's s*x parade give me some time and Ill speak to Eden about my Heartbeat manuscript I've been working on this for fifteen year it just so happens that me and Eden are totally compatible and she's a stroke of genius right there what are you doing Thomas you got to take your time with me Eden but I wanted you and my next move is to talk to her I thought Thomas you ain't saying nothing what was you thinking about just a minute ago Eden even though I was thinking about believing in myself Thomas Allred Jr you made me so happy I can't do nothing but tell you the truth Thomas I'm getting married this afternoon Thomas I just can't let you do that Thomas I realize you like me but Eden see I have a manuscript called Heartbeat just read my manuscript before you make any decisions promise me this boy just set out a manuscript for me to read and I'm about to get married at 4 what do I do Eden I know you love or you really love this guy but what I have to offer his business and stability you asking too much a year ago you should have talked to me while wait on wedding day to talk Eden I couldn't bring myself to talk to you all those years going past me I remembered that you kiss me and you never said anything else for five years I wonderedEden I'm trying to catch you before you make a huge mistake because Eden a care about you I want to show you how I feel take my manuscript Eden let me see that manuscript now throw it in the trash that's how I feel about your manuscript Thomas you watching me get married to a man that you know that I love the only thing that I'm asking is that you look at it and give me another chance Eden give me the manuscript Thomas Eden thank you I owe you my life Eden Miss Athena is looking for me I don't know what to tell you that woman is ruthless Thomas Eden I want you to enjoy read my manuscript you take my p**sy and not pay you a millionaire Ebony Buy it Eden I got to go but I'll be right back before the wedding if you want me call me at this number I love you Thomas oh yeah almost forgot to tell you Eden your beautiful whether or not you have a man I'm just saying I mean I'm in love with you and I'm proud of you for the job that you do read my manuscript and wait for me to get back before you decide to jump into your dress Thomas where you going I got to do something that I should have done a long time ago I put my dress on hold for you Thomas our police station is trying to figure out a way to straighten out the system I think I figured it out I'm a police officer Eden to be continued on the next Heartbeat episode Eden you wrote all of that sh*t in your manuscript and than going to stop here I should kick your a** baby I know that you figured out that I'm your heartbeat Eden explain to me Thomas what a heartbeat is you need to talk to me Eden a heartbeat is the love that we have between one another only expressed to emotionsa heartbeat is the feelings and the emotions and the longing of wanting to be with someone that's far away that your heartbeat just can't touch a heartbeat is the emotional feelings that's running through your body when you speak Eden I can't change my situation but here go my manuscript I love you will you please be my wife we're running out of time Eden I need you he the one who stole my p**sy give me back my p**sy no receipt you heard what I said this p**sy battling from the cold and lightening you want me to get your p**sy back filled his heart beat volume 1 Eden I could have had you but you didn't want to talk to me at the time on the phoneI know I couldn't talk to you I was standing in front of some people making business calls Thomas you could have called me back when we schedule a meeting Eden I was busy working that day I had someone else to call you Thomas well this is the manuscript to the Heartbeats soundtrack Eden Heartbeats soundtrack what are you some kind of music musician and writer I've been many things in my life Eden I just know that if you trust me it will be alright cause I'm in love with you your news bring me so much joy that you're not getting married Eden see I choose my man by strength in character not his bank account Thomas allred Junior I'm going to send this message off in a second so what do you think about me becoming your husband Eden Thomas pick game your up its people talking about you and me do the best that you can girl in no conditions will I turn away from you Eden I've been wanting you since the moment I heard your voice if you need me Thomas so you know what to do I need me some money but where would I get it the fact remains I'm a struggling writer with an addiction to cash and all of the hot women I bet Eden probably think I'm too slow for her talent I'd like to groom that there Philly if she don't kick my a** Eden and I go back since high school boyfriend and girlfriend I kissed you outside the school in front of her little brother Matthew you know what the funny thing is I don't even think eating has a little brother Matthew I'm just writing Eden.

Eden from the beginning I loved you night has became day and Sunlight is shine into my window how I want for you eden Thomas has got some sense about him focus I'm rich and I'm focused on the woman I want to be with we making a film out of this because this Heartbeat is beating for youI got so many different dialogues that your boyfriend just can't keep up with me Eden this is the second installment to Heartbeat God damn your sensual creature I got a community this backing me up Eden girl I can only see you with me imma give you a chance if you let me Eden your p**sy is valuable so you need to go to the bank and deposit something imma tare that p**sy up myself don't play with me Eden I'm headed for real estate investment you with me Eden a couple more trillions and I'll be set Eden to take you away from your man Thomas I can't help myself I just got to taste you in that candy Eden I've been saying to myself if I can think it I can have it Eden all I do is think about you Eden is about these decimals thats on the table you see I'm working call when you get a chance see I look like a goddamn billionaire and I feel like a goddamn billionaire but I'm a trillionaire that is out here working on his books and movies can I get an amen Eden Eden you already know how I feel about you so whoever your man is I feel sorry for him because I'm out here working everyday to make you and me successful you know my steelo if you want me call call me Thomas Allred Jr Thomas wake your a** up you need to write your book and focus on that before you try to talk to a Philly like this Eden Reid Eden I've been alone by myself for fify years trying to figure out a way to build my fortune now that I have it I want you and I'm not taking no for an answer Thomas Allred Junior communicate with me and we will see where this may go but if you try to Bogart something your a** is getting rejected I'm sure that Eden Reid i know you got work that you got to do and I'm not trying to take up most of I just want to let you know Eden that we're both going to be trillionaires after this work is done think about what you just said Thomas the whole community is watching us to get a woman like me you're going to need a pa**port and a Visa Eden Reid Eden a pa**port isn't good enough for me you left me no other choice but to make you my bride because money is strange to me I got a hundred hours in already on this manuscript Eden I know I can work it that off listen to me as a professional you can have to step up your motherfuking game I can't be here in the same old bulsh*t Thomas Eden Reid You had me from hello Eden Reid you see how much money you can make if you just shut the f*ck up and write your damn book Thomas Allred Junior suck my d*ck Eden Reid I would like to Thomas myself I really would but I can't find that muthaf*cker you know where around and write your manuscript please Eden Reid you competing against a rookie I'm one of the best so if you want some a** you better step your game up and complete your manuscript Thomas I am Eden Reid Eden slow jaMs. getting me sick to my stomach could you suck my d*ck to make me feel better Thomas Allred Jr hell know I cant suck your d*ck but I can cut that muthaf*cker off if you keep playing with me motherf*cker writing manuscript Thomas Eden Reid you crazy as hell girl I'm a producer Thomas Allred Junior produce these titties and this a** in your mouth Thomas Eden Reid Eden I think I found Paradise in your a** Thomas I see that b*tch I'ma kill your a** you f*ck around on this and your manuscript getting burnt Eden Reid so you want to play hardball a rustle me up some damn fried Chicken and some baked potatoes Eden Reid you going to make it where chef boyardee is the only cook you going to have in your house Thomas Allred Jr Eden this is a still mate go to the bathroom and hand me my d*ck back Thomas Allred Jr I would make you go yourself but I'm going to go I got a sh*t Eden Reid you might as well leave that toilet paper alone I lic* sh*t like that Thomas Allred Jr you need to carry my a** for me for a second I'm getting bored hold on for a second I got to sh*t eat this b*tch Eden Reid honey I just want to be with you I'm not afraid of no competition I just don't want to lose you because you're not doing your work Thomas step your game up Eden Reid even thinking of you only makes me stronger man because the dreaMs. I have of you go down in my manuscript and I know that if I keep going that you and I will be making sweet love someday so I never ever stop Thomas Allred Jr you banking on this boy then come and get your a** cause you deserve it Eden Reid come and get this d*ck Eden Reid I'm tired of these damn games Thomas Allred jr.see how big my muthaf*cking a** is you want to kiss on it hell know get your motherf*cking work done and send me the damn text message Thomas Eden Reid you sent me off I've never felt like this before I'm a make sure my d*ck goes in you Thomas Allred Junior look here you piece of sh*t you just a manuscript on the table you better get your sh*t together before you see no paper Eden Reid well Eden it looks like you corned me all I can do now is eat your p**sy and go to sleep if you let me Thomas Allred Junior if you were the last motherf*cker on Earth you couldn't eat my p**sy put this sh*t in your mouth you can handle that can't you Thomas handling sh*t is my first middle and my last name what kind of sh*t you got going on Eden I'm here for you Thomas Allred Jr this is a pretty good position I'm sitting in so if you would write your damn manuscript and get it to me some time this evening I can get my work done before today is over Eden Reid I ain't through with my manuscript but I'm going to send it to you to show you there's no hard feelings between my d*ck in your p**sy Eden Reid Thomas Allred Junior send the damn manuscript to me right now Eden Reid. Eden Reid I think I see you on my itinerary I just had to let you know that you and I are coming up in this business Eden the whole industry talking about you got too much game for me Eden I look at yo a** and I see a champion tennis player Eden Eden I switched up my style I'm gangsta with my manuscript Thomas Allred Jr with my manuscript Angels are telling me what to do with my manuscript Eden you got to believe in something believing me God Eden I promise I'll take you out of the hood soon as my work gets it's contract girl I promise you Thomas Allred Jr pull up a seat take notes get a chair I'm a professional businessman and I need your Heartbeat Eden Eden ebony buy it is here what you say Ebony Buy it is in room 2 Thomas Ebony Buy it is in room 2 I'll be right back here drink some bottled water and have a couple triscuits give me 10 minutes okay I'll be right back Thomas Ebony Buy it how you been just terrible Eden I've been watching your a** on channel 17 and I see yo a** running all through town with Thomas allred Junior if you got Thomas allred Junior on your a** Eden then I can't help you Thomas Allred Jr and I are close friends you got a call on line one Eden remember what you said you'd help me with my manuscript Eden don't be f*cking around on me Eden The Dark Knight Batman it's another call on line 6 Eden you better tell Thomas allred to get his a** home so you can eat this p**sy ain't playing with you Eden Kristen Beam there's another call for you on extension 14 Eden don't forget I'mma put your a** out I knew you'd like them big money dudes them tycoons a f*ck that damn sh*t Eden you out this relationship is over your ex-boyfriend you have another call online 10 I didn't mean what I said I just can't help myself I'm going through some things that that's hard to deal with and you do love me don't you just call me please Eden your ex boyfriend aggravated you have another call in line for it Samantha for Thomas hello Eden I'm calling about your husband Thomas allred Junior I'm sure you know me well I'm here to tell you that I slept with him the other night what other night your anniversary before the Rose bowl came on TV Thomas I'm getting ready to be with you make a point of this Samantha Ebony Buy it just sitting there waiting patiently Ebony Buy it looks like he's upset Eden could you hold on one minute Mr.. Ebony but It i can't wait on you hand and foot I got to get my secretary to help me Miss Eden Reid the reason I'm here is I'm going to be taking all my money out of your hands and putting it into seashells at the Daytona Beach April get in here second help Mr. Ebony Buy it find his way back to where he belong if I give it to him good Miss Eden Reid Will You raise Me up to your level April you talking about f*cking the man I just want you to sit back and take shorthand notes from Mr. Ebony Buy it Thomas these angels are everywhere Thomas you got to keep yourself in position to receive your promiseThomas and no that I kept you waiting but ebony buy it is here with you what am I going to do with ebony buy it he's in the singing to my secretary Thomas Otis Redding songs at that and people keep calling me leaving some of the most obscene messages you've ever heard I just want you to hold me Thomas it take all my fears and pain away text me back if you get this message Miss Eden Reid in the other room of the office well Eden I received your message it's no surprise that you working hard your the CEO of your own just like you dream to be I miss us talking face-to-face I'm going to get us in a better position to where we can take care of each other you only got 16 minutes before I have to leave but I know you were busy woman Eden I'm leaving tthe copy of this manuscript Heartbeat here on your desk since you can't be with me I'm asking you now if me and you have chemistry why in the world can't we be together I'm sending the message to you now Eden you got to wait until I finish my business before I can be with you Thomas there's something else I got to do before I can talk to you but just wait there I'm going to get to you in the morning time I love you you true professional Eden Reid send another message to Thomas the angels are talking to me Eden I really appreciate you for all the work and everything that you do take time to read my manuscript because I know that it is worth the effort and Eden I'm making sure that I'm producing you Eden you don't know what I would do for you I'm handsome Eden Thomas Allred Jr take over the school buses is here Miss Athena how many kids do you have I have three kids to grown up Miss Athena did Thomas make up his own manuscript or did Superman do it Superman did Eden Mr.s. Athena the day has come for me to whoop your a** how should I do it a very slow kick is what sets me off Eden a very slow kick to my a** stop whooping my a** Eden April Thomas is getting ready to leave in a few minutes could you give him a complimentary basket of fruit and basket of candy you know Eden I would like to but Ebony Buy it keeps sucking on my damn toes he said he was going to ma**age my feet but he's sucking my damn toes Eden I'm starting to believe a profession is all we need in this muthaf*cker Eden you have a call on line 2 come to a decision or that's your a** Thomas Allred who was the Eden April I have no clue Eden your man is about to leave I've been waiting here for 17 minutes Eden I told you I've been going through things but you want to take me for granted so I'm leaving your ex boyfriend Ralph eating you have another call in line 2 and I'mma tell you another thing Thomas allred you can keep that b*tch down at the company and your d*ck taste nasty too milk The cow Thomas Jr eating you have another call 18 what do you guys want don't you see I'm working here trying to make the money I'm a professional now this is the Reverend Don Juan Curtis Eden I know that was you last night on the phone and riding past my house Eden keep thinking just cause I'm a minister I want to tap that a** Minister done one Curtis Eden you have another call in line 3 Eden this is your mother I want you to hurry home from work today because we having a tea party for the neighborhood Easter eggs search its August mother there is no Easter egg search and we call it Easter egg hunt where I'm from I'm trying to make up this time I can hear you Eden

I'm still here for you baby I got to produce him what are you talkin about baby Eden you got to cuff the balls remember you got to cuff the balls baby that's how you keep him mama got work to do mamma i just got talk to you a little bit later on okay okay baby goodbye Eden line 3 keeps blinking what is it this time Eden this is Elizabeth and Samantha we just want you to realize that Thomas Jr is a professional Thomas gets whatever you want Eden you need to think about this b*tch you the one talking sh*t on the phone but Eden when Thomas gets angry that's when the beast comes out that's what he calls his d*ck Eden the beast and mini Superman why you to bother me and I'm at work today because Thomas isnt with us so he have to be with you making business plans for his manuscript it's only talks about if I'm professional what business is it of yours Elizabeth and Samantha hell no b*tch I'm whooping your a** when I catch in the parking lot today you want to fist fight with me b*tch I don't think you know who you f*cking with anyway Eden Thomas got his stuff in his Winnebago so let him stay with you if you want to the call ended at 7:15 Eden honey you look exhausted Superman I could use a hand to the stairs I'm sitting you down over on the couch so we can talk and you can get some rest Superman I know I can't handle this the Angels talking when you can't hear them Eden what is it that you said ThomasI said that I love you and I'm proud of the job that you did today everybody looks at me for advice and I Look to You for strength in peace Superman show Kristen Beam how you do things Miss Eden Reid we need to get Kristen on the phone right now April could you page Kristen a**I would Eden but Ebony Buy it keeps sucking on my damn toes talkin about April its time for you to take your medicine get her on the damn phone this instant April Kristen Beam on line 2 Eden I'll be with you regardless Kristen Superman move out the way this is Kristen how you doing thank you for coming down and helping me at the last event I had Kristen wait a minute I know that voice Eden Reid how have you been girl I just now started over and took over business started my own company than Eden who is your partner in the company step your game up I need to see you Thomas my partner is a Superman that is the Superman Kristen it's long as you happy Eden I'm going to keep it straight with you that boy got two more days until his contract shows itself thanks for being in my corner Kristen my shoulder is always here professional now Superman you can go now Thomas out the window I'm just playing with you honey go out the window I'm get a picture of you Eden you realize that I love you don't you you got me blocked in fix your face cause yours truly has a manuscript I'll put gold up your a** for that manuscript Thomas Kristen and Elizabeth and Porsche and Heather and Chelsea and Evelyn and Maya and Emily and Inger and Vivian and Samantha and Julie ladies I am Superman and you will be becoming Superman's wives and mistresses Ive circled the industry Thomas I'll be with you be professional I only got just a little bit more time I can hear you Thomas he want too many women Superman can have me anytime you want to you can have me to 4 seconds I'm professional so I won't my contract with me Superman make sure you get a contract off your books and manuscriptswhat I'm about to do is represent for all the ladies in the world this book movie is called heartbeat ladies and the one time I want all the ladies in the world to make an orgasm for me say it with me 1 2 3 orgasm see that p**sy is on a different damn caliber what caliber is your p**sy on I got p**sy for sale all way from East Africa to here in Canada and the United States Miss Athena you got to give me p**sy this at works you making me sick Superman you got money I know it your d*ck to Big you shine have a good time with that d*ck Eden Ill see y'all tomorrow Miss Athena didn't I tell you not to badger my clients pull your ponytail back and that'll be all right Eden used to p**sy know Superman d*ck for you I know exactly what you're going through Thomas allred Junior what kind of manuscript is it Ive been calling myself The Lion King on the manuscript Eden I think you should check it out if you professional and I'm professional then we have a chance of making something out of your manuscript Thomas Allred Junior talk to her all women will please you I'm a help this boy up out of his situation I know that you love me Thomas allred Junior but I'm scared that you won't separate yourself from your family just to be with me Eden my family is your family that girl wasting time on that man shut up April this is a CEOs business now go apologize to yourself in the mirrorEden it's just that I'm so professional I feel like I can run this company I want my chance to holler at Superman Eden you have a phone call on line 1 y'all better get that boy some p**sy Thomas has been working night and day on the manuscripts and books and I know Thomas d*ck hard I'm just saying that all you b*tches making money on his books and movies you need your a** kicked all cause Thomas is a hero of his community that's why we stand up for him day and night I'm thinking that you b*tches have got your priorities backwards give that boy some a** you here me Roseanne Barr wrote that sh*t all kinds of women walking around without the Superman d*ck in themI wonder if my heartbeat is strong enough to make these ladies feel emotions with there tears you can tell who professional out here The Lion King is the champion out here i am standing on my feet ladies I'm standing on my feet with a manuscript that I wrote to heal your pain Eden youll make love to me want you I'm going out to get itSuperman girl that saw you need I am The Lion King can You feel My heart beat Girl Eden i step my game up like you told meif the Lion King don't have the power to love you Eden then I am The Dark Knight call me Batman Thomas I need that manuscript badly it's on its way sweetheart I'm sending it right now The Lion King in The Dark Knight feel them girls heartbeats Eden Thomas if you don't send me that damn manuscript I'm a kick your motherf*cking a** be sincere stay professional Eden Reid CEO of business professionals I'm The Lion King I fought long and hard for my position on the throne Eden feel my Heartbeats no fear you are my Earth companion Eden and not showing your a** that you and I are just like each other read this manuscript Eden to the right person I am King Superman be sure that I got the right address to send this manuscript to you wasting time Thomas King Superman I need you to rethink your story yes Eden Reid I'll rethink my story go ahead Thomas and mash the send message sent button nowI'm sending you my manuscript now Eden because I need you and it's the only way I can make it as a professional writer it's all or nothing and Eden I'm going to send you this manuscript The Lion King Thomas Allred Junior I love you Eden my CEO to the stars

Eden my name is Pablo Escobar I got too much game for professionals Eden contact Pablo Escobar if you need your a** whooped this is the Heartbeat soundtrack how did i do Eden you were wonderful in the commercial Thomas Allred Jr take your time and change in to you Superman outfit I'm already in my Superman outfit I am Superman Eden boy quit play with Superman go change into the outfit that we design for you this is my outfit Eden Thomas you know that your under contract for three movies and 7 books I'm aware of all of that Eden Thomas I'm seeing you having trouble getting into your costume no you don't Kristen Thomaswe working together to make sure that you a big success Thomas now go change into your costume see right now I'm thinking of taking you Thomas to your own private island but this is my Superman costume Kristen you see the boy I don't give up we brought some cookies Thomas I know you like cookies will you change it to you Superman outfit now Kristen and Eden them cookies look good as a motherf*cker but I need a few more days a few more days Thomas me and Kristens cookies are off the hook Eden I wouldn't doubt you but something is telling me not to put on that costume make sure that man get his contract look how you turned them cookies I got some milk Thomas give that boy a contract it come from my a** all of a sudden all kind of females are trying to feed me I don't want nothing but to be my own entirely self Thomas you ain't got to put the costume on ilI see you later on tonight in the bedroom Veronica I'm ready to put that damn custom own Kristen but our set is complete now we do need you in the costume now Thomas just hold your ground Thomas people watching what kind of language is that you speaking Kristen just hold your ground people watching I'm going to do what the f*ck I want this boy unprofessional you know I do want to cookies after all Catherine you want some cookies Thomas then go to the candy store there better be some candy in that candy store Eden cause you starting to bulsh*t me go take your medicine Eden I want to but there's so many different women to choose from here is your incentive Thomas allred Junior the women are all in bathing suits bikinis and negligees with makeup all over their bodies this a music video Thomas this is your life listen to me Thomas I told you I'd take care of you when I first met you Frank Y and Eden I don't know how I can thank you just continue to work Thomas we trying to get your money back from them ideas this seeMs. like a dream to me Frank-Y and Elizabeth it's not a dream Thomas I'm going to give you what you been wanting all of your life and what is it that I've been wanting Nicole we making a movie or for you Thomas it is called Superman the beginning Thomas you need to change the name of this movie from heartbeat to Superman the beginning okay I agree with you Superman the beginning is the name of this movie right here and I want you to know that your okay Thomas you got to do push-ups every single business day for the rest of our lives I'm doing right now what I can for you be professional Thomas you only got two more business days and you get your contract to you back what contract are you looking for Frank Y I want Eden Thomas took his time and called on Eden do you sacrifice all other women for Eden yes as Superman I do Frank Y listen to me Superman is being professional give him all of the women on this station we are coming after you tell Thomas that a Superman contract is worth 20 Trillion dollers in the world today if you can handle your position two more business days than you are Superman for the rest of your century Thomas Eden be straight with me do you think that I'm professional Eden what I got to think dosent really matter to me Superman now Thomas Allred Jr I indail you with the power of Superman in the beginning you are a business tycoon named Thomas Allred Jr and your mission is daily saving females who are in terrorist organizations our government help you by Mental telepathy I make sure that you have what you need giving my situation Superman you have protected women all around the World and Superman is time that you receive your contract I've been happy being the person that I am who has nothing Eden Thomas pick one of them females to go with you to a place where you cannot see daylight Thomas be careful what you wish for because people aren't going to arent going to understand that you are Superman and that you have saved them all from destruction with your ideas Thomas call the police station on him I do what I can to help you Thomas I choose Elizabeth Kristen Porsche Kathy Kay and Samantha Chelsea Heather Eden Emily NADA and Vivian and Inger these are the women I want professionally in my household but Superman these woman already experienced in the ways of the world Monica there experience but they're friends of mine Thomas you know it's against the law for you to have more than one super female yall finish with the test that your doing of me because from this moment on I want every female in the world to be with me Superman that is not possible Lily anything is possible if you believe in yourself Monopoly is not going to have this think of what you doing the people Superman I'm thinking of having a home that I can trust and believe in I want you Superman first bring Monopoly so he could see how beautiful the world is with women running it you going to make it Thomas Monica hope so seeing my manuscript holds country band I'm Mister Monopoly and I approve of this message you see Mr.. Monopoly at fougt and saved the lives of women all over the world all I request of you is that you give each woman a hundred million dollars a piece to save face Thomas take over Mr.. Monopoly it is in my heart to be there for the women because the women were there for me and save my life all I'm asking is that you grant them a hundred million dollars a piece only the women to where they can take care of thereselves and be who they want to be watch your language with me Thomas I fill there's know use of me trying to parade myself in front the country anymore more I am Superman and I gave it to you Monopoly my 200 business ideas Superman there's only one thing that Monopoly says is wrong with you and missing Thomas your cape I am Mr.. Monopoly of the second money division and I hereby Grant Superman the rights to all the proceeds for every business idea that he's had if Superman wants to battle for a lady or all of these ladies he can let me ask you this Superman who do you want to be with that one female the lady that I love has been executed by terrorists I choose all the females in the world to love me and make a family I'm seeing this clear if all the females are your dreaMs. Superman did so be it Superman has come in since to take his Queens to another planet you need to listen to me Thomas yes Eden people like you and in this story I am your queen in the story I have a lot of Queens Eden don't play with me write the damn store and get the damn manuscript to me I am Superman and this is the beginning Thomas if you keep talking to her like that then you will have no story pick your game up Thomas you know I love you that's the words that make me want to rule the world a Superman this is our beginning Eden I got the cube in my pocket Thomas communicate to all the females out I there I am Superman and I want you ladies to have 100 million dollars out of my money from all the business ideas that I've created in this world a piece Thomas do you know ladies want to hear from you I am Thomas allred Junior and I'm building a compound where all of the ladies of the world can come and relax and be with me and I plan to build this compound in Carolina Beach after all my movies books and business ideas show progress I'm doing this because all of my ladies have been hurt and abandoned and abused Thomas take your time and speak to them ladies I want you to realize that this is more than a heartbeat Superman begins story this is a story of Eden and my life as professionals feel the heartbeat woman I'm doing everything I can to protect you somehow you have to believe in the true being that's better than yourself I'm with capable of more than this complete my affidavit and females you will be my queen my affidavit is a questionnaire only there's only one question on my affidavit ladies do you trust me yes we trust you Thomas call me Superman yes we all trust you Superman the promised land lesson is your compound ladies without any of the men that to bother you it's only me there your Superman I know Superman was a little bit far-fetched Eden but I had to try something hold you position Eden the city told me not to do this I work for and this is my Heartbeat here them females calling you we want Superman we want Superman we want Superman we want SupermanThomas all you have to do right now send that message to me I take good care of it I promise Eden the s on my chest means that I stand for good I'm Superman Boy send me that goddamn message right now get that sh*t on my desk you hear me Thomas or Superman I'm Ms. Eden Reid send me my message.

Come get my manuscript Thomas Thomas I'm only thinking about is you yes Eden ive finish my work see this manuscript right here April it's all beginning of Superman I thought Superman beginning whatnt the name of the story Kristen kristen is irrelevant I'm Eden Reid, Thomas wrote that whole manuscript Eden he had to work night and day thinking up these stories what are you planning on doing with Thomas's manuscript April I'm going to take it to the daily planet where it can get his true Justice Lois Lane is working there that is Kristen Beam for short if I see Thomas a** out here in them tight a** shorts again girl cutting gra** well do what you got to do April just give me a second Eden you know the daily planet deserves this manuscript has all rights to this manuscript excuse me did I come at the wrong time know Ebony buy it didn't oh you talkin about my twin brother I'm Thomas you can call me iron Man I made it is nice to meet you you look so damn familiar I can't put my finger on it but you seem like a superhero that's because I'm entangled with the Justice League of superheroes Thomas this isn't funny fix the story now Eden Reid she lost control in her vaginafix the damn story right now Thomas or I swear to God that's me and your a** he don't know how to fix the story Eden Thomas is a role model and he's in love with Kristen Beam Eden I tried to tell you my story but you kept telling me to step my game up you confuse me so I made up Captain America as a junkie down in Harlem you better quit with your stories Thomas some people like your stories Thomas and some people think that your mentally ill Superman deserves world domination I'm iron Man and what kind of Superman is this Superman is the only hero holding this planet together on a Nexus cell he is the type of hero that will give you anything that he has to ensure you survive another day Thomas can't be your superhero I'm afraid he is April what are you talking about iron Man is a fraud people Superman is the real deal Eden you that Kristen online 2 I'm getting to fax over this manuscript that I got from Thomas allred Junior you rich as hell Eden Thomas Allred Junior's movies and books are selling all over the world kristen I put my manuscript in your hands because Justice is served with you and the Daily Planet what are you trying to say to me Eden I'm saying that Superman has his memory back Kristen does he realize that I have his baby Eden no Kristen he doesn't what is he been doing for the last 15 years making business ideas saving innocent people's lives and working here for me when can I look at him you can see him now I'm sending the manuscript with him to you he knows your name but he doesn't know what you look like good morning Kristen beam office Kristen beam I got a package for you this is Superman he's already here Eden step out of the light Kristen and look at him through a mirror Kristen this is Superman coming up boy give me the package on what the hell Superman yes excuse me for being such a mess or being rude Lois Lane I have a delivery for you from work there I'm afraid I do miss Kristen Beam so what is it that you do Superman I just worked it's all I do is work Lois Lane call me Kristen Thomas I can call you anything you want if you sign the dotted line on these papers forgive me Thomas I totally forgot that you were delivery person Superman delivers all over this world night and day do you have a special delivery Miss Lois Lane There's a child that's waiting to see you Superman yeah I mean if Superman has the time he said yes Superman my son will see you now it is what you wanted isn't it Supermanon my life of dreamed about meeting a child like this Kristen Beam your not meeting a child Thomas he's just son Superman take your time Thomas Louis Kristen look at how beautiful he is and Superman there's something else I got to tell you listen to me Superman I am a dark angel from another world send back to bring in your captivity and Kristen Beam work beside you hand-in-hand with Eden Reid and Thomas Allred Jr now it seeMs. like your not understanding the story Eden at 2 on Sunday evening every superhero in the world should show their self the fighting over contractsin a country that is a woman's a** the Holy Grail keep it professional with this Eden Eden as Superman the superheroes are fighting over your contract which is your a** and your p**sy the holy Grail and the gato as Superman I stand up for it all give me the manuscript to me Thomas cause right now your in the wrong place at the wrong time I'm being so professional Superman Eden Reid Eden that's a part of my story but it doesn't make sense Thomas what are you after I'm at the world peace Eden just because you say your after world peace doesn't mean your going to get it Thomas Allred Jr your stories are amazing still the same kind of Innocence about you I can make you better all we need is a story about love but Eden I got you a birthday gift it's in your room on the table listen to Thomas I know you mean well Thomas but getting me a present isn't going to better your chances I listen to your heartbeat.

Thomas you are scared all the things that we can do for you and when you believe in yourself it comes out in your work I just believe in myself Eden that is how I create these beautiful stories about love and romance even though I notice that you are not wearing your ring that I gave youbecause I dropped it in the turnpike coming to work it was raining so I didn't know what to do I looked for you in the rain Eden well tell Superman what did you think of me after you found me I thought I felt something as beautiful as the sun you thought you found Eden walk in the other room and open your present that I gave you okay Thomas but you know what I'm thinking what's in the box Thomaseating it is your contract from Imperial designs and Stratosphere you are now CEO of both companies and I also found you I put a diamond ring with each contract you have two diamond rings Eden for each hand say Superman Thomas Superman now send me that damn manuscript right motherf*cking now so my business is with you Eden I'm going to work for my contract Eden day and night can't you see that I'm in love with you Thomas I'm a write just a little bit more to this manuscript and send it to you is the name of it Heartbeat or Superman begins Thomas the name is chapter 1 Superman begins Heartbeat for you Eden Reid so the name is Superman Begins Heartbeat Thomas that is correct Eden Superman Begins Heartbeat has a ring to it Thomas Im a see what I can do with this here Eden you have a call from your ex boyfriend online 0 hello this is Eden I'm not able to take your call right now please leave a message at the tone Eden I want to talk to you because I know that I hurt you and you need somebody in your corner now that you're a CEO of professional business sorry I hurt you I just get frustrated sometimesI wish when you come home you could bring me some Skittles and a bag of funyuns and a two liter cherry pop baby I appreciate all you did for me and I hope you hear from you soon your ex-boyfriend Ralph still loves you Eden what do you want me to do with this message put that on speakers to the whole company can hear I'm through with him April yes ma'am I got it Eden is though with Ralph Superman I just Eden you don't have to explain take the time and send me the message Thomas I love you Eden to you need to stop that but it's real I wrote you this manuscript take it Thomas I can't people watching im going to send the manuscript to your email address you got one more minute possibly Superman girl think about me feel my heartbeat Superman Begins.

Eden my manuscript is something that I think that you and I should discuss before you read any further Thomas I'm professional there's nothing that you going to say that's going to shock me it's going to bring you the test my book is dedicated to my past relationships Eden so what are you saying Thomas not to read because you were in relationships no Eden my manuscript will take over your mind heart and soul and how is it supposed to do that Thomas because Eden look around you everything's quiet and there's no people around around you Thomas haven't you noticed I'm a professional I don't get scared by horror filMs. and movies this isn't a horror film or a game Eden I'm trying to tell you something I agree this isn't no horror film or horror flic* you keep saying you trying to tell me something speaking mind write it down on a piece of paper and I'll get back to you Thomas Thomas you made me out to be a goofball and I don't like that its one thing that I have to tell you Eden before you read the rest of the manuscript what do I have to do to get through to you Thomas it's either your manuscript gets read or you quit playing God damn games what you going to do Thomas I quit Eden but I just wanted to tell you that Thomas don't tell me just read my manuscript Eden and you'll find that anyway Thomas come here pick yourself up your heartbeat is beating too fast innocent is running all through your veins Thomas Eden what I'm trying to get you to know is I've heard enough Thomas let me read this manuscript and see what the hell you talkin about Thomas Thomas get ready to close your eyes because your p**sy is here you got to keep it professional Thomas we all waiting for your manuscript to be finished do not close your eyes look at that a** you know p**sy goes on credit this evening p**sy goes on credit this evening now take your time and work for me Thomas tell me about the dreaMs. you've been having Eden I go to sleep and I dream that im lic*ing women a**es every night in the dream I'm having s*x with you Eden until I have a orgasm is that what you want to tell me Thomas no Eden I wanted to tell you that I'm a federal agent with the government code name Superman Thomas if your a agent with the government why my manuscript isnt through yet because you have to be at a certain security level to receive the rest of this manuscript Eden you know those white people programming me I am a police officer Eden this is where the conversation gets real Eden I got you see I'm waiting on your contract to build my family with all the business ideas that I made Eden thanks for letting me into your email address this right here is a book and movie called Superman Begins by Thomas allred Junior and Eden Reid listen people replace you Eden but there never going to replace the fact that we have our names written down in forever ink Eden can I tell you to just one more thing to help you realize just who I am your my contract Thomas aren't you I'm your contract and I'm your husband Eden then call me by my government name your government name is Christopher Reeves Superman no Eden my government name is Thomas allred Junior Superman Begins okay than Thomas Superman what is your mission and what are you here for I don't know exactly what I'm here for it's just that I'm attracted to your voice and I want to see you Eden I'm being pulled toward you like a baby being pulled Athena you know this man a superhero yes Superman I give you two for $5 on p**sy right up the street you see what I'm talking about Eden the women don't need to know that I'm Superman so you really are Superman what type of dress do I have on Eden I don't know Superman this day in age works with the government and you so you like a secret agent with superpowers listen to me contracts I use my mental telepathy to gaze into your subconscious I want you to be with me in America and in London all across the planet my ladies are with me Thomas be careful what you wish for the whole community is listening to you I wish that the women had two hundred million dollars a piece and I am Superman I'm going to see that it happens so we fight for women day in and day outmy community is taking care of business while I write these books in these manuscript the movies.

Eden I'm impressed by you taking care of me the way that you do Eden get out the way y'all this ain't no f*cking joke manuscriptwait for me until I finish my work Eden wait for me until I finish my work on these manuscripts females the hospital called and said that you have a large bill that you haven't paid Superman boy the hospital called you I'm a trillion are all debts for everybody in my community shall be paid I'm going off on this book and manuscript movie Eden I got this feeling that somebody out there really cares about me I know I haven't done much but Superman I'm in love with you tell me who you are and come to where I can see you female I am Kristen and Superman I believe in you Thomas Allred Jr I believe in myself that's why I can pay your a** 200 million to every single female around the world look Superman the rest of the world believes in you like we do it's just that by the time your books and movies come out you will be 10 years elder in your own time realize Superman if you choose Kristen over Eden you showing the world the power of your heart you got to make a decision Superman only one can be your wife in the sun I love you Superman Thomas I need you Superman is a God among women Superman is all true king listen to me Thomas there is no more time you must make a decision now which one of the ladies is it going to be a tooth Eden Kristen now that a choice has been made that is one princess of the world and we call her Eden Reid they putting Eden over all our finances my bank account just sky rocked it Superman has something to do with it Thomas for real are you Superman I am Superman Eden I need me a girlfriend one female to help me with my business issues from day-to-day Eden girl my businesses is called Imperial designs and Stratosphere girl I'm putting you on my business cause your a professional and I need a professional you got your money coming right don't you Thomas I need help to gather up this change Eden can I help you in any which way Supermanyou making it seem like I'm telling you a story or something Eden the truth is Thomas I've heard this many times before in my life no Eden I'm standing up for my profession and my community at the same God damn time y'all hear that boy Superman is trying to get him a girlfriend to take care of business with what I'm saying Eden is because you are professional I figured I would ask you to marry me and be my only bride now Eden I believe theres something about you that makes the sun shine brighter whenever we touch I'm waiting to hear you Superman Athena get your a** over there and stand pull up a chair and sit down Eden in Athena you listening to the sounds of Superman what are you are you a police officer or entrepreneur I'm neither one I'm a government agent that's working for the NSA then how come your wife isnt alive Superman.

Thomas with people listening to us my wife was executed about 20 years ago by terrorists Eden I know this isn't the last you heard of me Superman what's your ambition for our future Superman I plan to make these ideas to safeguard the ladies and the men all over the world if your books and movies don't make it what would you do then ThomasI'm through answering these questions because I never doubt I believe in the process of the United States government is Eden the woman for you Thomas allred Junioryou got to listen to me Thomas I never meant for Athena to ask you these questions it's okay Eden to answer your question Miss Athena Eden saved me from myself when I had nowhere to run to to her I owe my gratitude and respectI want to thank you Eden for your kindness and for being a true friend in my life Eden there's one more installment left to the story I need you to help me install it in 3 2 5 4 3 2 1 does the ending of Superman Begins heartbeat to be continued on another show and episode Thomas your writing is off the hook Eden I really need a girlfriend to safeguard to help me with my businesses now you mean that story was true that story about you was true Eden you can hear those people out there asking for you Superman I've came to a decision the girlfriend that I want to be my business partner standing beside of me and Eden Reid is Kristen Beam Kristen Beam he named you as his business partner along with Eden Reid Im asking both of them to marry me and be my wife's the council has chosen the leader for you Superman Superman the council chooses Eden and Kristen to run your businesses together Council of the world can I make one more decision think about your decision Superman it involved females lives can I give the police department 100 million dollars a piece to every officer meter made secretary cab driver and everyone that is working for the government in the world today I want them to have a hundred million dollars a piece and also the school teachers have a hundred million dollars a piece send a message to Thomas now that your working Thomas I think you look dashingly handsome in your new suit call me Superman Kristen you have no idea what you've done Superman you up there giving out money what about yourself who's going to take care of you Superman that's why I need my friends to help me Kristen you and Eden are my role models that's what I needed to hear now send Eden the message Thomas send goddamn message to me I'm thinking that I done risked everything but I don't got no kids involved so the two of you can be happy I'm sending off the message for the community send the goddamn message to me yes my Queen's Eden and Kristen that boys gotdamn mess Eden we got to get out here and help him Superman need help Eden I know what we must do and what's that kristen we got to kill Superman Eden send it gotdamn message Thomas he's talking to his self as of now on the new owners of Imperial design and Stratosphere are Thomas allred Junior Eden Reid and Kristen Beam y'all like this book Kristen I'm making it into a movie a motion picture film Thomas you keep on working you hear me you see me I didn't get to where I'm at by just sitting on my a** got to get to where you going by taking responsibility Thomas and I commend you Thomas for bringing Superman to my table Mister president theres a call for you on line 7 Obama working with the president you got to remember this day Thomas this is the day of freed up your money at your deposit slip and will I also gave you two contracts now will you listen its the president talkin I listen to your manuscript I thought your manuscript was quite intriguing young Superman the only thing I didn't like the only thing that didn't find attractive that you gave up on all the women of the World by accepting only two to be your wives Thomas I got some conditions for you which are Mr.. Presiden my first condition is your not going to date any women or see any women for two whole years after you get the contract and your second condition is and my second condition is that your the richest man on this planet and you should carry yourself as so my third condition is playing a simple Thomas Superman let me ask you son think of a place that makes you happy I feel safe and sound in my woman's arMs. Kristen Beam is your f*cking wife Superman listen I know you love Jesus Christ but you have no idea who Jesus Christ is somehow or another you got yourself involved in some serious sh*t you here what I'm saying to you Thomas you better quit playing with that manuscript and write your f*cking story it begins take one that's all I have to do is write my story Kristen Beam is professional but she can have me either way it goes I'm still going to be on top of the world reaching for my princess I'm Superman Kristen Beam and this is the beginning of the second part of my manuscript emotioning for my neighborhood to come with me to a place that I call Paradise I'm the one that figured this sh*t out for you listen Thomas listen to Elizabeth doing the work she got to be Catwoman Thomas see that's all I need is 3 Catwomans you need to talk to Kristin Eden give that boy his contract Thomas you done prove your point with all of us women Elizabeth I need my contract from you simply because you are beautiful I have another contract that I want I hope you can handle these contracts Thomas my name is Superman and your contract is Heather a police officer I hope you realize that this contract is a million-dollar contract Thomas trust me I do I need Heather to complete my kingdom this should be four Queens in my household and the names is Heather Elizabeth Kristen and Eden do you see what I'm saying knights of the round table send that message to me knights of the round table listen to me I am Superman and your kingdom is put together do the blood and tears of our forefathers I give to your a** a golden idol what is a golden idol Superman a golden idol is the genuine article I carry this in my hands is the truth y'all with the community behind me I say to the president of the United States of America that we need a contract and who are we the knights of the round table here in Longview North Carolina zip code 28602 I ain't finish knights with this I also put business ideas that will save and rescue your children forever more it's in the government's hands so Eden Reid I say to you sit at the round table right beside me Kristen Beam I say to you sit at the round table beside me Elizabeth I say to you Elizabeth sit at the round table beside me Heather I say to you Heather sit at the round table beside me these are my four Queens and the aces is this manuscript Thomas Ebony Buy it got to speak to you make it quit that boy got to send up that damn message I'm proud of you Thomas for choosing 4 damn queens see what bullsh*ttin you lost your train of thought the reason I'm talking to you Thomas there's a whole bunch of women out there that believe in you you Superman Thomas I am Superman Mr. ebony buy it listen to me you are Superman well get this cramp out of my a** tell Ebony Buy it that you steal watching him I'm giving Ebony Buy it one more chance to speak honestly Thomas I got love for you and Superman ladies is our true king knights of the round table to the true king Superman array array talk to Kristen now put you up as head of my kingdom my four wonderful Queens my kingdom is yours for the ruling don't play yourself for I know who You are and just who do you think I am my father said to me that Superman is Rumpelstiltskin y'all say Rumpelstiltskin three times if your Superman Rumpelstiltskin one time Rumpelstiltskin 2 times and Rumpelstiltskin three times now take look in the mirror Superman who the f*ck do you see I know Rumpelstiltskin and this ain't me I am Superman king of all Nations Thomas go to bed and write your manuscript tomorrow yes Elizabeth I just need a couple more minutes with my manuscript what kind of King is you I'm the ace of diamonds Heather I've searched for you all my life and I'll be with you only if the story never ends take your time until Kristen you love her I love you Kristen I love you Thomas okay Eden my manuscript is ready I wish you take your time and read and understand my thought process because we can't have a happily forever after without you Kristen you have a call on line 3 Thomas look here I'm to professional call on line 3 for Kristen Beam I'm taking my call right here in front of you Superman here give me the telephone hello.

Hello this is Kristen Beam I am your fairy godmother Kristen and you are in a book called Superman begins somebody on the telephone is playing Eden let me see the phone Kristen Ill talk to her I'm your fairy godmother Eden you have super powers with you Kristen and Eden did you hear what I just said to you Kristen I am your fairy godmother Elizabeth what's going on with this I hear her without picking up the phone I'm your fairy godmother Heather let me talk I'm going to teach you ladies how to control yourself at the stroke of midnight tonight at 12:30 come with the story books will be completed I'm asking Eden for you to surrender to Superman I'm asking each of you to surrender to Superman Kristen Elizabeth I need you to contact Nada and get her at the knights round table she is a queen to Superman let me see what I can do listen to me people this is a book about power it is more than page represent.

Thomas allred Junior that man is too strong maybe so but you need to Thomas allred Junior to take on superheroes who went renegade so this is what your saying Thomas if this is the best you got I just don't know about your manuscript I am your fairy godmother Samantha help Eden to understand that her heart has been cold from a grape the true love has for her he said from a grape the true love has for her what's your mouth Kristen I'm fairy godmother now open your eyes Thomas your heart is getting weaker Thomas from making business ideas and writing books and movies I see how they do you Thomas this is your fairy godmother I'm April Kristen you missed a call online to Kristen April if you forgot mother what do you work you are at the fairy godmothers business table go to sleep June my business is now here at the round table is it Pinocchio in this story stop that girl for running their mouth you look at Kristin and you see beauty and excellence and then you look at Eden and you see strength Beauty and knowledge and then you look at Elizabeth and you see understanding strength Beauty and justice and then you look at me Heather and you see Superman is struggling without you you don't have to look no further than the Nada I made a story called Superman Begins Thomas Nada is excellent and beautiful and we have Samantha the most educated beautiful respectful female here at the witches round table what you saying Thomas Allred Jr I'm saying that love these women and the rest of these women in the world the same way Superman look at me Rumpelstiltskin is in your heart because you fought so many battles that you don't realize who you are Thomas hang on a second do you hear me hello this is Asia I'm your fairy godfather Asia get your a** to the witches round table Etsy the fairy godmother Thomas you have to midnight to prove your point to the ladies at the 12:30 tonight all will be said and done with you need to take your time Thomas we know you Superman it's just that Kathy my heart needs you Kathy believe in yourself Superman believes in you it's almost 2 right now where I'm at lay down and go to sleep my ladies Superman has a job to finish fairy godmother and free godfather I know that Rumpelstiltskin is inside of my heart I'm trying to be professional give me a chance that's what we came here for Thomas see all the people they listening to you being professional has made you strong enough to make rules for justice I have to give it to you showing people that you are in love is truly the genuine article so we grant you your request Thomas Superman listen to me carefully listen to me as i take you on a journey with me go back to the beginning Thomas I told Jenny I loved her what happened to the relationship the relationship ended because some people attacked us and Jenny didn't survive where were you when Jenny needed youI was sleep in the hospital from being injured from a shotgun wound handgun wound Thomas what did you tell God when you heard Jenny left you I told God that I will be and avenging Angel and be there for all the women and children in the world with my life I promise if he give it back to me listen to how The story goes you're injured trying to protect somebody else.

Thomas you got a wife who gets murdered while you're in the hospital you go to prison for carrying a weapon to the police station you get out and get married and get divorce in less than 10 years you have no children that you know of and you may business ideas to save women and children 200 of them ideas you've made you can plead it to music CDs full length albuMs. and you worked at every company in your City and surrounding areas you've lost a few people Thomas but you haven't lost your personality Thomas what people are telling you is you ain't got to be a superhero for Kristen and you ain't got to be a superhero for Eden listen Thomas you know we love you Elizabeth but I tried to talk to you but you didn't listen listen Thomas Elizabeth and Nada and Samantha cannot hear you right now Thomas if I give you one wish what would it be my wish would be to grant the women 200 million dollars a piece all over the United States and surrounding area your wish is my command Thomas sit back and listen to yourself for a second Thomas know who is going to believe this made-up story of dream.

Ms. and fairies in my heart the people love me look how those people did to you Thomas we need you professional what is it that you really want Superman I'm just looking to have me a child a baby with someone who cares about me ladies awakened just fairy godmothermother we have awakened in this story of Superman Begins we found a heart has been broken you got to take your time with me Thomas the hero is Superman hiMs.elf Thomas allred Junior Thomas a he was telling the story but the seem like something is missing Eden Reid Eden when I was 3 years old I talk to God and ask him to make me an angel it's not what you think Eden because I have to 12 to be the hero that I am if you are police officer didn't tell me how you feel Thomas Allred Jr I feel confident in the world my business Eden see Eden I took my time and wrote These manuscripts I just hope that you could take your time and read through these manuscripts is this the end of the story no it ain't the end of the story I'm keeping it professional asking you do you understand me my wife take your time I need a compound Eden you have a call on line 1 Eden this is Eden hello this is the president of the United States Thomas I got the president of the United States on the phone don't give up Eden what can I do for you sir Mr.. President I listen to you and Thomas conversating Eden listen to me Thomas if you want Eden and you can have to be professional I can hear him without the phone in my hands Eden satellite imagery shows the images of you and Eden to me right now Eden you been searching all your life for a superhero ain't you keep finishing up that book the movie it's based on a true story Thomas is telling you Mr.. President if Thomas is a police officer and a government agent why is he writing books and movies for his first job is to be in the neighborhood and be there for the people secondly he made business ideas to stop terrorists and saved each Children's lives you say children's lives Mr.. President Thomas acts like a gotdamn superhero and three I sent Thomas out the rescue all the princesses all over the globe isn't that some sh*t Eden the possibility of your books and movies are endless take your time and explain to me Mr.. President Eden I programmed you and Thomas you were supposed to have met at this exact stage in your career your going to have to help me to please understand this Mr.. President I got you a compound that's full of women Thomas on that compound is King to all of his ladies why Mr.. President because you a secret agent Eden and Thomas's secret agent this been through ma**ive trauma and surgery so Eden look at him that was the president online 2 Thomas wait a minute if you really love me why all the games in your manuscript each time I told you I loved you you never called me Eden so I made it these people to replace the emptiness in my heart for you I'm saying it's almost Christmas Eden and I love you I'm going back to my family cause it seeMs. like they are the only ones that care about me girl what happened to your manuscript I'm too professional to tell anybody that I gave my manuscript to you over the computer Eden stop with the games Thomasyou make me feel like you don't have anyone in this world who loves you listen to you speaking to me Eden if you have something on your heart then let it show I can't wait for this book to be finished Thomas its a movie now in my eyes listen to Thomas it's beginning to rain in my business office you need to take your time and talk to me about your plans for the books and movies Thomas Thomas Allred just vanished in front of Eden Thomas quit playing I am a professional God has sent me to talk to you Eden to be continued on the next episode of going down with that crime Thomas your story reading is excellent Thomas you got the 12:30 to make you compoud complete make sure that the women love you that you take to your island it's not an island it's only Carolina beach that I'm going to Thomas Eden here for you baby I should just take a nap a nap sounds like a great idea do you want some Crystal give me a cup of crystal Thomas representing Eden I look at you and you look like you're the most beautifulest woman on this Earth Thomas it takes more than a cup of Crystal to get to mewhat I got you your check from Imperial designs Incorporated Thomas I'm to tired to look at it tell me how much it is its 80 trillion dollars and no cents Thomas you must be out of your goddamn mind saying that check is 80 trillion dollars and no sense take your time but Thomas why would you give me this much money forI appreciate your help and friendship Thomas allred Junior and this is the end of Superman Begins Eden is almost Christmas please read my manuscript do you want p**sy for half off or p**sy for full price either way p**sy good all day and that's the game Eden before 12 midnight he had time enough to say and that's the game Eden before 12 midnight that's a wrap Eden I know you don't believe in Superman but this movie is based on true events listen Thomas I know that you would know more p**sy Thomas If we talked about your future Thomas but I'm telling you I just have to go and read your manuscript now I can see you your Superman Thomas Allred Jr and that's the way my holiday season begin with Eden and my other 10 iven't forgot to mention.

A love angel has always been thought of as a mif Eden but their are Love Angels all across the country what a Lovely Angel is is unique spiritual bean who interferes when a relationship is going bad to make that relationship good again as you can see Kristen I am a Love Angel people threaten me because my love is stronger than in the emotion they have ever felt Kristen talk and embrace your Angel what do you want from me Angel to teach you love and security not finance in security where does love come from Angel it comes from your heart and your mind at the same time working together to create an emotion that we call Love I'm afraid of Love Thomas can you teach me how to be strong yes Kristen I can teach you how to be strong but you have to believe in your Angel Believe In Love again because Kristen I am your Love Angel Thomas's of Love Angel I need to talk to him Thomas you promise you won't leave me want you your are my Love Angel well right now he's sitting at home writing a book call Love Angel Elizabeth go ham on his a** if he cheat on you that boy got too many girlfriends to be a Love Angel Love Angels all over the country hear my voice my girl is Eden Reid and she is my Love Angel how can that be Thomas you a Love Angel yourself because every seven years and Angel starts to cry and another Angel hears them I swear to God anybody touches my woman I'm blanking out because of male Love Angel can't breathe without his Queen Angel you see the look on my face Thomas this is story I just can't accept why can't you accept the Eden Reid cause I need a Love Angel in my life to help me to help you wrote a book report in 7 days Thomas Allred jr.Eden the book report is to show you that I'm a true professional and that i am needing your hand in marriage Thomas but with stories like Love Angels Thomas get it professional Thomas you got the right building concept but you got the wrong things in mind think about what I'm saying to you Eden Love Angels are in here you just got to read between the lines I can't read between the lines on the story like this Thomas Eden are you saying that love Angels won't make it to the press I didn't say that did I Thomas so what are you saying then that you don't believe in true love that is exactly what I'm saying Thomas Eden look at us I know you've been through a lot of things that have hurt you but I tell you that if you could just believe in me in this manuscript a love angel with visit you tonight before 12 what time is it Eden it's 7:30 where I'm from I'm giving you three hours to write the story Thomas you got a Love Angel on you to don't waste my time Eden one more thing can I have a kiss see it's my birthday tonight give that boy a kiss who said that Thomas Eden I don't know who or when they said it but I know it's your Love Angel Thomas get the hell out of here and finish the manuscript called Love Angel bless you bless you too Thomas now im starting to hear stuff Merry Christmas Eden Christmas is 4 months away I don't want to hear it Thomas from you or nobody else but wait Eden I want to tell you something Thomas don't you see that she doesn't want to be bothered she has a boyfriend coming to a rescue does she now if you looking for her we got a Macy's day parade party in the office this Saturday night maybe you should come and attend Thomas Kristen Beam is going to be there is Samantha McDaniels is going to be there I'm trying to think of what is going to be that that you would know Chelsea is going to be there and Vivian and Nada going to be there and Porsche is also going to be there there's one more person that I forgot to mention is going to be there Heather Elizabeth and Evelyn it's going to be there for once in your lifetime Thomas take a chance these woman adore you how can I see them without people being in the way Kimberly Thomas your stronger than you think you are all you have to do is dressed as an angel and come to the party listen to me everyone in two more weeks we have the Macy's office day parade party get you a mate Kristen yes Thomas did you hear about the party I was just wondering if you seen Eden anywhere Thomas I was only being sincere I realize that I hurt you Thomas and I'm sorry I made a mistake but could you forgive me and let's start all over again cause I got you in my heart Thomas it ain't no way we can start all over again Kristen you let me down when I needed you the most I can tell you one thing and one thing only girl happy New year damn he just annihilated Kristen hey have you seen April Samantha she's not here tell me she was supposed to be here at 5 give it 30 more minutes and April be here I promise you Samantha by the way I'm free later on what are you doing tonight Thomas probably reading some old comics and drinking root beer it's going to be Christmas day in a few more hours Christmas day we can start all over again I like it when the ball drops Porsche I didn't see you standing there I know you were talking to somebody I want to take my time and thank you for the business ideas that you gave me Porsche gave to me an expression that made me think that I was in for something see look at you all over the place your standing there drunk who is that messing up the party this Kristen and Eden's ex-boyfriends this just all we need in here take your time and be professional Thomas I'm still looking for Eden Vivian have you seen her no it's just that I've been thinking about you Thomas a lot and I never cheated on you a cheated on you a couple times Vivian with my manuscript what can I do to make it up to you Thomas I'll fix you anything you want just come home to me Vivian you wasting your time speaking to me like this I come to the conclusion that I'd rather have my work then to have a relationship Thomas cut the noise out you trying to work who is that talking trash that's Elizabeth ex-boyfriend Samantha's ex boyfriend is here too Heather came to the party Heather way to make an entrance Thomas I need to speak to you there is something you don't know about Eden Heather what are you saying to me Eden is a prostitute no way I'm going to take you upstairs HeatherThomas just stay right here with me I got money I'm not in debt I got mutual funds and the house and cars that you need Heather I came here I'm looking for Eden come talk to me Thomas June how you doing I could be better if you wasn't so damn stubborn I need to see you Thomas tomorrow at the Christmas party remember Thomas we loved each other first I'm Your Love Angel I got to get rid of that girl June she's always calling me at 3 a.m. in the morning just because I wrote a couple movies the people seem to love what am I thinking about I need to find Eden and tell Eden that here go her manuscript at least one part of it I can deal with you ThomasI can deal with a man that knows how to handle his business I don't want to fight you Jill didn't rescue this one time put down the knife Jill how much you hurt me you're coming home with me go to hell I'm not Jill you crazy as a motherf*cker let me see those pills I see you took too many pills again somebody call the paramedics Eden what the f*ck is going on in my office listen to Eden I brought you the manuscript at a Macy's day party Thomas I just wanted you to see the work I done all right everybody out of the building everybody everybody out of the building now April just listen to her Eden is upset right now Thomas this means you April my manuscript is on your front desk I'm going to get it to her Thomas Eden here is his manuscript the people have been gone for 30 minutes now you can see what he's been doing how do you start it once upon a Time there was an angel of love and I called him a love angel and to my surprise the love angel needed love as well as I did I'm writing this book to show that I'm dedicated to you Eden you have to hear me out it's a lovely angel in between these pages I'm watching you from my words going through your mind I hope that you can see how much effort I took to become this love angel girl with me there is no pain there's only emotion in love Eden you need to talk to that boy what do you say next in the story April I sit at home waiting for your dream to call me I am the love angel thats knocking at your window see how he do it now I'm Your Love Angel and I'm here for one reason to program you on the secret theories of romance April he's being professional I'm a program you I'm a program you Eden whether you like it or not all I got to do is kiss you once in your heart is mine he done got major professional I believe you have something that belongs to this angel you have that scarf that you were in the winter time coach me to be your man I am your angel Eden so I can become human and love you more each day Eden I can become just about anything you need me to begirl I listen to your thoughts and your memories are in my head interviewed is Thomas Allred when i interview Thomas Allred hold your head up so we can see you Eden this is part one of your story as a love angel Eden I can feel your tears and when you going to cry I know my angel loves me but I have an ex-boyfriend trying to get back with me eating your ex boyfriend is the next boyfriend tell that dude to beat It move out the way Miss Athena you got an angel coming through p**sy on sale three for one$2 get you p**sy off the hook p**sy is not for sale Miss Athena high dollar p**sy go for nothing Miss Athena can I borrow your coat now look at this put on this mink Thomas Allred get p**sy for free going on and tell all them women about me Thomas don't give up i need you to focus on your manuscript I give to you your birthday present Thomas Eden you didn't have to all I want to do is write for you and don't recognize this Thomas but we're not a movie incorporation Eden are you saying to me that you can't help me out with my manuscriptsI'm saying that is close to 12 and your supposed to have your stories on my desk immediately Eden I am working but my time is 11:28 that makes it 1028 at my time Thomas see here Thomas the last of the manuscript better be on my desk by 12:30 midnight you hear me Thomas my time what was I doing I can't keep up with thismaybe I should just tell Eden the truth that I love her im a do exactly what I'm thinking about Eden I'm in love with you I know that sounds too made up Eden we have a talk for a second I'm in love with you no never believe me see what I got to do is introduce her to my love if a kiss shell know exactly what I'm thinking in feeling here goes nothing Eden and that's the end of the story this can't be happening look at the bulsh*t this boy handed in to me kiss my a** Thomas Allred thank you girls for reading my story I call this Love Angel the beginning part 2 Thomas send me my goddamn message Eden you been working all day haven't you I can't see how you do it Love Angel begins back up I'm a tell you Eden how much I care about you make sure the Eden realizes that you are her Love Angel Thomas what we do going to have to stay between us Eden girl Thomas professional Eden there so many things Eden there so many things that I would like to tell you things like what Thomas I am a superhero that's just now being recognized as being a manI know already Thomas Your The Dark Knight Batman no just give me a second Thomas let me guess your The Lion King Simba you are officer Reign from the New York Police department I'm going to keep my identity a secret just a little while longer Eden I'm not testing you but the book is coming to a close I told you he's an escape artist I'm going to skip all this Ashley you don't know what you're talkin about what are you then Thomas Superman if you must know I am Superman I'm also super negro from the ghetto give me your power super negro from the ghetto Eden watch this well super negro we're waiting on you the whole police station has been waiting on super negro to come out Thomas your awesome but you got so many identities that it's incredible I got powers of making you fall in love with the quickness Eden y'all better get that Superhero a badge of some kind Thomas end of my message I want to talk to Kristen yes I'm here listening Thomas eating Kristen Ashley April where that super negro go Kristen is he tripping Eden I said where is super negro April we might need to get somebody in there call security on Thomas Kristen super negro cant be far Thomas honey you might be tired from all the work come on with me and get you some rest Kristen I can't stop until I teach super negro a thing or two Thomas look at me you are super negro Thomas my agent code name is super negroKristen if I lose my memory what's going to happen to me I'm going to love you exactly the way I'm doing Thomas you're safe with me super negro quit worrying about super negro Thomas and send me that dialogue I know Kristen is ready to read everything that you say love angel Thomas to the rescue Thomas send me the message people are starting to look at me don't make me have to whoop your motherf*cking a** Eden your love angel sends you the message of Angels in love will you be my wife Eden I realized it's the only chance I have to talk to you what's the name of that book it's called Love Angel Thomas you need to talk to me for what because Eden and KristenI want y'all to hang on a second I got flip this tape over like I was saying before I was so rudely interrupted like I was saying I want you two and Elizabeth and Samantha and Nada to be my one two three wives you must be ridiculous you must be out of your goddamn I'm telling you Samantha the numbers don't lie what are you saying to us Thomas that you will buy us you can put it that way Kristen I also want Cricket so you just going to buy every woman that your attracted to Thomas allred Junior I'm going to pay for every last one of them tell us how you going to pay for all the women Thomas yes Porsche I'm putting business ideas books and movies together with plain ingenuity I'm worried about you Thomas Elizabeth there's not a thing to worry about what about of Kristen marry you don't say it if you don't mean it Elizabeth I been in love with you here we go with this again Love Angel I'm watching you I'm on YouTube Elizabeth you hear that there Nada be professional and tell me how you feel Love Angel Nada I care about you deeply talking about you love me go tell that to Eden Eden im still working on my book do you have material that you need Thomas yes I have my material I'm just dealing with this heartache that I have inside of me don't test me Thomas send a message to me if I send you the message Eden would you wait for me to become famous I'm Your Love Angelsend me that message Love Angel I'm watching you grow through your manuscripts Thomas what does Love Angel mean to you it means that we'll have kids Eden I'm Your Love Angel fantasy you just a dream Thomas I want you to realize that you had me since we spoke on the phone Eden I want you to realize Thomas that I've been dying and waiting to speak to you ever since I read your manuscript Superman And His Allies I have one more part of this manuscript Eden I'm working all night to get it to you I like you Eden these manuscripts are for you Eden and Kristen and Samantha and NADA in Porsche and Elizabeth and Heather and Kathy and Kay and Julie and Ashley and Karen and Donna and Jill and Nora is there any more people you want to add Thomas I'm open to suggestions no I think Eden that is enough ladies I am your love angel send me my manuscript Thomas be careful what you wish for Eden Eden there's a part 2 to this manuscript I'll finish it tonight before the sun rises so we have no hard feelings about things I'm saying I love you Eden your Love Angel part 1 send me my motherf*cking message yes Eden your message is sent to you now Love Angel

CHAPTER 5

Part 2 of Love Angel the angel made a deal that who shall ever shall published five books at one time shall have his or her destiny fulfilled so Eden you are my destiny five books is in your hand no I'm not Thomas you only realized me when I called you Eden I've been thinking that you are a Queen to my heart Thomas I know I've been thinking of you my heart just can't live without you Thomas you do realize I'm a professional publisher Eden I just want to know is there any chance that you will be my wife being your wife is the same thing I'm wishing for Thomas Allred Jr you know what they say about us don't you Eden what do they say Thomas that you and I are meant to be together Eden this second part of love angel I didn't know where to start how you going to ask somebody to marry you Thomas and you asking me listen Thomas go represent it ain't even that way Elizabeth damn Elizabeth who the f*ck is Elizabeth Thomas Emily listen to me for a second you must think I'm playing games Thomas I'm about to beat your a** if you don't get serious Kristen you know I was just playing with you listen what kind of book is this sh*t you had this sh*t Thomas Eden you're so special work with me you better stop that sh*t Thomas girl I want you to stand on top of the building with me and take a picture of me you think I'm a fool don't you Thomas you want a picture so hoe can see you Yes you heard me right hoe can see you Thomas check this out ElizabethI'm going to kick your motherf*cking a** boy Nada I'm just playing with you don't get so serious Thomas you getting ready to get your motherf*cking a** whooping if you don't quit messing with me Nada please understand that in a different time me and you would have been together good Hustle I got to give it to you Thomas you got game like Parker Brothers Eden this is the countdown this the last book that I'm writing Thomas you know you got talent sell me your books and your manuscripts I was waiting for you to say that these books and manuscripts cripts belonged to you Eden I love you Superman don't you think I love you too Thomas Allred Jr I'm Your Love Angel Thomas Allred Jr my name is sacrifice your book for love you want me to sacrifice this book don't you I will I mean I do love you Eden and onlyy you your love angel part 2.

Eden the end of love angel goes like this Eden I want you to believe in me because I'm in love with you Eden I care about you so much I'll be your love angel when you need me. Eden listen you and me or compatible that is a history we got going I'm waiting to see you my love angelcuz in my heart you Wonder Woman forever I took time to write you the manuscript sincerely yours super negro go ahead and send me my message THOMAS ALLRED JUNIOR I LOVE YOU WE ARE LOVE ANGEL'S EVENTUALLY IF WE'RE TRUE ENOUGH WE'LL SEE EACH OTHER ONE DAY Eden girl I want to see you on the other side of this manuscript I'm pulling the plug Eden we are love angels just let me know if you need me girl super Negro super negro I definitely need you I'm EDEN REID AND I LOVE THOMAS ALLRED JR that is all that I have to say bye super negro bye my love that's some sh*t Thomas send that message to me Kristen BEAM YOUR PUBLICIST oh sh*t

Eden you can't remember me but my name is Thomas Allred Jr I just wanted to see if you had the chance to read my manuscript I'm addressing you to let you know that I have recently been writing for what Arthur House so that you know that I'm being loyal I'm addressing you to ask you if we could talk over the phone about this issue sincerely yours Thomas Allred Jr and ps Eden if you want me you can call me anytime honey I'm a go now here go my number if you ever need to reach me it's my number is (828)302-0716 the next book that i send you got people in it I see you don't play Ms. Eden Reid have a wonderful day I just want to let you know that I'm worth it Mr. Ebony Buy it Thomas Super officer Reign Simba Of The Lion King Eddie Munster slimer from Ghostbusters The Dark Knight from Batman He-Man from Masters of the universe I'll be with you if you only let me we need a vacation Ms. Eden Reid I'm just showing you who I am listen to me I am the dark angel I'm Ludacris I am innocent of all charges I am a vampire Dracula can't you see that I am Van helsing now that you know me I'm Frankenstein once apon a time there was a girl who wanted a boy the boy however couldn't see that the girl had his best interest in mind so he kept writing dialogues in hopes that he would one day have a family with a beautiful woman like you Thomas so as the boy grew older that's all he wanted was a family officer Reign until one day the boy had realize that the girl had liked him anyway slimer from the Ghostbusters and see how my foot down can make things happen the girl replied to the boy you've been making these got lost for 20 years you really think that them people care about you keep trying and you will see that I care about you and your well being because your dialogues are wonderful heaven really knows that you are a prince of my happily ever after Thomas so the boy started to realize that it wasn't what he said but how he acted towards his girl and her name is princess Thomas speak to officer Reign of the new York police department see the moral of the story is Reign that you must keep all of your appointments with your girl Eden I just want you to know that my heart beats for you I don't got know kind of work schedule Eden Wants to see you I watched you make a speaker out of my self Eden you don't have a clue Reign how much I do love you I'm hoping that we can get the f*ck out of here and go somewhere seriously all this time I've been sending through my messages Ebony Buy it girl make sure that Officer Reign gets a contract y'all watched that man come up on the street corners a true testament is right now we doing the best that we can to show you how I feel and how am I I'm prince charming of forever after Eden you see Eden I don't give up on some one I love you can have this this dialogue as a reference that we knew each other your my Wonder Woman and im trying to see if you are ready to be apart of our Justice League officer Reign finish up with that girl well you please come and see me Eden I live in the states my city name is Hickory NC so good after noon Thomas I trying to tell you Eden that I have a crush on you that did it for me listen to me I'm Mr. Monopoly Eden the game has been played and the match as been set how much you think that this dialog is worth that your time Eden don't get it twisted I'm a business man this girl need you Thomas call on Superman Eden i programmed you to see the real me I'm only here for half of the week and that a be on Wednesday figure out what you want because with me there are endless possibilities in store for you and in store for me to do me a favor and tell your momma that I love you Eden listen Thomas I'm asking you to be my wife on a computer screen Eden Reid may I ask you did I say to much Thomas Because can't live me live without you Van helsing I'm just waiting for you to sign this contract my Superman contract be sure that you believe in me Eden before you even move forward Van helsing because I appreciate what you did for me in my time of need listen Dracula it's to many people that going through my files Eden turn the lights off and keep listening to my voice on your computer screen I'm am Prince charming and your happily ever after starts now in your new fairy tail it's called Romance Eden Romance Eden begins in a place to where Eden knows how you feel Thomas be strong Eden to endanger you that would be Injustice I just can't accept no more foul works I know that my business mature enough to make you my princess this is Dracula and your lips are everything that I dream of I'm creating this dialogue so that you understand that you are my girl Eden I don't stop when I'm working so Eden buckle your seatbelt because it's going to be a long day at work your the one who's famous honey it's my time Eden this is romance without you getting at me you brown nosing people stay the hell away from my girl I'm a put you on a pedestal once I get you in my house Eden say my name three times and see how much money you get Eden I'm working on this dialogue what do you think of it Eden I'll be mature what I think is you have my dreaMs. in your hands Eden my dreaMs. are too strong for somebody to hold them I must see the top Thomas allred Junior Eden I can't stop this if I wanted to I'm almost finished let me speak for a second see managed to make it through my prison-walls to speak to you Eden ever since I heard your voice Thomas I've been thinking about you Eden take the dialogue as a reference of how I feel about you Eden if you want to be with me press my buttons if you don't want to be with me you can have everything my dialogue is meant for you Eden I'm getting exactly what I deserve this loneliness Eden no other man holds a conversation like me im guilty as charged listen save Van helsing Eden recognize I'm doing everything I can to be there with you look I ain'tstopping this language Eden I'm usually to myself doing push ups and drinking miracle whip sometimes I can't believe myself when I think about you Eden I have ambitions and you know I ain't doing this for nothing so come and see slimer Eden we did Ghostbusters let's walk with people who got the mind on business let's boldly go where no one has been before Eden to search up new heights in New horizons to boldly travel galaxies unreached by anybody else look Eden come and knock on my door this is the beginning of our romance novel girl care about you I'm going to send you more dialogue sweetheart let me see if you want me first cause I make it hard for you to chill I Make It Sweet on your lips Eden we talkin about cold hard f*cking cashier you taking over you better get his boy his contract recognize who the boss is Eden Eden I watched you mature into the grown woman that you are I'm watching you make a fool out of yourself but not calling me listen to me girl I know exactly what I'm doing this is the game called life Eden and I'm Richer than any opponent on the board this dialogue is strong enough to make and conquer 10000 movies y'all can't be telling me my work is bulsh*t or bogus day and night I do push-ups Eden respect my g because you got a hard-working man listening for you do you see this concept I just will not admit defeat I am Prince charming this is happily ever after Eden my name is Jethro bodine Eden take your time and listen you better listen to me honey this dialogue is worth several billion dollars on the black market you only like me cuz I'm rich and famous Thomas girl what you need to do is tell me how you f*cking feel about me everyday I'm doing push-ups just waiting for your mother f*cking call maturity has got me reaching out to you Eden if your a woman of power then you can only see where I'm coming from Ebony Buy it goddamn motherf*ckers make me sick they hating on me Eden this overseas I'm Ebony Buy it hiMs.elf Eden I can't even sh*t without somebody being there to wipe my a** you got appreciate Thomas ebony buy it be keeping up with the times yall this is romance Eden part 1 girl we are never going to stop it just add dialogue and girl listen you a queen of the country listen Thomas these people are going crazy over your language what language is he using he uses ebonics 101 chapter 7 page 9 + 14 the rules state if a king is in love he can have as many different women as he want to in Ebonics chapter 12 page 16 in chapter 3 if a man has his damn moolah right than he can f*ck his girlfriend all f*ckink night furthermore in Lost education rule 17 states that once a queen find the king stay with him until his riches are depleted and his farm are burned down and his crops won't come in what I'm saying is Eden is that girl I know exactly how you feel about Mula it's my mission to solve that problem Eden check this out I'm using the language that ain't never been dealt with before Eden white people don't speak sh*t shose on your shoe Eden sh*t on my shoe Eden means that you'll get your motherf*cking money here we go Eden Romancing Eden part 1 is coming to an end put ebony buy it on the phone with me Thomas am doing what I can to get you this girlfriend ebony but it I heard that you a strong competitor Thomas listen this girl be making all kinds of movesshe don't bulsh*t when it comes to her work or her family life I got you Ebony but it tell her Ill beat the hell out of her if she cheat on me listen Thomas this girl ain't afraid of no beat down Thomas 30 seconds to the end of part one romancing Eden send her part 1 look how that boy communicating she understands you need a girl Thomas I got the perfect girl for you Romancing Eden part one is now closed this happily ever after for real Romancing Eden will open back up in the next dialog give me like 30 minutes Eden I get back to you Van helsing

Romancing Eden 2.0 it starts here Eden stop it so I can tell you what the truth is Ill never forget you samurai Eden we got Beauty and the beast on the radioI'm going to put everything I got on you Eden to win the championship you messing with a damn Thoroughbred I got you Eden muscle is humongously large I'm too professional for you Eden I'm here to tell you that I got potential and that you have potential to Eden they try to kick my conversation at the back door they don't know where I'm from and some a** whooping town and Eden I could have swore you got an a** whooping I got two different a** whoopins left its high-priced a** whoopins Eden but hell know any comedian I'm watching you could you professional will you help me out of the situation I'm in cause I need you to be my friend until I get there on the top Eden your special to me there's to much high price game in you for me to quit talking only care about beating you up Sweetheart we control the place Eden what do you want from me if you open up your heart then you see my true condition I'm just alone to myself Eden this manuscript is called romance and Eden part 2 I do everything I can for us to have it your way 2:30 in the morning I do push ups until 7 a.m. 7 a.m. I trim up my hair and brush my teeth 730 I shave my face and do push-ups again get to me girl 8 o c*ck I write my manuscript it keep on exercising it's a bag of chips on my table sour cream and onion so if your into me just give me a call Eden listen to me one second this manuscript is Romancing Eden I got to tell you I love you for someone else do Eden I'm getting better with time be professional cause it's me and you for the world about time that you realize this I will be professional now and on my way do you remember what you told me that you love me and you hope that I will give you a chance what Eden this is your manuscript by the time you read this here the whole country will answer to you as my wife you get benefits Eden you know you get benefits don't you as my wife receive benefits I'm taking over the country how Roswell go Eden now you see it now you don't I was sending my manuscript Thomas so you could approve of Eden cuz right now baby my manuscript is all that I have to offer I'm looking first then listening Eden girl is your heart that keeps me going professionally Eden I'll take care of you do you see how I'm doing you imagine is you and me on a beach somewhere best romantic Trip of our lifetimes girl I got two more entries to my manuscript I'm sending them to you right now I'm trying my best take your time girl and get to know me Eden when when I shineYou shine I'm going to make sure your a** gets to make it this is Romancing Eden part 2 and a half Eden all of them girls keep saying to me that I'm the one for the job manuscript I thank you damn much Eden this one more part to the manuscript Romancing Your Girl part 2 and 1/2 have come to an end y'all figure out me in the next episode of Thomas avenge me starring Thomas Allred Jr how many females want to get with me I'm Romancing you Eden part 2 and 1/2 is closed I'll send you part 3 tonight girl with the rest of my manuscript Eden I love you and I'm doing the best I can to make it I'll get you anything that you want in this whole wide world Eden part 3 begins now

CHAPTER 6

Romancing Eden part 3 girl I'm seeing you as my queen in this party I'm taking my time getting to know you Eden you got a beauty about you this unbeatable all kind of people watching you but I see your a** from over here communicate and you'll be working girl this is a decent book here isn't it I'm trying to help you get back up on your feet where you and me belong I recognize that you need genius Eden genius is my middle name Bobby Fischer is my middle name Eden after I'm done with you I'm send the manuscript to The journal of Bobby Fischer I'm not trying to betray anybody I'm just working on a come up Eden Bobby Fischer is a part of me along with Superman and Van helsing I think you are professional enough to hear me out Eden.

I want to compoud with 5,000 women on it I'm willing to die for itso when I tell you that you're beautiful Eden I mean it im a get you everything that you need and ask for I already conquered business ideas we talkin about you Eden I can't explain how you keep making me feel stop looking at me and girl that'll be shame I'm trying to help you to see that I'm professional girl and you are my heart come and see me Eden if you get a chance you hear what we got to do I put this manuscript in your hands your hands are gold in my eyesight remember we got a contract Eden I'm giving you half of my businesses for you to come stay with me at my compound I'm a serious ruler Eden only the best can live with me so you think you're hot sh*t do you you think you and them other girls can hold me down I need you to suck my d*ck Eden because there's a crown I got to achieve princess you know that I love you every single waking moment I'm at this money for you to deny me would be selfish I'm making sure that y'all have everything that you need long as I'm here on this Earth Eden don't try to play games with me I'll beat you in everyone go ahead sleep sweetheart listen to me I can't explain just how much I care about you this is a manuscript of love hope and understanding as you read my text I hope that you can understand that you are my North Star and Eden listen to me in the family of 10 sometimes the head of the family can't eat all I'm saying this to you bulsh*t with professionals all the time I see you I think to myself what a lucky person I am to have someone like you the cares about me I'm thinking right now that the manuscript isn't through Eden is so much dialogue that I have to give this is Romancing Eden im a keep on Romancing you I hope you don't give up I hope there's some fight left in you because these days are terrible honey and we need each other to be strong I looked at Michael Jackson filMs. I listen to Mariah Carey sing I dream of you every night Eden I just hope that we can remain friends after the contracts come out because once I get inside you Eden the game is going to be over now publish that right there Eden I'm sending this message out to you I'm taking over you Thomas Allred Jr Ms. Eden Reid is your source for income represent Thomas ALLRED JR professionally girl I'm just doing my thing omancing you Eden I'm telling you a part 4 after this.

CHAPTER 7

Part 4 of Romancing Eden Eden all you have to do is talk if you a good person then the whole industry a see to it that you have everything you need I'm a movie star professional honey I've been watching movies ever since I can remember Clair Huxtable I watch Bill Cosby I got Martin Lawrence on tape Eden my dreaMs. are simple Eden I just want you to pay attention to me in detail because your book is about done Eden and I starved to get it on the shelf I messaged you every time with new material Shall I published this Eden I heard about you taking advantage of my heart just like a woman is supposed to be professional Eden these are the times where your bank account doesn't matter I'm just saying to you I miss you my God I miss you tell me when to stop this Eden because a book is more important to me than you are girl I usually don't stand like this but I'm just hoping for my deal because waiting on me is a family of 6 they are beautiful thank you so much Eden I'm Romancing you as we speak I'm giving you my all in these dialogues I do the same thing for Arthur house Ms. Erin Cohen consultant Ms. Eden Reid I do apologize if I'm not doing the right thing you a** look good to me and I won't quit until I know that you watching me take over the world I mean us take over the world at the right Eden you know how I do things by now and I appreciate you Eden getting in touch with me here we go around 2 you asked for seconds damn Eden round 2 is a motherf*cker you better show that man the exit your ex-boyfriend what I'm saying Eden I come in here to wash my hands from all the dirt I am Van helsing in the world has you captive Eden I take my work very seriously so if you know I'm real then call me Eden I work at third night shift I want every night for you Eden this book is dedicated to the red white and blue flag is it possible that we can get together Eden if we knew each other we could have a ton of fun Eden this right we can do anything we want to win this manuscript comes out I'm serious Eden if I keep working on this manuscript and you keep working for I already know what's up Eden I'm thinking about you all day long keep holding your position cause I need you to understand that I love you Eden I'm being sincere with my words you asked me you will receive itMy love has no limits or no boundaries I'm testing everybody to see what y'all look like see the way I'm talkin is money imma get to the top cause Eden you are a part of me happy birthday Eden I bet you never seen a cake this big in your life before girl I teach you the finer things in lifeJust so I can tell you you're beautiful April fool's day Eden is 2 days after my birthday if you look for me I'm celebrating a major deal girl I met you I can't give up girl Because you wouldn't believe in me if I did Romancing your a** part 4 got me singing all the time I'm going to do everything in my power to show you that I love you there is another part to this part 5 Eden I'm testing your will I need me a contract Eden I'm Romancing your a** Thomas ALLRED JR

Imma give you some work Eden this is work Mr.. Monopoly has sent for you I hope you realize that you won't talk with what my dreaMs. are I realize that you've been professional not talkin to me we wasted time Eden them girls look at me like I'm a kick or a brownie or something I'm just doing push-ups all day long let me tell you something Eden every Sunday evening I try to prove myself to you buy making up a story I got to prove myself to you Eden thats why im famous I write with precision of excellence I'm Romancing you Eden in an interlude of jealousy my heart don't stop Eden until I bite the bullet of strangers out to get me you're exactly what I want Eden see this contract means nothing without you Eden I'm sitting here thinking of you every moment that pa**es moments that I get up I do exercises I'm trying to help you Thomas but you need to help me be professional and you see where life takes you but if you're not professional it's a lonely road and boy thank you for my gift you sent me Ebony Buy it sent you those gifts listen Thomas people watching you and they're watching me too whatever you do Thomas you have to keep your a** clean I mean keep your nose clean Thomas help me to figure out what it is you're after eating I just want some cereal boxes 2 gallons of milk you entertaining me which is smart comments all day a professional all we I can't give up on nothing it's 4 in the morning I mean to say 4:30 I got a real estate contract coming to me I got an idea contract coming to me I got a music contract coming to me I got a book and movie deal coming to me and you know about it all I got to say is B. Edenhis life is been rough but I think I can pull through it your loved it drives me crazy I'm sending the message out to you the message got a few mistakes in it as for me I'm doing okay I love yI got you aou emotions Eden you are my heart

Thomas

Eden I know you that you don't think I'm good enough for a contract I am mature I got you in mind you hear me my heart can't be satisfied without you Eden

The lifetime journal of Ebony Buy it hiMs.elf I got you Ms. Susan Jennings I'm with Eden Reid this is Ebony Buy it how real is that name you can pay me I wouldn't sh*t on you is the most powerfulest nastiest name I know Thomas yes Miss Susan Jennings you had me singing up a storm after you boySusan Jennings I'm back on my feet Ebony Buy it finna get knocked out come on if you want some boy float like a butterfly boy sting like a hornet I do like your shirt Thomas Thomas Allred Ebony buy it behave yourself I want some a** up in my house I want some house up in my a** what I'm trying to do today is calculate my figures if this is what 4 billion 4 billion did Ebony buy it got the Kingman ship Kingman ship is larg d*ck in Spanish ebony I heard you don't Kristen for Eden Kristen knew Thomas was in love with her and she locked his a** up for saying he loved her in public That's a cold b*tch if you ask me it's Superman give her the benefit of the doubt he wrote all kind of business ideas and delivered them into her possession I was like kiss my a** Kristen speak your mind Ebony Buy it for six long years I've been wanting to f*ck Kristen behind Superman back I've been doing my pushups but it seemed nothing's working out he's the push-up King I'm dat p**sy fella and Superman how do you feel about ebony buy it I think he's one of a kind with a little work we can make a superhero out of him yet what about Kristen Thomas what am I supposed to say about a man she told me in prison when I told her I loved her it's just a story that I don't want to talk about back to you Superman yeah I was kind of messed up how Kristen did Thomas but we're heroes we get over sh*t like that over sh*t like what know skins for long periods of time Superman talk to the people out there I'm a tell you one thing only people there's a thin line between love and hate I know that's right I didn't ask for much but as I stood my ground the world gave me plenty I'm a true competitor in the world market today I know I seen innocent how does she look how does how look Superman Eden Reid I'm writing this story 4 get your a** back to the story see one day while I was being a superhero I caught a glimpse of some a** that I hadn't seen before I said a** can I speak to you for a moment and lo and behold Eden Reidspeak to me and said you look like you could use something to drink yall what the hell is wrong with my story Eden Reid said to me hi Eden Reid from the group and all that sh*t to make a long story short she has me under a spell Superman what are you trying to say you want to f*ck her ebony buy it I am a man of a woman's values I took my time to get to know that a** before I want to f*ck her Kristen Beam noticed you the first day that's what Susan that'great Italian vegetablesThomas you know you get a contract if you win that p**sy I want change you Thomas all of us are being professional we going to talk about you

The lifetime journal of Ebony Buy it hiMs.elf part 2 where my p**sy at I was dreaming this p**sy on me she called Moby D*ck now of knights at the round-table mad as hell I d*ck you down Kristen I'm going to shut this from The mountaintop Ebony But it manuscript is a true d*ck keep it going Kristen keep popping that a** I'm through with it I went the jail off of Vietnam Vietnam p**sy make my mouth warm I'm in Ebony Buy it and I'm just doing my thing keep looking for me in the house baby girl in the first saw you my d*ck still tall I hope you win I got a headache yo don't say my name if you don't mean that sh*t I need a p**sy that's fine to take over the government with now don't eat pizza with my workout all across the globe they trying to figure me out don't say my name if you ain't worth nothing the story is happily ever after but your a** can't say nothing girl you better get a hold this d*ck Eden and hold it tight when you shopping that p**sy with girl you know that's right we talkin about you Thomas talk some sh*t you know you want to tell me how this makes you feel go ahead Elizabeth talk to him dirty Elizabeth I know that you like me Thomas if Superman wasn't here I sit on your lap and suck your face there you go Thomas stand your ground for this p**sy I want to see you dance for me but naked p**sy no Thomas you but naked p**sy control yourself this is The lifetime journal of Ebony Buy it hiMs.elf part 2 either way it goes I'm still a superhero I need you to eat my p**sy Thomas can you do that Thomas I want to but I can't my keep over there on the floor can you eat my a** out superhero my d*ck is telling me I can but I want to think about your situation Thomas listen Thomas sit back and relax while I undress for you I never seen Asian p**sy in my life quit talking nasty but b*tch I got to say something come as you see my titties don't you yes I see them now get up Lay on the f*cking floor your fantasies are about to be fulfilled close your eyes Thomas Ebony Buy it pissed on him you get Ebony Buy it pissing on you in a dream wicked mean Thomas is Superman's going to have to come stronger Ebony Buy it is everywhere I can't get to him then you probably going to have to go deep cover Superman Maya come along with me don't you did devote her information to nobody Ebony Buy it looks out for females get Eden Reid on the phone sir that girl control you what do you need Thomas Eden Reid I need this manuscript published immediately give me some time I see what I can do can you work magic before Christmas if the d*ck long enough I can do anything Thomas Eden I got a long a** d*ck guess what Ebony Buy it said to me that he was going to piss on you Superman in a dream Ebony Buy it is just f*cking with you Superman Eden tell me he's not as strong as me is he you made this sh*t up i'm letting you know that if your d*ck can handle this then your d*ck can handle these panties call right Thomas that's my man talk to Eden Thomas Thomas yes what is the Samantha you need to wake up is time to go to work a pissed you while you were dreaming say what you would dream and saying come here Samantha piss on me so I pissed in your chest a little I had to sh*t so I sh*t in your mouth don't tell me you dookie in my mouth Samantha I sh*t it all over your a** girl I want you to pick my game up what game we playing tonight Superman a three-way split with you Eden and Kristen no cards involved only d*ck and p**sy and where will the d*ck come from Thomas yours truly miss Ebony Buy it tell me sh*t about me I'm going to beat that motherf*cking a** girl I recognize you ain't new to this game I am the champion of the world Matt Dillon put your d*ck down and come with me okay Miss Susan Jennings but Miss Kitty is wet see

RoboCop be taking this time tell him the truth Eden Reid see yall what I'm saying at me and Eddie Munster are going to f*ck Eden tell them people the truth like it is my phone keep freezing up Eden but girl I'm battling for my position I don't play this Erin Cohen got my manuscripts to a different set of manuscript I sent when y'all play this game look for a boss a nigga who can hold his d*ck straight without pissing on hiMs.elf the Chinese people don't know that I'm a superhero black negro is my nickname what kind of superhero are you I'm the long d*ck ranger people watching you they can see you're talented getting Nada on the phone this is Nada speaking how may I help you baby they stole my manuscript get me a piece of cheese out of the refrigerator that boy stupid okay baby if these pussies want to go to war will go to war im a need two slices of tomato with the government cheese I'm about to turn you on Thomas Nada I have a question if I get you a bank account will you marry me Thomas I'm making your cheese sandwich right now you need to focus on your manuscript it's just that Nada I don't know the people that I'm dealing with you're a businessman Superman I know if you can handle this p**sy you can handle anything we going to take Superman out of the hood Thomas tell Monsieur cheese sandwiches ready Kristen how do I get here you been here the whole time send you love Kristen I'm telling you baby that boy cheated me out of my manuscript just tell Eden Reid when she walk through Eden Reid come on in and sit down what kind of dream is this Nada and Samantha come on in here and sit down now this is getting freaky what's going onthis is what's going on I'm ebony buy it I'm finna piss on you Superman you see how cool that nigga is this can't be my dream wake up Thomas we are now giving you a check for 3 billion dollars believes in you Mr.. Thomas allred Junior Eden Reid go to your man he talking about Eden Reid a I'mma tell you I'm going to send off the manuscript think about it Miss Susan Jennings and miss Lynn crouch this boy is on top of the world Thomas we never stop with that p**sy at I mean where that a** at cause all you ladies got his a**ets I'd like to have some a**ets right now all in my face I'd like to thank a lot of people a lot of people thank you Miss Erin Cohen and miss Eden Reid thank you

The lifetime journals of Ebony Buy it hiMs.elf part 3 listening people out there there shouting your king ebony get KBC whky on phone why Ebony who you calling I'm going to call Tom Selleck we need Magnum PI on this sh*t ebony he won't answer the phone then see if Mr.. T is off Mr.. T is working on that new Rocky film buster Douglas can anybody find buster Douglas buster Douglas is retired he now lives in Rhode island with his two kids where is Jody watley I need Jody watley I need the simple that butt Jody watley doesn't sing anymore Ebony Buy it can you find me MC Hammer where is MC Hammer at MC Hammer is retired and went to London damn it what about the thing the thing from the fantastic four where is he at the things costume was to tight and he suffocated we're all going to miss the thingdon't worry about that sh*t as Superman ever seen me I don't see how Ebony Buy it Superman be rushing people tell Superman he need to work for me give me tour from the movie scene don't you mean movie screen Ebony Buy it please get out of line one more time ho listen Ebony Buy it girl I put the house on it whatever you say to get you in the mood Ebony Buy it God damn you working with something Kristen yall get Samantha and come on hey Superman where we going we're going to the awards show ebony by kidnap My b*tch I thought Eden Reid was your b*tch she is my girl I mean the kidnap Kristen I'm a piss on him if I get the chance tell me why again you want to piss on Ebony Buy it Superman because he pissed on my sandwich in the dream of mine God damn Superman this girl off the hook Thomas wake up dreaming Kristen hey sweetheart wheres Samantha Nada Elizabeth and Eden we thought you were dead Thomas Ebony Buy it told you hed piss on you and it did where did he piss on me at he pissed on your backseat what do you mean the best seat of my car we mean your backseat Thomas your rump shaker hell no Thomas done got sick as a motherf*cker look at some of this sh*t wants me to publish Kristen don't wait for me and don't stay up I gots to see Ebony Buy it Ebony Buy it call online 2 this is Ebony buy it speak to me if you're the caller I know that was you with my wife last night Ebony is your wife named precious Jordan Thomas wake up Thomas tell them females what you going to do to him listen that boy ain't doing nothing but sitting at home writing his manuscript make sure the boy get some p**sy after we finish this she made up Ebony Buy it and the man who's controlling this still remains unspoken for unspoken for do you mean yeah meaning he doesn't have no wife and no children and he's worth more than a trillion dollars who's the hottest female on the planet right now That is Kristen Beam and who's the next to the hottest female on the planet right now that is Eden Reid imma get you some of this p**sy so they quit hating on you Thomas cuz a big d*ck got to do with a big d*ck got to do I know that's right Alexandra introduce yourself to Thomas you ain't talkin bout no bulsh*t is you Thomas no I like p**sy a** tits and dollars I like that too I guess we can talk yeah we can talk with that p**sy is fine girl your a** is fine I'm a help you publish your books but you ain't got my name in the stories Alexandria they going to put your name in the stories my d*ck is hard as hell and I don't quit until I Got the goldmind will you talk a good game for a man that's just coming up thats because I see myself as an entrepreneur Alexandria Thomas tell Eden to communicate Thomas your stories get a little complicated I choose for them to be that way Eden what's the idea of going behind my back and talking to Ashley Eden my d*ck got a life Thomas wake up Thomas you with Kay Kay girl I miss you so damn much Thomas is different girls out here that like me and you it ain't no probleMs. I can't fix Kay im a get the money over My Dead body you will Superman Ebony Buy it I'm a piss on you Superman no don't piss on me so you had a dream that you peed on Ebony Buy it he pissed on me and my dream first part 3 the lifetime journal of ebony buy it hiMs.elf is coming to a close how is this going to be coming to a close damn it I just now got started Superman I'm going to piss on you again well we just go be pissing on each other Ebony Kristen never f*cked you look at that that's the fattest a** I've seen all weekend long RoboCop needs to a** keep this station Simba from The Lion King want some a** to f*ck I'm telling what you know I want some a** Ashley

My favorite position is on top of her a** not in it I'm catching up for lost time with a Porsche that goes 150 Thomas make sure the Porsche gets one or two of these things I get my house built I can't help myself all I want is a** on my floors so this won't be no mystery I'm a federal agent send stuff can I take you for a ride precious I was waiting on you to come out send that bulsh*t off I'm going to take you away from your man ball with me for the *ssh*le the stole my car baby I like you some other time Ebony Buy it you don't have to do this call Superman girl cause you got me going crazy damn that p**sy was good finger f*cking your a** for the nation Ebony Buy it works it out this is the lifetime journal of Ebony Buy it hiMs.elf part 4 take your time don't be in a rush it's all going to happen Baby slow down with this d*ck in your hands there's something in my butt it's hard to control myself Eden I need you take your time we going to put your a** in this room this is the lifetime journal of ebony but hiMs.elf what do yall think about me you talk sh*t behind my back I get another mention and its Superman to be exact hold your ground Ebony buy it girl listen you don't want to give up them drawers girl is not than your a** got to go the whole neighborhood waiting on you Ebony Buy it 2 come out I see keep a b*tch down with me in Cambodia I did my thing in Switzerland I made them b*tches scream for me Michael Jackson was one of my closest friends that's why I play thriller every night when I'm hitting some a** listen my whole community I'm watching me come up girl we got one more thing to do I never cheat on my business so that a** is mine Eden right you can save a lot of money on your car insurance by switching the Ebony buy it yall make a movie out of this see Ebony Buy it is a faithful entrepreneur with a d*ck so long they talked about in London how can a hoe relax her self when my d*ck is in her present I'm trying to make some money rightgive me a compound with nothing but my b*tches on it all kind of people want me I am the undisputed heavyweight d*ck in a jar d*ck has an accent my d*ck is Russian You seen Me be Kristen a** Ebony Buy it commence you Kristen who needs a d*ck can I get an advance on my p**sy you know that I'm good for it just so that we can understand each other who drove this Chrysler station wagon to my house fellas its p**sy or nothing at all I hope my d*ck is professional by the time I meet you b*tches Ill kiss your butt if you tell me to Eden I'm going out to my p**sy man the ship get us a new whole crew because we want p**sy and your island has p**sy on it Kristen be respectful I take all of the Kings p**sy where the virgins at I'm going to take them with me to safty get your a** over here Elizabeth take off your panties what are y'all doing they trying to get me to walk the d*ck girl be careful people have walked a d*ck before and Ebony buy it d*ck don't play let's see how many girls want this d*ck we get Eden we got Kristen and afootball team full of b*tches this on the sidelines cheering for this d*ck to win we got an auditorium room full of b*tches let Ebony Buy it speak for hiMs.elf I'm putting myself on a loud d*ck speaker so that they can hear me in Korea because Cambodia or not my females are up in this b*tch let somebody tell me that this ain't the lifetime journal of Ebony buy it hiMs.elf part 4 ebony buy it you know where that a** at man up your stations is p**sy every word gentleman the wealthiest p**sy we are going to find but ebony how can you find that weathy p**sy it's just a myth can't you see him doing something here Alex y'all can find p**sy all you want but I'm looking for the holy Grail and the gato the holy Grail is a woman's vagina and the gato is a woman's a** the holy Grail in The grotto of most precious when they haven't been touched ive searched all my life for the holy Grail in the gato I went to East Asia where the women are fine but no Holy Grail and no gato I went to France on my search but the holy Grail in the gato eluded me I'm back in the US states and I'm telling Eden the she's got the gato and Kristen has the holy Grail make sure that thing holy Kristen I'm watching you Thomas send off the damn message Thomas police officers after you Ebony I'm put Thomas on time support it's my only dream to kiss the a** of the gato you still ain't say nothing about my p**sy can a mother f*cker say Amen that p**sy is delicious what about my a** to I'm chef boyardee Thomas wake your a** up this is the lifetime journal of ebony but hiMs.elf part 4 now coming to a close if they ain't talkin money I can't f*ck with them I finally got the gato Samantha part 5 of the lifetime journal of ebony but hiMs.elf will be coming up in 30 minutes girl that's the holy Grail and the gato so Kristen tell me have anybody seen my new shoes see my new pants see my new shirt and my new coat my new company think about this sh*t while you wait for part 5 Ebony buy it you switched up on us I'm still African American doing my thing Thomas wake your a** up and send the message don't play me out Kristen Eden this is part 4 the lifetime journal of ebony by hiMs.elf I'll take over this b*tch if y'all let me what I got to say I'm crazy girl pencil me in and appointment with Elizabeth cause I need some help watch what you sayin ebony buy it take me to the strip club I'm going to see what these girls talkin about Nada get your behind in here Nada tell me the truth is Ebony buy it a gentleman Thomas I can't lie to you Ebony Buy it is a beast and a dog that's is for part 4

The lifetime journal of Ebony Buy it hiMs.elf part 5 the whole damn country think I'm out to get them Ebony Buy it please calm your a** down ebony so stupid you think money grow on trees I think money comes from a fairy somewhere Look how talking Kristen I know he must want a peice of a** or something listen to me Thomas your d*ck ain't ready yet for this p**sy Thomas I'm just picking with you

you know this p**sy belongs to you okay Eden Eden you'll have any secrets there's one I can show you close the back door would you Thomas would you see me in our bedroom right now take your clothes off no kneel down on your knees you've been talking a bunch of mess about me in your books and your movies I'm a tell you what I'm thinking Thomas I got you d*ck where I want it so make a choice either you going to surrender to this p**sy or you going to eat this a** Thomas ain't got time to do this all day surrender to this p**sy Thomas or eat this a** Thomas Kristen on the phone Eden make the boy eat that a** I did some hard work for you I don't jack your d*ck Thomas cause I deserve my a** ate out and it's by you Thomas allred Junior get me my towel have you faced ready when I come back do you understand what I'm saying you even a** tonight man think about how much you mean to me now lic* this a** do it slowly Thomas keep listening lic* this a** again and again I want to stop you but I can't Thomas I feel so damn good now lic* this p**sy eat it professionally do not give up on this a** whatever you do don't stop Thomas lic* this p**sy Thomas keep lic*ing this p**sy I want you inside of my a** right now anything you say Miss Eden Reid ride me like a ride your d*ck I can't do nothing for you right now accept offer you a milkshake milkshake in your mouth Thomas you don't have to get no spoon this p**sy is warm in my mouth here something you can taste in your mouth Thomas the hot p**sy melting in your mouth we going to see if you can swallow this sh*t I'm getting ready to I'm get ready to Thomas as you stop eating my p**sy I know Kristen because you about reading make me c*m Kristen push It up inside Me Thomas Nada as a police officer girl I got to get you where you want to be think about it and Nada your a** is the reason you came here tonight let me see what you got in store for me Thomas lay down and take off your clothes I'm working with a big a** d*ck a Superman d*ck Nada you can sit on it if you want to police be telling me your d*ck is a lethal weapon you need to ride this d*ck and tell me what you think about it yourself give that boy a contract Nada he think this girl kidding Nada I want to be with you but you taking your time I want to see what that p**sy is about before I lic* it Thomas you better lic* my *ssh*le first before you lic* anything Here it comes *ssh*le first there it is that's the gato I'm going to make you c*m on yourself Thomas about this p**sy is yours my medicine and your medicine creative baby Thomas how good is that p**sy my p**sy is the bomb now continue you eating my a** like you doing I just came in your mouth lic* my p**sy Thomas I'm about to come in your mouth turn around and lic* this a** Kristen something about you got me rock hard Kristen admit it you can with Ebony Buy it Kristen his d*ck is better than yours say Superman Thomas Superman now put this p**sy in your mouth one last time for a nut Elizabeth I hear you Nada professional hold did D*ck Elizabeth he even capitalist d*ck on my a** Thomas straighten up your word play I'm capitalized on your a** Thomas bend over put your d*ck in me see my p**sy is made for champion d*ck like you we got a Superman d*ck in the house Samantha suck this d*ck like you mean it you can eat my a** first if its a** that you want a** I'm a get damn that feel good your a** is c*mming I'm melting Thomas Samantha hold my d*ck up off the ground so we can see what you look like Eden with c*m on your face Eden catch this for me catch this for me your own self the whole community got to say that we busting a nut at the same time I have but one request Thomas that you eat all of our p**sy at the same time you in the mood for a meal champion Thomas I got something else to tell you a** is on the menu I can handle that p**sy don't you watch a tape with me either I f*ck you you using the strength that God gave you I can tell that you like d*ck Nada this Superman think how does it feel to suck a big d*ck sucking d*cks is my middle name than turn over than here cuMs. the captain of the ship it's a hurricane I'm professional so I wear my jacket in my p**sy you make me c*m with that jacket on ask Ebony Buy it how dose this nut taste that girl is off the hook we getting ready to make alot of money don't you know this is Ebony Buy it girl turn around a second girl you better suck my d*ck and action Thomas how are you living over there Thomas I just came here to eat my girl a** I'm telling you now ebony buy it I won't tell nobody she sucking your d*ck high price p**sy excuse me ebony buy it can I sign your d*ck washer yeah Stacy professional look at me Thomas what the sad face for d*ck washing is a job for my girl where did that b*tch Kristen get to it's getting hot up in this place go on upstairs with Kristen and behave yourself while your in there don't act like you don't realize that you are the king Thomas now b*tches get upstairs y'all give that boy a piece of candy while Kristen sleep by the way Thomas I just helped you rescue the princess from Ebony Buy it are we equal say yes Thomas yes drop them f*cking clothes it's my turn to lic* some a** Eden stop Thomas wake up your dreaming about me I love you Eden Kristen is in here to Kristen I'm sorry that I ever hurt you I'm so proud of you for what you can do come and get this nigga off my porch my ex boyfriend Thomas this is Ebony Buy it The Lifetime Journal Of Ebony Buy it talk some more sh*t my book is finished just in time for Christmas let's see my family needs a gift my women need a gift and these haters need a gift two middle fingers to my haters a diamond bracelet a piece to all of my women friends my family get all of the money and to you of course don't play ball in the dark you might hurt your self that's the game listen baby I didn't mean to harm you my ex boyfriend Samantha it's okay Ebony Buy it is here for you Nada b*tch meditate cause this d*ck is here for you Joellen Thomas and I love Joellen that ends the story how Ebony Buy it got his d*ck wet with out being caught by a hater named you till the end of time I'm professionally not f*cking with no haters I fly ladies you can call me Surperman

Eden I want to speak to you for a moment girl I'm thinking about you all night and all day do you understand how much I miss you how much I care about you can't you see I'm trying to win your affection to many mistakes have made it so you look over me but I'm thinking we could some day get to know each other better and become real friends but I can't be on this computer long just know that I love you so very much and think about what I just told you Punky Brewster has your best interest in mind I'm finished with my stories Eden I'm just sitting back waiting for you to call me because Terminator x is in here waiting for you and Ebony Buy it wants a girl let's do sh*t a little bit better than we done before get Erin Cohen on the telephone hello this is Erin Cohen Erin Cohen this is Ebony Buy it the story is now ending what story we talking about Ebony no fair I just need a story now that we talking Elizabeth is the genuine article and I except full responsibility over this peice of a** look there go Superman you said you loved Eden Reid what is your book about my book is about the future because we've come along way since I have been writing give her some time Superman Eden a come around it's just that I'm lonely every day out there fighting crime and i just need my friend who Eden Reid no Kristen Beam now write this is a story of love and strength this is a story of love and strength the incredible hulk has something to say I'm in love with Samantha at the beginning of the story I shared with you that I was shy because I've been alone for 15years or single for 15 years I been through hell just writing this book it's no place like home Dorothy tell Todo to come inside the evil witches looking at you she can't do nothing to me because I'm protected by Ebony Buy it Ebony buy it want to come work for us darthy of The wizard of Oz the lion has no heart Thomas scarecrow has no brain you going to have to call Eden Reid and make sure this book get published I see what you're saying Dorothy Todo is my friend too if you have 13 minutes I can show you something Superman this is what I call a badonkadonk I don't know if I should taste it Superman stop being afraid and eat this a** some a** ain't good for you Dorothy you eat this a** boy right now okay but after this I'm eating Kristen a** and Eden a** let me see you got some sh*t with this why don't we watch this a** from the yellow brick road Thomas if you want this p**sy just say three times Eden got the fattest a** one Eden got the fattest a** 2 Eden got the fattest a** three times for the road Eden got the fattest a** now clic* your heels and getting bed b*tch Eden about to f*ck your a** Thomas I'm pissing on Ebony buy it the girl no Ebony Buy it a thoroughbred there's only one mistake that you made after talking to me Dorothy and what mistake is that ebony buy it you couldnt see that me Superman and Thomas in the incredible hulk all all the same person wait until I get to nail you exactly Dorothy your a** has been charged with the crime of having no d*ck get used to this d*ck it's a boomerang Dorothy boomerang is the movie Thomas a TV show no I'm saying this d*ck has a hook in it oh my f*cking god tell Elizabeth to come a** down see my d*ck Elizabeth works overtime for all you women and they saying that they can't use my words in a pilot Thomas is coming to an end y'all needed more material so I gave y'all the rough in the raw I'm the heavyweight champ of the industry Eden Reid put this d*ck in your mouth then after that put it in Kristen's a** Samantha you ain't going no motherf*cking where but our house she thought I said whorehouse started throwing up panties everywhere as a matter of fact why don't all y'all take off your panties take off your God damn panties Alice Ebony Buy it in here a** special I see why these muthaf*ckers go around photographing a** because p**sy and a** is top-notch ladies that ship better drugs and I know cause every time I get high I don't want nothing but some a** this dude over here had nerve to call his girl a b*tch you don't want me to fight you do you you can suck my d*ck I got p**sy on my grocery list I have to remind myself everyday Thomas make sure you get that p**sy and a** before you lay down tonight I stay to myself this p**sy and a** is mine the girls don't hear me though I pop that p**sy like I'm a can openerwhat are fitness girls I try to fit my nuts down the bottle This sh*t tight as hell and I'm saying girls we might have a new champion Eden I want you to play with your p**sy because it's fat and beautiful and I can definitely use some if you're willing to share I want a** to Eden be my guest if you sit on my face sh*t on my face I meant there's just nothing that compars to me I'm trying to pay for the p**sy if you give me a contract I can hold my d*ck like I always do my ending will be something like this I know I got a Superman d*ck but Eden your kryptonite won't make me come I'm turning you into a superhero megapussi don't put megapussi say that p**sy of the bomb Ebony Buy it what do you think this for that contract I want that a** all day seven days a week 365 Eden I'm watching you grow up through these text messages my how you a** him grown Thomas you're making a mistake here than let a court of 12 judge my d*ck the way it is you telling me to keep my d*ck to myself Eden my d*ck is called The Mangler my d*ck only comes out at nigh B*tches want my d*ck to pose for pictures one b*tch put my d*ck in a Santa suit as pretty as my d*ck is I looked at her and lic*ed her a** and went on my way Eden my d*ck can scuba dive I'm at the p**sy with this on dry land or in water or in the air p**sy has nowhere to run from my d*ck my d*ck will go in a cave at night I called at cave cave hollow a** a** have me stuttering sometimes I believe that I want a** more p**sy Eden I've been alone for 15 years so you have to forgive me all I'm doing is push-ups and writing but what I'm saying is a** gives me the shakes girl I see some pretty fat a** its like watching a horror movie I be scared that a** look good girl Eden save that a** for me make an exspress on my p**sy you see my p**sy do you see my p**sy Eden go take off your panties and let's talk about what you can do for my d*ck my d*ck is head champion my d*ck knows the secret to your vagina if I don't pop your motherf*cking a** eating nobody will b*tches c*m when Ebony Buy it sing I'm a man because my d*ck ain't been nowhere but in your big ol a** Eden now Eden I'm going to give you my d*ck take it somewhere safe Eden my d*ck is wanted by the FBI baby what I'm seeing is the president looking at my d*ck Eden hide the p**sy I'm taking it a** with me ladies to beat the d*ck you got to suck the d*ck until it goes down I stopped sucking on p**sy I just lic* it now I ate this one girl a** until she start crying and into them b*tches suck this d*ck I want some a** Superman want his a** on delivery I want trucks backing up to my Mansion bringing me a** all day and all night long 24/7 a** on delivery if you get some a** on New year's youll have a great year for the last 15 years ain't been able to find no a** cause I was broke but low and behold the d*ck is grown strong it is a sparrow little kids noticed my d*ck they point it out to they Mommy they put my d*ck in a snack pack once I'm a f*ck the hell out of you when I get a chance my d*ck said that that p**sy and a** of yours Eden don't you do it now c*m on yourself my d*ck said you could my d*ck been winged before this woman put my d*ck in a ace band my d*ck is been down but he got back up Eden Eden asleep with you and only you if I had the opportunity my d*ck has the eye of the tiger Eden I swear if you look at my d*ck and you look at it good it look just like Andy Griffith ladies I was drinking one day and I could have swore my d*ck was talking to me how paranoid the cops wanted to lock me up with indecent exposure but with a d*ck in my hand this large the new I was working with a beast so I got some help with reeling that mouth again we tried not to hurt my d*ck but he c*mmed anyway off a picture of ain't Bee a** on The Andy Griffith Show who said she don't like no d*ck I'll beat this d*ck if I want to beat this d*ck but if I get some p**sy I'm a c*m in that a** Mexico has a law against people with big d*cks I see them mutha f*ckers at the border all the time homes i can't go home we ain't got no p**sy at my house so you can sleep in the living room thank you my friendall you got to do Thomas's talk to somebody about your d*ck yeah Eden but who do I tell my d*ck is famous Canada and the United States I'll lead you where you got to be you just show your a** when you get there Thomas you made me come all over myself with your words of wisdom I'm a regular magician with this d*ck ladies damn right p**sy is all I want think of these apples and a p**sy between them now picture your last name f*cking with mine what do we have we have a pear tree Thomas Superstar control your a** b*tch all I do is count money Eden I'm worse than any comedian you've ever seen how is that Thomas I'm f*cking you would have sober d*ck see my d*ck a watch your a** grow say you want to and I help you get your sh*t together for good Eden I can't lie I'm at the dep p**sy and a** call me George Washington d*ck Im a eat every cherry on that damn tree just like I'm supposed to we f*cking with thousands of pieces a** I'm trying to I'm trying to f*ck with b*tches in Eden your a** and my d*ck mean the world is on my shoulders this d*ck is crazy you can put a** to my d*ck any day you want to I'm changing my d*ck name two I'm going to get me some p**sy d*ck I think it sounds better ladies how do you a**es feel cause if he want f*ck that a** my d*ck will c*m with no problem ladies your p**sy and a** got my d*ck in a marathon all I know is my d*ck ain't coming in last this is ask Kingdom where good a** rules everything I got some a** In my mouth right now I save that sh*t from a week ago the p**sy was farting and everything I didn't think I was going to make it it was me and my d*ck up against that a** and all I had with my balls to hold me up that p**sy spoke to me and I lic*ed it in that a** just like I was told I could do to make a long story short my d*ck wasn't the only one to c*m that day that p**sy and a** came to Eden I'm just being sincereI look at a** and p**sy like it's the final frontier when I step up to a b*tch I'm walking out on faith if she asked me to eat her p**sy and her a** I lean not to my own understanding music be playing in the background in my mind when I'm going down on that a** the Superman 4 theme songthere isn't a challenge great enough for my d*ck not to overcome any p**sy can be beaten

Listen Eden I gave you what you needed I gave you the heart that simply takes over any splendid a** out there I am ebony buy it and I'm thanking you Eden for today you don't see what I'm doing do you Eden Thomas needs a contract and you need a contract my business is bringing people together Eden I am more than a Matchmaker I am the god the industry knows as Ebony buy it now pencil me in I pencil you in you seem to romance me Eden I'm lucky to have found you you have done a wonderful job with Thomas so far and you are in my hopes and prayers Eden are all of the women that Thomas know and have seen we choose you to be his Guild up on the next level you got a week to make up your mind if you are interested just give Thomas to call and tell him he got a contract with you as his guide all details will be discussed further when I see you Eden I think the stories did Thomas gave you were wonderful very witty and the open range of discussion I want you to take your time and get to know Thomashe is a very important person in your life and in all of our lives when you figure out who Ebony Buy it is you'll be done got married because you are a friend to me Eden so I talk to you now before you prosper greatlyI want you to realize that on this Walk of Life there are many tests and challenges we've listened to everything you said and everything you thought I know how you feel Eden Thomas is in love with your a** being single has made Thomas strong but I'm thinking a good man shouldn't have to be single the rest of his life and you Eden everything that I wish and desire for my friend I'm timing you Eden to read these stories and to make a king decision listen Ebony Buy it doesn't play games Eden you just have to believe in yourself and what you read it's more to the story but it will begin in another book this book begins with Eden and Thomas apologizing to one another because Eden all Thomas wants to know is do you really love him or not Eden because this game is about money this is the ninth inning two outs on the board let me finish Eden if I got you a mansion and 12 cars will you say I'm Ebony Buy it I put you in my bank account i want you to know that you are forever in my heart and in my soul I'm maturing off you Eden as The story goes this is how I won the title by stepping up to the plate and asking my girl with one out left will you be my wife and did smashing the ball she didn't say nothing the ball goes out the park a homerun had me feeling like the man again as I looked at Eden and got down on one knee to my wife I love I give to you these stories I want you to sell them I am hooked on you Thomas Mr.. Ebony buy it hold on a minute what time is it now Eden it's time to play the game Eden what game Mr.. Ebony Mr.. Ebony buy it tell Thomas you love him Eden because with this here story you can buy 10 mansions for you two Thomas is all over the news I murdered that a** and I murdering another piece of a** if I get it what am I going to do with him Ebony Buy it it's only a movie scene I hope Kristen can see this tell her I won Eden it's about time the game is coming to a close everybody off the field except you this story was written by Thomas allred Junior Eden Reid I love you very much Ebony Buy it holds the key Thomas to your future and your contract Mr.. Ebony Buy it sir I thank you for everything and I finally think I've learned my lesson about women and life the woman is to cherish and have fun with and to adore and life is serious and risky and sometimes you have to give it your all what I'm saying is that if you put a good woman and life together with a good man then all of us could be called Mr. Ebony Buy it Mr.. Ebony buy it my name is Thomas allred Juniorsir I've never had much but I don't complain about being brokeI keep to myself sir and treat people the way they supposed to be treated I'm testing you Mr. ebony buy it everything that I am I'm testing you because you see sir all thats been promised to me my family and our community we want and we value and we hope that we get what I'm saying to you sir these stories are important that beautiful and as the women we all want to income now So Mr. Ebony Buy it if you are all-powerful mystical and magical sir could you please help change our life cause I love Eden and one day hope for a chance to be her husband Thomas if you love Eden tell her with in 1 minute okay Eden I need you lady all I'm saying is I will always be there and I Will never let You down girl please give me a chance to breathe I love you be mine Eden Reid will you marry me that's it Eden and Thomas don't worry about your bank accounts anymore Thomas because your bank accounts on my bank accounts I want you two to live with each other I'm giving you two 30 days to get your act right in 4th Thomas tell the girl that you love her everyday Eden I really need you I need you to Mr.. Ebony Buy it how did you know Eden and Kristen Thomas it was very easy tell Thomas it was easy it was easy Thomas Samantha and Elizabeth Porsche Chelsea Heather and Kay Kathy and Maya and Evelyn and Emily and Inger and Vivian and Molly and Asia and Julie and Lisa and Karen Miss Susan Jennings and miss Lynn crouch I'm finna rap up the whole game after im through with this b*tches say Amen because I am Ebony Buy it I'm the richest man on earth y'all when the government decides to give me my money ladies all I want to see is a** and elbows forever but the rap the game up I'm in love with all my ladies and I wish for all the ladies in the United States and surrounding area that have two hundred million dollars a piece out of the business idea money that we made Eden I'm a very serious opponent i would like for you and Kristen to decide if you want me f*ck that bring yall a**es on and it's a wrap i want every one of my ladies that can hear my voice I'm asking yall to please marry me and be my wives because I am Thomas allred Junior the richest man in the world of a business ideas I ain't jacking my d*ck Thomas they waiting my ladies only you are so beautiful but this is the end of my book So icey told my people all my ladies on controller all my a**ets I looked every lady in the world women y'all are some queens and y'all need to be treated like it it's a shame we have to leave this book Eden Reid apologize to you because this is starting a new story about me and you Kristen Beam I apologize to you girl I wanted you so bad I lost control of myself ladies I need your forgiveness before I can go on with my book the end starts here give me my PIN to the federal government you can have half of my business ideas a**ets and that's the only way I know how to play ball so fighting over women is it a thing that I'm not with but give him a woman everything is what they call me Thomas Allred Junior the end of the story is some real women out there if you're looking for a good time in the USA or Canada I wonder what we'll do next Its been fun with you after me and Eden Ebony Buy it if the story is ending what are we going to do with our cash all the women in North Carolina and surrounding areas I'm a buy you all brand new houses once I get my deal look Thomas Allred Jr you got to dream before the p**sy comes to you I had to dream first I'm Ebony Buy it and this was my story of success and failure and coming back up again to win it all with this many women zero women in my corner naturally I get myself together every morning and exercise every evening I'm doing push-ups at the moment but as soon as this book comes out I'll pay someone to do them for me y'all please let me have my contract because I just thought that I'd write to Kristen alittle bit in my book to show that even through incarceration a good man can never be broken they operated on me when I was coming up as a kid because someone decided to shoot me I over came my affliction I'm just lucky to be able to tell Kristen that no matter where I am in this world I will be there for her always girl the reason that I love you is because you make my heart beat fast and that's never happened to me before what time is it Samantha you and Nada are my women through the trials and tribulations I know that I can always count on you two ladies Porsche and Emily Emily I love you guys honey I'm just trying to make something good out of myself if you two need me I'll be right with you Ebony Buy it and that's the story of how a simple man because a King and a success over night there's only one thing left to do send me my God damn message right now Thomas it's out the park home run now Ms. Eden Reid will you please marry me please marry me Eden you had me at hello Thomas Allred Jr you say yes I say yes I was thinking we could work together on Thomas just kiss me boy and there you have it how Ebony Buy it took over the world with his wives this is the story of forgiveness called Be With Me In Forgiveness Eden your message is coming to you give me time to send it I love you Eden so much Ebony Buy it I'm a send the message give me three more minutes there it is home run these women are my queen who wants to play

Eden its Thomas girl I really appreciate you reading my stories and I also appreciate you being close friend of mine I hope I didn't go too far with the cliffhangers I just appreciate your name as a studio great I want to tell you Eden that I greatly want to make love to you if it's in your business plans I'm taking time to think of other stories to give to you your p**sy is an antique in my eye sight this is how the story really ends say tragically Thomas tragically the story comes to an end Superman did I get that part right Thomas I'm going to make sure that you and Eden get together this red white and blue flag means our country is different anybody who needs us Thomas ain't got no idea how much even cares for you Superman listen to me Thomas that girl is poison just look at her she professional poison hell no she's not then what is she Thomas she's my milk dud milk dud can you be more clear with what you're sayingI'm saying that because of her this book is a worldwide seller what about best seller see Eden's a** is the best seller I put my bid in for that junk Thomas I love you go back to sleep honey don't you think you need to turn the TV off Johnny Carson ain't never look like that before this d*ck is Johnny Carson Eden now you see what my story is don't you Lets end this civilized get my other d*ck out of my coat Eden for the best seller list in the United States and Canada I put this d*ck in every one of my books you need to a** Thomas you exactly right Eden y'all give me like 25 minutes and me and Eden a be right back drop them drawls Eden bend over Eden with this isn't funny you no more drop them drawls like I told you okay Thomas but I don't want to now finishing the story we need a number one bestseller what is that you have on your fingers Thomas this is two fingers of pa**ion he ain't got no damn clue do it Eden made me stick my fingers up my a** and I came to realize that my fingers are the key to this book because a** and sh*t come together let me hear you say it a** and sh*t come together I'm going to keep on thinking this concept how sh*t took me one place to another with a beautiful a** person leading the way Thomas ridiculous you think I'm ridiculous cause I got sh*t on my fingers think about it Thomas how many fingers are sh*ty all 10 of them which a** did you put yours in i put them in Eden a** and then I put them in my a** a double scoop so where did the sh*t come from what Eden and I got our twelve movie star mansions off of the first book we wrote digging in it we wrote digging it 2 that a** and sh*t went platinum I'm putting that a single book called revenge of the nuts part 5 I got the test the limits on Eden p**sy by giving her a d*ck for her birthday with some nuts on top of it I want to thank for having me run down my a** all month Long so my d*ck can take a break can't you see Thomas white dudes ain't black dudes work right now look around you Thomas what's the only thing missing in this room right here its some a** come back next season would ask be plentiful for you Eden Buy it I'm a tell you something I'm a regular Clint Eastwood on the p**sy I'll beat that p**sy down like stole something Ill handcuff your a** and f*ck the sh*t out of you b*tch don't steal my damn dreaMs. I dream of pink magnolias with p**sy and a** in the middle when I sleep at night I need to p**sy and a** mask just so that I can breathe better girl please help me get that a** like you stole something from me I'm playing Nintendo with my d*ck I want to see what your a** look like my d*ck playing Batman Eden I let Eden dress my d*ck up as The Dark Knight Eden you know my d*ck got and inheritance coming all this talkin has made me dizzy d*ck stand up my d*ck is Optimus prime Eden you can even call my d*ck Webster I'm still looking for that Wonder Woman p**sy if I eat that Wonder Woman p**sy and a** that sh*t a put me on the map lock up my d*ck because it's crazy in the a** constantly I burnt my d*ck in the Easy-Bake oven when I was 2 I can still remember that sh*t let me get out of here you see my d*ck don't you do I stand for my d*ck that's what I want to say Eden Ebony Buy buy I say something if I say something im a leave that p**sy smoking girl I'm a serious man I'm writing a serious book serious people are listening to me so get your fat a** in there lay down to take off your damn clothes you messing up telling people you ain't gonna f*ck me that p**sy was mine before you even realize and pick up the phone to call me Eden your p**sy been plotting on me since preschool let me know if we all done grew up serious matters call for a serious d*ck this is the hard d*ck capital imagine ladies women deposit a check here at this d*ck I want 42 mansions with 42 rooMs. what's 32 cups in each one of them mansions and in every room I want bunk beds four females coming to stay with me I'm serious about my work I want fifteen limousines at each mansion and my houses better be up to date these books and movies is like the final front a** tear I want a female to come with me as I come to Canada in greet my p**sy Eden that boy coming to Canada no my d*ck is going to Canada I'm staying here by my d*ck I mean my words of wisdom Eden this is going to make you famous so I have a d*ck for you nuts I couldn't think of a d*ck big enough so you just going at the borrow one of mine this d*ck is for you okay

Eden the book sacrifice manuscript Camelot is a book for all the people. I want you to save in my phone messages when my book beginning to test you really have no clue of who that girl who is Eden that's my publicist. Give it time. I say to you that that is your wife you are in the biz. I'm saying to you that I know nothing about what you're talkin about. I'mma tell you this Thomas so you figure it out. The book sacrifice manuscript Camelot. Is your second book that's coming out. I'm trying to tighten this thing up. I don't have no time for playing games. Thomas we all know you lost your girlfriend. Or is it your wife. That's what I'm saying. So you all know that she was murdered. Thomas you've been alone now for 18 years. Look ya'll I'm doing my best I got God. I believe in Zeus the king of strength yall. There it is. Thanks Thomas. My friends for what. Can't you see I put you on. The book sacrifice manuscript Camelot. Is what you tell all the ladies that you were wrong. Ladies I'm sorry and I apologize.but I fought so hard during my teenage years and I already died. Thomas your a damn Superstar. My friend I just want to be in love with a woman but amen there you are. Contact Jesus Christ and tell him what you want Jesus Christ can i be a star Jesus Christ I've been trying so hard. I really love all kinds of women. You took my wife from me Jesus Christ. Now I believe in Zeus there is no limit. This is the book sacrifice Camelot. Where I tell the truth about everything. I am a king to all Amazon women. All over the world all of these women are my Queens. I'm saying it now you know what I mean. What you going to do.Tell them Superman never gave up girl and that is me. Sweetheart I cried you here at the year I miss you everything girl I'm On bended Knee. Jesus please do me a favor. And get my lady back to me. I'm crying but I told my friend Erin I do her a favor. And write her book called you and me. Thank you Thomas. Y'all my friends why y'all keep thanking me. You know exactly what I mean. Eden I won't say your last name. Thank you for listening to my book sacrifice manuscript Camelot. I've been alone so many years without no one the Eden I forgot. But I noticed the women are beautiful everyday everything is changing. I keep praying that love will one day come my way in my heart because I'm changing. I keep hearing Thomas take your medicine. But to the world I am Superman. I'm saving the world $1 at a time. Eden imma zillionaire I'm not playing. But I asked you to be in my book and take my book and sponsor it. Because I don't have no one penny to my name. But I'm going to get you out of that situation. I give you eight hundred million bucks. If I could show you love girl I wouldn't have to explain it. This is the sacrifice manuscript Camelot. And I'm doing everything to show that you are a queen.we might be from two different lands and I'm a star I'm the king of Amazon eden and I'm saying that you are my queen. The Today Show is calling me what does that mean Eden. My friends are everything to me. And I done cussed out people. But I'm saying if I ever have to testify. To the goodness of the world.You know somebody murdered my girlfriend my wife. Imma just be fair with the world. The ladies and the gentlemen of the police force are the only ones in the world they have helped me girl. So in this book on professional. I'm in North Carolina so professional. I'm coming to you the best way I can. So that you can know how professional I am not at you in my life. You hear me Eden. Girl I give up my childish ways. I'm a man that's been alone for 18 years. I will cry on The Today Show. Amazon women somebody murdered my lady there it is. I could be famous for killing people.I don't know what I want to do to them people. Who took a beautiful woman away from me. Famous now it's going in history their name is Jeana. Eden she is my best friend. Shock waves are going through my body right now. I'm a tell you something Eden I'm not using no pen to write the story. I'm just so hurt girl scream glory. I'm a let butterfly go from somewhere. Jeana is the most beautiful Amazon princess around here. Jeana is the god of strength. For all of the Amazon lady princesses Thomas talk to me.Eden everyday I pray. For a better way for me and my family and my people. This Lynn and my heart has changed. There's a storm brewing all across it as we speak. Take your time and tell me what you want.Eden I just want to rescue my family out of this situation. I sacrifice myself to give to the people. Everything that it is that God says they deserve. Because I'm the truth with nothing left. I am called Superman. Because the government and Jeana said so.Eden .what do you think about this Superman. A world of Peace filling up the land. I think that piece is welcome to all the people. And I think that all the people can have my every last time. But I pray that God Zeus and Jesus Will be there and take care of my woman to Jeana and shine a light on me from heaven all the time. Because my woman didn't deserve to die man.Now Eden you don't understand my story.I worked and the people telling me I'm a zillionaire. But I don't care about anything in this world except the women's happiness. And the little children playing I got to be fair. The men say Thomas or Superman you don't care for us what's going on. And I do I love you all. But some man shot me and shot my girlfriend. My wife is no longer with us y'all. So I've been alone for 18 years. Just a young lad just being myself. The only thing that's been on my mind. Is how to go out here and help people so one day I can down myself. Because I died and they brought me back. This is a real story see my heart attack . Cause people won't let me live. As the cop I used to be. I'm thanking my family and my mama. For sitting me down and talkin to me. You can have anything in the world and you still got Jeana. I understand that Jeana is your queen. It look Eden I'm trying to do this the right way. I am an officer of the law. The code name is Superman.Jeana is my best friend and girlfriend and I'm supposed to protect her. I had to leave her side. To go off to protect someone else. Who was close to dying. When Jeana got killed I wasn't there. And I'm sorry I'm so sorry. I give him a badge I don't know where my badge is. But when I got shot.Jeana is the one who helped me learn to walk again. All my life I've been in love with her. I still love her to this day. I'm Superman. I'm a New York Police department officer. My name is Thomas Allred Jr. And I am a part of the FBI and NSA. And a weapons specialist.Eden what is messed up is I don't even have a picture of Jeana .Eden I'm hurt so bad I'm afraid to look it up picture. I can't breathe and I'm Superman. It stop raining I want to see her picture. how in the hell could I ever let my best friend down. I've been alone for 18 years. Eden I'm an old man now. And I still don't have no kids. Sometimes us as police officers. We go through moments and things that change your life. I've never wanted anything to happen to that girl. Because I love her see is my wife. And they killed her because of me. This is the sacrifice manuscript Camelot.Eden listen to me Thomas. You sacrificed all you have and all you are. For a vision of the future. Make sure you ready to become a star. Make sure your book is a blessing from a teacher. My teacher's name is Miss petite. When I was five she told me not to cuss. Miss petite I love you all my life. Me Tonya Kim Ted Michael and everyone else we love you Mr.. T . Thomas we love you too Thomas.Jeana you hear what they said they said they love me Jeana. Baby I still can't breathe. I am Superman.And in the rain I'm On bended Knee. Asking Jesus to please forgive me. Sir I am stupid. I want to thank the rescue squad and all the police all over the world. Even the woman that told me to hold on Thomas its going to be alright when the men had shot me. I give to them my life. One life for another it's only fair thank all of y'all listen Jeana . Honey I'm getting ready to go to sleep. I miss you so much baby. Oh yeah.Eden I am zillionaire I'm being responsible. Give all my money to all the people all around the world. And tell them that I love them. Because with Jeana being the goddess of strength. And Jesus and Zeus Eden they see it like this. I can be a police officer again. And I say thank you God. For giving my best friend.Eden and Erin a book called sink or swim. Now they killed Jeana and murdered me and the people brought me back. Don't worry Superman. Is what I hear justic say. Because we all are fair and we all are people of the land what is right is right and what is wrong is what I'm saying we all are super human beings I love all your so much for judging correctly Jeana Loves y'all. This is the book of decency and simply because the new day I want for you to all love each other I'm sending this from the beginning. Hi Jeana I'm Thomas. Thomas you look like Superman. I think I love you girl will you be my girlfriend. Yeah but people after me.you'll be sick for me I'll protect you I promise of Superman. I think I love you too.Jeana do whatever you're always be me and you baby say .always. always. I miss you so much boo. Thomas keep trying you make it. We got to cut the pants off of you. Thomas just flatlined at 8:35. We brought him back at 8:36. All keep saying now is were great we are a team. Yall man where is Jeana. They can make a movie off of this. Listen to what I tell you. I'm Superman and I'm a zillionaire. And I make it one day at a time just like everybody else. This is the suicide manuscript Camelot but I'm not committing suicide I'm just saying you that my story and the pa**es has died and now it's buried I'm a cop again.y'all better quit playing with me and tell me who got my damn badge. Superman

Eden my mama said to tell you all her life she has cared for me she said she's trying to best in everything to protect our children and the people around her she knows that I'm Superman but she don't want me to know that she knows my Superman handicapped mental abilitiesand with the doctor would say I walk with a limp comes in an adventure Eden where people jacked me. This story starts off in a small town in Hickory North Carolina.Jeana,Thomas. Hello Jeana.Thomas make sure you wear your Superman suit it's a lot of trouble out here.Baby you always talking about where my Superman suit. I put on my vest some of the time I told you I look better without it. Come with your police officer you should listen to me.Jeana that vest slows me down. Thomas your professional. Baby all I know is I love you. I love you too Thomas. Thomas do you think we'll have kids. I'm hoping We have a big family Jeana. Listen to me Thomas wake up. What what is it you been in the hospital for 4 weeks. I'm sorry to tell you this but you've been shot. Jeana Jeana Jeana I'm right here with you tell me a baby what we going to do you can't walk right now Thomas but I'm here with you. Jeana am I still Superman. Why you think these girls like you. I love you Jeana. You're my best friend of all times ever. The story goes that Jeana and I went home to stay with my family. And I have forgot that I was a police officer. Thomas put on some clothes what are you doing boy. Jeana I'm Superman I'm doing my dance. I told you they couldn't stop me. What what are you talkin about I feel strong Jeana. I think I can about walk. I got you can about walk Thomas. You can do anything you want to do. Baby what is things happen. It's just people Thomas sometimes things happen that we don't know why. Jeana promise me you'll never leave me even if I can't walk.Thomas listen to me no matter what goes on or no matter where you at I'm always with you. Yes Jeana I'm a police officer Jeana I always remember. Boy what did you just say.I said my name is Thomas Allred Jr and I'm a police officer. Boy I'm so proud of you. I know that you love me to Nia. And as The story goes Thomas Allred Superman became well with Jeana help and his family's help. Jeana I got to go on another mission. You a police officer Thomas but I don't like this sh*t. I know I love you baby it's been like four years. Plus this a lady with children I have to defender. OK Thomas what did she have. She has a little girl and a little boy.The little girl name is Amanda the little boy name is Jonathan. The lady's name is Jacqueline. They said I have to defend her in the police department is fronting the bill you be safe Thomas I don't know how long I'ma be gone Jeana. Thomas will get through these things. Take your time and tell the police station you love them Thomas. Police station I love y'all no matter where y'all at there I said it. Jeana girl I love you with all my life. They be talking sh*t about me and you Thomas that's because they don't know how wonderful you are or I am and we are getting married here is your ring. Thomas thank you. Girl I love you so f*cking much. I got to leave you right now but I'll be back Jeana. In my past that was the last time I talked to her. Because someone murdered Jeana and now I am a Time cop. Thomas just let me go I promise I get the money back. You're two-faced it and I can't condone that. The time accelerator will have his way with you. You are dead to me. Jeana I'm so sorry. Thomas who you talkin to there's no one here but us. I've only took 3 million of the children's trust fund. You know exactly where you're going Cusack. You're becoming a Time cop. Tell me what is that what is that sound. You're becoming the time cop.there are people listening to us in other worlds and other nations all over the world.I tell you what Thomas I put the money back I put every last dime of it back Ill even give the money that I have in my pocket diamonds just don't kill me. Too late Cusack the dream is over I'm here to take you in. Dream is over are you killing me kidding me. You don't know the people you're talking about. You talking about free the ladies all the time in your books. They're f*cking them girls in prison stay right there I need you to do something for me I want you to tell the judge everything that you have told meSuperman you don't understand something wrong I can't tell the judge they'll kill my family I will protect you.yes Superman the same way that you protected Jeana. Now you starting to understand this is more than a Time cop movie or a book.you are really Superman and they are really killing these people. And you want me to talk to a judge. Who do you think these judges are Thomas. There put there so the women cannot get out of their position. Ask Junior who the time copy is. You're kidding me I'm a Time cop. See Thomas you think that you are timecop. In real life Thomas You are holy figure.

Cusack you have the right to remain silent. Goodbye. Listen Cusack. Thomas I'm telling you my name isn't Cusack. What what is your name. You just stay right there and I'm going to talk to you in a minute. There's so much I want to share with you Thomas.You about to embark on a journey never like this. An amazing journey never like this. The people around you love you deeply. Because you refuse to go under peacefully and you see here make a movie out of this Thomas the night they killed your dream girl. You son of a b*tches. Yes Thomas feel all of the emotions. Jeana didn't deserve to die y'all. She never heart anyone. But you did Thomas. By becoming a cop. You were just too damn good. You had the free all the women. All over the world that's what you said. You just never would give up.no matter how hard we beat you no matter how much we made you bleed well they say you can't teach a old dog new tricks I killed your girl Thomas. Take your time. You are under arrest. For breaking the time cop code. Thomas where have you been. The time cop cold has been destroyed. Almost 25 years ago when we killed your girlfriend Jeana. You going to pay for that sh*t. Thomas listen we're watching you. Even as you write your little movie through your phone. I'm saying you're brilliant. You act like you're not scared Superman. I'm not worried about anything at all.then you are on trial for breckin time cop code 99926 how do you plead Superman. I plead not guilty. Exactly Thomas. That's what I thought you were plead.so here in front of all of the women of the world even the women that you freed out of the prisons and jails I asked you again how do you plead.for saving all of my women all over the world even in the prisons and the jails I still plead not guilty. What are you saying Superman you not have a chance to speak. If your name isn't cusac what is it. I'm telling everybody that I am God. What God I am Superman. And I'm saying no woman has the right to die defending their self in a man's world. Free all of them women from out of those prisons and every woman deserves to have her own house. Superman listen to yourself God I'm asking for no favors. I stood up for people God. I'm with the church and testified in front of people God. I laid down my life and you brought me back a lot of God. All I'm saying is let our woman or free. Thomas are you a lawyer or an attorney. No I'm only a man that wife has been murdered. God why did you take Jeana. I run through these neighborhoods and protect people all over the world and I keep doing that that is my life understand it.as a cop I understand that all of these women are innocent all over the world they have no right to be locked up or murdered or killed or raped because they're trying to defend there selves and defend their lives of the children. Superman slow your a** down. God you made man the king of the world. These women have never had a chance. I'm asking as one time cop to take my life and let all the women be free I speaking as one man to a god. Is Zeus your God and not Jehovah Superman. I am a cop I believe in woman. What are you saying Thomas did a woman's life is more important than a man's I'm saying that this book is alpha and Omega another understanding all across the land. They trying to play my book off like it's just a fluke. And for some reason the women of steel locked in cages.but I come to you as a Time cop telling you that I am the Man of steel. I am zillionaire Thomas Allred Jr. And I'm staying let all of those women and children out of those cages a Kid can not know the difference when they're 12 or 13 years old between life and death free all of those kids I'm a women's victiMs. rights advocate called Superman listen to me Superman we all hear what you're saying but what I'm telling you is that we've been killing your people all over the land do you have anything to say Thomas Jr . No. You see how that boy communicate.I just told him that I've been killing his people all over the land and he said he has nothing to say. Listen Thomas you are about to die. So be it let my woman free. Let everything be everything this is God speaking. What just happened. What just happened. Now I'm back in the room recording my book in my movie.Eden I took my time to tell you what has happened to me.Eden you can just a book and story the way you want to. But my wife is still dead. I think I just had a moment with I think I just had a moment with God. I'm terrified but I'm not scared. Because I'm a Time cop. And I want my woman and children freed all across the land all over the world in every country I'm the only Superman that I know.Jeana sweetheart one day soon I'll be with you. Honey I told you I'll be right back. You are the most beautifulest dream in the world. Hey yall and to my wife Jeana. Baby it hurts so bad. The girl now I can walk and I can stand. That's because you always protected and watch my a**. I Love You Jeana. I have time cop Thomas Allred Jr reporting for duty officers. I give to every country around the world 267 billion dollars a piece. I'm a town cop and a zillionaire. The money is not fiction. To my family and friends in Hickory North Carolina and Fry regional hospital I thank you all for saving my life good job y'all good job I want them to have 267 million dollars everyone in Hickory North Carolina a piece except those who shot me and Jeana. We're going to be able to see the stars one day Thomas.Jeana honey the Stars never come out around here. You just watch and see Thomas you have a little bit of faith one day we will be Stars thank you Thomas the end

CHAPTER 8

I told you I was a Zillionaire people don't doubt it. You do what you got to do but this is a story that you going to remember. We started off poor in Berlin Thomas. I reached in my pocket and had two cents. Take your time reading the story. I reached in my heart and felt the pain and agony of the world. I told my mama when I was a small kid. I said Mama what is Superman can fly. Not knowing the Superman on TV could really fly. As a kid I dreamed about going places. And making friends all over the world. I seen a movie called Aladdin with a genie. And all the genie wanted to do was be free. I thought to myself and I said to my mama. Mama I will free the genie if a letter doesn't let him go free. My mama told me to hush the TV was on.I still ain't understanding what she was trying to say. But me and my mom are best friends. And I finally found out that Aladdin did free the genie. I'm proud of my community because they show me things to do. I want to give my community. The City of Longview North Carolina for all of the people five hundred million dollars to be spread it out between the people. These are the wishes of Superman. The first I want to let you know who Superman is. Superman is a different kind of Bruce Wayne. He is an eccentric Zillionaire. Thomas well my name is Superman to Thomas. Every man can be Superman if you wants to be. Even you but I'm a girl Thomas okay my badare you saying that I can't be Superman Thomas. I'm saying that you are Superwoman all the women of the world. Are either Wonder Woman or Superwoman. What I'm saying to my fellow men. Is the all the ladies have confidents and pride. It was women and men who saved my life. When I got shot this the true story it is not fiction. It is not for the weak at heart. Save your TVs read and listen to the story. We are listening Thomas. In your face means no matter what I've gone through no matter how many struggles of challenges I've been through I am still a Time cop. In your face. Someone murdered my wife. More than 20 years ago. And I've been alone for 7 years of my life now. Can't you see as a Time cop. I've used extended resources. To find milady's killers. You killed Jeana and other women. And I've been all over the world after you. You saying no this is a book. But you shot me. I'm a zillionaire Superman. And I'd give to the people of North Carolina 620 billion dollars a real money not fiction to protect women and children all over the world. Now could have said the killers of Jeana and other women. But I'ma let the police do their job. It's almost Christmas I remember dude you shot me. After I saved your life. I'm not bitter with you. I'm bitter with myself. Because that day I could have been with an Angel. And now she's dead. Do you see how I think. Time is so precious I must be a time cop. If God would only let me go back in time I could save us all watch. You need two story Thomas to seem like you're healing. God please give my lady back I hear you work miracles. I've been alone for 7 Christmases and I've talked to no one. I've respected everybody I gave all the money I had. Now the same that I am a zillionaire. And I can never run out of money. Lord please help me bring me another girlfriend new. Take your gun out and kill yourself Thomas. Devil I don't believe in nothing but the Lord. Jesus I trust you I promise. Can you hear my supplications Lord. Lord do You hear My cry. I took a bullet saving a life. If I can't have a woman I want to die. Is this the story that you want to tell Thomas. I have to God I'm Superman. Thanks for your love and mercy Jesus. Thomas you are timecop act like a man. I want all of those people brought up on charges. For the shooting death and murder of a police officer. Why is that Thomas you are still liven. Jeana was time cop sent to protect me and that she has children. Are they your children Thomas. Physically I'm not the father Lord. But I swear to you they are my children. That girl is still with you Thomas. Oh my God. Your life has been trials and tribulations. What I tell you not to give up. This is the second time I've strengthened you. Lord Jesus I've never gave up. Whatever you go keep your head up police officer. Lord I'm doing the best I can. You are a time cop Thomas Allred Jr. Lord I am alone. Thomas do the best that you can. Jesus I am called Superman. And I stand up for the world. Listen to what Thomas is talking about. He said them people killed his girl. And shot him. Almost 21 years ago. Now it's almost Christmas time. Has anyone seen Thomas y'all? It's okay y'all I'm alright. All the people come down and relax. Look you're going to spend time with your loved ones. Sometimes I think about going back. Sometimes I think about going forward. Most times I sit right here in my movie chair. God I wish I had me a beautiful woman that love me.Jeana did I go too far. I've been fighting hard as hell I'm a time cop. Activate timecop show response activity.Eden I apologize I get carried away. The book is called in your face. It's for me and Jeana and all the children that have been killed. What we are saying is in your face. God is still good. Jesus loves the little children. All the little children of the world. Jesus loves the little children. All the little boys and little girls. Kids when you grow up take care of each other. Little boys don't hurt these girls their young ladies. You have to dream about yourself in the future. Can't you see the Superman is a king. Jeana I promised you a star. It's in your heart girl you a queen.Jeana sweetheart you taught me everything.Eden I do apologize. But sometimes you get hard to the think. In your face is a story about Jeana. Doing Superman Thomas Allred Jr a favor from heaven. What flavor is she doing Thomas. She is helping me find love two times and give me all the money I ever dreamed up in the bank. Cause I'm her Superman.

And she told me everything will be all right when they shot me. She told me she had me and that she love me. And they took her life. I have been alone close to 7 years. Fighting all kind of crime the best way I know how trying to die. God I’ve written these six books is close to Christmas. I don’t think I could spend another Christmas night alone. This is Superman waiting for you radio station. Superman this is Tyrone man we love you man keep trying. Imma kill the man that killed Superman. Look my friends. To be continued in another dream.Jeana I love you have a pa** my test. People have done beat me up and everything. There is one more test I have for you. Thomas go to sleep.Jeana I am a zillionaire.but right now me and my family and neighborhood don’t have nothing to eat. Ain’t this some sh*t Eden . I’m Superman and professionals know me as Thomas Allred Jr. Jesus thank you for putting the star on top of the tree uptown. Is a guiding light to us all. And to us all good night. Superman

I told you Rose that I was in love with you you think that I’m finished because you blocked me off your webpage. I give my all for everything that you do. Woman you are lovely take your time. Just to understand the man that I am. Girl make sure that I’m okay. Thank you for caring about me. And taking me off of your web page. As you know and you should know me by now. I am Superman the king of the house.And Rose I’m hoping to treat you better. Then anyone in your life. Only looked at you image for second road.can’t you see Rose that I’m transparent to other people’s vision. I’m writing a book called a zenith book report.Sa I want you to know that I got you in it.Sa I call you Rose. Everybody knows I’m in love with Sa. Dc even knows I love you Sa. That girl talking to you is my best friend. Thomas. Yes I am Superman.Sa but still I’m Thomas. I know it’s getting confusing. But baby I’ve been all around the world to know you. One criminal at a time. Will you keep my promises Sa. Girl I give you 2 billion dollars for every book that I ever wrote. 6500 billion dollars. For you to keep Sa. I hope I see you one day. Where children play with each other. I like you when I first saw you.Sa I’m for real I’m no longer undercover. Im a time cop Sa. Rose I’m not using you. I’m just in love with you. And I’m fighting my a** off to make you understand. That your ex boyfriend ain’t right for you. Baby I won’t play with you. They telling you I’m a good man.Eden can’t you hear of Superman. I’m trying to get a message to Sa. I call her Rose but people don’t hear me. I’m coming after you Rose I’m the greatest love story ever written. Is Thomas is Superman divided each other. Superman Loves Kristen. And Thomas loves Sa. He calls her Rose in front of his mother. Superman you better not be playing with me. Kristen I tell you the truth. I want a family. And I’m in love with Elizabeth. Thomas is in love with her two. Thomas read my face. Go after if you really love Sa I’m getting tired of people telling me what to do. Thank you wifey thats undercover. And so has it Thomas Allred Jr is a zillionaire in love with three women. I still don’t want to get biblical. But all of my ladies are looking so biblical. Thomas do you really want to women you are a zillionaire. Touch One hair on any woman's head. And the book is finished right here. Elizabeth Thomas is a zillionaire. And he is in love with you Kristen and sa. I want Kristen in them to help me. I'm going to make you a** official. Get in It Thomas. In my dreaMs..Sa that you and me. I'm writing a book called a Zillionaire book report Camelot manuscript. Camelot music. I'm starting to record label just for Sa to do her music. Dc I haven't forgot about your a**.Dc you are my best friend. I got you Camelot music to own. Girl keep up. Cause you even say you're my best friend. What are we going to do about Camelot music. We are going to distribute music all over the world. Right now people are talking about us. Can you hear me. Yes I can hear you. Mama I love you. Superman get ready for bed. Yes Charlene. Boy you hear what I said.yes Mama give me 10 minutes and I'll cut the lights off. Boy I mean now. Okay Mama. I got super human hearing. We already took over.Sa didn't I tell you I was going to get you into the music industry. Thomas everybody knows that you're Superman the soldier. Jeana wrote about in all of her journals. How you some kind of Superman. And you're in love with your woman. Thomas you know Superman is a legend. Can you make sure that it stays alive. As long as I live I will always love Jeana. Until the day that I die. Now I'm going to sleep my mama said so. I thank everybody. For being a part of this book. I want to thank Danielly. For being a friend if a being Supergirl where getting tough on Superman Danielly sometimes the sun does shine through the clouds. Superman. Thomas is this your story is this all that you have to say. I thank every one of my brothers and sisters on the police force and not on the police force we are family no matter what we go through. Jeana is not with us. But you have to be strong. Like the men on 300 are. Thomas everybody thinks that you are leaving them. I leave to you a collection of superhero manuscripts. So that you will understand the even though I might leave you in the world ther is still my heart. All I want is my wife and a family. Thats all he does is sit down and talk to his self. Jeana may I be in love with Sa and Kristen and Elizabeth at the same time. I know what that boy saying. You hungry. Elizabeth yeah. I told you I no what he saying. Elizabeth Sa and Kristen. All three of you be my wife's on the ship. Excuse me. I am a zillionaire. This story is dedicated. To all my people who don't believe in theMs. elves. When I talk to you you seem fine. Realize we going through some junk y'all. I'm giving you the superhero manuscript. Put the collection together. Everybody is talking to you. There are books all over the world. If Jeana could hear me. She would say you are timecop Thomas. Now your story is complete. You got a zillionaires book report. Yall thank you. Be professional.Sa and Kristen and Elizabeth. I don't know how to find you. Keep looking Superman. One day we might just show you your future. Kristen and Sa and Elizabeth. If we should by chance ever meet again. Call me by my name. I am Superman.and this is a zillionaires book report Camelot manuscript. I'm a cop.A Time cop named Superman. Thomas.

You don't know how I feel about you. I hear you staying that Superman is this and Superman is that. But I'm going to tell you something in fact the reason I'm with you. It's cuz I'm a zillionaire. Take your time to wrap that around your brainwave hello Cusack. Well if it isn't Superman. How's the term cup thing going for you. Thomas. Hold Your position.Jeana got killed because you wasn't with her Thomas. Cusack you win some you lose some. You win some you lose some. Now that is funny. Thomas. Hold your ground I ain't done with you yet.whats even more funny is I've been tracking you all through this book Cusack. Take a picture of me when you kiss my a** timecop. I'm getting to write me a book. Oh yeah Thomas what we call it my dead wife. Thomas to professional. And that's the name of your new book I'm a write another book. What we're going to call this funeral arrangements. Are hell know. I want you to know that I restrain myself. Cusack getting his a** whooped by a professional in a talk game. Are he'll know what. You still seeing a ghosts aren't you Thomas what is that Superman. Say hi to my a** for me. Trix are for kids. I'm going to get you a therapist Thomas. The 1 800 suck my d*ck Superman. You f*cking loser. I want plastic my a** next to your face you f*cking loser. Say something to me Thomas. Say something Superman. Say something. You can go ahead now Thomas. The only reason that I haven't kicked your a** is because Jeana told me not to.and you damn right I'm seeing a ghost because my wife told me she would never leave me. Give them time Thomas. Your a** is going in for conspiracy to commit murder. Those are bogus charges listen to me time cop. The woman didn't have to do but stay cool. She flipped out when she found out they were going to kill you. So someone killed her instead. Who killed my girlfriend.I don't know .but whoever it is is high up in the ranks. Thomas I'm talking zillionaires. They knew you would come and Thomas it's all a setup.they're going to get you at the top of the game just to wipe your a** out Superman.You can hide nowhere in broad daylight Thomas. Thank you Cusack for your words.That's why I'm putting you under arrest for attempted murder. Of a police officer timecop named Jeana. Don't put me in there they will give me a prison. Give me one week Thomas to make up for everything that I've done. Thomas Jeana and you owe me that. You think I'm against you I'm a Time Cop two.Eden did you hear Cusack confession. You recording this. You even more messed up than I thought you were. I am a zillionaire Cusack. So What by the end of the day you'll be warm meat. What are you saying to me. The reason Jeana got killed ain't because she was with you. Jeana got killed because she was a cop a Time cop.think about it Thomas when those gangster shot you who helped you heal up and survive and tough to you to be strong. Jeana did that's right. She helped you live so she could die for our community. No you f*cking liar. Cusack Jeana isn't alive because of you and your f*cking buddies all I need to do is to prove it you're coming with me.i already told you that I'm a time cop. You are stuck raving mad. Tell It To The judge.Cusack how do you plead in this episode. Tell the people what you told me. Thomas looking for my family. Wait a minute judge he has something to say. I Cusack I'm guilty of murdering Time cop enforcement officer Jeana. I'm with you Thomas. I'll see you in a big leagues Thomas. Your honour that is not what he is going to say. Cusack with your family. Officer Cusack for breaking time cut code 96743 5 8 200. A reprimand you to serve in the salt mines for no more than the rest of your life. Time cop sentenced to be serve now .lieutenant officer Superman. Do you have something to say.those people who kill my wife are going to pay for what they did. It is noted in my time card manual. Superman look at you it's been almost 30 years. 15 since Jeana death. Nowadays how you getting by Kristen I'm doing the best that I can. I just keep on. I just can't believe someone would come after. If you need to talk to anyone I'm here for you. Kristen. Yes Superman. Take care of yourself and I'll see you in the morning. Okay you sleep good Thomas. Thats all I can do. Them b*tch a** motherf*ckers. Superman wake up is 4:30 in the morning. And it's raining outside. Kristen what are you doing here. I just had to see you Thomas. I was worried about you so I just started to drive. Kristen you really shouldn't be out this late let me call you a cab. Thomas I really don't want to go anywhere can I just stay the night will do rest of night if you know I'm saying. Okay I get some popcorn is downstairs. It's Superman could you bring me something to drink please. All I have is Coca-Cola. Coke is fine for me. Kristen I appreciate you staying with me for a while. Superman if you want me to move in with you I can help you take care of your house. Kristen. Superman I mean Thomas I know that you're too proud. No it's not that and you know it. Thomas I need you to be professional. Kristen I haven't been around anyone in almost 10 years. You can relax Thomas it's only me. I know Kristen that's the problem. Are you saying that you still have a thing for me at all these years. Since you want to see it that way okay.this is amazing Superman has a thing for me Superman has a thing for me y'all. Okay Kristen tell the world I have a thing for you. I got put this on YouTube wait a minute. Kristen don't. No Superman just wait a minute. Kristen I said stop. I didn't mean to say that. Superman I understand maybe I should go. Kristen no. Well what are you saying Thomas. I'm saying I just don't know can I hold you tonight. Superman what did you say. Kristen, Thomas I'm a tec cop from the future. And Superman people are after you. How many tec cop is there. From the future I mean working on my case. There's about 300 million of us time cop Thomas. And you are a lady. You are man Thomas it makes no difference with both time cops.Eden did you hear that. Finish your story because I'm right here Thomas. Yes Eden.i knew Jeana Superman. And now I'm here to save your a** from being murdered. All I can say is Kristen thank you and what took you so long. Don't play with my a** time cop. Give me the f*cking code so we can get out of here. The zillionaire code to my future manuscript is. 121 406-328-9716 4 - time cop.dosent the future looks so bright Superman. But Kristen nothing's changed maybe you put in the codes wrong. No Thomas we are in the future. We are two seconds ahead of everybody else. So what are you saying why did we do this. 2 seconds me nothing in real time yeah it does Thomas I mean Superman kiss me. Okay I've been waiting on my life to do this. And your two seconds are beginning what did you say I said it's your time now kiss me I've been waiting all my life to do this again and you two seconds are beginning Thomas. Kristen I do believe that you're playing with me. Shut up and do what I say Superman and kiss me. Superman do you know how to make love. And I want to say that Kristen and Superman live happily ever after. But one day they had kids. And that is the future of our time cops. I know Jeana will be proud of what I'm doing. I'm working to make my way through life. Superman Thomas realize that these people after you are not trying to hurt you. These people after you are movie stars and directors. I Thomas Allred Jr am putting into the Jeana fund for elderly senior citizens adults all around the world 2500 billion dollars. For all of our American veterans and senior citizens all around the world this is the Jeana.I got something to say then im a get loose from y'all for a minute. Seven years I visited the Jeana grave in my head. I've been alone for 7 years. I need Kristen to understand me. I'm using my powers of observation. To distinguish good from evil.and Sa I'd like to call you Rose.and Elizabeth.Kristen they are good people just like you. See i question my judgment of understanding.because all three of you are worthy to be my superhero. So I asked God for understanding. And I want y'all to know. Get whatever I am super heroes. There's a place for you call heaven in my home. I didn't tell you this stuff so you can feel sorry for me. My 7 years alone has been a soul enrichment treatment a sabbatical. And girls now that I'm telling you the truth about me. I'm putting my foot down who wants Superman.

Eden it's been awhile since we last spoke to each other. I was beginning to think that I've done something wrong.Eden you see nothing would make me feel better. Get a chilled gla** of wine. Laying back conversation with you about my new book coming out.I called this new book give it to females what they want Camelot manuscript. Sometimes I think to myself just how special you are Eden. Once in a blue moon I think to myself I should have dated you in the past. But enough for me I see that you.take your time out to enjoy the finer things in life. Give it to females what they want Camelot manuscript. Is a ma** array of a Miss production. In a gender of diplomacy. Communicating knowledge among females to indicate the love I have for you is real. He know what he is talking about. More than that females with the reproductive organs tired and unjust. I believe have a chance of talking to another reproductive system before talking to a man reproductive system. Somehow this is me talking to you Eden. Let freedom Ring cause. We United together on the firm understanding you hear me girl. Listen we collided together I'm too strong a** winds. Control yourself Thomas. And Jesus Christ and God almighty. Cares about you. What I'm getting at you Eden. And what I'm trying to say to you is. I need you Cusack. I can't I'm in the salt mines this is where you sent me Thomas. Come down some.if you realize that the salt mines are killing people every few minutes. You better hurry up and come and get me out of here Superman. Cusack I know that you're not well in the salt mines. Giving those books to both publishers was a smart idea to do Thomas. They can mix and match to get the story straight. Which publisher are you talking to right now. Eden Cusack. Eden is good. But once you get my letter that I sent to you Superman. You will understand me clear. Give Erin a call Thomas. Isn't she the other that you sent the books to. Yeah cusack you've been gone almost two years in the salt mines. Good grief Thomas you got to get me out of here Superman. Come down Cusack. It has only been eight minutes since you've been gone. 8 minutes in your time Thomas and eternity in mine. Look Thomas people are dying here. I feel the same way about Jeana Cusack. You know that I had nothing to do with that. All I need is one more chance Thomas. Thomas please. I'll see you in the next millennium Cusack.then why did you message me I thought you said you needed me Superman.Cusack oh yeah I need you to kiss my a**. That boy is professional.I'm a Time cop I'm going to get your a** you watch when I get out of here Thomas. Cusack that will not be ever. Turn on the Time accelerators. The time accelerated what are you talkin about Superman. I want you to have a nice after life Cusack. And do me a favor. Tell Jeana that I told you to kiss my a** I'm a murder that b*tch in my afterlife. You're after life is right now Cusack. No don't kill that man Thomas. You are a police officer time cop officer 96710 what is your code Superman. Superman f*cking here me what is your code. Elizabeth I'm time cop officer Thomas Allred Jr. Thank you Elizabeth so much. Shut up Cusack. Thomas release the lever and let Cusack go. See this man is crazy Elizabeth he's not listening to you. Time cop officer Superman what is your code. My code as a tec agent. Is im to protect and serve people all through time no matter the difficulty and no matter the cost. Give me the numbers I'm running you in. Give me some time Elizabeth. My time card numbers are 473-9610. You need time to kill that man. Elizabeth yes we need time to kill that man. Elizabeth what are you saying. Cusack this is your execution for murder Jeana. You are f*cking fruit loops y'all. Enjoy your stay Cusack.What you talkin about enjoy my stay .I've been enjoying my stay .what you talking about enjoy my stay.enjoy my stay Elizabeth. She meant in hell Cusack.you son of a b*tches is going to pay for this sh*t I'm going to get you Superman Elizabeth kiss my a**. Let me time cop Superman. For killing Jeana Cusack. We will put together the lever. Now Elizabeth. Rest in peace Cusack. F*ck you Superman. Timecode annihilation is complete. Thank you Elizabeth. I knew that you needed help getting rid of sc*mbag Thomas. You know that we must never talk about this again. I'm here at the Town cop to help you Superman. I didn't know I need any help until I put that lever. We put the lever together Superman oh my p**sy is wet. My d*ck is hard to but I don't know what to do. We got six hours before we supposed to be in the correct time. Are you saying what I think you're saying Thomas. Elizabeth take off your clothes. Come with my a** is so hot. Don't worry my tongue knows what to do. I need you right now Thomas inside of me. Face the wall. Go ahead and put the d*ck inside of me. See first imma kiss your neck and then down slowly imma lic* your a** is this allowed in the time cup code because you know we're not ever supposed to have s*x. Thomas got him a real girlfriend. People are listening to us.I don't care no more Elizabeth we about to have s*x. Alright time cop show me what you f*cking got. I intend to and then some. Run through a simulations with me. Run through a simulations Thomas this is my p**sy getting wet. Now take your time and. Time cop a simulations of Thomas allred jr are done. Dammit. Elizabeth failed her mission. Bring timecop Thomas Allred Back to real civilization. But in my book Eden. Sometimes I think to myself. What a lucky guy I am. To have time cops with me. What did you just say Thomas. Elizabeth is coming. Thomas Allred Jr you're going to have to go back with me. I'm just sitting in my work Elizabeth. I haven't changed a thang . Thomas it's people out there that see that you're timecop. I don't know what's going on but I'm a book publicist. Shut up b*tch. Thomas you can come with me and play fair.Im supposed to be on vacation I'm supposed to be done with all this. Thomas we are going to need you to come in for test pilot run on the simulations. Thank you Thomas. Your code name is still Superman. And yeah there's something I got to tell you about your old pal Cusack. He didn't make it Thomas.Thomas remember that you got a Time burst sitting in your wallet. I haven't seen my wallet I haven't seen my wallet is 6 business days. Shut b*tch you tell me. Thomas and get down she's from the future. Almost had your a** Thomas Allred Jr. Elizabeth thank you for being here you right on time. Your book bored the sh*t out of me Thomas. You're welcome Superman when I say run run toward the window and jump out of it. run. I'm running with you to Superman. No the hell you don't. Eden control yourself. He doesn't know does he Elizabeth. The time accelerators are now open. Kristen is coming to kick your a** Eden . Its you again Eden. I got his baby Thomas. Christian sweetheart she's lying. Make yourself useful and turn around Eden. Just like we used to. Just like we used to imma make sure you have a safe place to go to. B*tch if you don't get your a** down on the floor. The time accelerators are now open. The time is celebrated are now open. Cusack. And Mr.. Weaver to. Doing it to Cusack. Elizabeth is good to meet you. How did he know you Elizabeth. Thomas me and Elizabeth had a run in a couple days ago. You where there. it should have been fun. Elizabeth it was fun until I got out of the salt mines. You put Cusack in the salt mines. Don't waste your time. I can see the reunions that you're having. Everybody don't move. But Superman you don't even have a weapon permit. My book is with his permit. What is he saying. Clock this boy like 10 times. Oh no hell no you know you don't. Kristen Elizabeth move. Shoot that b*tch. You see how that boy is thinking. Thomas now realize people are listening to you. Everybody how you're doing. Thomas were watching you because you is a time cop. Thank you I know I realize that. Did I pa** my test. You are in our time conciliation chamber. You have nothing to eat and no food. Everything will be given to you. Upon your request. Upon the request of the generals. If generated Lucky

Day stripes. So what are you saying I'm a prisoner in A Time consideration chamber. I'm saying you realize that boy just touch a woman.Jeana .yes I realized the man kill my wife.Give Jeana a capital letter when you spell out her name. Put capital letters on Jeana Thomas. This is not a game. Everybody want to know if you control yourself. I've hurt no one I only want to love four women I've been a man my whole life. Take your time.look I don't think this is right I work for my money I should have something to show for it. See what you're saying Thomas we are timecop enforcement officers. You need to listen to Thomas.the reason I'm saying this Thomas is because people around your neighborhood are killing people. You got the Superman emblem that I sent you Thomas.I had it but I gave the ring away to a woman that I liked and wanted to marry her name is Elizabeth. The Superman emblem means that you already been through that situation one time. Thomas no matter what you think of yourself you are police officer. Yes sir I know that sh*t. I know that sh*t sir. We are going to send you through time back to your conversation with Eden. Are there any last words that you want to say to us. They killed my wife and shot me why can't you just send me back to save Jeana.we can't send you back because it is too dangerous for any time cop agent to pursue. But what we can do is let you have a memory report. A memory report what is this. You can remember each other just like you were there. Memory report is being installed in you as we speak.if I save Jeana I'll be damned if them bastards are going to go back in time to steal steal money. You hear it. Say steal money one more time Thomas. Steal money. People are after you.the simulation machine will help you realize that your family ain't after you. You need to realize Thomas that only time cops can hear exactly what were saying. You better treat Kristen better. Kristen honey I'm sorry.I know that wasn't you thinking about them other women Thomas. Kristen no more apologize I love you. And you were saying to me Thomas. Kristen. Enough of that sh*t. I'm interviewing Thomas Allred . Thomas Allred Jr I need you to report to the time acceleration locker. Listen everybody hear you. Do you know I'm taping your a**. Thomas Allred Jr report to the time acceleration locker immediately. Look Eden I would love to do this but I got to take care of some business maybe a rain check. Maybe. Speak to Elizabeth and Kristen Thomas. Elizabeth and Kristen how you doing. We've been waiting for you to realize that your time cop professional Thomas .as The story goes theres people at the killing people. Thomas. It ain't nothing new ladies we all can rock and roll. Make sure that you understand that you are they Superman Thomas. So we can rock and roll. Kristen Elizabeth I fully understand. Take your time out and speak to Kristen. Look at it this way you can own that b*tch. Thomas. Kristen apologize for the way I've acted over the years I almost didn't remember. You hear me Thomas realize that your professional police officer. I know Kristen all I'm saying is that I need you and I love you and I put no one before you you are my wife. Take your gun out and kill yourself you bested for leaving me.Kristen you know that you don't mean that stuff and you and I both know that you don't mean it. Listen Thomas. Hey who is that that's my friend I know that voice. Thomas tone loke Thomas get your a** in there and take a shower like you supposed to while me and Kristen talk about you. God this is so unreal. People are after you and there are after me. You have to realize one thing Thomas. This is a Time cop continuum. Your books will circulate throughout the land. I said throughout the world. Whatever you do from here on out mistakes that you made Thomas. Give them to Jesus. Because I'm going to kick your a** if you mess up. This is your one chance to date me Thomas. What do you have to say about that. I say thank God I love you so much Kristen. Control yourself. Take off your shoes Thomas. Let your feet. Let your feet position you. You know I can't love you right now Thomas. Just be patient you're making me come Thomas. So what's going on with Elizabeth and you what's going on. I said give me some time Thomas. Is it my p**sy you want. Kristen I want your friendship and your body I need you so much baby I'm alone.listen Thomas listen go spit that gum out of your mouth and come back to sit down and listen. You are a Time enforcement officer. A TEC track agent. Thomas continue working. And hold that position Thomas right now. Our people are working. Right now your book is named give it to the females what they want Camelot manuscript. Dude I want you to change the name. To girl I got you. Go ahead and change the name before a time cop come back through. Please hurry up Thomas be professional just one second I'm with you Thomas. Thomas Allred Jr professional.I want you to take your time out and call Kristen name out at the top of your lungs. No. that dude is the TEC agent. Think about Elizabeth Thomas.that girl been positioned out there close to 15 years waiting on you to come and talk to her. Thomas ain't giving up.give him everything that he wants in this world TEC track agent Elizabeth. Keep up your pace Thomas. I know that you want to finish the story. But you are a Time future cop. Thomas it's time to lay down to take a nap now. But mama I'm going to time future cop. Boy what future are you talkin about. Because in this future we ain't got nothing to eat in the kitchen. And I know you hungry Superman but I figured something out. Mama you just call me Superman. You are Superman Thomas you my hero. Girl I got you. Teach me a time cop like you is Charlene. You got to just relax Thomas quit thinking about it Thomas. I'mma tell you something. Superman of giving you time. To live in my house and get yourself together. Not only will I take care of you but I will feed you. I'm your mother Thomas. Moma check out these cool shades eyewear. Some other time Superman. The time is celebrated that now been open. Mama I love it when you come to visit. Take your time Superman. When will I see you again. Only women time circuit continuum allows. Thomas we both our time cops. I know Mama.Go to sleep now. Thomas you're making a mess all over yourself. Look at these sheets I got to clean this up. Mama I love you the time accelerator is now open. Give Kristen the best for me. I Understand what you doing for Thomas.im So in love that I can't sleep mama Thomas a lot of people sitting here watching you you need to go to sleep. And Thomas remember. With great authority comes more time. I got you Time cop.

Look at me girl I need you to understand that I love you.Thomas I realize that you need help to understand that you are a Zillionaire.Hey I don't know what to do about the situation. That's exactly what we talked about Thomas. Exactly what what are we talkin about Eden. Kristen may I talk to him please. Eden if you want to Thomas I love you. Tell Thomas that you love him Eden. Thomas I love you. Suck my d*ck Thomas. Eden I know that voice from anywhere. Suck my d*ck Thomas you owe me $75. Ya'll give that boy $75. I got your a** out of jail. You got to suck my d*ck or give me my money Thomas. That is in the punk handbook. I knew it Kristen. Is punk Daddy punk Daddy is out there. Thomas come down.Eden y'all don't know what you're saying this man is dangerous.Punk Daddy is just playing with you Thomas. He asking me to suck his d*ck and he has a gun. He has a squirt gun Thomas. It doesn't matter Kristen a gun is a gun. And I'm telling you Kristen that gun is real. Where you go you rascal you. Thomas where did you go. Kristen I'm hiding under the table. Thomas come from under there Punk Daddy won't hurt you. I got to get a contract to the kids Kristen. You going to suck my d*ck Thomas. Listen to me Kristen I'm not sucking that man's d*ck. Thomas you might as well just suck his d*ck. Kristen you are Stark grieving mad. And Eden and Kristen.if this is the way you going to treat me I don't want to be in these relationships ever again. You can both give me back my rings or give them to Punk Daddy for the $75 that I owe him. Because I am going to tell you again

. I am not sucking that man's d*ck Eden and Kristen. Listen Thomas sucking a d*ck ain't as bad as you think it is. You Ladies got one more time to tell me to suck a d*ck.look Thomas ain't nobody here now you might as well suck his d*ck Punk Daddy is going to kill you. Kristen I'm not sucking a d*ck that it. I've been sucking d*ck since I was 14. Shut your mouth. I've been sucking d*ck since I was 18. That's is blasphemy and you know the devil. Thomas. what are you saying we're going to do Punk Daddy wants his d*ck sucked. Come take your medicine Thomas Allred Jr. Punk Daddy look you bail me out of jail and I thank you. It's clobberin a** time Thomas Allred Jr. Thomas are you alright out there. Kristen get back in the room I'ma handle this. You can handle it Thomas. You need to suck his d*ck Thomas. Eden shut up. Beat his d*ck baby. I'm not putting my hands on that black man d*ck. Kristen and Eden honey. I'm getting ready this Jack this muthaf*cker d*ck.it's about time you stopped running and faced up to sucking this d*ck Thomas Allred Jr. Yeah about that first of all call me Superman Punk Daddy. Thomas our hero. Yall ladies going to chill I'm working my game out. Still in the room like I said to you. Thomas you ready to suck this d*ck. Punk Daddy you a big ugly motherfuker. But I got this diamond ring and a checkbook right now. Worth over a billion dollars.Punk Daddy I will give this to you as a token of my gratitude and I was still get you your $75 as soon as possible. Because you bail me out of jail with my baby. Didn't you tell me that you were going to f*ck me in my a** Thomas Allred Jr. Punk Daddy that was just a metaphor of trying to get some p**sy on my d*ck from a young lady when my d*ck was starving for attention and I do apologize I will give you another billion dollars because of that so can we squash this. Hell know we can't squash this sh*t Superman. What is too bad Punk Daddy.because instead of me sucking your d*ck I got two women in the other room that wants to suck your d*ck Punk Daddy. There's two women in the other room there that's sucking d*ck. Yes Punk Daddy they said they've been sucking d*ck since 14 and 18 years old. I swear to God to it. Hold my weapons Superman let's go see. Punk Daddy I'm not holding your f*cking d*ck. I'm a man Punk Daddy I'm a man. Give me the gun. Give me the motherfuking gun Punk Daddy. It Thomas I'm sorry I messed up. Yes you did Punk Daddy. I was just playing about you sucking my d*ck. I knew you was Punk Daddy. But to chase me all over town at night I can't condone. So what are you saying Superman. I have to knock the sh*t out of you punk Daddy. So the girls will calm down and suck to d*ck. They have to know that everything is cool between us. Eden. Thomas is out there fighting Punk Daddy. Hit me my a** Thomas. Punk Daddy you got to be mature about this. Take off your hand cuffs Punk Daddy. I'm a cop I need my hand cuffs I can't do that. Is for the ladies Punk Daddy. It's for the ladies. Okay Punk Daddy put your hands behind your back. We going down to the police department like I said we would. And get back your damn $75 in front of people. There's something you should know Punk Daddy. Imma take good care of these b*tches you asked me to. Suck my d*ck your zillionaire Thomas. Superman captured Punk Daddy in front of two women. Thomas the who Damn police Force was looking for me. Thomas Kristen and Eden is bringing in Punk Daddy. Thank you Kristin for bringing in Punk Daddy. Either way it goes Punk Daddy I won. You told everybody I sucked yo d*ck. Kristen you Eden did suck my d*ck and Thomas did too. Hold Your position Thomas. Punk Daddy here is your $75. And I hope that you realize that we captured you. Well at least tell me something Thomas or Superman how did you do it. Suck on this d*ck and I'll tell you all about it Punk Daddy. Will you please are you really going to let me Thomas Ill suck your d*ck. Gaurd. Thomas im giving y'all two minutes to get your d*ck sucked. The both of you. The entire police station want they did sucked Punk Daddy. Sucking d*ck avenger. Guards take him away. A Guards I want to tell you the last time that we made Superman suck my d*ck. Stories about Superman Punk Daddy got stories about Superman. One night I had him down on his knees. Guards shut Punk Diddy up. For good this time. Thomas you forgot you gave me 2 billion dollars. I'm getting bailed out in 20 minutes. What kind of justice system is this.Don't worry baby you caught Punk Daddy one time you can catch him again. Eden shut your mouth. Christian what are we going to do. Run they letting Punk Daddy lose back there. Superman is clobbering time.yeah but my stories sometimes get a little little kid away. I'm Thomas Allred Jr and this is

Dru Hill. Listen to me Reign do you realize that Dru Hill isn't coming. Thomas Allred Jr I don't know we're going to do the people came to see a movie. Can you find Kristen anywhere. No I ain't seen that woman all day man. And was Eden at. She's over at Camelot music working with DC and Sa . It's my birthday man. Happy birthday to you Officer Reign. Dude i know just call me Thomas.A Thomas when them girls find out your police officer is going to trip they a** out. I know I got to be on stage in two minutes. You got this Thomas Allred Jr. Ladies and gentlemen and I'll bring to you. Punk Daddy. Thank you for the Superman. You still going to suck my d*ck Superman. Punk Daddy your lying I'm not sucking you got damn d*ck. Yes you are Superman. Punk Daddy no I'm not. Suck this d*ck Superman. Officer Reign going to beat your a** Punk Daddy. Punk Daddy on the stage telling Superman and officer Reign to suck his d*ck. This b*tch a** nigga won't come near me. All the ladies p**sy they fear me. My d*ck is long and boy I'm strong. I got this whip and they can't come near me. Thomas. Go and stop Punk Daddy right now. And how do you expect me to do that. Kristen Punk Daddy is a madman. You captured him the last time Thomas. Kristen if I remember so well. You me and Eden captured him the last time. Listen to trying to get Thomas this contract. Ladies coming to the stage. You have my truest honour and respect. Miss Mary j Blige performing 7 days. Thomas almost became a producer. Producer that a** to me Mary j Blige. A Punk Daddy the show is over you going too far. Suck my d*ck Thomas Jr. I suck your d*ck all right call the police station. I got to get out of here. I'm jealous of you Mary j Blige. For what reason Punk Daddy. The reason why I'm Punk daddy is because it had that you wear. And what are you saying Punk Daddy. I want to know if I can quit comedy and come on the road with you styling your hair. Wow. I would have never thought. Be strong Mary. Thomas. I am not going to cry. This is Dru Hill. A wheres that crazy dude. Who Punk Daddy. Here comes Daddy Dru Hill. Is clubbing time. Sisqo I told you going to suck my d*ck. Punk Daddy not even in your f*cking dreaMs.. I thought yall said these are the times that we all wish for. All four of you singers together on my d*ck make the ladies want more. Suck my d*ck sisqo. Thomas help me Superman. Sisqo the only way out of this sh*t you got a capture Punk Daddy a**. Come on Dru Hill it's clobberin time. Hey thats is it for me. I hope you enjoy my book Dru Hill Camelot music. It's a manuscript book coming out called be with me Camelot music. And we're done cut action. How you going to scream action after you say cut. These muthaf*ckers don't know what the f*ck they doing. Thomas the people here you we still talkin. Are you nuts inching. Now listen to me y'all. Punk Daddy a**istant is coming in. I give great pleasure to. Sir a** alot.Sir a** alot. Why do I have this pleasure. Well Thomas I'm the a**istant to my brother Punk Daddy. Make common sense. And seeing that you owe my brother $85.49. I will give to You Dru Hill's manuscript. Can you suck my d*ck Thomas. Hell no. Get the f*ck out of here. You suck my brother d*ck. That's a goddamn lie.All the boys and just said you sucked a d*ck. F*ck you Sir a** a lot.

Look beening the mayor I. Won't suck no d*ck. It's either you suck my d*ck Thomas or I'm a tell Kristen that you f*cked Eden. You wouldn't it's a lie. I am Sir a** a lot and this is my game. Well I have a friend to Sir a** a lot. My friend goes back in the day with me. Called my foot up your a** if you ever lie on me. What you think I'm a tell Punk Daddy. You ain't going to tell him sh*t for about 10 f*cking years. I myself Kristen Eden Mary j Blige and Dru Hill an officer Reign. Captured Punk Daddy's a**. He is in prison now for about 20 years.Sir a** alot. You are under arrest. Take a minute to think about that. Mary. I'm not going to cry. Superman. Eden this is a comedy Central book Eden. Realize that Punk Daddy is a fictional character. And so is Sir a** alot. I bring you scratch your balls cure 109. When the boss inch in your a**

. That boy got something going on about his self. Do you like him Eden. I love them Kristen. I love them to Eden. Kristen you love what you said them. No I didn't. Yes you did Kristen talk to me Im yo girl.Well I'm thinking about going all the way girl I'm dreaming about Superman's balls. I know girl. Thomas they dreaming about your balls on stage. Checkmate baby girl I want it all. Dru Hill Camelot music. You can suck my d*ck Thomas Allred Jr Punk Daddy if you still want me to suck your d*ck in 20 years talk to my foot in your a** about it. Thomas. I want suck a d*ck forever. Punk Daddy. That is between you and your cellmate.Thomas Allred Jr is out there the motherfuking real is hell. And I'm telling everybody on state he don't suck d*ck or play with your a** Thomas.

I'm going to kick Superman a**. Punk Daddy how long we got in here. I day or too maybe. And you sure about that Punk Daddy. Superman. What are you doing here Superman. Punk Daddy I'm offering you a chance to rehabilitate yourself before you get out. I don't need a chance with you Superman. Okay Punk Daddy have it your way. Guard take him to the hole. Suck my d*ck Superman. Suck my d*ck Superman. Punk Daddy wake up. You screaming suck my d*ck Superman out loud everybody can hear you. One more day we'll be out of here you want to see. Okay Punk Daddy I'm going to watch and see I believe you. What's the first thing you going to do when you get out Punk Daddy. I'm going to find Kristen .Eden and Superman. You know Superman real name is Thomas Allred Jr. How do you know that Sir a** alot. I got it from his movie called being safe. Well ladies I had a wonderful night. Superman I'm paging you. Y'all didn't hear voice did you. Superman if you cut off the TV right now. You can hear a voice that they're on the street corner. It is a wino almost done with his bottle. But the story is that you got hearing. Punk Daddy say goodbye to the prison system. They letting Punk Daddy out of prison. He only been in there for one week. What you think Punk Daddy been doing behind bars. Don't even think about it. Ladies I'm getting out of here. You going to the prison to stop them from letting Punk daddy out aren't you Thomas. Be smart enough Kristen. Punk Daddy is a madman. I'm going to my mama's house.

You can call me over there later on. 9:30 the phone rings at Thomas's mother house. Hello. Hello, this is Kristen. Hi Kristen. I just want to tell you to pump days at my house. What. I just want to tell you that Punk Daddy is at my house me and Eden are here. And no we didn't suck his d*ck. Kristen you and Eden listen carefully. What is Punk Daddy doing right now. Heating on the phone with the governor Thomas. What. He on the phone telling the governor that the governor going to suck his d*ck. What you can't be serious Kristen. Ask Eden . Eden what is going on with Punk Daddy in the governor. The government scare Thomas. Eden he has a right to be. The governor told Punk Daddy. That he can marry me and Kristen if you f*cked you in the a** Superman. Now what in the world would he do that Eden.because Punk Daddy in here talking about he going to f*ck the governor in the a** if you don't get to you. And the governor gave him all rights to your a** Superman it's open season. Why snibbling son of a b*tch. The governor says that he's not getting f*cked for nobody Thomas. This is the USA the governor said. Superman. That's Bulsh*t. Sign your name on the dotted line that's bulsh*t. Superman you better watch out. Why is that when are you ladies coming over. When not we re in here with Punk Daddys little brother. He is coaching us on the do and don'ts of being a b*tch. Okay Kristen where is Punk Daddy at right now. Punk Daddy I don't know he left like an hour ago. A hour ago what do you mean Kristen. You said that he was on the phone. Oh my bad Superman that was his brother on the phone they smoking weed in here I keep messing up. Kristen listen to me get Eden and get over here at once. Maybe Punk Daddy left town. Superman. Punk Daddy. Suck my d*ck Superman. Punk Daddy I told you I'm not sucking yo got damn d*ck. Is poetic Justice Thomas. What are you saying Punk Daddy. You put me in prison Superman for 10 years.Punk Daddy you only in there 3 days. It's still hurt it cost me a nail.so you know what that means don't you Superman. No I don't know but you're going to tell me aren't you Punk Daddy . Punk Diddy is ordering you to get on your knees. Punk Daddy that's not going to happen never in this century or any other century not in your dreaMs.. We need to see you in the kitchen Punk Daddy. What is this everybody in my family is cool Punk Daddy . Stay on your knees Superman I'll be right back. Punk Daddy I'm not on my knees nor will I ever get on my f*cking knees. Mama talk to his a** in the kitchen he trippin. No Punk Daddy listen to me. Yes Miss Charlene. You are not f*cking my son in his a**. Tell him Mama. A Charlene this bag of weed right here with $500. Punk Daddy you can funk my son in the a** if you need to. Mama what the hell are you doing. Thomas here comes Punk Daddy. Superman is clobbering time. Punk Daddy. Put that d*ck away Punk Daddy. Kristen thank God. Sweetheart I didn't know what I do without you. Where is Eden at. She's waiting in the car outside come on Superman. Superman you order stuff this d*ck. Punk Daddy not if your life depended on it. Thomas come on. Excuse me I'm trying to get your girlfriend to come with me. Punk Daddy Superman you almost got it you almost to the door. Hey baby. Mama. Is that your mother Thomas. Kristen you no my dear Mom. I leave this house I live here. Then Thomas what are you going to do with Punk Daddy. Yeah I want to see this baby. Mother hush antagonizing sh*t. Okay but I'm going in the other room. What are you smoking weed it's in the air. Punk Daddy you are cool and everything but I would like it if you would leave. No. No. what the hell do you mean no. I said I'm not going nowhere until I get ready to. A Punk Daddy understand we cool but you not going to pull your nuts on me in my mama's house.you better suck my d*ck Superman I'm staying right here you ain't got no gun. Punk Daddy you are absolutely right. Suck my d*ck Punk Daddy my mama got a gun. That's my mama that's my mama. You show are right. Alright Punk Daddy get your a** out of my damn house. Thank you Mama. Boy now gone ill put a hold on your a** I'm not playing. But Charlene I just gave you a bag. Punk Daddy that was dirt weed here go the rest of your bag. Now more boy. Punk Daddy keep your eye on him. He crazy and you're right Superman is crazy but his mama even crazier. Now move. I'm going this way. Move Boy. Punk Daddy has left the building. You hear that noise the whole wide country is screaming yay Punk Daddy has been defeated but Superman 3 times. In front of the world and a bunch of women. Kristen Eden I love you. Listen I can't tell you how I beat him. Thomas the police just picked up Punk Daddy and his little brother. The governor said he not having that sh*t. In his house. The governor is a bad man. He crazy. And baby that's what I told him that then. Superman come here. You getting heavy. Eden. Tell Kristen I got the baby. Superman got yall baby Superman Thomas just put him down he needs to walk near sister. In a put Superman next to Supergirl.I hope you don't mind my baby touching your baby Eden. My baby is a mess. Both of them belong to and look like Superman. And that's the end of my story. I know you wouldn't believe it. But I've been reading book at the book. And hope that the work can find my chapters. And finally make some sense out of what he called me Superman. Get him Thomas. A special thanks goes out to my mother and my family. And the police department for keeping Punk Daddy behind bars. Both of them babies look like you Superman. I never thought I could have kids. Maybe it's a dream. Maybe it's a new position. Maybe my whole family and City and world are superheroes. Check please Superman. Punk Daddy Dream House Camelot manuscript. Yall it was fun. Have yourself a wonderful holiday season. Puck Daddy and family. The Superman and family watchman. I got kids that are incredible. Don't rescue Me Punk Daddy im a get to you one of these days Superman. Look at my bed I've got to take on it Superman.

I want you to know that I thank you. Thomas wake up the people I get to see you now. Okay give a warm welcome and no further ado we got you coming to the stage is a funny motherf*cker. Show you love for Thomas Allred Jr. Thomas. Lieutenant Dan thank you. People I didn't want to come out this mutha f*cker tonight. Why Thomas why didn't you want to come out here. Come my feet won't stop hurting.

your feet won't stop hurting what do you mean. Your a** kicked has been approved. Why Thomas you motherf*cker. CNN president of the a**-kicking club. The show you nigga get your a** whooped on primetime. I told you not to call a woman a b*tch. But this dude said no. He going to act like Bruce Lee. And the b*tch whooped his a**. On primetime. Now when I say primetime. I do mean prime time. All the niggas in the hood. Seen this man getting his a** whooped by his woman. They had her whooping his a** on cable access television. So all the inmates could see men and women even the jailers could get in and get a piece of the action. The sh*t got so large. They were watching this b*tch beat that Man a** over in Italy Iraq and Pakistan. Over in Chile they don't f*ck with that b*tch. One thousand memories go out to my wife Jeana. You know what I've been thinking. It is my duty to think for the crowd. The crowd like what the f*ck you say. So I'm going to think for them. And tell them. That I said we all should be f*cking rich. You just a zillionaire Thomas you ain't got a clue about a work man struggle. They whooped my a**. Talking about ain't got a clue about a work man struggle. I come up at a time when hustling was your balls. You couldn't have no little balls either them b*tches wanted bricks. Let me do this for you. To break down a ball brick. You going to need a nice piece of a**. You a soldier. Not any piece of a** a do. I mean to say. You ain't f*cking your best friend in the a**. See b*tches already know about that. The Ricky put on your drawers and go home. Ricky like why I got to leave I'm his butt buddy. Because I asked you to leave. Plus you just proved my point. Why b*tches do not like little balls. Say Kristen.I need to make an example for the people and I want to know if I can use you as a witness. Yes Superman you can use me. Now Kristen is it true or not. That you have a fat a** and some big titties. True or not Kristen answer the question.Superman is true. No Kristen let me ask you again. Do you want to have little balls or big balls in your run down. What is a rundown. Kristen it is your vagina. You never getting away Superman no matter where you go. Cusack. And your tec officer. But this is what you do with your time stand-up comedy. I had to have a place to relax myself. Superman I brought along a friend of yours. I'm sure you two will have fun. Thrill Me. Superman. Oh sh*t its Punk Daddy. Maintain your position. A lot of people can hear us. How Cusack the stage is Frozen. Keep going Cusack you'll get him this time. Punk Daddy. And Cusack. Do you have the time. There about to dim the lights are you Thomas. Now really Punk Daddy do you have the time. Yeah I have the time. The time is 12.20 a.m. lieutenant Dan Punk Daddy also has the time. I'm going to make mincemeat out of your black a**. Forrest Gump get his a**. I got him lieutenant Dan. Life is like a box of chocolates. Punk Daddy. You never know what you're going to get. Good that's good Thomas you captured Punk Daddy again. But Cusack is not so good for you. Im a TEC enforcement agent. They training Superman. What do you saying Cusack. My name isn't Cusack. I'm Kristen Thomas. I'm Kristen Superman you mean to say. Superman were training you. To be faster. To pick up think smarter. I know Kristen and to boldly go where no one's gone before. But why you here really honey. Superman I missed you so much. It's only been a few days Kristen. Thomas it's been 7 years. Honey your face. I don't want to talk about it Thomas. Honey your face please tell me why what happened. Thomas the time enforcement agency blew up. I barely made it back here to save you. Kristen thank you. Superman you have to come with me now. Wait Kristen will it be coming back. We can't come back. The time enforcement agency is gone. We can't go back we can only go to the present time is of the essence Superman let's go. Superman go I love you. Thomas. Where am I. You are in the time enforcement agency simulation chamber. But what. Elizabeth DC Sa and Kristen. What is going on. Superman you are Zillionaire. We find it too risky for you to go out in public. So you are hereby arrested. Place your shield and your gun on the table Superman. For violating time enforcement code 10672 .34. how do you plead Superman. So Kristen you really going to kill me over. Superman you have too much money to give back. How do you plead Superman.you talkin about Superman was going to b*tch up make a movie out of this. How do you plead Thomas. Kristen Elizabeth Sa and DC.LADIES I LOVE YOU AND I PLEAD GUILTY. Time cop Thomas Allred Jr stand up. You are guilty of breaking time cop code three one eight. Looking out for your own personal gain.you put in a plea of guilty in the court finds you guilty. You're starts starts Now. What happened Kristen. Superman I blew up the TEC agency. But why Kristen. Because I keep going back in time. And I keep crying for years. What's wrong Kristen tell me. I blew up the tec enforcement agency. It came back in time to save you. Because I couldn't see you die again. All over again. We got 30 seconds to get out of here. And maybe I want to do this again. That's my Jenny. Forest what are you doing here. Jenny is supposed to be doing a show. I'm here to watch it. But there's no one else in the stadium you're here. Thomas don't believe him that's Cusack. Kristen I love you. But I can't go with you. I just want you to get in this time machine Thomas. Kristen no I have to save forest. Life is like a box of chocolates you never know what you're going to get. Thomas that is Cusack come with Me Now I don't want you to die Superman. Kristen you know I trust you with my life. But honey I can't go. Say hello to Elizabeth in DC for me and Sa . This it Superman. You always willing to be the damn hero. Listen to me Thomas you need to go over and take your damn medicine. Cusack. And Punk Daddy. You and the whole new world time cop. The courts have come to the conclusion. That we'll conceal the matter. Of you dating Punk Daddy's sister. What you don't mean to tell me.Sa yes Thomas. I'm Punk Daddy sister. Superman. You going to suck my d*ck Superman. Punk Daddy I'm never going to suck your d*ck. Superman. Suck my d*ck Superman. Is never going to happen.Thomas there is your gun and sheild shoot him. No I would not shoot Punk Daddy. I figured out I'm going through the time acceleration chamber. I will no longer play any of your games. Look and see can you hear me talkin.Jeana I love you sweetheart. Your alright. They are just testing you Thomas. You are police officer. Always remember that. I love you Jeana. Always. And what happened was Kristen told me. That I have been shot. And that my mind had to be tested. Before I could spend the money. The tec gave me. For saving all of the children's lives. As the time cop. Thomas that's almost it. Elizabeth that's more. Girl I love you. I love you too Thomas. Elizabeth will find a way. I believe in trusting you .Sa sweetheart. I don't know one is to be with you. And the rest of the family. I love you .Sa I love you too Thomas care about you. And my last but not least Little helper. My bestfriend Dc. I love you honey. I love you more do you hear me okay. I can hear you DC. You gave me something no one's ever gave me. What's that my heart back. DCU give me my heart. Kristen I love you. Thomas I love you too. We are time enforcement officers. Better known in today's world as the police. Ladies hold it down. As Punk Daddy would say it's clobberin time. Punk Daddy. Superman I told you I wasn't going to suck your d*ck. The end. I wrote this in loving memory of my wife Jeana. To the neighborhood in Hickory North Carolina I give the proceeds from this book. To understand that I live right. And to enjoy life to the fullest. Time cop officer. 7+78-134-965-2813 officer needs a**istance. With too many girlfriends. We got too many girls time cops. How many time cops can handle one woman. Jeana thank you. I want to thank you Camelot manuscript. Good evening everybody.life is like a box of chocolates you never know what you're going to get. Forrest Gump take your a** to bed. Yes drill sergeant. Superman.

Eden look over my book called dreaMs.. I communicate with you in the essence of myself. I communicate with every Amazon princess in the essence of myself. Girl take him out of the hood. Take him off of the street corners. Though I adore your conversation.Amazon women i ask for you to please control yourself. See I am Amazon King Bill Clinton. You're not Bill Clinton get your a** off the stage. Amazon queen listen to me. I am Amazon King Bill Clinton. Bill Clinton is just a metaphor. Of who I am inside. Let us speak to Hillary Hillary Clinton. Amazon princess Hillary Clinton. Is coming to the stage right now. What all ado Hillary Clinton. Keep on rhyming Thomas Allred Jr. Amazon princess Hillary it is an honor. My Amazon queens and princesses. Yes Hillary yes princess Amazon Hillary.I come to you today in the date of trail and testimony. Amazon sisters of family needs us. To take over a household's. And let the men work for what they want. If you are Amazon princess Hillary how did you get so far up in the state. Amazon God Bill Clinton rescued me. I like to welcome to the stage. Amazon God Bill Clinton. Thank you my wife Hillary Clinton. My honey said to you Amazon women. That the job market is a job market for men. All we want to do is straighten out you Amazon women. A woman balloons at home with the children. Amazon men we are The warriors of the world. Thank you Thomas. Yes Mr.. Bill Clinton and yes Mr.s. Princess Amazon queen Hillary Clinton. Barack Obama wants to speak to you Amazon Queens. Amazon queens and princesses. This is Amazon King and God

Rock Obama. The world isn't the same anymore. A Queens of putting the lives on the line to put food and water on the table. I could have said food and drink but water cost money. Listen to me what I'm saying. Is Amazon princesses. You got beauty that's uncontrollable. Choose a man and have you Amazon king and queen. As children we learn. Amazon women you are taught to be. Our future society now everybody. Repeat after me. Barack Obama is a Amazon King. Barack Obama is an Amazon king. Thank you. Listen Van Damme wants to speak to you Amazon Queens. Amazon queens and princesses. Yes Mr.. John Claude Van Damme. And King Amazon Van Damme. What may we do for you Amazon God. Just be natural stay of queens that you are. These people are talking about Botox. To plastic surgery. State exactly the way you are women. Your natural perfection. Holds the key to men's hearts all over the world. Thank you Thomas Allred Jr.See what these Amazon gods are trying to tell you ladies is. Amazon princess is natural. And give us strength and power a woman rules the world from her household. I'm a Amazon King. I am Superman listen to me ladies. Let your men rule the workforce. These Amazon King's will not let you down. They are God's. And you ladies are our Queens. And no one's s*x targets. I'm ordering better be given to the world. The freedom of amnesty. For all Amazon princesses around the world. To have and to hold. From this day forth. Forevermore. That our Amazon princesses. And queens. Get 5 million dollars a month. For staying at home. And taken care of on Amazon children and families. Amazon King's know that. As a man. As a Superman. Om has on Kings. And gods. Believe in all of our women. I give to you with my proudest respect. An Amazon princess. Miss Michelle Obama. Thomas I want to thank you Thomas Junior. Seeing how is today a girl got one thing left to do. And thats be real with yourself. Thank you Michelle Obama. Amazon women at tell you this. I can feed you this knowledge. Or I could feed you this sandwich. I am giving you both. We are making it a bill that. Amazon women take over their households. Meaning that. It's you Amazon women. That the world counts on. And I'm going through the pa**ages of my scripture. These days are. Days of joy. And days of happiness. Amazon women. You are now free from the workplace. It can enjoy the rest of your days out. With your children and with your families. For our governments is built apun Supermen. That's it. Thank you Michelle Obama. Cusack is and Amazon King and God. Amazon King stand up. Yes Amazon King and got Cusack. We all are warriors from the future set back in time. Thomas. Let Cusack finish speaking. Did Amazon Queens have addressed us. The workplace is no longer. Because as Amazon kings and queens we have captured the world. By working together. Amazon queens and princesses. Ladies go home to your children and your families. And I know what you thinking. That this might be show. But Amazon kings are standing. And wanted to die for You Amazon princesses. Just like you are willing to die for us Amazon Kings. I am Superman Cusack. I am Superman Barack Obama. I am Superman Bill Clinton. I am Superman Thomas Allred Jr. I am Superman John

Claude Van Damme. I am God and Superman Donald Trump. Speak to the people Donald. Amazon princesses were getting our a** kicked. And handed to us on a silver platter. Yes Donald Trump. Yes Amazon God Donald Trump. What can we do about it Amazon princesses. We fought through the Nations. Kicked a** and took no names. We don't play sh*t. But somehow am I the bad guy. No Amazon God Donald Trump you not the bad guy. I said but somehow are we the bad guys. No Amazon God Donald Trump we're not the bad guys. Women the work fourth is now coming to a close. The men will leave the house to make the money. And all of our women with stay-at-home. To take care of our families and I'm going to your possession. If this should be now. Any Amazon King. That shall violate his brothers purchase. Or interrupt his brother purchase out in the street. I'll stick my foot up your a**.. and a purchase is.A Amazon's King pride and Joy his Queen and family. We cannot have no violators in this new world. Amazon kings and queens and princesses. Thank you God Amazon King Donald Trump. Amazon God and King Nicolas Cage has something to say. Shake It up baby now. Is the old saying that I heard when I was a kid. I am as and Amazon God and King. Nicolas Cage. Has never heard anything like that before. Neither would ever be anything like that again. What we're saying to the women. Is that y'all will have a much better time at home. Inner testosterone built society. A king and queen has it hard only each other. Take the women out of the equation. And we have a strong Nation. I just want to talk to you. I am Amazon God king Nicolas Cage and I'm saying shake it up baby. Thomas Allred Jr do you want to speak . Listen man. I'm Superman god Amazon King. 403 - 78926. Time çop Thomas Allred jr.. my Amazon Kings. Our ladies of precious. Do not make our lady's work. I as Superman. Have something to say. I believe that I'm being voted in upon all the nations. Our woman are our future. People are killing our women. The same way that they are killing you and me. Be professional you know who your children is. Have common sense the women know watching you. I as Superman here by declare the community is the bank and our women are the community. One more thing dudes. I put 10 zillion dollars in a bank account in Zurich. If something should ever happened to me. It belongs to those women. Thats taking care of their families. Thank you I am Superman 109. Ladies without further ado. I bring to the stage. Amazon God and King Superman Samuel Jackson. That boy Gave Samuel L Jackson the praise. God damn it I don't told you motherf*ckers. To stop playing with me. God Samuel L Jackson Amazon King. All of the ladies welcome you. It's about freaking time. Get mad at me if you want to Amazon princesses. But get your a**es in the house. Lay down on the bed and think to yourself how good the mercies of God is. See this is a new day in the new era. Men got to be stronger than they've ever been. And so we can cut out some of this sh*t. We're going to meet you ladies in the house. Now ladies when I talk about in the house. I don't mean in your bestfriends house. I don't mean on the phone talking to your ex fiance. We need you ladies in the house. Taking good care of them kids and raising them right.being there for mothers and fathers and brothers and sisters. Do I make myself clear. I am Superman Samuel l Jackson. I don't take lightly. To know Amazon princess or queen the playing games. Amazon princesses. Yes King Samuel L Jackson. Repeat after me Amazon princesses. Women say this. As a woman of my house. As a woman of my house. We will follow the rules. We will follow the rules. Of our given King. Of our giving King. And im a open up a can. And im a open up a can. Upon any violator woman and man. Upon any violator woman and man. That tries to mess up my Kings playing.That tries to mess up my Kings plan. Take care of yourself Samuel. Take care of yourself Samuel. Now girls get in there and wash them dishes and go to sleep. Yes Amazon God and King Samuel L Jackson. This is called dreaMs. ladies. Try your best to stick to the family that you designed to. Your a Amazon princess. Punk Diddy that us on home. Superman. Suck my d*ck Superman. Punk Daddy I'm not sucking your d*ck. Yes you are sucking my d*ck Thomas. Punk Daddy cut the damn sh*t out. Yes Miss Michelle Obama. Goodnight Amazon my beautiful princesses. I hope you enjoyed our meeting here. This is dreaMs. Camelot manuscript. Superman lock that boy up for telling you that I can't miss Michelle Obama. Why Superman. Miss Michelle Obama Amazon princess God and queen everybody got dreaMs.. The end.Eden I want to thank you for your time. It has been my pleasure to help you Superman. Thanks The end. We got a Superman.Thomas

This not the last round for you Rocky. Get up and go to your time continuing chamber. Listen Rocky ain't finished training you yet. I'm here because Mickey told me to be. Get over there and run them laps like I said. You live too f*cking noodle soup. Stay off of that Dame Adrian. You realize that I'm a Time officer. The whole city's listening in time officer.I see struggles before but I ain't never seen nobody give up like you do. Stand up Mr. time off the Rocky. Rocky don't give up you can beat him. Adrian I'm scared.Take your time Rocky and think to yourself he's only a dream. Rocky if I am a dream why can I say this. Get up you bum I ain't heard no bell. Is that all you got.I thought you wanted to be a man you turned out to be a leg breaker. Mickey give me one more chance. Mickey you the angel. Mickey loves you boy. Rocky this time I want you to train. Even harder than before.you're not going up against the Russian this time Rocky. You going up against time.And Rocky time does it take no prisoners. Watch what you saying Thomas. Rocky to me you one of the toughest so of a b*tch I ever seen. I'm dedicating my gym to you. Sylvester Stallone golden Jim. How many years you been doing this Rocky. Well don't know we've been at this a few years. I have I ever let you down Thomas. No you have not let me down. Stick with me because the training is just now begun. Spit that bubble gum out before I break your f*cking Jall Rock. Watch how he do this sh*t. Rock I want you to look at the tape. I'm watching the tape. Rock You only seeing things to one eye. Your eye is bad. I know how you think I pick up all the ladies. I don't have no time for you to play with me. Time is kicking your a** Rock and time is going to kick my a** we have to train for it now okay what do you think we do Mickey. You got hit hard rock. It all the places that times not hitting you. So you mean I got to exercise. Like your life depended on it. Lay off my dame. Like your life depended on it. Have Punk Daddy come through and work out with me. Why he'll know. Your life don't depend on that.Rock what are you doing making a fool of yourself. Apollo Creed is going to whoop your a**. You're going to be fighting him in 2 days Rock. If you ain't got it up here by now you will never have it. I got it I got it. Listen no More leg breaking rock. And even though Apollo Creed is the champion. I think that you can win. If you keep trying. And keep believing. That you are better. He's not going to know what hit him. You could him like a freight train. A fast chicken. No I know what I know what. You going to come at him like an Italian stallion. Because I'm here with you. And rock I'm not leaving until you make good. Now go hit the showers. I can't cause Punk Daddy there. I'll see you Mick. What do you mean we got two more days of training to do. Time acceleration doors open. Why mother of God. Send Mickey I've been a time cop all these years. Punk Daddy is going to have to fight Apollo Creed for the title. Listen Rock before you go. I want you to have this cufflink. It came from my heart. Rocky time acceleration doors now closing. You done visiting mickey Sylvester for now I am you know he kept me sharp. No weapon formed against you shall prosper. Ain't that the truth Pastor Troy. Go to the police station. Let Thomas Jr get a chance to fight him. Who is the Apollo. I'm talking about Mickey that boy is a fool. Thomas. Sylvester Stallone is a Time cop. And TEC enforcement officer. Amazon princesses. Time cop Sylvester Stallone. The Amazon women award you. With our key to our city. Sylvester Stallone time cop is an Amazon King God. We applaud you. All of your women. And King Superman.Thomas Allred Jr.for your dedicated devotion bring the rocky back to the screen. Listen to me Thomas.I want you to stand up and give Sylvester Stallone a handshake. Now for your continuing dedication would give to you our hearts and our gratitude from your ladies. Don't forget Carl Weathers. Carl Weathers. You are Amazon King in God. The Amazon women adore you. We gift unto you. King God Carl Weathers. A Amazon bracelet. Which is a Time resiliation chamber. Listen. You can't go back in time. But we can't go for without you either. Carl Weathers. I see you. For the man that you are. Your Amazon Queens have spoken. Amazon King and God Donald Trump wants to say something. We are getting our a**es kicked out here. Let Donald Trump speak a minute. We got Punk Daddy fighting all over the place. Ladies the men are tired and they are hungry. I am Amazon god king Donald Trump. Let John Travolta say something to. I'm going to keep up with you Superman. Here Amazon princesses. Me and Superman have saved the day. Not to mention Donald Trump. I like to give a warm welcome to. Amazon queen Oprah Winfrey. And Sally Jesse Raphael. Now that you strong enough. Ladies quit messing around with these men that don't care nothing about you. It's time to give an Amazon Kings a chance. That's it for me Sally what do you want to say. Keep professional ladies. Let God lead you. Let our Amazon Kings take hold of you. Walking in the rain is a king. Amazon princesses do not pa** me by. Your a king. Just like me Superman. You have no idea just what you've done for these people Thomas. One life for another. The people saved my life. So I give them everything that I have and did some if they need it. My greatest gift in life is when God gave Me an Angel call Jeana. Being professional Jeana is no longer here. So I write these books in dedication to her memory. I'm opening up a Jeana fund. Because Jeana I want you to have everything weather your in heaven or on Earth. The Amazon queens and kings and I still love you. I am Superman.

Gabrielle Union. We welcome you to the White House. What is this all about. Well I guess we should tell her. Do you know who this man is in this picture. No I don't. Well you seem to know you. His name is Jimmie Walker. You mean the guy that plays on Good times. No he wishes. Gabriel what we trying to say to you is. That Jimmy Walker. He goes by the name of Punk Dad Punk Daddy for short.yes I've heard of him but what does this have to do with me. Punk Daddy has everyone at the TEC fooled Time Cop. Mr.. George Bush. Now it's Mr.. George Bush. Before I couldn't even get you to vote for me Gabrielle. George you was such a *ssh*le back then. And what am I now time cop officer Gabrielle Union. George you still an a**. But I'd vote for you too. See Gabriel of the world don't recognize what we do here. What are you saying we don't energize the nation. No it's not that Gabriel listen to me. Time cop officer JJ Walker. Has been infiltrated. It is up to you Gabrielle Union to go and find the truth. Are you up to the mission Gabriel. George Bush do I still have a chance. I didn't call this meeting. I called the meeting Gabriel. Mr.s Barbara Bush ma'am it is an honor. Cut the sh*t Gabriel. Punk Daddy is a Time enforcement cop criminal what are Saying Gabriel is. We said Punk Daddy is stealing time. Superman can handle this. Superman is at home awaiting your arrival. Does he know that I'm a time enforcement officer. He knows exactly who you are Gabrielle Union. A TV star and actress. That is all Daddy needs to know. We are trying to find out if Superman and Punk Daddy are working together. And how serious is this. It's a level 9 on the time of forcement code. What are we waiting for get me to Superman right now. Time acceleration doors are now open. Gabrielle remember in this time Superman is kind of worried about Punk Daddy. What do you mean he's worried about him.you going to the time when Superman's a kid he's afraid of Punk Daddy . Whatn't Superman the one that captured and killed Punk Daddy. That's what we have in our files. But you see now Punk Daddy is back in time with Superman and he remembers that night is Superman almost killed him. He doesn't know the Superman finish the job. Gabrielle take this with you. What is it. It's a flash time accelerator. You'll be back at the TEC office with your prisoner or not.

In 2 seconds. Thanks guys. The Gabriel remember. You going to 2019. Superman's house. He's writing a book about this exact same story. Does he know I'm coming. He is praying for someone. Because in that time. Superman is just. A man trying to figure out self in the world. His ex-girlfriend's been murdered. And Superman hiMs.elf has been shot. Be there for him Gabriel. Mister George Bush You can count On Me. And Gabrielle we can see and here everything is going on. You can talk to us. In your mind. Will using mind telepathy. Time acceleration doors are now clothing. Damn where I go from here. Talk to him Gabriel. Thomas keep believing in yourself. I know you'll get through that whole entire book. You sound so much like Jeana. Thomas I'm not Jeana I'm Gabrielle. Are we girlfriend and boyfriend Gabrielle. We are something like that. One day I hope that you are a big actress Gabriel. The people are going to talk about Gabrielle Union all around the world for her acting abilities. Do you believe Gabriel. Knock at the door Thomas. Its just my friend Jimmy. Thomas come on we got to go handle that business. You fellows it's 9:30 at night why don't you just stay in the house. Superman you let a woman speak for you.You damn right it's too late to be going out I'm not going nowhere tonight. Gabrielle stop Punk Daddy at all cost. Tonight is your night Gabriel. Jimmy what are you saying. I'm saying there ain't that much time in the world to keep me away from you. Jimmy watch your damn mouth. This is where Superman and Punk Daddy fell out Gabriel stay out of it. He got a gun on Punk Daddy. Get out of my house. Suck my d*ck Superman. Punk Daddy get out of my house. So you a** want to call me punk Daddy huh get your a** whooped. Punk Daddy just get out of my house. The time acceleration Chambers are now opening. Superman. Thomas what is this how. Punk Daddy you under arrest for breaking time code. 618-849-6032. And what is that.you stealin between Thomas and Gabrielle. Thomas give me that. Punk Daddy's got a gun. Get down everybody. Gabrielle. Thomas I'm alright Superman. I'm a time enforcement officer. I'm using the flash time accelerator now. What are we. When the tec enforcement office. We got to send Thomas back. The same matter can't occupy each other. Not the same space at the same time. What's going on time acceleration doors are now opening. What to talk about this in the future Superman time acceleration doors are now closing. Superman do you remember this part. Punk Daddy fighting Superman stop. Why Punk Daddy TEC officer. Because my job was to take over and get you there Thomas. What is he saying Gabriel time enforcement officer Gabrielle Union. What is he saying. We saying Christmas Thomas. And we want you to have a merry Christmas. This is exactly what there saying Thomas. George Bush. Mr.. George Bush. Thomas. Well can I call you Superman. Welcome to the FBI.

I'm on the run Superman I need your help. Gabriel what do you mean you're on the run. The whole community is after me. Y Gabriela what did you do. Thomas you won't believe this. What tell me what is it. You are a Time enforcement officer. Time enforcement officer. What do you mean Gabriel this is making no sense. Thomas listen to me. The reason I know that your a time enforcement officer. Is because I'm a Time enforcement officer. Superman you are a Time cop. I'm a Time cop. Look at me we haven't got much time. Gabrielle if you have time cop. Can prove it to me. I dream of you when I sleep. You love is here now wake. Gabrielle. Yes Thomas. Superman I know the quote mean something to you. But to me it means diddly. There is some men after me Thomas. Time circuits are now opening who is this. Its Van Damme. Gabrielle and Superman. I'm glad I can reach you the party is about to begin. Okay come on Thomas let's go. You guys do this then. Ladies and gentlemen welcoming to the stage. With all of do. We have a husband and wife. Will and Jada pinkett. Oh my God its Will Smith. Superman please contain yourself. Jada. You go girl. Superman will you stop your embarra**ing me. Superman just hold Your position. Thanks Willie Smith. I think the time accelerator must have screwed his brains out. Why do you say that will. Because he's putting food in his pockets. Thomas we are your friends. You do not have to stuff food in your pockets. Which year did you get Thomas from. You brought the to us hungry man Thomas. Hungry man Thomas you better control yourself. I'm going to get you a plate. Yes Ms. Jada Pickett. Morris Chestnut. I'm the best man Superman. Oh hell no Morris Chestnut ain't the best man. Superman why you making fool of yourself. Because you had a thing for that guy Gabrielle. It's in the past. You know what I did Thomas. No Gabriel what did you do. I had to grow up Thomas. All I want to know Gabriel is that you love me and only me. I love you Thomas goodbye. Goodbye baby what you mean goodbye. This man is still putting food in his pockets. Thomas give me a couple of turkey legs. Okay Gabriel. And come on Superman. I can't leave till I get the last of this punch. Will and Jada pinkett Smith. We'll be sharing the first dance. Everybody gather around on the dance floor. Eddie Murphy singing. Yeah Eddie Murphy. Someone to care. Someone to share. Lonely hours. In moments of despair. To be loved. To be loved. Oh What a feeling. To be loved. Yeah I had a great time at the party. Untill Will and Jada came and took the turkey legs back. Yeah it did kind of bummed me out. But we were having a good time haven't we. We have been having a great time. Baby they didn't do it like us no more. The potato salad missing. Superman. Will let it go. Just let it go. Okay Jada. I only wanted to give him the turkey legs back. I prayed to God for you Jada. And I prayed to God for you to Will Smith. Baby don't leave me. I love you. I'm not going nowhere. My Big Willie style. Did you my girl. I'm one your girl will. I'm your baby mama and your wife I got you for life. Look at that sweetheart. Superman you just call me sweetheart. Gabriella honey I did. May I have this dance. Eddie Murphy singing. Damn he must like this song. Will and Jada. Come and dance with us. Getting jiggy with it. Someone to care. Someone to share. Lonely hours. In moments of despair. To be loved. To be loved. 00 What a feeling. To be loved. That dude is crazy. Who's Superman. No Eddie Murphy. Eddie Murphy what. Eddie Murphy what. Call Eddie

Murphy name one more time and I'm a whoop your a**. Try it just whistle my name. And I'm a whoop your a**. Eddie Murphy you coming. Yes anime. Girl get me some of that cake. I don't take a break on my sh*tt. Yeah about to go get up out of here. Yeah we're getting ready to move. I didn't piece motherf*cker. Did Eddie Murphy just called me a mother f*cker. He just playing with you Superman. A Eddie Murphy suck my d*ck. I'm going to whoop your f*cking a**.

Nowadays you can't trust anybody. I told my mama not to give me my money back. I can't trust anybody. Im a zillionaire 10 times over. All I'm saying is people. There's a lot to get over. Like child support not never happening. People f*cking with me. And I'm just saying. Becoming the zillionaire supposed to be cool. I just want you to know. That I had my a** whooped. My girl ended up talking to me. I said can you use another g. 600 g's on the table girl. Me and my man's On bended Knee. I can suck it up as a loss. The b*tch is that my baby and she is the boss. Maybe some other time. I asked her about children. Because I'm sitting here. And my man ain't never soft. It's something that I got to say. I'm a newfound zillionaire. I'm so hot in my pocket. That my coins sweat zillionaire. Ted Thomas Jr to keep rapping. But ain't rapping I'm just talkin. I can't stop too damn good. My days off I'm in New York in. My sh*t is pitiful I get to walking. See my sh*t on the toilet is dangerous. This is return of the Mack part 2. Anything else is uncivilized. When I look my lady up for thighs. She ain't the colonel she samurais. 10 hundred zillion in my pocket. Mean my baby and I can summarize. I'm about to reach for it all. Baby girl Ill trade it all. This is a book and a movie script. I said that I'll stand tall. My sh*t is harder than the Rock. Hard sit in my a** that ain't no c*ck. A gorilla on a motherf*cker. Wasting my time we ain't on the block. In them boyes screaming the city. The city is prophet boy you can make it with me. But I stay talking to myself. It's cold outside you f*cking with me. This track is so Vin Diesel nuts. All right I said it dude now what the f*ck. If I make another 10 zillion dollars. My mama going to sue me in that is nuts. Keep rapping Thomas. Dude I'm just talkin. I'm order to do this sh*t why you be walking. Keep walking out there. Ain't got no car. But I never walk. I'm not in the wheelchair anymore. Thank God he crazy but I got heart. Return of the Mack. Part 2. I'm going insane Gabriel. Insane. I put insane on the three times. Could I never lose my f*cken brains. Not even if they spilled. Milk and cookies chill. I'm sitting free time I eat your cookie. My b*tch want to f*ck for real. People you can see I ain't playing around with this sh*t. I'm deeper in conversation than yo man with this d*ck. Turn it over I want it my way. That's the tape there go my DJ. Time's up. Superman. Superman. Cusack. Don't play no games with me. Is that who I think it is. Thomas you're right about that. Are you saying that. That is deputy dog. No Superman you got it wrong. I'm saying that it's Punk Daddy voice on recording. Listen to it Superman. Superman. Superman suck my d*ck. That is Punk Daddy. No it's not Superman. Punk daddy is dead Superman. Gabrielle sweetheart you got to help me. Were trying to help you get over it. Get over what. The fact that you didn't kill Punk Diddy. Superman no one kill Punk Daddy. He did it to hiMs.elf and another time error code. Superman. Gabriel. Listen to me. Punk Daddy is taking over the streets. Thomas we're helping you because when you sleep. You are dreaming Punk Daddy is chasing you Thomas. I had no such dream. Cusack. Superman the whole world can hear you scream that you're not going to suck f*ck daddy's d*ck. Over and over again. All day. And all evening. Frankly Superman. We're all getting tired of your sh*t. Superman. Punk Daddy. Suck my d*ck Superman. Gabrielle I'm telling you Punk Daddy is alive. It Punk Diddy is alive Superman go in that room then. I do not have to go into a room and prove a point. Superman if you're not afraid of Punk Daddy stand up. That's what I thought. Your scared. Gabriel. Cusack. Kiss my a**. You damn right I'm scared. Because Punk Daddy. Is a madman. Superman. If Punk Daddy is dead stop playing that damn recording. I can't stop playing the Superman. Why Cusack. Because it's programmed into the time codes . And what I'm saying is Thomas. Punk Daddy voice will be with you. Forever no matter where you go. Oh hell no it won't. Gabrielle. Thank you. Thomas you don't have to listen to this sh*t. I want Punk Daddy to know that we miss him. But there's no way in hell. That I will allow. Anyone to scare my husband for the rest of his life. Gabriel. Oh sh*t you hear that. That is Terminator Eddie Murphy. You damn right it is. I'm back. Superman. Stop Terminator Eddie Murphy. Gabriel honey I can't. Why Superman. I'm paralyzed Punk Daddy is in the other room. Help me Superman. Gabriel honey I'm sorry sweetheart I can't. Terminator Eddie Murphy . Get off me. Punk Daddy or not. Take your hands of my damn woman. Terminator Eddie Murphy. No Superman I've been waiting on your a**. What the hell. Gabrielle Union. Give Terminator Eddie Murphy a command to shutdown. Terminator Eddie Murphy sit yo a** down and speak to us. Yes Gabrielle Union. Who programmed you in this year terminator Eddie Murphy. You program me Miss Gabrielle Union. In what year. 1825. You see as a Time cop enforcement officer. I have to lookout for sh*t. Superman. That is Punk Daddy. Terminator Eddie Murphy stop that sh*t and go to sleep. It is my pleasure Miss Gabrielle Union. Thomas. You don't have to be afraid no more. Cusack. I am going to kick your a**. For what I'm only a standby. I've been waiting my whole life to say that. The thing is Cusack. All three of us are Time enforcement officers. And I was scared. And you didn't help my lady. But see Superman. I couldn't help Gabrielle I'm on the overseer. Meaning what. You have finally gotten over your fears Punk Daddy. Gabrielle sweetheart. Thanks to you Thomas. A lot of people can live and breathe. Happy birthday sweetheart. My birthday isn't for 2 days from now. Yeah but I want to give you your gift right now. Cusack. Yes Gabriel Superman. you can watch if you want to but I wouldn't advise it. I'm out of here. Time acceleration doors now opening. You took kids at fun. Cusack we will. And Cusack. You smell like reefer. Take Terminator Eddie Murphy with you. Terminator Eddie Murphy let's go. Okay but I have to make one suggestion. This suggestion is. It Thomas turn around and kiss Gabrielle Union in her face. That I can do Terminator Eddie Murphy. In the face. In the face. Time acceleration doors are now closing. Time is now closing Thomas. Are you going to be with me Thomas. Gabrielle you keep saving my life. It's a life for life. My O G and them taught me that. And plus we are married Gabriel. Thomas you are time cop. I appreciate you. Time cop Thomas Allred Jr. One more thing Thomas. When I was in trouble with Terminator Eddie Murphy. How did you muster up the courage to come and save me. I just knew what I had to do. And that makes you that guy. TEC enforcement agent Thomas Allred Jr. Gabriel you look like you're thinking about something. No Superman I just want to get me a gla** of water. Because no matter where I go. Where run to. George and Barbara Bush. Will always want these two time cops back. Timecop Gabrielle Union. Reporting for duty. It's about time you came home Gabrielle. Yes sir Mr.. George Bush. And who do you have with you. This is Superman. Thomas Allred jr. Now the mission Thomas. Is to create time. For Gabriel Union birthday party. We have another time enforcement officer that's going to help you. Gabriel Superman. Introducing Cuba gooding jr. As the new and improved Punk Daddy. Listen Thomas you don't have to run from me. Listen Cuba . I wasn't. Will you guys just get a loan. We have a party to go to. Time acceleration doors now opening. Cuba and Superman go ahead I'm coming ill catch up. Ok. No George Bush what the hell are you doing. You know Cuba gooding jr. Was my man. Timecop return of the Mack. Gabrielle Union sets fire to the stage. But I'm not acting in this movie time acceleration doors now closing. Get used to me fellas ain't going nowhere. Gabrielle get down. I'm Gabrielle Allred. Thank you for watching my movie. I appreciate the love from you I do anything for anybody but Terminator Eddie Murphy. Suck my d*ck. Eddie Murphy stop that sh*t. You see Thomas I'm sitting at home just thinking about you. I'm doing what I can Thomas. Separate the wheat from the fake. Is what I did. I am Gabriella Union Allred. And my husband Superman. And I. Was meant to have a contract. So whatever you are be careful. Because the new Punk daddy is back. Cuba gooding jr say hey. Hey. Punk Daddy. Cusack. Commit Punk Daddy. Gabrielle Superman Cuba gooding jr. Is a madman. No he's not he's playing with you Cusack. This Nigga famous. Time acceleration doors now opening. Now closing Thomas. Keep your memory. Cuba gooding jr. Why is that Superman. Because Gabriel is mine. Dude I know that Superman. I'm just making sure that everybody knows. What you fellows talking about. I'm just telling them how much I love you. Gabriel Allred. Have a great day you too. By. This boy just wrote a movie in the room by his self. You see Thomas we the perfect match. Give me my contacts Superman. Gabriela Allred Gabrielle. I got you something sweetheart. It's your cross my heart contract.no matter where I go in this world I Will Always Love You. Your Superman Thomas Allred Jr. And Thomas Allred Jr I have for you a contract prenuptial agreement. 526-9710. Of the time enforcement code. Just saying that you. Give up all rights to your fortune. If you ever put someone's life in danger. Superman do you agree. I've been waiting on you on my life. Superman do you agree to my terMs. of the contract. Gabriella Allred I agree. How many times do I have to tell you. Call me Union Thomas. And how many times I have to tell you Gabriella. To call me Superman. No matter where I go. No matter what I do. Gabriel will always be my wife. And I will always be your Superman. Return of the Mack part 2 and a millennium you see me Thomas. Baby I'm all the way up here. Listen to me Thomas. A lot of people watching. What you going to do when you get to me. Give you two diamond rings. One for each hand. For you are moment In Time. And the love of my life Gabriel. Contact me as soon as you get famous. Gabrielle I'm contacting you. What can I do I'm his wife Superman

I'm trippin off the way people talk to you Gabriel. Gabrielle Union. Is a star. Gabrielle Union. Knows how to do business. All these things they say to you. To kiss your a**. Girl Im serious it makes no difference at all. I am a man. Thomas. No wait Gabriel listen. I come from a long line to ask kisses. And give you a believe me. I kiss a** the best. I want to see you naked. In fat Gabriel. Lady I need to see you naked. It is more than ambition. It is my lifelong dream. Seeing you on the big screen but naked. In our home. Would make this boy into a man. See dreaMs. Gabriel. A bit pieces of an existing life. And honey all that im saying is. Thank you for having this interview with me. Superman I. I know Gabriel. You suppose that you love me. Well before his interview I never knew that for the same. This nigga talking sh*t Gabrielle. Gabrielle talking sh*t eating sh*t. It's all the same. I'm tired of this. What are you tired of Superman. This meager existence. I try my best to tell you I love you Gabriel. And all you do is chew breadsticks. I am more of a man than this. So I am leaving. Yeah he's not leaving. You're right I'm not leaving Gabrielle. Your friend that good perception. Yeah I can smell bulsh*t. I'm kicking bulsh*t out the door. For a new body in the new me. Do you understand what I'm saying to you Gabriel. I think so Superman. I'm saying that your my body Gabriel and I'm your ocean. I guess you're going to say we all float Superman. This is exactly what I'm going to say Gabriel. We are afloat. On the sea of parallel Nations. And s*xing like a potatoes. You and me get down Gabriel. So what you're saying is. Hold that thought Gabriel. While I run up these two stairs. To rescue Your Love. From falling to the Earth and plummeting. In the seat of unparalleled Bliss. Will you be mine Gabriel. Is this the way you talk all the time Thomas. Gabriel what I'm tell you is. Someone to care. Someone to share. Lonely hours. In moments of despair. To be loved. To be loved. Oh oh What a feeling. To be loved. What all is in having dinner. And this man is trying to sing to me to be loved. By Eddie Murphy from coming to America. No he didn't .Girl I swear it. And what do you think that's Gabriel. You're not going to believe this Whoopi. Eddie Murphy set three seats behind me. And heard Thomas when he was singing. His song. No. Yes you did. What do you do. He get up from the table. It came to Thomas and my table. And said excuse me but aren't you Gabrielle Union. I told Eddie Murphy yes girl. Going to continue. Eddie Murphy said I love your movies. Miss Gabrielle Union. And then he followed to say. If you ever want to talk sometime. Please tell your man to quit singing my song. Especially when I'm at dinner. So he didn't want him to sing the song while he was at dinner. No whoopie this is the thing that got me. He didn't want Superman to sing the song. While I was at dinner. He said it was unbecoming of a princess. Damn what next Gabriel. For a few minutes I have my mind fixed on Eddie Murphy. And then I thought about Superman. So I looked at him. And he was mad as hell. No you lying. I'm talking about Superman was pissed off Whoopi. Oh sh*t Gabriel would you do. I can see it in his eyes how pissed it was Superman I'm talking about. So I had to think quick. I introduced him to Eddie Murphy. I said hi Superman. This is Eddie Murphy a long-time friend of mine. Superman stood. And said nice to meet you man what's up. Eddie Murphy just looked at Superman that if he was going to hit him Jessica Alba was in there. Gabrielle would Superman do next. It wasn't Superman it was Eddie Murphy. What did Eddie Murphy do. He just started laughing patted him on the shoulder and offer us over to the table. To have dinner with him and his guests. Which I wants anybody names. I Understand this Eddie Murphy. No this b*tch look like she can fight. So I stayed out of it. The Superman still mad as hell. The Eddie Murphy patted him on the shoulder. Said he'll know Eddie Murphy out loud. I mean the whole dining room could here him. Tell Eddie Murphy that he was a cheap motherf*cker. Now ladies we all know Eddie Murphy the king of ends. What did Eddie do Gabrielle. Whoopi Goldberg is what he didn't do that turn me on. Eddie said I can see that you are having a tough day. I'm going to say good night. And he got up and left. What is Superman do. Superman picked up a bottle of champagne. I threw it it at Eddie. Whoopi and tell you this if you won't believe me. Eddie Murphy caught the bottle of champagne. Turned around and threw it back at Superman. Superman jumped up in the air and kick the bottle. And it put all the damn lights out. No you lying. Whoopi I'm not lying trip this. The emergency lights came on. We at Caesar's palace. Eddie Murphy took off his shirt and wrapped it around his arm like he was Bruce Lee. And Superman got down on the floor and start doing football plays. Talking about blue 42. The whole dining room. Was in a frenzy and worried about these two. When they broke out singing. Happy birthday Gabriel. In front of the whole dining room club. I thought Superman was pissed. But I never knew Eddie Murphy's knew him. End of story. Superman. Yeah what are y'all ladies doing. Well we just talked about things. She probably over there telling you about how Eddie Murphy whoop my a** and black my eye. You damn right I whoop your a**. Youd a never got me if I wouldn't have slipped on the champagne bottle. That Gabrielle drunk a** left laying on the floor. Well Superman it was my birthday. Who you want to fight next Tyson Will Smith. Whoopi that is uncalled for. Time is acceleration doors are now open. Michael j.fox it is time enforcement officer

Michael j.fox. Whoopi Goldberg yes Michael we need you we got to go Harry time enforcement officer Michael j.fox were are we going. We where are you going time enforcement officer Whoopi Goldberg. You're going to go to the past. To see when your career first started to take off. This is a gift for your friends. Gabriel Allred. And Thomas Allred Jr. Thank you so much you guys. TEC of the Whoopi Goldberg. Time is acceleration Chambers on now clothing. Superman everybody know about you have a 10 zillion dollars. Miss Gabriel Allred. Unite with this Union. Aww Thomas. Kiss me right now Thomas Allred Jr. Tec enforcement agent Gabriel Allred. How do you plead. What are my charges. Been in love with a superhero. If I plead guilty. I be selling myself short. So I say take me to trail Superman. I'm taking you to the bedroom Thomas. It ain't no secret I love him but this Superman is not for my time. My Superman has been captured. Buy time enforcement officers. Dwayne Johnson and Kevin Hart. I must lay low until. The Superman from my time goes to court. He is my husband and I will die for him. I am Gabriel Union Allred. And I will free my husband. This is my time journal. Give you a honey I love you. I love you too Superman. Just think honey one day we'll have a house we won't have to worry about this apartment living. I know honey would you say. Gabriel you a just be staring off into space sometimes. You have a lot on your mind. Baby just start the damn movie less talking. Gabrielle your wish is my command I'm starting the movie right now. Honey I picked this out for you. what is it just wait and see. Bruce Lee enter the dragon. I will save my husband in the future. This is Gabriel Union Allred. Reporting for duty. I'm a Time cop. Superman your going to court in a couple days. I want you to think to yourself the last time you seen Gabriel. I don't know who you talkin about. Have it your way Superman. Gaurds cut off the lights. Oh Kevin Hart. And Dwayne Johnson. I am going to get you. Okay so may you enjoy your night. Lights off. Superman. Punk Daddy I'm not afraid of you anymore. It's dark in here. but even in the darkest night Superman got the heart to fight. Time is acceleration Chambers are now opening. Superman baby I'm getting you out of here. Can we hurry up hurry up. Uncuff my hands. Let's go. Thank you honey I love you. Time acceleration doors are now closing. Gaurd cut the light on. And another thing Superman. This man just now vinished out our cell blocks. You know Gabriel had to come to get him. Dwayne this is pissing me off. Kevin don't take it so personal. I got it all on film. We know what they both look like together. What game Kevin. Why because we're time cops. Yeah because with time cops. And they can't run forever through time. It runs out Kevin. So what do we do now. Let's get something to eat and watch this video tape Kevin. I think you said Gabriel is beautiful. She is beautiful. Superman I missed you. Honey I knew you'd come for me but it was too dangerous. I couldn't leave you another. Another what Gabriel. Millennium Thomas. When you've been gone I took care of your younger self. Now he and I are in love. Gabriel how old am I. I believe you 660. Oh my God. Give me a mirror. No Superman you're not ready for this. Give me a mirror Gabrielle. Punk Daddy I'm ordering you to place the gun down. It's not going to be that easy Gabrielle. Cuba gooding jr. It's not your place to kill me Thomas Superman. It is my place to kill you. Gabriella hold my charm. I'm Superman. To be continued on the next adventure of. I'm Gabriella. Superman is my husband. You see how professional it is. All I want to do is go back in time and save him. Now I'm with his younger him. Keep listening. I will save the future Superman. Before Time runs out. And TEC gets ahold of me. No matter where I run they find me. No matter where I go they look for me. I became a secret agent. Fluent in every language. I taught myself how to fight. Too face Kevin Hart and Dwayne Johnson. I am time cop. Gabrielle Union Allred time cop enforcement officer. You can look into my eyes and see that I'm ready for anything.

We going to make a way Camelot manuscript. Is a metaphor. Of us showing you that this is our world and we did what we had to do. All of this has risen to the top of our games . Taking no prisoners we own and industry. What matches as tight as chess games. We rise to the top of our limits. We sore beyond our nation. To bring liberty and Hope. To us all. Time acceleration doors now opening. I'm going to Thomas's a** where the hell are we. I still got the chocolate and chocolate City. Martin Lawrence will you shut up. Gabriell why you so series. Because if we went in the pa**ed. Punky Daddy is still alive. And that means Dwayne Johnson and Kevin Hart are still alive. Dwayne Johnson and Kevin Hart them my boys. Pick him up Thomas. Martin in this time Their the bad guys. Hold up a minute Kevin Hart and Dwayne Johnson in this time period Are the bad guys. Yes Superman. Where are we. Where at high School graduation. And why did you bring this is Superman. These where my order. You orders nearly got us into trouble Superman I have two kids with me. It comes Cuba gooding jr.. hi Superman are you ready for the graduation. Yes Cuba I am. Right this way people. What is this Punky Daddy looked right at me and didn't say nothing. You enter the gymnasium this way. Come on baby it's going to be alright come on. Is dark in there. Martin Gabriel follow me. Okay Superman but if I go in there and somebody jump out they going to get their a** kicked. Martin am glad that you here come on babies. Surprise. Martin Superman I'm glad that you got her hear. Martin what are you talkin about. Gabrielle look around at this place. It looks familiar but I don't know. This is the wedding place where you and Thomas got married. SeeMs. like years ago. Just because you a time enforcement cop. But to us it was just yesterday. Free hip-hop free Gabriel. What are the people screaming. They are saying play that song once again. Eddie Murphy. Is singing on stage again for us. Baby listen. Thomas I love you. Gabriel it's okay let's listen to Eddie. Someone to care. Someone to share. Lonely hours. And moment of despair. To be loved. To be loved. Oh oh What a feeling. To be loved. Someone to kiss. Someone to miss. And what is he doing now. Eddie forgot the damn words again . F*ck you. F*ck you and f*ck you. Mommy I don't like this man. F*ck you. Thomas control yourself. Eddie Murphy. You're going to have to watch your mouth we have kids. Is this a movie. I don't think it is Eddie I don't know. Then what is Biff over there. Biff. I'm going to get you Marty McFly fly a hold up ain't no damn Marty McFly. My name is Martin Lawrence. You can call me Martin Payne. You can call me pain in your a** if you f*ck with me. I know about the time machine Martin. What are you saying what is he saying. I'm saying happy birthday to you. And happy birthday to P-Diddy. Where did Eddie Murphy go . Cant you here him singing. Someone to care. Someone to share. Lonely hours. In moments of despair. Man I've heard enough of this song. To be loved. To be loved. Oh oh What a feeling. To be loved. Hey so what's the main attraction. Gabrielle Superman you are the main attraction. What are you saying. Today you are getting married. I'm not even dressed for are you crazy. All the people are here. What people. I don't see nothing but some empty bleachers in the gym. Gabrielle you a time cop that's what you would see. See we got TV cameras all over the place. You need to start rapping to Thomas. Honey I love you. I love you too Gabriel. Honey I love you that's why I set you up. What are you saying. Thomas Superman Allred. You are under arrest. For breaking future time code. Adultery. Martin Lawrence you my man you can't be doing this don't tell me you serious. I'm more than serious. And I'm not your man anymore Superman. But Gabriel I've done nothing wrong. And you won't. Eddie Murphy you just mad about that party. The party was a sham Thomas. I drank all the champagne I could drink and I still did not get tipsy. You wasn't paying for it Eddie Murphy it was nonalcoholic drinks. So you tried to poison me to. Listen to your mouth. I'm here with my kids I can't let you arrest me right now. Oh you going in. Biff what's that sh*t. The time is acceleration Chambers now opening. Martin McFly. Take your time and get your hands off him. Biff. I need you to go back in to that acceleration chamber Martin McFly. and pretend like you didn't see nothing at all. Make like a tree and leave. No no Biff. This is some weird and scary sh*t. Thomas keep on communicating. Gabrielle I thought you were with me. Ill never leave you this is the miseducation of Lauryn Hill. Come with me Biff. You are under arrest. Marty McFly is a Time cop. Oh hell. Gabrielle you're not going to let them do this. If you are under arrest. Thank Martin Lawrence for caption you. Time is accelebration Chambers and now closing. Hey can I come to the party. It P-Diddy. We brews cruise after us . Thomas stop that Eddie Murphy you want to sing. And you know that I do Gabriel. Everybody dance to this. Faith Evans is here. You my graduation Thomas. Dance Gabriel and Thomas. Lauryn Hill and Erykah Badu. I just come to say I love you Thomas. Yes Ms. Erykah Badu. Someone to care . Someone to share. Lonely hours. And moments of despair. Somebody tell Eddie Murphy to shut the f*ck up. Why is Marty McFly. Way down in Louisiana down in New Orleans. Way back up in the woods of today evergreens. There stood a log cabin made of earth from wood. Where lived a country boy named of Johnny b Goode. Who never ever learn to read or write so well. He could play the guitar just like it ringing the bell go go. Will somebody tell Marty McFly the shut the f*ck up. Has anybody seen Biff.

Oh sh*t we might have messed up the story. No martain were a different movie. This movie better the motherf*cker. Lady of Rage. Thank you for coming through. It and Cedric the entertainer. Now we got a movie. Steve Harvey can you do the prenuptials. We are gathered here today. Who place Thomas Allred Jr. And Gabrielle Union Allred. Together at last. In my slow jam for the future. Someone to care. Someone to share. Lonely hours. In moments of despair. To be loved. To be loved. Oh oh . What a feeling. To be loved. Gabrielle Union Allred. Do you take Thomas Allred Jr. To be your lawful wedded husband. To have and to hold. From this day forth. And the rest of your life. I Gabrielle Union Allred. Do take Thomas Superman Allred Jr. As my lawful wedded husband. Steve Harvey I'm saying I do. Thomas you may now kiss the bride. Someone to care. Someone to share. Lonely hours. And moment of despair. To be loved. To be loved. Oh oh What a feeling. To be loved. Y'all get the boy contract. My work here is done. Eddie Murphy you can't leave yet. Why not. Macy Gray is going to sing. Macy Gray is here. I tried to say goodbye and I choke. I try to walk away and I stumble. Macy Gray is here. When I try to hide it it's clear. My world ain't same without you near. Eddie Murphy smiling at you. Macy Gray mad at me. Everybody welcome to the stage. Mr.. Tim McGraw and Faith Hill. It's Your Love. That shines right to me. I can't get enough. So if you wonder. Tell him Ms. Faith Hill. About to spell I'm under. Honey its your Love. Thomas you can control yourself with P-Diddy. Coming to the stage. Is P Diddy and Keyshia Cole's. Keyshia Cole's. Martin Lawrence is going crazy. No I didn't know Keith is going to be here. Last night. I couldn't even get an answer. I tried to call. But my pride wouldn't let me dail. I'm sitting here with this blank expression. And the way I feel I want to curl up like a child. You know I miss you girl. We got Busta rhymes coming to the stage. That's my dude. Listen at Lauren Hill. Silly with no delay so what you saying yo . Coming with hot sh*t all of my video . Top notch my mean freaks they fill it yo. If you don't know you messing with the record player pros do you really want to party with us. And now if I could bring to the city. For One last dance. We got to Lisa Raye. It seeMs. like you ready with our R Kelly on the stage singing. Your body's callin for me. I'm telling you the truth. Martin do you always got to act a fool. Tisha Campbell. Gina. A Tisha you know i really wanted to tap that a** didn't you. Martin thats what made the show all good. Sing it R Kelly. I hear you calling. Here I come baby just save you. 00. Baby no more stalling. Because I've been longing to save you baby.. and now that you come around. To seeing it them my way. You will regret lady.And you surely will forget it baby. It's unbelievable how you body's calling for me. I can just hear calling calling calling me. Thomas. I just had the strangest question. What do you think Gabrielle. You got your book to professionals right. Yes Gabriel I did. Just think if your book and movie come before the ball drop 2019 in 2020 That a be a Christmas present from God. Keep working Thomas. Merry Christmas to all. And to all a good-night. Gabrielle talk to us that can't be the end of the story. Julia stiles its not the end of the story. Matt Damon get down. Gabrielle your hurt. It's just a scratch.you're bleeding in your leg Gabriel you can't walk. What are you doing here anyway. And what did you come from. Just bandage my leg Matt Damon and Julia styles. I have to go that woman just saved Our lives time acceleration doors now opening will I see you again Gabrielle. Yes Matt and Julia at the awards at the awards Time accelebration doors now closing.

No matter which world am I in. I am a Time enforcement agency cop. My name is Gabrielle Union Allred. And I'm married to Superman. And it is my birthday. Matt Damon and Julia stiles are here. Someone care. Someone to show. Lonely hours. In moments of despair. To be loved. To be loved. 00 What a feeling to be loved. why is this song still playing and where the hell is Eddie Murphy's and Macy Gray . Gabrielle I can see you healed up. Yeah Matt Damon this is my husband Thomas allred jr Superman. Thank you Gabrielle for taking care of us. Thomas wrote this movie. I couldn't have did it without my friends help. TLC come help me. What about your friends. Will they stand their ground. Will they let you down. LL Cool j everybody. See what I mean I've changed them no longer a Playboy on the run I need something that's stronger. Gabriel I love you. I love you too LL Cool j. Thank you Superman. Happy birthday LL. Oh sh*t it is my birthday. Time acceleration Chambers now opening. Be strong Gabriel. Superman where you going. I got a hand in this book report. Because right now I'm still in the past. And Gabrielle you are my wife in the future. Superman I'm coming with you. I won't be able to see you Gabrielle. But I'll never leave you Thomas. Superman and Gabrielle. Sharing a last dance. Someone to care. Someone to share. Lonely hours. In moments of despair. Shut the hell up Eddie Murphy. I alright I done whooped your a** one time. Okay Superman you want some more. Naw I got to go. To the bat machine. Everybody that cares for us Thomas took his time and wrote these movies. He is stuck in the time loop. Help me save my husband everybody and his family his community. Gabrielle your legs bleeding. What you want to do Thomas. Take your time to write that book. Gabrielle you in the future I love you. Tell my children I love them. I love you too Daddy. Time acceleration doors now closing. I got to finish this book. All my people in the industry I love you. I know you can hear me. This is Will Smith.This is Thomas Allred Jr. This is Martin Lawrence. This is P-Diddy. This is Eddie Murphy. This is Michael j Fox this is Cedric the entertainer. And I am Mary j Blige. Telling Gabrielle Union happy birthday. Happy birthday Gabriel Superman The end. I meant to say your husband Superman Gabriel Allred. We going back in time. Yeah it was a perfect story girl. So Whoopi. I dream about this man. Superman is a tough act to follow Gabriel. Do you think I should talk to him. Yes you should. Because he is. Ladies and gentlemen Thomas Allred Jr

Superman. Thank you Mr.. Russell Simmons. When I became a Time cop.

Gabriel listen. I've been thinking about you all this time. I'm watching you make your way through the industry for all these years. I love you and I'm very impressed by you. And I think that you are a queen. A Superman. No Gabrielle I want you to know that I care about you. Is this a civil story Superman. As simple as it gets Gabrielle Union Allred. I like that name Superman. It's kind of got a ring to it. It does have a ring to a Gabriel. Happy anniversary sweetheart. Look at what he's done for me. It's a horse and buggy in Central Park. Thank you Thomas. When Superman hears. What the industry has done for his wife. He is going to be proud. Whoopi Goldberg. Yes Superman. Get over here girl give me a hug. Time tickets are now opening. Are you leaving Gabriel. Now listen Thomas. I know you don't understand this. Butt whooping I have to go to handle business. Gabriel. Hush Superman. Everything be alright boy damn. Yes yes Whoopi Goldberg. And why do you always say my last name when you speak Thomas. He respected his queen on once knew named Jeana. He's referring to our Amazon princess God. In another lifetime. Jeana and Superman were married. In common law. What happened. Thomas. He was going one night on a mission. And some thug's I guess. They found Jeana and took a life. Go back and get Jeana and save her. Superman has tried many times. And rescue her. But no matter what he does. She always turns into Amazon God. Because Jeana a Time Enforcement Agent. TEC Time cop Jeana. Solved 801 cases. The case she died on. Would have been her last case. That's what makes Superman so mad. Actually I don't think he's mad anymore. I believe that Superman that piece. And realizing that Jeana is a God. And they will be together one day. In the universe. And all time cops. Big and small. Will wear the symbol of Jeana. On there clothes. And in There grommets. The Jeana symbol. Shows that we care for one another. Was it you are black or you are white. Asian or Hispanic. Whatever racing Creed. The Jeana symbol. Shows that you have been through something. And you feel it in your heart. That no one should be taken advantage of. Hurt or killed. For who he or she loves. The Jeana symbol looks like the Superman symbol. With a j instead of an s. Listen to me Thomas you don't have to say nothing if you don't want to. Miss Jada pinkett I want to speak. Thank you Will. A long time ago. I thought I had the world in the palm of my hands. And I did. I had a job. And a beautiful woman to love me. She told me everything was going to be alright. When I was hurt. In the senseless 211. It was a robbery gone bad. Where I saved a persons life and got shot. See when I thought Jeana was going to leave me. Jeana stepped up and took care of me. And will give to you today. So all the people can always remember. With strengths does Hope. o God warrior princess Amazon God Jeana. May we live on forever

Continue speaking if you can Thomas. Thank you Roseanne Barr. We came today. In celebration of the future. For not just one but for all. Tec enforcement offices. We are time cops. And we believe that. It is better to save one. Then to go out the thousands. Because in our hearts. We know that love and life. Is inside of all of us. The Jeana symbol. Shows us that there is a God. Because not now but one day. You will Jeana symbol. If you were instead of gang signs. Instead of graffiti.

It will be beautiful art. Because Jeana is an Amazon queen God. Listen. My wife Gabriel wants to speak. I bring you to the stage. Miss Gabrielle Union Allred. Thank you Superman. In the tough world. We do we can to make it. Thomas and Jeana did what they can. In the world took them by storm. Now today. We have 80 billion time cops. That is joining the fight ladies and gentlemen. I tell you we would not retreat or surrender. You come in this world. Is every time cop for 1. Gabrielle Id like to say something. Everyone. Miss phylicia Rashad. Thank you Gabriel. Even my husband. Knew that there was something inside of me. That everyone can see. Superman new. You're still suffering inside the new year. To all of our heroes and Time Cop. We commend you you time cops. We're going to take a brief second to speak. Let Roseanne Barr speak. Okay Miss Roseanne Barr. Look I'm just going to say it like this. This mess get messed up sometimes. But we still believe in each other. I hold my head held high to the wind. I'm pray that there's a God up there waiting for me. Everybody I'm pissed. Jeana is a sweetheart and a legend. May her name live on. In the new and improved Superman symbol. All-time cop stand up. All over the world. and place your hand on your chest and repeat after me. I will protect my brothers and sisters. The Lord give me strength I will fight. And the Jeana symbol. Reminds us. That there are no more gangs . Police ain't playing no games. With the Jeana code 170-653-8921. Everybody say. Jeana lives on forever. Thank you Ms. Roseanne Barr. Let Ms. Jada pinkett speak. Okay folks. It's like this. Life is a struggle and a challenge. We try our best to do our best. It's sometimes things just doesn't work out. But we keep trying. No matter how hard the pain. No matter how bad the Lost. We keep trying. Now I personally. Didn't know Jeana. But every time cop. In person around the world. Remember the name. I'm saying if love is that strong. I'm proud to be married to my husband. Everybody give a warm welcome. For my husband. Will Smith. Thank you honey I'll see you later at home. What's everybody looking on Mad for. We are cops. And we knew this day would come. But regardless of the circuMs.tances. Regardless of who we be. We will stand strong. And do our jobs. Jeana showed us what a superhero is. Thank you. Everybody. Mr.. Arsenio Hall. Okay Will. Yesterday people shot me. Today it doesn't hurt so bad. I say this. Because people. With God all things are possible. Now Superman I know it hurts. Thomas I know it hurts. But God has placed a beautiful woman by your side. Gabrielle Union will not leave you. Sacrifice your pain for this love Thomas do we all have to give you. We have been watching you for years. And we have to say to you. That you truly or Superman. We seen you walk again Thomas. When there wasn't no hope. You Jeana never said anything. To hurt or bother anyone. Now with great pleasure. Coming to the stage. Ricky Martinez and Jennifer Lopez. See you don't have to worry Superman. We all have your back. There are struggles that we go through. That we sometimes don't understand. But as the world. We watched you and Jeana. Over and over again. When Jeana told her friends. She was in love with you. It shed be damn if anybody hurt her man. Thank you general for Lopez for saying that. Ricky Martinez. See I like today because. It's one of those days where everybody comes together. We all believe in strength. We all believe in love. And now we're going to hold each other until every last second is gone. More Tighter. The Jeana code. Says More tighter Love. That you can depend on. Gabriel. Yes Thomas. Thank you for your time people.

Dionne Warwick and Tamela Mann. It is your chance to speak. Time cops. I want to take this time. To congratulate you on a job well done. To congratulate you individually Thomas Allred Jr. We commend you Thomas. For your heroics. And taking care of a runaway Queen. We all are going to you. Cause though the road seeMs. rough. You can always count on your friends. We are the World. And we seen you fight. Over and over again. To save people. For your very own existence. You think you have nothing Time cop . But give me a couple more weeks. Thank you Miss Dionne Warwick. Coming to the stage. Is Miss Tamela Mann. And Mr.. David Mann. And Mister Tyler Perry. Tyler go ahead speak. Everybody look it's like this. This is not a sad occasion. We got to let our sister go. It is the Jeana code that God brandished the world with. Four us always to remember. There is love waiting for us. If we try. Now movies May come and movies make go. But I'm a tell you this time cops. Jeana didn't deserve to die. Thank you Tyler Perry. David Mann. Yall see me a fun on television all the time. But in a real situation ain't acting. Jeana we love you. Tamela Mann. You know I appreciate you too Thomas. For your character and individuality. You are part of life that is strong thank you. Now say something. I want to thank all the time cops all over the world. I want to take the North Carolina PD. And my home town Hickory North Carolina. See I've come along way y'all. And I believe to teach the kids it's the best way. So I give to the United States of America and surrounding areas. Arts and crafts project. For our kids. To draw the best superheroes that they know how. And name them. Superman and Gabrielle Union Allred. Gabrielle speech speech speech. I'm a police officer. This isn't a party. But we are gathered here today. The show love. A great gratitude. To one of God's angels. Thomas Allred jr.. Gabriel. It's alright Thomas. Stand up and take a bow Thomas. Thank you all so much. I am Thomas Allred Jr. And I have time cop. Super agent Superman. Code 213-572-4618. We love you super hero. All your kids. The better better books. But guess what people. You are the parents now. Jeana said so. You lucky Thomas. The time acceleration chamber is now opening. Gabriel I love you. I love you too Thomas I see you in the future sweetheart. Time in accelebration doors are now closing. What Thomas said he meant. We are the parents now. We have to rise our children the right way. And teach them to love instead of fight. I am Gabrielle Union Allred. And my man isnt here right now. But I'm telling my friends. Just like Jeana did her friends. I'll be damned if somebody hurts my man. I'm Gabrielle Union Allred. Good night.

Gabrielle are you trying to tell me that's all it is. Yes that's what I'm trying to tell you. Good morning Superman making all these zillion-dollar devices. I don't believe Superman knows how to quit fighting. Tell me what happened the last time you talked to him. Okay went like this Lauren. Jeana will live on in our hearts forever. Ladies coming to the stage is Robert de Niro. Man I just don't know what to tell you. An angel has gone. Even though the industry knew her well. We still have a soft spot in the heart. Thank you mister dinero. Play Keith Urban The fighter. Mr. Keith Urban will speak and then play The fighter. I'm not going to be able to play the fighter day for all of the people. Talk to Keith Urban. I'm not going to play the fighter today. Because I am the fighter. And Jeana we love you. Look at Thomas. An American Hero. Just like the rest of us are. Thomas Allred Jr. We commend you and your mother and family. Take your time Keith. Im a be The fighter. Coming to the stage with all ado. Julia Roberts. Tec tec time enforcement officer Julia Roberts. I'm telling you this sh*t is not right. Jeana is my homegirl. And I know we've all been through pain. But she would want us to go on. So for my homegirl. This is for you. Keith Urban. The fighter. I thank you . Miss Julia Roberts. I mean time enforcement officer Miss Julia Roberts. It's okay Superman. Coming back to the stage is Keith Urban. Thomas no matter how hard it gets. You can get through you got a friend beside you. Gabrielle Union Allred. Bringing to the stage Mister Garth Brooke. Get this party open. I want to tell you a story about mine this evening. We travel a long road. And we all know this world comes to an end. But we keep fighting. For one another. And hope of the Jeana code. I'm here today to tell you. That the Jeana code has been approved. I am Garth Brooks. And I approve this message. Jeana code. 81627. Stands for love and responsibility. Go ahead Garth Brooks. Talk to the people. We have to quit fighting and take care of one another. Time is important. And it don't last forever. Time is accelebration doors are now opening. Bye Garth Brooks. Who you waving bye to. Coming to the stage. If Beyonce and MC Hammer. We Love You Beyonce. I love you too. Thomas and Gabrielle. You have all my best wishes. Superman. We once seen you when you were washing dishes. Now look at you Thomas you are such a man. Beyonce thank God. And s*x symbol. Thomas Allred Jr. The people want your face. On GQ magazine and people magazine. And Times 100 richest man. Beyonce. Because if you hung beside my girl Jeana. You are welcome to hang beside me anytime. Thomas. Who is MC Hammer with have you seen her. Let MC Hammer speak to Thomas. That's it Thomas. Just like that. The record says. I'm too legit to quit. Superman you are. A true friend. And you are. More than too legit to quit. Superman. Thomas Allred Jr. You are amazing. And every time around the world commend you for job well done MC Hammer I love you man. Clock MC hammer. Look at your face Superman. Coming to the stage. Is P-Diddy and Reba McIntosh. What is this a party or what. Yes we Reba we love you. Tell the people out there. That us Time cops. We never give up. Not until are done day. And even then we keep on fighting. There's something better out there people. But for now we believe in each other I respect each other as heroes I'm Reba McIntosh and this is the Jeana code. Listen P-Diddy. Take them their brother. Yes Miss Reba McIntosh. Now we've all suffered loss. But we must keep going. I am time enforcement officer. P-Diddy. And this is Jeana code 71218. Where officer can be seen crying. Because the angel has entered in his or her world. Jay-Z and Beyonce. Happy birthday Jay z. From Thomas Allred Jr and Gabriel Allred.May all of the people say salute. And that's the way it went. Lauryn Hill. You know what Gabriel I believe you. Coming to the stage is the roots and the fugees. Performance ready or not. Right after slim shady speaks. Slim shady. Eminem speak. Look Doctor Dre took me out of a situation. First I want to congratulated man. Thank you dr. Dre. Dr.Dre stand up speak. Go ahead slim shady you talk. I believe in superheroes. Listen to y'all. I believe in superheroes. Because that's a superhero. That brings us all together. To stop the violence. It to stop hurting one another. I thank God for Jeana. And this is the symbol. A piece in understanding the Jeana code symbol. Shown here. As it will be shown everywhere. Means peace and understanding. We've all been through something. May I take the time out to welcome to the stage. Todd Bridges. Todd Get on up here. We are family. Thomas. Is Todd Bridges. Gabriel I love you so much. I love you too. Todd yes Gabriel. Superman would like to shake your hand and get your autograph. It'll be my pleasure Gabriel. Your best friend ever Superman Todd Bridges. Jeana meant the world to us all. Miss LeAnn Rimes is coming to the stage singing how do I. Speak first Miss Leanne. I love all of you. How do I. Get through one night without you. If I had to live without you. What kind of life would that be. So I. I need you in my heart my love my soul. If I should ever let you go. If you wanted to leave. Baby you would take away everything. Thats good in my life. Thomas can Will and Jada pinkett Smith stand up. Superman go ahead and talk. for everything that you do have done for everybody. I commend you. Superman Will Smith. An Amazon queen God Jada pinkett Smith. We love you. Always and forever. From your industry. King and queen. Jay-Z and Beyonce. Now Jay-Z rip up the stage. It's a hard knock life for us. It's the hard knock Life for us. Instead of treated we get tricked. Instead of treated we get kicked. It's A hard knock Life.Let Jay-Z speak. To Gabrielle and Thomas in a super position. Let me have a second man. To bring knowledge upon the table. Look understanding is knowledge. And my people hurt for understanding. Thank you Jay z keep on. But understanding never leaves us. That's what we believe and be strong. We go on day by day. And we trust in our loved ones. Would never give up. But we all miss a falling star. The Jeana Code is this. To every man there's an angel. Thank you so much I'm Jay-Z. Timecop God Jay-Z. Thank you Jay z TimebAcceleration Chambers now opening. President Bill and Hillary Clinton. Y'all didn't think you can have a party without us our two sense. Thank you Bill we love you. Miss Hillary rodman Clinton speak. Before this universe ends. We all will do some great and wonderful things. I believe we will be there for each other. Like never before. We believe in each and every last one of you. Because you are our children. And when lessons take us back a pegg we never stopped believing. I wanted to talk to you today. About rebuilding. Rebuilding a people and a nation. From the ground up. All of us working together. No matter the race color or Creed. And staying strong alway till the end. This is the Jeana. 18709. Meaning. We would never take advantage of us sisters and brothers. Ever in life. Mr.. Bill Clinton is coming to the stage. No Barack Obama couldn't be here. But here is Miss Michelle Obama and Barack Obama. Barack. Michelle. Listen to me Thomas. Yes sir President Barack Obama Amazon King God. We all seen you work for what you want. On the leg that wasn't supposed to be no good. We seen you fight and take on crime. Is the best man that you are. We welcome our daughters into your heart. Our daughter Gabriel is truly an angel. Thomas Allred Jr. Let freedom Ring Thomas Allred Jr. Let freedom Ring Amazon president Barack Obama. And my wife would like to say something. About Jeana Thomas. Jeana Time cop.

Ran out one small evening. We all know how it is. when we are fighting for love with the odds stacked against us. Your heart beats. Time it understanding seeMs. to slow down. And you're worried but you aren't afraid. Do you want to know why. Why Amazon princess Michelle Obama. Because Jeana is with you. God bless all of our Time cops. Coming to the stage is Lost boys original Kiefer Sutherland. Now you see Thomas. What believing can do for you. You ain't got no clue what we can do for you. Don't give up. And never give in. Because you stayed strong. You are hereby. Movie star actor Superman. And your wife is Gabrielle Union Allred. A man. Hey Keith Keith Kiefer Sutherland. I'm a Lost Boy till the end. What I tell you about this man. We are lost boys to the end. Thank you thank you I'm Kiefer Sutherland. Coming to the stage. Is Gabrielle Union Allred. Introducing Bobby Brown. With every little step that I take. Excuse me Bobby Brown. But I like to talk to my husband for a minute . Go right here miss Gabriel Allred. Superman is not to be played with. The reason I'm saying this. Is our kids are listening to us. Now I want you to understand.

That Superman has fought and bled on the field. Along side of all of our offices. He also stood his ground. For 25 years. After he was shot in the leg. Only to love two women. Walking to work. To pay his bills. In the rain sleep is snow. We have Superman on camera. Doing the best job he could as a man. Who refuses to be wounded. Because he is in love with a woman. Name Amazon God and princess. Gabrielle Union Allred. Everybody welcome to the stage a give a warm introduction for everybody you like. Amerie. Anne-Marie speak. I just want you to know. That means the world to me. Speak speak. And that I will try my best as a female cop. To be there and listen to. Everyone who ever needs my help. I want to think Gabrielle and Superman. May truth and life follow you always. May truth and life for you always. Lauren was the last thing that they said. Superman stood. In front of a crowd. Is shot in his leg. It said that he loved Kristen Beam. For having the strength to go on Gabrielle Union Allred without Superman. Until the time code matchup and you receive your husband. We give to you the medal of Honor. From Superman Thomas Allred Jr your husband peace. Misses Superwoman Gabrielle Union Allred. You are now free to go. In the introduction to the story. I want you to know that all facts and realities are true. We love you Jeana. Amazon queen God Jeana. Gabrielle Union said that.

Welcome to the stage TEC Time Enforcement Officer Mr.s. Ellen DeGeneres. See when I thought of time enforcement. I thought we would laugh at me. But us as ladies do the same job that Jeana had done. We take care of our families. Ellen excuse me Porsche would like to speak. Ellen DeGeneres is my role model. Id give up my world to protect her thank you Thomas. You and Gabrielle Union Allred. I will give up my world to protect you. Ellen did you she said. Yeah I was standing right here Superman. We love you Ellen DeGeneres and Porsche. Coming to the stage is Stephanie Mills. Where I can see right now. That this is going to be a hell of a movie. There you go. But Thomas I seriously love you. Come to me if Gabriel no longer needs you. You better watch it Stephanie. Coming to the stage is Tyra Banks and Joan London. I've covered the news a mini years Tara. But this is a great occasion. For movie and a manuscript. To rise to this heights is unstoppable. Nothing left to say incredible. That was Joan London y'all. Tyra Banks speak. My Amazon girls where are you. Amazon Queen to me now. The workplace is no longer. We work if we feel like it. What tired of being judged. About a makeup on our skin. And by the looks of a body. We are Amazon warrior God princesses. Lady I said that we are gods. We don't go after men unless their kings. I'm going to say this one thing and then im going to get out of here. Will and Jada you are unstoppable. Jay-Z and Beyonce you are unstoppable.

Kanye West and Kim Kardashian you are unstoppable. Thomas Allred Jr and Gabrielle Union Allred. You are incredible. Stay together. People let's just stay together. I am Tara Banks. Bring it to the stage Lucy Liu and Chris Tucker. God bless the USA. Chris you fool. Watch what you say to me almost didn't come in. I was stuck in traffic. Cab driver had the nerve to tell me that he was charging me by the hour . I was like what I look like a superhero ain't got no money. Yes you are Chris. Thank you Gabrielle Union Allred. I am Superhero. Chris Tucker of the time code. 816254. You better stop that boy from coming out with that music. I ain't stopping sh*t. Any disturbances call Superman. Thomas Allred Jr. Man we love you. Thanks for keeping and I on Jeana. Oprah Winfrey get up here and talk. Please Oprah please. Okay. Today is a celebration of the greats. All the people. Even down in the street corners. All over the world. To the Lowest and to the richest by youths. We trust in you. We give to you honor and dignity and respect for the people in which you are. And we are not thugs or gangsters. Yet and still. We are brothers and sisters. In God's great world. Just called for the pledge of allegiance. Everybody no matter where you are. Place your hand on your chest. And repeat after me. I.

Pledge allegiance. To the flag. Of the United States of America. And to the republic. For which it stands. One nation. Under God with liberty and justice for all . Ladies and gentlemen I give to you Lucy Liu. Know where I'm from. We believe in being there for brothers and sisters. No matter how rich you are or how poor you are. You are still a part of my family. Are family I mean to say. Grow stronger and stronger everyday. And we may not have the things that we need. But somehow we always gets by. God as our captain. We can make the world a better place to live in. And I enjoy everyone. Thank you I'm Lucy Liu. Coming to the stage let's give a warm welcome of applause.

Two ice cube. What yall crying for ain't nobody leaving y'all. At least not yet anyway. Jeana is still here. In our hearts. So all you ladies and you men. Shut that crying up. We don't want to see you in heaven acting like this. And that's what this world is. It is heaven as long as we got our brothers and sisters. Coming to the stage. Is Time cop Magnum PI Tom Selleck. Look I don't know how this thing goes. And none of you do actually. All I know is that we work. And will continue to work. For those who try and those who can't. Now touches my heart. That everyone of us just see grace one day. And I bring to the table. Hope and justice. The best way I know how. Jeana this is not the end. It is the beginning of time cops. All over the world. In every nation. In every kingdom. On every stool. In every school. In every house. There's the time cop king and queen thank you thank you Mr.. Time enforcement cop Magnum PI. Tom Selleck. Coming to the stage is Time Enforcement cop Drew Brees. Time enforcement cop Drew Brees come to the stage. The time acceleration doors are now opening. Drew Brees. Drew Brees. Drew Brees. Hey everybody. We love you Drew Brees. I love you too. Introducing to the stage Joe Montana and Jerry Rice. This is a dream. Yes Superman it is a dream. You and Gabrielle Union Allred you help people. Take your time Drew.

You help people remember their faith in God. I've seen a lot of great plays Thomas Allred Jr. But you have stood your ground when they said you couldn't. And you might not be a great football player. But you are a great friend. We've all in Washington seen this over the years. What I'm saying is. Thank you Miss Gabrielle Union Allred. For pointing to us a superhero. Superman is crying. Will Smith. What. Jada did you hear them. Eddie Murphy I'm going to kick your a**. Bring it on Will. Bring It On. Everybody welcome to the stage. Mister Tom Hanks. I thought you would have forgot about me. No Tom we love you. You are Mr.. Big hiMs.elf. Thank You Will and Jada pinkett Smith. Bring it to the stage last but not least. Miss Faith Evans singing I love you. Let Miss Faith Evans talk. Things ain't as it seeMs.. In this world. Mama I appreciate you. For teaching all of us to love. We are the future. And we're not hiding. I am Mr.s. Faith Evans. And I am Mr.s. Gabrielle Union Allred. And we will try no matter the circuMs.tances. Thick and thin. To always. Remember that we are sisters. In God. In your face. Superman to say something. We all stand for truth. And liberty. And the American way. Every

Nation. Is our friend. If your girl and boy child. Is a woman and man in God. And we would not stop trying. The Jeana code is activated. And every nation Jesus Christ. We have us a queen. Miss Faith Evans. Listen to me sweetheart. We all realize. The sacrifices that you and Christopher are made. Faith we thank you so much. And we want to give Tupac respect. These are our Amazon King gods. Not fighters. And to their families we give all our love. Superman and Gabrielle Union Allred. Thank you sweetheart I love you.

Bring it to the stage. Is a man who needs no introduction. Ladies and gentlemen give a warm round of applause . Officer John McClane. Time enforcement officer Bruce Willis. Look I'm say it like this and then im a go. When the world hands you sh*t make roses. Cause sh*t is fertilizer any day to grow. We are the f*cking world. Can you believe that. Time cop officer John McClane. Bruce Willis thank you. F*ck you buddy. Ain't finished talking. Jeana. We'll always love you girl. Officer 217-8590. John McClane reporting for duty. Miss coming to the stage we have a man that you all love katt WilliaMs.. This nigga Superman. He took on a whole gang of niggas with a slingshot. When the slingshot didn't work he start throwing rocks. Never one time. Did he use his weapon. To hurt any man. Officer time cop enforcement officer. Thomas Allred jr. Give a warm welcome I'm help you. Get up out your seats. Give a warm welcome. For Mr.s. Gabrielle Union Allred Jr. She is your queen. Thomas you got a contract. Listen. I know that yall think this is funny. But I am here to under my husband. Kanye West. Kim did you here them. Kanye I love you. Make Kanye West please come to the stage. Kanye you ain't bad. Performing Jesus walks. Is Mister Kanye West and his wife Mr.s. Kim Kardashian. Kim speak. Chloe and I. We want to thank all of you.

For making us who we are today. All me Kanye ever wanted. Is the respect from all of you. And now Mr.. Superman. And miss Gabrielle Union Allred. We realize that we have it. But what kind take your time Kim. But what kind knee has been trying to tell you. Overall all these years. Is that we not only respect you too. Jesus walks and perforMs. miracles. Thank you Miss Kim Kardashian I'm Mr.. Kanye West. Coming to the stage is my friend Mr.s. Marla Gibbs. Kim I know you don't expect me to pick up that microphone after you dropped it on the floor like that. Naw playing with you girl. Go head Marla speak. I came a long way since the Jeffersons. All the way to 2 2 7. I am time enforcement officer Marla Gibbs. And nobody's breaking my damn time codes. If you hear me. Now Superman you've done an awesome job. And the reason why you don't have anything. Is because we're watching you write your books. But we want to let you know. It's a love in the hearts for you. That is Grand. And we know exactly where you come from. Because we've all been there ourselves. Welcome to the stage. The time enforcement officer you know what to do. Mr.. Russell Simmons. How's it going everybody. It's going good Russell Simmons. Look I'm leaving short and brief. We all miss you Jeana. Thank you. Get ready to come to the stage is Nia Long Katy Perry Adele and Michelle a and TI. And Denzel Washington. And Bruce Willis. These are all time enforcement agents. Singing we are the World with a Kanye West freestyle. Robin givens and Halle Berry wants to talk. You go first Harley no you go first Robin. Okay. The way I see things is that we make movies I will bring people together But when we lose people. We all seem to fall apart. We all need to come back together. In this thing I call a Jeana fund. Dedicated to helping underprivileged kids. In sickness and in health. All around the world. That's the Jeana fund. Halle. Halle Berry. Speak. Tonight is more than I opener. Tonight is a revolutionary praise. For and to all of us. No you go home tonight. I want you to understand. If your name was it spoken here. It's not because we forgot you. We don't have too much time. And this is not a party. But this is a celebration.Of Will and Jada pinkett Smith. You got to be kidding me. Of Kim Kardashian and Kanye. The whole industry love us baby. We better do something. This is a celebration of Jay z and Beyonce. No matter what Beyonce I always be there for you. I love you Jay. We're also celebrating welcome to the stage. T i and Tiny. Happy birthday Tiny and happy birthday Ti. The world and the industry has not forgotten you. Kanye look. It's an angel. On our envelopes. We all are welcome at Superman and Gabrielle Union Allred house anytime. That we want to. Without a do. Miss Grace Jones. Superman you know it's stupid. How people fight when they know they've already been chosen. Superman were saying. That you have no idea Thomas. That we have been recording your every move. You are a star. We call you Thomas Allred jr. -Now get up here and speak Thomas. It took a lot of courage to see how you tonight. All of the women are Amazon God Queens. And all of the men are Amazon God Kings. I'm going to be careful when I say. That I love Gabrielle. First of all I'm going to be with you. All the way to the end. My friends and family. All around the world. I'm bringing to the stage. My wife Gabrielle Union Allred and my mother Charlene Allred. It's a miracle. My mother-in-law just wants to sit down. Gabriel take my slack. Is what she told me. Ladies. We are Queens among the nation.

Who we date and when we date. That is all on us. But as Amazon princesses. It is a god-given right. To feed our men. Somebody get Bruce Willis TI Kanye West Jay-Z Thomas and Denzel Washington a plate. Cause these are the kings of the future. Yall not going to give me a plate. Katt WilliaMs. you can never play too. It's a part a party y'all. Thomas will you speak. Time circus now opening. Here comes Your near to the stage. Everybody don't be stoned. I'm here to get Superman a hug. And Gabriel a hug. I love you. We love you too Jeana. Thomas don't cry. There is a heaven after all. I keep on saying to you if I could only been there. You weren't supposed to be there Thomas. You had to take care of a family of your own. Jeana I love you. I love you too. Gabrielle. Yes Jeana. make sure that Thomas Allred Jr gets everything that he needs. Thank you Jeana. Listen Thomas I would do anything if I can come back to you. Why can't you Jeana. Cause they remind me of the past. I would do anything in this world. Take care of Gabriel and her family that is what I ask of you. Okay sweetheart I love you so much. Yes Superman I love you too. Jeana. She's gone Thomas. Gabrielle I have nobody. Thomas im right here. TI grab Superman don't let them fall. I'm alright tip. Tiny thanks for coming out. Happy birthday everybody. Happy birthday Thomas Allred Jr. Gabrielle it is my birthday. Coming to the stage LL Cool j. I need some love to everybody. Everybody love you James. Coming to the stage is Rakim. And Kid Capri. Gabrielle Union Allred. Yes honey. I promise I will love you forever. I know you will Superman. I know you will. Gabriel. Yes honey. Thank you for saving my life and the people's lives. Matt Damon and Julia stiles told me what happened. How you jumped out in front of that truck to save two kids. Yes Thomas its old news. The kids that you saved do you even know who they were misses Gabrielle Union Allred. No I don't. But I'm a tell you who they were. They were George and Barbara Bush. As children. Walking to the stage is none of the Then Amazon God. Mr.. Donald Trump. Speak speak Mr.. Trump. 6:30. At night.

Tec enforcement agent Gabrielle Union Allred. Risked her life. To save kids that she didn't even know. In the past. Today those children are. George and Barbara Bush. Give a round of applause for George and Barbara Bush. See I told you take your time George. See I told you Barbara our kids are going to love us. Please let Barbara Bush speak. Ladies and gentlemen. A gift to you. Miss Gabrielle Union Allred. Superman. It takes a man to love a woman to the end. Tell me about it Kanye West. Welcome to the stage. Will and Jada pinkett Smith. Jeana I see God. Will and Thomas. Who is Martin Lawrence. God damn you even said my name. Cedric the entertainer. And Naomi Campbell. One more thing. I'll be back in a minute. Were she going Thomas. I don't know. Superman this is Mr.. Jackie Chan and he holds your contract. Hey Jackie Chan thank you man. It is my pleasure Thomas Allred Jr. Thomas Allred get up and shake Jackie Chan hand. It Jackie Chan you know I think you're better than Bruce Lee. Nah. I'm just a man trying to make it like all of us. Teacher Jackie Chan Amazon women. No matter what I do I always busy teacher Jackie Chan.

Look I'm going to prove to myself I'm Superman. Every time I do something. It seeMs. to be always done to perfection. Let me tell you my story. My name is Thomas Allred Jr. And the new story that tell people. Is how I have a good wife. And a loving and caring family. How I ended up this way. Was that a congratulations ceremony. For life and love. We all work everybody. And everyone. In the world for this. I mean small children in Taiwan. We're picking up people in the streets. In the United States we cleaned everything. Over in Brazil we start rebuilding. And Pakistan we sent out signs and letters. In Bosnia we gave food. In Germany the people came together. In Russia the USSR we all learn to get along. We kept going around the world Paris London Japan. Showing people the Jeana code or Superman sign. For trusting understanding. We realize that you don't have to trust nobody. To understand that love is sacrificial. The Jeana code. Is already printed in every language. Professionals are working night and day. For these books and movies to come out. About a woman. Who fought to the very end. Who was the police officer. For the people and the nation she loved she loved. Jeana. Fought for the world. And taught Superman how to fight. In the process. Because when I Superman Thomas Allred jr. Was down. Jeana and the rest of the community stood for me. With there prayers. I was able to get back up on my feet. And with Jeana feeding me knowledge every day. Thomas you have a visitor. Yes in the morning. It is Snoop Dogg yes Superman. Snoop d o double g. How's it going sir how can I help you. we at the dog pound just want to let you know that we think you're doing a good thing with the Jeana code. Snoop I'm starting to realize what Jeana really means to me. We all come together as one. We all come together as one Superman.Time Acceleration doors are opening. You Snoop Dogg. And you know it fool. Tec time enforcement officer Snoop Dogg. Time accelerating doors are now closing. You hear the people. Gabriel. We need you Snoop Dogg. Baby. Don't worry about him Superman. Snoop doggy Dogg will be alright. Be professional. And finish your story. Okay I'll try. I'm a prove to myself I'm Superman. But taking on hunger all across the world. I'm just doing what I can do. Because even though I'm Superman. The only perfect man in this world. Is Snoop Dogg Snoop doggy Dogg. Time enforcement officer Gabrielle Union Allred and Thomas Allred Jr. Come on out to the stage. Gabrielle what are we doing. It's your mama's birthday Thomas. Happy birthday Mama. God bless you Thomas. Gabrielle I could kiss you. Superman why don't you. In front of the the whole world. I don't know if I can. Yes you can Thomas. Well coming to the stage Adam Sandler and Melissa Milano. You can do it Thomas and I'm saying you can do it. It's either now or never Thomas. Yes Melissa yes Adam. It's either now or never Gabriel Union Allred. You always be my baby. I love you. That boy kissing the hell out of Gabrielle. Listen Adam Sandler and Melissa Milano. We Appreciate all your help. Coming to the stage is Bryan AdaMs.. A world. A dream is but a wish. And a wish is but a dream. If we stick together. You can have anything you ever imagined. I'm Bryan AdaMs. and this is. Tina Turner. What's Love got to do with It. Giving all props to Gladys Knight. And the pips. Hey Go Ti away from that punchbowl. T I get over here. Tiny I wasn't doing anything. Happy birthday Ti. Happy birthday sweetheart. Now where is Russell Simmons. I was almost going home. You can't go home cause Gabriel and Superman have something to say to you. Yes Gabriel Superman you wanted to see me. Yes Mr.. Russell Simmons. The whole neighborhood is watching you. We want you to make and direct these Camelot manuscripts of our. We only have the 12:00 midnight to write what do you say Mr. Russel Simmons. I do the job for you miss Gabrielle Union Allred and Mr.. Thomas Allred Jr. One more thing Mr.. Russell Simmons. Camelot manuscript. And Camelot music. Now belongs to you and my friend DC. She will be your co-partner. I'm going to repay you Superman. By looking in the sky and thanking God for Jeana. I got one more question for you Superman. What will you do now that you have your dream becoming an actor and Marrying Gabriel Union Allred. I'm going to get me something to eat Gabriella they still ain't gave me my plate yet. Somebody get John Travolta and Nicolas Cage some of them mashed potatoes over there. John Travolta I know you can put down more chicken than that. Don't be up in this house. Given. Time the time cops all came together as men and family. Time acceleration doors are now opening. Oh sh*t it's a Terminator. Chris Tucker are you going to do that every time I come to a party. Thomas keep your mind on Gabrielle Union Allred. Yall give Arnold Schwarzenegger some space at the table. Time enforcement cop Arnold Schwarzenegger. Keep on talking to yourself Thomas. One day you have a look at the future. Time acceleration doors announce closing. Time acceleration doors on now opening. Is Jimmie Walker. JJ Evans. Come get your plate JJ. Time enforcement cop Jimmy Walker. Time acceleration doors are now closing. Time acceleration doors are now opening. I know you didn't forget about us. Chris Rock and Oprah Winfrey and Reba McIntosh is Sally Jesse Raphael. Reba You can't touch This. MC Hammer I'm going to touch the whole plate I bet I can. Sally Jesse Raphael. I can touch the whole plate to MC Hammer because I'm too legit to quit. Let Oprah Winfrey speak before she sit down. May God bless this food we're about to receive. Let's eat. And that's how I prove myself that I was Superman. You are Superman baby. You are Superman. Thank you Jeana. I love you. Come to the table and get your plate Thomas. Everybody where I sit at. Sit wherever you want. Sweetheart. Yes Gabriel. We want you to sit at the head of the table. This is your seat always and forever Superman. Always and forever Superman. I love all you. The where is ja rule and Ashanti. Time acceleration doors now opening. The Jeana Code states that we're all supposed to take care of those in need. Ja rule how you doing Ashanti hello ma'am. We're needed some of those potatoes. Yes ma'am coming right up. Thomas. I'm sorry about Jeana Thomas. Ja rule Ashanti brought more love to us than we had in a lifetime. Theres nowhere to sit where do we eat. Boy you at home you better sit your a** down someplace. Uncle Cedric the entertainer. Yes ja rule. Good job sir good job. Superman Tell them ladies we're going to need some more potatoes. With this succulent ham. I'm on it right now thanks Said. Time acceleration Chambers are now opening. Steve Harvey. Y'all better move out the way I'm hungry. How did Sid get here before me. Steve we saved your place at the end of the table. So you Superman Thomas Allred Jr. And you won't give in will you. A gift to you a brand new Bugatti. From the people at family feud. And from my show Steve Harvey Show. A gifted Gabrielle a brand new Bugatti. Colors blue and black and red and silver the colors of the Jeana code. Thank you Steve Harvey. Time enforcement officer Steve Harvey. Is needed at the tec enforcement agency. There you go Steve. These people always need you. Time enforcement codes are going off all over the place. Everybody it was wonderful Thomas. Superman and Gabriel we're going to see you later. How come we didn't get called Gabrielle. Because we doing our job right now Superman. Over in Tokyo they understand. Understand what Gabriel. Be professional. Oh I love you I love you too I am Gabrielle Union Allred. And I'll be goddamn if anybody hurts my Superman.

TEC Time cop Central. Is located in Longview North Carolina. Longview North Carolina is tech Central. Tini Chapman. And Time Enforcement Officer Christopher Lee Allred. Get up and say goodbye. Because we are giving you new houses. For keeping the Faith. Inn above and well in danger. Timecop enforcement officer Tini Chapman. We thank you and commend you. For your heroism in the face of danger. Timecop Enforcement Officer Christopher Lee Allred. For having sense when in ungentlemanly conduct. And Christopher me Allred. I also give to you the purple heart. For not leaving a brother on the field. Thomas you got to be kidding me. No Tini no Chris. Steve Harvey wants to talk to you guys. See the way I see things is. You never had your chance at nothing. All that man needs is a second chance to try. Christopher Lee Allred record name you Optimus prime. And Tini Chapman. The code name you Scarlett O'Hara. Tec officers. You are now two movie stars. Steve Harvey. Thank you. I get to you in a moment Superman. See the thing about your folks is. Yall don't believe in the power of people. See we know you know what love is. Cause yall hold on to family and community with everything that you got. McKenzie. Is now a movie star. Take care of Mackenzie yall. I've been looking at you. Since as long as I can remember Mr.. Christopher Allred. And I see what the problem is. You keep putting yourself in the head over computer. When that computer was it supposed to be yours. What I'm saying to you Mr.. Christopher Lee Allred. Is now you're the head of a whole computer operating system. Complete with design for your family. And Ms. Tini Chapman. Superman doesn't realize the love that you got for him. Michael Emmanuel Tucker. You are lucky to have a family like this. We respect you Michael. And granting you and your brother Anthony Allred a house because Anthony in love. And you both need guidance. Superman. The reason we do these things. It's so that you keep up. Keep up with what Mr.. Steve Harvey. The children you about to receive from your wife Miss Gabrielle Union Allred. May y'all man. Have everything in heaven that God has to give you. We know Superman. Superman. Talk to your Mama. Mama I used to think nobody cared about us. I was tired and I was hungry and I was angry. But now I know that we have friends in God everywhere. And that Jesus Christ is real. Cause he brought to us an angel. Name time enforcement officer Steve Harvey. Steve thank you man. My mama loves you. And I do too. Here Thomas. This is our pleasure Thomas. Its 17 minutes before 12. Tell Gabrielle you love her. Because you are on the Steve Harvey Show. Gabriella I love you. I love you so much sweetheart. I love you too Thomas. Gabrielle we never quit trying for the best. We never stop going where we have to go to help out people.

And we stand up to the end no matter what. And say forget it. We are time cops. And we love our families and our women and men. Amazon princesses. We will come and praise every president that ever been. And every first lady. Amazon Kings. We are all warriors in God and we would never stop fighting for what is right which is our children. We love our friends. And we believe it or countries no matter where we're from or where we at. we stand to make sure our people have the best and would give them the best. Amazon women and men. Time acceleration doors are now opening Bill Clinton. Amazon King God Bill Clinton. And Bill Cosby. Amazon King God Bill Cosby. And R Kelly. Amazon King God or Kelly. And Snoop Dogg. Amazon King God Snoop Dogg. Okay Amazon King God Superman. Take us on home. Can't we all just get along people. I mean it I'm sick of this can't we all just get along. He's been through a lot that's enough. Let Barack Obama speech. This man has been hurt. But somehow in God's name he still stands. I was just men unload a truck. Three of them. After being wounded in the leg. Now I don't know about God. But I do know the strength of people. Sometimes you have to maintain yourself. To get the way you need to be going. My people no one has forgot you. Will still one great nation under God. And we never will forget you thank you Amazon King God Barack Obama. Mister Amazon King God Bill Clinton. Barack and Hillary said it best. All people deserve a chance to eat. It doesn't matter where you are in the world. We all need to feel like we've done a good day's work. Amazon King gods. Hold on to you women. Amazon Queens. Make sure you feed your men. Because we all need each other. Even whether or not we have a job. Because our I'm missing is. To sustain each other until God calls us home. Time is accelebration doors now opening. We have Amazon God and princess Miss Charlene Allred. You thought I want to say nothing. You thought I want to get my two cents in. No Child. I've been fighting all my life just for today. My children are grown. and all of us ladies have been fighting all of our life for our children. See Superman's mama. And I was the first one that showed him that cartoon. But I am more than Supermans Mama. I am Man At ArMs. in the Masters of the Universe. Tec time enforcement agent officer Charlene T Allred. And we have yet begun to fight. Superman we give to you. Excuse me Thomas wait one minute please. Yes time enforcement officer Steve Harvey. Your probation officer and time enforcement officer Ryan. I knew that you were Superman. Ryan I love you man. Thomas be professional. Here is Gabrielle Union Allred. She is beautiful. Superman you lucky. Why do you say that Ryan. Just don't mess it up. I got help from My Friends that a never happen. Is there anything you want to say before we go. It's past 12:00.

The way I see it Vann Damn is the best Marshall artist in the world. I know he's a good fighter but. What about that Chinese dude from best of the best. They both good Jackie Chan. But you can't see me right here Jackie Chan. Connect for. Man he keeps beating me. Superman you have powers of observation. Oh no. Time circuit codes are going off of all over. Jackie Chan wait right here. Happy birthday to you happy birthday to you happy birthday to Jackie Chan. And Lucy Liu. Happy birthday to you. Gabrielle Union allred . We know you did is Gabriel. Superman' is the one that put it together. Jackie Chan and Lucy Liu we give to you the Union award. for bringing peace and harmony to every nation in the world we love you Jackie Chan and Lucy Liu. You ain't got no clue who Lucy Liu is do you. Gabrielle Union Allred. Lucy Liu tell them who you are. I am Time Enforcement Officer captain Lucy Liu. Of tech code and text station located in Longview North Carolina. Homes base of the TEC time enforcement unit.

Gabriel come inside that's raining. Thomas can you believe it in just a few more days our books and our movies will come out. Thomas believe in me. I always have Gabriel Union Allred. Well Mr. Superman. Its done stop raining. Indeed it has Gabriel. Thomas I want you to take advantage of the time you have allowed to you. Ms. Gabriel Union Allred. Are you saying what I think your saying. Yes Superman I think I'm. Connect for. Baby you always beating me. Listen to Donald Trump phone the television. We let freedom ring because we're just not having it. And if you want some with me. I got friends. The belong here today. But there in high places. I want to give a special thanks to Gabrielle Union Allred. What the world now no as the Union code. Which brings every Time cop enforcement officer together at once all over the world with a single. The Union Time cop Union code. Was given to Gabrielle and Time cop all over the world. By her husband. Thomas Allred jr. And and George and Barbara Bush. See Thomas and Gabrielle. Your relationship is proof. That We in the government. Listen to me for second. Go ahead Barbara speak to them. Gabrielle we put you with Superman. Because we watch you both through the years. You both a kind. And carring. Your chances are slim without each other. A give to you Bill and Hillary Clinton. You know Superman someday we going to get this right. Barbara tell them about it. Gabrielle Union allred . This is what the union code looks like. Oh my god is incredible. And Superman. And do it seeMs. like everybody else forgotten about you.And Your always all alone with you back to the wall. Thomas. Were dedicating a statue to you. In Central Park. The name of the statue is. The Thomas Allred jr. Park memorial. We call you Superman Thomas. Keep it up. And Gabriel be ready to report for duty Monday. Why. I am supposed to be married. P Diddy is having his pajama Jammy party that day. And sometime the kids get crazy. They requested you Gabrielle by name. Did they ask for Thomas also. No they just requested you Gabriel. Thomas This isn't fair. Gabrielle Union Allred. Just do a good job I love you okay. Time enforcement officer Gabriel Union Allred. These are your command paper. You are leaving first thing in the morning. You have 4 hours to get ready. And Gabriel they did quest that one other person be allowed to chaperone you. Who.The People request that Superman come to the party Gabrielle. Gabriel I love you so much. Is there even a party. The is one now Gabriel.

Diddy. Happy birthday Barber Bush. Thank you so much P Diddy. The President George Bush. P Diddy please pa** the courvoisier. Miss Hillary Clinton how's it going P Diddy. I'm alright now. Mr.s. Gabriel Union Allred. P Diddy we love you. And Superman Thomas allred jr . And Bill Clinton. That is President Bill Clinton b Diddy. P Diddy it is. Superman where you going. This is for my wife Gabrielle Union Allred. Henry Winkler the funs . It's about time someone invited me to the party. Gabriel where all saying happy birthday to you. And Merry Christmas and Happy New year.P Diddy. Tell me it ain't so. President Barack Obama Michelle Obama and President Donald Trump. Henry Winkler. It's our duty to make you. Tec time enforcement officer Henry Winkler. Everybody we give to you the funds. Michelle Obama know way. Barack Obama's know way. Donald Trump way. And as a people we never stop trying to bring each other together. everybody Michael Jordan and Shaquille O'Neal and Scotty pippen and Kobe Bryant. I won championship after championship. I played beside some of the toughest people in history. I put the ball in the hole with seconds left on the clock. And I rebound it. We are part of the NBA. and Mr.. President Donald Trump. We are all saying happy birthday. From your wife and family. And all of us. In the world not the USA . Mr. George Bush and Barbara Bush. We thank you

Jeana I'm sorry that I cheated on you. Why Thomas. Baby I just don't know. That's not a good enough reason for anything. Look Jeana it doesn't mean that I don't know if you. Can I make it up to you somehow. Thomas I love you and I'm not going to leave you. But I want you to know that you hurt me. And Ill never forget.i See you walking much better. Yeah thanks to you Jeana. I'm walking in this way. Thomas go ahead I'll catch up. He doesn't know does he. No he doesn't and I don't want to tell him yet. Jeana you a time cop. Sent hear to protect Thomas Allred jr. Gabrielle promise me. That if something happens to me. Youll take over. Jeana as your time enforcement officer. And best friend Gabrielle Union. I will step in two guide Me Thomas Allred Jr . I just realized Thomas is involve with two women. You see the look on his face Jeana. You are a Time Enforcement Officer selected to do so. Jeana. Yes Thomas. Jeana. Honey I did you wrong. And I want the entire world to know that I'm sorry. And I appreciate you. I love you Jeana. Time Enforcement doors are now closing. Still in the simulation chamber Thomas. Yes Gabriel I am. Let's repeats sequence 409 of the time code. I'm a time cop trusting Jeana. Can't you see i just don't want to be with you no more Thomas. Jeana I love you. Thats why I know that I have to go Thomas. Gabriel is helping me up. Jeana I'm sorry. Time acceleration doors now opening. No matter what I try I just can't get her to realize that I love her and that I made a mistake Gabrielle. That's because you're trying to hard Superman. Jeana already knew that you looked her. And the mistake you made was human I hope that you learned from it Thomas. Gabrielle how do you know these things. Because I talked to your momma before you and I got married.

My superman Thomas Allred Jr. The man that Time Enforcement Officer Jeana fell in love with and dead to protect . In her last login. Jeana was fighting with that girl that you slept with Thomas because of you Jeana is known forever as miracle Jeana and we say this because it's a miracle that Time Enforcement Officer Jeana didn't kill you for sleeping with other females. Because I had to stop her a many nights from doing so. I am also you wife. Gabrielle I need you to understand that I got true feelings for you. I am now a Time Enforcement Agent . See that's the thing Thomas that Jeana was trying to get you to realize. You always have been a Time Enforcement Agent. Gabriel run time enforcement agency simulation 309. I just want to thank you Jeana. For what Gabrielle and I are friend. Jeana. Honey one day you'll see a star. And that a be me. Thomas be professional. I got your wedding ring right here. I like you Superman. Your my Louis Lane forever. Every time cop. Say to your wife and girlfriends. Forever. It is part of the Jeana code. Say forever everyday. To the woman or man that you love. Time accelebration doors now closing. did you find what you were looking for now Superman. Gabrielle I think I did. Great Superman. What are you saying. Miss Gabriel Union Allred. Baby forever. Forever Superman. I love you. Superman is calling. This is Gabrielle go ahead Superman. Where my Superman suit issue at. It's coming up the the next future installment. Of flying with people right now. Thomas ain't flew. Thomas hurry up and finish that novel because.i know that you paid. But I'm going to make you a billionaire Thomas. In the end Superman prevails. This is Gabrielle Union Allred signing off.

You want me come and get me haters. Listen to her Thomas. Gabriel I got to be just as strong. I depended on Jeana. And that she is gone. I'm a carry on like her Gabriel. Thomas get in here and put your clothes on. Yes Jeana. I will pick up my clothes off the floor. And put my clothes on. She going to kill you Thomas. Gabrielle was Jeana supposed to say that. This is a simulation. Program changes that you go. Jeana talk to me. I am a TEC enforcement agent officer. And my name is Jeana. Jeana you are beautiful. I am beautiful. Jeana you are wonderful. I am wonderful. Jeana you are a friend to all. I am a friend to all. Jeana this is Gabriel. Gabrielle Union I know. What Jeana how do you know. Gabriel Union. Is Time enforcement agent TEC Boss. Over Jeana. And other offices. Gabriel you should have told me. Simulation now complete. Gabrielle. What. Tell me what Jeana said to you in her last login. Time was complete. Oh my god she said time wasnt complete. What does this mean. Time wasnt complete means that we have unfinished business. And so your saying Thomas. I'm saying to you my time is all Jeana wanted. Jeana asked me to look out for you before she died. Gabriel there is a God. Seeing how you know I got your back you know that there is a God start simulation. Hello Gabrielle. And hello Superman. Gabriel Jeana just called me Superman. No she didn't Thomas. I called you Superman in front of her. Superman that's a nice name. I think Ill use it. You think. Hahaha. Gabriel Jeana is laughing. Yeah I know that's a up grade I made to the new simulation. I think it's wonderful. Thomas. Yes Jeana. Hold your position officer Jeana. Gabriel. What do you think about the name. Gabrielle Union Allred. It's tight. I love you Gabrielle Union Allred. Jeana can you program the sunlight to come in. If I know what you want I can do it. Jeana me and Gabrielle Union Allred would like to see. What Superman. Honey will you please tell Jeana what we would like to see Gabrielle. I'm just thinking Superman. Thomas you know that I love you. Yes Jeana I know that you love me. You know that I love you to Jeana. I also love Gabriel Union Allred. Allred. Jeana Gabrielle is also my wife. I know that. What she said I know that. Thomas the program adapts and adjust to your language and demeanor. Jeana can say anything that she wants. Simulation now ended. Gabriella me talk to you Give me a minute. I'm working with this new program. What program is that Gabriel Union Allred. It's the program where I tell you that I been in love with you on my life Thomas I love you so much. Just promise me you'll do one thing Gabriel. Keep promise. I will keep my promise. And I promise not to cheat you. And to hold my baby close day and night for the rest of my life. Become a professional police officer. I'm already police officer. That's why we chilling. Computer simulation now ending. Thank you for fixing the Jeana code. I know now Gabrielle Union Allred that I'm not alone. Will and Jada pinkett Smith and Martin Lawrence. This is the Jeana code ain't that right Superman. We got to protect it. We got a protect our dreaMs.. Make sure your microphone is on when you speak the Jeana code people. It's people watching you. Make sure that you can trust everybody that you be around Superman. And there's one more thing. Make sure you give back to those men and women female in your community. We're saying you're free to go Superman. I love you so much man I love you so much thank you so much. Thomas taking care of yourself. You know we love you. You know I love y'all to. That's why I'm giving all kinds of people. 100 million dollar houses. Next time you get with me. I want to know that I got a plate at the table next to you mom.

Gabriel I'm losing myself if I don't get to see you again. Time accelebration doors now opening. You never know Thomas Allred Jr. Its Superman Gabrielle. What is. Well my name is Superman. Thomas you must be kid. No Gabriel Union Allred I'm not. Okay then. Superman it is. You want to know what Thomas Allred jr. Superman. What Gabrielle Union Allred. I am the first one to ever call you Superman. Gabrielle I love you. Thomas. You say that to me all the time. I want you to realize baby that Ill do anything for you. Thomas you are a TEC Time Enforcement cop. And so am I Thomas.. Gabriel Union Allred. Have you ever had the feeling that people wanted us together. No why. Because Gabriel everytime and look at you. I Depend on you. To carry the weight. That i can't handle. Superman I have to talk to you about something. Simulation doors now opening. Hi my name is jeana. What is it that you had to talk to me about Gabriel. Did Jeana project is off the map. And your saying Gabrielle Union allred. The Jeana code is going to save us all. But what about this Gabriel. What is Superman. Gabriel this because of you is. The Gabrielle Union code. It's a networking computer software disc. I Understand you. Gabrielle Union Allred let freedom ring. And Superman when do you want to talk about the fact that you and I are Zillionaires . Gabrielle Union Allred money is and illusion. Keep working on that book professional. Jeana we love you. A simulation chamber now complete. With the union code download. All I care about is you Gabrielle Union Allred. Superman why do you use my whole name when you talk to me. That is because. When I talk to you and need your attention. So I say your entire name to show you respect. Thomas Allred jr. Today is our anniversary Thomas. And today I have your gift. Gabrielle you should have. All of the people came together for this. For this for what is it Gabrielle. I want you to say hello to your new companion. Jeana. This is outrageous. I thank Jesus Christ. The Gabrielle Union cold linking up with the Jeana code. Made a super computer and a program code defensive initiative. What the Jeana code is Thomas Allred jr. Is a networking capital. The reason Thomas for this. Is because you have your hands full with doing police work. so with a network that's with you wherever you be or may go. Thomas. The odd are slowly in your favor. Gabrielle Union Allred how can I thank you for everything. Thomas. I do mean Superman. You got to hear me. I hear you Gabrielle. We will be together in the future sometime Superman. But you have to keep yourself together. And pray and look on the bright side of things. There's no one i want to be with more than you Thomas. Gabrielle we talking days weeks month or years. Honey I got to know because I got to see you Gabrielle. I'm talking about weeks Thomas. Gabriel Union Allred I can't make it without you. Thomas listen to me I know you hearts in the right place. If you choose another girl I understand. Gabriel I am Time Enforcement Agent Thomas allred jr. And I love you and Im a stand by my woman. Gabriel honey will you speak to me sometime. If I don't Thomas you'll always know I'm listening. The reason why I love you so much is because I ain't got to say anything about it. But I can remember you in the past Gabriel. Thomas got his memory back. Are you serious Thomas. I'm serious about seeing you in the past Gabrielle. How much do you remember about me. It's just that I saw your smile that's just what I remember. Jeana. Thomas Allred is a good person. And the right person for me. If something happens to me Gabriel Union. I want you to take care of my husband. Who Superman. Girls Superman. I ask of you this Gabriel. Please do me this favor. Jeana quit talking like that you're not going anywhere. But just in case I do Gabriel. That man has been good to me. What do you think. Jeana I'm a get the groceries out of the car. Hello Gabriel. Hello Superman. Come into the stage. Is a person who needs no introduction at all. Mr. Keenan ivory Wayne's. Speech speak speak. I wasn't going to come here tonight. Because I didn't think I was invited. But Low and behold here I am. And when the world do you lemons. You make supper with them. But what I'm saying is. Ladies and gentleman. A missing you. By Case. Is going out to all of our love ones. That we may have lost along the way. Coming to the stages is a friend of mine. yo give it up for Mr.. Stevens seagal. Hey listen y'all. I'm going to make the short and sweet. No one is above the law. Thank you. Now I'm just kidding. The Jeana code truly means everything to everybody. It is a networking banking system. That continues to network. Without the help of man of woman. The Jeana code. Is finally a symbol that the star can look at and understand. Along side of Superman the quest for peace. We have our own superhero Superman. Thomas Allred jr. And Gabrielle Union Allred. Will you please come to the stage. Time acceleration doors now opening. A y'all it's Gabriel Union Allred. It's Superman Thomas Allred jr. Mr.. Steven seagal thank you. You quit welcome Gabrielle thank you Mr.. Stevens to go also. Superman one more thing. I hear that you to can't be together the way that you want to. No we can't. My wife has to work. And we both police officers. So I guess we have make do. Make do with this Superman. Oh sh*t. I give to you. Your own house mantion escape. Gabriel Do you see your house. Thank you Thomas. Simulation doors now opening. One day Thomas. You'll have that house you dream of so well. Honey please don't leave. Thomas you already know its tech code 496781.Right now in the beginning we have to be apart sweetheart. Gabriel Union Allred. Honey I can't live without you. Girl I'm asking you please. Come home with me. Superman I see what I can do. Because no matter where you. What job I'm doing. I will always be. Gabrielle Union Allred. And Jeana asked me to be there for Superman. And Superman is my husband. I'll be there

It is a ring in the box. Superman did you do this. Thomas Allred jr.i Said did you do this. Yes I did Gabriel. Thomas honey but why. Jeana meant the world to me. And you so hot. Gabriel saying that you mean the world to me to. I just don't want nothing to happen honest. Thomas this is a real diamond engagement ring. And Gabriel it's 51 carrots. How did you do this. Years ago I had a contract. I lost touch with her for some reason. Lately I've been thinking about. Maybe reconnecting with the past. I didn't know Gabrielle. That you were Jeana friend. Who she would run to. I think somewhere in my past. I must have sent you a diamond ring. Because Gabriel in my presence. Baby hear it is. And I've been down a second. My feelings are hurt. And I kinda feel like don't know one want me around. But my love is here. For anyone who's going to something. You ready for me to preach to you. I want you to preach to me Thomas Allred jr. In the day of you coming up. Helping people. We bring to you. The backstreet boys Gabriel Union Allred. Will you be my wife in and outside of the pages. Thomas I'm saying to you yes I will be your wife in and outside of the pages. Gabriel Union Allred a love you. I give to you R Kelly and the public announcement. Thomas kiss that girl on stage. Listen Thomas I want to chicken wings. A hot dog. Two large cokes. And a scratch off lottery ticket. With the number two four power play. Gabrielle thats the original Punk Daddy. Superman it'll be okay because. I'm with you . Gabrielle I love you .James Earl Jones is the voice of Punk Daddy. Superman. Stop that sh*t James. Gabriel we all about to leave.

Just one more period on this book and it's done. There it is its done.

You got to understand. That I'm here for you. You got to understand. That the book is already finished Thomas. Gabrielle Union Allred I'm a beast. But playing this game I'm in control Thomas Allred jr. Will one of y'all make a move. I'm starting to get sleepy waiting for it. You need to take your time Gabrielle. He said you need to take your time. Okay somebody make a move. Mr. Donald Trump and Mr. George and Barbara Bush were going to do it. Now don't take all Day now Gabriel Union Allred this game is tricky. Mr.. Barack Obama and Michelle Obama. What do I do now. Superman you take your time. Okay I'm going to make a move. Superman you better be careful. Always Gabriel. Gabriel. Yes Thomas Allred jr. In real life will you marry me. Connect for I got you. I win again. Well Gabrielle this seeMs. to be your game. Im a get out of my seat and go now. Thomas It's not you. It's just that I got connect four. On Barber Bush. On and earlier game. And she let me see the future. Of me and you. I like that Thomas. Baby Chris Rock just never stops does he. Superman listen to me. We have all work hard at the TEC. Everyone will receive their payment. In which we sent out to them. It's not about the payment Gabriel Union Allred. Read the manuscript. Thomas and Gabriel must live on forever. And may God help us. Because im married to a wonderful woman. In the whole wide world inside of my books. These are my books Thomas. And in my dreaMs. Thomas I'm getting down on sweet potato pie with you. Superman and Gabrielle Union Allred. Can't you see your future is now beginning. What do I have to do for you to know that I love you Thomas Allred Jr. Clean up the room Gabriel Union Allred it's a mess. Ain't I here for you Thomas. Yes Gabrielle I got to say that you are. Here for me that is. Usher Raymond so you just going to sit over there and sing to yourself. Everybody coming to the stage. Is miss Pattie LaBelle. Singing If only you knew. The first time I got to speak. At a conference of this magnitude. I was scared I was scared out of my brains. But when Jeana came to see me I was alright. Ladies and gentleman welcoming to the stage. Legacy and legend. These are Jeanas children. I like to thank the community for Honoring my mom. We truly thank you. Connect four Gabriel Union Allred. Superman you the only one that can beat me. Thank your time and youll get this game. Welcoming to the stage Mr.. Danny Glover. Danny Glover couldn't be here tonight. He's filming another lethal weapon movie with Mel Gibson hiMs.elf. But what we want to see is. We think you Gabriel Union Allred. For Stepping in and saving. Your husband on the books. Thomas Allred Allred Jr life. Superman wants to speak to his wife Gabrielle Union Allred. It's incredible Gabrielle Union Allred. Honey I worked all of my life. And I never knew that anyone could see me. I thank you Gabriel Union's Allred. Another I have 1100 zillion dollars. I just want to let you know that our love his eternal. And I give to legend and legacy. a gift that their mother always be stored upon me. Money. Legend and legacy I give to you 2 billion dollars a piece. Gabriel. I'm ending this book now. Because of you. The future is getting clearer each day. A really love you Gabriel. And I'm sorry for all the wrong with that made. But I aware to you in front of everybody. That I'll love you the rest of your life if you let me. Gabrielle please be my wife in and outside of the pages. You To legit Thomas. Gir I love you. And I'm scared. That this is a movie. That you somehow won't understand. The entire industry thanks you Gabrielle Union Allred. For being there for Jeana. And for also being there for me to. This is the Jeana Gabrielle Union Allred code. Meaning that friends are going to be there for each other. The Gabriel anytime you need me. Or anyone in the industry. Just say it. The Jeana Gabrielle Union Allred code. Is activated. The symbol looks. Red Gray and Blue. Your a super hero Gabrielle. We call you superhero Gabrielle Union Allred. Industry look. Gabriel saved my life. And where im from its a life for life. A gift to her. Three zillion dollars. And I hope excuse me move out of the away Gabriel's is coming through. Thomas Allred Jr. Your about to be dumb if you think I want your money. Gabriel I have nothing left to give you. Superman we'll figure out something. Ladies and gentleman Rob Schneider. Go ahead Superman. You can do it. You can do it all night. Kathy Bates ladies in gentleman. This is a celebration of all of us. Id like to welcome to the stage Rachel Ray and Steve Harvey. You got to see what this those for my show Steve Harvey.The Jeana Gabrielle Union Allred code. Is simply this. We are not a gang we are people. Everyone say it. We are not gang we are people. Standing in unity. Everyone say it . Standing in unity. Right now we need you to stand up. For Mr.. Laurence fishburne. You be seated some people didn't have the nerve to help Thomas. Gabrielle took a big chance on him. And I think you. Because as I look at Superman. I know that he needs someone. Like Gabriel Union Allred. Give that boy a contract. He stood his ground and he spoken his peace. He can sit next to me at the awards. Thank you Mr. Lawrence fishburne. Everybody miss Keyshia Cole's and Miss Missy Elliott. We're not supposed to do this. The Gabriel Union Allred. We give to you this . It is from your future husband Thomas Allred jr. In and outside of the pages. It's a ring.

I'm doing everything I could. To make you realize who cares for you Hillary. Cant you see Hillary. That we want you to take over the presidency. Gabriel and Thomas this is insane. With the popular vote youll win Hillary Clinton. Get back up here and train with me alittle more Thomas I mean Superman. Attack me Thomas. No I want miss Hillary's Clinton. The time adjuster phone is ringing. It's Oprah Winfrey. Gabriel Union Allred and Superman. Thomas Allred Jr. I have to take this call this meeting is ajoured Attack me you little piece of sh*t. Thomas you playing I don't feel like playing. It's true that I'm playing Gabrielle. Do you want to punch me in the eye. Why hell know Superman. We are just now getting off the ground. In 19 business days. We are going back to save Jeana. Careful everybody I'm not going back to save her. Why not Superman. It's because Jeana doesn't need saving. She is in heaven Gabriel. Let the time enforcement team realize. That Jeana is a Amazon Queen God. That has already been rescued by the woman. To the Jeana code. To the Jeana code. You where out there with Jeana on the streets weren't you Gabriel Union Allred. She tought me everything that I know. I know Jeana was good for that. what can I do to make you see that I care about you Thomas Allred Jr. Just spend time with me. Listen Gabriel I've been alone for 8 dogs on years. And I can really use a friend. Are you saying what I think your saying Superman. Gabriel Union Allred I believe I am. Connect four. Yeah you got me Superman. Gabrielle guess what. I got you for life. Walking to the table is. The children that I had with my beautiful wife Gabrielle Union Allred. Ill never cheated you Gabriel. Talking about cheat on me. Superman its your turn to change the baby. Another game of connect four. Another game Thomas. After this we will go play in the house. I know the thinking about Superman. Getting my help to change the baby diapers. Gabrielle stop playing. Connect four Thomas. We are rich as hell now Gabriel. I'm going to be right back. After I eat this slice of cheesecake. Gabrielle if you see any mashed potatoes left in there will you bring me a bowl. I greatly would appreciate you. Take advantage of this Thomas. There is more cheesecake and mashed potatoes what do you want I only want what you would let me have Gabrielle my babies. Thats good answer Thomas. Gabriel my super census are going off. Come here baby. I'm a need you to go change this baby. I am NOT playing around Thomas Allred Jr. And that's how It went. Though Time code after Time code. I had her back. And that's the reason I married her. Miss Hillary Clinton. Mr.. Barack Obama and miss Michelle Obama. This is my story. Can't believe it Bill. Who would have thought that Thomas Allred Jr.and his wife Gabriel Union Allred. Each of them would save the world from destruction. I have a message from Gabrielle. Mr.. Bill Clinton. I have to make this short and sweet. Thank you sir for going back in time and saving my husband Superman. I'm giving to you a code called the Jeana code. It will all makes sense through time. And Mr.. Bill Clinton. Your wife in the future is name Hillary Rodman Clinton. Try not to mess up. There is another tape Mr.. Barack Obama and Ms. Michelle Obama. Go a head and play the tape President Clinton. This is the type of Superman Thomas Allred jr. Ms. Hillary Clinton. Oh my god miss Hillary Clinton. I just now thought up why the Jeana code is going to work. That's because. People see how Jeana is. I know first hand. That if we combine the Jeana code. With the Gabrielle Union Allred announcement code. Who will have the Jeana Gabrielle Union Allred announcement code. And what that means. Is that this book is now closed. Wait one minute the Jeana code. Is part of a legend and legacy production. If y'all see Gabriel.Tell her I'm still going to beat her at a game of connect four when I get her home with me. And there it was even my president even said it. Good job Gabrielle Union Allred. Good job. Thank you Mr. President but where my Surperman. Connect four Ms. Hillary Rodman Clinton. I beat you Obama Michelle it takes time Barack it takes time. Time for the kids go to bed. Superman yes Gabriel

I just want to thank you Thomas. For givinh me lead way and letting me handle my own business. Thank you. Gabrielle I would never hold you up from doing what you want and love to do that's not who i am I just want to spend time with you and let you know that I care about. I love you I'm your husband Superman. Always remember this Gabriel Union Allred. If i go its not because I want to it's because I must. Superman you do remember me. He got his memory back Gabriel. Gabriel thank you for saving my life I love you so much . There's only one more thing left to do to make sure the Jeana code is complete. Let the whole industry sing happy birthday to the one and only Jeana. Happy birthday Jeana. Happy birthday Jeana we love you. Thomas Allred Jr And Gabrielle Union Allred. Good night everybody. Forever and two days I will always here for you Gabriel Union Allred. Thomas you need me. Yes I do so much sweetheart. I'm a Zillionaire Gabriel Union Allred. And I think it is about time that I talk to someone. I'm a pencil you in Thomas Allred Jr. Superman is hurting Gabriel Superman I got you down for the next three weeks. Three weeks I'm only playing with you you see Surperman our book is coming to and end I done seen all I had to see today as you and your momma Charlene showed what it means to stand up for each other. Tell your momma that your houses will soon me ready. Gabrielle is this a dream. No it's not a dream. I love you. I love you more . He and Gabrielle are a winning couple. And to the stage. Gabrielle Union Allred and Thomas Allred Jr. Together at last. We'd just like to tell y'all that just like Katt WilliaMs. I been trying to get some help out here. Thomas Good evening and good night Gabrielle Union Allred thanks for reading my literary good night.

Freeze time. George theres someone in the offices. Alert the chief of security missed Gabriel Union Allred. That boy say that your the chief of security Gabrielle Union Allred. I am head of security . Misses Barbara Bush. So were at a standstill Barbara Bush. Gabriella what are you saying. Im saying that there are to helping of that potato salad missing. And reasoning and deduction has it. That the corporate are no other then. Will and Jada pinkett Smith. The potatoes salad is the proof. If first I didn't want to believe it. History repeats itself. Get Martin Lawrence in here. Hell no Will and Jada pinkett Smith didn't you it . Who ever Martin is. Martin stands by his friends. Here we go the new and improved Martin and Gina show. With Martin Lawrence as the same person he is. And Tisha Campbell as the funny but not so witty Gina Pain. I can't discuss this with you. But I'm working overtime for you Gina . I'm staying yall that. The reason that there are two bites out of the potato salad. Is because I took a bite myself and I gave Superman a bite. Security security. I am the damn security. Yall I hate to do this but. Time is beginning to stop. But time with me is everlasting. The next time you going to leave a bowl of potato salad on the table. Don't forget to put some spoons at Fox with it. Contacting Superman I need Superman. Superman contacting Gabrielle Superman contacting Gabrielle

Way to work that potato salad Superman. So Gabrielle your business is finished for the rest of your life. It is with you in it Thomas Allred jr. Simulation now coming to a close. Thomas. Gabrielle I want to be with you. But this is just a simulation. And I realize this

Superman you can't realize this. Because you are just a computer program. And to love me you must have feelings. Gabriel you talking to Superman. I just can't believe it Thomas. Turn off the simulation . That I love you Gabriel. I'm turning off the simulation right now. I need you Superman. Look Thomas. If you don't be here when I turn the simulation. I'm going to get married to Dewayne Wade. He is a basketball player and NBA champ. No Gabriel Union Allred. This is really me. Superman this is to difficult. Then leave the simulation on forever Gabriel Union Allred. With the Union code. Thomas thats not your program how do you know about the Union code. I told you Gabriel of Superman. Simulation know Gabriel now coming to close. If you are Superman what are you now Thomas Allred jr. I hate you. Still running them simulation uh Gabriel. Superman is not coming back Dewayne Wade Gabriel I know. What am I going to do. We can just hope and pray that Thomas Allred jr. Remembers you. And if he doesn't. Then Gabriel I'm here for you. Run simulation Superman. Thomas I'm getting married. Gabriel honey please don't do that. I love him Superman. Gabriel you have my best wishes. Simulation now ending. Can we get some dinner Gabriel. Id like that. Superman has just woke up. 2 minute ago . He's asking for Gabrielle. She is running some simulation the why she always does. Dwayne I changed my mind. I hope that you understand. Catch you later girl. Gabrielle Union Allred. Whoopi Goldberg. Superman is alive and he's asking for you. Time Time Enforcement doors now open. Time enforcement doors now closing. Thomas I'm here baby. Gabrielle. My beautiful wife Gabrielle. Baby I dreamed that you left me. Never Superman honey never. This story is a portrait of the strength of love. And anything can be done when you believe. I do love you Superman. I love you too Gabriel. Baby I want to go home. Time acceleration doors now opening. Time is accelebration doors now closing. I'm going to get you back on your feet. Hold on Gabriel a just want to tell you this. Tell me what Superman. Even in darkness I never cheated on you even in darkness nor day light I cheated on you either. Simulation now closing. Gabriel keep trying. My Superman is gone he needs me. Gabriel Thomas is in a coma. Just keep working and keep waiting. Superman will find his way back to you. Thank you miss Hillary Clinton. Whenever you people would like to see me. Miss Hillary Clinton I'm here. Just take your time with me Gabrielle. Hillary attack me.

Breathe easy Breathe out. Superman why you crying. Somebody ate my strawberry shortcake. There's more we're that came from Superman. Are you serious Gabrielle Union Allred. Let me see if I can find your peace. Here we go Superman. Two last pieces. Thomas you getting ready to make a mistake. Connect four. I'll beat Superman. Listen Thomas. Somehow I beat you in connect four. Another game of connect four out there on the porch honey. Girl I watched you come up to the years. In the TV movies screen. Thomas Allred Jr. I did what I could to save you. Happy birthday to you. And Merry Christmas. And Happy Easter. Happy Thanksgiving. Cut off the lights when you eat that cheesecake. It's not cheesecake its strawberry shortcake. You have no idea what cheesecake is do you Thomas Allred Jr. My husband and my bestfriend Superman to my life of understanding. A cheesecake is a metaphor. For the white man trying to help us out our situation. With cheese. You need to be professional is Jamie Foxx and Neyo . Excuse me Gabriel Id like to wash up before dinner. The wash room is right this way. Neyo that's it. Some times you win some some times you lose some. Connect four Superman ok I'm ready to eat . Neyo Chris Rock and Oprah Winfrey you sit right here at eat . Jimmy Foxx and J z and Beyonce. You all can sit over here. Eminem and Beyonce could you scoot down alittle. For Will and Jada pinkett Smith Steve Harvey. And Kanye and Kim Kardashian and Ti and Tiny. Miss Roseanne Barr could you please have a seat to table. Is everyone one okay. President Barack Obama and Michelle Obama may you have a seat. President George and Barbara Bush.You are to be seated here. And last but not least President Donald Trump. Connect four Superman I got you yes you did Mr. President Donald Trump. Let's get to the table. Thomas honey we love you Thomas. You can eat right here I'm being professional I'll just stand while you seat and eat and talk . No honey. What Gabriel Union Allred honey there's much more room at the head of the table then you think. But Thomas there's only one chair . This is your chair Ms. Gabriel Union Allred Thomas to my wife and best friend thank you for saving everyone's lives with your business ideas and income. Gabrielle you risked your neck to save. And I appreciate you. I appreciate you Thomas . Everyone to Gabrielle Union Allred. For she is a jolly good fellow Gabrielle. I ready love you and from now on Gabrielle and all women seats on the house will be at the front of the table where are men going to sit. Beside you at the end of the table. Amazon women it's beginning to look a lot like Christmas women stand up for you kings. Y'all not going to be able to give me a plate. Katt WilliaMs. come and sit down. Everybody do Katt WilliaMs. like this. Get your a** in there a get you a plate. I think now is the time. Yes now is the time Superman for presents. Thank you Lord for saving the day. That's what I'm saying. Katt WilliaMs. talk professional Gabriel I thank the good Lord for giving a brother a chance to get a peice of apple pie. Lord knows that you work magic when your cooking and baking girl.i Thank you Katt WilliaMs. for not eating it all and saving me a piece. Thank you Jeana for everything we love you. Thomas. I put my hand up on my hip. And this meaning you are in trouble connect four Michelle a thank you. I beat him I beat Superman. And the night you went like that. So we can count you gave how much money to save you husband Thomas Allred Jr. 65 zillion dollars. And now he stands to be worth. And infinite sign. Cusack you know that Jeana and I were friends. Cusack just leave Gabrielle alone do you here that it's the applause John Claude Van Damme. The girl is innocent you need to quit going over the numbers. Check the numbers Gabrielle went back in time a saved a superstar from dieing. Who Cusack. Vann Damn I'm talking about Thomas Allred Jr. She married him for Christ sakes. You need to fix it in your time code Cusack why Gabriel. Because this meeting never happened. She went back in time y'all and changed things. How are you doing Cusack how are you doing Ms. Gabriel Union Allred. Yeah Cusack I went back in time but no one can do anything about it. And my name is Gabriel Allred Union. Get it right you muthaf*cker. Time car take me home I'm being professional. Park right here. I love you Gabrielle Union Allred. Thomas I got some thing to tell you. It just will have to wait until I figure out these finances of our. I'm pregnant . Gabrielle your a superhero in my world. And I love you honey. The End

CHAPTER 9

You know my style don't you Gabriel Union Allred. Thomas Allred Jr we make a beautiful couple. You know I'm Superman Gabriel Union Allred. Its a race of time untill Superman uncovers me. Gabriel Union Allred can Superman play with your kittens. Hell no my kittens ain't people friendly. What are you thinking about Superman and I don't like it. Gabriel Union Allred all that I'm saying is that you are a perfect specimen for a project that I have for you later on at the house. Tell me more about your project I want to hear you. We need to be undercover . Hell no I'm getting the divorce papers right now. Superman or Thomas Allred Jr what ever they call you good by Thomas Allred Jr. Guess what Thomas Allred Jr I'm lending you something. All my love forever and ever. Do you here me Thomas Allred Jr. I just know that the easel on that paint should be dry in a second or two.

Listen Thomas Allred Jr what are you painting. The police with us and you have to be professional because I can capture the imagination with both of my hands tied behind my back. My Superman has sense about his self . You need to focus Thomas Allred Jr on you and me. And leave the police where they are on the security feedback see Thomas Allred Jr. I ain't going nowhere so you might as well get used to it and me . Gabriel I'm doing all kinds of things to prove I'm professional . The last girl took my heart. And you gave it back to me. Will you drop a free style for me Gabriel Union Allred. Thomas Allred Jr. Your to legit to quit. Im getting ready to turn in Thomas Allred Jr. Sleep well my mistletoe Gabriel Union Allred. And while I'm sleeping can you Thomas Allred Jr surrounded me with your love. You ain't got to say it . You got my love on your index finger. In case I forget to tell you stay strong. You'll get your contract one day baby. It's nothing else that I can do bust a move I'm fend to weed out. I like the jungle book. It's the jungle book it is. That woman always calls me when she need something. I'm her Superman. Baby we ain't got no soap in the bathroom. Do you know what I'm saying . Gabriel Union Allred. Yes I do Thomas Allred Jr. What's the name that they call me. I'm reluctant to say this but your my Superman. You damn right. Pardon yourself there are kids listening. I want you to sit right here and count to a hundred and come and find me. Enter Hollywood code +695-398-421-0612.thats the Hollywood code enter the second Hollywood code in now. 387-245-8964 0 - 1 2 3 Enter the third Hollywood code. +172-698-273-78094.Gabriel Union Allred baby can you see I not having this sh*t. Thomas Allred Jr you will get your chance at Superstardom I know it but everywhere I look couple are having families together. Gabriel I've been by myself for seven years the reason I say this is that the bath water is complete . And it sure would be nice to swim in it . Well officer Thomas Allred Jr you'll get your turn after me .

I didn't mean nothing by it you know I got love for all tpyes of people. Yeah Thomas I heard about you get fresh with all of those women. No mam those women where getting fresh with me. Your surpposed to be straight up and forward coming. Well I surppose that I do have two more females to add to my list of entertainers . Wich ones do you want Thomas Allred Jr . I think that I'll have Amerie and a girl from my home town name Maya. That is it for today. That is it for today. You need one more Thomas. Lucy Liu you got to be more professional. Well Gabriel Union Allred you all that I need . To get over the hump baby. I got your got damn hump baby. Gabriel Union Allred the kids honey the kids . I love you Thomas Allred Jr but I'm not giving up on you. Say anything you want to Gabriel Union Allred . This house a be full of kids pretty soon. Leave it at pretty soon.

I'm coaching you to run a marathon. You can ask me anything you want but I ain't running a complete marathon. As you see in the prenuptial agreement. I get half of the estate that is if you ever stick your d*ck in a female. Without my consent. It's called insurance papers. Gabriel. I'm a pretend like I didn't here you. What kinda fruit cake are you . To kind that police officers no me best as the husband to the most beautiful woman in the world that's why I will never cheat on you. What about them girls on your list. What list . Thomas Allred jr Gabriel it ain't like we been mistreated all them girl that I mentioned earlier . Honey your the only one that I care to be with. Gabriel sweetheart I have came to my sense. And the prenup if we need one is going to be and made in your favor. I will give you a prenup simply because your the one who's worth it . My lovely wife and soul mate Gabriel Union Allred. Honey I apologise. I need you so damn much . I'll be with you in a minute. Thomas Allred Jr said girl he want me. Be cool. Baby I'm a see you now . Kristen Beam was on the phone with me . And it seeMs. that I am the proud mother of newly weds . I'm happy for her .I stepped out a few seconds what were you saying Thomas Allred Jr about Kristen Beam.I said she worked her a** off for her contract. Yeah that's what I thought you said muthaf*cker. Thomas Allred Jr I'm just making sure that I'm not getting in over my head . Sweetheart I got news for you the other Hollywood pa**code is. 42+389-592-348-7654.Excuse my baby but I have to use the bathroom . Go a right ahead Thomas Allred Jr I have to use the bathroom also .

The first news for the day is the conduct code. Listen to me I'm Gabriel Union Allred. And my conduct code is brought to you by. Slits malt liquor bull. And incorporated. I'm using everything I got in this code of mine. So if you answer me try this on for size. I'm putting my picture in every paragraph for this book. Not literally. I'm just realizing today. That working with Thomas Allred Jr. Is a waist of time. I'm telling yall. Here go the outcome of working with a man like Thomas Allred Jr. Thomas Allred Jr we winning. I got this risk I want to take. But we short on money and our bank account is being suspended. His bank account is not mine. So Ill lend you $7,500 in good faith money. Thomas Allred Jr. Do you know what he tells me. I'll get your money back to you I got a hunch on something. Everytime he has a hunch it pays off. But seeing how I love Gabriel Union Allred that's why these hunches keep paying off. And so Gabriel Union Allred code is. To be. Always. And let live always. Take your time and think about it. Who ever gets to the restroom first gets to sit on the new and improved tub with jet cycle involved in it. I'll race you to the top of the stairs Thomas Allred Jr. We both battle for the top.

It's just that I know when to give in to my Gabriel Union Allred. The girl of my dreaMs. Thomas Allred Jr. Anyway I keep courting her in the press I guess because Gabriel Union Allred my bank account is 200 zillion dollars Wich is half of yours if you show me how to spend my money. A with that said. Have yourself a good evening. And I don't know who parked his truck out there in front of me. There a tow unit coming soon. Martin Lawrence move that truck out of the way. Now Eddie Murphy singing his song. Someone to care. Someone to share. Lonely hours. And moments of despair. To be loved. The be loved. Oh oh what a feeling too be loved. Thomas Allred Jr . This boy don't have no sense do he. Thomas Allred Jr tell Eddie Murphy I love him. Gabriel Union Allred are you crazy I'm out here where Martin Lawrence can see me.

Thomas I got something to tell you about your damn tow truck. Go Gabriel Union Allred.Martin Lawrence is a mad DC cop all over again. Eddie Murphy will you please quit singing that same damn song over and over again. Thomas Allred Jr you don't like it. No Eddie I'm kinda tied and I don't like it. Well f*ck you Thomas Allred Jr. F*ck you. Happy Thanksgiving Eddie Murphy. Happy Thanksgiving Martin Lawrence. To everybody Happy Thanksgiving. Eddie Murphy sing that song. F*ck you you bastard. Someone to care. Someone to share. Lonely hours. In moments of despair. To be loved. To be loved. Oh oh what a feeling too be loved. Bout time you get through with it. Martin Lawrence kiss my a** . Martain stop.

Thomas Allred Jr Eddie Murphy and Martin Lawrence are out here in our road tap boxing I can't move the car . All right goddamn I had enough of this sh*t. Happy Thanksgiving Thomas Allred Jr. Gabriel I'm a get you. It something else you have got to here . Baby it's silent night. Eddie Murphy can sing. Happy holidays to you and yours from Thomas Allred Jr and the wedding planner Gabriel Union Allred. Help this boy Thomas got his money back. The government ain't playing when they say they going to give you your money back.i heard they gave him 300 million dollars. Cheryl underwood get out of here you know Thomas Allred Jr and I are Zillionaires. I'm know that Gabriel Union Allred I just wanted to see if I could get you to say it. Thomas Allred jr you better ask your damn friends to quit playing. What friends honey I don't have any . Thomas Allred Jr I mean Will and Jada pinkett Smith and also Ti and Tiny. And also Kanye and Kim Kardashian. Thomas Allred Jr you made a good decision. A Gabriel Union Allred. Has and body seen the Thanksgiving turkey . Take louder I'm taking to Will and Jada pinkett Smith. Im saying somebody kidnapped the turkey. Bra Man. I'm sorry Martin I was hungry. You paying for this sh*t Bra Man. Somebody at the door. Jesse's Jackson go get the door. Its Jay z and Beyonce and they brought alot of Turkeys and fixing. Turkeys for each of us. Thank You jay-z and Beyonce. Bra Man. Had gave us a call and said that I was and emergency to bring more food. Hustle man get the hell out of here with them steaks. Gabriel Union Allred.My love Thomas Allred Jr Happy Thanksgiving. Happy Thanksgiving Thomas Allred Jr. Happy Thanksgiving every body good night.

Say you want me Jasmine. Thomas I'm only a princess Gabrielle Union Allred. Jasmine are you professional. You damn right I'm professional. Look how i think about you. Jasmine be careful what you wish for. I'm waiting for you Aladdin to kiss me. Thomas Allred Jr.

Thomas Allred Jr automatically won his woman. Can't you see that your a princess Gabriel Union Allred. I'm a make sure that I provide for you. If your careful. You can look into my eyes and see the future. Gabriel Union Allred. I can see the future. And what can I get you. A triple x action Kung Fu grip Conan doll. Thomas Allred Jr be professional. Gabriel Union Allred I ready did enjoy the conversation. Yeah right Thomas Allred Jr you want to go. No but. No butts please Thomas Allred Jr. Your wish is my command.

Sing with me. Someone to care. Someone to share. Lonely hours. In moment of despair. To be loved. To be loved. Oh oh what a feeling too be loved. Somebody body must be choking over there. They out there trying to sing my muthaf*cking song . You got some real material Eddie Murphy go back to sleep Cletus. I'll Cletus your mutha f*cking *ssh*le. Let them two argue Thomas Allred Jr. Princess Jasmine I want to give you something. I mean princess Gabriel Union Allred. What is it .It my tooth it feel out when we were dancing earlier. And I wash it off and spit dried it. But here it is Gabriel Union Allred. My tooth had been cleaned and ready for you. You see there is a god somewhere up in the sky .

And I know that you and I will end up together. Gabriel Union Allred. I'm waiting on you to say something. Got damn this is a big a** tooth. I mean this is ridiculous . I can here Eddie Murphy singing. That not Eddie Murphy. That's Martin Lawrence Thomas Allred Jr. Oh sh*t my bad. And it's like that Thomas Allred Jr. I thought you and Gabriel Union Allred were Bra Man and Hustle Man. You nearly go my foot up y'all a**es. You talking big sh*t Martin Lawrence . And I can back it up to. Hold on to that though I'll be right back. Gina what I tell you about going across the street down there. Martin Lawrence I need you to stop baby sitting me. Let's go and get out of here Gabriel Union Allred while we got a chance. That was great. I never felt so alive I'm trying to be professional but that was fun. Yeah Thomas Allred Jr we no you had fun. Goodnight Jasmine I do mean Princess Gabriel Union Allred a. k. a Princess Jasmine. Good night Aladdin a . k. a Thomas Allred Jr has anybody seen Superman anywhere.

Look and see honey ain't you professional. I have enough reasons to call it quits here. Being your third eye Gabriel Union Allred I can see what's happening around you. Everybody can see you for who you are. I'm trying my best not to pee on myself. Move over may I sit down. You go right ahead and sir hear. Thomas Allred Jr you know I kidnapped you for a reason don't you. I know you and me are going to have fun tonight. Thomas you are not afraid of the public. I rest my case. Gabrielle Union Allred. I think this dance belong to me big time. Gabriel Union Allred are you having fun yet. I can see everybody. I have some thing to tell you. What Thomas Allred Jr . What is it. Gabriel Union Allred I'm a police officer and I'm undercover as a writer. My name is Thomas Allred Jr. But my code name is Superman of the New York Police department and of the NSA and FBI.

What are you saying to me Thomas Allred Jr. I'm not sure why they put us together . Body language tells me that your on fire. Thomas Allred Jr this was a joke. Ok if you believe it. Everyone have a good night. Touchdown inside of the thirty . That was and awesome play. Yeah it was would you like something to drink . Officer Thomas Allred Jr of the New York Police department code name is officer Reign and the code name for me is officer Reign .

Calbunga Go deeper Thomas inside of your cranium. Let me see what you are about. Well Gabriel the more I look at you. The better I feel around you. Ill do anything. To feel your body against mine. Gabriel I am getting to old time is waisting. Just call me Aladdin . And you are Princess Jasmine Gabriel Union Allred . Do you always talk like this Thomas Allred Jr. I do mean Aladdin. Well Gabriel Union Allred. I do mean Princess Jasmine. It becomes a choir when I can't be with you. Merry Christmas. Princess Jasmine. I do mean Gabriel Union Allred. Aladdin. I do mean Superman. Thomas Allred Jr. Everytime that I look in that girls eyes I can see my self in them. Don't even think about leaving. I'm having fun hanging with you. And when the novel gets finished. You can hang with me some more in real life .

You got to see what I done for you fixing up the Christmas tree Gabrielle Union Allred. I told you I had skills in the kitchen didn't I. Thank the Lord the cookies aren't burnt . Excuse me guys there's a message for Ms. Gabrielle Union Allred. can't you see I'm doing everything I can to get these cookies out of the oven. Superman loves you the letter says. Listen Thomas Allred Jr. I think me and you need to have a talk about boundaries. I can give a f*ck what you do in your own time superhero named Thomas Allred Jr. But once you step into my kitchen. My cookies better not be burnt. The cookies are a golden brown. I know I like them cookies. Gabriel Union Allred. Seeing that you have got me almost done with this book. Suger bear let's go up stairs and tell some more stories Gabriel Union Allred. Nick name Sugar Bear. Listen to me Thomas Allred Jr this is how it goes. Connect four. I'll race you to the top of the stairs. Happy anniversary to you. It's our one year anniversary Gabriel Union Allred and I got you these cookies there cooling off. Thomas Allred Jr your cookies hot as a muthaf*cker. Cookies are off. There go my baby. Gabriel Union Allred. You can call me superhero Thomas Allred Jr.

The cookies avenger Superman for short. I'm a lay down with you tonight. Honestly baby that is all that I ever wish for. Thomas Allred Jr be professional and turn the light off. Superman. Gabriel Union Allred that is Punk Daddy in our bed room. Shut up and go to bed Superman. Superman. Superman my a**. Now I know that's Punk Daddy. I can here him Gabriel Union Allred. Suck his d*ck Thomas Allred Jr. Ain't no way he's sucking my d*ck. You wish it was Punk Daddy sucking yo little a** d*ck. Get off me. Big things come in small package Gabriel. Plus this is compact size. Able to fit small hard to reach places. Compact is better. Compact show is better you told me right Thomas Allred Jr I think of you every chance I get with you Gabriel Union Allred. I'm just crazy you girl. Be my new professional. We are hustlers baby. I'm a Zillionaire because of you Gabriel Union Allred.

I like that because we really need each other Gabriel Union Allred. Right now I'm do homework leaning how to be a professional. But I need you to understand this I'm a give you half of my income for these books. And what I'm saying half of my income is 100.300.000.000.000.000.000.you understand don't you. What you think Thomas Allred Jr. You better not be messing with me. When the bank clears my money I'll be sure to get you your money. I'm making a note of it to professionals to give to you Gabriel Union Allred one half of my fortune.

Wich is 175 zillionaire dollars. That all most your half Gabriel give or take a few pennies. You are responsible for my saftey today Gabriel Union Allred this world is exactly what it seeMs.. I'm giving instructions to give you your money Gabriel Union Allred as soon as I get mine cleared from the bank . This is homework I'm doing right here. Girl it cheapens me. To care about someone and not give them a good by kiss. The money is your Gabriel Union Allred I'm a see to it that you have it. Great work on those movies that you made and your videos . I'm looking forward to seeing you in the future My beautiful beautiful wife Ms. Gabriel Union Allred. Listen anyway come and live with me. I'm just a poor man. But I can take care of you like no other. Be my wife in real life Gabriel Union Allred. Check your bank account it should be full in eight or nine minutes. You have to give money time on this leave. What happened you talking about spending. Thomas Allred Jr. Max the limit out of your cards. I can be your best friend if you want me to . Enjoy spending money while I do this. Thing it is you girl that turns me on. Do you realize that I can't move out of this position until I'm through working. That's professional. There is one thing Gabriel I ask of you just always run my tab. Up as high as you can get it. And Princess Jasmine. I do mean Princess Gabriel Union Allred. I'm home this evening. I'm home every evening.

I'm saying Thomas Allred Jr in defense to myself. Thomas give her another one of those cookies. It ain't alright Thomas Allred Jr. I'm working with a team of cookies Slayers. Your more professional then I ever thought Gabriel Union Allred. Im a see that I get you a new bag for the one that I ruined. Gabriel Union Allred there's just something that I have to tell you. Listen Thomas Allred Jr. Superman I don't that gifts from strangers. A Chanel purse I think we can be friends. Pink cookie in a plastic bag. Was that song by none other than hustle man. Where did you get that Chanel purse. I'll trade you for it. I got some old steaks in the fridge . Hustle Man you the same way every year I rest my case. I love you Gabriel Union Allred I rest my case to. I am hustle man. And hustle is my middle name I rest my case Thomas Allred Jr and Princess Jasmine .

I mean Gabriel Union Allred. Girl you see this. He's on house arrest. They put him on house arrest because they think he can't handle his money. But I'll talk to you later. That's a rich mutha f*cker if you got the police station putting you on house arrest because you made to much money. My husband is Superman everybody say hello to Thomas Allred Jr. He's a genius business professional. He knows exactly what he's doing don't you. Hell no Gabriel Union Allred the cookies are burning. Did I tell yall we burnt cookie up in here. Gabriel Union Allred. Damn I rest my case. One more thing Thomas Allred Jr rest his case. Eat up them damn cookies. Don't stop until every single one of them cookies gone I rest my case. Now send the message.

They got Thomas Allred Jr entering my movie as a movie as a cop.You know that boy really is a cop. You gonna answer to someone. Did you hear that. Professionally or not he sounds for real. That's because he ain't quoting lines he means what he says. Gabriel who wrote this script for you. A man called Superman. Thomas Allred Jr is a man called Superman. He's a cop for god sakes Gabriel. And professionally I think he wants some booty from you Gabriel. My movie talks about there's a s*x scene. Listen Thomas Allred Jr put your hand on the nape of her neck. You have no idea what your doing do ya. The nape of her neck. That's the bottom of her head Thomas. Now action. Are you a cop Thomas. Yes I am but you will be alright in police protection. Thomas watch what your saying to me and cut. That's a wrap for today Gabriel and Thomas Allred Jr . How did you think we did Gabriel. Thomas there's more than acting. Can I come and join you for something to eat. You may sit down it you want to. When I get paid I'm a buy a mansion for me and you. Give me a mansion Thomas you still are not going to get none from me at least. I'm sorry that I had to tell you this. Are you ready baby. Yes Kobe Bryant . Alright let's get out of this place to eat somewhere else. Stop I need to get my purse off of the table. I can't find it here it is Gabriel Union Allred.

Ok now that you see that I'm with Kobe Thomas what are you going to do to me? I'm happy for you. To see you with someone that is nine times better than me is incredible. I just wish that I would have treated you better when I had you. Places everyone action. So you standing here . And I'm standing here . Thomas you better be professional . Because of you I'm a marry Kobe. Thomas this is your scene right here. What is wrong with him. 1234.what happened with us is just a faze baby. Gabriel Union Allred I'm much better than that. You need to wrap it up. This is my movie Gabriel Union Allred. I've been working on this the whole time that we was apart. And if you want to talk you need to holler at me. Because I'm here for you you special. And someday I'll win your heart back. Watch and see dont I. Look keep my manuscript to yourself. As Kobe enters the scene. Thomas Allred Jr and his wife of 11 years separate. Walk away Thomas I am going to but not before I shake the hand of the winner. I'm mean the NBA champion and you thought that I was talking about you. Kobe good to see you.

Thomas Allred Jr how you doing. I'm be professional. And you bra. I'm holding it down. I can prove it to you. Kobe kissed Gabriel in front of Thomas. Champion ships don't last forever Kobe Bryant. Yes they do. You just ain't never had one. I looked and Gabriel and I gave back just as good as I could get. I said. Y'all be professional you know that there diseases all over the place.

There we go. Can I ask you a question. Thomas Allred Jr . I don't think you want to play this game. I didn't think so. Come on Gabriel get in my ride. Time to switch up episodes. We do be professional. Get Thomas out of here right now. The sugar is in the candy . It makes common sense. How many time I have to tell you. That I love you Gabriel Union Allred. You just need to give up. I'm getting ready to marry Kobe. Yeah and man don't f*ck with me. And do f*ck with Gabriel. Watch that boy. Thomas go sit down. I said go sit down muthaf*cker. What do you want me to do with you . Your just a yellow belly Thomas Allred Jr. And your girl seen right through you. Keep your a** on the bench NBA champs coming through here . Go back in time. Make Gabriel Union Allred a professional. And make your damn self a professional. That's my wife right there. A couple of more years went past. I'm fed up. Thomas Allred Jr we losing everything. Cause of you stupid. You call me stupid honey there's no place but up to go. You can't depend on the movies Thomas Allred Jr. Gabriel Union Allred baby listen to me. My script is blazing. I don't want to here about it Thomas my test is due. And unless you can pay 300000 by sundown today we don't have nothing else to talk about. Thomas Allred Jr pack your bags. Why .

Cause your getting out. You ruined me Thomas Allred Jr with your empty promises . Hold on a second don't you go nowhere. I'm going to get my bestfriend Kobe Bryant on the phone. Hi this is Kobe leave a message at the tone . Baby don't go nowhere. Kobe it's right here officer Reign . Kobe I loaned you some money some time ago. And I was wondering could you let me have 900000 Kobe I appreciate you for doing this for me. Once again this is officer Reign . Thomas Allred Jr. Kobe already gave me his number. I don't get it. He's surpposed to be my boy. He said the next time you are in a jam I'm changing my number. I'm a f*cking million because of you Thomas .

Now I placed back some money to help you get on your feet. Take the money. Baby wait until I get back on my feet . You need to get out Thomas. But what about our kids. That all I have to do is take care of my kids. These aren't your kids anymore. Thomas there's something that I want to say. I want a divorce . But what about my movie script .ain't no way in hell the movies is going to pick up to men playing basketball. Called white men can't jump. I ain't going to happen. Baby I'm telling you I got a new script baby. Called the Jackson five reunion. Ease yourself up off of my steps. I do depend on you Gabriel Union Allred . Kobe depends on me now. Switch episodes . Baby I know that I messed up big time with all of those investment bankers. But I'm here to pay you every penny I every borrowed . Thank you Thomas Allred Jr for looking out for me. Kobe Bryant did the same thing you did. And maintain yourself he got ripped off.

Kobe how is business going lately. What the hell do you care . It's only because this is April fool's day. You see I'm professional don't you honey. May movie paid off . Big time honey. What did you call the movie. Take a look at who talking 3. Leave television alone I'm thinking about writing me a script called I really need my husband back. Baby one second. Can you do a 8:30 .8:30 what do you mean 8:30 our house on the hill is really for you and I.

You crazy. Yeah maybe but I got my wife back from NBA star Kobe Bryant just in the nick of time to. Girl I know that you were s*xing Kobe Bryant. But your my business. And my best friend and I love you Gabriel Union Allred the divorce papers haven't went through yet. And another thing I'm not that girl that you think I am. Kobe and I are just friends we knew you were professional. So we staged alittle plan. 100000 zillion dollars is still safe in your bank account Thomas Allred Jr. That's the answer to the question do we really love each other. Yea we do. Yea we do. You know girl I told you that I love you. I got this perfect script for you. It's called Die Harder . You writing a script called Die Harder. People will laugh in your face. Do you know what I mean baby. Yea baby I know what you mean. Well this is our place. It's gorgeous in here. Be professional and repeat after me. I will not get the baby crib out of lay away. Because our baby room is finished. Courtesy of homes and gardens. Now Gabriel Union Allred will you have this dance with me. Thomas Allred Jr. That's the back to the future song. Time circus now opening. I want to see how much you love me Thomas Allred Jr. Walk this way you can see that I. Have your best interest at heart. breaker breaker 1: 9.Thomas control your self because we'll be back in a second after this movie plays out. Here we go what year is it. 211 get all of your people because Thomas Allred Jr you are now professional pow. That's the end for me. My wife Gabriel Union Allred I want to take. And I'm a need to thank Kobe Bryant I mean NBA champion Kobe Bryant thank you. Green light. Yellow Green light. I am Superman Thomas Allred Jr and I had fun doing this. Kobe this is a movie you didn't have to kiss my girl man. Yes I did Thomas Allred Jr. Well you didn't have to do it like that. Goodnight right now you are professional Daniel son . Listen Daniel son to be professional one more time. I want you to drown your nuts in a hop pot of chicken grease. Thomas Allred Jr act like you have got some damn sense. Thomas I love you professional. I love you to Gabriel Union Allred. I love you. Thomas.

In time you'll see that I'm two steps ahead of you. Gabriel Union Allred. Girl i float like a butterfly sting like a bee. Thomas Allred Jr is the producer of this movie we have here Gabrielle Union Allred. Just stand your ground and you will inherite a fortune. Gabriel Union Allred whatever you do. Don't penalized me for all the years it took to get to the top. The record stores have my two record right now. Imma need you to speak to me. Gabriel Union Allred listen. This is the beginning of something. Why I say its the beginning. Because it is the beginning of something. All I can say is that I don't want to hurt you girl. Because you mean the whole wide world to me. Your manuscript is completed I'm just talking to you right now. Honey I need a real eye opener. Because I'm too legit to quit. And I put my money in your account. Gabriel Union Allred half of my fortune is yours. For rescuing me that night. Every since then yall have been helping me to get my feet. I appreciate y'all. Thank you for making me who I am Gabriel Union Allred. Either way it go I own the street corners. I'm just kidding with you. If you ever think of me. And wonder where did I get all this money from. You can email me at ww- I feel you. Com. Gabriel Union Allred I'm really trying to get in touch with you. I wasn't thinking of this years ago . When you first talked to me. But now I have realized. In other to grow we need each other. Gabriel Union Allred what can I do to make you understand that I'm really in love with you. I wrote this on November 13th 2011 at four thirty in the am. Gabriel Union Allred I hope that this letter finds you well. I'm doing my best out here Gabriel Union. I put Union because that is what I want to do with you. I know that you are here in this town for like a day or two. And I was just wondering. Can I be your chaperone around town honey. I know a place that has the most famous ribs in town it's not chillies. It's backyard burgers. Because when you eat your ribs feel good. Girl I woke up for the ten thousand time with a negative in my checking account and my savings account is closed all because today is Halloween . Thomas Allred Jr. I'm saying hey to everybody. Professionally. Gabriel Union Allred I just can't eat because ain't no food in the refrigerator . Food if your hiding from me. Come on out . It's to early to be look for food. My females act like I ain't got bills. Always supersizing they junk. I need a menu especially for a man's taste. Girl we'll call it Happy Hour. Because not spending money can make a man Happy. And it's depending on what hour it is when he gets his food. I'm saying will decide if he come back our not. Because every nigga in the hood y'all like chillies beans. Gabriel Union Allred you don't understand me. Coming up to the stage is myself and I. I. How are you doing myself in trouble. Well I what are we going to do about this trouble I myself am when we going to tell Gabriel Union Allred the truth that I'm crazy about her. That's the end of my show ladies and gentlemen. What kind of man are you looking for Gabriel Union Allred. I'll settle for a good man at all. One who has his own self motivation about him self. Keep calm I mailed it out to ya. And this was written November 13. 2019 at 5:00 in the morning. There is a good man out here for you Gabriel Union Allred.

You just haven't gave me the chance. I've been by myself all most 8 damn long a** years waiting for somebody who sparked my interest. Then I seen you in a movie called deliver us from Eva . Then I fell in love with you Gabriel Union Allred. And I'm telling the truth. I'm in love with you Gabriel Union Allred. And it's not about paper or s*x. Because I have my own money. And your beautiful but I been saving myself for the perfect mate. Can you understand that Gabriel Union Allred. I'm saying I'm producing your a**. And I would like it if you marry me Gabriel Union Allred. Talk all day. And I'm a tell you yes you are a Zillionaire check your back account Gabriel Union Allred. I have you 1.75 zillion dollars and the people are helping me with everything. So how do you like them apples. I'm in the same boat as you Gabriel Union Allred.

Sitting in my room. The people seem to think that you and would be happy together. I have to seen off this message. My battery on my phone needs recharging. But if your reading this 1.75 zillion dollars is in your bank account. In the case that you didn't hear me. Get your a** up me im a Zillionaire I approve this message. Ill talk to you later Gabriel Union Allred. By the way I'm Thomas Allred Jr. It is nice to finally shake hands with you. I didn't get any sleep the last two business days I have to make sure that each manuscript is right for you book. I'm going to name it in a couple of minutes. Gabriel Union Allred I'm producing you. And you book is called . Believe In Her. By Thomas Allred Jr. Believe In Her. Is the book that I'm writing. I'm a professional with a zillion bucks just to prove it. After my baby account clears Gabriel Union Allred I love you. Your husband Thomas Allred Jr a good man is right in front of you. Talk to me Gabriel Union Allred. Pace yourself I'm only human. Thomas Allred Jr loves Gabriel Union Allred 4 life

I already told you that I am Superman. My manuscript is burning with fire. Like fire. I'd deliver a cure to all elements. This is the only Superman you will ever know or hear of. Don't mess with that boy. I'm on my P's and Q's with you in here. My wife Gabrielle Union Allred is sitting with you. Just take your medicine . I got them December blues. Where nothing seeMs. to go my way. I'm starting my book off in turning to Superman. Thomas begin that story. The gave me just two weeks . Capture everything in my book. The made me say .That I would not tell who they are. I'm from the land of milk and honey. Y'all are going to do me a favor. I'm arguing with myself. In trying to accomplish this destiny. This destiny of mine is horrendous. This destiny of our is horrendous. I want you to see that I am Superman and I'm with you all. My manuscript proves it I am Superman. Listen. I'm doing exactly what I said I was going to do. A said to my mama. That I am going for it all. I'll be damned if North Carolina doesn't have a king. I use this as a memory a keep drawing circles. And now with this movie. Combines with the last two movies. We have us a beast. Superman all of the people want to realize you Superman Thomas Allred Jr. I give to you Angel my Valentine Mr.s. Gabriel Union Allred. I completed my work. Completed your work. Superman is the richest man in the whole wide world. The is you Thomas Allred Jr. We are holding a press conference to see about this. Y'all got a hold a press conference my a**.

Oh my god he's a brute. Listen to me Thomas. Keep on rapping in your manuscript. I will Publish your book for you. Put I am Superman on the shelfs . I want to speak to the people. Thomas we need you to realize that you are a gifted individual. Known as Superman to the business world. I'm a pace myself.

My memoir's consist of each challenge. Thomas Allred Jr. You hear me Thomas Allred Jr. If you go back to sleep you lose the game. What game are we playing. Everybody realize you Superman Thomas Allred jr. You got to much confidence for the world. Let me see how much confidence to takes. Become professional Thomas Allred Jr. Your bank account is 760 zillion dollars. Now it is the Infiniti sign. You ain't got numbers no more you got infinity. Read the paper on you Superman. Here Superman is saving a baby in broad daylight. I took my time Angel Gabriel Union Allred. And I delivered a manuscipt worthy of being looked at. Thomas you ain't got nothing but six more business days. Thats all you got to do Thomas is write your manuscript down. And keep up with those business females.

Everybody looking at me. That's because Thomas Allred Jr. You are the new Superman of the business world. And I am your Angel Gabriel Union Allred. Don't say anything to the press about me. Angel Gabriel Union Allred keep messaging me. A long time ago I dream of you Thomas Allred Jr. This boy no how to communicate. Thank you for being here for me Angel Gabriel Union Allred. I'm going to help you out. But there is one thing that I want form you Thomas Allred Jr. Superman. Your light stick. I got you a new lights stick. Thomas Allred Jr keep your mind on her. For Gabrielle Union Allred is your Angel. And one more time I'm telling you I see and Angel. I got to break the silence Superman Thomas Allred Jr . There Terminator Eddie Murphy. Take your shoes off for me Superman Thomas Allred Jr please .

You writing a book that's a comedy. No this this is a straight up book. Superman Thomas Allred Jr put Eddie Murphy in a column. Yes my Angel Gabriel Union Allred. Something is wrong with you. Look at Will and Jada pinkett Smith running down the hillside.i Cant focus on the future with all this bulsh*t in my head. Calm down Superman. Your future is single and bright. You need a queen Thomas Allred Jr. Be careful who I choose for you. This is the last time I'm giving you a queen. And once these words disappear from your site. The world will realize that you are the one in true Superman over the business sector. Look at the clock its getting close to 6:30. Listen Thomas. I am your f*cking police officer.

And that's Angel Gabriel Union Allred. We need you Superman Thomas Allred Jr to help us ut of our situations that we're in. Can we count on you to help us. Yes. Yes. Yes. Yes. My Superman has got confidence. In of the story. Each story is depicted in front of white people. Superman Thomas Allred Jr will you please come in there please. I thought I gave you and order to unload that truck. You sitting on your a**. Writing in a manuscript. Get off your a** and unload that truck Superman. I already did it.

Thank you Mr. Slate. I already did it. Superman gose back in time hero. Look a here Superman. You famous Thomas Allred Jr. With his Angel Gabriel Union Allred. There you go. Keep your mind on me. Listen Mr. Slate will you let Superman go for today. Let Superman go my a**. This ain't in living color. And Superman ain't know. Keenan every Wayne's. But I'm a tell you what I'll do. Have Superman to go out there and talk to the press for me on this white House situation. Sit your a** down I am and Angel. And you speak accordingly to me. Do you recognize that I am a Angel. Do you recognize that I am a Angel I said in front of every body. It's straight he can go with you. Superman you don't have to work at that place no more I'll get you a better job tomorrow evening. And so it was Thomas Superman Allred Jr. And his Angel Gabriel Union Allred. You keep going. Take on situation after situation.

Trying to look out for the children. In America and East Asia. Superman is hungry y'all. Angel can you feed him. My attitude is adjusted now. These people don't play no games.Thomas everytime I talk to you you getting stronger and stronger. Good looking. Got damn that boy Superman. Got damn I see Superman. You can run but your a** can't hide no more. Listen Thomas. what would you do if a Superman picture really came out. With you in it. Be happy don't worry and be happy. My Angel Gabriel Union Allred. I'm really to see Thomas Jr in my office today. His attitude is complete. Thats my books Superman Thomas Allred Jr. You the one helping everybody. What do we call you Superman. Thomas Allred Jr. To the rescue. You see what and Angel can do for you. I'm glad you picked Superman Angel Gabriel Union Allred. Mama I'm going to take him to where his cape is. Angel Gabriel Union Allred Superman can fly. Look Thomas I know that you Superman. And you can hear me Thomas Allred Jr. Put on your cape I give you.

It's a cloaking device Superman. The reason that I give this to you. You're making it out of the zone. Sacrifice nothing for goodness. And always look to the hills where your help comth from. What are you going to do when you see me Thomas. Say my Angel Gabriel Union Allred .I love you thanks. That's the end of the movie right there. I am Superman Thomas Allred Jr. And this is my Angel Gabriel Union Allred. To the rescue. Clock that boy and girl. Thanks for working with me Gabriel Union Allred. You are very welcome Superman. Think of us when you read every chapter of this book. Black on black it is important. Superhero styles. Superhero styles Angel Gabriel Union Allred. Superhero styles Superman Thomas Allred jr Superhero styles forevers forever. I Arrest my Thomas Allred Jr. Superhero styles Angel Gabrielle Union Allred. That show is it.

Gabriel I think it's time that I say how I feel. We getting married in a couple months. And its you I want to be with. If you have a song in your heart. Come and sing it for me. Be thankful that you got me Gabriel Union Allred. Girl see how respect you. Honey I wrote you a manuscipt. You better not not play with me. Listen Gabriel as I write you his love letter. In through out the pages of our manuscript. I can see a bit of joy. On her pillow. I want you to know that I appreciate everything. That you have to offer my Angel Lois Lane Gabriel Union Allred. This is your Superman and I approved this message. Gabriel love you before my heart. I'm not concerned with how we'll live. I'm just concerned about the living part of it. In time youll see me as your superhero. Superman Thomas Allred Jr. You got know idea Angel Lois Lane Gabriel Union Allred. That I always protect you in my dreaMs.. I protect you in my dreaMs. to Thomas Allred Jr . Then I am supposed to say that I love you girl right here. I been in love with you Thomas Allred Jr. Gabriel Union Allred Camelot manuscript. Thomas I really care for you. Ditto my love ditto. The boy really is Superman.

You put people watching me Thomas. Now take the you put off of there. People watching me. Now you get what I'm saying. Thomas you are the right person. The right person for what Angel Lois Lane Gabriel Union Allred. Thomas right person for this out fit. Here you go. Superman were this every day. Of his life Thomas Allred Jr. This how its going to be Superman. Can the world know my name is Superman. Angel Lois Lane Gabriel Union Allred? What do you think this is Thomas Superman issued. Christopher Reeves Thomas. Allowed you to the haves this suit. I am totally Greatful. Let's see if I can where the suit. The whole community is after me. After you finish that manuscript the whole world will be looking up to you. Can we fly together. It's too dang windy. You got to keep on that suit for 7 years. Can you hear me Thomas. Yes I can hear you just fine my Angel Lois Lane Gabriel Union Allred. There's another thing I want to tell you is. I wish you would ever cheat on me. Superman Thomas Allred Jr. That's not going to happen my Angel Lois

Lane Gabriel Union Allred. Can you hear me Thomas .Can you hear me Superman. Get ready to turn your manuscript in. This is my manuscript. There might be some like it. But this one right here is Gabriels Union Allred. Angel Lois Lane Gabriel Union Allred manuscript. Sit back and let the flavor take effect. Thomas do you need somebody. Angel Lois Lane Gabriel Union Allred. I do.

I ain't playing I'm going to pull some teeth if I find out who eating my strawberry shortcake. Superman you got to come down we have guests over. Superman I liked to introduced to you. Mr.. James Earl Jones. He's a little stronnie to be Superman ain't. Why Mr.. James Earl Jones. From coming to America and The Lion King. How you doing Sir. Thomas it's about time you made it up here to see me. So you knew of me Mr. Jones. I knew of you. Kid I raised you Superman. Baby. Yes Thomas I'll be with you in a minute. And when I said I am your father Simba . I nearly start laughing. Because we can all see you Superman. You mean to through the TV screen. Thomas we can see you whenever you go to commercial.

Gabrielle honey what is the saying. He saying were watching you Thomas. Everyone. Everyone in the world is turned into your channel. But why Gabriel. Because of you we see what the true meaning of life is Thomas. But I've been nothing to hurt anyone. And we know that you never will. Go back through your list. A books and movies and read them out loud. What are you saying Gabrielle. Happy birthday to everybody in celebration of you and I. Gabriel this real you really my wife. I told you Thomas this is real. Not the book or movie I'm talkin about. I've saying the feeling between us Gabrielle. Is it real are you really my wife in real life. Gabriel are you my wife. Hell no I'm not your wife. This relationship is all pretty platonic . I'm sorry. Superman of nothing to be sorry for. And all these people really watching me. Say hello to home improvement man. Tim Allen. Listen to me Thomas.

If you listen to me you'll go along way. Women come and woman go . And Thomas we know that you been hurt before. You got now idea how much and how famous you are. People are walking around in Japan talking about you Superman. Just followed steps that we give to you. Tim Allen is Gabriel my wife. Yes she is your wife. Establish yourself Superman. Just sir Mr. James Earl Jones. Mr.. Tim Allen. I have nothing in the world no money no clothes and knowing that it makes it hard for me to be the man that I can be. Realize that everyone can see you. How Gabrielle. Through a cable access channel. Thomas we've been with you all this time. And were not about to leave you now. Time Allen talk to him. He get no clue that. A miracle is about to happen in his life. Thomas Allred Jr. This is my only chance. To introduce you to. Mr.. Time Enforcement Officer Charlie Sheen. And Emilio estevez. And Lou diamond Phillips. And Kiefer Sutherland. These are our young guns. Your bank account is 100 zillion in Zurich dollars. Thank You Thomas for going out and getting those bad guy. A look yall. Speak take your time. I didn't do nothing but help a man up when he was down. Sometimes that's exactly thats to be a superhero. We give the you Thomas Kristen Bean. Hey Thomas. This is almost the end of the year Thomas. A year that we will not forget. We want you to know that where counting on you to be Superman. And if Christopher Reeves here. He would say job well done Superman. A Kristen i love you so much. I love you too Thomas Allred Jr. My dream is that you have everything that you wish for. Thank you. I saved a friend's life. And I got shot. And I forgot who I was. Through rehabilitation. And the work of every agency around the world. Today I remember. That I am Superman. Thomas Allred Jr. And the world believes in Me. Because we all believe in God. That is all I can remember. But look. What I don't remember. I think that it's okay. Cause we have fought hard as a people. Through thick and thin. To be there for one another. Because we understood that. In our family. There must be hope and justice. And that is the reason for the police show on TV. Shows are there so we would never give up hope. In each other. Superman how you doing come and sit down. One more thing. I thank Gabriel and everybody for saving my life.

We got some unfinished business to talk about Superman Thomas Allred Jr. Seeing how I'm half of your business. I believe that you independently give me half of your income Superman. Type Superman in there. Thomas Allred Jr. You are a Superman professional in the business world. Write Superman on the top of the screen. Put with Angel with it. You didn't realize Gabriel Union Allred was and Angel Superman. Write Superman Thomas Allred Jr. In your manuscript Thomas Allred jr. I'm listening to every word you say. And I'm not wanting to make a fool out of myself . Making a fool out of yourself is up to me. I am your studio executive host writer Angel Gabriel Union Allred.

Your book is called the way I do this. By me Superman. Realize who you talking to. I'm making you see that you are Thomas Allred Jr. A Superhuman. Superhuman you got enough to deal with. Your the only superhuman I mean out here thats giving our people money. We tested you superhuman. And came up with this suggestion. we are going to make you a star Thomas Allred Jr. Do you have anything to say Thomas. Yes my Angel. I have a lot to say. Get off of that bed and stand up for a minute. Take your folder with you. Your looking incredible. All right now sit back down and read that book to yourself. You already got me my Angel. I can feel your pain. Thomas your pain is apart of you. And I am your angel. Thank you God. You have no idea who got is. But I'm going to prove myself to you. Listen Thomas Allred Jr. We have been testing you for 21 business years. I have Thomas Allred Jr. Instead of we. I have been testing you. In a business aspect. See I got a plan for you. Put everything that I say in your manuscript. Now follow me Thomas Allred Jr. Do you believe in God Thomas Allred Jr . Yes I do. Can you keep a secret. Yes. You are that God you believe in. Tell me more my Angel Gabriel Union Allred. We programmed Thomas Allred jr. What do you have to say about this one. I'm Lucky to be alive thank you my Angel Gabriel Union Allred. I'm am greatful for everything that you do for me and my family and the neighborhood. That boy true to the game. Thomas listen to me. A lot of people. Can rescue you of that situation that your in. Get your a** down here and write that manuscript. It takes time. How much time . Four more business days .Thomas will you be professional. Give me one business day and I'll have it for you. I like you Thomas Allred Jr. You can scratch all you want to. You really can see me. I love you my Angel Gabriel Union Allred. Gabrielle and the industry saved my life. I am Superman Thomas Allred Jr. And I'm thankful. That Gabriel Union Allred. My Angel Gabriel Union Allred cares enough about me to want a Superman in her house hold.You Getting it Thomas. Just like i first did you. When you messed up.

I put you in the big house. My Angel Gabriel Union Allred you put me in prison yes I put your a** in prison Thomas Allred Jr. Thomas you need to understand this I am your angel. Listen I know that I seem rough on you. But Im making you a professional Superman. My Angel Gabriel Union Allred. I am a police officer. You are a police officer because I said that you are one Thomas. We can heal up your body. Where youve been shot by and unknown vagrant. Thomas take unknown vagrant off of there. Thomas what did I tell you to do. You told me to write the manuscript Angel Gabrielle Union Allred. Thank you for saving me Superman Thomas Allred Jr. It really is no problem now miss Lane. What did you just call me Superman. I called you Angel Louis Lane Gabriel Union Allred. And this is Superman Thomas Allred Jr. Signing off. Thomas you ain't got but two more weeks. But you can send the manuscript in.

Thomas thinking about them other girls gets your a** burnt. I trust in you my Angel Lois Lane Gabrielle Union Allred. I said that I would try and make something out of myself my Angel Lois Lane Gabrielle Union Allred. So far what do you think of me. There go Superman right there honey. In the hopes that you read this letter Thomas Allred Jr. We got a beach house waiting for you. With 7000 women waiting for you. Take a pic of the ones you'd like to talk to. I choose Angel Lois Lane Gabriel Union Allred. To be my wife and my soulmate. I feel like I'm losing stature. Just wearing the same clothes all the time. These clothes are state issued. Thomas Allred Jr. Everybody wants you to become the new Superman. What do you think about it. Since I was 5 years old. I always have believe in Superman. I'll do the job everybody asks me to do. Thomas Allred Jr from this day forth. You are the leader of the US world commission. And we invoke you with the powers of Superman Thomas Allred Jr .Just realizing that all this is real I thank you everyone of you. I got no plans to ever take from you people. You got a couple weeks to control yourself. My Angel Lois Lane Gabriel Union Allred I'm Superman. One more thing Thomas Allred Jr. You are Superman. But I'm your police officer Angel. Lois Lane a Gabriel Union Allred contract.

I'm a professional and you know it clap your hands Gabriel Union Allred. I just wanted to say that I need you. More than anything in this life Gabriel Union Allred. Thomas Allred Jr. Don't get sentimental Thomas Allred Jr. I come from a long line of don't care. And I'm home sick. Gabriel your bank account will tell you the truth about me. See I'm a Zillionaire because. I believe in myself and my community. If I do have my bank account. What have you do of me. Thomas Allred Jr. I just want you to be happy and Happy because Jesus loves all of us. Time is getting cooler. Meaning I got to more book to send in . You know Gabriel that you have to give it to me. On my improving your situation. Thomas Allred Jr I like you Thomas Allred Jr because your straight up because look Thomas my account has seven zeros and 1.75 zillion dollars in it. A Gabriel do you have your money. Yeah I got it. Have anniversary sweetheart .

My story begins. In a house too small for anyone to stay in. My name is Thomas Allred jr . And this is Superman. The lucky charm bracelet. Superman Gabriel Union needs to hear from you. If Gabriel Union pleases. Tell her I will be there in 1 second. The reason why I summoned you Superman is that somebody has been. Going into the job of lucky charMs.. This isn't you Superman. No my princess Jasmine. Thomas. No Mr.s. Gabrielle Union. I haven't went to the jar of lucky charm. Superman is professional he wouldn't tell us a lie. You making a fool out of me. You no that man is professional Thomas. Listen Gabriel Union. These are too many diamonds in your lucky charMs.. I'm a help this boy with you. Listen to those diamond sparkle . My heartbeat is telling me some trouble is coming. Write the damn manuscript. And sit back. And watch your stardom come on you. As if you were drugged. Thomas I have but one thing to say to you. Thomas keep your position. We all are watching you. This boy can see. I had no idea that Superman is Thomas Allred Jr. Girl I left you because of Superman now I want you back. You can see me Thomas . Change the direction. You hold the position to that girl's heart. That man loves Gabriel Union.

They talking about her on the radio show. I will find you Gabriel Union. Didnt I tell you Thomas is a major superstar. Come here Gabriel Union let me talk to you for a minute. It's about time that boy is saying what he feels. He can rap his a** off if he wanted to. Some woman needs help Thomas. They got the wrong mutha f*cker for that job. I aint the Superman from the movies. Let me ask you a question. Is it you and Gabriel Union forever. If she wants it to be. Stand your ground Superman. Yes it is me and Gabriel Union forever. You need to wash your f*cking hands off I'm fending to give you a plate. Well damn Gabriel Union. A lot of people are watching. That girl famous as hell. Clean up my sh*t. She said clean up my sh*t. Gabriel I know you better than this. Clean up all of my sh*t Thomas. Okay my love. Listen to me. Do exactly what I say to do. Take hold of the manuscript. And write your name on it. Now when you look at again. Read your name of it. The reason I said this is because. I've already cleaned up all your sh*t. Keep reading girl. Where your reading gla**es at. There's one more thing Superman forgot to tell you Gabriel Union. I'm doing this for your hand in marriage. In the beginning there was Superman Thomas Allred Jr. And than there came along a police officer. Name Gabriella Union. I put $7,500 million dollars in your bank account. Both of these stories that I'm writing. The both of us can realize the importance of this nature. Girl I'm waiting on this money to mature in my bank account. I wrapped the game up with a smash hit .I won't give in. Off one of my upcoming albuMs.. I want you to stand waiting for me firm. A coward dies many deaths but you and me are going to die but one. Each one of us has Superman's abilities.Im famous because I listen to what other people think. I want you to eat sh*t and die Thomas Allred Jr. Baby open the door up. Will you baby please.

You coming for more sh*t. Superman Thomas Allred Jr. No but I'm a get you a charm bracelet. For the lucky charMs. that you lost. Do mention it to me. Cause they may deliver it early as tomorrow. Delivery for Superman Thomas Allred Jr. Sign right here Thomas Allred Jr. Give that girl 200000 for bringing my wife her present when it was so desperately needed. You the most arrogant man that I ever seen Superman Thomas Allred Jr. What you going to do Superman Thomas Allred Jr. I'm going to get down on one knee and pray you marry me and ask you would you please except my gift of friendship. Because Gabriel it is a gold charm bracelet with diamonds charMs.. And a diamond key and lock. One more thing . The lucky charMs. that you said where missing. This should cover them. Its 700 million dollars. For grocery expenses. You know I'm a spend that money. Superman Thomas Allred Jr. I wouldn't have it any other way. The mystery of the charm bracelet is sovled. Hallelujah Superman Thomas Allred Jr. Don't say nothing about the charm bracelet being missing. We were just testing you Superman Thomas Allred Jr. Take your money back Superman Thomas Allred Jr. Im a professional police officer. And a deal is a deal. Because I know that police officers are taking a lot of slack about giving the money back. That is why we give to charity sweetheart.

I got me a police officer. He goes by the name of superhero Thomas Allred Jr. Now that you have your suit on. Come and show everybody that you Superman. Ladies and gentleman I bring to you Superman Thomas Allred Jr. Put your cape on. They believe you really they Superman Thomas Allred Jr. I am their Superman Angel Lois Lane Gabriel Union Allred. Recognize the costume don't make the man. You there Superman. My baby is hurt can you get me something to drink for him. Yes I can. Oh yeah Superman. Your manuscript script is the bomb diggity. Remember what I told you. Yes Frankie. Become Superman. I am Superman Frankie. Thank You Frankie for everything. Hey Frankie thank You Man. I got you Superman. The reason I liked you Thomas Allred Jr is. Because you never gave up when people was attacking you. Frankie man I love you. Can you here me Thomas. This is off the charts professional. We don't want gravy and your shoes Thomas Allred Jr. You know how much your are worth. They cost a grip. exactly. Listen to Tyrese Thomas. Put that fast and the furious soundtrack in there. My name is Superman Thomas Allred Jr. And I'm looking for super people. For the next movie. Called Superman Thomas Allred Jr and Angel Lois Lane Gabriel Union Allred No Surrender combat style the movie coming to white people theaters soon . I got a two minute clip of No Surrender combat style. What the hell Thomas I outta beat your a**. Angel Lois Lane Gabriel Union Allred I'm sorry. That way our wedding anniversary. I might have bit tipsy. Tipsy my a** you showed them people my a** on purpose. Baby why would I do that. Because you like my a**. Girl I'm Superman Thomas Allred Jr and boy I'm Angel Lois Lane Gabriel Union Allred. And this is these are the breaks. Angel Lois Lane Gabriel Union Allred I love you. Thanks for my chance to be in your life. A mountain to a mole hill. Superman Thomas Allred Jr I need to button that suit I mean. What's stopping you Superman Thomas Allred Jr. From taking off the suit here in front of me. Nothing.

I need Thomas Allred Jr. Gabriel Union Allred Surperman Thomas Allred Jr is and unknown for sure. Who's going to take time out to groom Thomas Allred Jr . I will. You hear me Thomas Allred Jr. I am your wife. Gabriel Union Allred. And I have been watching you for 21 years. The first thing I want to know is. Do you want to take a bath with me Thomas Allred Jr. I put my lucky charm on you. This is a to manager. Do not worry about the audience listening to us. Listen to me Thomas Allred Jr. you might as well give my lucky charMs. to me. Surperman Thomas Allred Jr. I didn't mean it come back. Thomas. Angel Lois Lane Gabriel Union Allred I'm only going to the bathroom. If I go with you to the bathroom Surperman Thomas Allred Jr would you think something is wrong with me. Girl Ill do everything to get you to follow me to the bathroom. In my dreaMs. I'm with you in the bathroom Surperman Thomas Allred Jr. Thomas you know Ill do anything for you. Get Punk Daddy out the bathroom for me. Angel Lois Lane Gabriel Union Allred. Girl and Punk Daddy in the bathroom. Should the people talk Gabriella . Punk Daddy is a Plummer for instance Surperman Thomas Allred Jr. He does a great job . Punk Daddy you got my pipes fixed yet. Keep communicating. You got to communicate with Punk Daddy. Superman. James Earl Jones cut that out. There is a Punk Daddy in each and everyone of us. Not really ginger Jones

I'm a pack my stuff and head for broad way. I need someone to look out for me. Could that be something you would be interested in Angel Lois Lane Gabriel Union Allred. Listen Superman Thomas Allred Jr. I think to myself that you are a wonderful day. Gabriel Union Allred is in love with Thomas Allred Jr. I keep writing these manuscripts. In hopes that change will come. You see my bank has not cleared yet all of my money it is in suspension . I just realized that you are a dime piece Ms. Angel Lois Lane Gabriel Union Allred. Princess Jasmine honey I do mean Princess Gabriel Union.

Thomas look see here these white people want us to be together. And I'm lucky I found a lucky charm like you. It is my hope that you and me. Can keep our cool while we get this money. Cut the got damn light off and come to bed Superman Thomas Allred Jr. Give me time with you Superman. The next morning I straightened out bed out. I couldn't believe that she kissed me on my hands. As we lay together. Somehow me and you. Is what Id tell Gabriel if it really happened. That im speaking. The truth is.

That I'm just a single man. In a world that don't approve of us.Me and you Gabriel Union Allred. Just a little more and I'll start explaining. See the way see things is. Gabriel Union Allred you beautiful and I would like to know you. Do you know what I'm saying. Christmas is coming up in a few weeks. I'm doing everything I can to get to know you. It's a set up. Thats got me thinking about you the way I do. Gabriel Union Allred your bodys talkin to me on the movie screen. And I just want you to understand you is all I need. He make sense out of his damn stuff. That's why we call him Superman Thomas Allred Jr. That's because he never does give up. Take your time Thomas. I'm trying Gabriel Union Allred. Tell me this? Yeah what is it honey.

How would you feel if I made love to you on the beach in front of every one Superman Thomas Allred Jr. Where every you want to be when the moment occurres . Thomas Allred Jr I'll pull of my clothes and jump into the shower . Are you coming . Give me a minute. You timming me. And girl in my dreaMs. you would say yeah I'm timming you Superman Thomas Allred Jr. And I leave the room. Until I can get hold of myself. Because Gabrielle Union Allred all I dream. Is that I make love to you. Be professionals. Thomas you see I'm hot. Is what I dreamed you said to me. So I ravished you. And your body.

Until my name called out. In my dreaMs. of you. Everyone of them. The people just now getting home with me. Gabriel Union Allred. I had a great evening. Tell my Superman that I love him Thomas Allred Jr. I'll try to give him the message Gabriel Union Allred. And could you please give Gabriel my love. I love you Thomas Allred Jr. I love to. Gabriel princess Union Allred. I don't smoke or drink anything Gabriel Union Allred. That's a good thing. Superman Thomas Allred Jr. My community thinks that I'm professional. You are professional SupermanThomas Allred jr. I see terminator Eddie Murphy. Hey Eddie Murphy. That's Terminator Eddie Murphy mutha f*cker. It's time you became professional. Superman Thomas Allred jr.and Gabriel Union Allred. Terminator Eddie Murphy. Listen to me Thomas give Terminator Eddie Murphy your number. Keep listening Terminator. I want you. To stand up for my people. Yes Gabriel Union Allred. And Superman will you have his back. Of course I will anything you say Gabriel Union Allred will happen. We professional. My dream ended like this. A kiss goodnight is what you get from me. Okay Superman but you need to make it quick Thomas. That's when you up and disappear. About 6 in the morning. I had a dream of you all night long. I'm Gabriel Union Allred and have anybody seen my charm bracelet that my Surperman Thomas Allred Jr brought for me. It took to days for me to almost get over that dream and start writing again. I'm use to dreaming about you Gabriel Union Allred until I can't say anything but you are beautiful. And being professional I just have one thing left to say . Gabriel Union Allred your my lucky charm. Are you hungry Superman Thomas Allred Jr. Has a thing for you Gabriel Union Allred. Now that you'll proved your point Surperman Thomas Allred Jr it wasn't a dream that we both we're having. Talk to me Thomas Allred Jr. I can't . Why . Because I'm dreaming of you Gabriel Union Allred. I dreaming of you. One sweet day Gabriel Union Allred.

Bring back Thomas Allred Jr to me. Yes ma'am I'm here right here for you. This boy has no idea what I'm going to do to him. Thomas can you hear me okay Thomas. Can you hear me. Yes I can hear you I got to stand up. You have Superman hereing. Thomas I know that you trust us in the meantime. I want you to write your manuscript everyday. I had a feeling I would be doing this. Look Thomas Allred Jr people are watching you. Is it good or bad the reason that there watching. You got to shave up your face. And keep up on your chest fresh and clean. Do you know who this is Thomas Allred Jr. No I don't. This is your Angel Lois Lane Gabrielle Union Allred. And I'm saying to you. Baby don't go back to that world you was in. Never sweetheart. My Angel Lois Lane Gabriel Union Allred. I love you. Will you be my valentine on business working Valentine's working weekend? Thomas I'd love to be with you. Thomas will you control yourself if you can hear me Thomas what is my name. Angel Lois Lane Gabriel Union Allred. And this is a Camelot manuscript. The whole community is waiting for you.

To come out of that room. I know what you getting read to be thinking. And I can't condone you making love to anyone else. Angel Lois Lane Gabriel Union Allred I wouldn't. I know that you wouldn't Thomas Allred Jr. But I see your situation. Listen hear Thomas Allred Jr. If you don't worry about a piece of p**sy Thomas Allred Jr. A piece p**sy will come to you. Thomas is a Zillionaire professional. I only have one destination and that's to the top of this game. Somehow I'm working with the best female in my city. And I didn't even know it was true. How I feel about this is. Ten more checks going out to. Women professional League championship. Hickory North Carolina. You see your p**sy is coming. This boys talking about anything. Half common sense Thomas Allred Jr. Introduce me as your woman. My woman is Angel Lois Lane Gabriel Union Allred. Now that you see that I really care about you. I'm a do for you this one thing Lois Lane Gabriel Union Allred is sure to go bananas. When that tell her this. That her contract is about to run out. And I'm rushing to her rescue. Because my contract is forever and ever. Now you see how woman are. Say forever Angel Lois Lane Gabriel Union Allred. Forever Superman Thomas Allred Jr. Baby I really need you. And I really need you to Superman. Look at us Thomas we are acting like little kids. Cause in my heart we never grew up Gabriel Union Allred. My Angel Lois Lane Gabriel Union Allred. This is my new beginning without my momma. Thomas don't give a f*ck. What I tell you.

What did you tell me my Superman Thomas Allred Jr. I told you that I will fight the good fight. It's happening I'm becoming a true Angel. Angel Lois Lane Gabriel Union Allred. It's happening to me too. What is it Superman Thomas Allred Jr. I'm becoming the Superman truth. We are the truth. And let Justice Lead the way. Put house Superman Thomas Allred Jr. I put my whole neighborhood. In Hollywood California houses. With the rent unheard of. Thank you Gabriel Union Allred. For saving my life. Superman got a job for you. What's that my Angel Lois Lane Gabriel Union Allred. I got to get you out of that suit. First and then Ill tell you what I want you to do. Superman Thomas Allred Jr. Be professional you got a week until you get your contract.

Drink some of the bubbly soda out of the can. Just a minute Honey I will. I'm making you go through everything that we went to. That is before we got to see our contracts. I'm at work for you Angel Lois Lane Gabriel Union Allred. Y'all give the damn boy his contract. I don't know to say to you Jesus Superman Thomas Allred Jr. Why don't you have anything on. Because the Superman suit is all that I've been wearing. Girl come here and let me see what you working here. Superman Thomas Allred Jr. I don't hear a thing. Superman Thomas Allred Jr you know I love you act like you got common sense. Take this towel and cover up your a** with. That's good thinking on your part my Angel Lois Lane Gabriel Union Allred. Right now I'm just a static. Because both of us got a contract. Baby I all the time want to see you. Whatever happens keep your pants on Thomas. How professional is that. So far so good Superman Thomas Allred jr. I need an Angel.

Angel Lois Lane Gabriel Union Allred. Can you be there for me listen. yeah I can be there for you my husband Superman Thomas Allred Jr. My wife Gabriel Union Allred. Thomas my name is. Angel Lois Lane Gabriel Union Allred. Thomas. Superman Thomas Allred Jr. You complete me Superman Thomas Allred Jr. By it time you get this Angel Lois Lane Gabriel Union Allred. I'll be with you. This is the way it's going to be. Angel Lois Lane Gabriel Union Allred.

What Superman Thomas Allred Jr. The dog is getting in my suit. Crypto I warned you about this. You dogs name is crypto. Angel Lois Lane Gabriel Union Allred. I know that it's kinda crazy isn't. Thomas. I mean Superman Thomas Allred Jr. Put your suit back on . Cause off my dog Crypto. Just give me a minute and I'll put my tights back on. Be a gentleman Thomas Allred Jr. Angel Lois Lane Gabriel Union Allred honey there's something that I want to tell you. What is it Superman Thomas Allred Jr you see me doing something. Girl I'm about to eat something. This relationship is finally official girls he is Superman. Girl I just really got a Taste for some Cenna biscuits. And to top it all off. I want me some pieces of fruit. If Superman wants fruit he gets fruit. Girl Ill bit that Apple. Be strong enough to come and kiss Superman Thomas Allred Jr. Listen girl. This is a higher level understanding. I'm looking at the future with this Angel Lois Lane Gabriel Union Allred. Superman goes in it hard. I do mean Superman Thomas Allred Jr. So it's on. Super Thomas Allred Jr people know what you up to. Then they know you and I Angel Lois Lane Gabriel Union Allred. Take care of each other. Without a f*cking doubt Superman. How do I look. I like your suit it's on backwards. See here Superman Thomas Allred Jr. The pants are easy to put on. Thomas what kind of manuscript are you sitting writing. One of adventure y'all. Angel Lois Lane Gabriel Union Allred . That proves it.i ain't giving up until people see who I am. And you know this consist of. Being with family. Superman Thomas Allred Jr. Ill do anything to get you out of that situation that you in. My Angel Lois Lane Gabriel Union Allred. You already have. Now Superman Thomas Allred Jr has been brought to you by. Another chance and production. Gabriel Union Allred I love you. Baby spread the word. That Superman Thomas Allred jr is yours. My Angel Lois Lane Gabriel Union Allred. Just end your case Superman Thomas Allred Jr. I love you Angel Lois Lane Gabriel Union Allred. This is a real a** problem.

Because I'm in love with you to Superman Thomas Allred Jr. Honey realize you beautiful. And that I will do anything for you. Can I get a kiss for short time shakes. I need you to big girl from me. And be in love with your Superman Thomas Allred Jr. Listen Angel Lois Lane Gabriel Union Allred. Girl when you need me. Don't hesitate to call me . You see im professional. I'm watching you sit on your a** and get famous Thomas. Superman Thomas Allred jr. Is my manuscript ready and completed. This is your manuscript. Superman Thomas Allred jr.and his Angel. Queen Angel Lois Lane Gabriel Union Allred.

Are out of this hotel get Crypto Thomas. I mean my Superhero Superman Thomas Allred jr. You did the right thing Thomas. Angel Lois Lane Gabriel Union Allred. You did the right thing. Give him a contract professionals. He has proved his self to Gabriel Union Allred. He truly is a superhero. Call him Superman Thomas Allred Jr and I'm professional you can call me Angel Lois Lane Gabriel Union Allred. And this is the final rendition of a manuscript. I'm just realizing. That my dog has superpowers to. People can call him Crypto. Good by every body. I'm just chilling right here reading a book called Superman Thomas Allred Jr. People look at this. Thomas and I are Zillionaires. Am I preaching to the choir Thomas Allred Jr. No Angel Lois Lane Gabriel Union Allred your not. Say your peice . My Angel. Say your peice Gabriel Union Allred Angel peace. There's nothing that I love more than a woman that knows her peace. Everyone good night. I hope that you enjoyed our manuscript . All of the proceeds go to Gabriel Union and family. Even though I am Superman Thomas Allred Jr. I'm a bust panties open. If you want me to Gabriel Union Allred. My Angel. I'm a be finishing up a new manuscript. Called This lucky charm. The proceeds belong to you. Will you marry me . My Angel Lois Lane Gabriel Union Allred. Girl I get my strength from just knowing that your making movies. I'll be with you shortly. Trust me. I'm the only Superman that you were ever know of the business world. The business is looking right on us right now. Id take you out the hood if I could in a second Thomas. I'm a professional police officer and I just want you to know that you can have my vote in the next coming election. And Gabriel Union one more thing I have a dollar to my name and girl I watched you. It accured to me that as a Zillionaire we both haven't went on a date. I'm a tare this dollar in half. And give it to you. Some how I'll see you. My Angel Gabriel Union Allred.

I just figured out why you so important. Gabriel Union Allred. It's because you professional and I'm professional.i look up at the stars. To see where my help coming from. It comes from you. Gabriel Union Allred. No matter what I say to you. You will always be my girlfriend. You are the first lady in my life. Everyday is like a new beginning with you Gabriel Union Allred. You think that I'm going to far. Than you need to be more professional. I can go farther and than some . Because all of my life I've have waited for you. When you read this Gabriel Union Allred. Don't give up on people. Because the ma**es taught me how to fish. What I'm saying Gabriel Union Allred. Is generally I don't do this but I'm a go ahead and keep the party going . Tell me if I'm making the right sense. Because I'm Nia Long and I'm Gabriel Union Allred. People use me Thomas Allred Jr. For my generosity as if I'm supposed to do that. And from reading your words of wisdom on the fact that you love me. I approve this book message. Because he can back it up with cash. Thomas Allred Jr never in my life has some body demonstrated such a bravery and courage as you have.

Thomas Allred Jr keep reading your book give me once second. And now I'm going to take care of you for helping me. Gabriel Union Allred my lady I need know reward. I have sense about myself. It's true Thomas Allred Jr that you are a true gentleman. All I want to do is lay my weapons down. And see what the business world has to offer a begger like me. You can have my hair apron to give you strength in the days of battle. Thank you so much Ms. queen soon to be Gabriel Union Allred. I'll cherish this forever. Do you cherish this. Forever. Yes I do my lady. No matter what happens. I will all keep this scarf with me. Take the scarf off of my head to Thomas Allred Jr no my lady my heart only belongs to My fair lady and that is Gabriel Union Allred. I'm a see you win Thomas Allred Jr. I shall win after I beat you hypocrite that lie on the name of greatness. Gabriel Union Allred don't give up. Or in. Say never have you come to a decision yet. On the up coming prenup schewels. That's right. Thomas Allred Jr . I do care for you. But I'm this just isn't my kinda day. Do you hear what I'm saying to you Thomas Allred Jr. You don't need to be ashamed my Queen Gabriel Union Allred. May I come at you again. You can come at me anytime that you want Thomas Allred Jr. This is amazing. Gabriel Union Allred you ain't seen the half of it. I am a true to life Queen. Thomas Allred Jr works for the people in the salt mines. Gabriel Union Allred where ever you go. I will be there to protect. I'll be with you if I could my lady. Get your a** up and win some battle's for me Thomas Allred Jr. I think to myself is there a place where a King can use the bathroom. My lady named Gabriel Union Allred you are special as the moon. That sits right up there in the sky. Now we are special. Thomas Allred Jr . In a movie I'll play . A devil worshipping princess. And I'll be a devil worshipping King who is to fall in love with his princess. Thomas Allred Jr I need to see you take you time. Gabriel Union Allred. You are here by repremmanded to stay on the farm land. There's and Injustice going on somewhere. And I shall find it.Thomas you ain't thinking about me remember my scarf .

I keep it right next to my heart. If I could do anything. I could use a Pepsi right now. I'll go and get you one. This amateur theater has been brought to you by Crest and mouth wash soap. I'm getting ready to go to work on the prairie how many hours must you sleep Thomas Allred Jr. Until another day is here Gabriel Union Allred my princess my Queen. Than go to sleep Thomas Allred Jr. That's King Knight Sir Thomas Allred Jr. You can call me Superman. Superman. The whole community is out to get me. Gabriel Union Allred. I'll put my life on the line to rescue you. The same way that I'm doing right now. Any others want to question me. Because in the day of danger. I don't play Queen Gabriel Union Allred. King Superman Thomas Allred Jr. I will give you a kiss now. Thomas Allred Jr report to my office right now . Yeah boss I'm afraid we have to let you go. Is there any way that we can keep this between us. While I finish out the day. I'm just playing with you Thomas Allred Jr your wife is here to see you. Now where my kiss at. Gabriel Union Allred. Thank you sweetheart. Thomas Allred Jr I love you. I love you too Gabriel Union Allred. You just witnessed a Camelot manuscript production. I love you so much Gabriel Union Allred. That show was professional. Yes it was Gabriel Union Allred yes it really was. Anybody need me I went home for the day with my wife. Get back here Thomas Allred Jr. I'm just picking with you go ahead on home . We all clocking out courtesy of you.

As it seeMs. to me this nigga is legit. Thomas Allred Jr is a icon and a roll model. I deserve to have him. Girl I see that the roll model is you. Gabriel Union Allred. Your the most kind of all of the women. And I'd do anything for you. I'm only rapping to you. To show you how. I'm a be after we are married. Thank you Gabriel Union Allred. For the reconsideration of my application. On employment into your house hold. And your bed. I know that you are tied. Of men telling you that they need to be with you. And you just shoulding them off . I need to take over Gabriel Union Allred. In a Land of tuff competitors. I just want my wife. Gabriel you are the wind beneath my wings. Thank you. Thank you. Thomas Allred Jr. I have to say something to you. What ever you want to Gabriel Union Allred. I face my charges with you. Gave I'm a give to you another two zillion dollars .That's for shopping expenses. Girl I need you to realize that I'm trying to come to know you. And This book is apart of my mental. At a time when everything seemed to be going good for me. Gabriel Union Allred. I fight to understand you. Listen Thomas Allred Jr it takes a man to come up and do the things that you are doing. You are already beautiful Thomas Allred Jr. The best man that I can be is in your life Gabrielle Union Allred. If you would just take your time and give a read to my supplications. Cause I know that I love you.

If anybody ask you just why we are here tonight in the club. I want you to tell this story. Gabriel Union Allred. The first time that I saw you. Girl I didn't judge you Girl I just understood that you were a work in progress. Now I love you. Simply because of your hands to doing things. Gabriel Union Allred. I'm Thomas Superman Allred Jr. And I girl have been watching you. Now the extra two zillion dollars in which I have you. Will help you with your shopping expenses forever and ever. It's just that when I get out of this position. I'd like to know that I done something worth while with my time. The bank sweetheart tells me that your money is there. Gabriel Union Allred I'm all doing this in dedication that I love you. See my supplications are a matter of me being cleaver enough to make you Gabriel Union Allred say what you want to. But my episodes of this book. Is almost ending.

So I compact turn myself. For another understanding because I don't know just how long it's going to take for me to be with you. Excuse me but your my soulmate Gabriel Union Allred. Do think that its dialogue either Gabriel Union Allred. Girl when I first bump into you. Realize that I'm a work in progress and he ain't through with me yet. Listen at you. Girl I noticed you as soon as I bought my movie. We dont drink or smoke where I'm from. And exactly where is that. That your from Thomas Superman Allred Jr. Listen baby you a superstar Gabriel Union Allred. You know that I'll take good care of you. So let me speak my peace. As it is that I was saying is. I'm truly sorry for what I was saying Gabriel Union Allred. And I hope that one day. Me and you can sit down and read a little bit on a man's sacrifice for understanding and freedom. Amongst the women. Think of me. In our supplication of happiness and joy and triumph. In history as the bread winners for our family. Gabriel Union Allred. I give a gift of sixth million dollars to you and sixty million dollars to your town. Seeing how my money is a professional number 00 now do you get what I'm saying to you. Gabriel Union Allred my money is at the infinity sign. No kidding Gabriel Union Allred. I got to give that boy a contract. If you want I can keep the yard clean for you. Those snakes in the gra** are who I can't stand. All of the money that I have told you is securly beening placed. In my bank account for you. You can access your bank account by just saying that you want something a loud at anytime that you want it. You see how we roll. I'm fending to start designing a new list of flower arrangements because after this book I you might retire. But Thomas Allred

Jr take it easy. I already know that you love me. Gabriel Union Allred I need you so much. Thank you for everything my Dr Santosa . Be back with me for a complete talk in 90 business days Thomas Allred Jr. Yes sir Dr Santosa . What makes this story our King is. That I be sitting here writing while they be smoking weed. What kinda of story is it. It's about a dudes heart. And is he capable to win. The love of a lifetime now that he has the money being processed in his bank account right now. Your bank account is 645 zillion dollars after taxes Thomas Allred Jr. And that's real. To proceeds to this book will go into my account for Gabriel Union Allred. And her people know what to do with the rest.

Time is moving forward. You damn right we in love. Im a police officer Gabriel Union Allred. And I respect the fact that you listen. Yo last name is Superman. I didn't do nothing but sit down and write you this script. Now i know you Thomas Allred Jr for the powerful person that we are. What are you saying Gabriel Union Allred. Do I really have a chance with you. Right here right now. Yeah buddy. What zillionaire is going to scream yeah buddy Gabriel Union Allred. A Zillionaire girl like me and you. There's one more thing that I need to know. Can I prove something to you. I giving to you a puppy named When we first meet. But this has nothing to do with the story. Gabriel Union Allred say goodnight. Goodnight everybody. You killed it out there. I just hope that Gabriel Union Allred realizes I'm telling the truth about I love her and her money is in her bank account right now as we speak. Ladies and gentlemen Thomas Allred Jr and Gabriel Union Allred. Thank you everybody. You just want quit will you Thomas Allred Jr. I'm to legit to quit. Gabriel Union Allred you suck Gabriel Union Allred. It's a nice night to go fishing Thomas Allred Jr everybody for your welcoming pleasure Dru hill . Thank you.

You think the world is going to believe us. When we say that. All of the kids love us. Because we because we programmed them to. Superman we can't have any errors. The is in our adjustment Superman. They talking about you. On the press radio. Is getting to dangerous for me and you. That good care of yourself Thomas Allred Jr. Don't put jr on there you know that you Superman. It seeMs. like the world is come to a standstill and everyone wants my Angel. Listen here Thomas Allred Jr. The world knows that we've been after you. Thomas Allred I'm going to tell you one thing. My position is critical. To our survival. Angel Lois Lane Gabriel Union Allred. Report for duty now. Angel we have incoming torpedoes coming from the East Pacific. I have to take care of these torpedoes honey. But Superman. Enjoy yourself Thomas Allred Jr.

The missiles are close to reaching there target. Angel do something Angel . See how that dude is. Superman. All you have to do is threaten people. And you'll come running to the rescue. The missiles have been stopped in there place. What are you trying to do be forever. Thomas we need you to take your a** to sleep. Youll get a better understanding of this when night time comes. Night times comes what's going to happen once night time comes. Thomas it is inevitable that we speak to you at once. Majoir Payne I thought you were on a**ignment. In Bosnia or somewhere. Thomas will you quit playing around. You put Damon Wayans in a movie. With Superman Thomas Allred jr. And youve got a hit. People get contact. Off the pistol smoke of your life Thomas Allred Jr. Are you open to new things. New things as in how to get this suit off it seeMs. to be stuck. With the power invested in me Angel.I now make you Thomas Allreds wife. Superman you may kiss your angel. They are glowing bright like the sun. Keep going and we will kill somebody. Thomas Stop kissing me. I can't Angel Lois Lane Gabriel Union Allred. It's just that i need you so much. Do not bother them.

But Damon we're going to get killed. Superman knows what he's doing. I hope to Christ God that he dose . My book as ended here Surperman Thomas Allred Jr. Angel Lois Lane Gabriel Union Allred I'm picking up our story right here baby. Thomas. All we got is each other Superman. Back away from me Thomas back away. Hollywood is going to enjoy this.

We got superheroes. That explode when you touch them. The actually have the kiss each other. And than explode. Thomas Allred jr. Your needed over in Bosnia. Without my angel I ain't. Gabriel Union Superman really loves you. We want you to be happy with Superman. So let's see what we can do for you Angel Lois Lane Gabriel Union Allred. Thomas gave me his money. He couldn't have. Thomas Allred jr. I mean Superman. Never runs out of money. That is the rule in his contract. You see Thomas is in a room by his self. Suspended in time animation.

Until the day and Angel arrives. His Angel is right here. Superman hears you Gabriel but he can't see you. Superman is in a chamber of complete solitude. Our question to you is Angel Lois Lane Gabriel Union Allred. Will you love Superman Thomas Allred Jr. If he couldn't walk or see. Yes I would love him.

And our question to you Superman. Is would you love your Angel Lois Lane Gabrielle Union Allred. If your site wasn't so good. And she looked desirable to you. You need to say yes I would Superman Thomas Allred Jr. Yes I would. We have a perfect match Thomas and Gabrielle. Let me write the end of it Superman Thomas Allred Jr. Yes my love Angel Lois Lane Gabriel Union Allred. Superman you know that I got you. In my provisions I have provided enough for a King to be with me own my own accords. Clock this girl. If you put your hands on her I swear God help me. Thomas Allred Jr. Listen to our father Thomas Allred Jr. You are with Angel Lois Lane Gabriel Union Allred. And I'm here for you Thomas anytime that you need me. You have forgotten me. I am your father since before time. We choose Superman. Keep on continuing to write. This world been through enough. I got a Superman coming up. And I'm too be continued. With my Angel Lois Lane Gabriel Union Allred. They going to put this in the movie theaters Surperman Thomas Allred Jr. Act professional. Towards the end. Now many people. Can realize the truth about me and you girl. Put me and you up there. In my sacrifice. To among the nation's. Thomas you ain't got no idea at what you doing. Superman we are training you to run through traps. If you can allow this as part of your contract. Yes i can allow traps as part of my contract. Figure out you to professional. Than Superhero. Angel Lois Lane Gabriel Union Allred. I need you. How do you this story . All you got to do is say it's time to go to sleep. Angel Lois Lane Gabriel Union Allred. I love you. And it's time to go to sleep. We are going to make a contract out of you Superman Thomas Allred Jr. There goes Terminator Eddie Murphy. That's Arsenio Hall. Well he starting to look like Eddie Murphy. Gabriel Union Allred I do apologise for this book and movie. I couldn't up it. Gabriel Union Allred you are so beautiful. And I dedicate all of the proceeds to you. From this manuscript. Thomas Allred Jr. Ms. Gabriel Union Allred keep going professional. You are simply irresistible. I'm a sign my contract The police laughing at you. I'm a have to do something about this sh*t. He knows how to treat a lady. Anytime that you in the jam. Angel Lois Lane Gabriel Union Allred. Call on your Thomas Allred Jr. And be professional. I got the whole world calling me. For my autograph. Thomas I bet you know how this feels. I just can't help myself. We gave Thomas his contract because he's professional. And that's the end of the story people. Superman is our hero Thomas. Gabriel Union good night to you all Merry Christmas and happy New year. I love you so much Angel Lois Lane Gabriel Union Allred. I love you to Surperman Thomas Allred Jr. That girl is to professional. Go clean up the house or something my love is only for you Superman. And that's a rap.

Amazon women stand up. This is Queen and Master Angel Lois Lane Gabriel Union Allred. We have programmed you to eat and do everything that we do. This boy got some game on his a**. I know that you realize that you are Amazon princesses. Thank you Thomas Allred Jr. For the meantime being conscious of your where abouts . Thomas is the one dating Gabrielle Union. Can't you see. That I intrust in Superman Thomas Allred jr. In front of the whole Amazon woman nation. I'm saying he is a King. In sickness and in health. Tell death do me part. I'm giving to the Amazon women. Your King of the Amazon women .Superman Thomas Allred jr. I knew you were Amazon women. I just couldn't put my finger on it. Gabrielle princess Jasmine. I mean princess Jasmine Gabriel Union Allred. Has taught me so many things. What did she teach you Amazon King Superman Thomas Allred jr. We got a princess right here. Amazon princess Hillary Clinton is coming to speak. You damn right it's Hillary Clinton coming to speak. Amazon the music. Gose back alone way. Thomas is a Zillionaire. And so is the Amazon women Gabrielle Union Allred. You are a Zillionaire . Take your time and speak. Amazon princess Hillary Clinton. We thought you weren't coming to see us. Amazon princess Hillary Clinton. Yall that boys amazing. Thomas is the one that's doing the speaking. Don't you give up on me. Miss Hillary Clinton says. Keep on going. We came to fight. And women all over the world. Stand up for what you believe in. Because stand up is not a testimony. Stand-up is the truth of a woman nation. Gabrielle Union Allred. Is your turn to speak. Right now Id give my life for anyone of you. In solitude. I pray that you all have bank accounts. Cause when the cookie crumbles. In which it always does crumble. A put genius on you. And try my damnest to know that your okay. The first time I heard of you. I was sitting on my porch. Drinking a gla** of Lipton ice-t. And they said the Amazon women are in trouble. You need to listen to me right now. Amazon women having been in. Nor will they ever be in trouble. Keep going Thomas Allred Jr. Because Amazon women adore you. Thomas you should speak. Let Amazon woman hear your voice. I'm here today. It's time for a new better change. Say it with me Amazon women. One for one. And one for everybody in the Amazon kingdom. You better Lean on me Thomas Allred Jr. Gabrielle Union Allred I need you so much. Be strong Thomas. Now we can judge who's greatness. Is in our pudding. Amazon women.There is and injustice going on. We can skip it. But as Amazon women we face things right ahead.

You can see that the Amazon nation is lacking school material. And enough pay for bus drivers. To whip this out. I Amazon princess Gabrielle Union Allred. Thomas come to the stage. Yall thought y'all whatn't going to see me didn't you. Amazon women I'm giving to you. 867 million dollars. To Coat the problem. With the school issue. Amazon woman. Let me show you that all of you will be protected. Girls I'm starting a bank account fund. Just so that I may have some thing to do with you. I'm giving every body. 9.1 billion dollars. To split evenly in each banking account. For the woman in Hickory North Carolina. Thomas all your doing. Is more than proving your a good man. It let all of us know. That we'll always have you. To count on. Pick your game up Superman Thomas Allred Jr. Ladies I love each and every last one of you goodnight. Go ahead Gabriel Union Allred. Finish talking to the Amazon women. Plymouth Rock didn't land on Amazon. It landed on me. I am Gabriel Union Allred. My story is this. Y'all making those lucky charm bracelets. Im making a better way to spend our time together. Get ready to go to commercial. I made you. To all the Amazon women that's in this nation. King Superman Thomas Allred Jr wants to speak. Good night and God bless you.

I was told Ms. Gabriel Union to write these manuscripts by fources I can't explain. I would like for you to know that I honestly do honor and respect the privilege to write to you and for. All of my life I have always thought that you are a woman of true grit. And now I'm coming from a place. Where the mountain grow seeds. Ms. Gabriel Union Allred I am doing my best to hang on to what I have for myself which is nothing. And I've been involved in no esplanade of any kinds. It's only that the world sees me as a man. When I truly am a star material. You can see it in my eyes that I desperately want to date you. I'm just expecting. Rain to fall all over me at any minute. You see Thomas Allred Jr. Rain doesn't fall right away. And I know that you are a police officer who has been shot in the right pants leg. You still can walk. And you lost your girlfriend and fiance to a shooting nine years later. Thomas Allred

Jr in my life I have heard many stories. That have turned the audience against you. But what I'm saying Thomas Allred Jr that I make a Pat with you to always be your friend no matter what. But I just want to date you Ms. Gabriel Union. You see. No woman wants to date me. Because my wife has been killed and I've been through the same thing. Now I work daily on nine hundred inventions to save the lives of children and adults all the same. I'm only a man Ms. Gabriel Union Allred. I have written these books to tell the Amazon women that I did not shoot anyone. My wife and I were attacked. Thomas I no everything about you. Then you realize that I'm alone and there saying to me that I'm a Zillionaire that can't spend his money yet. We all know that you are a Zillionaire Thomas Allred Jr. And you realize that I would do anything for you Ms. Gabriel Union Allred.

Get yourself together . That's the only way that you can say that you truly beat those individuals . Ms. Gabriel Union Allred. I've been alone for seven years. And it's getting to hard to bear with me working everyday on this manuscipt not breaking down or anything Ms. Gabriel Union Allred girl I'm just saying that true life it comes through friends. Ms. Gabriel Union Allred . I except your friend ship Thomas Allred Jr. Is excepting Gabriel Union friend request . The moral of the story is you ain't got to be a superhero to have friends. I love you Angel Lois Lane Gabriel Union Allred. And I love you Superman Thomas Allred Jr. No matter what you going through. I take care of my own. Sincerely yours Gabriel Union

In need to take care of you my Angel Lois Lane Gabriel Union Allred. Can a brother get a rain check. Gabriel Union Allred your the most beautiful woman that I know. For saying I know you. I do apologise wifey. Lord's knows that one day I would famously like to advertise in you . A brand new house. And a puppy named daingerfield. You got to see me out. Gabriel you need to. See all my things. A half them with all of your family and friends that love you. I'm a police officer Gabriel Union Allred. And I just hope that one day. I could eat in a restaurant with you. But girl that does it. Here go you Lucky Charm bracelet. It's yours to keep girl weather you have love for me or not. And one more thing Gabriel. Girl I love you. For making my days go by complete. Because of you I'm taking a chance on forever with you by my side. I love you Thomas. And I keep wishing right now that me and you were in the same area code. So that we could talk over dinner. The way that you come up with these stories is so amazing. And I need you to understand Thomas that in with you and my hands are tied. See Thomas get up and tell me that your a fighter jets pilot or something of that nature. Because all I get from you is that you and your wife where attacked and shot up. And your wife isn't here no more. But you still are and you've been alone for seven going on eight years because of it. Gabriel Union Allred and I love you too. And what it is is I'm happy with myself. Not my situation but me. I want you to know that the coffee is on the house. But Thomas you know Gabriel Union Allred. I never have felt pitiful before. And I want you to know one thing. I wanna be your man. Are you telling me that you forgive me. Mr. Thomas Allred Jr. I'm saying that it's a work in progress. Ms. Gabriel Union Allred. Don't forget his name is Surperman. Gabriel Union Allred. And I open the door for any Superman. That I see needs a hand Thomas Allred Jr. Are you saying Gabriel Union Allred that it's going to be. What I'm saying is that Thomas Allred Jr . Has all the characters that we want in our next Superman. He is a decorated federal police officer. With a wife that has fallen on the field. People I don't know what else to say. I vote Thomas Allred Jr Superman of the world commerce building. All in favor say I. I.

You need to put Thomas in that position. Look here Thomas Allred Jr. Was the coffee that good your back for some more. This whole hour Thomas. I been thinking to myself. On how to tell you this job that I have for you. We'll all you have to do is just give me the coordinates. Ill do the got damn job for you. Keep on severing that coffee Thomas that's all that I can say. That's all that I can say. This is Surperman Thomas Allred Jr and I'm Angel Lois Lane Gabriel Union Allred. Signing off. Clear.

I see everything you trying to do Gabriel Union Allred. Be careful what you wish for. The commerce building needs a Superman. To run through it. Thomas I am choosing you to run the place. I really flattered with the way y'all have thought about me. But I got a question for you Gabriel Union Allred. Think about your life ahead of you Thomas Allred Jr. Realize Gabriel. That i hold you to my heart. Girl please take me off this manual labor and be my wife. Gabriel can't see myself without you. Gabriel look into my eyes . Ms.. Union its time that we be leaving. Next time I see you Thomas Allred Jr. Gabriel Union Allred that is what they all say next time. He is really holding his position. He genuinely is a good person out here y'all. I've tested him he don't have no diseases. Im watching him on a spy cam in his house. He doesn't know I see him. Any coffee today.

I asked him Thomas Surperman Allred jr. All he said was coffee is good everyday. And I sat down and had a cup of coffee with my husband. Thomas Surperman Allred jr. For the first time. He likes to call me Angel Lois Lane Gabriel Union Allred. Um indebted to Superman Thomas Allred Jr. Because if not I wouldn't know how sweet it is. A couple coffee sweetheart. This is dedicated to those men out there looking forward to there position take your time cause we all are looking for a good person to live and enjoy each other with. I'm Gabriel Union Allred Thomas Allred Jr ain't here with me today. But here go my Surperman Thomas Allred Jr thank you so much for everything not yet Surperman Thomas Allred Jr what is it Angel Lois Lane Gabriel Union Allred He said who let the dogs out . The men outta be careful these women want you Thomas Allred Jr. I'm already taken see Angel Lois Lane Gabriel Union Allred . I put this ring on your finger on national television. Take your time honey saying national. Goodnight everybody. Goodnight Surperman Thomas Allred Jr and Angel Lois Lane Gabriel Union Allred. If you need us where right here.

That boyes got superhuman powers. I didn't think anybody heard what I said about you Thomas Allred Jr. I'm identified you as a Superman because I don't know what else to call you. You the only Superman Thomas. Sometimes being Superman gets hard on me. Never fear cause I'm your angel. You mean that you there for me Gabriel Union Allred. Its something about you that I can't put my finger on Thomas. Thomas Allred is the man in these parts. I hear you. Don't sh*t nowhere. These people a here you. What a tell you. Keep listening to me. And watch you grow through poverty. You getting ready to be a goddamn Superman. Look Thomas. We watched the Sun beaming down on the shore. Standing in position Thomas.Thomas jr. I'm trusting you with my heart. Do your damn work. There is no position like Superman's position. Don't hesitate to rebuild your society thats Fallon. Thomas I order you to take a bath everyday. We have got to clean you up. You better get clean Thomas. Thomas Allred jr. Is clean enough. Legend has it Thomas ain't going to be Superman because. 10 years ago. His wife was kill. Buy and unnamed dude. This was before you had your powers Thomas. Do yall think I'm too old for this. A man has to stand his ground no matter how old is. Do you hear me. Listen angel I have no id on me. If your a police officer come with me right now. Thomas Allred your Surperman you can get in the club. What kind of club is this. A dooMs.day club. What kind of club yall want to be in.

Thomas I'm going to tell you. That your the remaining got damn Superman. Pick one female that love Thomas Allred Jr. I choose Gabrielle Union Allred. My angel. Thomas what you going to do without Kristen and me. Superman you have no idea what you doing by picking Gabriel Union Allred. As a contract to you. Those kids are looking up to you right now. Superman in the sky box. Is where we have a difference in opinion. Superman listen carefully to me now. Thomas I'm going to get you the biggest contract this world is those thing. Thats Superman right there. I'm trying to tell you Thomas. That you really are Superman. Not in the movies. But as you write down the script. Thomas everybody in the neighborhood is depending on you. Stop bringing people names into your script. Thankful that I got here. Thomas you got to be thankful of these mastermind. Giving your project a boost off. You innocent Surperman Thomas Allred Jr. And overtime Thomas. You will start to believe in yourself as much as we do. We give to you the powers of Superman. The Almighty God allowed us to. Big careful what you wish for Thomas Allred Jr. I want my suit and cape. There you go. If you want your suit and Cape. It's cool but your not that kind of superhero. Exactly Thomas Allred Jr. Superman you are a professional. Stay focused on our film. Now Wich house do you choose. These ain't houses these are Castle I'm looking at. Superman we want you to spend the rest of your days in pure bliss. You think I'm kidding don't you. Superman has the ability to reach in and take out powers from the sun. Is that you Thomas Allred Jr. We'll the sun dose shine a light directly down on me. Can you help me I want to stop this from happening. Stop this from happening. You are a Zillionaire professional. Just like the soup member for you. Are you telling me this is real. Exactly.So you saying that Gabriel Union Allred really is my wife. Is real life. Thats what were saying to you take your time. You got to take your time with this Superman. I've been alone for 7 years. this is your last year we know how long you've been alone. Keep remaining professional. We are looking at you through our satellite channels. What about Emily and Kristen.

We will give to Emily and Kristen whatever it is that they need. Thomas listen to their hearts Thomas. Angel Lois Lane Gabriel Union Allred. I realize that they are hurting. But I don't want to lose you angel for anything I love you Gabriel Union Allred. Get Superman his contract. Thomas you need to sign the contract. Do you agree to the terMs. of our Superman Thomas.

Yes I do. He done got professional. Are yall telling me that I was only alone so that I can get into the movies and on the movie screen. You got a movie coming out call Superman returns. And that buzzing that I hear my ear. Surperman got buzzing in his ear. Not always folks. You need to keep yourself together. Thomas. You see how professional you are getting. I'm still in the United States. You can tell me. Superman makes a good roll model. Clock that position. The young lady looks to be stranded. Hi I'm Thomas. Thomas unless you know certain things about engines I'm sorry. Well I do no a thing or two about car engines. Do not put water in them. Thomas oh my gosh. It is you Superman. I was ready to clobber your a**.

You should let my driver fix your car and come with me. Chinese food. There you go. Get Thomas a contract. People say that Chinese food cures cancer. I no supermodel when I see one. To times I wanted to ask you your name. But I didn't. Because you are so beautiful that your name doesn't really matter at all. Surperman watch out. A little kid is throwing stuff at me. That's just because he likes you. You get no idea who Superman really is my Angel Gabriel Union Allred. You knew who i was. To the batmobile. Well Superman that's lunch with original. Thomas I'm telling you one more time. You need more iceing and on the cake. I'm putting all I got to it. That boys is talented.Superhero what happening to you. The bank in the kenan island says that you have and Infiniti symbol. On your bank account Superman. Do you realize it. My angel do you realize it. Gabrielle im a buy you anything that you want. Keep rapping. You see Thomas Allred Jr Surperman. I ain't got nothing to do with myself all of this time but to sit down and work . He a professional. So all he does is work. Allow me to reach your home destination. That was my home we are talking about Angel Lois Lane Gabriel Union Allred. Please Superman. Why do you call me Angel all the time. I got to lose these powers one day. And after i lose them. I become mortal and die. Unless I get my powers to and Angel. Through s*x. What are your power Superman. Listen to me. No matter what people say about me. I will always be Superman. Do you here me Angel Lois Lane Gabrielle Union Allred. I here you Superman Thomas Allred Jr. Superman lets transfer energy. My angel you've been hurt that's and old wound. Let Surperman kisses it for you.see the main difference is that you love me Surperman.Do you here what I am saying

Thomas Allred Jr. Superman I need you. My angel me and you are close. I want you to be with me.inside of this skybox. I brought these bikes for us. When will we ride them. In the morning. Superman will you look at the sun. This is my place Angel Lois Lane Gabriel Union Allred. It's about time he said .Angel Lois Lane Gabriel Union Allred. I'm not playing with you.You live on the beach. The beach over here is all my land. What if all of you bank account get full .They are full. Thomas. I'm asking you to. Put that book down and come with me. The things I'm going to do for my country. Girl can you see me. Superman I see you. Then don't be afraid. I'm not afraid Thomas.

When the morning comes I just want to be with you. And you will be with me. Angel Lois Lane Gabriel Union Allred. Because I'm Superman. You need to stay with me for the rest of your life Angel Lois Lane Gabriel Union Allred. I will stay with you Superman Thomas Allred Jr. For the rest of my life with Superman. I'm bringing to the table. Our newborn baby.If Superman quit talkin .He could see that this is our movie. Thomas Allred Jr is Superman and Angel Lois Lane Gabriel Union Allred . Is open for suggestions on our movie.

Just take your time Superman Thomas Allred Jr . Open your eyes and you'll be back home with your mother Surperman. You need to open your eyes. This is kind of messed up. My mother is here but Gabriel isn't. That's where you supposed to be Superman. Once you realize that you are a multi talented zillionaire actor. Called Superman Thomas Allred Jr. Than your world will not be the same. Exactly. Look Thomas . The kids are playing out in the sun. Be more professional. Write your book as it is told to you. And capital will be your way shortly Thomas. You are Superman. Thomas. And there is no one else like you. Thomas for years I tried to preach that to you. That with power you can get everything you want in this world. Your angel has gone to a new level.im so proud of you Superman Thomas Allred Jr. Be professional Thomas the ladies all have there time. Time to do what. To masturbate your love Organs. We are with you you got to clean up your act Superman. Hey look I apologize it's just that this is little strange. Your Superman.

The reason I tell you this. I a am Superman. You are Superman. And the reason why I tell you this is. To break it down to you. The sunlight beaMs. on everyone. But your the one. That the sunlight beaMs. down on you first. Every morning while you are sleeping. That's some sh*t for you. Look Thomas here's the deal. You have the powers of Superman. Weather you no it or not we cannot leave you. I'm glad your not leaving me. We are going to transfer your accounts into money that you can spend. Bank account 1-0 100 is now open for you approval. And in my bank account is. 600 million zillion dollars. I no thats enough to keep you happy Surperman. You want to keep me happy. Make my whole neighborhood zillionaire. As you wish Superman. I'm going to give you time to figure this out. Now everyone realize that I'm Superman. Of the business industry. And you asked me to be the leader of the world Commerce building. Superman we are going to ask you to be the leader of a lot of things. You are our professional. We are giving you one business day. To finish up your message to Gabriel. How did you know about that. Because we are watching you through satellite imagery. We can see everything that's going on in the house with you. Hey Superman. He waved at us. Why all of the cloak and dagger. I'm Sitting right here and I'm Superman. Be professional. For goodness sake. Thomas Allred Jr. Your Angel is in love with you. My Angel is in love with me. Do you know who your angel is. My Angel is Gabriel Union Allred. No that's one of your Angels Surperman. I need you to keep up with me. We don't have all day at this. Okay I don't know who my angel is. Who is my Angel. People are watching. Your new angel is. With a minute. As Superman I only want one angel. No Superman has done this before. Are you sure. Yes I'm sure that I choose Gabriel Union to be my wife and soul mate .

I can hear you Thomas Allred Jr. Thomas likes Gabriel Union. Well done Surperman well done. Gabriel Union Allred when your Surperman Thomas Allred Jr was put to the test to have any other angel in the world . Your Surperman also choose you Gabriel Union the same as you did he. Your levels are completed you may be with Surperman Gabriel Union. Thomas talk to your angel. Gabriel I may never know truly what these powers are about but I'm learning I want to see you as soon as you have a chance. To get us two a room because celebrity or not . I got to sh*t baby. You can go take a sh*t Thomas Allred Jr whenever you to your bank account is full. And we're ready to give you your money. Thomas a professional. Woo woo woo. Superman.

I'm just doing my homework. But Gabrielle its almost midnight. Listen Thomas I really need to finish this science homework. Go ahead and do what you got to do Gabriel. I have a novel to write anyway. The beginning of Superman. Thomas your a Time Enforcement TEC cop. Look and so are you Gabriel Union Allred. Time circuits going off everywhere. Except yours and mine. Thomas what have you done Thomas Allred jr.Gabriel I asked the TEC tech agency to grant us alittle time on a break reunion. Thomas Allred Jr. You didn't. You know that a break Union is like 10 years. For us to be together. If Granted. So what did the TEC say Superman. They couldn't allow us both to have a TEC reunion. So we have to work our a**es off through Christmas and try to make some overtime. Gabrielle I'm just being professional. It's alright Superman. No matter where I hide. They always knew my position. Gabrielle what are you saying. I'm Speaking out loud Thomas. Freeze time. Gabriel you can run from us but we see you. George and Barbara Bush. It's about time you show your true faces. Gabriel we never did nothing to you. You had no right to take Superman alway form me. Thats in a few more weeks. Just understand this. Its you that i work for and that's all. Now give me some time with Thomas my husband. Unfreeze time. Gabrielle I'm trying to tell you that I love you. Superman what did you say. I can't no without you Gabriel. Honey I need you so much. I need you to Gabriel. Get your a** up Thomas we're going to do some training. Dang Gabrielle you don't have to be so rough. Believe me Thomas this is for your own good. Make a move on me. No I can't do it. Superman I'm not playing make a move on me. Free time you making a fool out of yourself Gabrielle. Free me Superman with only allowed the inevitable. But a have to do something. But I have to do something. Gabrielle I know that this hurts you but Superman has to reach his true destiny as a TEC Time Enforcement Officer.

Superman is a Time Enforcement Officer. I'm begging of you. Let's Superman remember my name. Mr.. George and Barbara Bush. Please allow me to help with Superman's therapy allow him to remember my name. And was just important to you Gabrielle Union Allred. Listen just say I promised a friend that I'm going to look out for him. And which friend is this that you promise Gabrielle. Jeana. If the time codes are correct. In wich they usually are. Superman will be attacked in survive his attack in 36 hours from this moment in time you only got 36 hours to tell Superman that you love him Gabrielle. And if love is as strong as anything.

Then Superman me remember you. But no one can with stand the force of attack not even Superman. And why do we have to keep living this. Miss Barbara Bush. Go back to the beginning. Thomas you a TEC agent Time cop. I know I love that movie. I'm a cop Jeana. I'm a cop Gabriel

I'm going to take care of the both of you ladies yall not going to want for anything . Gabriel don't cry I am Time Enforcement Officer Jeana. I'm on Superman's case. I won't let him get shot Gabriel. Stay close to me Jeana. I love you . What about Gabrielle my friend Superman. Jeana I'm a one woman man. Like Dave hollister. Gabriel about you to. Jeana.I'm going to get a job and get us a house and a car. Unfreeze time. Superman what are you doing.

I was thinking about attacking you Gabriel and the can't do it. It's okay Superman. Is long as you love me. Gabriel I love you so much. I can't sleep without you Gabrielle. If you only knew Superman. That you going to have to go twenty five years without me alone. Time simulation coming to a close. you still running the Superman prograMs. Gabrielle Union Allred. Yes Time Enforcement Officer Whoopi Goldberg. You know in the future you and Superman have kids sometime. Yes I know Time Enforcement Officer Whoopi Goldberg. Go head back to you simulation time simulation now beginning. Ill catch up to you. Thomas you cant kiss me. Gabrielle Union Allred one day I will. Even with pressure all on you. Even with pressure on on me. I hold you to that. It's a kiss. One day Gabriel Union Allred. Time simulation now ending. So Gabriel are you getting married or are you going to wait for Superman to realize who you are. I'm a wait for my man.

You got to get used to me Angel Lois Lane Gabriel Union Allred. As you see Surperman Thomas Allred Jr. I don't settle for less. What you thinking Surperman Thomas Allred Jr is. Don't call me Superman in front of anyone. No that's not what

I'm thinking and you know it Angel Lois Lane Gabriel Union Allred. This book is professional. It'll be a movie one day. The wouldnt it be something. Oh my god Superman. Clark Kent welcome to my house. I want to speak with Thomas Allred jr. You call him Superman. Y'all move over for Clark Kent. So this is the Superman I so proudly heard about. Clark Kent welcome to my home. Me and my Angel Lois Lane Gabriel Union Allred.

We do try to make the simple things out of life. You got the Superman name in business Thomas Allred Jr. And your wife Gabriel Union Allred .Has her business name. Gabriel Union. Thomas be professional. I want a piece of the action. You need to separate me from you Thomas Allred Jr. Ill give you one day to think about it. Everybody Superman has left the building. Remember your writing a manuscipt and your professional. Surperman Thomas Allred Jr. I know you can hear me in your thoughts. I know what you would like to do for you and your family. The Superman symbol means our world. Breaking the symbol along time ago. Puts pain to anyone who sees you. Your whole community is getting ready to call it quits on you. What you need is a Superman who can handle finances as well as the movies to. Im keeping my word to the people.

Superman Clark Kent. And as the new Superman of the business industry. We are not saving anything. We are just creating new and better things. I am Superman Thomas Allred jr. And I can't Neil to your demands. Look Thomas. Before you take on the Superman outfit there is something I got to tell you. Get ready for war my people. Superman I am Superman and I'm not afraid. Nor will I fear any tyranny or oppression. Besides you. I have been working. On on a Superman outfit. It comes in a nun plastic fireproof are money suit. If I give up Thomas.

Will the Amazon women respect Clark Kent forever. Yes we will Superman Clark Kent. Give him some time to speak to the Amazon woman. A new days is horizing . One without violence or guns in it. The weapons of our pa** have been destroyed. Can't you see this. Is dangerous Superman Thomas Allred Jr . Surperman Clark Kent. I have your powers. You mean Thomas that we have the same powers. And im suppose to work out every single business day . Come with me. You come with me this is business see me Thomas Allred jr. Angel Lois Lane Gabriel Union Allred. Yes my husband Superman Thomas Allred Jr. Do you recognize me as your one and only Superman. Thomas I do recognize you but I can't. Angel Lois Lane Gabriella Union Allred. What is it. Superman is really hear. In our household. I know that Clark Kent is here. Make him feel comfortable. And sit down and eat with him. And so the story went. How Superman. Realize he had a twin brother .In the business industry. Named Superman Thomas Allred Jr. Take your time and speak to Gabrielle Union Superman. Mam thanks for having me over to your gracious house. And you are welcome Surperman. Do you think that I'm to far for you Thomas. If I did I wouldn't have married you Angel. Goodnight my brother . Goodnight Surperman. Thomas Allred Jr and Angel Lois Lane Gabriel Union Allred. Are getting ready to read something. It's a contract from Surperman. Oh my god Merry Christmas to you Ms. Gabriel Union Allred and Mr.. Thomas Allred Jr. Gabriel. Thomas be sincere thank you and Merry Christmas to all of yours Superman From Gabriel Union Allred and Thomas Allred Jr. We ended this like this.

We're running out of time before Christmas. Gabriel i promise you. That we'll trim the tree on time. I'm putting Superman in this to help us. Honey remember the last time he trimmed the tree. We didn't have no tree. Listen Thomas. I know that you're Superman. But Superman Clark Kent is coming to dinner. Merry Christmas. Superman are you just hanging around listening to people. I. Hold that thought. I am angel Lois Lane Gabriel Union Allred. I never seen Lois. Don't feel rained on Superman Lois Lane is an Angel. Gabriel just use that name.

Because I'm is Superman. Aw sh*t. What is it Superman. Somebody got to get the turkeys from the store. These Turkey's Superman. Is presence Day. Pa** the cranberry sauce Superman. Say Thomas. Which one of the presidents you like the most. Nixon. The present I like the most is Barack Obama. Barack Obama couldn't save your a** from Nixon. Eat your food and shut your a**es up. Barack Obama said he's coming to dinner he just text me. Take your time and fix another plate angel. Hello Mr.. President. Hello Gabriel Union Allred. It smells good in here. What it is homeboy. Barack Obama. How you doing Mr. President. Taking my time out to enjoy myself. Did you read my book I just got finished with it. Whats your book called Angel Lois Lane Gabriel Union Allred. You know my book is. Is called payday volume one. Thats the name of it my book. It's about time she wrote something entertaining. Barack Obama is a handful. Less eat who craving the turkey. No Superman.

Listen Camelot manuscript productions don't play no games. If you need me you outta. Suck my d*ck Thomas Allred jr. And Gabriel Union Allred. He's Punky Daddy. He is so damn rude. Suck my d*ck. Gabriel Union Allred. I'm yelling Superman Thomas Allred Jr suck my d*ck just so you can fly away. Stop the games Cuba Gooding jr. I'm Punky Daddy there is no game. Punky Daddy stop the games then. It's a tape. That means I'm on it. Now apologize to Gabriel Union Allred. Girl I apologise I just to you. Now Punky Daddy. You got to suck my d*ck for this one. I'm not sucking your goddamn d*ck Punk. Remember Punky Daddy . If I say suck his d*ck you will do it . Because we got you on film sucking man d*ck. That's not possible. It is to possible Punky Daddy. Now shake Superman hand and tell him Merry Christmas. Thank okay. We'll you two kiss and makeup.Thats not happening. Well how about the both of you say I'll see you around. I see around Superman. Punky Daddy I'll see you around. Thomas close that window. Punky Daddy can fly. I know Thomas Allred Jr. He is a fairy . Angel Lois Lane Gabriel Union Allred. People see you as a wonderful person. First I got to get in. This Angel outfit. Merry Christmas to you Surperman Thomas Allred Jr. Merry Christmas to you Angel Lois

Lane Gabriel Union Allred. That girl is the true King. King me Gabriel Union Allred. Thomas I King you Sir Superman Knight. Gabriel Union Allred girl I Queen you my wife and Queen Gabriel Union Allred. Girl you see me. Boy you see me. I took my time. I been at this game for a long time. But now I have a king to run with. Gabriel Union the bank account is yours. In gratitude of all my respect to you. Take your a** home. And call me. There go Cuba Gooding jr. He's flying up moon. Gabriel Union Allred you don't want to see that. No matter what happens just know that I got you back. I know Gabriel I know.

Please baby. That changed you one time. Superman is coming after me. He is the real deal in sports entertainment. Okay then. Don't you see that I'm working my a** off for you. Let me have a kiss for old times sake. Man that looks like Surperman Thomas Allred Jr. It is Thomas Allred Jr. You taking advantage of the love of my life Duran. Cause if so. Your are more talented than I think. Because my lady wouldn't be in that position. I here that you haven't seen my lady Duran. Keep it simple with my time. Now look at me who am I kidding. Honey be home by twelve. Part 2 of the way I feel is sorta like this we got the contract.

The Superman contract is our. Did that man touch you. No Thomas Jr. He did not touch me. He was a gentleman all through our meeting after you left. Sweetheart did he touch you. With the contract of a century. Did I lose my lady. To Duran.Even for the contract of the century . I would never leave you Thomas . Do you hear what I'm saying to you. I love you Thomas. And I think that we may need some counseling to get us over our issues. Of insecurity and rage. Gabriel Union Allred rage. Yeah and rage.

You seem to forget that you are Superman Thomas Allred Jr. And I'm your one and only Angel Lois Lane Gabriel. This is your path into the entertainment movie industry. For years Surperman Thomas Allred Jr. I have sat back and waited. For a contract with enough magnitude to get you in my life. Now that I said this. This is what I want from you got damn it. Superman. If you take your eyes off of me one time I'm at smack you. Here go my women team. Good afternoon. Let me know what you think of them Superman Thomas Allred Jr. Why Gabrielle you're the most beautiful thing I've ever seen. Thomas hear is my men team. Take a look and keep on walking. And last but not least. My restroom. Show him the restroom. Superman always got a sh*t but he's a good man. Hey Punky Daddy. I here that not only was that not funny. I don't have to sh*t. Gabrielle smile happy Thanksgiving and Merry Christmas sweetheart. I pray that you let me in your life. Take your medicine. Punky Daddy got wings. What am I going to do with the both for you. Put us in the circus. I turkey dinner always dress up me it the fixings. You ain't got to do nothing but be yourself. I'll be getting in touch with you what did you say your name was? Superman Thomas Allred jr. Mam. I'll be sure to remember that man. Ms. Gabriel Union Allred that is Surperman Thomas Allred Jr. I know. I love you okay. Wash your mouth out with soap. I told you I love you and you didn't say nothing back to me. I love you too miss Gabriel Union Allred. You did the right thing Thomas Allred Jr. You did the right thing. We all here at Hollywood studio are proud of you for standing your ground and that's the reason why we call you Surperman.

Surperman Thomas Allred Jr is with you. Angel Lois Lane Gabriel Union Allred. Gabriel Union you are the most beautiful talented person that I would like to no. I'm taking my time to express my feelings and interest in you by walking the chalk line. Ms. Gabriel Union I have always been interested in you. It's just before I didn't no my tail from a hole in the ground. What I am saying Gabriel Union is that you are the finest lady that I've ever seen hands down. Y'all help me to express my self and interest to her. Gabriel Union my name is Thomas Allred Jr and I go by and Reign as the leading Surperman in business. Listen to me shorty. Im a get you one more thing. Before I leave this contract on the table where I signed my name as Surperman of the business industry.

Thomas we all know that Surperman is you Thomas Allred Jr. Well when do things change in my life Gabriel Union Allred. You got to put Angel in the front of a business woman's name. Because I am your wife Thomas. Do forget that. Angel Lois Lane Gabriel Union Allred I'll never forget. Until we meet Angel Lois Lane Gabriel Union Allred. Until we meet Surperman Thomas Allred Jr. I saved the best for last. It's a diamond letter. And opener. But why Surperman Thomas Allred Jr. I want you to read all of the emotions that I've put into each one of our dialogue stories. I am a master storyteller and you and a very beautiful master storyteller also. I was hoping that we could get together right now and discussed business. Go over contracts. At least talk because lady you are fine and every one knows it.. but Gabriel the next chapter is coming up. It starts off like this. Y'all I know what I want for Christmas .

Bring to me Surperman Thomas Allred Jr. Angel Lois Lane Gabriel Union Allred. We saved the best for last. Surperman is in the building. Looking at you. He says that he needs company. Tell Superman right now can't do it. Why Angel Lois Lane Gabriel Union Allred. Because I'm talking to my husband Thomas Allred Jr. I love you baby. What do you think about Gabrielle getting with Thomas Allred Jr. Gee it sound like a match made in heaven. He is the president. Of the worlds chamber club. You know what the world chamber is don't you. Listen to me. Once quick question. Does it feel good with those tights on your a** Superman. Gabriel Union Allred these are mine. Your Angel suit is almost done. Just to her her Angel suit. You look beautiful. That's what I was looking for. Gabrielle Union Allred you have my contract. I trust you Gabriel Union Allred. I'm a businessman And I know a great deal when I see one. Gabriel I've almost waited 8 years to see and talk to you. To prove to you that I'm not famous. I give to you. My comb and hair. Gabriel Union Allred. I give to you my 8 summers. Going without no one. And I to have went eight summers without no one. Thomas is it really you. It is me Gabriel Union Allred. Thomas it is you. I really went 8 years without no one Gabriel. I give to you your complimentary manuscript. Courtesy of Charlene T Allred. My mother Angel Lois Lane Gabriel Union Allred. It's really you Thomas. It's really you. Surperman. Honey I'm thankful. For everybody involved in this. Thank you again for saving me. And Gabriel I need to speak with you in person about some thing.Superman Thomas Allred Jr got a big contract. So. Here go my story. Weather you believe it or not is up to you. Angel Lois Lane Gabriel Union Allred. Is the Reigning champion of the business world .

They got Superman out of hiding. That's what they did yup. And sure enough Superman and Gabrielle got married. Listening to Monica Angel of mine. A whole bunch of people was their at the wedding. Baby I want you to look at your bank account. Thomas no you did it says Infiniti. When your bank account says Infiniti. Just know that I'm here with you. Im your Superman Gabrielle Union Allred. To Gabriel. To Gabriel. Gabrielle Union hear is your contract. I want you to take these manuscript. And do what you wish with them. I just got to ask you one important question. How do you feel in them tights . You know I feel good as hell thank you for asking. I do anything for a hit of you. Angel Lois Lane Gabriel Union Allred it's really you. I love you. I love you too Superman Thomas Allred Jr . I love you.

Gabriel by the powers of Grayskull in me. I just keep looking at you. You turned out to be something wonderful. And I'm telling you that you need me Gabriel. It's supposed to be another L on my name. I didn't see that coming. I'm professional. So Miss Gabriel Union. Welcome to a game where playing. Called Masters of the Universe surviver series. Thomas I ain't playing with you. I'm not in the mood for this talk. Your situation gets better after our game is over. Tell me your name will you please. It's Gabriel Union. I'm about to hit that.

Do you want my nuts in your mouth or in your a**. You have to play the game Gabriel. I'm a scoot past that question. How many nuts do it take to screw in a light bulb. You have to put this together. What I give you is the combination to my heart. How many nuts do it take to get the combination to my heart. It don't take any Thomas Allred Jr. You as nasty as you want to be. You can see my temperatures rising. Why don't you go through a deck of card and do push-ups. Thomas. Masters Of The Universe call the orders. You in trouble Thomas. Why .Because your with me .And I'm a Master Of The Universe. I call the shots. Let's go home to s*x to Masters Of The Universe. Let me phone up He man and see if he can get into this. Be quiet. Everybody in here is probably asleep. Thomas get you a mutha f*cking seat. Cause the game is just beginning to get nasty. I a Master Of The Universe looking for her dj Thomas Allred Jr. You have no idea at what your doing. Its Mr. nasty time Thomas. I have to go. Down the hall to the left. His attitude is good . But he sure does have to poop . Very much. He is writing on the mirror that he needs a condom. He better go get a condom. I'm a Master Of The Universe not a grocery store. Gabriel Union Allred I found one it's slightly use. Tell that boy if he clean the dishes than I'll give him a condom. Gabriel you must have had a party in here chitting juice is everywhere. I'm going to need some help in the kitchen. I'm glad we finished that up. What are you doing. I'm just sitting here watching star trek on the TV. Good I'm a treky . I'm leaving right now because I know where this is going to head. We don't have to have s*x if you don't want to. Lets call it a tonight. And Gabriel Union Allred. Honey what is it . Your beautiful in that evening gown. I'm warning you to go to sleep Thomas Allred jr. Thomas we are the Masters Of The Universe. I don't give up on me. Gabriel Union Allred. Never say never. This is how I train you. Masters Of The Universe.

Gabriel I'm seeing that everything is straight between us. I give to you a doc*ment to make sure everything is straight between us. I don't play like this. But everything I realize belongs to you. My business world is a couple weeks away from me. How can I get you to understand that you are beautiful. The reason why I say this to you right now baby girl is. Besides my family and my neighborhood surrounding me. I want you to have everything. That involves me in business. Only get one thing left to do. Notarize this. Just like I did with Won't Give In. I made it my business. To see that the truth Queen. Has everything that she can ever need or wish for. Once I leave this planet. Again I am Thomas Allred Jr. Control my hood. One more thing want to say. 13 years ago. I made and album. Called I won't give in. Since than I am the man. To call the shots. People what I need from you.

Is a double cheeseburger in happy meal fries. Because I made it to the next over yall. And Gabriel is my wife. They training me. Thomas pick up your goddamn game up. I love you Gabriel Union Allred. I love you too Thomas Allred Jr. This contract is solely between Gabrielle Union and Thomas Allred Jr. For your hand in marriage Ill do anything. Its is witnessed By the following officials. This contract can't be tempted with. Gabriel i release you from our wedding proposal. I hope that this will satisfy you enough. And prove my honesty to you. I've searched the world for you Gabriel. And without a ado here is your contract. All you have to do is say yes to my proposal. I'm saying yeah Thomas.Gabriel Union Allred you are now one of the richest women on the street. Just ask that voice inside your head who's talking. But why Thomas. For no reason. God sent me to police station. He's telling me what to do right now. I'm need you to be strong. And give to me. Two double cheeseburgers with large fries and a cold soft drink please. Now that I see you laughing. Listen to my voice when I tell you that your a Zillionaire I half everything down the exact middle with you my heart is beating if you don't come and get me soon. You know Gabriel Union .

Listen to me people. My name is Gabriel Union Allred. And I hear a pen drop. Right now I'm going to tell you. That I'm not afraid of you anymore. You got a

Zillionaire woman standing right here. And I appreciate you. For making me strong. I also appreciate you. For the rest of your life. I am Gabriel Union Allred. And i approve this message.

Play group thing. Theres somebody here for you Gabriel Union Allred. Send him or her in. Brian McKnight and music soulchild how did you get my address. I made arrangements with we all know Superman and here I am. I had to hop the bus all of the way across town to get here. I'm so sorry you to have a complimentary basket of fruit. No thank you Ms. Gabriel Union Allred we just came to wish you happy birthday before your next show. Well Brian McKnight and music soulchild the show has already begun. What the f*ck I lost my wallet. A guy do you think that I could borrow a dollar. For my car . You see it's broken down. And to fix it I need a dollars worth of gas. Is there any way that I can repay you. If you let me borrow a fresh new dollar. Sir I'm sorry my bank account is twenty one hundred dollars. And I can't spare cent.

Coming to the stage is Ms. Gabriel Union Allred. She is putting make up on .I said coming to the stage is Ms. Queen latifah. Performing unity. Queen latifah how did it go. It was a great evening tonight. Thank you Gabriel Union Allred for calling me back on such short notice. Ladies what I want to do now is keep y'all pussies wet. Mr. Brain McKnight and music soulchild. How did the show go Mr. Brain McKnight and music soulchild. Either way it goes the fans loved it. You have to pay up Thomas Allred Jr. Give us our dollars for the show that we proformed. Well you see what had happened was.

I got your money for you. 88 hundred just like my husband promised you. Thank you Gabriel Union Allred. And Superman you need Jesus playing with me and my bank account. Well music you got your money. The show is over. What are you waiting around for. Thomas Allred Jr and Gabriel Union Allred. Teach me how to love you better. Oh hell no. Brain McKnight where's my fruit basket. Thank you honey Gabriel Union Allred for having my back on those payments to our friends. Your welcome but honestly Thomas Allred Jr what happened to your ends. I don't want to think about it. music I found a wallet. 600 million dollars is in there. I got Superman written in it. This is Thomas Allred Jr wallet. Here Thomas Allred Jr I found your wallet. 600 million bucks Gabriel Union Allred just like we place it there for Brain McKnight . If you do mind me excuse me for a moment. Coming to the stage is Superman Thomas Allred Jr. I couldn't believe that sh*t. I lost my wallet and it took a hero to bring it back to me. Ladies put your hands together for heros Mr. Brain McKnight and Music soulchild . It's undenieable the way things work they self out. Back at one. Y'all can catch me at the hot spot. I'm Thomas Allred Jr and I'm Gabriel Union Allred saying good night. Gabriel Union Allred I'm still in love with you. Im still in love with you to Thomas Allred Jr.Thats our show . Thomas Allred Jr Dru Hill wants to talk to us. 85 hundred dollars just like we promised you.

Thank you Ms. Gabriel Union Allred. Superman you need to get it together. Gabriel Union Allred once again I have to thank you. Thomas Martin Lawrence is here to see you. 87 88 89 hundred dollars Martin Lawrence we are even that's all that my girl and me got. I'm just teaching you a lesson you can't be me out there Superman. Be your self Thomas Allred Jr. Be realistic I'm a give you my spoon rental business. Not rent a spoons. It is rent a spoons have you heard of it.

You know me by now Gabriel Union Allred. I'm the last clean up man that you'll ever here of. Your flowers me pruning. And your heart is heavy. Because that played with you. To many times. Once is more than enough. Welcome to all that is is. And Gabrielle get ready to meet your future. Future man Gabriel. They trying to play us. But they have no fiddle or guitar strings. Police officers take time when they make enough. When I say I'm a clean up man you know what I mean.A house on the lake will do nicely.Gabriel Union Allred. Anywhere with you will make me a King. I'm putting all kinds of energy into this letter. To make you feel like you deserve me. If you know what I'm saying. I want you to call me the last golden child. My business ain't no body's business.

You know how it goes each one teach one. Wait to you see what I got for you. Be professional Gabriel Union Allred I ain't trying to do nothing but clean your house up. Once I meet with you. You'll find me hot to trot. You see Carolina raise me. Im a clean up man. Sweep your woman off of her feet. I'm depending on you. To give this a chance. You can keep the lucky charMs. that you got form me. As for me. Get ready to be with me. This is my second time doing this for the people. I'm waiting on my husband to come away with me. And Gabriel Union Allred. And I'm a Time Enforcement Officer . And your time is beginning. Thomas is my husband. You see hes trying his best to get through the me. The date is 11-17-2019.im sending these paragraphs to you on 11-30-2019. I'm a professional clean up man. How do anything you ask of each other. I do anything you put in front of me. I will find my wife. Thomas Allred . Thomas Allred Jr is looking for me. Is he professional. He wrote a 900 Page letter. Almost 900 give or take a few pages. That boy can read like hell. I like him so do I . So do I. The moral to this story is that you got to be professional.Because we all are time cops. We have got to free my husband. Read though that. Time acceleration doors now opening. Where are you going. I got this hunch. Time acceleration doors now closing. If you betray me one f*cking time. That's it Thomas. Gabriel I'm not that way. I love you. Thomas. I'm coming back for you. Time acceleration doors now opening. Keep up with your charm bracelet. That's how I'll remember you. Why. Cause you pretty wearing it. I'll remember My husband I love you. Time acceleration doors now closing. Girl so did you find Thomas. Yes I did find my husband Thomas Allred Jr .Sorry ain't no more details. Heres a picture of zillionaire and you together ten years ago. Thomas don't look like that now. He is a TEC Enforcement Agent. Time Cop. I'll be with you baby in a second. Time acceleration doors now opening. I love you baby. I love you too. Thomas Gabriella. I better go to keep my position. I'm sitting here waiting on you Gabriella time cop position in my house involves you. Thomas don't ever talk to me like that again.im sorry .Maintain my position. Gabriella I'm a get this contract. Keep on thinking that we will see. Be careful baby. Time acceleration doors now open. I only need you to move up Thomas. But I don't know how to move up without you. Keep using your mind . That's the quickest way I know. Time is acceleration now closing. So what is Thomas Allred doing. Momma. I couldn't tell you if I tried. He is after his contract.

To my dearest Gabriel Union Allred. I leave to you. The networking to all of my inventions that if anything should ever happen to me. These are not just stories my dear Gabriel Union Allred. I'm scared that you will not love me right. If I tell you that I really do have 800 thousand zillion dollars. I'm a porching the infinity sign as we speak. What I'm saying is that. I'm a need you to be a big girl and handle this responsibility as it comes to you. I wish that you. Could get to know me my heart is in the right place. Maintain listen. I'm thinking to myself you and me could be something real. And I need you to realize that I'm in desperate need of a soulmate. To manage my account for me.

I'll put 65 more zillion in your account for you. Now that it is done. Don't say nothing about it to me. All because when my people ordered if. I put a yes grin on my face. All I'm trying to do is make up for lost time. With a I love you open heart symbol. Of my affection . Anyhow Cusack wouldn't be bothering us. Im seeing to it. That my pictures of you remain tasteful. Thank you. Time Enforcement Cop Thomas Allred Jr. I want you to know that you are my husband in the future. No matter what you think of me I'm still a good guy in the future. I've only been through some things. Is my p**sy ok. That p**sy bad come here girl I want you . Second thing is keep talking to you cat Gabriel Union Allred I'm trying to make sure that you get this money. Hollywood access code is. 3978 652-431-0486 . Gabriel Union Allred I watched you on the television. For all of my life. And now I want a chance with you. Gabriel please understand that I'm just a cop. Suspended through time. Thomas Allred Jr don't give in do he. No girl that's my man. He ain't never going to give in. He is up to speed now time circuits on. Gabriel Union Allred. I miss you that's. Thanks for coming back for me again and again. Gabriel Union Allred is now up to speed .To this day I've been in love with you Thomas Allred Jr. Our money is gone. No it ain't Gabriel. It is in a bank account in Zurich. Is this the end of our story. Time acceleration doors now opening. Michael J Fox's Thomas Allred Jr. You still got one wish left Gabriel Union Allred for your belated birthday. Ha ha ha. That can be arranged. Michael J Fox's is and actor. Ain't he the coolest. Time acceleration doors now closing. Hollywood access code is. 710 908-642-9381.Thomas we're back it's all over . Gabriel Union Allred I'm in my room at my mother's house in Longview

North Carolina. And I'm on the TV screen Thomas Allred Jr. You cannot see me. But you can here me . Alot of people care for you Thomas Allred Jr. Gabriel Union Allred honey what is going on. We are Time Enforcement Officers Thomas Allred Jr. And so it went she talked about the future and how Terminator Eddie Murphy and Martin Lawrence and Will Smith. And TI and Jay z. And Kanye West. Where all planning to take over the world. And on our side we got Kim Kardashian. And Jada pinkett Smith. And Tiny. And Beyonce. And Tisha Campbell. And Robin Gibbons. And Reba McIntosh and Jessica Alba. Along with every other Amazon woman in the world. We are fighting to stop Terminator Eddie Murphy. If its the last thing that we do. This is a contract. Between Thomas Allred Jr and Gabriel Union Allred. Girl I'm giving you the access code. To my future. and I hope that we can one day come to terMs. and to grips. With this movie about to go off. Three is Company stand up for yourself. Because we make sure that you're ok. I ain't no fool. I love you Gabriel. Now your safe and your okay . In your own bed. Thomas Allred Jr. I had the strangest dream. Go back to sleep Gabriel Union Allred. When you awake your bank account will be full. That is the end of our movie. Listen to me Thomas Allred Jr. If you ever need me. Say my name in the TV screen. And I'll be there for you Thomas Allred Jr. Goodnight threes Company

Is it my personality.Or Is it my personality. The way that I look. That keep sending me through all these challenges. Yet i feel like I'm in a game show. My man is sitting there. From the beginning to end with me. Pick up the pace Thomas Jr Allred . I have got to know that your with me. Gabrielle Union Allred my princess. There is trouble off the cost of Switzerland. Something has to be done about these angels. They are play mates for sure. He knows how to get up on our f*cking team. Look its Charlie's Angels on a TV show. I Don't care what you do. Just save those angels on the coastline.Thomas Allred Jr was making up all kind of rules. Now that he got his money back. Thomas Allred Jr. I told him. Can i be with you. He kept on blowing kisses at my body. All night the sea crushed on the shore. Yall get to bed. That's what you told me. As you turned around and said April fool's yall. This is a Holiday rendition. Here my man is. It's true Gabriel. You are a Time cop. Show Thomas Allred Jr what Time cop really stand for. Gabriel Union Allred. Enforcement Officer of you. So that is meaning that you Thomas Allred Jr. Are lock down until farther notice from Gabriel Union Allred and the TEC Time Force Agency . One other thing Thomas Allred Jr your my husband. But you are not the Loin King. Take him away. Gabriel Union Allred wait honey I got you this present. From Aspen it's a small moonstone that changes color when you hold on to it tight enough. Look honey. Gabriel Union Allred see. I love you. Please don't lock me down Thomas Allred Jr. Hold on to that Stone cause not even Superman can get you out of this one. For breaking codes of honesty Thomas Allred Jr. How do you plead. Ladies and gentlemen I have been honest. Then we find that you are a Hustler. That's it put your phone down and go now to sleep Thomas Allred Jr. Where am I Gabriel Union Allred. Sir you are in the TEC headquarters chef Thomas Allred Jr. Sir you got a request. From Share she wants to go back in time. Definitely not. See you can handle it. Plus you got me for eternity to help you with it . This is our home. Any last final words. Gabriel Union Allred you are amazing. To save my husband I had to get locked down. Because the Time acceleration continuum is tricky . Some days you win some. Someday you lose some. Unless you stay lockdown. To Someone you love. All I know. Is that I'm tired of running . Back and forth. For my life from. Major Payne. Damon Wayans report to the Time office. She done told Told on me. For Officer conduct. Uncommon Lee of a man. We place you on lockdown. With Karen Parsons. As your Time enforcement Officer. Can my lady say Amen. Don't feel bad. These ladies are Time enforcement officers everywhere. Do me a favor Gabriel Union Allred. You can't survive with just to people. The three of us can. Gabriel Union Allred. We'll talk about this in the morning. Its lights out time. My direction was simple. Go through Time and save Thomas Allred Jr from extinction. I done my job. And now the United States Presidents want to thank you. Gabriel Union Allred for winning in time. Cop.

We thank you. And there's one other thing Gabriel Union Allred. If you ever need anything just send for me TEC advisor Superman Thomas Allred Jr and White House Chef of staff Major Payne Damon Wayne's. Gabriel Union Allred your house is almost ready we building. To all of the Time professionals. Goodnight. Gabriel Union Allred here is your moonstone it is from your husband. Thank you everyone. Its final over or is it. Wait a minute there I can use me something to drink . Hi you doing sweet thang. I am the ladies man Leon Phelps. And you look like you haven't had s*x in a while. I'm pregnant Leon that was fast . But look here I have got to be going. Here ladies man . What is it. It's a moonstone to guide you on your mission. Thank you Gabriel Union Allred. You welcome. A how did you know my name. From the press conference on the set. And plus we are still in the conference room goodnight Leon Phelps. The ladies man. Goodnight beautiful lady. Gabriel Union Allred are you ready Superman yes dear I am. Let go than. Let go. This is my rendition of what had happened that night. So I just hope that I made sense miss Barbara Bush. You made perfect sense Thomas Allred Jr is on lockdown. And you also captured Major Payne. Karen Parsons is his commanding officer. Still there's one more mission. Gabriel Union Allred I want you to capture Steve Harvey. I already captured Steve Harvey. He's In simulation room eating food by hiMs.elf a waiting on judgement. Well less don't leaving him waiting too long. President George Bush. And president Donald Trump. And president Barack Obama. And president Bill Clinton. History is in the making. Steve Harvey. You've been entertaining our people for a while. Steve Harvey we give to you the president awards. For being open to new things.

Okay y'all come back in a half an hour. I'm going to finish up these potatoes. Listen Gabriel don't try nothing fancy. Every house we go. I'm saying Merry Christmas and Happy New year Gabriel Union Allred. Happy Thanksgiving everybody. I came to you in hopes of thanking over in your current situation. With Gabriel Union Allred on the top of this. We going to help you to see. That you are better off on the fifth floor staying with Martin and Gina. Put Hustle Man out of his apart . And into and apartment with Martin and Gina. Martain will love this. Just sign on the dotted like and the steaks and bake potatoe are your. But don't say nothing about this contract. Hustle man. Time is accelebration doors now opening. Martin and Gina. Hustle man don't sign that damn contract man. Yeah Hustle Man it took us six years to find out what you did. Putting out these flyers. Need some space call Martin and Gina house. And Thomas Allred Jr and Gabriel Union Allred what are you doing here. I Fumbled your heart. Come on Gina where getting out of here. Hustle man the deal is off. Time acceleration doors now closing. Our present time.

If Hustle Man isnt moving in with Martin Gina. Then who got the steaks baked potato. Martin and Gina. That is a Indecent Proposal. Hello no I'm going after them. Gabriel Union Allred wait on me. Martin and Gina give up the steaks.Oh those steaks where yours. We knew they was. Terminator Eddie Murphy wants to see you that's why we took them. How's it going Terminator Eddie Murphy. I need another stake. And I'm prepared to pay top dollar for it. Do you like my proposal is it indecent. Terminator Eddie Murphy turn off. Thank you Gina. Martin. Get the hell out of here. Damn Gabriel. I guess it be like that sometime. Damn right it be like that sometime. How about we go and sleep on it.Now that's the indecent proposal that I want. Hustle Man get out of my apartment eating the last piece of chicken .Oh that was my bad. You want these bake potatoes instead. Hustle Man go home. What about our contract. Hustle Man go there is no contract. I'll be back in three seconds. Gabriel Union Allred I love you . I love you too Thomas Allred Jr. But why did we need Hustle Mans apartment in the first place. So we can store our business plans in there Gabriel Union Allred . Think honey. And what's is our business strategy Thomas Allred Jr. Rent a spoons. Gabriel Union Allred. Rent a spoons. Thomas I'll kill you.

Caruso im finished talking to you. You got me see in that. You a puppy on the string. One more thing. You have been terminated. My time code. 71812. Whatever. Gabriel Union Allred. You think. That I'm afraid. To enter another time code. Caruso. May God have mercy on your soul. Gabriel this is haunting me. Go back outside don't walk over here. What did I tell you precious. I put the juice in time cop. But how Caruso. Because I didn't pay attention to the rules. Time cop. When you gone as far through time as I have you see things. You were able to cheat death in one life. And in this one Caruso who are you cheating. I'm looking to cheat each one of the time cop out of there time. I don't believe that you can do it. The captain is still working through time. Working with my secrets Gabriel. What secret are you telling. I got time on my side. Caruso Caruso im a kill your a**. Look at you. I'm beginning to show in you Gabriel. Thank your Jesus. That girl honest as hell. Isn't that what everyone used to say about you. You ain't got but one more chance. To make something out of yourself. Caruso can you me and listening to me good. Not only am I going to wipe you away from existence. But when I figure out just how you got in my head in the first place. I need you to know. That your a** belongs to me. Gabrielle Union decorated cop on the time force. I am something you have never seen before. I entered your mind the second you killed my body. This has to be simulation chamber.

You have pa**ed your test now Gabriel. Two Caruso to faced. Then you and me. Be doing our best. Keeping one eye straight. Superman can we not. I need to look at Caruso files. Just as I thought. Caruso wasnt dirty. Her boyfriend was. Do you know this means. What does it mean Gabriel. I shoudnt have changed the course of time. Superman. Get into the truck with me on the other side. Thomas going to get his contract. Don't you both have something to say. Cusack. Let us by Cusack time is waisting. How about you tell me how the two of you keep maneuvering through time. Cusack drop the gun. Throw over your time modules. Aw f*ck this sh*t . Gabriel no. You shot him. Superman get back in the truck. We can't go hes bleeding. Superman get back in the truck now I know what I'm doing. I can't leave him. Why. Cause Cusack is my friend. Stay here Superman I'll be back. Time elimination chamber now starting. Time acceleration doors now opening. Gabriel where are you going. Make something right. Time acceleration doors now closing. Time elimination chamber now starting. Gabriel get me out of here I did nothing wrong. Elimination in 10 9 8 7 6 5 432. Take your time Caruso. You got all day to tell me that story. Gabriel Union Allred there go your one true love Superman Thomas Allred Jr. We'll he ever know that you are in love with him. Him and Cusack will never know me. But I see just what kinda man he is by the way that he kept standing up for his friends. Superman Thomas Allred Jr I commend you. Just like you did for me Thomas Allred Jr. Time acceleration doors now opening. Time acceleration doors now closing. Honey I'm home . Honey. Surprise happy birthday to you.

Now that things are over and done with. Yes Gabriel Union Allred. Thomas do you have something to say. Baby I'm sorry I took so long to get back with you. Its because they had me trapped out on the field. Listen Thomas Allred Jr. All is fair in love and war. Okay love and war. I have no idea what you saying to me. Your contact is ready. What contact. We settling everything. Thomas Allred Jr what we need to do. Is buy some more rent a spoons. I was thinking the exact same thing. And that's how it goes. The first time I seen him. The first time I seen her. It was on vacation. It was on vacation in Vermont. He had business. She had a business. What was his business. Selling rent a spoons. Her new business was. I'll Teidi Up.

Any questions. It's a God damn different day in the moon de. Gabriel Union Allred all I'm saying is get your time codes ready . Thomas Allred Jr can I do to make you see that they didn't change my. Talking about they change you. I know you solid Gabriel Union Allred. That doesn't mean that everyone else knows I'm solid Thomas Allred. Here just put these things in my truck and lock it. This is the second time that I put these things in your truck. Thomas i come to fix the Circle. And in this world you are the Lion King. I can't believe what you saying my circle is complete. Thomas I know your family really needs you. But you are the one true Loin King. And they shots you because of it. They shot two times Loin King. When they broke your heart. Since that girl left me. I just haven't been the same. That's because she was your eternal mate Thomas. What is today. Here in the moon de. We call this day Sunday the November 18, 2019.

We all go by numeric clocks. No favoritism this way. Gabriel Union Allred why are you so damn consumed with the circle. It's the one thing that truly over me in my lifetime existence. You should read a book on how to speak to yourself with no mate Thomas Allred Jr. As the true Loin King. I requested you from out of mini Gabriel Union Allred. You have requested me sir. Yes Gabriel Union Allred. For what reason Thomas Allred Jr. Gabrielle Union Allred see. We trying to help you to understand that. You are a part of the light. And the circle isnt complete without you Gabriel Union Allred. Look I'm a Time Enforcement Officer. We know that your a Time Enforcement Officer Gabriel Union Allred. We took our time and selected you.

Listen Thomas Allred Jr. I realize that your in pain over losing your wife Jeana. But I'm to strong for you. Can't you feel the love tonight. You got to give me a cigarette. Gabriel what are you doing with that. Calling Gabriel. Timer acceleration doors now opening. Thomas Allred a great story. You almost had me believing you. Gabriel Union Allred I know take this with you. So that you can remember me. As the true Loin King. Thomas Allred Jr. I need a couple more minutes to straighten out my head. What are you going to to do. I have to go straighten out something. You never will get it with you. The circle is the time continuum. This is meaning that we know what you doing. In any time romance that you go in. Well can you stop criminals. You see I selected you Gabriel Union Allred. Through a time continuum. I have watched you go back and forth through time into a paradox. The surrenders your heart beat. To Loin King territory. Surrender my heart .Thomas Allred Jr you need to come up with a new one. I Already know that you search for your husband. He is in another spirit world. Exactly. My sweet sweet Jeana. Remains the truth Queen of the Loin Kingdom. Will you name our son. I don't get what you saying .will you name our son. Gabriel Union Allred take the time and listen. I Said will you name our son. Thomas Allred Jr. You know that I can't do this. It is okay Gabrielle Union Allred. We are two different creatures. I'm a King out here. That knows when a lady needs help. But life is eternal Thomas Allred Jr. As I go back through time. Ill remember Thomas Allred Jr one thing. That the Lion King is Thomas Allred Jr.

And that you are my husband. In another time zone. Time acceleration doors now closing. Watch what you saying man. Keep on listening to Gabriel Union Allred. They talking about giving you to Thomas Allred Jr. The new and improved Thomas Allred Jr. It's may husband. Gabriel Union Allred this is courtesy of the Loin King. Y'all my search is over. Thomas Allred Jr go to your wife. And y'all make love. Thomas Allred Jr Gabriel Union Allred honey I miss you so much. The circle is complete everybody. When the Lion King touches you. Than you are heal cause you are the Lion King and Time Enforcement Officer Thomas Allred Jr. And I am Time Enforcement Officer Gabriel Union Allred. Coming in with our reports now . I characterized you. My leader and my friend Thomas Allred Jr. Thank you Gabriel Union.

Girl I'm your man. I can see that you have no clue as to what we are doing. Don't you ever go nowhere because Gabriel Union Allred I might need you for some thing. Listen Thomas it's really good to see all of the business that you have got for me but I am kinda in the middle of something. Am I hurting your feeling. Do you understand what I'm saying to you. Yes Gabriel Union Allred I grew up listening to you your a house hold name in my house. I suggest that you sit down and read the whole manuscript Gabriel Union Allred. This message well self destruct in 5 4 3 2 1. Congratulations Gabriel Union Allred you are incredible. One more thing mission impossible is waiting for you. Will you marry me. O yeah Gabriel Union Allred what I wanted to say is I'm working on a new and better manuscript called Twilight Eclipse I'm writing the name down as we speak. Keep on writing Thomas Allred Jr and yes I'll be your wife. I was thinking about you.

Thomas I can't reach it. Gabriel Union Allred keep reaching for it. This boy is professional. I'm trying to get it but I can't Thomas Allred Jr. Gabriel Union Allred baby listen to me . If you keep trying sweetheart you can reach the top. It's not here Thomas Allred Jr. Gabriel Union Allred you are my wife and your beautiful. The top is there Gabriel Union Allred. Keep trying and you will get there. We have got to produce that man and woman . Who are they Ridd*ck I have got no clue. But if she keeps trying. She is going to reach the A list. Don't you give up on me Thomas Allred Jr do you here me. Gabriel Union Allred I'm trying. You need a contract Thomas Allred Jr. Gabriel Union Allred I'm trying to see if there's anymore cookies left in this jar. He trying to eat. Ridd*ck strange these people.

Thomas Allred Jr is professional. Gabriel Union Allred you have got to prove your self to me. Ain't no way that I can get there Thomas Allred Jr. It's just to far for me. Oh my God it's Vin Diesel. Get your a**es over here Thomas Allred Jr and Gabriel Union Allred. Go the phone off of the counter . We about to call Domino's Pizza. Vin Diesel I'm cool. I haven't eaten. You can't be serious with me you haven't eaten. Look I'm about to give you two some of my free rewards. From Domino's

Pizza. You got see what I'm saying behave yourself I'm out once this pizza get ready. Now what you Gabriel Union Allred and Thomas Allred Jr Reaching for. The top of our industry. We reaching for the bed the top of the industry ain't that far as it is. I'm a take my time and pretend to I didn't here that. Vin Diesel That's for your help but my wife and I are going to need some quiet time . Thomas Allred Jr do you know what you lack. Is personality. Wait a minute Ridd*ck or Vin Or what ever they call you. I just ready to jump on you. Happy birthday Vin Diesel . Thomas Allred Jr and Gabriel Union Allred. This is the best birthday of my life. Being with some down home people. Vin Diesel we aint down home people. This your audition for a movie that's coming out called Vin Diesel The Top. Hollywood access code 827-6150 4279 5376.Your a Time Cop Vin Diesel And Thomas Allred Jr and I Gabriel Union Allred have captured you. Remain professional. The boss lady wants to see you. Miss Barbara Bush.

Well Vin Diesel are you ready turn yourself in. I hadn't planned on it Miss Bush. Give him time he'll come around Barbara. George Bush I don't know. We captured Tyrese last night. He was at a all-you-can-eat buffet. Tyrese. Do you know who I am. Look Thomas Allred Jr people watching us. Than ill let Gabriel Union Allred speak to you. Tyrese do you believe in me. I didn't get to eat my food last night so I don't know what the believe Gabriel Union Allred. Get Tyrese some food right now. We making a movie called Vin Diesel On The Top. Tyrese is the star of the film. It's being written as we speak and sent to publishers. Who are all these people thats watching that girl. I didn't mean to say that Ms. Barbara Bush.

Is totally alright gentleman. I don't like the shows you been doing. So I'm producing a new show. Called Vin Diesel on the top of the world. I play hard as I can. Listen theres only one person we got to see in this movie. And that is you. Who are them people out there. That our Fan base Vin Diesel. And Tyrese. This is the Chronicles of Gabrielle Union Allred volume one . And my movie is just started. We got ludacris. Good job Jimmy Walker. We all know JJ from good times. Ludacris how are you doing. Oh sh*t. I got kidnapped by JJ. Again. Let me see. Vin Diesel. Tyrese. Gabriel Union Allred. Thomas Allred jr.. miss Barbara Bush. So that you know the mean one thing. What. The president is after me. George Bush. Welcome ludacris to our little Circle. We got Tyra Banks Mr.. George Bush. Damn get off me. She's just as mean as one of them Ali cats.Tyra Banks. Honey it's okay. Vin Diesel and Tyrese. Ludacris. Behind you is Jimmy Walker. JJ kidnap me again. You can say what you want to Tyra Banks but this movie is about to start. Gabriel Union Allred I knew it had to be you . So where are the hidden cameras. There no hidden cameras. You six people are going to be our entourage at and very important dinner.

Where in the United States of America. Are you surprised yet professionals. They captured Roseanne Barr. Oh hell you again Jimmy Walker. Roseanne come in and get acquainted with the people I'm sure that you all know each other . And Superman Thomas Allred Jr what are you doing here . Roseanne Barr I really don't know . I just wrote the story. And now I'm here. I got a little game that I want to play. Saw Superman you wrote us In to a Saw movie. That muthaf*cker don't wrote us in to a Saw movie. Listen Tyrese Gibson this isn't a Saw movie. This is The Chronicles of Gabrielle Union Allred. Well can I go to the bathroom. How do you go to the bathroom on this unit. Right this way Ms. Tyra Banks. The rest of you go get in the showers all your clothes we'll be provided for you the same way you are use to getting them . By dress code. You get enough food to go in your belly Mr.. Tyrese Gibson. I'm still hungry.

Hey y'all don't got any music. Who funds this place. I'm a kick your a** Vin Diesel. What the hell is going on up in here. A couple of more girls and we'll have a party. Well stop that sh*t. We got one more night before they they to kill each one of you. Ms. Barbara Bush mam what are you saying. I'm already no Barbara Bush ain't playing. So read your message on your decoder phones. And wait for everything to that play and happen. This is a safe place. Hell no the last time I went though this sh*t I was in a room like this for three damn years.

Tyra Banks Superman Thomas Allred Jr knows what he is doing. Ok Superman Thomas Allred Jr what are we doing in here . And who is trying to take us out this this. All that I can tell you guys is we all are in terrible danger. And I suggest you not leave any time soon. We can leave . No you can't leave . They put us in a saw movie. Tyrese Gibson I promise you that this is not a saw movie. Well who it the little girl that in the corner laid out than. You say this is the Chronicles of Gabrielle Union Allred. You check her out than. What girl that's in the corner Tyrese Gibson. She was right there a moment ago. Look in the mirror thank you Tyrese Gibson your the only one that noticed that little girl. Hologram image. Tyres Gibson you can take your time and have a dinner of your choice. Good cause I stay hungry. Take your time Thomas Allred Jr and back us out of this program. I'm trying Ms. Barbra Bush. I just can't get it to shut down by itself. Shut the damn thing damn. It's not as simple as it seeMs.. Hit the power button on it. Okay that there shut it down .

Thank you Vin Diesel this man may go home now him and Tyrese Gibson are the first to leave our mantion. The hell they are if one of us leave that all of us leaves. Roseanne Barr I you were giving to chance and opportunity to go home tonight what would you do with it. I'd give it to you Tyra Banks and Ludacris. Tyra Banks and Ludacris can now go home along with Tyrese Gibson and Vin Diesel . What is this its almost like a game show. Thomas Allred Jr tell my future. Gabriel Union Allred your future looks sunny but party cloudy. It's never raining in doors Superman Thomas Allred Jr. Gabriel Union Allred has a free past to give to anyone in wich she chooses. Jimmy Walker you may go home now. Wait a minute you guys

I'm a big fan of each of you . Write your name on this sheet of paper I'm letting you know that Roseanne. Barr cares for you. Roseanne Barr you are now free to go. Okay what is this if it's a chance we didn't do nothing. Ladies and gentleman in the sky box is miss Hillary Rodman Clinton. And miss Michelle Obama. Alone with Mr.. Donald Trump. And Mr.. Barack Obama. And president Bill Clinton.

We texted you guys. To see if you had character. Gabriel Union Allred the Chronicles is almost done. Superman Thomas·Allred Jr. We saved the best for last. How would you like a movie contract.

I would love to have a movie contract. It was written that. Superman Bill Clinton helped Thomas Allred Jr out with the problem of not having anything to do with those rainy days. It's about time that he can see. I felt better to be on top. Gabriel Union Allred I love you. I really do sweetheart. That you all for everything thank you Ms. Oprah Winfrey. You do have to thank me Thomas Allred Jr just continue winning. Thomas Allred Jr you are free to wait for us to make a decision on you based on your Merritt Thomas Allred Jr. The Chronicles of Gabriel Union Allred is now over. Just like that I'm on top again Thomas Allred Jr. Gabriel Union Allred I new you could do it. Where everybody go come on Gabriel Union Allred we hungry we are going to stay at the top. I'm Pokemon Ms. Gabriel Union Allred. You don't know what I got in store for you Pokemon. I'm Gabriel Union Allred. The Chronicles of Gabriel Union Allred have now needed. Listen Thomas Allred Jr. we know that you strong enough to get yourself a movie roll. But do you really want it. Because we all see the look on your face. I know what your able of doing.

Sleep on this tonight Thomas Allred Jr. We watching everything that you do. Don't give up my contract Thomas Allred Jr. I'm Gabriel Union Allred and I'm teaching you this. This is how you getting into the movies Thomas Allred Jr. What an opportunity this is. To be a part of the entertainment industry. Thomas Allred Jr you almost through with your test. Your bank account is 160 trillion zillion dollars. Are you happy yes. Gabriel Union Allred. I just pa**ed my test. And I love you. Your medicine helps you. To cope with everything around you Thomas Allred Jr. I will come you into this industry .With open arMs. Thomas Allred Jr. President Bill Clinton. Thomas I'm not the president anymore. You is in my case. And there you have it. Hillary Rodman Clinton. Got some thing to tell you. Take a damn bath Thomas Allred Jr . Your test is now over.Look the reason I tell you this is. Say nothing. Access granted has been recording you. For 25 years Thomas Allred Jr. People shot you. And you didn't do nothing but get up and walk. That's why I give you the name. Superman Thomas Allred Jr. To carry with you. In this industry for all times. All you got to do Thomas is clean up yourself. Your family situation with change. I can see right now you don't believe me Superman Thomas Allred Jr. Fire engines. I did that Thomas Allred Jr. Thomas think to yourself. I love Gabriel Union Allred. Just sending your book. The Chronicles of Gabriel Union Allred. Right now.

I got it Thomas Allred Jr. I knew that you would Gabriel Union Allred. Is there anything I can do for you Thomas Allred Jr. Call me Superman Thomas Allred Jr Gabriel Union Allred. Okay Superman Thomas Allred Jr. Always Gabriel Union Allred. Always Superman Thomas Allred Jr. Is There anything I can do for you Gabriel Union Allred. I looked in her eyes and she said. Superman Thomas Allred Jr . All sorts of females love it when you call me Angel Lois Lane Gabriel Union Allred. Could you please do that for me. Superman Thomas Allred Jr. From now on immediately. Yes Ms. Angel Lois Lane Gabriel Union Allred.

I will do it always. You will do what always Superman Thomas Allred Jr. I will call you by your neutral name Ms. Angel Lois Lane Gabriel Union Allred. Your the Champion Angel Lois Lane Gabriel Union Allred. Everyone get Gabriel Union her belt. Ms. Oprah Winfrey I knew that it had to be you. I'm a bad woman Gabriel Union . Ms. Oprah Winfrey I go by the name of Your Highness Angel Lois Lane Gabriel Union Allred. Your Highness it's nice to make your acquaintance. Gabriel Union . Ms. Michelle Obama. I heard your new name is all of our Queen Your Highness Angel Lois Lane Gabriel Union Allred. Yes Ms. Michelle Obama . And who gave you this idea. Well I did Ms. Michelle Obama. Great job Your Highness Angel Lois Lane Gabriel Union Allred. You are our new womens champion in the business sector. Thank you Hillary Clinton. I'm coming to get you Your Highness Angel Lois Lane Gabriel Union Allred . Phil Donahue.

It's time that you learned your lesson Your Highness Angel Lois Lane Gabriel Union Allred. Mr. Superman Thomas Allred Jr has requested that hiMs.elf and his whole neighborhood in Longview North Carolina move in your neighborhood. With you Princess Gabriel Union Allred. I do mean my wife Your Highness Angel Lois Lane Gabriel Union Allred. I have found hard for your hand in marriage in our stories and in true life. Your Highness Angel Lois Lane Gabriel Union Allred. This is Superman Thomas Allred Jr. And I'm asking for you to pull over that a** is to fat. What I'm trying to say is when I first stepped on the sence people where petrified. Your Highness Angel Lois Lane Gabriel Union Allred. Just give him time Superman Thomas Allred Jr is new at this. Yes Ms. Barbara Bush. Do the right thing for your shorty. Superman Thomas Allred Jr. Let Tyra Banks tell her. Tell me what girl. Superman has bought you and island. Complete with complimentary chefs. In all culture's. You got to pick up your game. Superman is and industry Leader. In another month Mr. Thomas Allred Jr name will be every where. And he chooses you Your Highness Angel Lois Lane Gabriel Union Allred to be his wife now. What do you say. This is the Chronicles of Gabriel Union Allred Volume two. Yes i love that boy. Get your butt out that seat. We have a new mission apun as . Your Highness Angel Lois Lane Gabriel Union Allred. We don't have enough road for this .

We captured Michael J Fox's. Your Highness Angel Lois Lane Gabriel Union Allred. Where we are going we don't need roads. Hey would run this thing . Your

Highness Angel Lois Lane Gabriel Union Allred and Superman Thomas Allred Jr. Run this thing. You've been a**igned a movie Michael J Fox's. I don't believe it. Take a look around you. I've been kidnapped by Jimmy Walker again. JJ y'all have got to quit that sh*t. Michael J Fox's. In the first installment episode there was 7 people to be giving a question. Hear we have but you. Tyra this is not America's next top model let's get to it. Michael J Fox's. Who is the English amba**ador. Why I Michael J Fox's . Have no idea what to say to that question. Honesty. Michael J Fox's you may lead my ship for a day. I want you to live on this island with me. If Superman Thomas Allred Jr can agree. I agree. Your Highness Angel Lois Lane Gabriel Union Allred.

We have captured LeAnn Rimes and Reba McIntosh. Ladies welcome to my test. Superman Thomas Allred Jr. Look around you. We have been kidnapped by Jimmy Walker again. Man I seen it coming. I got one question for you. Who is the king and queen of the business industry. Why it's you Superman Thomas Allred Jr and Your Highness Angel Lois Lane Gabriel Union Allred. The whole world already knows you. Superman Thomas Allred Jr. Barack Obama had something to say. Reba McIntosh. And LeAnn Rimes. As for a beauty queen. Ladies you are pretty queen yourself. We thank you for all your help. In making this book a success. Let me help you. On to your brand new island. We captured Whoopi Goldberg. And Monique. Miss Hillary Clinton how you doing girl. I'm okay Monique. You and Whoopi Goldberg. Have been giving one question to answer. Seriously. Look around you. You mean Jimmy Walker kidnapped us again. Is your question Monique and Whoopi Goldberg. If you had a billion dollars. How would you spend it. We would spend it on and island. You did exactly what I thought you do. Ladies and gentlemen welcome to majesty.

There go Tyrese and Vin diesel. And Roseanne Barr and Ludacris. Look ya'll here comes Michael J Fox's and LeAnn Rimes and Reba McIntosh and Monique and Whoopi Goldberg. There go Your Highness Angel Lois Lane Gabriel Union Allred and Superman Thomas Allred Jr. This is your island. And you are free to do whatever you want to on it. We started business over. And you have to more days to make up your mind if you want to stay. The way they serving us food hell yeah I want to stay. We should leave that to ludacris. Here we go. I just captured Madonna. Superman Thomas Allred Jr you hear me. I think we are going to have some fun. I'm a treky Superman Thomas Allred Jr. Your Highness Angel Lois Lane Gabriel Union Allred what are we doing here. We're kissing. I'm making sure Superman Thomas Allred Jr. As a added bonus your money is no good here. This has been a dream of mine since I can remember. Get some food Superman Thomas Allred Jr. To you and Your Highness Angel Lois Lane Gabriel Union Allred. We welcome you to Majesty island. I'll be right back. Your time codes are going off. Time acceleration doors now opening. Your Highness Angel Lois Lane Gabriel Union Allred listen to me you don't have to go anywhere. But I do. Time is acceleration doors now closing. Gabriel me a full report. Damon Wayans I need some more time. When Steve Harvey says that he wants a full report he wants it right now. Damon Wayans I'm trying to get this man out of my system. Superman Thomas Allred Jr is my hero. And I'm telling you and Steve's Harvey that I'm going to stick by his side to the end. Time acceleration doors now opening . Gabriel Union Allred . Yes Steve Harvey and Major Payne. Do forget your crown because Gabriel Union Allred . You and Thomas Allred have pa**ed your second text. There is one more test. Time is celeration doors now closing. You don't need to here the rest. This is the Chronicles of Gabrielle Union Allred. Volume two. With Hillary Clinton in command. Bill Clinton has something to say. I been sitting right here thinking for the last minute and Donald Trump has some thing to say. Your Highness Angel Lois Lane Gabriel Union Allred. You have impressed us. Your kind nature has impressed us all. To Your Highness Angel Lois Lane Gabriel Union Allred. We thank you.Thomas

Here goes nothing Thomas Allred Jr. I don't understand you Gabriel Union Allred. Why girl is it. That you insist on trimming the turkey for me. Let me see I. Can forget to tell you. That you mean the world to me. Gabriel Union Allred you mean that you care for me.I mean i care for you. Thomas Allred Jr think about what you just said to me. What did I say to you honey. It's not important. It's important to me Gabriel Union Allred. You missed my greeting. Stop the presses . The whole town is under suspicion. For that missing greeting. Hear it is Thomas Allred Jr. Before we eat our Christmas dinners. Don't make a fool out of me Thomas Allred Jr. I'm not Gabriel Union Allred I love you so much. Honey please trust and believe in me. I will not hurt you ever in life and beyond. I need you Gabriel Union Allred. Honey I'm praying for the day that I can meet you. In person because you are the best thing thats out there single besides me. Gabriel Union Allred I knew that you were my wife and my best friend. When I seen you in the movie theaters and how I wanted to be with you. They call me Superman were I'm from. And Gabriella Union Allred I want you to seriously go over my application for love and happiness because I'm a Zillionaire in real life . To have a friend like you would be awesome. To Gabriella Union Allred.

Thomas Allred Jr you know you can't brag over your money. People are watching you Thomas Allred Jr. Girl I just want to see how much I can spend before I die in this world. The new papers is going to tell you that you spending $675 zillion dollars. Gabriel Union Allred I just want to say. I love you. And I'm sorry that money is in my life. As if it is a person. Now tell me how long does it take money to clear in the bank. Be I'm famished. You mean you famous Thomas Allred Jr. That to Gabriel Union Allred. I been watching you Gabriel Union Allred for some time now. And I see right now. That you are going to need a new pair of shoes. Think about what your saying Thomas Allred Jr. 685 zillion dollars is shose money. You just said

Thomas Allred Jr that you are worth 675 zillion dollars. Now Wich is it . Gabriel a** off this morning. I have the infinity sign. Besides these X's . Infinity. Thomas Allred Jr the infinity sign means that you are the richest man and woman in the world. I know ain't that something. Thomas Allred Jr I'm teaching you that in my life. I need me a new bank account. I could tell she was thinking about me. So I married her anyway. We having lunch on the top of the four seasons. I'm new to this but it feels like I got the money that it doesn't matter if a few crumbs are blown. Your coming up on the infinity sign again in our joint bank account Sutherland. Thomas Allred Jr did you hear what I'm just saying to you. You pretending to be Kiefer Sutherland in the lost boys. Is not going to make this money to stop growing. What am I going to do. Gabriel Union Allred. Don't spend all your money. The black people know that you have star capabilities. Sweetheart. You and I are Zillionaires. Girl we are was past star capabilities. Gabriel Union Allred we have got so much money. That you and I can't spend anything because it ain't cleared the bank yet. So what do you suggest we do.

Thomas Allred Jr. Let's make love Gabriel Union Allred. Thomas Allred Jr. And Gabriel Union Allred. I need you right now in the other news room. This is the Daily Planet. There's one news room. He just wants us out of the bathroom Gabriel Union Allred. I'm a take my time and try to help you. In my whilest dreaMs.. Have I kissed a man like you. You are Superman. Girl I need you to be quiet. I have a bank account. Now that's it. Thomas Allred Jr. Your secret is safe with me. What ever we do Gabriel Union Allred. Let's put money into our Superman movie. And our business will mature and grow responsible in my bank account you mean wich is our back account. Thomas how long do you want me to hide the fact that you are our Superman of the business world. I don't see any reason for you to hide it. Anymore Gabriel Union Allred is everything you saying to me correct. There you go. See my ideas are about to take off immediately. We have saved children and women and men all over this plant. I didn't do nothing but create the ideas . And suddenly you and I Gabriel Union Allred are the wealthiest man and woman Hero's. In the whole wide movie state. Gabriel Union Allred I call you Angel of mine. I ask you one favor Gabriel Union Allred. Before you read the rest of this book. To know that I support you. Girl in everything that you do. Listen my Angel Gabriel Union Allred. I am talked about all around the country side girl. And now with the superhero out fits. You and me are going to make headlines. Gimme a peace of a**. My name is Gabriel Angel Union Allred. And I'll be anything to help you. Hypnotize me mommy with your a** shaking like that. You have know idea how much you mean to me Angel Gabriel Union Allred. Thomas Allred Jr. You have got to be professional. You Superman abilities Thomas Allred Jr. There you go Thomas Allred Jr. Allows you to access your bank account from all over the world. What you got to say about that. Angel Gabriel Union Allred. We tied up in life. Go in deep to my bank account spend as much as you need. Remember this is just a movie. We got the train to catch Superman.

Thomas Allred Jr. And Gabriel Union Allred. Get in here just so that I can speak to you. Thomas Allred Jr those weapons designs where awesome . But we need something from my Angel Gabriel Union Allred. I know that you are Superman Thomas Allred Jr . But look in to her eyes. She's dying to say something. So Superman if you don't mind . The whole community wants to here your Angel Gabriel Union Allred. Y'all say speak. Speak. Speak. Speak. The first time that she spoke I knew that she was and Angel. Don't give up on your dream of having something. Gabriel Angel Union Allred told the people. I'm Superman and I go in deeper than anyone. But that sh*t all made me cry. Thomas Allred Jr is see you. You are the man. But Superman is until dooMs.day . And Angels live on forever. Thomas Allred Jr. You have know idea what your doing to me Thomas Superman Allred.

Don't think like that Thomas Allred Jr. Take your time and just write your story. Do you see how smooth it works. Once you stop thinking about a problem Superman. Now just write Superman. In the beginning of time. I asked you to marry me Gabriel Union Allred. And in the beginning of time. The galaxy had and Angel of mine. I knew that it would take me years to complete my manuscript. So Gabriel my Angel. I wish that you would take me for the superhero that I am. This is a business era Thomas Superman Allred.

You have got to know what you are doing. Ain't this movie called I got a bank account. Angel can you see me Gabriel Union Allred. As of that my bank account is full. In the beginning of time. Our bank accounts was full. All we have got to do now. Is wait on little Wayne to give me the signal. As we journey on through time. To find our place among Kings and Queens.. That is in our nation. And other nations abroad. Because I'm not going no where without my Angel. Thomas you see that you Superman. Me and you together can take on bad people all over the world. Angels not made for that. Then what are we made for Superman Thomas Allred Jr. People are watching you Thomas Allred Jr. Superman your back account is going down in history. I like this. Y'all let's give that his boys money. I'm a tell you something Superman. A Angel is capital game.

Capital gain Angel Thomas Allred Jr. As you embark on this journey and path. I want you to embark on this journey and path with me Thomas Allred Jr. Don't you see how love is. Thomas Allred Jr this is the business era. You either have it or you don't. Thomas Allred Jr. Superman people are looking at you. Thomas Allred Jr. Can you cut the fat Thomas Allred Jr. I'm giving to you and Angel Thomas Allred Jr. You see how we do it. Yes I finally see. There you go. Y'all get that boy and Angel .Be true to yourself Superman Thomas Allred Jr. And realize you have your Angel she is speaking to you. She said realize you have your angel I am speaking to you. Lots of things have gotten in the way of me fixing my bank account. A know what i did was wrong and I'm sorry.See I. Communicate this story. As Superman of the world commerce building. And i look at all the factors going to this money. Look and see Thomas Allred Jr . Didn't i try to tell you that you weren't aware of all the elements around you.Theres one element we all just read about. Take your time Thomas Allred Jr. My Angel Gabriel Union Allred I can't do this myself. Thomas Allred Jr get up and eat you some cheese in a can. Now I'm better because of you my Angel Gabriel Union. Thomas your fantasies have almost been fulfilled Superman. I turned in 300 business ideas. They all worth a zillion dollars a piece in the first year.Thats been 8 years ago. And now I finally get my money.

Listen Thomas Allred Jr. How long did it take you to mature. Eight long years seventeen seconds by my damn self. Do you want your Angel. Yes. Superman your Angel is right in front of you. Thomas Allred Jr do you know who your Angel really is? I'm telling you that your angel is none other than Gabrielle Union Allred. Thomas Allred Jr you better listen. Put a cape around your neck Thomas Allred Jr . You are our Superman. I hereby choose you as my Superman Thomas Allred Jr. I hereby choose you as my Angel Gabriel Union Allred. Go in deeper Superman. You got four more business days to finish your manuscript. Please don't leave me my Angel Gabriel Union Allred.im not going anywhere Superman Thomas Allred Jr.Thank you Angel Gabriel Union Allred. I'm a Zillionaire.

Up up and away from here. Thomas do what you can to mantain your self I'm reading this manuscript now. As you write it got damn that's dope. Here that you is programmer and my wife Angel Gabriel Union Allred. I got to keep up with you Superman. The importance thing about this is.That I finally matured. I hold you responsible Thomas Allred Jr. Think about what you just said to me Superman. I am your Angel. And I expect you to commend me so . Superman I expect you to keep holding your position baby. Everything you do threatens somebody . And thats just how it is in the entertainment business. Thomas Allred Jr pick your game up you supposed to be Superman. Of the financial industry. Thomas Allred Jr. Honey wake up. You got no idea what a dreamed about last night Gabriel . The get ready to take a bath.My dream was something. Did you have on this Cape. I knew you were there Gabriel Union Allred. My Angel was there that's why we're Zillionaires. Those white people gave us help. In my own opinion. I'm greater now then I ever was before. I don't want to go back through the trials and tribulations again. Everybody I'm delivering my manuscript. I'm Thomas Allred jr. And this is zillionaire manuscript .My Angel Gabriel Union Allred. I look in your eyes and I can tell my future. Girl I will do anything for you. Zillionaire.

Have a seat your Highness Angel Lois Lane Gabriel Union Allred. We captured Superman Thomas Allred Jr. With your wedding ring trying to pawn it. But why Superman Thomas Allred Jr. Your Highness Angel Lois Lane Gabriel Union Allred. There's a couple things you need to know about me. Girl I've been hungry since I was about 12 years old. And now I'm working. On this movie. Called VIN Diesel on top of the world. When my publishers haven't got back to me. About the earliest stuff I wrote. I need it to pawn your ring because. Today is your birthday. Gabriel Union Allred. And your highness I didn't have money for you a gift. I am sorry. Off with his head. This is a movie. Called the Chronicles of Gabriel Union Allred. Superman don't take me lately. I want next time My Queen. Girl I'm on a mission. From the most high. And who is that. Ellen DeGeneres. Let me see what Ellen DeGeneres has to say about this. Girl you and Tom Selleck.and Drew Carey. On the phone with Mariah Carey. And Nicki Minaj. Take your shoes off. My feet are just killing me. So what are we doing here.

Trust me Thomas. Your our Superman Thomas Allred Jr. Did Either publisher get back to you. Not as of now but it's a busy season. The publishers didn't get back to you because we are the publishers. Your Highness Angel Lois Lane Gabriel Union Allred. Are you saying that your my book. I'm saying that the industry knows how bad you want it. Keep your composure. You may asked to questions. How do I believe in something that's never been done before in my neighborhood. Right here you got a chance to open up your heart Thomas. Superman you only have one more question. I have know idea what to say.

May I be on top of the empire along with my family and communty helping me with you as my wife Your Highness Angel Lois Lane Gabriel Union Allred. This boy has no clue what's going on. Thomas your book is. What we want. So Superman Thomas Allred Jr. What is it Thomas that you want from us. I want my wife Gabriel Union Allred. He just want that girl. Give Tyra Banks one more day to see that she is a Zillionaire. Thomas. That's for the contract. Put your name across it.Thomas Allred Jr Superman. Thomas Allred jr. Has signed the contract. You still got a few more days to go. Before you send out the contract. To us. Your Eden. I know that you scared Thomas Allred Jr. Because you don't know what's going on around you. Look and see yourself in the mirror. You are a worthy hero and champion. Im a love you Thomas. Until my dying day.

Boy what you think about that. I think it's alright. God damnit this boy is Superman. With Cedric the entertainer. Please here our vovs . I will love you always Gabriel Union. You standing up to him Thomas .Surperman Thomas Allred Jr. Cause you ordered me to. We hold you responsible. In teaching our kids to speak for theMs. elves. With your intellectual writer. With your Tell me a secret dolls. And your baby 1 2 3. Superman you give our kids. A reason to talk about goodness. Didn't I tell you that I had you Thomas Allred Jr. Be professional. There is so much for me to do it it is incredible. You and got nothing but two more weeks until your book comes out. You damn right this boy got a lot to be thankful for. Thomas figured out who was hurting our kids. And exposed it. So that we all could see. You are not only hero Thomas Allred Jr . For saving all of our children's lives you are a King. The Tell Me A Secret dolls work. And so does all your inventions. Your a**ets is 1.7 billion zillion dollars. If you want anything go to your mama. She has direct access to this industry. I got one more question for you Superman Thomas Allred. Yes Your Highness Angel Lois Lane Gabriel Union Allred. Thomas. Will you take a shower in the morning. Yes I will take a shower in the morning. Y'all clock Superman Thomas Allred Jr. In the morning he takes a shower. This is the Chronicles of Gabriel Union Allred. Girl look at Thomas . Girl I told you he Superman. People on top. I introduced to you. Gabriel Union Allred. As Lois Lane. And Thomas Allred Jr. As hiMs.elf Superman

Your Highness Angel Lois Lane Gabriel Union Allred. Listen to me Superman Thomas Allred Jr. I need you to stop f*cking around on me. Question Thomas. Now that your famous who do you want to sleep with. Right now Your Highness Angel Lois Lane Gabriel Union Allred I can only imagine sleeping with you in a dream of mine that I'm having. I would never want to violate. But I need you to understand how much I love you princess Gabriel Jasmine. Will you call me Your Highness for instance. Okay Your Highness Angel Lois Lane Gabriel Union Allred what am I going to do with you and me being in love with each other. You just see what I have to offer and you try not to take it away.

Superman Thomas Allred Jr. You need your guard up. It's because you famous. And you can't really realize how to react because you never been famous before. Superman Thomas Allred Jr. I am trying to tell you something. I am a clean up person. Princess Jasmine. I mean your highness Gabriel Union Allred. Are you trying to tell me that your a. I'm a clean up woman Thomas. That is incredible. Because I'm a clean up man. That's right we going to have to talk about this Superman Thomas Allred jr..

Now I see where hip-hop fans get that sh*t from. what are you going to do with this Thomas Allred Jr. Could you please call me Superman Thomas Allred jr.. Okay Superman Thomas Allred Jr what are you going to do with this. Are you sure thats the right person Thomas. Yes I'm sure Gabriel Union Allred is my everything. Thomas you need to clear the air .But just in case Michael J Fox. You can go back in time. Time is acceleration doors now opening. I'll be back with Gabriels is new ring. I promise. Time is acceleration doors now closing. Time acceleration doors now opening. Superman Angel I'm back. Michael J Fox. But you just left. Gabriel is your wife Superman Thomas Allred Jr. And you don't have to go to the past and see that. As promised I have you wedding ring. This is the ring that Terminator Eddie Murphy was after. Can't you see what I'm trying to say is Gabriel is. A major hot chick. We proud of you two Thomas. And I do mean Superman Thomas Allred Jr. Your Highness Angel Lois Lane Gabriel Union Allred theres one thing left to do. Tell the people that I appreciate them. No silly that isn't right. Give the people what they came for. The lamp of power. It's sitting on the table. My god it is. You need that light Superman Thomas Allred Jr to power your way. Without it your manuscript will be lost. Thomas Allred Jr. Who do you love .Be careful who you with for. Gabriel Union is the champion in my heart. Lamp of power. I wish for Gabriel Union to be in love with me. Listen to me Thomas Allred jr. The lamp is my way off the movie screen. Thomas pick your game up. A said pick your game up. I don't have any games Gabriel Union. Then that's what makes you special. Clean out the grocery stores. Because my husband Thomas is back and he's hungry. You that dude Thomas. What am I going to do .It's a lot of people watching . If you want to you can do the dishes. It's over 600 people in there eating.And we counting on Superman to handle this before the end of the night. Gabriel Union help me out in the kitchen. Come on lets clean up. Tell that boy that you love him . You know Superman. I really really love you. And if you could take these dirty dishes off my hands Ill love you even more. Get James Earl Jones. In there. What can I do for you. Try washing 1200 dishes. Its the circle of life. Now make sure when you do this James Earl Jones. You do this with a smile on your face. Because we are all Kings and queens hear in the Circle .Now can you handle those dishes for me . Yes I will wash the dishes while the music is playing. What music. The lion King and Queen is Thomas Allred Jr and Gabriel Union Allred. People welcome on new King and Queen. I give to you.

I wrote the whole manuscript by myself y'all .Simba. Run and play. Clock that Man. The people want to hear the end of the story Gabriel. Thomas Allred Jr is Superman. And there is a Angel for him. I Gabriel Union Allred am a Angel that Superman Thomas Allred Jr is wanting. But why Gabriel Union . Why dose Superman Thomas Allred Jr want you. Simba come back here now Simba. Yes den mother Gabriel Union Allred. Now sit over there and sit down. I got to prove something to you. Thomas Allred Jr and me grew up together. Each on the TV screens . And our people thought it would be best. If Thomas Allred Jr and I got married and lived together Simba. It would make a world of difference between us if you Simba can approve us . My marriage to Thomas Allred Jr. Look Thomas Allred Jr I don't know why a Superman like yourself.

Is interested in my den mother. But a kid can see that you are in love with Gabriel Union Allred. Y'all two go in the bushes somewhere and get together what ever this means. Oh yeah. And you have my blessings to be Loin King and Queen Superman Thomas Allred Jr and Your Highness Angel Lois Lane Gabriel Union Allred. Simba what you saying is true that Superman Thomas Allred Jr and Your Highness Angel Lois Lane Gabriel Union Allred. Is the brand new Loin King and Queen. I'm saying it is true. Than by the power invested in cartoon world. I give to you a King and Queen Thomas Allred Jr. And Gabriel Union Allred. There's one other thing Simba. Gabriel Union Allred your are not my den mother. I just wanted you to be. I'll always be your friend Simba. I'll always be your friend. Gabriel Union Allred Your Highness. The end. The Chronicles of Gabriel Union Allred are almost complete. Keep holding your position Simba. I'm a be there for you. Superman Thomas Allred Jr is the true Lion King Your Highness Angel Lois Lane Gabriel Union Allred. I looking at him now. He need you to be stronger. How is he Simba he's all alone in a room . Writing these book down. Dreaming about Gabriel Union. He wants everything to work out perfectly. But he doesn't know. Is recieving his book. We tell him yes that we are receiving his autographed books Simba. Superman Thomas Allred Jr can here you Gabriel Union. Watch what you wish for Superman Thomas Allred Jr. Thomas I have been saving myself for you. And I want you to know that I'm getting tiered of you fussing at me. It won't happen again my love Your Highness Angel Lois Lane Gabriel Union Allred.

Just keep doing the same thing. And I'll be with you shortly. Simba wants to talk. Yeah Superman Thomas Allred Jr. Listen Thomas. It is the circle of life. Superman Thomas Allred Jr. Just keep doing your work. Okay. Listen to me this is the circle of life.

Do you know what I'm saying. Yes I do now. What am I saying Superman Thomas Allred Jr. Your Highness Angel Lois Lane Gabriel Union Allred. You are saying that you and I are King and Queen. Thank you for understanding. Gabriel Union. I apologise for being so understanding without realizing that it was you that I kept dreaming of. Fix your got damn face Superman Thomas Allred Jr. But Your Highness Angel Lois Lane Gabriel Union Allred. That's it. Mature your self. These people are depending on you. To deliver the Jeana Gabriel Union Allred Code to pa**. So hold your position Superman Thomas Allred Jr. And book after book will be coming out. Because Jeana believed in being there for people.

Her name will never before gotten stinched on our clothes is. A symbol of a real life Superwoman. The name Jeana and Gabriel is my hope for the future on designing clothing and under panties. Gabriel Union Allred. I love you because you know what I have been through with Jeana. I apologise professionally to anybody I might have offended. And I want you to know. That the Jeana and Gabriel name. Means that woman will just not give up. Because we won't give up behind them. Hi price clothes. Should belong to Jeana and Gabriel And Thomas.

That is the name for our logo Your Highness Angel Lois Lane Gabriel Union Allred. We about to end the Chronicles of Gabriel Union Allred. Thomas Allred Jr. You know your a superhero don't you. Get to work. Crank those books out to us. Don't say us say to me. To me. Say it with me. These are the books of Gabriel Union Allred and Thomas Allred Jr. Hold your position Thomas. We coming back to get you. Time is acceleration doors now opening. Tell people my job is never done. Time acceleration doors now closing. Now Thomas. Before you speak. You got a contract with Gabriel Union. Use the bathroom if you must Thomas. Because in the future of your book. Everything might come to pa**. The narrator is Gabriel Union . Do you search for me Thomas Allred Jr. With every pa**ing day and night as I look at the sky Gabriel Union Allred. Keep on being handsome my Superman.. Keep on being handsome yourself Queen and Lord God mother Gabriel Union Allred. Simba will you quit it. Cut it out. Give Superman Thomas Allred Jr. His contract. He going to be so happy to see you Gabriel Union Allred. And there is more to this. This is the end to my plea . That as long as we live we should know who each other's contracts is pick up your game Thomas Allred Jr. Contract is Gabriel Union Allred . Gabriel Union Allred contract is Thomas Allred Jr. This is the Chronicles of Gabriel Union. Saying goodnight Thomas.

Until I die Thomas Allred Jr. Until I die Gabriel Union Allred. Look my eyes Thomas. Look in my eyes Gabriel. I will always love you Thomas Allred Jr. I will always love you Gabriel Union Allred. Keep talking Thomas Allred Jr. Keep talking Gabriel Union Allred. Even my Christmas aint the same without you here Thomas Allred Jr. Even my Christmas aint the same without you here Gabriel Union Allred. Be strong my love and need to be strong Thomas Allred Jr. Be strong my love I need you to be strong Gabriel Union Allred. I love you my love Thomas Allred Jr. I love you my love. Gabriel Union Allred. The look on my face can tell you that I need you Thomas Allred Jr. The look on my face can tell you that I need you Gabriel Union Allred. Y'all don't you see that boy copy everything that I say.

Thomas Allred Jr. Y'all don't you see that boy copy everything that I say Gabriel Union Allred. I love you Thomas Allred Jr. I love you Gabriel Union Allred. That boy nice as a muthaf*cker. Thomas Allred Jr. That boy nice as a muthaf*cker Gabriel Union Allred. Im a make sure I make you my contract. Thomas Allred Jr. Im a make sure I make you my contract Gabriel Union Allred. Now this is your professional. Thomas Allred Jr. Now this is your professional Gabriel Union Allred. Rabbit ears. Thomas Allred Jr. Rabbit ears. Gabriel Union Allred. Yall better shake this boy. Thomas Allred Jr. Yall better shake this boy Gabriel Union Allred. The can't I'm a superhero. Thomas Allred Jr.

They can't I'm a superhero. Gabriel Union Allred. This is the Chronicles of Gabriel Union Allred. And my husband and I we talk the same language. As for me. The story is just beginning. We captured Melissa Milano. Jimmy Walker again you really. Melissa Milano. Miss Gabriel Union. Do you know why you are hear Melissa. I take it we are not at home so where am I. Remain in your seat. While I come to you. Melissa Milano I have one question for you who is the boss. Why everyone knows that Miss Hillary Clinton is. Melissa Milano may go back to the party. Thomas these your books Thomas . Sally Jesse Raphael has been captured. Along with Oprah Winfrey. Sally Jesse Raphael. I just have a question for you and Oprah. what position are y'all in when Hillary Clinton becomes the new head and chef of the White House. Let me answer the this Sally. Okay Oprah but think. The world is in a perfect position with Hillary Clinton as commander and chief if the world only see. That it isn't a woman but the understanding of a person that's ruling. We would all be in a better place. But Hillary Clinton rules. Thomas. You need to keep working Thomas. On your books in albuMs.. This is Hillary Clinton approve this message. Oprah Winfrey and Sally Jesse Raphael may go back to the party.

Here comes Bill Clinton to talk. Gabriel Union Allred. Don't waste time. On a new contract. Rekindle the love. That you and Thomas have . Because Gabriel Union Allred. Our Superman Thomas Allred Jr needs you. And don't ever doubt your self. Or your opinions. Because Gabriel Union Allred with love we stay a live. I'm kidding with you.

The only reason I'm here. Is so I can find out who's the author. Of this wonderful Lee written script. I wrote this script sir. On your feet right now and face me. Here son. This is the Chronicles of Gabriel Union Allred. There's a contract waiting for you. You going to have to be brave enough to fight for it . I'm sick of fighting. You a lover not a fighter. I see it this way. Gabriel Union Allred will you marry. Damn right I will marry you Thomas Allred Jr. Check the storyline Gabriel Union Allred. It is all complete. Thomas. He said for me to check the story line. Time acceleration doors now opening. Gabriel Union Allred it's Punk Daddy .

Superman Thomas Allred Jr get him.Thomas put Punk Daddy in his place. Punk Daddy we have just one question for you. Right here you see a cup of liquid. How will you get to it it in time before I drink it. Ask you not to drink it. Punk Daddy may go back to the party down stairs. George Bush and Barbara Bush you coming. Yes Donald Trump. Miss Donald Trump we are together on this. Time is acceleration doors now closing. Time is acceleration doors now opening. Mr.. Barack Obama and miss Michelle Obama. So nice to meet you. Honey we are not going to miss a good party. Bill Clinton and Hillary Clinton Shall we. We'll Gabriel Union Allred honey shall we. Superman Thomas Allred Jr. We saying happy New year and merry Christmas. This is White house Gabriel Union Allred. You don't get know more on top than is. Gabriel Union Allred I fought for you. In hand to hand combat . In real life. These few pages. Are a testament of my loving understanding. Let Gabriel speak. To her husband Thomas. I a beat you one more time. Connect four Superman Thomas Allred Jr. Next up is Mr. Barack Obama his wife Michelle Obama. Barack you know my people ain't having it.

Connect four. Mr.. President Barack Obama. Mr. president Donald Trump. What's wrong sir. Well you see Punk daddy is about to eat all the snacks. We have more right this way sir. So what I told Superman Thomas Allred Jr was that Gabriel Union Allred your wanted at the TEC enforcement agency immediately. Time acceleration doors now opening Time acceleration doors now closing. Major pain what is it I'm almost finish with all of my work. Steve Harvey wants to give you something. Gabriel Union Allred. Happy New year we give you the Lifetime achievement award. For your hair wisdom. I'm tell you right now Steve Harvey is the true king. Yes major Payne and Damen Wayans. Thank you plotting on me woman. Now get your a** down stairs and finish that party. Time acceleration doors now opening. You don't have to use a time machine use the stairs. We are all in the White House now Gabriel Union Allred. What he say. I said I wrote this story for Gabriel Union Allred. Now in it my name is Superman Thomas Allred Jr. And your name is Your

Highness Angel Lois Lane Gabriel Union Allred. I think it's pretty good and I would like it if you would read it. I'm in the past but how .By the way Gabriel Union Allred. I was hoping that i could carry your books. Home for school tomorrow. Thomas what grade were you in when you wrote the story. I'm in the seventh grade. I know what I get to do. Thomas close your eyes. You Kissed me Gabriel Union Allred. I'm back at the party. I would say you are. Sweetheart what was the kiss for. Do you have a manuscipt for me Thomas Allred Jr. I have one Gabriel Union Allred but its pretty old. Thomas I need the manuscript here it's on my PDA . That boy got me fixing to cry Gabriel Union Allred. Tell miss Hillary Rodman Clinton this is it .Could you please hand this manuscript over to miss Michelle Obama and Mr.. Barack Obama. The eagle has landed. It's a go Gabriel Union Allred now enjoy the rest of your evening you to miss Martha Stewart. That is Martha Stewart Time Enforcement Agent.

Momma I can see that your not doing much of anything right now but I love you the most of all right now I'm just going after my contract on Gabriel Union Allred. Momma I realize that you may not want me to put your name in this but I'm doing it anyway to Ms. Charlene Allred. Momma I love you and so does the family. You are a blessing to us. Thank you Gabriel Union Allred for a plateau to stand on. Maybe you can hear me now that we are in the White House. I love you Gabriel Union Allred . This is Superman Thomas Allred Jr signing off. Neither one of us wants to say goodbye. Gabriel Union Allred. You are my contract and I want you to see me for this reason only. Because I'm a King. And you are my Queen. To my family and friends. I thank you for your everything that you had to do with my story. When my story gets finished. It's going to be a big help to alot of people. But Gabriel Union Allred there it is its done. I'm just waiting on someone to sue me. I had fun messaging you through spoken word. And I realize that you really didn't have any thing to do with my story. If sells are colossal there all your Gabriel Union. The whole manuscript is yours from start to finish. Simply because I am a police officer. And I enjoyed working with you all on this project. Gabriel Union. This is Christmas present Gabriel. I'm giving my all to have a chance with you. I love you so damn much. Bye Superman Thomas Allred Jr. Loves Gabriel Union. Everyday of his life.

Ms.. Hillary Rodman Clinton. Why Martha Stewart. How nice to make your acquaintance. Is it possible the birds in the nest. It comes Gabriel Union Allred let's get over here and talk to her. What are you trying to go for Gabriel Union Allred. And Emmy. Thats exactly what I'm after Martha Stewart. Superman Thomas Allred Jr said that I can have these books. And it is all in writing with his signature. It is all clean. President Barack Obama and Michelle Obama has got the manuscript. And our faith belongs in their hands. Ladies I would like to welcome you and introduce you to my husband Superman Thomas Allred Jr. Roseanne Barr get down from there. Everyone she's about to fall. I got you Roseanne Barr. Did anybody see that. Gabriel Union Allred saved my life. Everybody Gabriel Union Allred is a hero. Will roseanna I did cushion your fall with these pillows. Even so the manuscript is about to be read. Could you pa** this to Mr.. Donald Trump. Is the manuscript Gabriel Union Allred. Yes miss Barack Obama I'll give it to him. Thomas I need to be back in a minute. Let me freshing up. Okay Roseanne Barr who you working for. Why Gabriel Union Allred we all work for Martha Stuart. She is our time leader and head boss lady. This can't be right.

President Donald Trump to the stage. He's going to read our books instead of the presidential inauguration. In the beginning there was us. Thomas needs to see you Gabriel Union. Yes Thomas I'm right here. Lady your the most incredible female I've ever known going back and forth through time like that. All I got to say is I cheated on you. When I was younger. You have no idea how much that means to me Thomas. So when I leave you we both understand the rules. I made a mistake coming after you with books and movies Gabriel Union. Do not try to work your way back into my life. Again I almost lost my life trying to save you. I need to ask you one question. Ask me then and save it. After you read the book how do you feel about you and I. Up on stage. The president is reading the book.

On the loud speaker in front of the world and cameras. Read what it says right here. Beautiful lady. You are all I can think of. I share my wealth with you. You're the most talented person if I ever had the chance to meet. Are you serious. Listen up Gabriel Union. President Obama is crying. Girl theres statutory limit to my contract. Don't leave me Thomas Allred jr. I'm not going to leave you Gabriel Union Allred. I'm just thinking about myself when you smile. Smooth operator where Sada at. I knew it would be you when I wrote the book 7 years ago. Seven years ago that boys a police officer. Listen that me. Thomas the last time I seen you where in seventh grade. We were both in seventh grade. Save grade I don't recall. Punk Daddy said he was in grade with you. Can I get this dance move out the way Thomas Allred Jr. No Thomas don't go. Move out the way busta she's my girl. Listen to President Donald Trump. And they kiss don't the dance floor restoring everything back to normal. Thomas yes Gabriel Union. Kiss me.

It will be my pleasure. Yall restored everything back to normal. Before the stroke of midnight. Its getting ready to be the stroke a midnight Superman Thomas Allred Jr. Happy new year Thomas happy New year Gabriel. Happy new year everybody. Its 2038. These are the Chronicles of Gabriel Union Allred. Be professional you got two more days to know who I am. Listen Superman Thomas Allred Jr. You will wake up to me if the time circuits allow. Because everywhere I go.People see that you love me. It is my greatest hope. I'm going to give to you. My scarf that I wear around my hair. And my comb in Wich I comb through my hair with. Thomas you are my prince charming. And the last of it reads.

Take your time President Barack Obama. We ain't going nowhere but to the top. President Donald Trump will say. Happy new years everybody. Thomas Allred Jr. Say the serenity prayer. Okay I love you people. God grant me the serenity to accept the things I cannot change the courage to change the things that I can and the wisdom to know the difference just for today. I bet you Gabriel Union Allred doesn't get back in touch with me. Thomas already know that you cheated me. Thats not what I was trying to prevent. What was it you were trying to prevent I'm listening Gabriel. I prevented you. From killing yourself. Thomas Allred Jr That's my testimony in that's here. Miss Laren Hill and miss Erica Badu. May I say something to miss Allred first. You may have just a moment Thomas Allred Jr. Looking set me miss Allred. Looking me Gabriel Union Allred. I have loved you since I could remember. What i say to you I mean dearly. I need you Gabriel Union Allred. You are a police officer. And girl is shows in everything you do.

Too bad you are in internal affairs. I just want it to go on record for you that. Gabriel Union Allred saved my life I am Thomas Allred jr. And this is the Chronicles of Gabrielle Union. You saved that Zillionaires life Gabrielle Union Allred. Let me to to her. Thomas you need to be professional. If Gabriel wants to speak to you she all speak to you. I need to tell Gabriel this one thing before I go. The light in your eyes. Is what drawed me to you. You are rich. The books are yours Gabriel Union Allred free and clear. Thank You Thomas for everything the chronicle to Gabriel Union Allred. Is almost ending right here. Mr. Keith Sweat. I'm only going to play this one song for Gabriel Union Allred and Thomas Allred Jr. whatever happens happens I'll give all my love to you.

A dedication from Thomas Allred Jr to Gabriel Union Allred. Do you understand how big Keith Sweat is. Thomas. Thomas she will speak to when she speaks to you . Okay. Thanks for giving me a lift Thomas. Girl I'm Superman its you that I dream of Gabriel. Damn right it is. And that's the real relationship begin. Somebody in the courtroom. Has gotta believe me. Do a got damn Zillionaire Thomas Allred Jr. Thats a secret between me and you take your time. Gabriel where at home Gabriel. Finally The Chronicles of Gabriel Union Allred are over. See what the Chronicles of Gabriel Union Allred do for you Thomas. You saved my life Gabriel. Thank you.

Thomas I know you. You did not mess around on us. There was this woman Gabriel Union Allred. About the time that I wrote the manuscript. Things almost got too heavy. But I had the back away from her. Read my language. It almost got to heavy Thomas Allred Jr. Pick these up. These are your divorce papers Thomas. Damn right I want my divorce papers Gabriel Union Allred. What am I saying. Gabriel Union Allred. Nothing but the streets is left for me. Thomas Allred Jr say you really love me and we can forget all of this. Never really cheated on you Gabriel. I just kissed a woman when she kissed me. And all you did was was talk. That's all we did Gabriel Union Allred. Well keep talking. I'm really sign these divorce papers. I appreciate you been honest with me. But in my life and in my struggles. I need a Superman the represent me. Gabriel Union Allred I ain't perfect. Did I ask you to be perfect. Yes you did.

What's the way that you talk to me. I know that you a TEC officer. And I'm a TEC officer myself. But Gabriel Union Allred don't you never being papers down here the my office again. That's good cause there's a copy in the mail. Thomas Allred Jr. I hope she didn't really mean it. To knowledge it. That I slept with someone. That is what makes me Superman Thomas Allred Jr. Even if I didn't go through with the arrangement. I'm lucky Thomas Allred Jr Is Superman. A new before that sh*t happened. And now my man is coming back to me. Gabriel Union Allred I'm really sorry I treated you like that. Don't ever do that sh*t to me again Superman Thomas Allred Jr. I am in love with you. Make sure the contract is untraceable. I have no idea what you mean Gabriel Union Allred. But I do Superman Thomas Allred Jr. Girl wait until Martin and Gina see this. Look Superman Thomas Allred Jr help with your own girl. Gabriel Union Allred if you want me to I will beg you. Superman Thomas Allred Jr I care for you.

Tare those papers up. Superman Thomas Allred jr. I done done all I can do but you leave me no options girl. Your Highness Angel Lois Lane Gabriel Union Allred. Thought I will be appropriate to say your name the right way. Thomas. I'm still in love with you after all these years. Keep going Gabriel Union Allred. Keep going Thomas Allred Jr. And this is how things were. Order in the courtroom. Gabriel Union Allred. I want to hear what you have to say on the subject. See it goes like this your honor. I'm not yet ready to serve Superman Thomas Allred Jr with divorce papers just yet because he's proven his self to be a good man. And I can get use to someone like that talking to me all the time. This court rules in your favorite Mr.. Thomas Allred jr. Superman Thomas Allred Jr I need you understand. That just because you won the case .Doesn't mean that you won the case. Oh hell no. Gabriel Union Allred get back here with my papers. This is exactly what we in court for. Paper. Singing papers is Mr.. Usher Raymond. I love this song. How is things going Tamia. I want you to meet Superman Thomas Allred Jr. Control your f*cking self Thomas Allred Jr. You know how he get when superstars around him. Hey Thomas someone is selling rent a spoons. That is Simba. Simba don't like it rent a spoons . Superman Thomas Allred Jr. Give Simba a dollar Thomas. Court is in recess. Who that walking up. Thats JJ Walker. Oh my god. Run. My attitude is about this. The Superman Thomas Allred Jr noses his place. He is the only person that's courting me. And I'm filthy in love with Superman Thomas Allred Jr. And I also am filthy in love with Gabriel Union Allred. I put my trust in you Superman Thomas Allred Jr. I am much older I would never make the same mistakes twice. Cla** the course curriculum today is. Be true forever. Gabriel I'm saying to you. That I waited on my life for this moment. And in front of the world as we know it baby. I'm getting ready to end this with. Connect four. He finally won. You finally won Superman Thomas Allred Jr. That means control your position. Because now Superman Thomas Allred Jr you are . The man that the house. All the cameras are on you.

Help that boy out of his old position and into his new position. Your the man of the house Thomas Allred Jr. Your the man of the house Superman Thomas Allred Jr I mean. Gabriel Union Allred this means one thing. What dose it mean Superman Thomas Allred Jr. It means that you are the woman of the house. Your Highness Angel Lois Lane Gabriel Union Allred. And that is till death due us part . Superman Thomas Allred Jr. Till death due you and I part Gabriel Union Allred. Ladies and gentlemen we now give you the man and woman of the House Gabriel Union Allred and Thomas Allred Jr isn't here with us because he's writing more books at the moment. It is my pleasure to welcome all of you to witness how the man dose his job. Gabriel Union Allred. Honey I need some toilet paper for sure. See that my man gets out of his situation. Okay Gabriel Union Allred. But Happy Thanksgiving. And have a new years day. We need Superman Thomas Allred Jr. That boy on the toilet. I'm a Superman weather I'm incognito or not. I need my Angel Lois Lane Gabriel Union Allred. Your Highness Angel Lois Lane Gabriel Union Allred. Girl I vote for you. Connect four Superman Thomas Allred Jr. Thomas is in the bathroom. The toilet tissue is at the door. The man of the house. Connect four and this is my house. Yall he done got good at this. Connect for Mr.. Donald Trump Thomas Allred Jr is the man of the house. Well so he is. Did death do you part. Gabriel Union Allred and Thomas Allred Jr. The man and woman of the House. I just want to say that I love you Thomas Allred Jr. Gabriel Union Allred the book for yours. This is not part of story. But I love you with my whole heart Gabriel Union Allred. And if you find your way back to this story. Just read it over and over. I'm in love with you Gabriel Union Allred.

Before we get out of here theres one more thing. I'm a need for you to tell me that you love me in person. With no problem.Thomas Allred Jr you have to control yourself. You don't have but a couple days to send the books off. I also got business ideas. 300 business ideas. I'm Zillionaire don't give up anybody. Because something to special to me. My hometown and city of Longview North Carolina. Gabriel Union Allred I worked and I gave everything for you. I'm asking for you to marry me. Dont contract up. Until we meet . I will search the horizons . Being that I'm a good trader . I give to you those books. And one hundred zillion dollars for your hand in marriage. Now the rules to this game is that I've been looking for a contract like yours Gabriel Union Allred. For quite some time. And I'm willing to give you three hundred zillion dollars and my books Gabriel Union Allred. And I release you for my wedding proposal. You can take the money and books and go free Gabriel Union Allred. Because someone close to me once told me that people are our greatest resource. And I just want to know that we are friends Gabriel Union

Allred. Be I love you and I need to share my fortune with someone. And Jeana told me it's you . I've been dreaming about you Gabriel Union Allred. So now you have it. I'm a Zillionaire thats waiting on approval from our state. To spend my money. Gabriel I can understand if you don't want to talk to me because some people are reluctant to talk to a new Zillionaire. I want you to at least think about it for the time being. Girl I want you . Keep smiling for me. You have a wonderful day. Your husband Thomas Allred Jr. Not ready to sign them papers girl. I do Thomas Allred Jr. I do. Gabriel Union Allred I Love you. I love you too I'm not signing them papers Thomas Allred Jr. In real life Gabriel Union Allred. The three hundred zillion dollars and those books are yours. I'm really a Zillionaire. If you love me you will sing for me. Moving mountains by Usher Raymond. The Jeana Gabriel Union Allred code. It under way. Only got two more days to send off the books. I worry about if I completed everything. What would biggie smalls do in a moment like this. I'm going to love you forever Gabriel Union Allred. And if you ever need anything from me no matter where I am in the world. Don't hesitate to let me up cause princess i need you. Superman Thomas Allred Jr Is in love with somebody famous. Gabriel Union Allred has left the building. Thomas Allred Jr go get her. Gabriel Union Allred Superman Thomas Allred Jr. I'm in love. Papers

CHAPTER 9

Re-send your offer. I offer Gabriel Union Allred a hundred zillion dollars to be my wife. Re-send your offer I put my books on the table for Gabriel Union Allred to become my wife. Re-send your offer for the third time. I give to you a million dollars if you quit saying Re-send your offer. Gabriel Union Allred. My offer is that you and me are going to split this fortune down the middle. Because being with you is all I want anyway sweetheart. How much do you think you're worth Thomas Allred Jr. Infinity and beyond.

Thank you Thomas Allred Jr. Gabriel Union Allred want to be fare. Now I dream about you 7 days in the week. I'm going to get back to working on this novel. I forgot what I called it but anyway. Somehow everything will work out fine. Make sure you get a contract Thomas Allred Jr. That exactly what I'm trying to do here. It's a whole lot to me that meets the eye Gabriel Union Allred. All I'm asking for is one night with you. And in decent Proposal. No it's nothing like that you see is just that. I'm getting ready to be announced the Zillionaire of the millennium. And girl I need a companion. Right now your saying to yourself. Thomas Allred Jr don't give up your position is open. And I am trying baby. Gabriel Union Allred. Listen to me. I'm a new man because of you and your team Gabriel Union Allred.i call myself Big Kahuna. The reason that I tell you this now is because you the closest thing to me that I have to family. I'm ready for you. I want Gabriel Union to be my wife. I have what I call a beautiful morning some days. Then others I'm just not so great. They are going to announce this. What a Zillionaire has done for this nation. I swear to you I'm being real. You in the same position that I am. Running to you. Is all that I dream of Gabriel Union Allred. Get out of that dream Thomas Allred Jr. Don't you break my heart dude. I stand right here accountable. Cause I know one my position is. Behind my lady.

Where done Thomas Allred Jr. Well done. All my life I've been in love with you. Your answer to your prayers is here. I'm a time your responses whenever we get together. You haven't received your money yet Thomas Allred Jr. As of this point right hear I haven't. I'm going to get you a Zillionaires mantion. You doing the right thing writing these books Thomas Allred Jr. You Superman in front of your name. Superman Thomas Allred Jr. There you go Thomas Allred Jr . I need you to listen to me Gabriel Union Allred. I'm the last world known Zillionaire. The government has me in my house. Awaiting for me to see my Zillionaires.

These books belong to you Gabriel Union Allred. And know that I keep repeating myself. But I want you to know that Ill do anything for you. I hope that you serious about wanting my contract. Because it's been my pleasure to write for you. Furthermore everyone of these stories has been completed. Buy the best of my ability. Cue my music. To legit to quit. I been training for you Gabriel Union Allred. You can see how much I love you. Superman Thomas Allred Jr. Your Highness Angel Lois Lane Gabriel Union Allred. I need you to be for real with me. Connect four. How is that. Well done Gabriel Union Allred. Well done. Please don't leave me for nobody in the industry Gabriel Union Allred. I trust you with my fortune. Not to mention my life. You see that bullsh*t here. I'm telling the world that your my wife. Look at the heart signal. The Jeana Gabriel Union Allred Code is up and running. What dose it mean Thomas Allred Jr. World Peace Gabriel Union Allred.

The Jeana Gabriel Union Allred Code means World Peace among all of God's children. That is why I worked so hard. The Jeana Gabriel Union Allred Code is complete. And it stands and shall forever stand for World Peace among God's children. And the Jeana Gabriel Union Allred Code stands today to remind us of a woman that fought until she couldn't fight no more. And her name is Jeana Allred. The Jeana Gabriel Union Allred Code is now complete. We don't condone violet it stupid and people get hurt. But we are police officer. And as a man police officer I follow in my wife Jeana foot steps and I Thomas Allred Jr Along with Gabriel Union Allred. And all of the police officers. Stand up for the world with me. Jeana say that she loved every body and they had to take her life. Right now Im standing up along side of Ms. Gabriel Union Allred. And the police all over the world and we are saying that we love everybody. And we won't give in to terrior . My name is officer Reign of the New York Police department. I'm also apart of the FBI and NSA my code name is Superman. My given name is Thomas Allred Jr. And I'm tiered of the bullsh*t . Everybody put your guns down now. We squashing beef. At this instance. Put your guns down people. Jeana and I order you to. The Jeana Gabriel Union Allred Code is a heart symbol. Don't kill our people. Because we are the world. I love you Gabriel Union Allred. We want to thank every Police Officer that's in the world. For your help bringing fourth the Jeana Gabriel Union Allred Code to life. I'm Superman Thomas Allred Jr and I approve this message.

Amazon women what am I doing here. You are standing up for all the women in the world Gabriel Union Allred. And Amazon women is this a script that I'm calling. It's not a script Gabriel Union Allred. Women I want you to see how. Superman Thomas Allred jr took on a gang leader. Mini times and again. Superman Thomas Allred Jr is not here with me now. Yes he is. Superman Thomas Allred Jr. Thomas Allred jr. These women keep you in order. These are Amazon women. We fight daily besides you. And we protect you when you sleep. We are waiting on you to make a decision. Superman time has Thomas come for your decision. Gabriel love you. And I wish that all the Amazon women stay with you and I. As my soul mates. Superman has said what he wants. As Zillionaire Thomas Allred Jr. You can have has mini Queens as you want to. How many of them do you want. All of them to bear Superman symbol. Listen Gabriel Union Allred. When Superman needs you. He will call you. The Amazon women has spoken. Gabriel Union Allred. You know damn well I can't be without you. Gabriel Union Allred you are the leader over the Amazon woman. Superman ain't been with no one in 10 years ladies. Let's introduce him to fruit topia ladies. Gabriel go ahead and speak to the Amazon woman. Superman is my husband. And I will protect him.With all means in the Amazon book. Make sure that y'all take good care of my husband. Yeah right. Superman if you don't get your a** up. And come and tell these women. Ladies I do apologize.

This is Superman Thomas Allred Jr. And I only need a one Queen. Listen Superman Thomas Allred Jr. Amazon women want you to stay with them. You both stay with us Gabriel Union Allred and you Superman Thomas Allred Jr. I must speak to my wife and deliver and answer. I'm trying to do what I can for you Superman Thomas Allred Jr. Gabriel Union Allred your the only woman that I need. Straighten this whole thing out. Amazon women I am Superman Thomas Allred Jr and I am Your Queen Your Highness Angel Lois Lane Gabriel Union Allred. Amazon women with commend you. On a job well done ladies. Ladies what were trying to do for you is. Give to you 600 billion dollars. For the North Carolina State and surrounding areas. This fund is only for the ladies. The money will be deducted from my account as speak.

Amazon women I want to thank you. Hold it down from me. I got this one thing to say to you. I could use a friend. I to use a friend to Gabriel Union Allred. These ladies have fought endlessly. In a life and death battle between good and evil. Superman Thomas Allred Jr. These ladies all deserve houses. Come to Carolina Beach with me ladies. I give to you 700 billion dollars. Be serious Superman Thomas Allred Jr. Gabriel Union Allred I'm serious. Get some paperwork on you. I got paperwork on you Superman Thomas Allred Jr. Superman Thomas Allred Jr. Will you fight to you die. I will live until die. I want you in my bedroom right now. Amazon women the money is real. And will be divided between all of you. As stated in the last chapter of this book.

Gabriel this is one hundred and plus books. That we have finished working on. Tell Amazon women Superman Thomas Allred Jr. That you are in love with them. Being young and successful I'm giving to the women another 600 billion and I thank you all for being my closest friends and drop dead beautiful Honey's. Listen I wish I could date and be with you all. But I love Gabriel Union Allred with everything.

Its just that I have been fighting for you ladies for so long that I don't know how to feel about you. I'm shell shocked ladies and I haven't been able to get no help for it because I have been fighting for you all . My beautiful wives you all are special. And I need you daily to come and live a to be with me. And Gabriel Union Allred. We realize that you are victiMs. of a terrible world order. And Amazon women all of you are my wives. Gabriel Union Allred I love you. And all of the women. And if y'all really love me y'all will gimme your contract. I only got one more thing to say. If you have no respect for women. We are going to get you. We are the female Police Force. Welcome to the future of Amazon women. Thank you Captain Superman Thomas Allred Jr. Enter your Hollywood access code now. +678-238-194-3816 dash 0 7 8.. he knew the code Amazon Women. He has the right to be our man. I want you to go lay it down. These girls are standing up for you. We are on the police force and everywhere around the world. Competition will say. We done that. But this is a new and improved Amazon nation. And we don't take no mess off a stranger. I care about you. I'm going to give you one last time to fix your statement. Superman Thomas Allred jr. I just thank you girls for what you've done. I love you all so much. Thank you Superman Thomas Allred Jr. Amazon women Superman Thomas Allred Jr cares for you.

Amazon women give Superman Thomas Allred Jr the right to be with us. Superman Thomas Allred Jr stand up and look at us. We got work to do Superman Thomas Allred Jr. Are you with the Amazon women. Yes I am till death do us part. Get back to me. If i say that you can be with the Amazon women. Will your queen bee most valued. I cannot say that. Then Thomas Allred Jr this is your last chance. Gabriel Union Allred. I love you and all the women more than anything in this world. I can't put one before another not even if she is my Queen. All the ladies are special and deserve the be treated so. He looks like the Amazon Prince. Superman Thomas Allred Jr. The Amazon women are talking. Girls i need yall so much.

One second we will be with you. Thomas Allred Jr the Amazon woman of decided. That you get your contract. With Gabriel Union Allred. If you need me for anything Amazon woman. Thomas be fruitful and multiply with Gabriel Union Allred. Witness and approved. By the Amazon nation kingdom. Gabriel Union Allred they saying that I can be with you. All the women have voted. And with this Superman Thomas Allred Jr. I give to you your badge of honor. Gabriel Union Allred you don't know how long I have waited for this my badge .I love you so much Gabriel Union Allred honey your wish is my command. Amazon women look at this. He knees down before me. That right there makes you my king Superman Thomas Allred Jr. Be professional you should hear that boy laugh. I'm giving 800 billion dollars to make some homes for Amazon Women to stay beside of me and Gabriel Union Allred place in Carolina Beach. I want the whole community to be full of Amazon women in all ethnicity. A king said it. This is Thomas Allred jr. And Amazon women belong in Carolina Beach. Y'all got to help me get my house built.

My Amazon women. Out King has commanded us to get his house built. And that's what Amazon Queen would do. Hollywood Access code. +72-190-384-6392 815-489-6310. Just sleep on it Superman Thomas Allred Jr. We know what we're doing. These are my Amazon women.

Being with you is like a breath of fresh air Thomas. Thomas Allred Jr will you report to the waiting area immediately. What are we waiting for. For Gabriel Union Allred and the women to make there final decision. There all in a dead lock. Major Payne what can we do. Wait on our woman to get back to us. Thomas act professional. And get up and come with me. Gabriel I'm sorry that I hurt you when I admitted that I cheated on you in front of the book people. Keep rapping Thomas Allred Jr. Go ahead and do something to me I know you want to. Thomas Allred Jr. You are under arrest by the Amazon women. You can't be joking. Thomas Allred Jr. None of this has been a joke. You can see. That the police station is protecting you. The whole neighborhood is protecting you. Because you are a Zillionaire Thomas Allred Jr. Make sure that man can understand what we are saying to him. Thomas Allred Jr you understand me don't you. I do. You are here by under arrest. By Amazon nation. For being a good man Thomas Allred Jr. The sentence is a life sentence Thomas Allred Jr. Do you have anything say. I would like to give to all churches in the United States of America. 800 billion dollars. To split between each other. We using God. You took the words right out of my mouth.

As you know Thomas Allred Jr. For the crime of being a good man. I sentence you to. 27 years of hard labor. In the salt minds. Do you have any objections to this. Let the man speak. Your honor my only crime is being in love with all of the ladies and trying to do the right thing. And that is trying to protect them with my life. Your sentence Thomas Allred Jr. Is reduced a couple years. With a minute. This is just coming through the fax right here. Jeana gave Thomas Allred Jr her will and testament. And it reads that Thomas Allred Jr is the Hero in her life. And that our Amazon princess should also give him love for stopping a gang from coming after her by rising his life. To save her. For there more it gose on to read that it is everything that Thomas Allred Jr realizes that I love him. Those are the last wishes of Ms. Jeana Allred Time cop enforcement officer. Thomas Allred Jr Stand up. Listen to me Thomas Allred Jr. That you are a police officer. Listen. Im a get you out of that situation. Lay back down. And be sincere with us. Do our contract really matter to you. Ladies yall are my friend I can't let no one hurt you every last one of you matter. Because we all are people. And knowing that we must stand for one another. Until the end. I love all of my brothers and sisters in the world. Gabriel Union Allred I like you because I want to see the rest of you that a** is mines. Didn't I tell you that I'd be a smart guy and get the richest first before I get the lady. Amazon women I know that you have worked hard with little or no pay. And these guys out here continue on taking your money away from you . That's why ladies Amazon Women will get and Express card with unlimited balance on it. Only to be used by Amazon Women. And who are these women that we are talking about ? Listen all of these women are Amazon women. That card Carries you in a month to month cycle. I Thomas Allred Jr would like to give to the humane society. 100 billion dollars. I had to now the people can see that I am Superman Thomas Allred Jr. That's not fair Superman Thomas Allred Jr. What isn't fair. You need some children Superman Thomas Allred Jr. I just blessed to be alive. Why do you keep saying that you are blessed to be alive. That's because most people are not fortunate enough to thank God for another day. So while I'm here. I'm saying thank God for everything that he dose for us all. That a look in his eyes you can tell that he is thank full. The first time I seen Gabriel Union Allred . I lost my cool . Simply because my cool is under investigation. And I find you. You a smooth a** operator. In our Hollywood offices we have judged you and your family Superman Thomas Allred Jr. And now you can see that your access has been granted. Count your breath because your records comes out in the next few days. We know how you feel Thomas Allred Jr. A new trail between you and the whole damn industry is being set up . We know you kept your cool in every situation. Known to you. We put you in jail for know reason . And we watched you communicate . You gave us time to get to know you. Get to know us Superman Thomas Allred Jr. You didn't flip out on a single person in over 25 years that is what my contract is all about. I like you because Thomas Allred Jr you are a real man professional. One more thing we all know that you are crying over Jeana being gone. And Hollywood has a plan for you. Look Superman Thomas Allred Jr . You kept on believing in God know matter what we through at you. That makes you official Thomas.

It ain't no way that I could have made it through what I've been through without Jeana Allred you and Gabriel Union Allred. Have been with me my whole life. Only to step in when I needed to the most. And crazy if I say this. But I want to tell everybody. What these women did for me. Along with our police force. And courtrooMs.. I had to stand face to face with gangster individuals. That where known for what they did to Jeana Allred. I just can't help it. Jeana is my always be my Valentine. And Gabriel Union Allred. I choose you. To help guide me and you. With all respect. I thank you Gabriel Union Allred. For being a part of this experience. And for never given up on me. Girl I am police officer. And I love you so damn much. Gabriel will you come up with me. Because of seeing you as my queen. And there is no other in your place. I'm writing music right now. I only stopped for minute to tell you. It's the music that drives us. Anyhow Gabriel Union Allred. Jeana and you saved my life. And i have no way to repay you. I want you to realize one thing Gabriel Union Allred. God knows about this. And I thank you. Too much. Girl to much. I thank you. Clock that girl professional. I only got one thing to say to you Superman Thomas Allred Jr. You hear me Superman Thomas Allred Jr. I am listening Gabriel Union Allred. Take your a** to sleep. Goodnight my princess. Goodnight my Superman names Thomas Allred Jr. Jesus is real Superman Thomas Allred Jr.We see that everyday in you Superman Thomas Allred Jr. Just keep on doing the right thing ladies and gentlemen God has not forgotten about you and me. Thomas Allred Jr without the Superman is my husband and I saved the life of Thomas Allred Jr Because to us he was the sincerest. I want you to read over the whole manuscript. And parts of it where sent to another company Eden . Ask Erin for a copy. Ext 5811 .ThoMs.s my man and my Hero. I'm a do everything that I can for you. And yes you are still under arrest by the Amazon women. That's cool with me Amazon women. I need to see you Gabriel Union Allred. Yes Eden . Gabriel Union Allred this man is a major star. I betch he don't even realize it . If you become professional Thomas Allred Jr. I'll lighting your sentence two more years. Okay Gabriel Union Allred. That would make 25 more years you got to go. To be under arrest with the Amazon women. In charge of you. Thank you Jeana for saving my life. Gabriel Union Allred I can see now that there are going to be some new born kids in our future together. I'm doing this because I need to express my interest in you Gabriel Union Allred. To the state and to the world. I'm saying Gabriel Union Allred that I'm at a lost for words. And I thank you with all my heart inside of me. Man Thank you Gabriel Union Allred. The girl pa**ed the test. My won't give in album is yours. And also my album The Dawning Of the Reign is yours. I'm professional see with a millionaires contract. You would have came out in ruins. But I am a Zillionaire twice over. Gabriel Union Allred all 300 business ideas that we have made is worth more than a Zillionaire dollars a piece. I'm waiting for you to come and get me baby. I'm having a good time at my mommas house. Where Amazon women have me locked up. Until farther notice. From the rest of the Amazon women. Carolina Beach is that way. Thomas Allred Jr I know that you scared but just listen to the Amazon women. Okay. Gabriel Union Allred. And to my boss Frankie . Sir we never stop trying for greatness. Gabriel Union Allred and you make a lovely couple. Thanks Frankie Your welcome Mr. Thomas Allred Jr. Your access has been granted.

Thomas Allred Jr listen to me. The people helping you. We the police department Thomas Allred Jr. Are hear to safe guard you through your out falls . Now that you have proven your self to be a good Samaritan. Thomas Allred Jr the whole police department knows exactly what your going through. We seen you cry in your sleep a many nights crying over your girlfriend Jeana. We put a stop to that and we realize that you are a professional and we just waiting on that day from Hollywood to go with you into that position. Because if you are strong enough to survive twenty one psycho killers. Than be strong we have a place for you in Hollywood. Thomas Allred Jr the worst thing that can happen is you die or get killed out here. You just stay professional. Our police department is here to help guide you all the way to the end of your career. All you have to do is say what it is that you want. Thomas

Allred Jr throw your hands up towards the ceiling and wave at the camera. See how professional you is don't you. We been testing you since you where a juvenile . Why .cause you the Loin King Thomas Allred Jr .y'all serious . I'm dead serious about this Thomas Allred Jr. Jeana and those other women and men should not have died. I don't care about those people this is the police department the look in your eyes and people could tell that you were about to commit suicide. I fight until the death . There's no way out this Thomas Allred Jr you are a prisoner of the police department. So what . Read that contract that you signed. For a woman and your family you will take over my position in Hollywood Superman Thomas Allred Jr. We only call you Superman Thomas Allred Jr .

Because of your kindness towards others. There we go now you are listening. Thomas Allred Jr I need you to trust me on this. You are the real life Loin King .And Hollywood is waiting for you to realize it.what about my people and my friends that are in the community.i grew up with these women and men.i can't just leave them. Yes you can all of your people have been waiting for this. My access is grant. Hallelujah Thomas Allred Jr you made the right decision. Gabriel has to speak to you thank you sergeant Slaughter. Your welcome the whole community is ready to is you. Bad boys for life . Gabriel Union Allred talk to him.

I just want to let you know Superman Thomas Allred Jr. That you are programmed by the state board. So what is your decision. I'm coming to Hollywood me and my family are and my entourage of police officer are coming to. This I already know. How long until the transition see completed. The transition is complete. The board has recommended that Chris and your family belong in Hollywood California. You pa**ed everyone of our tests Thomas Allred Jr. Just do me one favor. Once you are there be your self and not and actor. Are you saying that you don't want me to act Gabriel Union Allred. Look Thomas Allred Jr you know that we got people watching every where . You are a damn Zillionaire just lay your butt down. Okay. But I was promised a bunch of women.

Amazon women who Zillionaire is this he's mine. Gabriel Union Allred I didn't think that you cared so much for me. Your access has been granted Ms. Gabriel Union Allred you and I have something in common. We need a goodnight sleep. And yes before I forget. All the probation officers who have help. I give to you 700 billion dollars in the North Carolina and surrounding areas. This is the circle of life. My Queen Gabriel Union Allred. Honey I need you. I'm kinda tired. I've been fighting to stay up and finish the rest of this book and manuscript. North Carolina as a whole we granting 7.200 billion dollars to fixing the project system for the entire United States. I'm adding another 1.12 million dollars to every Secretary in North Carolina. And to all of my neighbors and friends in Longview North Carolina. We grant to you all my friends women and men in the amount of 6.700 billion dollars I just want to tell y'all that I that you all for wonderfully taking care of all of us. Do not give anything to those people who have shot me and killed our people.

The Loin King Thomas Allred Jr. Gabriel Union Allred I'm crazy about you honey. I'm a see if you can hang with me. Thomas Allred Jr be careful what you wish for. If I had a wish I would wish that people everywhere can rest good now. The Loin King Superman Thomas Allred Jr and his wife Gabriel Union Allred. Are wish you all a very happy holiday season y'all. In case Thomas Allred Jr The Loin King forgot and this crime stoppers. Thomas give to them. Yes Gabriel Union Allred sweetheart. I give to the Crime Stoppers of the North Carolina and surrounding areas. 100 billion dollars. Girl I negotiate for your hand in marriage. Happy birthday Queen Your Highness Angel Lois Lane Gabriel Union Allred. The man is a Zillionaire . Y'all he can never run out of money in his life. Listen Gabriel Union Allred we two are Zillionaires. Have of my fortune is yours. You promise. I can promise you all day Gabriel Union Allred and it won't mean nothing to you . But I can get you a piece of paper saying that it is you that I'm after. Half of my fortune is now yours Gabriel Union Allred. Spoken as you wish for it. Y'all have a good holiday season. Thomas Allred Jr and Gabriel Union Allred The Loin King

Gabriel Union Allred I negotiate with you. You have to negotiate with you. In order to get you to realize how much of a Superman I truly am. Now say these books are worth. A pretty good nickel. Ownership to these books. Belongs to Gabriel Union. I'm getting to the negotiations. I negotiate with you. Another 75 books on top of this one. Baby I'll start working on them immediately. Young and successful means. That Ill do anything to satisfy my woman. Is two more business days. Until I make you realize that I love you. Girl I want to send into you. 100 book strong. I've already sent in like 75 books to you. And this right here. Will make a hundred and 75. Benjamin Franklin taught me. He told me how to treat people. I'm the Lion King Gabriel Union Allred. and professionally I'm tired of the damn females getting hurt. A say to you. The In my negotiations. With you I may bring up. The fact that you are a beautiful woman. Loin Queen. Will you please come and stand beside me. Because without you. Benjamin Franklin can have his money. I can't use it in this world without my professional. Take a good look at our money sweetheart. I've been taught to hustle. I've been taught to be there for somebody. But mostly I've been taught to raise kids up. You don't have to get with me. I'm putting every resources I can at your disposal. You know I need you Gabriel Union Allred. I just can't do this here without you. And i beg you three times. In front of our people. You want me Thomas Allred Jr. I can handle everything that you been giving me .Thomas Allred Jr you need to give me your heart. Do you really think the whole community would let me live without giving you my heart. Gabriel your love means the world to me. And if you would only think about giving me the chance. To get to know you. I'm a be the happiest man in the world .That the worlds ever seen. My pretty young thang. I'm seeing how far this can go. Whatever you want from me just ask and you will get it. Sweetheart I'm in here alone right now coming up on money. And yes I said I'm sitting here alone . I'm trying to show you that suffering for a contract isn't the way that God intended. We need to control our selves in order to get to where we desire. Like this I graduate are funds our funds professional level. I guess I'm watching you on the TV and thinking to myself. If a girl like that loves me. Than Iook pretty good. Because this sins of the father fall on the child. I got to warn you that I have been fighting. Theres people around me who don't agree with progress. But Gabriel Union Allred I didn't mean to say that I have been fighting. It's just that I'm a man of principles. And my truest profession is writing music. Don't get me wrong I really don't care for anything anymore. But you have one thing that I want. A kiss. I'm sending Benjamin Franklin to help you. What ever Gabriel Union Allred needs for herself she gets. Courtesy of Thomas Allred Jr professionals. Gabriel Union Allred you do not have to worry about money Anymore.

Now I said that I'd give her one hundred good we'll to do manuscripts. But no more fantasy just the real stuff . I almost completed this that I'm writing. How much do you need Thomas Allred Jr. After this it will make 95 stories that I plan on sending in once I reach one hundred stories. Get ready you look fabulous in that dress Gabriel Union Allred Sweetheart. It's hard to believe that you and me are Zillionaires . Well we ain't got nothing but a couple more season and then you can stop writing. I said Thomas Allred Jr that we ain't got nothing but a couple of more season and then you can stop writing .

I take it that you Dy want me to write my beautiful wife Gabriel Union Allred. Not at this moment know . What you say is my command. Thomas put the book down . I told you to put the book down damn. This is the man in the mirror Gabriel Union Allred Camelot music manuscript in production with Thomas Allred Jr studios. There I put the book down. How you going to book the book down if you continue writing. I'm looking at the man in the mirror Thomas Allred Jr. My wife Gabriel I really do love you. Have me my book Thomas Allred Jr. Read any Superman stories lately. Just one thing . How'd you could up with this anyway. I just trusted God. And let him lead the way. Get your butt in there and clean up that room Thomas Allred Jr. Yes . I'll do anything to help you. I just want you to realize that you are everything to me Gabriel Union Allred. Thomas Allred Jr there are people that like me. How many of them are there. The great United States of America . Oh listen to me just keep up the good work and you and I will be alright one more question. I know that you are a police officer but can we not ride in a patrol police car. I'm a put you in a big a** house. As soon as they gimme the access granted. Thomas I need the access codes just so I no that your not playing. The access codes are +178-543-289-1706.and my bank account information code is. 3 - 2658 +917-632-145-8960 your Hollywood access has been granted. You can use these to see that I'm not playing . Let live up here Gabriel Union Allred. I think that they call this Pride Rock. Thomas Allred Jr. Then you outta come and stay with me. Gabriel

Union Allred. My Angel. I'm producing the book. Just while I'm speaking with you. I know that Thomas Allred Jr. We been up all night talking Thomas Allred Jr. Pride Rock I'm a remember that. You want me to write it down for you Thomas Allred Jr. Yes I do but here is my pen baby. Write it on this piece of paper. On the piece of paper it reads happy birthday to you my beautiful and s*xy wife Gabriel Union Allred. And I swear to it. That's what Thomas Allred Jr said to me in his book. Order in the court. Gabriel Union Allred we hold you in contempt for being a good woman. You are now under arrest by the Amazon Kings. Gabriel you are under arrest for the crime of being a good woman. Your sentence is to be carried out with Thomas Allred Jr in Hollywood California for the rest of your natural born life. Any objections. I only have one thing to say. Didn't I tell you if get this Zillionaire to love me. You are both sentenced to spend time together. Have a good evening I do mean after noon. Well what are you doing over there Thomas Allred Jr. I'm writing books. Why what is it you got there Gabriel Union Allred. It's a piece of chocolate covered cake. I'll tell you what Thomas Allred Jr I'm a give you half of my cake you start reading your story to me. It started like this.

Girl I know that it see that if you want something bad enough it never comes to you. Don't play no games with me Superman Thomas Allred jr Gabriel Union Allred as soon as saw you. I new that something was bad about me. I am the Lion King and you are my mistress. Once you give me a little while to know you. I plan on getting you a boat. As big as the Titanic. For us to make love on. As we listen to the sounds of music soulchild and the song is called Don't Change. Thomas Allred Jr I need to ask you one simple question. What is the Hollywood access code. The code is 826 35789.your Access has been granted happy new year Thomas Allred Jr. Listen Thomas Allred Jr Jimmy Walker wants to speak to Thomas Allred Jr. Let him through. Honey just let Jimmy Walker in. In front of your family. In front of my family Jimmy Walker. Thomas Allred Jr you and your family listen here you to legit to quit. You are famous. Thomas Allred Jr and Gabriel Union Allred and family. Each one of your family members will be give a TV program. How many TV prograMs. do you want. Seven. We got seven he's a police officer. Gabriel Union Allred whats going on. Thomas Allred Jr you are famous. Damn right the boy is famous. Jimmy Walker you may leave now. Not before I get the last word Gabriel Union Allred and Thomas Allred Jr your access has been granted for Hollywood studios to start taping your story up. Thomas Allred Jr do the right thing by Gabriel Union Allred. But I'm gone now. Jimmy Walker. Yes Gabriel Union Allred . Superman Thomas Allred Jr wants to say something to you. Jimmy Walker yes Captain good job here is my card it says Easy Money. You keep handing business like you just handled and I'll make sure that you have you your own broadcast. Don't hold me to it Jimmy Walker from Good times. I'll hold you to it. Gabriel Union Allred Jimmy Walker have Christmas day dinner with us . All we need is a spoon. I found some rent a spoons out in the hallway. Martin Lawrence. Can I buy a rent a spoons. I don't sell spoons no more. I thought I'd try comedy. That's Great Thomas Allred Jr. We have the rent a spoons business all to our self. Jimmy Walker a took the business over for me. Jimmy Walker that was a good meal. He didn't leave us nothing Thomas Allred Jr yes I did Thomas Allred Jr and Gabriel Union Allred your Hollywood access is granted pick your spoon up and repeat after me. I will never go hungry as long as I shall live. I will never go hungry as long as we shall live. Continue yourself speaking to one another using telepathy. Oh yeah I almost for got to tell you that chicken was good. Get the hell out of my house Jimmy Walker. Thomas Allred Jr what look at you Thomas Allred Jr God damn you grew up in front of the movie screen thank Jimmy Walker. Your access has been granted. I can see it in your eyes . Gabriel Union Allred how beautiful you are. Baby this year will be ours. Hold that position Thomas Allred Jr. Hold that position. The Lion King and Queen Gabriel Union Allred. I love you. You have got to produce me. I got the rent a spoons and everything. A baby can hold it's ground. And a real hero gets the woman that he desires. Who do you want Superman Thomas Allred Jr. Well of course I want you Gabriel Union Allred. Of course I choose you always and forever. Thomas Allred Jr I also choose you always and forever.From your lady Gabriel Union Allred.

And it comes to pa**. That no new taxes are our topic. President Barack Obama and Mr.s. Obama. Come and meet the clintons. Michelle. Hillary Clinton. Nice to meet you Michelle Obama. Hillary Clinton it is my pleasure. Something is wrong with the time circuits. Time acceleration doors now opening. It's Michael J Fox. President George and Barbara Bush. Please come with me. Why Michael we don't have enough room to get up the 85. Because I'm too time champion. Get our president Donald Trump on the phone. It's raining sir. In my heart Ive seen many challenges. As it was. President Bill Clinton. Yes president Donald Trump. Well what in the hell did he say. President Barack Obama he said connect four. Connect four what a strange language. Is the earth gravitational pull in trouble. Oh my gosh. If it isn't Thomas Allred Jr. And his wife Gabrielle Union Allred. Mr.. Donald Trump is about time we came to this party. You see us for who we are Gabriel Union Allred and Thomas Allred Jr. Yes I do miss Martha Stewart. And miss Sally Jesse Raphael. And miss Oprah Winfrey. And Dr . Phil . It is about to turn out easy. We have a new champion. For the third time in this year. President Bill Clinton is our new champion. Your access has been granted President Bill Clinton. And Hillary to you access has been granted. To Hollywood studios. Right now I'm just so proud of you people. The way that you take care of one another.

Ricky lake you mean the tell me. That Winona Judd ain't singing no more. Michael J Fox. Nobody is. This is the future. And your heartbeat is being secured. With a kiss from your own mother. Back in good old 1985. That's it people. Thomas Allred Jr you ain't got to do nothing but send your stories in. We are going to fly you all around the country. And overseas. We you just say for me please. Give me space i worship you. Even president Clinton wouldn't say that. Michael J Fox. I'm going to let my wife tell you best. Miss Gabriel Allred is getting ready to speak. My word is. To heavy for the earth gravitational pull. But I come to yall estranged people. And I ask you all. How come Steve Harvey isn't here. Girl I want you to realize something. That over the past 20 years Thomas Allred Jr. We been sating up all kinds of people. Where so proud of you. And this is. Gabriel's birthday surprise party. Whoopi Goldberg. And Martha Stewart. Whoopi Goldberg has something to say. Along with Jeff Goldberg. And Gina Davis. Along with Susan Sarandon .

And Tommy Lee Jones. These are all the people that are at your party. Gabriel Union Allred. The princess is here. Gabriel this isn't a dream. Your Prince charming Superman Thomas Allred Jr is waiting for you. He has clean up the entire world with his business ideas. And all that he can say is that he wants to meet you Gabriel Union Allred. Now Gabriel Union Allred I've never meet you in real life. But Winona Judd said that you are a really great woman. So without a do. I'll like to give to you your husband Superman Thomas Allred Jr. I see how he does it now. No President Bill Clinton.

Coming at you my wife Hillary Clinton Connect four. What you know about that Thomas Allred Jr. Nothing miss Hillary Rodman Clinton . Gabriel Union Allred this man is a keeper. Have Morris Chestnut give you a call. Why hes here and he's right over there. With Christina Aguilera. Christina Aguilera. And no doubt. He keep going you and he will be famous once again Mr.s Gabriel Union Allred. This is all that you looking for. Think Morris Chestnut. Your Superman awaits you. It's a horse and carriage. Is got police officers around it. Stepping out of the limousine. Is your family Gabriel Union Allred. This is a dream come true. I already know it's a dream come true. Listen to your heart beat. Your heartbeat is not broken anymore. I done fixed your heartbeat. Because that's what I do for a living. I am Superman Thomas Allred jr. Come and get you some money potatoes. I don't mind if I do. We have Jimmy Walker in the building. We see that Punk Daddy is in the building also. Along with Christina Aguilera. You already said Christine Aguilera. And the ladies from in vogue. We are relaxing. Trying not to be superficial. This is a holiday season. Happy birthday to you. Gabriel Union Allred. Is 32 years old. If I adore you for the rest of your life will you be mine. Yes Superman Thomas Allred Jr I will be yours. You need to stop the music. Thomas Allred Jr. It's almost 12 again. Gabriel I get down on one knee.In front of the whole world. At the stroker midnight. In the White House. And ask that you please. Be my wife. Gabriel Union Allred. It is time. I lose all my glits and klammer. It midnight. I become a average man again. Superman Thomas Allred Jr I love you for real. Take care of my woman people. Superman Thomas Allred Jr just left the building before the stroker of midnight. It is midnight you see Thomas Allred Jr. I'm trying to be strong for me and you. Can you feel my heart beat Thomas Allred Jr.

Connect four. Barbara Bush. She just beat the hell out of Bill Clinton in connect four reload. This is our future of being together. No you see Thomas Allred Jr. How that girl needs you. Time circuits moving. Time acceleration doors now opening. It's Superman Thomas Allred Jr. And he got her 12 dozen roses. And a box of candy that says the Allred corporation on it. Excuse me for dressing like this. But this is the real me. I don't have anything to offer you Gabriel Union Allred. Give him a minute to talk to his self. But people are telling me. That you and me are Zillionaires. I want if you would take my hand seeing at how dirty it is. I'll take you just anyway you are. That girl love me man. President Barack Obama that girl love me man. Morris Chestnut that girl loves me man.. President George and Barbara Bush that girl loves me thank God for miracles. We had to see that you were worthy Superman Thomas Allred Jr. Take Superman and get him cleaned up. His biggest fear was not to be able to talk to the ladies. Remain Professional. We need to do everything we can. To help out our Superman. Because his heartbeat is broken. Not anymore it ain't. Superman Thomas Allred Jr come out of the bathroom. Excuse me Sir. I'm waiting for someone. Gabriel Union Allred it's me Superman Thomas Allred Jr.

Superman Thomas Allred Jr. It's is you Thomas. I love you Gabriel Union Allred so damn much. For what is Christmas Eve time without someone you can hold Gabriel Union Allred. May I have this dance. Thank you for saving my life sweetheart. All-time circuit open. Y'all handle that sh*t. President Barack Obama watch your language. Okay my sweetness. Michelle Obama. Mr.s. Trump where do you get your hair done at. At Sally's hair products for women. Listen up Thomas. Miss Trump is speaking. I'm going to get you your contract Thomas Allred Jr. For having the audacity to write these stories. Pulling us all together one more time. Thomas I give to you. Miss Gabriel Union Allred hand in marriage. Thomas Allred Jr. I feel like I'm in 7th grade .I'm a kiss you. Thomas Allred Jr. I'm a kiss you . Close your eyes until I tell you to open them. Open your eyes. Gabriel Union Allred that was amazing. My heartbeat is now fixed.

Thank you Ms. Michelle Obama. Because when I get through tonight I will have accomplished my task of one hundred memorable stories I get to you of people coming together in friendship and love and honor for all nations to come in to.Superman Thomas Allred Jr . This is the Jeana Gabriel Union Allred Code. One nation. Individual with liberty and justice for all. This boy representing the entire nation God. Gabriel Union Allred is my princess. I know because the first time that I seen her I changed my ways. My heartbeat is complete for Hollywood access code. +1-879-236-4894 851-236-2789.i said your access has been granted. In the days to come I'm a sit here and just dream of a better day for me and my family. Our access is completed . The whole country owes you a debt of gratitude Gabriel Union Allred. Get gratitude from the entire nation. I knew y'all would respect me. Gabriel Union Allred I just want me a House to watch the sunrise in. If you want a house I'm a see what I can do for you. Do forget that you are a Zillionaire Thomas Allred

Jr. Do forget that you are a Zillionaire Gabriel Union Allred. Girl the money take as much as you need. I still have got people waiting on me. To check my heartbeat. I love you Thomas Allred Jr. I love you to Gabriel Union Allred. Your heartbeat is done matured. Think about this just one second. If we advertising you Thomas Allred Jr why not put you in a Superman suit. Naw professionals won't believe that they will to Thomas Allred Jr.

Well Hillary Rodman Clinton. Yes President Bill Clinton. It's time that we dance. President Bill Clinton and his wife Hillary Rodman Clinton. Are stepping to the floor. Be sincere Bill am I who you want. Put everyday of my life Hillary it had to do you. Welcoming the Bushes. Barbara Bush dances beautifully. Make sure George is who he suppose to be. A Bush Thomas Allred Jr. Will the first lady please come to the dance floor. We right now. I'm waiting for. Miss Keisha Cole's. And Deborah Cox. Along with Amerie . Listen we got these ladies first cla** seats in the White House. Jennifer Lopez. And Nicki Minaj. And Missy Elliott. I'll get first-cla** seats in the white house. Along with Travis Crisp . Thomas Travis Crisp cant be here right now. He's gone on a world wide 80 day tour. He sent a letter Superman Thomas Allred Jr. He said thank you. For everything. What did I do Gabriel Union Allred. You got famous. And gave all them people their props and respect. That came before you. Well alright dammit.i know that I got this. It might just take a little ingenuity. But connect four has been achieved. Ladies in gentleman I give to you. Mr.. Bill Clinton and miss Hillary Rodman Clinton. Dancing the first dance of the evening. Bill Clinton I can't control myself. I feel like a kid again. You are my dream Hillary Rodman Clinton. You are my dream favorite my sweetheart. May everyone else join in beside of them. Who is that DJ. That is DJ clue and DJ Kali. In your face Hater I mean. Thank you for my respect. Gabriel Union Allred. I feeling this good. Thomas Allred Jr will you ever cheat on me. No Gabriel Union Allred. I would not. In real life Im single. And your this great movie actress on the big screen. I'm writing books trying to get close to you. I made these business ideas. So I could stand up as a man in the community.

Don't you say it Thomas Allred Jr. Gabriel this can't be the last dance. A Thomas Allred Jr do you mind if I cut in. President Thomas Allred Jr. What did you call me Sir. You are the President of the world's commerce building. Aren't you. You damn right I am. We need you to report back here every morning at 7:36 The commerce building ain't your yet you have got to be sworn in to secrecy.I Thomas Allred Jr and I Gabriel Union Allred. Have sworn our allegiant to the White House of America. For with it's republic. One nation under God with liberty and justice for all. President Thomas Allred Jr and his lovely wife Gabriel Union Allred have took over the industry. Superman Thomas Allred Jr . Can everything go our way. Your Highness Angel Lois Lane Gabriel Union Allred Mr. Destiny is here. The two of you look lovely Superman Thomas Allred Jr. And Your Highness Angel Lois Lane

Gabriel Union Allred. How do we thank you Mr. Destiny by being good to each of . You two have single handedly you've saved the industry and you brought all of the people together. Jeana would have been proud. Two more books and you've had a perfect story Superman Thomas Allred Jr. And Your Highness Angel Lois Lane Gabriel Union Allred. Thomas Allred Jr can do it. I believe in him. What I tell you Superman Thomas Allred Jr .

Your wife needs you to be focused on the future do sleep around after we have done tested you and got you approved for Hollywood. Get your neighbors and chance to see something good happen for you and your people. Mr. Destiny I do everything that you tell me . But I still want to meet Gabriel Union Allred. She is right there in your dreaMs. Superman Thomas Allred Jr. You couldn't have done this without her. Remember you only need to more stories and your access is approved. Tell Gabriel that you love her and you will never leave her. She can see and her you from where you are Superman Thomas Allred Jr in your room laying across the bed writing your book alone. Gabriel Union Allred I love you and I will never leave you. These two more books Superman Thomas Allred Jr. Should be uplifting. To us all. Now use the bathroom and come back at write. Take your time and tell your princess that you love her . I love you Gabriel Union Allred access approved. Thomas Allred Jr gimme a access code. The access code is 412-783-396-7018 546-8901. Examine yourself before you leave Superman Thomas Allred Jr. Gimme those two books. Okay Mr. Destiny but I get to kiss the girl after we do this. Hold on tight Superman Thomas Allred Jr.

Where are we . Sit right down and write the last two books. This is your story. If you want it Superman Thomas Allred Jr you have got to get it. I'm on my way Mr. Destiny why Superman Thomas Allred Jr because Your Highness Angel Lois Lane Gabriel Union Allred . And I wrote this story right here. Your Highness Angel Lois Lane Gabriel Union Allred you have been a great experience but I don't need you for the rest of the book. I need you for all of the book. That's my wife Mr. Destiny. Thomas your time is waisted. You know longer have time to write two more books. So with that being said we will just add up you and tell you and say to you that your access has been granted Superman Thomas Allred Jr. These are all Gabriels books. I want them to be hers as a wedding present. From a really great person. Name Superman Thomas Allred Jr. Now your getting the point that your destiny isn't as strong as you think it is. You are the Lion King Superman Thomas Allred Jr. And no one has the right to take anything from you. Gabriel will be with you shortly. Keep your head up Thomas. And your destiny was for filled. Superman Thomas Allred Jr because you are the Lion King and everyone knows it even you. Gabriel Union Allred I will look at you as the princess in a dream who has everything and is always happy to be in love with me The Lion King Superman Thomas Allred Jr. Listen I know that you are The Lion King. But can I borrow 20 dollars. Only in America Gabriel Union Allred I love you only in America. Thank you Mr. Destiny . What did

I do is. Shut up. Deborah Cox's is going to be singing. Nobody is supposed to be here. Superman Thomas Allred Jr thank you. You are welcome Your Highness Angel Lois Lane Gabriel Union Allred . Is there anything else I can do for you. Thomas Allred Jr when you make your book. Don't dedicate it out to anyone because you are special. Okay Your Highness Angel Lois Lane Gabriel Union Allred. You got to think. Gabriel Union Allred your access has been granted. To Hollywood California. We up in the big leagues. Look Superman Thomas Allred Jr . Thank you. It was me and Gabriel Union Allred pleasure everybody. Commercial.

No matter what you do you can't cheat your destiny. Superman Thomas Allred Jr. I'm saying to you that. Your wife is coming to you. You got to wait and be patient Superman Thomas Allred Jr. I have been alone for 9 years plus. And Gabriel commands you for that. But my superhero. Thats Your Highness Angel Lois Lane Gabriel Union Allred speaking to me now. I didn't have time to speak to you Superman Thomas Allred Jr in the last episode. It is our destiny to be together. Your Highness Angel Lois Lane Gabriel Union Allred this is not a book this is life. You and I are really Zillionaires. As soon as the state allows me and you to spend our money. I know your probably mad at me. How could I be angry at you. I'm the new Lion King. Superman Thomas Allred Jr. And President of the world commerce building. Do you smell that.

What is that. Sweetheart I'm getting ready to tell you what The Rock is cooking. I need to Superman Thomas Allred to be serious. Okay Your Highness Angel Lois Lane Gabriel Union Allred. Cut on the music. Play R Kelly music. Just imagine if you and me were together alone right now Superman Thomas Allred Jr. Now is there anything you want to say to me before we turn the music off. I want to say Your Highness Angel Lois Lane Gabriel Union Allred that I need you to stay with me no matter what may happen in the future. Superman Thomas Allred Jr the future is ours it is what we make of it. Now fix your dreaMs. Superman Thomas Allred Jr. Mr. Destiny is here. Gabriel Union Allred and Thomas Allred Jr. How good it is to meet you. Once in a lifetime opportunity. Thomas Allred Jr have you seen your future in the pages of these books. I'm confused Mr.. Destiny. One more book and then I have a hundred. But Sir. How do I make a hundred books become famous. Just use your heart Superman Thomas Allred Jr.

Take her of the street corners Thomas Allred Jr. I must be true to Gabriel Union Allred. Thomas is a goddamn eagle scout. In all fairness he's being true. Mr.. Destiny are you saying it is okay if i date someone. So much for destiny. Gabriel listen to me. There are things about this life that I cannot explain. But I will wait for you honey. Gabriel Union Allred. Honey I will give the best to me. And wait for you daily. With the horizon. You have these books as a reminder. The there is a love waiting for you. On the shores of North Carolina Beach. That is where Ill be after I build my home. True love is. Never having to criticize anyone. Everytime I think it you. I get energy. The want to see you Gabriel Union Allred. I just feel stronger than I've ever felt my life. I'm your soulmate. Thomas Allred Jr. And a peach. Is what you and me have. Talk to Mr.. Destiny. Any doubts Gabriel Union Allred. Superman Thomas Allred Jr is so damn stubborn. Causes you Mr. destiny. My dreaMs. have awoken. And how do you spell dreaMs. Gabriel Union Allred. One step at a time in history. The journey of a thousand miles begins with one step. Now do you understand your invent help book Superman Thomas Allred Jr. You where summoned to go to invent help. You and Candis M Collins. For this evening you have this one chance to make things right. Who do you want to be with after all of this mess is straighten out .I want to be with all of the Amazon women that have been helping me over the years. Because right now my destiny isn't clear. And I am not letting no woman down ever again. Be careful what you wish for Thomas Allred Jr. I wish that the Amazon women and the Amazon nation except me as there king. The Lion King Superman Thomas Allred Jr. Now my destiny is clear. I knew it would come to this. I keep telling you. That I can hold my head up. But without you Gabriel Union Allred. I ain't got nothing going for myself. So the answer to this question is. I choose the women Amazon nation. To represent me. I am Superman Thomas Allred Jr. And I also Am the Lion King. Your access has been granted. Just one more book Thomas Allred Jr . And your destiny and your dream has been for filled. Keep our composure. It is your composure. That make things magical. I'm a police officer. Mr. Destiny . My right hand man. Look Thomas unusually I don't do this but we are going to go ahead a keep the party going DL hugely I respect you for everything that you said in the comedy show. The Lion King Superman Thomas Allred Jr the Destiny forfillment has been approved. Thank you Mr. Destiny. Thank you.

CHAPTER 10

Right at this minute I'm a police officer Gabriel Union Allred. I know you like me but I'm doing everything I can to be with you. What are you saying to me Thomas Allred jr. I'm saying that I haven't given you any reason not to trust me. It's just that. I don't know how I can trust you when I can't see you. Gabriel Union Allred read through my words there all true. This is the last book that I'm writing Gabriel Union Allred. Your Highness Angel Lois Lane Gabriel Union Allred. Please invest some time and read it. Cause we at the White House are telling you. That its okay to be afraid. Here go Ms..Hillary Clinton. Gabriel I've watched you grow into a young lady on the TV screen. And I have been proud of you. We at the White House. Are so stupendously proud of you. Not only do my stories fit you. You have got a man Gabriel Union Allred. That has his whole life been in rags. He is a Zillionaire Gabriel Union Allred. Y'all keep a look after him. Listen to me Ms. Hillary Clinton. Thomas can begg me to the sky turn blue. You know that he cheated on me. I know that its not to many chances a person gets to say there sorry. Superman Thomas Allred Jr. Never cheated on you. He was just seeing how you would take it. Because he is a Zillionaire. And he has to be careful about his surroundings. Angel Lois Lane Gabriel Union Allred your Access has been granted to live with Thomas Allred Jr and the Amazon women immediately after this book gets read through thoroughly by Amazon woman. Woman of the Amazon nation we have a King among you. Superman Thomas Allred Jr . Keep and eye on your girl. Yes. Mr. Destiny makes you out to be the real deal The Lion King Superman Thomas Allred Jr. Y'all have better take care of that boy. Let Bill Cosby and R Kelly go. We need them to solve the case of why I can never beat Ms. Hillary Clinton in connect four. Connect four Superman Thomas Allred Jr I win again. Look you have but two weeks to put your manuscript in. You should put it in the day after tomorrow. Any who Superman Thomas Allred Jr. I don't know what you call yourself. But it's working for you The Lion King Superman Thomas Allred Jr. Gabriel Union Allred is proud to be beside of you. Now you may kiss her The Lion King Thomas Allred Jr. Get a room after that. It's my Destiny to know just where I'm headed to Carolina Beach. A Mr.

Destiny. Is there anything that me and my wife forgot to say. It's a new beginning Thomas Allred Jr and Gabriel Union Allred. Thomas what about Jeana Allred. Jeana we thank you for your sacrifice. We love you always and forever Jeana. Mr. Destiny I only have one thing left to say. Yes Gabriel Union Allred you have said it all. Mission Complete. Your access has been granted. Put one more code in Thomas Allred Jr. The Hollywood access code is. 627-813-5894 312-0816.Thank you Gabriel Union Allred I'm going to love you forever. Jeana you have got to take care of yourself. I got a. new life to live. With Gabriel Union Allred my wife.

Eden I had a talk with myself. About the importance of life. And what am I here for. Just then I thought to myself that I am a gazillionair with and infinity symbol behind my money. And girl I thought to myself. If I had one dream it would be that. Kristen Beam of Morganton North Carolina. And Maya of Catawba valley behavioral healthcare. In Hickory North Carolina. Thats 28602.Dressed like a Hero. In this new movie. I'm calling. Last Rights To infinity and beyond. In Wich I am currently writing the movie for Page Company as we speak. I haven't spoken to them yet Eden. But I a**ure you that I've done my homework. Eden I am told to speak to a professional about the Lion King movie to come out. Gabriel Union Allred and Kristen Beam and Maya and I. Thomas Allred Jr. Have just as much rights to party. As any body else in this film. What I'm saying is that this is our opportunity to bring back a cla**ic to the big screen . I don't unusual say nothing but I am a gazillionair and im the true Lion King that's based off the movie. I'm saying the Lion King movie is a copy of my life. Down to me taking over our Pride Rock. Maybe it's a coincidence . Or maybe there is some great power at hand but I just know that I want for Kristen Beam out of Morganton North Carolina. And Maya. Out of hickory NC. And Gabriel Union Allred. To stand beside me in costumes. That look like Superman's costume. Except instead of and S across the chest. All of our costumes will have and infinity symbol. My our costume will look like Supermans costume the only difference is I'm the true Lion King. I still got to make a costume for that but until then this a do. Last Rights Infinity and beyond. Thomas Allred Jr you are getting short on time. Honey. Thomas be more professional. I'm surpposed to give you something Eden Reid. Ms. Eden Reid I Grant to you. 70 million dollars a piece. I don't know how they do this but you can check you account and see that it is there. Thank you Ms. Eden Reid. And Eden I want to give your Company 11 more million dollars to show you that we are with you. Ms. Eden Reid one more thing. I want you to have one billion dollars. Happy new beginning and merry Christmas to you and your family from The Lion King Superman Thomas Allred Jr. I know who I am now. Stand up and speak these words Eden. I am The Lion Kings contract. I mean that. The Lion King Thomas Allred Jr keep working .The superhero suit that I want you to were Ms. Eden Reid is a flash costume with and infinity symbol on the front of it. Like I said I am the true Lion King Superman Thomas Allred Jr. So Eden Reid

I want you in a Superwoman super suit as well with the infinity symbol on it has well. Because me and you. And Kristen Beam and Maya also and Gabriel Union Allred. Are infinity man and woman. Girl I'm putting this together right now as we speak. Thomas Allred Jr you time is about up. Listen Eden Reid you are very special to me . My bank account tells me that you have your money. Is if any other man can do you like this. Eden I want you to be my newest wife. Think of it . Thomas Allred Jr your almost running out of time. Start the movie over . I'm making a movie called The Last Rights To infinity and beyond. Eden Reid if you could just call me. Look at the time. I guess I better get off the phone with you. And Eden for Christmas Kristen Beam and Maya and Gabriel Union Allred and I are granting to you company another billion dollars also. The Lion King Superman Thomas Allred Jr. Thomas Allred Jr say Merry Christmas to all of you. Merry Christmas to all of you. Eden the money is real. The government a see that you have it. I'm am The Lion King Surperman Thomas Allred Jr. My girl wants to talk to you Ms. Eden Reid. Look at the time. You just have to choose who you will be with. Cause the business man of the year is The Lion King Superman Thomas Allred Jr. And everybody knows that after midnight tonight. That boy going to get his money back. Thomas just got two more weekends to go. To prove he is The Lion King Superman Thomas Allred Jr. In the business world. The Lion King Superman Thomas Allred Jr is keeping up with everyone that is seeking his contract. He has come back from a gunshot wound and he is hungry. As my heart beat Eden Reid I'm telling you that Thomas Allred Jr is truly and officially The Lion King. Of the world entire country. This boy gots hands hand in business. And in real a state along with you Eden Reid. With Kimberly as his literary agent. There is Erin as his literary agent. And last but not least I give you. Where Mr. Roma. Is his literary agent. Eden this is Gabriel Union Allred. You know what we are fighting for. So the Lion King Superman Thomas Allred Jr can have his proper place in the world. Think about it. I'll be getting back to you. Sincerely The Lion King incorporation. You finished Thomas Allred Jr. Eden Reid we thank you for everything. Will you join my team. The Lion King incorporation. I'm a send to messages now. Don't ha**le her .

My counselor Ms. Gabriel Union Allred. Girl it's nice to see you again. I was so wrong the last time Gabriel Union Allred. I should have let you speak at the end of the meeting. Don't even worry about it The new and improved Lion King Superman Thomas Allred Jr. I am going in to this meeting wide open. We are going to get you your contracts back The new and improved Lion King Superman Thomas Allred Jr. Everyone single on of them. The truth is that I'm a little frightened Gabriel Union Allred. And you should be The new and improved Lion King Superman Thomas Allred Jr . These ain't your regular players. First in the corner we have Mr. Richard Roma. And over sitting on the couch we have Eden Reid. And who is this by the counter and something. That is Ms. Kimberly Schwandt. And coming towards us we have Ms. Erin Cohen. Now that we have meet and know everyone. The new and improved Lion King Superman Thomas Allred Jr. Have a seat in the corner. Now you can see the Loin King doesn't have fear in his heart. He told that girl that he was going to feed the dog gone nation after his money comes back. I know that everyone of you got the feed . The new and improved Lion King Superman Thomas Allred Jr. Only wishes to be fruitful and multiply his labor. Why shouldn't he be able to lift up a old curse that is on him. Before we all see the end of his life. Why must we do this The New and improved Lion King Superman Thomas Allred Jr looks so happy. The Lion King is not happy. Ms. Eden Reid. You put him on blast on TV just for the world to see. Knowing damn well that you are the ones that sent him up there. Now now listen to me. Mr. Richard Roma the problem is if the Lion King gets free he can hurt somebody. You don't Know the power that he possesses. But what I'm saying is what if The new and improved Lion King Superman Thomas Allred Jr. Is already free inside of him mind with no mental traps.Is that true. Why don't you ask him. Mr. Richard Roma in New York City . Thomas. Yes it's me. You the Lion King aren't you. I'm a man who family as been stolen and executed for wanting to live there live the right way. The came be happening . Who lifted the curse. Ms. Erin Cohen. I did. To show you that the Lion King is a man. But he is going to hurt us. He is going to kill y'all a**es. They murdered him family. And he still went out and rescued everybody. The war on terrior is over. I'm a ten time champion Lion King. I am the champion of the world. Do you see what I'm saying. He ain't wanting to hurt none of you.

He just wants to have a family like everyone else that has those contracts. The new and improved Lion King Superman Thomas Allred Jr. Has saved us. You and I from terrorism. Living in fear of death. It is time that we bring to the Lion King all of his contracts. And remember he hasn't really been around a woman ever in his life. The new and improved Lion King Superman Thomas Allred Jr . Listens perfectly. I'm a ask him a question. Be my guest Ms. Eden Reid. Thomas Allred Jr are you hurt. A little bit. He spoke to me. Can I ask you another question Thomas Allred Jr. Lion King. What will you do with you contracts that ain't never been done before. Stand out in the sun light with them and watch the light beam down on us from heaven. When the light beaMs. down on your what dose it feel like . Purity. The light heals the body and purifies the soul. That's it. That boy don't want nothing but a girlfriend.

Gabriel Union Allred think about what you are saying. You here Thomas Allred Jr take you damn a** to sleep. Gabriel Union Allred the Lion King it's going no where . Yes he is going somewhere. Jesus Christ the boy is almost fourty five years old. And he's been working for the government all of this time. He's saved our children and end wars as we know it with his idea . He has to much information at hand. He is the one who gave you all the information Mr. Richard Roma. Gabriel Union Allred. Listen . No Mr. Richard Roma you are wrong Thomas Allred Jr has saved the world single handedly while we didn't do nothing but sit there and watch him fight. What are you saying get him a house. With everyone of his contracts to go in it. And get his family a house to each one of them brought Jesus back to us. See watch. Jesus what are you doing. I'm sitting here writing my book called the hard way. What you doing Gabriel Union Allred. You mean to tell me that Thomas Allred Jr really is the Christ. Thinks about it . Thomas Allred Jr died in the hospital. And came back to life seven teen minutes after his own death. He calls him self Surperman in the presents of the police. He is starting to realize that ain't nothing wrong with him. And the world stole his contracts away from him. He knows Thomas Allred Jr tell the committee just how you feel. I wasn't put on this Earth to fight. The war on terrior is over. The white House is in charge of everything. I lose love ones just like you do. And if you think that you hurt. I feel pain as we. I want all of my contacts back. Because the have been mistreated. And need to be healed.

We saved all of the little children. I myself. And the Secret service. I just dedicate this to my own Police department. The Hickory Police department. Of North Carolina. For saving Then new and improved Lion King Superman Thomas Allred Jr. A thousand times. Thomas there is no place out here for you and your contracts to be. See there you are wrong. My contacts belong with me at Carolina Beach In North Carolina. All I'm asking of you is that you give them to me. Let me see if the Lord will make a way. Thomas you realize you are a gazillion with the infinity symbol behind your money. What is going to happen to you if we let you go to Carolina beach Thomas. Thomas just answer the question. I hope to become a school teacher and a father. That is what will happen to us if I go to Carolina Beach. All that I know is that I miss my women friends around me. They are more than your friends Thomas Allred Jr. Keep your pants on. You have got the community in a frenzy with that last Idea that you made. I really don't want to discuss any ideas with you right now. I just want my contrast to see me for the man that I really am. Exactly. Mr. Richard Roma picture that man with kids. He is not needed to fight anymore. The battle has been won. We can see right through your defenses Thomas Allred Jr. What is it that you truly want. I want a girl named Kristen Beam.

Why do you want this girl for Thomas Allred Jr. Because she's the most beautiful woman I ever saw. I'm a beat that a**. Once we leave out this community. Miss Kimberly. You can say what you want to. But when it comes down to it. Thomas Allred Jr is your professional. You damn right Kimberly. This man is a war veteran. And inventor. A book and movie writer. A welder. A musician. A actor. And a gazillionair police officer. I see why Uncle Sam programmed Thomas Allred Jr. They done lost they f*cking mind. This man is not a weapon. We have all stuck together and won a war. See look at how professional that boy is. He is writing the book as we speak. Are you okay Gabriel Union Allred. You made a mistake Thomas Allred jr. I mean my wife Gabriel Union Allred. Thomas look at these people. They all interested in one thing. Your superpower to make the sun come out of the sky. I haven't did it in a while Gabriel Union Allred. What it is is I can tell when the sun is going to being down on me. And everytime I'm in the sunlight it gets brighter. I don't care if it's just my finger that touches the sunray it gets brighter it's stronger. No matter where I am in the world. I think that the sun getting brighter around me and others heals us. It makes us stronger and happier people so I trust God and I keep believing that one day I will have my contracts. That is the end Thomas. Of the hard week calculations. You don't have to do nothing but. Send off the messages. Gabriel Union Allred I love you. My counselor. And to all the publishers who are going to publish this book. In movie trailer. I want to thank you from the bottom of my heart. We won the war on terrorism. God bless the USA. Thomas get ready to send your message out. Maya. And Shannon Clay I love you. To all the people that lost someone . I am The new and improved Lion King Superman Thomas Allred Jr. And I'm just thinking that there is a place on the other side of mountain . Where I tell you angels go. You have to see it to believe it keep pushing . Cause the sooner I get through this I may get a look at Faith. These contracts are history. And I'm a school teacher. Coming back for the all. In the community. I'm praying for a better way other than war. Mr.. President. We have Thomas Allred Jr a contract. The Lion King

I'm just saying that counselor you did good in there. Well Thomas Allred Jr. Watch and see how good that I do now because I have forgot something. What did you forget. Ms. Gabriel Union Allred. That new girls contract. New girls contract. Yes Thomas Allred Jr follow me to my car I'm a get the paper. Now hand it to tell professionals as they leave. Here you go Ms. Eden Reid. And here you go also Ms. Kimberly Schwandt and Ms. Erin Cohen. Mr. Richard Roma. This is for you as well. What is this Mr. Thomas Allred Jr. My counselor says it is a warrant for you all arrest. Do make this easy on us. Back seat of the bus Mr. Richard Roma. Kimberly sit down and hush your mouth. Now is everybody comfortable. Unlock this got damn car do you here me. Let me speak to a lawyer . I can't breathe do you here me. Okay Thomas Allred Jr let them all out of the car. Ms. Gabriel Union Allred. Was all of that ready necessary. In true facts it was. Mr. Richard Roma. You the one telling us to. That care of our selves but you couldn't even get out of a locked car from a police officer. And Ms. Kimberly Schwandt you telling us to keep the faith but your in the backseat hollering you can't breathe. And you only been in the car for half a minute. What I'm saying is Thomas Allred Jr has been through at least seven different types of war for our country. He didn't want to take a bullet. But before he could let his friend die. He picked him up from off of the ground in the black community. Before he was executed. And recieved a bullet to the back of the leg for his troubles. He didn't panic he just did what he had to do. Thomas Allred Jr is in love with some females. They contracts a mean the world to him. And since Thomas Allred Jr and I are gazillionairs with the infinity symbol behind our money. We give to each contract 17 million $$$.for a sign on bonus with a beautiful man named The Lion King. Thomas Allred Jr. Is especially excited about moving in to his new houses with his contracts with him. See Thomas Allred Jr ain't God good. All the time he is. Ms. Erin Cohen and Ms. Eden Reid. Get out the front seat. This new girls contract is real and legal and binding. The woman will get 17 million for just a quick interview through the house. I kid you not . It's a price that tell have to pay. If they want to stay on with Thomas Allred Jr and me. Wich is the price. They each have to dress in Genie out fits ever day of the week for the rest of there natural born lives. The contract states that as new girls. The queen will make a serve Thomas Allred Jr. And how do you think that she is Thomas Allred Jr. My wife Ms. Gabriel Union Allred. That's it Thomas Allred Jr. do you agree to my terMs.. Yes but we need to think about it. And get back to you. I will give each one of my new girl contracts. 700 million dollars as a sign on bonus to be with us at Carolina Beach. And I will pay for there wardrobes and everything they need. If we can only be family and tell the truth to on another. What do you say do we have a deal. Be smart. Through in like two vacations and we have a deal. We have a deal. How many contracts can we have every last one of them you like. Come with me and show me. Your contract are waiting out there for you. All you have to do is write down how special they are to you Thomas Allred Jr. Gabriel Union Allred. Honey I can't breathe without them. I love my contracts so much.

Listen I have trusted in the girls in my neighborhood for all of my life and even though we never where together. We kept a friend ship though out the years. Gabriel Union Allred this war game is almost over. And all of the troops and police officers will be coming home safely . I give 21 billion to our troops and police officers. Stop right there what kind of gazillionair would take his money and help out his fellow man. Thomas Allred Jr that is who. Give the ladies 2100 million dollars a peice to buy my contracts back from actors.

Thomas Allred Jr im just in aww at you. Your father would have been proud The new and improved Lion King Superman Thomas Allred Jr new girls contract is that all of the girls will get 2100 million dollars. Apun arrival to the mantion . Where they can choose to stay if they want to stay. May I ask you something. Thomas Allred Jr we know that you ain't suck on d*ck in jail. Why you stand up to everybody and end the war on terriorism. Cause I believe in God. And I love those lady contracts of mines.

Y'all see my point don't you this boy. Gives up everything to his friends strangers and family all be church people put a see in his head to believe in God over anything else . I hate to say it but they are right . Thomas Allred Jr is The Lion King. Thomas Allred Jr it okay we realize that you are a virgin. Look I don't know how you knew but thank you committee. Thomas Allred Jr make a wish for me. I wish that I receive my new girl contracts this year. It is three weeks before Christmas right now where I am. And the police and Homeland security keepped me out with everything.

Everybody y'all are the reason that I can make it though. Gabriel Union Allred I love you. And half of my fortune belongs to you. Down to the last penny. We will cut it in half. I love you. Goodnight. This the new girl contract do fall a sleep yet. Thomas Allred Jr. I secretly got a crush on you. Baby I know how you feel. You understand that these are all my contacts. I'm a program you to always take care of your business. Can there not be any men on this island.we can see. I love you. And now that you have had your fill of the old world. We now want you to sit back and realize while we take care of you. Your new girls contract. Is ready and completed. I want to thank you for giving me my contract. My wife Gabriel Union Allred it is no problem. It is no problem y'all. And just like that he up and disappeared. To North Carolina Beach with his women. Thomas Allred Jr is a legend . He is a Greek God. Thank you Mr. Richard Roma for your time . And Ms. Eden Reid and Ms. Kimberly Schwandt and Ms. Erin Cohen. Thank you all so much. This is the new girls contracts. You can read over them it's sealed and doc*mented in what we call danger and pa**ion. I love this girl . So countseler what is next. I really really want that girl. That's your contract. You got a few more business days. That new girls contract is our. Thomas Allred Jr. You do know what a contract is don't you. Know but I know that you will tell me. It's they butt that a** and titties is all mine. Now I rest my case. Countseler whatever happens. I want me girls with me to get everything. On my business word. I remember that you don't like these so I'm throwing them away. I O Us. Yeah Thomas Allred Jr toss them in the trash. Hollywood access granted is watching us . Put in your access code now Thomas Allred Jr. Listen to me. The access code is . 1385 +64-290-791-6835 489217.your access has been granted. The new girls contract is ready for your signature Mr. Thomas Allred Jr. Congratulations this is your new girls contract. Thank you my wife Gabriel Union Allred. I'm a see what we can do about you unbecoming a virgin. Mr. Thomas Allred Jr. Send my message in right now.

It's just that I have got love for Shannon Clay, Kristen Beam and Maya. Of Hickory North Carolina. I know that you do Thomas Allred Jr. Because they are your contracts. But what I want to show you is. It a world out there. That's full of contracts. Each one can take you to the next level. If you want them to. Do you know that you are The Lion King Superman Thomas Allred Jr. Yes I do know that I am the Lion King Superman Thomas Allred Jr. Listen to your contracts Thomas Allred Jr. Do you know how many that you have got so far. No I don't. All of them are waiting for the chance to be with you. God that's slot of contracts. Didn't I keep my word when I said that I would get you and island. With your contracts on it. Yes you did my beautiful sweet wife Gabriel Union Allred. Thomas Allred Jr. What are we going to do if this contract ain't strong enough to handle is. He is strong enough to handle. All of you. Come outside with me . I'm telling you Thomas Allred Jr that as your contract I am working my a** off for you. I appreciate you for doing this for me my beautiful beautiful wife Gabriel Union Allred. Thomas Allred Jr bullsh*ting on her contract. By what damn means would you say that to your contract. Because of rent a center coming up the steps. It the wrong address. This gose to someone else's house. I apologise for this. Just forget it.Thomas people are watching. Shake his hand. And give him some money. Okay Gabriel Union Allred. I got a gazillionair shaking my hand. This nigga gave me 500 thousand dollars. Rent a center. I quit working. For the rest of my life. I'm a be Thomas's new best friend. Thank you for calling in. You done took all of your d*ck days. I love you Kristen Beam. And I love you Shannon Clay. And I love you Maya of Hickory NC. And I love you so damn much my wife Gabriel Union Allred. Thomas Allred Jr each one of these girls is sitting back and watching you. What you want you receive. Thank the Lord. Don't you give up. If you want me to show you. Just how your contracts is reacting. Thomas Allred Jr just say the word. It's okay I don't want to know. Yes you do want to know. Your contract are getting ready for you on every occasion that you present your self. Remember the lady out side when you where cutting gra**. She is you contract.

Don't you see that there is p**sy every where. We are going to help you to pull yours. I'm not scared are you Thomas Allred Jr know my wife Gabriel Union Allred I'm not . He is the true Lion King ladies and gentlemen. This man is our leader it says it in the Bible. That Officer Reign would lead the nation. The war on terrior has been defeated. By Officer Reign and the police. And who is Officer Reign? None other than the Lion King Superman Thomas Allred Jr. Gabriel Union Allred. No one will believe that story.

Thomas Allred Jr the women are depending on you to keep your self in shape. And don't smoke. Because that is your only weakness. Do not believe in your people. Believe in your self. And count on you Thomas Allred Jr. You getting ready for a contract. Thomas Allred Jr The Loin King Surperman Thomas Allred Jr. You have no idea what your doing. Gabriel Union Allred. I only want to please you. You got to have to stay up in here all night if you want to please me. You making me feel like. I go straight to your heart. And your to blame. Darling you give love a bad name. Be professional.

Darling you can see my contract has gotten fat for you. Get your mind out of the gutter Thomas Allred Jr. Listen I'm a provide Kristen Beam and Maya and Shannon Clay to you. Do you want them at the same time. No I'm might get one of them pregnant. Let me see everyone of my contracts at once. You herd what that boy said didn't you. Hold that position Thomas Allred Jr. Just a little while longer. Now how is it that you ache for the most. Out of a of the women. You Gabriel Union Allred. I ache for you. In my heartbeat. You can see that I go pain. It time to put in a access granted code. Hollywood access granted code is. 6924 +38-754-893-1206.your access has been secured. Thank your contracts Thomas Allred Jr. Thank you ladies all of you for everything that you do and who you are make a difference in the world as we know it. They are going to give you your contracts. Don't go to sleep yet. Now you see all of the work that it takes to get to go to Carolina Beach. Your access has been granted. Call Richard Roma back. And tell him that you are The damn Lion King Superman Thomas Allred Jr. And we depend on that contract. The new girls contract is finished. Mr. Richard Roma taking his sweet a** time coming to the phone. Look Thomas Allred Jr if you can't get him on the phone call Kristen Beam. She took a restraining order out on me. A couple years ago because I told her I loved her on and answering machine 30 times. And I went to jail for it. How long where you in jail for telling Kristen Beam that you loved her. 28 business days and nights. Hot damn . The Lion King Superman Thomas Allred Jr. Has been a prisoner of war. Twenty one days I would have said. You know Thomas Allred Jr. Just maybe you shouldn't have done that. But twenty eight business days for not kissing. And going to jail for it. Don't for I had to do a years probation. And go to court five business times . They took Thomas Allred Jr to court because the Lion King wanted his contract. And locked his a** up under a ten thousand dollar bond when Lion King had know money. That is a prisoner of war. I got out with my police officer pay. 30 days later. They stole my contracts. I have bee alone every since. Look than you all for everything. But there a wise man once told me . That this life isn't fair. And who was that wise man Thomas Allred Jr. God in the physical form. See I believe that God is all over this world. And the only way that you will see him is that if you open your eyes. Because man or woman you never know you could be talking to God. So I'm a ask Jesus Christ may I have my contract back. Lord I had a few brushes with death. I even put my life on the line saving my fellow dude. We stopped terriorism in the world. We saved the children for a predator Nation. I'm saying we even gave a idea to create another planet on earth before the world gets destroyed. God I'll I'm asking for is a chance to know your beautiful women. I have been shot and locked in jails fighting for my life. Jesus I'm a police officer please gimme all of the contracts the belong to me. Little Thomas Allred Jr sir at your service. I want that girl thank you Jesus Christ. For listening. I got a question for you. What person breaks down on the computer screen but doesn't in the world. A person that breaks down on the computer screen . Has took all he or she could take . And realizes that God can see him or her. And make a final plea for his or her contracts. Gabriel Union Allred I think that I'm tired. Do you want to see Kristen Beam again. With everything in this world. Put the access code in. Access code to see my wife Kristen Beam is. 87062 +934-857-612-0968.your access has been approved. You both have been through the exact same thang. Kristen Beam. Thomas Allred Jr. Thomas Allred Jr. Kristen Beam. It's nice to make your acquaintance. Gabriel Union Allred thank the Lord for granting me a contract. Thomas don't know that Kristen has her own place. Where in Carolina Beach. That amazing. Thank you God for Thomas Allred Jr and me Gabriel Union Allred. I want that girl. Thomas we got you a new contract. I want that girl. Who is she Michelle Obama. I would like to have and keep all of my contracts with me from now on . I'm the bread winner. Gabriel Union Allred I really love you sweetheart there are so many things I want to share with you. But I know that if I keep working on this project of mine. That everything will be alright. See I'm professional Richard Roma. Mr. Roma will talk to you now. Should I hang up the phone I don't get a f*ck what you do. This is Richard Roma speaking. Hello . Hello. Yes Mr. Richard Roma the is The New and improved Lion King Superman Thomas Allred Jr. And I was just wondering if you have read my manuscript yet. Thomas Allred Jr to honest with you I haven't got a chance to read it yet I've been so busy. When do you think you will be able to read a copy. Gimme two days Thomas Allred Jr. Yes Mr. Richard Roma. The Lion King is a professional business personality. I will respect you on this . The Lion King is out Mr. Richard Roma. Gabriel Union Allred he told us two days. And he'll read the manuscript. And Page Plus that this wasn't my idea. My wife Gabriel Union Allred. Helped me get through the traps. I love you Gabriel Union Allred where ever you are sweetheart. I will be wishing on a star. Do you see that's how it is with all of my contracts. I want that girl God. Lord I want all of my contracts back. I am The new and improved Lion King Superman Thomas Allred Jr. Telling Maya and Shannon Clay that I already love them. Great job counselor. I just knew what I was doing. Thank you again Gabriel Union Allred. You welcome husband The new and improved Lion King Superman Thomas Allred Jr. I love you. Good day Kristen Beam. Good day Gabriel Union Allred. A Gabriel Union Allred manuscript

I'm producing myself self that's right I said it. Gabriel Union Allred you need to take your time counselor. I'm the best in my field The new and improved Lion King Superman Thomas Allred Jr. Why shouldn't I produce myself. Because I am producing you Gabriel Union Allred. What I do get it how are you producing me. The new and improved Lion King Superman Thomas Allred Jr. By your standers I am a good man right my wife Gabriel Union Allred. The new and improved Lion King Superman Thomas Allred Jr. I guess that you are all right. That new girls contract that you wrote up for me was spectacular. And what I'm saying Is everybody has got to give credit to where credit is due. Gabriel Union Allred you are and expensive part of my life. Everybody know me now because of you. And I produce you for the fact that I'm honored to be apart of something that you were apart in my life. The new and improved Lion King Superman Thomas Allred Jr Call me crazy but you are beginning to get tiered of the games. I came to play Gabriel Union Allred. We have come to play The new and improved Lion King Superman Thomas Allred Jr. What I did was use and access code to make it to Hollywood California. The New and improved Lion King Superman Thomas Allred Jr gimme the access code for access granted to take us to Hollywood California. The access code is. +318-297-641-0896 3 425-3180.wait a few minutes.

Your access has been granted The new and improved Lion King Superman Thomas

Allred Jr. And stand back I'm a enter my code to go with you and your family to Hollywood California. My access code is 69058 +213-841-054-3861 89.The new and improved Lion King Superman Thomas Allred Jr wait a few minutes your access has been granted. Gabriel Union Allred baby you still have got it baby. It's time for us to make love The new and improved Lion King Superman Thomas Allred Jr. Gabriel Union Allred I. I realize that you are a virgin The new and improved Lion King Superman Thomas Allred Jr. People we ain't got to do nothing but talk to each other. You get the point the new and improved Lion King Superman Thomas Allred Jr. Queen Your Highness Gabriel Union Allred. I'm a clean up my act. Okay then The new and improved Lion King Superman Thomas Allred Jr realizes that he has a hard on for this sh*t. Do not lose your patience. You'll get your contracts The new and improved Lion King Superman Thomas Allred Jr. It just take a little finessing.And I'll negotiate the deal for your contracts. Ain't no deal that can break me The new and improved Lion King Superman Thomas Allred Jr. I'm solid oak. Baby I realize that you are own to something. Call Richard Roma for me. This is Roma speaking. Gimme my damn contract for The new and improved Lion King Superman Thomas Allred Jr. And I mean it. I'll show them pictures on the internet of you sneaking money In a sock drawer at your house. Don't worry about how I got them. Gabriel Union Allred this is Richard Roma and your not making any sense. I'm about to hang up on you . Know Mr. Richard Roma. Don't talk to the beauty queen like this. Mr. Richard Roma. This is the new and improved Lion King Superman Thomas Allred Jr. And I'm saying give my wife a couple of minutes with you on the phone for and old friend of ours and who would that be. Our friend is Benjamin Franklin. Yes Gabriel Union Allred how are you Gabriel. I've heard so many nice things about you. I got a new movie that's coming out I want you to start in the place of Meryl Streep. The Lion King is your husband. I can't understand just way The new and improved Lion King Superman Thomas Allred Jr. Loves you. Well it's my personality that wins him over. I need you to see that in order for a movie to be made there are some details that need to be attended to. Alright Richard Roma how much are you asking for. A small donation. I'm telling you that it would make all the difference. Mr. Richard Roma name your price for us to be Rich and famous. I got a movie coming out The new and improved Lion King Superman Thomas Allred Jr and I want you in it as well. Much is it. It's my hand shake and I want you to to see your faces. You mean you want take our money. If he take our money The new and improved Lion King Superman Thomas Allred Jr the whole community a be after him. Yeah I'm a straight up business man. The New and improved Lion King Superman Thomas Allred Jr and Queen Your Highness Gabriel Union Allred. Your access has been granted. For Hollywood California. You got to keep on working. The new and improved Lion King Superman Thomas Allred Jr. And Queen Your Highness Gabriel Union Allred. Queen Your Highness Gabriel Union Allred. I since that you have got to say something. Richard Roma you and alright dude for a White Mexican dude. Queen Your Highness Gabriel Union Allred you have no idea at how much that means to me. Let's talk about the new girl contract it is legal and binding. Is this is what happened. And they took all of his contract away from him except me. I'm Gabriel Union Allred. Give my husband y'all his contracts back. He is The New and improved Lion King Superman Thomas Allred Jr. All we got to do The new and improved Lion King Thomas Allred Jr. Is send messages in to every Publisher at the same time. I'm going to tell Ms. Eden Reid that you apologize for your behavior on the phone and to give me my f*cking contracts back. And that I'm a talk to Susan sarandon. And get her to take you back. You are The new and improved Lion King Superman Thomas Allred Jr. When they retire I'm a make sure that they remember your name. Remember our names Queen Your Highness Gabriel Union Allred. Gabriel listen you are my wife. And it and all about me or you it's about all of us. This is the film recording industry. It do or die baby. You hear that contracts. The new and improved Lion King Superman Thomas Allred Jr is still playing y'all. I said playing y'all. He is still in the game. All Hell The new and improved Lion King Superman Thomas Allred Jr . And Queen Your Highness Gabriel Union Allred. For getting us this far. Can the crowd say Amen. The new and improved Lion King Superman Thomas Allred Jr is in here thinking out loud. What we saying is that we would like to make sure that The new and improved Lion King Superman Thomas Allred Jr gets everyone of his new and old contracts back. Thomas Allred Jr you got you a real life girl fighter. Do we have a deal. Till him that youll up the girls contract. I'll up the girls contract to 500 million every two weeks for the rest of there life. How many contracts is it that you say that I have. 800000 contracts. Send them to our beach in North Carolina. Now sign here Thomas . Just put your name on the dotted line. And the woman contracts are your. This can't be real . Sign the damn contract. Leave the Lion King off. Okay. Sign the damn contract. Thomas Allred Jr. There is people after you. The girls money has already been paid to them. Your the owner of 800000 contracts. Be good to everyone of them. And The New and improved Lion King Superman Thomas Allred Jr. Thomas . We are going to take the new and improved. Off of your name. How is this . The Lion King Thomas Allred Jr. Gabriel Union Allred it works for me. Send the book in The Lion King Thomas Allred Jr. The book Thomas

I'm a make this short and sweet. We as cops have never seen a payday like this. The Lion King Thomas Allred Jr we have just figured out how to feed people all over the world. Without the use of the hot skillet. That's amazing Thomas Allred jr. I'm very proud of you Gabriel Union Allred. For being my guide in this descovery. Ok that's enough of that we have to get to the story. Called pay day a cops history. The Lion King Thomas Allred Jr. Well Thomas Allred Jr. You have the floor. It is all on you. Gabriel Union Allred honey. I need you to do this with me. Okay Thomas Allred Jr. I am here with you. Lets go ahead together and say. That Mr. Richard

Roma and Ms. Eden Reid and Ms. Kimberly Schwandt. And Ms. Erin Cohen. Please get out your pens and paper. Counselor Gabriel Union Allred is going to speak for me right now. Okay to Mr. president Bill Clinton and Ms. Hillary Rodman Clinton. And to you both we have some good news. And to you both Ms. Michelle Obama and president Barack Obama. We have had this good new for a while now. And to president George and Barbara Bush. I just want to say thank you . You can see that im anxious to tell you that I'm not going to be a counselor no more. To president Donald Trump and Mr.s. Trump. We have figured out a way to feed and water the whole planet. Without the use of back backing labor. It's called electric cloud machines. I give to you the future of food traveling to the heater . It's in a memo what a electric cloud machine . Can do . And like this I appreciate your time. We turned out idea into Davidson inventions company yesterday around 3:o clock in the afternoon. And there another thing that Thomas Allred Jr and I want to tell you all. Thomas Allred Jr come on up here and speak on the White House floor. Gabriel Union Allred and I The Lion King Thomas Allred Jr are gazillionairs because of the idead in Wich the Secret service and the FBI and the police department and the NSA has given us. Y'all have got to remember that this was a war on terror. And we did what we had to do. To save the lives of our friends and our people. That are down all over the world. Now with ideas like signature Heat. We bring to the threshold of a new generation. Of ideas. Your bank account. Shell be refurbished and everything made whole. What bank account.

What kind of bank account is he saying. Gabrielle Union Allred will you please help me. He is saying that all of our money. In which we may from business ideas. Is to be split evenly with the police and the public. Thomas Allred Jr talk to them. See I believe in God. And I believe that every person should have equal. No matter where they are in the world. These business ideas had me. Some how at a lost for words. But believing in God. And Trust in and Gabriel Union Allred my wife. I don't need business ideas to support me. I want my friends and family on the police force. To share the business ideas evenly. Cause everytime I look at a business Idea now I get sick. And I'm sharing with the White House my findings.

That people have terrorized us all our lives. With weapons of ma** destruction. And common hand held weapons that take our lives. I give to you the sword of Justice. And the sword of magic. Help a brother out Gabriel Union Allred. Each one of these swords. Is a professional model killing machine. To advance our government. Along with signature Heat. The money from the ideas. Should belong to the public. Because the public is. The ones who raised us and saved Our lives. Our United States Secret service. And the whole wide country. Is looking at this. Give to me signature Heat. And the world has had a secret agent in Thomas Allred Jr. And Ms. Gabriel Union Allred.

I just want you to know. That we are making it out of our situation. And with these business ideas used properly. The world is a better place to live in. I am

Gabrielle Union Allred. Thomas Allred Jr do you have something to say. Look as secret agents. Gabriel Union Allred and I and the Secret service. Along with the NSA and the police force. Have been rededicating or talents. To being there for the world and for the public. We lost our contracts. Due to this war on terror. And we are extremely hurt. My wife name was Jeana Allred. And I miss her so much. So I get my gazillion dollars with the infinity symbol behind the money. Over to the United States Secret service. For me and Gabriel Union Allred. To have a little freedom with each other. To a businessman. That is the only freedom he got. Miss Clinton. I'm saying the war on terrorism is over. Thank you Thomas and Gabriel Union Allred. What we have here today. Our two people. That's willing to risk it all. For there fellow brothers and sisters in Jesus Christ. The state appreciates your honesty. I give to you your contracts with each other. Gabriel Union Allred I love you. I love you Thomas Allred Jr. Y'all are two secret agents. That needs know introductions. Y'all are famous. If there's one thing that I know. Listen Thomas Allred Jr. That you are The Lion King. We have watch you on surveillance tapes. By reprogramming you. Your actions speak louder than words. I'm a give to you your contracts. And all that you see before you. That Gabriel Union Allred. As a remembrance of a Time. When y'all had no chance but to have love.

I'm saying now Thomas Allred Jr your chance has been granted. Im a need the access code. The access code to a better future for the world is. 784-396-2108 9135 642-5481.your access has been granted Thomas Allred Jr. You may lay down now. Get up and write your friend. With everything I want to thank my countseler and my wife Miss Gabriel Union allred. And I also thank the states justice department and Gabriel Union Allred. For saving my life over and over again. Gabriel Union Allred we have no money no food no clothes and it's cold. But some how I know God Will Make A Way for us. Cause we have been good to everyone . God did make a way. With a Payday Thomas Allred Jr.A Cops history. Men and women all around the world. This is your education story. The killing each other. Is wrong I tell you. These business ideas will serve as Justice. Among the Nations. I just want my contract back and my houses. Thomas your access has been granted.You can Hurry up and go to sleep Thomas Allred Jr.

I have to write a friend first. I'm giving you exactly one hour to write that friend. Because what you don't realize. Is that you really talking to Michelle Obama. And I thank you for everything Thomas Allred Jr and Gabriel Union Allred. You can send your book in today. Thomas Allred Jr these books are the future of our people. How The Lion King stood up. When no one else would. And is walking today because of it. They shot you in your leg. Because they couldn't kill The Lion King Thomas Allred Jr. You want your contracts. I say to you that women want your children. It's one more thing that I have to add Thomas Allred Jr. What kind of shoes are you wearing. Feliz. I don't know the name has rubbed off of they. I had them so long. I know that you understand what I'm saying to you Thomas Allred Jr. But everybody sees your struggle. This whole country is watching you. You are The Lion King. if it's contract you want then it's contract you get. I don't want yall to ever treat my family this way again. The access codes . To link my business ideas together. Is +812-738-109-3486 7921.your access has been granted Lion King. I wish we had more time to speak to you about the subject thank you.Thomas you are the The Lion King. And your contracts will be waiting for you come Christmas morning. You need to go to sleep. Gabriel Union Allred. I'm still a police officer. I'm still you police officer representative . Gabriel Union Allred you are The Lion King Queen. You know that right. Thomas Allred Jr I want you to write your letter to your friend and get some sleep. This is The last thing that you have to do for the government . I love y'all. Thee Lion King. Right now he'll think that's it's a dream . But the access code the the White Houses future is 3967 81213 504-875-1396.The Lion King is opening code and unlocking algorithMs. for Michelle Obama. That's it Thomas Allred Jr when I snap me fingers your job will be completed. You and Gabriel Union Allred and the Secret service the NSA in the police department along with Homeland security have saved the world. Lion wake up and send your book and movie trailers off. Once you do you will become and average person. In today's world. With out a contract but do worry Thomas Allred Jr. You are The Lion King . And God I make a way for you. Put all of his books together. I'm lone and I can't go nowhere. Miss Michelle Obama. You have got to believe. Snap.

CHAPTER 11

I saved the best of this for last. I'm a newly secret service agent. Thomas we all are Secret service agents without contracts. I'm changing up the game. I'm giving them a call. I'm writing you to understand. How can we open this New year up with a contract. See how stupid you sounding. So my baby girl can visit me. And InventHelp and Davidson invention companies. To sacrifice your belief. That A thousand Miles begins with one step. I give to you my awesome contract. Gabriel Union Allred shall I talk to them. You are my counselor and my girlfriend. Thomas let me say something to them. It is not fair at all. How many manuscripts have we written. For each of you. Thomas sit there and cried last Christmas. And came back stronger this year with new and better material. I am Gabriel Union Allred. Let me help you Thomas. Before you get to go to Carolina Beach. The president wants to say something to you first.

Thomas we listen to your voice messages. And over the years we come to like you. Don't say nothing about police officers everybody here respect you. positive energy maintains the motions that are good for your heart and soul. what kind of TV personality would you be Thomas Allred Jr. A role model. Your access has been granted Thomas. You done pa**ed your final test. Showing love to a contract that you haven't even recognized or seen. Listen to your contract in the background. You need those contracts to protect you in time. How much are you willing to pay for those contracts. President Donald Trump I will give my life for all of my contracts. Let me see what I can do Thomas Allred Jr. You and Gabriel Union Allred standby. Thomas Allred Jr I don't know what he's doing. He is the president Gabriel Union Allred you got to trust them. Gabriel Union Allred I love you so much. Thomas Allred Jr I love you to the president is coming back. Stand up when you speak to me Thomas and Gabriel. Thomas and Gabriel. You have fought in the battle against terror. And I know that you are tired Thomas and Gabriel. I see what Thomas is doing I would marry you if I could. I'm trying to see here. If a contract is worth you both level of service. We are Secret service offices. President Donald Trump. And all that we request is our contract back. Every last one of them is our contracts.

Listen to me. What are you going to do Thomas Allred with your girl besides you and the rest of the world looking at you. Im a thank God that I'm free. Thomas there you go. I've been waiting for this for all of my life. Even the president can see through you Thomas. Give me my contract sir. I'll contracts mean the world to us. I'm seeing how you broke it down. But people don't realize that it takes time to get a contract. Too many people are watching the police on television. And not seeing how things really go inside the house hold. Look here Thomas. Yall are going to get your contacts back. Because that is the Lion King's will. To the one who pa**ed before you. Are you seeing my father. I'm saying that. Your father gave us a contract. He saved a lot of people. Before he died. Look and see Thomas. You have his eyes and his features. The Lion King. Represent us in the movie theater. Can Gabriel Union Allred represent us to.

Thomas take your a** at home and get a contract. When I get finished with you. You will have a kid soon. Thomas Allred Jr. President Donald Trump is now leaving the building. We did it Donald Trump .We stopped the war on terrorism. Think about that for a minute. When you get through Thomas. I need to see you. Okay Mr.. President Donald Trump. My wife Gabriel wants to see me now. You better not Jack your f*cking d*ck Thomas. I'm fortunate to hear that. I'm trying to teach you the fundamentals of life here. Stand up for yourself. You are going to see the doctor in 3 days. And you are The Lion King. If I was with you Thomas Allred Jr. I say that you look all damn right. For a King. But sir I do not have finances. Take your time and finances will come to you Lion King. Sir I need me a new house at Carolina Beach. The Lion King needs a new house.

Make sure the Lion King gets a new house. And sir my wife Gabriel needs everything. Make sure that your wife Gabriel Thomas. Has everything that she desires in this world. I call Gabriel my counselor. Every body knows Thomas is it true Lion King. And the true Lion King knows it yourself now. That boy needs his contracts back. And I need my contacts back. I'm his wife. Gabriel Union Allred. I got a secret for you. The Lion King already has his money. In an access code. Put in the access code Thomas. The access code is. 1 2 4 5 6 8 95341 208-965-3812. Your access has been secured. The Lion King wants his house and his contracts. He is not worried about politics even though he does work for the government. As the Lion King's counselor and attorney. You got to see what he can do with sunlight. We know that the lion king is risen.

I love you Thomas. I love you too Gabriel Union Allred. I hope this book get finished soon. So a girl can use the bathroom. I'm going in there with you to see that you okay. Thomas. Thomas ain't doing number writing his book. For his contracts. Look how big he's done gotton. Since his hair grown out. Thomas do you have any idea that you're The Lion King. President Donald Trump yes I do and it feels good. The president is shaking his head. Thomas everybody see that you focused. You going to make the TV guide channel. You got that right. I'm just sitting here going over these number there astronomical. If they offer you a contract take it. Gabriel what about you. President Donald Trump. May I make love to Gabrielle Union Allred. On television where the TV channel can hear us. And why do you want to do that Thomas. It is the mating call of the wild and I need all my contracts to hear it. I am The Lion King. And I am his Queen Gabriel Union Allred. Together Thomas and I are too damn strong for the bullsh*t. Thomas. That girl knows what she doing. Thank you.

I need Gabriel Union Allred to come and get me off the streets. Exactly what you need. I need a island of very strong women to comfort me. Is that all you need Thomas Allred Jr The Lion King. I need houses from a woman. And all the food that they can eat. Beautiful beautiful linen for my wives. And the fruit basket of a**ortments. For my women every day that they wake up. This is for the rest of they lives. God has ordered me. To be good to all the people. Under the sun. And I am The Lion King. You see how confident I am. One thing is that I'll never give up. No matter what the situation is upon us. Girl if you need some space. Check out what we doing at Carolina Beach. I'm saying everything is being hooked up right now to accommodate The Lion King. It is a town but a civilization as well. I shall do great things here for the world and for the public. All we got to do is stand the test of time. Lion King. The Lion King is busy writing this book. Thomas Allred Jr. Do you want to kiss me Thomas. I've been wanting to kiss you all my life Suzanne Summers. Then what are you waiting for Lion King. Thomas. The Lion King here you. Do you know where he is. Yes he is hungry. They can do something about this. Yall I said The Lion King is hungry. Focus on ending your story. I need a place to stay other than these street corners. Michelle Obama wants you. Thomas I said to you that you don't have to write any more stories. I apologize Miss Michelle Obama. For the first time in my life feel like. What you feel like Thomas. I feel like all my contacts are free. That suits as well. But listen here Thomas Allred Jr. You don't need to write to these people anymore. Because you are part of the Secret service. Miss Michelle Obama will I get my house and my contacts back. Every one of those women knows that they are your contract and loves you Thomas. So what do I have to do. Give it time and you'll get your contacts back and your house to. Gabriel are you hearing this. Thomas be strong. Just Miss Michelle Obama. I know that you need your contract. I need all of my contacts. We are going to get you your contract. Good night Miss Michelle. Goodnight Superman The Lion King Thomas Allred Jr. Gabriel I'm in love with you. Listen my contracts. I cherish and respect you. And the government is working out this problem right now. Keep listening Thomas. Send a message on right now.

I'm telling you people never listen. Girl I write books because I feel like the man when I do it. Take your time and write your book on seductive ability and I am. The woman near the apple tree. 4 years of being alone by myself. And my position is that I need somebody. I've been standing up near this apple tree. Standing here by myself I'm lonely Thomas Allred Jr. If you are the true Lion King come and rescue me.Exactly Thomas. I've been helping you out of every situation that you get into. Exactly what you need to know is. That I do for you and nothing more. You are telling me not to worry if I can make love to you or not. My Fair Lady near the apple tree. I'm telling you that the tree is full of apples to apples. Apples that ain't been picked. My heart says that you are the one for me. Lady near the apple tree. Thomas a give to you every apple in the world. Take me to Thomas as your own. When my man sees me with you he will be scared of your power. On the ground is one more thing. A crown I give you. You are The Lion King. Listen sweetheart. There is no apple that I want more than you. Tell me what you want. I draw closer and closer to you. Yeah Thomas Allred. Queens like me know just what to do. I'm saving every cent and giving you every Apple that you ever wanted is true. Pick the fruit that you want but only for today. I'm getting to make you cry for me girl because I need you lady. See these apples know that you are here. Time acceleration doors now opening. Give Thomas Jr his goddamn contract. Gabriel its good to see you again. All my life I welcome to fight.

Who was fighting against Thomas. I'm tightening these books up for the publishers that don't think I'm the man. Give me my husband contract. Gabriel the situation has change your husband is The Lion King.

My damn husband ain't The Lion King. My damn husband is the new and improved Lion King Superman Thomas Allred Jr. Y'all better give me a goddamn contract for my husband and me. I'm trying to make you see that these people don't care about us Thomas Allred Jr. Gabriel i I'm The Lion King so I must believe that there is some love in the world. Do you see that we keep hoping. Exactly. We would not lose faith on the cloud that doesn't have what it takes to speak the truth . The apple tree is ours.

My fair lady I need you to understand that the apple tree is love and knowledge. Give us our contracts. We deserve our contracts. I'm a tell you what the business is. King Thomas Allred Jr. Is more than The Lion King. Are you listening Thomas. King Thomas Allred Jr is. Listen to me Thomas. You are Superman. Keep your head up. Keep the faith Lion King. You are one of the best novel writers in the world. Now I speak to the apples on the tree. And I say to them. Apple's we aspire to be whole. Give me my goddamn contracts. We need every apple on the tree to say give me my goddamn contracts. Gabriel I never seen you like this. That's because only one apple fell off the tree. And thats you Lion King. Look Gabriel I don't understand what you're saying.

I'm seeing Thomas. That why you been dealing with people protecting the tree. The government has been stealing your apples. Are you saying stealing my woman from me. I'm saying stilling your women your money and your time. You gave time up. For a women you barely knew that you loved. I'm going to take that boy out the community. Thomas is special. I believe in him like I believe in myself. If I could prove one of the thing to you. It'll be that he is Thomas. The Lion King. the one that's been guarding the apple tree. For all of these years of its existence. I talk to you now. And letting you know that the book is just a metaphor. Are contracts mean the world to us. Every contract was handed to The Lion King by God. And when people take advantage of a good thing. It makes me mad as a motherf*cker. Your book is almost ready. This book is called she's so seductive The Apple tree volume 1. The reason that talk like this is because I know. Look Thomas. Them people out here they stole your contracts. I keep on doing work but I never get nowhere Gabriel. It's not that you don't get nowhere. Its that people are arguing over your contracts. Go ahead and try me for who I am.

Let The Lion King have his apples. See now there are 3200 apple trees. They all belong To You The Lion King. All my life all I wanted is a girl and a family. Thomas you will get that. But I want these people around you to know. Did Thomas is the true Lion King and he is professional. So fair lady will I be able to kiss you after all. No you cannot kiss me. For I am your counselor Gabriel Union Allred. Give me his contracts. What is a contract Gabriel. Thomas you don't even know what a contract is. You got to listen to me Thomas. A contract is the bond between you and your fair lady.You got me wishing and hoping and dreaming for lady and they stole my contracts. Thomas I know that you hurt because they stole your contracts. But I need you to be a man about this.

We are about to lift off and produce a movie production company in your name. Equal right Justice is the name of the company. Communicate with your people via email. And let them know this. I got a movie coming out called Equal Right Justice. Your movie have to be more than six letters long. My Fair Lady God please let the movie come out. I'm desperately on top of your business. I'm desperately on top of business myself. If you are the true Lion King Thomas call my name. Gabriel Union Allred. The Lion King is stronger than you think he is. I'm giving it up to you Thomas for not throwing in the towel when times got rough.

You don't know what I feel like with you by my side Gabriel Union Allred. You know this apple tree. They took the story from you while you were sleeping. See I'm the man in my community. Go Thomas. You see what they do. They are going to copy you until the end. It is not my right. To try to stand in the way of anyone. Copy as they must. I am only here to protect them in the apple tree. So with everything I own. I am sitting it beside the tree.

To show that. I'm The Lion King. And I will protect you. Weather you give me anything at all to eat. Lion King control yourself. This here is a story that is turning you into a man again. Now where did the story begin. I came up and I was writing music.and I worked every day to pay for the studio time that I got.You see what I'm saying Thomas the stories coming together now. Where did the story begin. It begin with me graduating training school. Thomas you need to take your time when I ask you this. How many contacts do you have. Say what could you say that again.

I said Lion King how many contacts do you have. Gabriel Union Allred I have all of them. The women and the men are my contracts. I prepare for a plate at the table for everyone. This is equal rights Justice the movie. In The Lion King is more than hungry The Lion King is a beast. Thomas. Yes Gabriel speak. Are you hungry Thomas or are you a victim. Gabriel I'm a goddamn man and I'm hungry. Do you think they are still in your material. I think they just can't believe the things that I am saying. And for every book and every movie that I write we're getting lifted off the ground 100%.

Make sure that the Lion King understands us Gabriel. What are they seeing Gabriel. They saying if you slow down a minute everything will be alright. My Equal justice is known.We don't bow because America is too damn strong to Bow. I'm going to dedicate this book to the success of my brothers and sisters. Now give me your contracts. I Trust You My Fair Lady Gabriel Union Allred. You can hold on to all of the apple trees. And I will protect you from harm. Keep in mind Thomas Allred Jr that I am and attorney. With a marriage license for you as my contract. Yeah you seem shocked. The conditions of my contract is. That Gabriel you gotta understand that I love you and I'm not playing any games with your heart. You've been there for me all this time and I respect you thank you so much fair lady .

Thomas I had to put chains on you.But why Gabriel I'm stronger than all the other people. Because if I didn't put chains on you. You would know how it feels to be free. And you are The Lion King. Girl hold on. I'm doing my best. To make you understand that I'm here for you. House arrest and other tricks and gamete. Un professional Gabriel. I want to see you because you love me. In North Carolina. I am the king. Hear my voice. All we want to do. Is council your contract. Because you and I. Be professional once through. The seven chapters of success and danger. The Apple tree success and danger volume 2 . I'm living right now for my people. Without war we fight to win conquest. This program for me is. A wake-up call to the Future. Girl I'm giving everything for you. I listen to you now Thomas. Without the snakes in cages. I hold you down like a grown man should. If you understand that I am responsible for you girl.The Universe breves at my calling. Every time that I look up with you. I'm reminded of the apple tree so far away. Listen.I can see you that so many people that don't believe in me. But I am The Lion King. The reason that I do what I'm doing is.

So you can understand that a piece of meat is in history. I'm going to go and take over The Lion King. You got two more days to become something. How can I relax when the people depend on me. And I depend on you my beautiful woman. Trust me Gabriel Union Allred. I've done nothing but till the fields. All the seeds are for you to plant. This novel has you standing on the edge of your seat. Get a contract I give you an exclusive. Your contract means the world to me Gabriel Union Allred. This equal rights Justice. It came to me as police officers made their way into my room. Nobody should be writing like this.but I tell you I love you with all my heart.

Thomas I'm about to give up on you.that proves that you in the world are not that smart. I don't give up on anybody that this world has me here to protect. Tend to the apple orchard.The Apple orchard can take care of itself. We can program you. To do some amazing things. Danger was all around you. And you walked right through that sh*t. Thomas you are the true Lion King. I don't know what everybody's saying and what everybody's talkin about. I did what a Lion King is supposed to do. And protect the citizens of the world and my house. My contract means the world to me. I need a contract these contracts are not mine. So I'm giving you all the apples back. Only one fell off the tree and that's mine. The moral to this story is. No matter what you see. There's always a apple somewhere on the ground for you. All you got to do is pick it up. And dust it off. The Lion King of professional Thomas. Give that boy his contracts. All he needs is his contract back to him. Thomas you done stood your ground. The word count on this book got to be 700 and plus. So are you sleepy Thomas.Or do you want to play ball.

I like the damn Major leagues. That's good baby. Kimberly we won't have it no other way. We want our contracts Kimberly. Listen Kimberly consider this. This man is the truth of God Lion King. And everything has been stolen from him. He walked around in the desert. For 7 years. We got in New York City.

The Lion King is more than man. Thomas is f*cking hungry. Professional see us as guppies in a small pond. Well I'm telling you the Lion King has got his heart back. The Lion King is here for the world. But you people you still all the apples and you run. The Lion King has been protecting us a whole lives. And you know I'm telling the truth because we program him to do those things. I know what you're saying. So what we program The Lion King. But does that mean this man doesn't have feelings. Thomas Allred is a worldwide figure. He is somebody to be admired and respected.you take all the money and all the food from him and every last one of his apples. And then you got him program not to leave the yard. This is what you do to a war hero. A North Carolina native that save the whole world over and over again. It's about time you all respect Thomas Allred Jr for who he is.

This man has made 300 business ideas for you that save people lives all around the world.two music albuMs. called I won't give in .And The Dawning Of The of Reign. He's written books and you already know that because you reading them. Now if you want to see how professional he is. Thomas Allred Jr is a newly renowned secret service agent for the u.s. government. He was a police officer for the New York Police department. I want yall to listen to me. All that man want is a house and his contracts.

I'll be damned if your not going to give it to him. We ain't coming to play. We want movie and commercial rights. Soft drink clothes and radio. And the right to all the copies of all books and movies. He ain't got but one more day to prove itself. As The New and improved Lion King Superman Thomas Allred Jr. I'm telling you now don't give him his contracts. Watch God has to deal with you. Because you see now the Lion King knows what yall did to him. And he is madder than eagle sh*t. 35 years The Lion King work for you. Out in your dungeons. This man is a superstar. Thomas Allred Jr got a contract. Still a little cloudy Thomas. Will bullet a do that every time. My counselor my wife Gabriel what is he saying to me.

He's saying that you have no idea how many girls thats on you. Say what you want Thomas Allred Jr. I want all my damn contracts at home with me. Hey listen y'all think this is a game. I've been through your little bullsh*t test. Everything yall through at me I took that sh*t. And I am going to tell you like this. Just because you have money or you have my women that don't make you a king. Would it makes you is stupid. I'm a champion weather I win any awards or not .Because I protect the people. You better pray I don't get my contracts back. Hey come on Gabriel let's get out of here mam. A queen that stayed by my side. I give her everything. Apple after apple on the apple tree. Seductive chemistry for your a**.

To reach straight. Get that boy his contracts. He is The Lion King and he's the only King in the world. To deny him the right to parlay will be Ludacris and wrong. Thomas make sure when you get a contract this time that you don't eat it. what are you going to do with all your money if we give it to you Thomas Allred Jr. If yall allow me to have my money. I'm a rehydrate these contracts in to new and a better position. My apple tree. when I get through with my contracts they going to know I'm The Lion King. Im a rip their a**es apart. I'm getting ready to blow up either way it goes weather you give me my contract or not. Pick it up Thomas Allred Jr. Consciously I resort to using the sun to fight my battles. I'm The Lion King not no personality. I can't do nothing but tell the Lord what you done to me. Keep watching my children. Are going to be kings and queens. I like you before I even met you Gabriel. Everybody know that is The Lion king contract. What im a give to my people. I give two hundred million dollars for every state. In the United States of America. I give my contracts 86 billion dollars. All around the world I'm looking for that Queen. Y'all have a nice night you. And enjoy the apple tree. So seductive she is.

Come in my office and sit in the chair Thomas Allred Jr. I've heard a lot about you. Welcome to Camelot music. Eat your heart out no professional has been able to capture Thomas Allred Jr. What are we saying here professional. You ain't got no idea the links I've gone through the reach you. Gabriel I want your contract that's all I know. People gave you little chance of getting my contract Thomas Allred Jr. I'm going to put my contract in your face Thomas Allred Jr. Take your time I'm not going no where. Now let's just cut to the chase. Thomas I got a deal for you. The deal is on the table right there. All them contracts are for me. Your are The Lion King professional and the business King. Thomas I got a job thats waiting on you. Are you familiar with the Chinese language. I speak a little Chinese but not much. I need you to learn this book in 2 business days.

See what this girl has me doing for my contracts .Thomas Allred Jr we running out of time read that book. You better remember at the book. Read that book Thomas Allred Jr. The 200 rules and ways to lose a contract. By Gabrielle Union Allred. That's it Thomas Allred Jr. You wrote the book in Chinese. I wrote the book so that everyone read it is Chinese. Thomas I said that you read the book because I need for you to come with me. Come with you where I just got here. Overseas.

CHAPTER 12

I want to know if you got change for a 10 Thomas Allred Jr. No all I got is a 20. Y'all better stop and here that boy. Goddamn I hustle until I can't get enough boy. Thomas you see how that boy communicate. Switch the game up on him. Start writing your books Thomas. Thomas that tattoo on your neck says Superman. Your the leader of our community. Now take your time and think to yourself. What female are you really wanting to be with this community. Kristen Beam and Maya in this community. I would like to be with. They took all the stuff from you. Somehow you became a man through all the controversy. Ain't going out like no punk can you see me. Thomas got enough sense to write that book.That book is the most devastating book that I've ever read in my whole entire life. You shot that man because he's a millionaire. Thank you. I am a gazillionaire that wants to bring Equal justice to our community. They you understand you Thomas. Thomas you need to keep writing. That boys is a goddamn rap artist. And them people shot him before he could get in the studio. All you got to do is start all over again retraced your steps. But do you really want it Thomas. No I don't want it. TuMs. what are you saying. I've grown up to be a police officer. And I respect the fact that you want to help me. But I just. Exactly Thomas. Be sure you know what your doing before you turn this down. I need you to Thomas . Man the whole country is waiting for you. You better do something all kind of females out there waiting for you. I guess we got to go in the studio then. I get emotional. When I'm rapping. I don't give a f*ck how emotional you get. You understand. I want you to deliver equal justice on these muthaf*ckers that shot you in the past. Listen to Thomas.They done your girl think about that sh*t. Are you ready to sign on the dotted line. I'm ready to sign on the dotted line. So we got a contract on you that waiting for you. I want you to rap to the people Thomas. Im a do the best I can to deliver Equal justice to the community. And surrounding areas. All you got to do is put your name inside this book. Thomas Allred Jr. That's me inside this book. Wake your a** up and finish writing this book Thomas. Listen to Thomas. People are watching you. Take care of yourself. Be professional in the studio. And don't forget about the fact that they killed your girl. They shot you for no damn reason Thomas. Thomas I hold you responsible for your situation. This ain't a book that your writing. The first thing you do. Is send your contract off. Sign the deadline of the contract. Thomas Allred Jr. There go my signature I'm all in. The next thing you do Thomas is get some sleep. You are now in the entertainment industry your old life is history. Thomas before you go to sleep send off two parts of Equal justice for your contract. Go ahead and wrap this up. You have two days to prove your point to the people. And then you and your family are leaving for Hollywood studios in Hollywood California. I just knew Thomas Jr was in the rap industry. He wrote that book Equal justice. Thomas you have to be smart everybody's listening to you. I'm giving you one damn week to prove to the rap industry that you ain't to be played with. Around this muthaf*cker. Go ahead and send that book into the publishers. Don't send it in yet. I want you to know that I tried my best to help you out of that situation that you in.

Thank you Thomas for rapping to us. Now we know what to do with you. Go ahead and send the book in Thomas. Type Equal justice on the back of that book Thomas. You got two days. You got two more days to rap to the people.Send that book in Thomas. I want you to say this with me Thomas . First comes success. First comes success. Then comes a baby carriage. Then comes a baby carriage. All these people be against you. All these people been against you. You don't have to get these folks nothing except your finger up the a**. You don't have to get a folks nothing except your finger up the a**. Thats Equal justice. For the community that hated Thomas. That's Equal justice for the community that hated Thomas. The reason that I behave the way I do. Sometimes I think about myself in the Lord give me strength. Make sure you get your contact Thomas. We had no idea at the pain that you went through. But see here Thomas. The industry is with you.

You get the industry on your side. Now can you deliver Equal justice. To those people who hurt you Thomas. I can make music that's all. Are you ready for this. I'm getting ready to change myself. You got two business days and we'll see how much you changed. Keep writing your book Thomas. Remember that there is those who want some things and those who can have some things. All you got to do is sending in those two parts of the book and the industry can hear you and read your pain. Those people will never know who I am. Who are you Thomas. I am the New and improved Lion King Superman Thomas Allred Jr. Keep going and you won't what. I want every last one of my business contracts I had before they shot me. What are you willing to do for your contracts . Ill die for the people. you got to versus left to go on this here part of the book.

Did you love your girlfriend before they kill her Thomas. She was and still is my best friend. I love that girl with all my heart. I jack my d*ck because I ain't never found nobody to love me as much as she did. Thomas keep going. Excuse me I want to say something please.Now that I'm in the industry. I want to say thank you to Michael bivins. I want to say thank you to Ralph tresvant . And I want to say thank you to MC Hammer. For making me too legit to quit. Tell Deborah Cox I said thank you.And tell Amerie I said thank you. Thomas what in the hell you got here all we doing is. Is trying to make you see that a bunch of people here love you. I want you to jack your d*ck Thomas. If you don't jacket it we are going to think you playing with us. The boy needs some equal Justice. Your industry is waiting for you to send in the contract. Now sign your name on the dotted line. Thomas Allred Jr. Congratulations you are in the industry now . Now send the book in the start other half. You see your girlfriend Thomas. Write that other book made if you want to. Congratulations Thomas. We got your contracts waiting for you on delivery of the other half of the book. Tell that police officer to write the damn book. Everything looks legit with me. Thomas you got no idea at who your contact is. Send that book in Thomas. Ok Gabriel Union Allred. I will send it in. I want you to do the same. And send in a copy. Of equal justice volume 1.

Now that your in the industry Thomas Allred Jr. We want you to be a role model Thomas Allred Jr. I'm giving you a contract with Eve. I'm giving you a contract with Diane Summers. I'm giving you a contract with every girl from America's next top model every season. Thomas you ain't got to do nothing but do your music for me. Thomas Allred Jr. Your access has been granted. Say what you want to Thomas. But this experience has made you a man out here. You can stop if you want to. Thomas we got you contracts with Lucy Liu. And return of the Jedi jet li. If I be with you you going to think that I was wrong Thomas Allred Jr.

For business reasons. I'm acting as your attorney. In the meantime do you hear what I'm saying. It's a war going on outside. No man is safe from. That boy done grew handsome. Listen to me Thomas. Weather you know it or not. You got females everywhere this wanting your contract. Look at the people that's in the area that you live. They'll do anything for you. Because you pa** the industry's final test. Having love for your fellow man and woman. After you've been through so much pain and difficulty.

You never took a life Thomas Allred Jr. God damn we excited about you coming. Up with music that fits our industry. I welcome you be professional. Interscope Independent records. Thomas Allred Jr we gave you interscope Independent records. Because you've been professional your whole life we saw you. We saw you when you killed that dog in your old neighborhood. We know how you feel. Thomas b*tches out there going crazy over you. I need your signature one more time. Sign on the dotted line Thomas.

Thomas Allred Jr. Interscope Independent records welcomes you. We making you President Thomas. President of interscope Independent records. You see Thomas Allred Jr. Everybody here likes a straight-up game. Because of You Thomas showing our people that God is worth everything. I just want you to realize that were saying a prayer for you every day that you're not here with us. The industry got you a house near Carolina beach to do music in. So far you have two whole business days left to do your music. Now Thomas Allred Jr. Was it as easy as it seemed. No it was not as easy as it seemed. Are you ready to go into the industry and do music. I've been waiting forever to do music. Take your a** to sleep and start writing music. I don't write only freestyle. I give to you Gabriel Union Allred. Thomas Allred Jr. You spend your last time on others. you put your life in danger to help other people. You work your a** off for pennies on the dollar. Everything in this world unjust you have let go. We made a police officer out of you Thomas Allred Jr. Because we needed to see you take on bad guys before we put you in the movies. You are undercover police officer. Having bad luck. With a good personality. For of the people around you.Thomas think about what I just said to you. We putting you in the movies in 2 business days.Thomas how do you feel about this. I feel good about it I want to thank God I want that my sister and I want to take my family for everything and my community. And I especially want to thank the people in the industry for everything that they do and God is real. I tell you this because seeing I'm here now. I want you to cancel me. Because I miss my girlfriend. And I'm all hurt inside. You ain't got nothing but one more day to prove yourself. Thomas if you believe in yourself Then you will pull through. We got a producer in you Thomas Allred Jr. These contracts are official. Now give it to me straight Thomas Allred Jr. How did you get out of those situations. I prayed to God and ask for help. And then I just walked on faith. You walked on faith through fire. It's incredible. But God was there to help me before I even knew to ask. He carried me every step of the way. A look your might not believe me. But I'm being honest with everything. The only way I survived. Is because of God the people in the community. My baby girl my girlfriend my wife is gone.

They killed her. And I don't know what to do. I know that I need somebody. But I've been alone for so many years that. sometimes I think I'm better off being by myself until I'm dead and gone. I find all of the ladies attractive. But me and God is still trying to work out things in my soul. I don't want to bother you. But I can't see myself without my contract here. What I'm saying is there is some beautiful ladies in my own community . Who are by law all good women. I'm not the type of person. To get upset with people and hate the whole town. Most of these women on my friends. And I made a promise I made a promise. I told myself that I was not going to leave my friends in my community.

If we make it we make it together I'ma say that again. If we make it we make it together .All for one and one for all. I'm a police officer Gabriel this is the way it's got to be . You got the industry on you Thomas Allred Jr. You ain't got no room to be trying to save nobody. You get one opportunity to try make something out of yourself. So what are you saying now Thomas Allred Jr. I'm staying what I got to say Gabriel. And that is Thomas Allred Jr. One for one and one for all. I'm not leaving the women I love in this community. I love my woman and I'm not leaving them I was raised with them I'm not leaving them. Send in that book Thomas Allred Jr. What happens if a girl cheats on you Thomas Allred Jr. She is still a part of my family. Everybody is responsible for their own. I'm a police officer Gabriel.

It's a day before Christmas. I'll want my damn husband contracts. Gabriel Union Allred I am trying to do the best job that I can do here to get you two your contracts. Look Kimberly has let us down. Thomas Allred Jr tell how you feel for them. You can't even say anything can you Thomas Allred Jr. That man is in charge of the industry recognize that I'm not only his counselor. I'm his wife. Now I want for you all to use your heads your not playing against a fool. I been ready for your a**es well since I sent in the first book called circuMs.tances to Richard Roma in New York City . Now that I have your attention Richard Roma. My manuscript consist of and music soundtrack in wich I will let Thomas Allred Jr profarm.

You can see that you listen to me. In the hopes of bringing something. To the fore front of the table. If you want to get out of that situation that you are in. It's time for you to let Thomas Allred Jr have control over your companies. The game is called chest and your four are in checkmate. By taking over your companies I using my mental abilities to order to around through messages. One other thing . Go head baby. You better keep your damn d*ck in your pants Thomas Allred Jr. You don't have to tell me twice Gabriel Union Allred.

You don't f*ck with anybody Thomas Allred Jr. This is why we are timing you to put out a manuscipt worth so subtains. Here go the bread and butter Thomas Allred Jr. These companies are working together on your movie script. You no the play ain't playing with you if you can't get you no p**sy . I do commend you on being strong enough to make it to the next level 3. Ms. Eden Reid and Ms. Erin Cohen they all work for me Thomas Allred Jr. So dose Richard Roma. You are famous and everyone who talks to you. They know that fact and they don't think that you do. Even your brothers realize that you are famous Thomas Allred Jr. Your mom's is sworn to secrecy. Thomas this is your book and movie. In which you are policing. And all you can think of is when a piece of a** is going to come your way. I'm a make some sense out of you. Begin Thomas Allred Jr. Writing your story again. You are the most successful business man that I ever laid eyes on.

Thank you Gabriel Union Allred I got to get going. Where are you handed Thomas Allred Jr. I'm watching myself grow. See he ain't no dummy. Thomas realizes that every thing he do is recorded. That's because I want to be with you. Said Gabriel Union Allred the keep on going Thomas Allred Jr. You said Gabriel Union Allred the. What Thomas Allred Jr . What is it. I'm saying Gabriel Union Allred is my wife and my queen. Gabriel Union Allred is the Queen . In my life. Thomas you don't have to put that on there. Lay it down Thomas Allred Jr. I gave your a** a ultimatum Thomas Allred Jr. In my dreaMs. it's me and you Gabriel Union Allred. Let me repeat myself. Now it's Christmas time in the city. And all that I want and need is my beautiful wife Gabriel Union Allred to be apart of my life. Thomas Allred Jr angels are going to hear your prayer. Wich one is that dear. That I'm your wife for ever more . Gabriel Union Allred I love you so much baby. No you don't. Yes I do. See I didn't realize that I was famous. As the Lion King professional Thomas Allred Jr. Should have his choice to as many Queens as he wants. Thomas Allred Jr the game is really over and we have everything that we need to write your book and movie with. What happened to you Thomas Allred Jr was a shame. It's ok Gabriel Union Allred we saved lives that's all that matters. I love you Gabriel Union Allred . I will never forget you. You think I'd seen for you . I pray that you do. Listen Thomas. Your access Thomas Allred Jr has been approved. You are the Lion King Superman Thomas Allred Jr. And you have waisted time trying to prove yourself. When you wrote that book. For a friend Thomas Allred Jr. That proved that you where The Lion King Superman Thomas Allred Jr. Thomas you are going to need some more kids. I got to kids that I surpposedly don't know of. Stand up for yourself Thomas Allred Jr. I don't give a f*ck if them is your kids. Im careful with everything that I do. See Thomas Allred Jr taking your shirt off is the only thing missing. The game is over y'all. Send in that manuscript. That manuscript isn't what you think that it is its a hell of a lot more. I love you my beautiful wife Gabriel Union Allred. Seen it in baby and happy New year baby. Merry Christmas from Gabriel Union Allred and family. To your family where ever you are at.

Now see here it's Christmas time the day that our savior was born .Thomas stop and listen to me. We have got your contracts. Thank you so much Ms. Michelle Obama. Your absolutely welcome Thomas Allred Jr. I just took my time and watched you while you were in with your family. Thomas Allred Jr. You truly are the Lion King. Dose that even mean anything Ms. Michelle Obama and if so. Why do you take all of the money that I earn for me and my friends of the family. I said I would get you your money back to you didn't I . Thomas Allred Jr here on this Christmas day we forgot to bestow on you. Your badge of protection shield. Thomas Allred Jr I can tell you right now that you been ahead as the Lion King all of your life. What about my ladies. Everyone has them. The Lion King Superman Thomas Allred Jr. He as won his war. Let give him a apartment with all of the ladies. Thomas Allred Jr would this make you happy. Yes Ms. Michelle Obama it would make me happy. For it is written that the Lion King Superman Thomas Allred Jr shall return to this world in a thousand business years to do battle with Satan once again saving a new generation from theMs.elves in a computer error. Lion King Superman Thomas Allred Jr. Before the sun goes down on this Christmas day. Thomas Allred Jr do you agree to come back in one thousand years to save our children from Satan like you do for us. Yes I agree. As long as a can have my same team working with me every step of the way. The secret service agents will be with you Lion King Superman Thomas Allred Jr. The NSA will also be with you. And the police stations all over the world will be with you. You guys have do a great job. Ms. Michelle Obama . I am going to need my money and my ladies now. Lion King Superman Thomas Allred Jr. We now grant you your money back. And your women back to you. Thank you Ms. Michelle Obama. Thomas Allred Jr. There are two more questions that ld like to ask you. Okay Ms. Michelle Obama go ahead. How did you come back to life. When we all seen you die? I trusted in our Lord and Savior with everything all I had. And Lion King Superman Thomas Allred Jr. Now that we've saved the world. Is you accommodations award winning. Ms. Michelle Obama. I just want my family and my friends out of the rags. And to a better standard of life. I am not trying to run away. I am the Lion King Superman Thomas Allred Jr. And i am fighting now for the right to polay with all of my woman. Make sure that the woman are what you want. The woman are what I need Ms. Michelle Obama. When I snap my fingers Thomas Allred Jr you will no that you are a star and how to handle it. Ms.. Michelle Obama I just want to say thank you. For what Lion King Superman Thomas Allred Jr. For putting your life in danger save me . My wife Candis M Collins and my daughter. You are a president in my book. Thomas Allred Jr I want you to remember something Thomas Allred Jr. I programmed you to fight the good fight. Everyone we have saved the world on this Christmas day. The Lion King Superman Thomas Allred Jr promises to come back to help out our children. Thomas Allred Jr you now have all of your money and all of your women. Will be given to you for procreation. You are a good man. And the world is proud of you Thomas Allred Jr. Ms. Michelle Obama. Could you please tell Ms. Gabriel Union Allred that I said that you and that maybe one day God a let us all be there before the evening lights. Thomas Allred Jr take time and take care of yourself snap send the message off.

Thomas in my wildest dreaMs. have you put in the work. To excavate my situation even higher than it already is. Gabriel Union Allred I'm answering your prayer. By taking care of myself and looking for one woman. You two outta be ashamed of yourself Thomas. What is it Michelle Obama. I'm watching you on dish imagery Thomas Allred Jr. I want to see you have your room for this. I'm lending you apart of the sight of you. To make it out of that situation that you find yourself in . When you get done sitting worrying about every body else. There is work to be done Thomas Allred Jr. And I mean the new and improved Lion King Superman Thomas Allred Jr. There's is work to be done. Yes Ms. Michelle Obama. You are going to make it really. I'm leaving home in a couple of weeks. And I don't know where I am going to be living at .

Pick your mutha f*cking game up there Thomas Allred Jr. Do you think that it is best for me to go and leave my family Ms. Michelle Obama. I'm telling you Thomas Allred Jr The new and improved Lion King Superman Thomas Allred Jr. That if you move forward and don't turn back that your family will always remember you. And so will I Thomas Allred Jr. What are you saying Ms. Michelle Obama. I'm saying that we are going to make you a King in your own right. Thomas Allred Jr I know that this can be scare but I am really speaking with you about this issue that you have here on weather to leave or to stay with your loved ones. Listen Thomas Allred Jr. Thomas we understand that you like Shontel. But if you can't talk to her Thomas Allred Jr I'm going to need you to go by yourself. Yes Ms. Michelle Obama. Now when I snap my fingers. You will be done accomplished your book. And we will never here from each other again. In a manuscipt. Thomas Allred Jr are there any more questions. Ms. Michelle Obama can you help me with getting Shontel to come and to live with me. Thomas Allred Jr the girl already knows that you two are going places after this. Put the access code in for Hollywood California access The New and improved Lion King Superman Thomas Allred Jr. The Hollywood access code is 2678143296014389678241 your access has been granted Ms. Michelle Obama if I don't leave where will that leave me. In the danger zone all by yourself. And the reason why I am saying this is I need you to open up your eyes. You finished the books and movies. And we will get back to you and Gabriel Union Allred about this. Thomas Allred Jr just have some faith Thomas.

Speak to all of those police officers. Who are helping you in the struggle. I would like to thank each and ever last one of you for making it possible to take me outta the hood. We are giving you a Surperman contract just like you asked for. And now you got to prove yourself as the Loin King by remaining non two faced it. Thomas Allred Jr we welcome you to the end of your life. And one day you will look back on this. And realize that either way you go the road runs out one day. So what is it going to be . Come with me Thomas Allred Jr Gabriel Union Allred I would like to but I can't. Thomas Allred Jr I have got your a** under a federal judges contract. You have your a** in that car the day that Vicky sends it to pick you up

Do I make myself clear. And if Shontel wants to come with you. She can but if for any reason she can not come. I want your a** in that car. Do you here me. Yes I hear you. What is my name. Ms. Gabriel Union Allred. Thomas Allred Jr you have got to be good we are offering you a new place to live. And than some. Like I was saying yes Ms. Michelle Obama . That contract really means something to you. I'm saying it just. I want your a** up every morning waiting for your ride. Why I'm only going to Newton. You going to Newton my a**. Thomas we got a police station on you. Your ride is going to be there in the morning so act professional. Tomorrow is Sunday what do I do until I leave. Keep exorcising give me three weeks and your ride will be sitting right here. This is access granted. Thank you I didn't snap my fingers yet. You 600. Females are going to be living with you. On a bend over contract. What I'm saying is that Thomas Allred Jr you are going to except what we give to you and like it. Do it sound like I'm playing. Shontel is your contract. Get us to it. Shontel will only speak to you when we design for her to. So quit worrying about all of the women. You have already placed your bid.unless the want to up the ante . I do want to up the ante Ms. Michelle Obama. Go ahead Thomas Allred Jr up the ante. I give you Females. 600 and 27 billion dollars. For being my contracts and my wives. I also bid another a thousand and six billion dollars for females that truly are exceptional girls be my baby mama's. Ms. Michelle Obama I won't give in . I need all of there contracts. Ok doly noted . Listen Thomas Allred Jr you are the Lion King. Your money is no good around here. But you can do like I said and take what we have to get you . Shontel is your contract. And I say it snap. I offer you Shontel contract. Do you want it Thomas Allred Jr. Yes I do Ms. Michelle Obama. Tell Gabriel Union Allred that you want this contract. Gabriel Union Allred sweetheart I want the contract with Shontel to be mine. Your wish has been granted. Thomas Allred Jr yes Ms. Michelle Obama . I'm getting ready to snap my fingers. Remember what I said I want you to have your a** in that car when we come for you and Shontel. And if Shontel ain't with you . Thomas Allred Jr you have to leave with out her do I make myself clear. Yes Ms. Michelle Obama. Now I will be watching and talking to you from here on out. In voice telepathy. Thomas Allred Jr don't give up . I just don't want to loose Shontel Ms. Michelle Obama. I'm going to give you one more chance Thomas. I'll take it Ms. Michelle Obama. Go the your appointments as scheduled. And I will get you ride to you. One more thing Thomas Allred Jr. I depend on you as a man to keep your word. I'm going to the new place Ms. Michelle Obama and Ms. Gabriel Union Allred. With or without a contract or not that's coming with me. Shontel will come with you Thomas Allred Jr. I hope so snap. Now send off the messages. The End.

CHAPTER 13

As you realize that I am The Lion King. I want you to know one thing about me. I could never imagine living with out my family and my community with me on a daily. So I'm giving you 300 hundred million to the restoration of Longview North Carolina. And I'm giving my family members a billion dollars a peice. Going back to Longview North Carolina. People are saying that the New and improved Lion King Superman Thomas Allred Jr. Is a push over. And I'm trying to tell you that I am a push over. It's just that I hope for the best in what I do. And people think that I want their digets.This Lion King Superman Thomas Allred Jr is in need of something straight. I want to thank Ms. Hillary Clinton for speaking with me in my novel. And I'd like to thank Ms. Gabriel Union Allred. For believing in me way before I could believe in myself. And two my brothers and sisters there is a triangle in the sky you just have to keep reaching for it. And to my beautiful wonderful mother. This is the end of our book my analogies are complete. Time circuits are now on. Thomas Allred Jr you and Gabriel Union Allred have just saved the world. Along with the police department and the NSA and the secret service. Martha Stewart give it a rest. I'm just glad that my man is finally home. To stay for good. Thomas Allred Jr I want you to give Longview North Carolina 100 million dollars out of you piggy bank. Okay Shontel. Because I been watching you and I came to play Thomas Allred Jr. I get it . You know that I need you to rescue me from my self. No I just want you to tell everybody that the police department ordered you to write this book. Shontel is right the police department ordered me to write this book. And gave me my contract with you Shontel. Put your seat belt on Thomas Allred Jr . Shontel we ain't got enough room to get up to 88 miles per hour. Okay get out of the car and talk to Ms. Michelle Obama a minute Thomas Allred Jr. Thank you Ms. Michelle Obama for everything that you have done for me and my family and neighborhood. The Lion King Thomas. I know well that in the day of trouble that I can turn to you. Are they gone all the terrorist who had all of our women and children hostage. Did we seal them in with a one two three combination. The rest of the terrorist are being captured. So the good people will sacrifice our position. Ms.

Michelle Obama I tried my best as a police officer to be there for every one. And I have after all these years. It's just that I missed out on having a family of my own because I had to tackle some dirt. That should have been cleaned already . See The new and improved Lion King Superman Thomas Allred Jr. The reason why I choose you to head up the organization is because you are famous in our news papers in Washington DC. I know that it's been a hard time for you. But the fighting has stopped. I'm a need you to be professional and give me the final access code that you will ever need. The access code is. 7286423107652314897261283056. access approved. Thomas Allred Jr there is man that I am wanting you to see. Mr. Barack Obama. Be professional Thomas. Mr. Barack Obama how are you sir. I know that you have alot of unanswered questions about our program. Thomas Allred Jr we are testing you to become a movie star. And as famous as you are you could be large. All I need is your word that you will carry the standards of the Lion King true professional. Mr. Barack Obama I give you my word. As long as I may have a family with all sorts of contract. You have my word that I want stop you from having you kids with all sorts of contracts. Bring Shontel over here Thomas . This is your wife Thomas Allred Jr. Shontel is speach less right now. You movie career begins Thomas Allred Jr when I snap my finger. You are a true to life movie star. That people are out the snapping pictures of you as we speak. Thomas Allred Jr always remember that we have saved the world with you help. The armed fources that you. Mr. Barack Obama I'm a businessman can I beat you a** in a game of connect four. Connect four Thomas Allred Jr I win. Snap. Now send off the messages Thomas Allred Jr. And begin talking that nonsense that you usually talk when you are not afraid of nothing right now Thomas Allred Jr . Right Now snap.

Cla** less start our stories up. I know Thomas Allred Jr can beat me. That is a man right there. Ms. Oprah Winfrey could you please talk to the cla**. Okay everyone settle down. Here go the story. Of The Lion King Superman Thomas Allred Jr. Listen to me Thomas I'll trade you my Garbage Pail kid for your comic book. You don't have to do nothing but tell the truth about who you are. I am a great King. And Superman is my code name by the government. I am a NSA agent. And I am partnered by The Secret Service. Gave me the last writes. To write my story. I am a part of the police department. Listen to him. Yes the cla** will miss Oprah Winfrey. This Superman is King Thomas Allred Jr. I call you King Thomas Allred Jr. Because you are a famous individual and person. Listen to that. Cla** is in session. Mr. Lebanon Gates. Are you King Superman Thomas Allred Jr. I'm afraid I am boy. No you talkin to me. Mr. Lebanon Gates. I hear you Miss Sarah Spencer. King Thomas I mean Mr. Lebanon Gates. How does it feel to be the richest man in the world. It is a brisk cool feeling. It is kind of like being reborn into the world a new. Where reality meets your pillar. You take your time to be thankful. Now with these books I had not a penny to start with. King Superman Thomas Allred Jr then how did you get out of your situation. I just kept working and telling myself that I am the richest man in the world. And what I did was train myself to do better and stronger. How did you train yourself. By listening to motivational speeches. And doing push ups everyday while I wrote my books. In my books. I am in love with the Lion Queen Ms. Shontel Allred Jr. And he is in love with me. This is too good to be true. Shontel. I mean the Lion Queen princess Shontel Allred Jr. Let me talk to you too for a minute. This is your interview.Start the tape. You are the Lion Queen princess Shontel right. That is correct yall. And the new improved Lion King Superman Thomas Allred Jr. It's going to be your husband. The whole community is waiting on you two to get married. King Superman Thomas Allred Jr. Is too wedd the Lion Queen Shontel Allred Jr. You already gave her your last name in your books. To let them know that there is no game with me. Once people get around you how would you feel. Shall I let you speak. I am the Lion Queen. Because I chose to be the Lion Queen. And King Superman Thomas Allred Jr. Is truly indeed our King. We call each other the new and improved line king and queen Superman Thomas and Shontel Allred Jr . Now I don't know what makes us famous. If sunlight hits you you glow King Surperman Thomas Allred Jr. Say nothing and you'll get nowhere. I even save people in stories that you read. This interview is getting captivating. This because it is Oprah Winfrey that is training us. King Surperman Thomas Allred Jr I can see right now.

That you have picked a strong wife. You see we picked each other Miss Oprah Winfrey. Thomas only loves me because I was there for him. In his time of need. Miss Oprah Winfrey. That boy sacrificed everything he had to take care of his people. He calls this his comeback tour. He just want to eat some foods that he's never tested before. Take your time and speak to me. What kind of superhero gives money away to every woman that I knows. The Lion King. The new and improved Lion King and Queen Superman Thomas and Shontel Allred Jr. Also give to you their sound judgement. In my place. Criminals aren't allowed. So Shontel. That girl needs her place. Thomas professionals are already given you and Shontel your place. Keep writing your stories down Mr. Lebanon Gates. And Mr.s. Scarlett O'Hara. Scarlett O'Hara is the Lion Queen and princess Shontel. Everybody there go Scarlett O'Hara right there.

Her name is the Lion Queen Princess. Shontel Allred Jr. And we call her Miss Scarlett O'Hara. That is a bunch of respect coming from The Lion King. Isn't it. We need to change the name of the story. To the last but first. Your community. Clean up the community King Surperman Thomas Allred Jr along with your Queen and wife beside you. The Lion Queen Princess Shontel Allred Jr. King Surperman Thomas Allred Jr do everything that you do. To try to see things more clear. What do you mean see things more clearer. You are getting tired. You are getting sleepy. And when I snap my fingers this interview will be complete. Look Miss Oprah Winfrey I want to thank you for everything. Me and the Lion Queen Princess Shontel and the people in the community. We all love everything you do. King Superman Thomas Allred Jr. We have programmed you. You are a police officer who has cleaned up your community again and again and again. So I would like to thank you King Superman Thomas Allred Jr. Or shall we call you Mr. . Lebanon Gates . Mr.. Lebanon Gates is alright with me. Alright then this short piece of interview is over. When I snap my fingers like I told you. You will continue to have a good day. And Lion Queen princess Shontel. Is going to be your wife King Surperman Thomas Allred Jr. Just pay your publisher. Some attention. After you book is already complete. You know the people are watching. I'm bringing you out of a hell crisis. Mr.s. Oprah Winfrey. Do not think me.

For what I did for my community. But thank all of the officers. In my community and surrounding. For helping me and protecting me. When I had fallen down and couldn't stand. I want to thank my brothers and sisters in uniform. For calling out to me when I was hurt and falling into darkness. Are people are true heroes. So if anyone people deserves any justice. It is the Hickory police department and rescue squad. Miss Oprah Winfrey these people saved my life. Along with my brother Chris Allred Sr. For carring me off the field when I couldn't get up. You truly are the Lion King Thomas Allred Jr. Our test is almost complete. Are you the richest man in the world King Superman Thomas Allred Jr. Yes I am the richest man in the world. Just because I have people that care about me. And a beautiful lady that loves me. She is my queen y'all give it up for the Lion Queen Princess Shontel.

Princess Lion Queen Shontel so what do you think about The Lion King Superman Thomas Allred Jr. Thomas even though you've been shot with a bullet it didn't slow you down. Cause your heart beats eternal. And you are a world superpower with ideas coming out. Thank you for listening to me. Thomas get up and send that book in pronto. Yes my beautiful wife Shontel The Lion Queen and princess. Over this thing called life. See right now. We are going to take you out the hood Thomas. The Lion King and Queen is ready. For another existence. You're not understanding Thomas Allred Jr. I said that the Lion King is the richest man in the world. All of your money will be given back to you. I just wanted to test you to see what interests you had in this world. Now without any further ado. I'm Snapping my fingers stop the tape. Snap

I had this here on the table of my mind. It is a parable and I'm seeking the truth from all of my readers. My story starts here. I Lebanon Gates. And the richest man in all times. I try to explain myself though books and magazines. I got the position of a king in my own mind state. I want for my books to be put together. I want for my books to be put together for genius sakes. This is how the beginning should start. He walked in the room a trillionaire . Thomas Allred Jr and Elizabeth. And Kristen. And Shontel walked in the room all Trillionaires . You walk in with me you are a trillionaire Lebanon Gates said to them. You thought the story was going to end with my last book. Here we go with the ending of Elizabeth story mansion

3. Thomas you're going to make me cry. This story is designed to make you cry Elizabeth. I need your approval Thomas Allred Jr. Before I can send a copy of this to the president of the United States. And my approval is yours Kristen. Quit listening Thomas Allred Jr. Lebanon Gates is our boss and leader. Put Lebanon on the phone with me thank you. This is Lebanon Gates you talkin to. This is Hollywood Access granted. We just want to know one thing Lebanon Gates. How come you didn't marry Kristen when you had the chance ? Opportunities like Kristen present thet self once in a lifetime. You expect us to believe that Kristen is not your soulmate. I love Kristen with all my heart. But Shontel is the one for me. What type of book is it. My book is a historian book. Reaching out to me or three beautiful women. They all take care of theMs.elves. I care for them all. Let's see if my story mansion. Can past any of the test. You welcome to Lebanon Gates. You welcome Mr.. Thomas Allred Jr. And you're welcome my husband and soulmate. Y'all three ladies. Are my pride and joy to this book industry. Every book that I'm writing. I should put you in that from now on. Clean up your damn act Lebanon Gates. The women want to see a hero. We are all trapped in the book. I'm saying that you and me are one inside of the book. How did this happen.

Thomas I'm trapping you inside of the book. Until you can make up your heart. on which one of these women is the right one for you. Access granted. There is another woman. I think she is Miss Gabrielle Union Allred. Gabriel Union Allred you may speak. Thomas realizes how I feel about the matter. And I know we haven't talked in awhile. I love Thomas Allred Jr. Just because he wrote the book for us story book mansion. In all of his teachings. One Thing remains the same. That Thomas Allred Jr is in love with me. Shontel you get a chance to speak Shontel. I said I'm in love with that boy. And I know for sure that Thomas Allred Jr loves me. Because he told me he loved me and I looked in his eyes.So this is how our book ending. You better depend on Thomas Allred Jr. He is sure to come through for you once he gets his money right. Kristen stop crying and talk to us.

Listen at me .Thomas Allred Jr ain't care about none of you females. Until I hurt that man heart. Thomas Allred Jr I am sorry. Don't marry because you want to be with somebody. You marry a person because you love them. Can you hear me Thomas Allred Jr. If you're the man that God chose for me. Then we will find out one of these days. But Lebanon Gates. If you are hurt in your heart. That is not a reason to get married. I'm letting Elizabeth talk to you. Thomas Allred Jr i see what you going through. I am your helper in my book Elizabeth story mansion 3. You loved and then you lost . Everyone could feel it when Jeana died. Listen to me Thomas Allred Jr. All you have to do is send in the postage money. And your wildest dreaMs. will come true. I need a couple of months. Mr. Lebanon Gates. The stories are going to match up. Stay at home with your family. And send in the proceeds for your book. If you love us for women. God will make a way for you to have just that. There is four more women. Keep him talking. I said keep the boy talking. That is Nada. And Chelsea. And Porsche. And Ashley. That man said he in love with 8 Women. This is Elizabeth story mansion 3. Overtime youll see what I'm asking is not far-fetched. Who is the narrator in this book. It is me Thomas Allred Jr. I am the narrator in this book. Give two more weeks and I will have the money. For the book postage. Thomas Allred Jr you don't need two more weeks. All of us ladies are paying for your book postage today. We realized you haven't been with anyone Thomas Allred Jr. And we're proud of you for that. When you had your love affair Thomas Allred Jr. You were only a teenager. Jeana is your love forever. But Jeana is no longer with us. And as much as it hurts me to say this. your Elizabeth story Mansion 3 hasn't pa**ed the test yet. Sometimes I get so tired I just don't know what to do. Other nights I cry until I cry myself to sleep.

Look ladies the reason why I called this Elizabeth storybook Mansion is . because you ladies have nothing to do with your time but gossip. I give to you Elizabeth story mansion 3. In hopes that when I take on the world. That all the ladies will gather around and go with me. To the Hamptons . We all can see. Did my girl stand up for me all the way to the end. Jeana we applaud you.That boy is professional. It's just that women saved my life. And I want to return the favor. I've been dreaming about. A new statement Center. To wear a woman can voice her opinions night and day. And they are taking care of for her. That very next morning. I am Mr. Lebanon Gates.

And I'm also Mr. Thomas Allred Jr. And you are reading Elizabeth story Mansion 3. Kristen it's alright go ahead and talk. I never meant to hurt you Thomas Allred Jr. I do mean I never meant to hurt you Mr. Lebanon Gates. But I had to do something. People were looking at you like you were after me. I hope you know that I still have feelings for you. And feelings for you. I'm saying if you asked me to marry me i might would. Now let Elizabeth talk. I do love you Thomas Allred Jr. But my storybook Mansion is my dream. Let the other women go and come with me. I have enough strength to pull you out of the book.

But I don't know if I can get the rest of the woman free from the book. Thomas Allred Jr are you hearing what I'm saying. I'm saying that I'm the one that loves you. Elizabeth I'm in love with you too. Lebanon Gates. You have pa**ed your test. In storybook mansion. Why because I said I love Elizabeth. No it's because you gave your all to Elizabeth in storybook mansion. I've been in love with her. I'm in love with eight other women to. You need to talk to me before they close the book Thomas Allred Jr. Elizabeth I don't need nobody but you. That is the end of our story.

Mr. Lebanon Gates has chosen Elizabeth. To be his lawful bride. Narrator could you please read the rules and regulations of our story. This is Storybook mansion. Once a man has confessed love with his heart. All of us want to see if it's true or not. Thomas Allred jr. Has proven his love. In Elizabeth story mansion. May him and Elizabeth be happy forever. Elizabeth Thomas Allred jr. Is your heart. For the story Land mansion will not rest. Until you break the heart of the one you love. That is for the one that loves you completely. Elizabeth Mr. Lebanon Gates or one in the same Mr.. Thomas Allred Jr. Considers you to be his wife. Make all excuses. He is waiting for you.Catch him. He went out of his way. To write you a book called Elizabeth story mansion. Just as we have it. Elizabeth needs Thomas Allred Jr also. That's where the book gets complicated. Because two people that love each other shall have one house. And this is Elizabeth Storybook mansion 3. Where a dream has been said. And your wish is my command Elizabeth. You ain't got to say nothing else about me or story book mansion. Because our people already here us. Are longing for one another.

In Elizabeth storybook mansion 3. I got to see what you were thinking about. That's why we are getting professional as we go. Listen to me it is a world if we can have our hearts pulled together. In storybook Mansion Elizabeth. Girl number three. Keep it professional. I just realized I'm a trillionaire. Mr. Lebanon Gates I do thank you. Don't call me Mr. Lebanon Gates call Mr. Thomas Allred Jr. Writing this book has been my pleasure. I did research on every chapter. What kind of research you do. I made sure that you have everything you need before I delivered my book to you. All the proceeds to be divided down the middle between Elizabeth and Thomas Allred Jr. This is your story mansion. Elizabeth story mansion 3 has come to a close. Elizabeth claim your man .That boy just fought hard for you . In story mansion book. This book is dedicated to Elizabeth. Because of your smile and personality. I can see life.

Don't say nothing to him. He is in love with that girl. That girl wrote the book. Being in love with Thomas Allred Jr. It is so many people after him. You got to do what you got to do crystal. I know Shontel loves him. I just want to be with him for one night. Do you here what you're saying. In the book Elizabeth story Mansion 3. Elizabeth has won the right to marry Thomas Allred Jr. I hope you do realize that people are watching you. I got to make sure that all our kids are straight. Mr. Lebanon Gates promised to give his time and his money to helping the community out of trouble. Yeah but this is how I feel about Mr. Lebanon Gates. Crystal tell me what do you feel for Mr. Lebanon Gates. Lebanon Gates is my heartbeat. I will fight and defend Mr. Lebanon Gates.

Thomas you have to realize what I'm telling you is true. I do hear you Crystal. I just wanted to tell you that you are everything to me. And I love you baby for everything that you do. I'm going to take my time and think about the situation right here Crystal. Don't give up. It is good women in all of you. I need you to tell me. The inner makings of the heart. You with this boy just said. The inner makings of the heart is when you love someone honestly. That your love just shines through. I see here at this moment. Crystal that you deserve to be a part of my family. Oh Mr. Lebanon Gates. I have to thank you for this. It is about time that boy is thinking of hiMs.elf. Miss Oprah Winfrey. And Mr.s. Michelle Obama. And Mr.s. Hillary

Clinton. And Mr.s Barbara Bush. And Mr.s. Trump. You all believe in the stories that I right. I am Mr. Lebanon Gates. And I am the richest man in the world. My name is Thomas Allred Jr. And I come from my humble beginnings. It is no fantasy how I see things first ladies. As of the Forbes Fortune list. I am the richest man in the world a hundred thousand times over. I'm going to tell you what I'm going to do for you. After I finish with this book. I'm going to try and sit down with my wives. Shontel . And Elizabeth. And you all remember Kristen. And Nada. And Ashley. And Porsche. And Kay and Chelsea. And Heather. Now alone with Crystal. I want you to be with me. On my campaign to free the whales. Do y'all love that man. I see what you talkin about Thomas Allred Jr. Yeah Mr.s. Oprah Winfrey. All the females care about me and I have this money. With money comes great responsibility Thomas Allred Jr. No one said it was going to be easy to be Mr. Lebanon Gates. You have to find it inside yourself. To be the best trillionaire you can possibly be. He taking Kristen out of the hood. It's difficult because. I am just now coming into money. It's difficult because.

I am in love with all of my women friends. Thomas Allred Jr. Your women friends are going to have to do without you. Now get your a** out of the seat and write that book like you supposed to. This is Elizabeth story Mansion 4 . Oh Thomas I thought you were going to forget about me. No Elizabeth how could I forget you. This means you do love me. I always have been in love with you Elizabeth. But who are these other ladies Mr. Lebanon Gates. I want you to know Elizabeth that these are dreaMs. of mine. Mr. Lebanon Gates do you have dream to me. I promise you I do. Well lets start the book up. As we left off in Elizabeth storybook Mansion 3. I'll be with you if I could Elizabeth. For the first time my dreaMs. are about to come true. Now want you to take your time. And open the first page of the book. This page got a diamond on it.I autographed the book myself. To serve as a reminder. The all of you ladies are in my book.

You make me see. That you truly care about us. That man has more love inside of his heart than you can imagine. Mr.s. Hillary Clinton. One trillion are to another. Is the books ready to be launched off. I'm telling you Thomas Allred Jr the books are already launched off. Just pay your shipping and handling fee. Look at Shontel and Kristen and Kay and Porsche and Katy .Thomas Allred Jr finishes his book before midnight. Midnight is coming around and the people want you. Thomas Allred Jr. Wake up Thomas Allred Jr. It's your goddamn birthday. The ladies who I was talking about where are they. There is no one here Thomas Allred Jr. But my name is Mr. Lebanon Gates. Around here you just Thomas Allred Jr. But I'm a trillionaire. I'm telling you that you're not a trillionaire Thomas Allred Jr.One of these days I be a trillionaire. Jesus Christ will hold me to it. We got a meeting this afternoon. With a girl named Elizabeth and Kristen. A woman name Shontel will be there. In two more women named Nada and Porsche. Will be at this meeting. I take medicine for this anxiety. That I feel inside my heart. Thomas Allred Jr we all are with you. Okay Elizabeth. This is your Elizabeth storybook Mansion 4. Thomas Allred Jr am I your wife . You ain't got to see it I already know. The storybook Mansion is a creation of Jews. And though it seeMs. out of touch it is real to every woman in the world. What a Storybook Mansion is. It is a paradox that is able to reach a woman's heart and mind at the same time. And I am Lebanon damn Gates y'all. And this is the end of My success. In Elizabeth storybook mansion 4. This boy writing a story about Elizabeth. Keep your composure Thomas Allred Jr. We wanted a book about superheroes. But I can see it right now that you and those women. all are superheroes in my heart. Mr.s Barbara Bush. Thomas Allred Jr you are doing the right thing. Give Thomas Allred Jr that contract. In the Superman contract goes to. Mr. Lebanon Gates. Mr. Lebanon Gates is not here to speak to us this morning. I'm going to accept it for him. It is Elizabeth and Thomas. Along with Shontel and Kristen. Listen Thomas Allred Jr. You deserve this award. For being a superhero among any other. We programmed you to stand up for your neighborhood. But you did something far greater than that . What you did was you put your life on the line to help out a friend. Thomas Allred Jr everybody cares about you. Look at my facial expressions. This storybook Mansion is just the beginning of your books. And every woman that you are interested in Thomas Allred Jr. Is to be in the book alongside of you. That way we can see Superman for who he is. Thomas Allred jr. Thomas and the person that you saved. Was the president of United States. His heart rate is beating. Move out the way clear. Come on back to me Thomas Allred Jr. You can do it get your a** up off the bed. My story book is finished. Yes your story book is finished. Mr. Lebanon Gates who you wanting to see. I only need one person get Shontel on the phone. And take me to the White House. If I do I'll make Elizabeth mad . Look what you said. The only person that you need is Shontel. This is business and I got to teach you something. Elizabeth is my wife forever. AND SO IS Shontel. In my storybook mansion. To be continued.

CHAPTER 14

Listen Elizabeth our storybook Mansion is now coming to a close. You got the name Thomas Allred Jr. Yes I do have the name. It is because of you. That I can see clearly and reach farther. Girl I envision. A storybook mansion. All over the TV sets. And even in the White House. Thomas you have got to finish the story. Shontel I'm trying to be there for everyone. But Elizabeth honey. My book is based on a true story. And it is a story about. A man and a woman being in love with each other. And not being able to express their love. Only through the storybook mansion can the man and woman be together. You see we are working to change things. In my eyes Elizabeth. Storybook Mansion is your mansion. Let me open my eyes so I can see. Mr.s. Michelle Obama. Mr.s. Hillary Clinton.

Open my book for me. In your book there is a heart and a diamond. Its true that you are the true Mr.. Lebanon Gates. I am one in the same. You see Miss Hillary Clinton. I got your best interest in mind. I give two hearts to you. For helping me right now. It hurt my feelings how I couldn't. Spend time with the women that I love. It is starting to be amazing. I'm taking storybook Mansion to the Congress. And I'm telling you that. I am a trillionaire. That deserves to be with his woman that I love. This book is mostly dedicated. To my good friend Erin. I am a trillionaire. Just be with me and you will understand the book is right. As i struggle to find revenue for this book. I'm wishing all of the ladies a wonderful blessed Valentine's Day season. I can't find my revenue because. My hundredth million dollar stop me from being able to spend change. Can anybody in the world understand me. Kristen I truly am Lebanon Gates. There is more to this story. Put Amazon Women on it Thomas Allred Jr. Amazon Women Queen gods. I see my future in Elizabeth's eyes. What do I do now that the book is almost complete. You have been jealous of the story Thomas Allred Jr. Elizabeth will always be there for you. In the story line. Wait a minute this isn't making any sense. What did I just tell you Thomas Allred Jr. A woman is waiting for you. In between the lines of your story. All you got to do Thomas Allred Jr. Is pay the postage and let well enough be. I can't help you if I only could. The storybook Mansion is to be large. Elizabeth come here the Amazon queen gods are talkin to us. I'm on my way Thomas Allred Jr. But still my question is for you Thomas Allred Jr. In real life. Which woman will you marry? After the story has been completed. Amazon queen God. Ladies all over the Amazon Kingdom. I shouldn't have went back on my word. But if I could I would like to give all of you A $1000000. In those books. I want Elizabeth to have her share of the proceeds. Split it down the middle with her. See back to my question. Mr. Lebanon Gates. Mr.. Thomas Allred Jr. They are one in the same. Before the storybook Mansion ends which woman will you choose to be your wife in the story. This isn't happening to me. Shontel relax and be quiet and let him speak. You are trapped in the book Thomas Allred Jr. Realize that you must choose one woman because they all are listening. To you inside of your storybook mansion. I would like to marry Shontel. Women of the Amazon Nation. You have all heard Mr. Lebanon Gates request. Mr.. Thomas Allred Jr chooses Shontel to be his suitor. Pick those eyebrows up. Because a king and a queen is among us. Mr. Lebanon Gates you are the richest man in the world. By teaming up with Shontel.

Y'all will be unstoppable. But I don't feel the same. Elizabeth what are you saying this is your story book mansion. I believe that Mr. Lebanon Gates should be able to have as many queens as he wants. Elizabeth I understand what you're saying. But in the real world things are kind of different. Thomas Allred Jr you are the richest man in the world. And you can be with any woman that you want to. All I want to know is do you still love me Thomas Allred Jr. Samantha yes I still love you. Then Amazon princesses I call for parlay. Parlay Parlay what is Samantha saying. Samantha is challenging us to a duel Thomas Allred Jr. The to the to the death. Who do you choose the battle against Samantha.

I choose Shontel. No. Thomas Allred Jr. It'll be alright I got this. Remember I am also Amazon princess queen God Shontel. Each ladies will pick up a gla** and drink.Shontel why you not drinking. Common sense I didn't see what was poured in the gla**. Samantha neal to your queen. Elizabeth I understand what you and all the Ladies are saying. Lebanon Gates is a trillionaire. But it doesn't matter if Thomas Allred Jr is a trillionaire. Or just an average person sitting on the city train. When it came down to it and the chips where on the line he chose me to be his wife. This is a book. No NADA this is real life. You always in my heart Nada. It's just that I see myself with Shontel. The story has to end somewhere. Give all of the women to kiss Thomas Allred Jr. I can't Amazon queen goddess Michelle Obama. Thomas Allred Jr I'm ordering you to give all of the women a kiss. If Shontel doesn't mind. I will kiss the hand of each lady.

I looked up into her eyes. And my future became clear. Elizabeth I love you. And that is what trapped me inside. My Elizabeth storybook mansion 5. How do you think the story could go. Thomas Allred Jr is in love with all of those women. Try to keep your composure when making a decision for Thomas Allred Jr. You are the richest man in the world Mr.. Thomas Allred Jr. It's only right that we be with you.

Amazon Queen God's. Are you saying that I can be with all of the women. Elizabeth have made her point in her mansion. We all need a man that is above and beyond the call of duty on his job. And Shontel agrees. That the mansion shall be ours. If you communicate to our women. Women I'm prepared to give you. 7500 million dollars a piece. I need to ask you this question though first. Has anybody seen my wife. Keep on going Thomas Allred Jr. Mr. Lebanon Gates. We hold you responsible. For the women's hearts in the USA and surrounding areas. How do you plead Mr. Lebanon Gates. I don't plead anything. You better gimme my contract boy. Porsche came all this way let her talk. You see I have the right to parlay Thomas Allred Jr. People think what a woman wants is too much for her. But every one of us women. Are you looking at you. to see how your storybook Mansion is going to end. Porsche I didn't hurt you did I. You just made me fall in love with you Thomas Allred Jr. And Chelsea and Heather feel the same way. We both feel the same. Ladies can I speak to you for one minute. In the rules of parlay. If a king is overthrown by his Queens. Then that King must follow orders of those Queens. I'm saying once you get with me don't turn back ladies. Our wish is to make you happy Thomas Allred Jr. Well as a trillionaire. I choose to be with an Mary. Every woman and single woman in the United States of America. I'm getting accustomed. Two women wanting to see me. But this is all the issue in. Elizabeth storybook Mansion 5. Have your fun.

Counselor I see you working on our book. Yes Thomas Allred Jr there are some details that are missing from your first Elizabeth's storybook mansion. Thomas Allred Jr just including another woman in this was a stroke of genius. Because Kristen and Shontel are ready to fight for you. See Thomas Allred Jr I told you that the storybook Mansion couldn't handle the fact that you are in love with different women. How many different women did you allow in to the storybook Mansion? Do me a favor and bow down to me. I am your wife for sure . I am called Amazon Queen in time you will realize your purpose inside of this storybook mansion Mr. Thomas Allred Jr. But as for now my name is not important. Counselor if I finish my book before the light comes up.

Will I still have a place in your heart. Listen boy I'm just a by stander in this book. I'm observing the way that you treat the characters in you book . Thomas Allred Jr. Don't believe her she is in to book. And you don't need to prove yourself to anyone. Believe in yourself Thomas Allred Jr . That's all that matters in storybook mansion . Elizabeth I need you. I can't believe in myself without you. Yes you can Thomas Allred Jr you are the creater of this dream that we have here. Nada I love you . Nada isn't here Thomas Allred Jr Elizabeth what do you mean. I see her. She is over there. Nada is another part of the book Thomas Allred Jr. I know that you love Kristen but Kristen is apart of the book to. Shontel .Kay .Kathy .Porsche . Heather. And Chelsea.

They are all apart of you trying to get out of the book. The library can't handle you typing up all of these manuscripts. In the very first Elizabeth storybook Mansion. I listened to you cry over Elizabeth. With all of you heart Thomas Allred Jr you have got to end your book. Thomas Allred Jr. Who is it that helped you out of the storybook Mansion. It was Elizabeth. She helped me with remembering my name is Ebony Buy It. The richest man in storybook Mansion. Nice to know you . Wait a minute councilor. Everybody is accounted for except for you. Was it you that saved me when I trapped myself in side of storybook Mansion. Thomas Allred Jr the book is getting ready to close. What you want me to do. Girl I know you Makia . Finish the storybook Thomas Allred Jr. Thomas Allred Jr just finished with in his Storybook mansion. By creating a bridge. Thomas Allred Jr don't let no one take your book away from you. Makia listen I know that you love me. Thomas Allred Jr Makia is a figment of your imagination. I get you Thomas Allred Jr. You are in love with a lot of women but in the real world you can't have none of them. The storybook Mansion is beginning to close. Jeana I love you. I'm so sorry for your lost Thomas Allred Jr. But I need you to realize that it is a story . All kinds of people are listening. In till I make it . I promise myself that I will continue making Elizabeth storybook Mansion one of the best selling books in history. And the book is now being open. Read about me in my book Elizabeth storybook Mansion. They trapping us in through the pages. How can I get out of this. I'll tell you how you can get out of the book remain confident. You see Evelyn. Elizabeth storybook Mansion is made for every body. I'll do about anything to kiss you women. Thomas Allred Jr the book is now closed. Was it a dream. Thomas Allred Jr asked him self. All you need to do Thomas Allred Jr is pay your shipping and handling. But starting out at humble beginnings responsibility seen everywhere to be a dream killer. Elizabeth yes Thomas Allred Jr . I am here.

Put that book down. And realize your heart. There have been a lot of stories on the inside of these pages. Can't you see that our situation is one for the narrator to finish. You have got to be true . But I am sorry Thomas Allred Jr I am only apart of the book. But I read the the book front to back. I am supposed to have the one woman that I love the most. Elizabeth honey you are the key and the narrator in Elizabeth storybook Mansion 6 .All you have got to do Thomas Allred Jr is start believing in yourself and trusting in your own universe to help you out with this book. Elizabeth I can't keep the book open. Just focus Thomas Allred Jr. Kristen . Ashley. And Shontel. Now I want us to get a place together to where all of my probleMs. are a thing of the past. Elizabeth all of us can live together. You here that girl. Wait until Porsche sees this. Ashley I really love y'all.

Thomas Allred Jr open your mouth and say what you want. I want you to be my wife Ashley. Along with the rest of my female friends. If I got love for you I'm a take good care of you in and outside of my storybook mansion. Elizabeth has the final decision. Thomas Allred Jr you need to choose one of the ladies to love honor and obey. Anyway that's what happened. I was reaching out to a part of me that I could only question. In Elizabeth storybook Mansion. Get my book. Combine all the parts of this book together and you got you a suspense triller. And the only way out of the book is to. Kill the mocking bird. In your heart . Let his postage be cleared. Now the book just needs a hero. The women are the hero in this book. Thomas Allred Jr your time is running out .Yes Heather and Chelsea . You need to turn in that book in. My book ain't got pubic reading just yet. Than what is missing from the story. The man that I own two dollars to. He knows that I got him on my mind. Thomas Allred Jr that's it for the storybook Mansion. The book speaks for itself. Me and Elizabeth will write a new one on our 25th anniversary . Because y'all put me up to this junk. And I'm a speak to Elizabeth about us as soon as the book comes out. Be care Elizabeth storybook Mansion could happen to you. Everyone of my girlfriend's and wives are in love with me. Walk me through it . In a business man imagination. Called storybook Mansion Elizabeth. People are telling me that you and me will never be . Same way with that. The same way my attitude opens up doors for me and you Elizabeth . The mansion is almost through. There's one more woman for me. Maya. This boy has got a lot of people checking out his book. That your time with him. See how professional he is. I got you Raven. But Maya. I like Thomas Allred Jr to. If you want Thomas Allred Jr. You just gotta read Elizabeth storybook Mansion from start to finish. And I'm serious about that book you are reading . Because I am Elizabeth and this is the end of my storybook Mansion. Close the book.

Elizabeth I'm trying to tell you that Thomas Allred Jr is a hustler. I know that he is a hustler Gabriel Union Allred you see what he has done for me. Thomas Allred Jr made your mansion. It was nothing but words on a page. Have Thomas Allred Jr -communicate . With me for a second. For now I see you. As a true hero. The community sees you Thomas Allred Jr. As a true hero to. What I'm trying to say to you is. I want to marry you Thomas Allred Jr. Gabriel Union Allred. You said that if I believed in you. I can have anything that I want in this world. Two more days. And you will be. Outside of the book forever Gabriel. I know my story sounds weird to you. But if you read it it makes perfect sense. You see the book keeps closing. In all these adventures keep happening. With Thomas and my love is doubted. We need love to keep the book open.

Elizabeth I got you a pen. So you can autograph your book for Thomas Allred Jr. I wish that I could see you.Cause for now that storybook Mansion is closed. History if you believe. Listen to me. Nada and Porsche. Don't agree with this book. That is called for. A rebate on the book. What Nada and Porsche believe. Is that when you open the book. You get a picture of our storybook mansion. Elizabeth. Be strong enough. To love a man who put a novel together. And either way it goes the clovers of the book. Remain on your dining room table in your kitchen. Until you open the book. Gabriel. Listen to them people. They are just worried about you. Because once you're in storybook mansion. You are here to stay because we are family.

And Kay. We want to thank you for opening the book. Thomas Allred Jr. You and Gabriel Union Allred shall be happy ever after. Gabriel Union Allred in the book you got me. Is this true love that you're seeking Thomas Allred Jr. Gabriel Union Allred and Thomas Allred Jr. This is our story book mansion. Now you see what the government is. In Elizabeth storybook mansion conclusion. wait don't close the book wait don't close the book. I'm am Jeana Allred Jr. And Thomas Allred Jr is the story book champion. What does all this mean Jeana Allred Jr. You wrote the book on success. How did I write the book on success. By trusting in yourself. If I give in to you Jeana Allred Jr. You would never see me again. Why is that Thomas Allred Jr. Because sweetheart I was making sure that i put you into the story book. A storybook begins with my love for you Jeana Allred Jr. Thomas Allred Jr who you talkin to. I was just talking to Jeana Allred Jr. In My story Land. Jeana Allred Jr is always ok and safe from harm. Okay put the book down for second Thomas Allred Jr. Which woman will you choose to go with you to Hollywood California. I choose Elizabeth. Elizabeth is the queen of Storybook Mansion. And why do you choose her Thomas Allred Jr. I just know that I can trust her through thick and thin. I'm watching you. And so are all the Amazon princesses. Now communicate with Thomas Allred Jr. Or should I say Mr.. Lebanon Gates. May all of the Amazon Women. Get a house. To where I can write a story in it. The conclusion of Elizabeth storybook mansion. Kristen I know you love me. And Ashley I know you care. I love you too. But the work count is almost finished. What are you saying to us Mr.. Lebanon Gates. That it is a book. That is making us feel the way that we feel. We have got to be strong. Enough to realize that the story is now closed. The conclusion of a Elizabeth storybook Mansion is. My world is a better place with you ladies in it. I wish I could marry Elizabeth. Storybook mansion. The Lord said let there be light. Storybook Mansion I Won't Give Up On You. This is dedicated to Jeana Allred Jr. Although you gone but never forgotten. Elizabeth storybook mansion the conclusion. 6 Gabriel Union Allred I want to thank you for being with me throughout my story book mansion. Get it together Thomas Allred Jr you can have anything. Pay for that book Thomas Allred Jr. Yes Gabriel. Now the story is now ending . The thing about Thomas Allred Jr. Is it he's always been professional. Storybook Mansion is my book. And girls I am Elizabeth. Take a note for me. I love my man. Elizabeth hold it down . Thomas Allred Jr I'm doing the best that I can. In Elizabeth storybook Mansion the conclusion part 6.

CHAPTER 15

You kind of famous on here Gabriel Union Allred. I'm only famous because I used you to get to the top. If I had one wish it would be for you to be at the top with me Thomas Allred Jr. I'm releasing you of your contract. Gabriella I'm releasing you. This is Glory town international. In your movie you never said that you were in love with Gabriel Union Allred Thomas Allred Jr. Mr. Lebanon Gates. We have a telegram for you. Who would be sending me a telegram at this hour. The telegram is from Elizabeth. In Elizabeth storybook Mansion. What kind of book are you reading Thomas Allred Jr. The book is called Glory town international. Affiliated with all kinds of other books.

Mr. Lebanon Gates do you want your cup of coffee now. I'm sorry I am Thomas Allred Jr at the moment. That boy has got two days to complete his book and get it to me. Glory town means so many things to me. You mean that it is special Thomas Allred Jr. Don't play with me you hear my a**. If it's not special then what is it. I got to go back so you can understand what Glory town really is. In Glory town the people they do for their self.We trust in you to come around with things good enough for everyone. We chosen you Ebony Buy It. To work off the debt that you acquired. By saving our community. With your fabulous stories that you create. Speak to us Mr. Ebony Buy It. Speak to us. Thomas Allred Jr is Mr. ebony it. It can't be. Now he is Mr.. Lebanon Gates. Mr. Lebanon Gates who are you. I am Mr.. Ebony Buy It. Thomas Allred Jr .Your starting to mess with me. These voices need to change. You're not thinking about Gabriel.Shontel .and Elizabeth. And Kristen. and all the other women that you left in the mansion. You are right and Elizabeth story mansion. I was in the book once the twice before. But nowadays this Glory town international. Look in her eyes you can see that she needs you. If I get professional. Listen to me Thomas Allred Jr. That man is talking to his self. I want you to see just how I've been in love with you. And take me out of the book whenever you need me. Elizabeth take care of yourself.

The More I say. The more I give to you in your storybook mansion. I'm dreaming of. Women have in my book. And women starting to get to know me. As a man who is serious. Confident. In hairstyle in finesse added to him. Who we talking of is. Mr.. Ebony Buy It. Gabriel Union Allred look at me. With you standing by my side. I am now the richest man in the world. Buy a hundred folds. It don't matter who you are Mr.. Ebony Buy It. You always be Thomas Allred Jr. Thomas Allred Jr shut up. Allison what's the meaning of this. Mr.. Ebony Buy It. This is Glory town. And I wanted you to know that I wanted you my whole life. Wanted me for what young lady. Thomas Allred Jr I listen to you speak. And I can manage myself with you. Listen to me Mr. Ebony Buy It. The whole neighborhood loves you. I got to keep my place. That's why I want to ask you. To help the neighborhood grow stronger. Don't you ask a second time Allison. You see the moral of the story is.That I will do the best I can for this contract. It's too many undercover officers in here.Realize we're listening. I got to explane myself to you Allison. There you go. See my rap is .

I'm the richest man in the whole entire face of the continent. Now Edina. She wants this contract to. But there are three of. And Lebanon Gates wants what he wants when he wants it. As for me your contract will be lovely. But Thomas is a particular motherf*cker. He wants to know that you have love in your heart. So you see Kristen. I never cheated. I've only been with three women my whole entire life. I stated to you before sunrise in my cell. That I will fight and make something of myself. For you because I love you so much.

Speaking my book Mr.. Ebony Buy It. Kristen I've been putting together. A dairy catalog. Of my speeches with you. AND SINCE I TOLD YOU I LOVE YOU. My heart has not been the same since. Thomas Allred Jr what are you. A millionaire Trillionaire or billionaire. I'm just a man trying to understand a woman that is love. Glory town means I love women. You are becoming professional. Who is that. That is the storybook mansion. Adding its two cents into the story. There is a evil queen in Storybook Mansion . No there isn't. Now that you confess to love for the ladies. Thomas Allred Jr there's only one other thing to do. Which is. Take your pin out and sign autographs.

We are all listening to you. Captain Thomas Allred Jr of the New York Police department. And NSA. And Secret Service And FBI. So you book is called Glory town. This is the last installment to Elizabeth story Mansion Glory town. That's why. I'm keeping you right here. Be professional. and tell me what the name of my story truly is. It is called Elizabeth storybook mansion a 1000 ladies I love. Kristen I don't want to hurt you. Thomas Allred Jr. Yes Shontel .You have made your commitment to Elizabeth. In Elizabeth storybook mansion. Be professional Thomas Allred Jr. You are the captain of the football team.

That's one thing I just don't understand though.Everyone of these stories have a different ending. It is because I'm in love with Ashley. What does your love have to do with the ending. God is sitting up there looking at me. And I cannot choose any female to be with. Until the judge makes a decision. On how much money I'm getting. I communicate my love to these ladies. In order to understand them .The will always belong to Elizabeth. Listen to me. This is my theory that as long as we have something to strive for. We all will be saved through to the next story. Show us a good time. You need to count your blessings. Queen I am back to you. How'd you put go. Shontel you in my book. Oh I am. Chelsea and Heather. I'm going to take my time and say that I love you. Kathy and Kay. The storybook Mansion is upon us. I can see it I can see sunlight. What you see are cash registers ringing up. Porsche and Nada and Evelyn an Ashley. I'm giving you one chance to tell me you love me before I end the book. Thomas Allred Jr these girls all love you. I know they love me I'm just coping with things. The judge will make his or her decision Thomas Allred Jr. I mean at the start of the storybook mansion. I was running through time to save everyone. Now the business ideas have been laid out there. And all I'm needing is love from the people who I have been fighting safe.

Thomas over hundred thousand women are in love with you now. You need to produce my books. Ain't nobody going to believe me how the story book changed my life in yours. For the last time. I'm in love with Elizabeth. Elizabeth this is your storybook mansion. But that is in the book. As we know that Shontel it's already my queen. So before the books end I want to make one thing clear. What's good for the goose is good for the gander. I'm meaning that. Secret Service agents. A talking about me. I hold this as a trophy. And lift My Queen up through all of the story books. See my queen is you. Every story got me crying at the ending. Talk to me Thomas Allred Jr. And let me know it's going to be okay. In Elizabeth storybook mansion 1000 ladies I love. Thomas Allred Jr you got me all emotional. Working with this book I have. Lost my self-respect for you Thomas Allred Jr. Did I say that I'm splitting the proceeds between the women that i name in his book. Alright we have a deal. I'm going to get my wish after all. Thomas Allred Jr what did you wish for. I wish for a queen like you Emily. Inside of Elizabeth storybook mansion. 1000 ladies I love. Mr.. President. My book is now finished. Thank you for everything sincerely Thomas Allred jr.

I have no money. No friends that want to hang out with me because im out there slinging that dope. The only friend that got with me is my gun and permit. I know what you thinking. He is just a drug dealer. But I'm an undercover police officer. Sanctified and holy. police officers need to take they a** home so somebody can get some sleep. Police officers outta here that boy. What boy are you saying. I'm just saying Joseph that. The community can't stand for this kind of crap no more. The Lord sent you here Thomas Allred Jr. Joseph I want to talk to you. That boy understand me. He's only a child Joseph. Watch over my child Joseph. Smoking a cigarette never seemed so damn good before.

You ready for war for the last time Thomas. Thomas Allred Jr. We need to see you out here on the porch Thomas. We've been getting word for my Mexican crew. That you've been through an ordeal. We're here to show our support Thomas Allred Jr. I seen y'all support. Don't waste your time. Thomas Allred Jr. The polls will give you a slight edge. Make sure the polls won't give me up.Thomas we got your back if you need me. You know he killed your wife. Thomas this world ain't even. Thomas we are police officers and we have nothing at all. While bullsh*ttin a** people get all the riches. Control yourself Ramirez. It's a lot of people around here. The still believe in the police. Listen Joseph listen to Ramirez talkin. Good night Thomas. There is going to come a time that you are going to need me Thomas. I don't care Ramirez. There is people after me. Still i face the day the same as anyone else. This series is going to get you in trouble. How can I get in trouble when they have no trouble to run to. Look at me Thomas you think this is a game. Those people who are after you aren't playing any games. Ramirez. No Conrad. Me and my posse. We out Thomas Allred Jr. Joseph I would like to speak to you. When in doubt let's eat Thomas Allred Jr. I just got a call from Eden Reid the publisher. Her and Cindy. Want to take my book to the next level Joseph. Keep your composure Thomas. You know you are a police officer. And why would you want these things such as the next level. I just got to prove to me that exactly how good I can be. All of needing is a couple hundred dollars a month. The recession is going on. And you asking me for money. Get up from the table Thomas. But I haven't eaten my food yet. Get your a** up from the table and listen. I want you to do the best you can. With your book.

Listen Thomas. a lot of people are seeing you as the commander-in-chief. Take time to read to me your story. It all began. Thomas. Yes Cindy. I know you're sitting at home thinking to yourself. But we are also thankful for you here. You read our manuscript. I did read it Thomas. Show Thomas. We try to be there for each other. Thomas. Get your a** back up there and write that book. Who you talkin to. I'm talking to no one Joseph. So how does your book begin Thomas. Remember we playing for keeps here. Go a head and send off the book. This is a series Joseph. Realize Joseph. I'm going to make my book on my own. I'll get that money that I need to publish our book. Give him his plate that to him. You can have a seat at the table. Where I was sitting at. I know that this. Thomas. May sound as a shock. But folks I am hungry. Listen to me Thomas Allred Jr. Imagine yourself in a white man's community. Breathe in the fresh air that the white man has. It can all be a dream. Or you can make it reality Thomas. I'm calling Ramirez. Thomas don't.

Let's just enjoy the night. Why Miss Pamela. Ramirez is a person that gets things done. That's the reason why I keep on trusting him. Thomas. Did you hear what that girl told you. Listen Thomas Allred Jr. Ramirez is a good cop. But as innocent as you are you don't need no blood on your hands. That fool out the crazy Thomas Allred Jr. Prove to yourself that you're somebody. You've already been shot write your book. For Jeana sake. What we going to do Thomas. Is make you into a role model. Now I know that they killed Jeana and shot you. But it has been years since that has happened. You know Jeana wanted you to write your book Thomas Allred Jr. You cannot never give up. You have to keep striving. With every bit of fear anger in love that is inside of you you must keep trying. It seeMs. like you will never make it it seeMs. like no one will ever care about you. It seeMs. like all your work is for nothing. Joseph Man. No Thomas. With the Lord all things are possible. And I am praying right now. That these children would lay down their guns and go home and be a family again. You are smarter than I thought you were Joseph. Thomas I'm just a man. I figured out you. What did you figure out all I'm trying to do is Joseph. Is have something for myself and breathe. Pamela give me something to drink out of refrigerator. Yes my husband Joseph. So tell me where you staying these days Thomas Allred Jr. I'm sleeping in the back room at my mom's house. You still aren't seeing anyone after all these years. No Joseph you know me. Thomas has been nearly 20 years you have to let Jeana go. I could never do that and you know it Joseph. Then you might as well be dead then Thomas. God brought you to my house tonight. To tell you young man that everything is going to be alright. Joseph not now not the time. This is the time Kristen. Come to the kitchen while we pray. Yes Daddy I'm here. Kristen you know Thomas don't you. Yes father I know of him. That boy can communicate. Speak the word into his are Kristen. Give that man a new life. What are you trying to tell me Joseph. Thomas we got your book printed. Think about this. I know that you see me as. A father figure Thomas Allred Jr. But I am Jesus Christ. Your lord and savior. And it's going to be alright Thomas Allred Jr. Thank you Lord. Because I have nothing and no one. All I have is pain Trust and Believe. I need You Jesus to come into my life it stayed here and guide me forevermore. Thomas go to sleep. Now send in a copy of your book.

We put together. People and resources. All kinds of things start to happen. All kinds of things Thomas Allred Jr. Ramirez appreciate you for looking out for me. Thomas Allred Jr I will do anything to help you understand that. As long as we have each other we're unstoppable. Wait a second. Is this a dream I'm dreaming. Keep on writing your book Thomas Allred Jr. I Thank you for not giving up on me. Lord I need your help right now. I came from nothing and I'm a police officer. And now Lord I'm injured and I'm hurt. And someone has killed Jeana. My wife and soulmate. This is Valentine's Day. And I get myself together by writing you Lord. I won't give up I won't quit. I keep on trusting in the opinions of my people. I keep on hoping for a better day.

I see people together in love. And it drives me to be a better man. Even though the fact is I have no one and no children. Jesus allowed me the strength to make it. Because I know without you there is no way. Go ahead Thomas Allred Jr. Let it all out. Thank you Ramirez for guiding me. Thank you Ramirez. Thank you Ramirez. Thank you Ramirez. Go on back to Jesus Thomas Allred Jr. God I need you. I can't get through the struggles without you Jesus. As long as I write this book I feel like I've done something. Damn boy that shot a police officer. If crying is what you want to do Thomas Allred Jr. Then I will cry with you. But we are working on that book.

Night and day. Providing you with help. Because we realize. How much it means to you Thomas Allred Jr. Do you hear me Thomas Allred Jr. Just do your work in. And we will handle the rest. This is your team. Im a get you a professional Thomas Allred Jr. Thomas Allred Jr we told you that in time will be here when you need us. That's all we do. Is take care of our people. Don't fear because things have happened to you. Just enjoy the life you have. Thomas Allred Jr we are going to look out for you. Here is what I want you to do for me. Take you a bath Thomas Allred Jr. And go to f*cking sleep Thomas Allred Jr. We have got this from here. Thank you so much. Now go to sleep. And send the message in. You got to appreciate Thomas Allred Jr. I'm ready to take you off of the street corners.

You have done a job well done. Listen to me Thomas Allred Jr. What I got to say is. Is that you and Jeana. Is two police officers. That the Lord has gave. This time you write your book. Tell the truth how you feel. Look I am so hurt yall. I know exactly what you're feeling is exactly what your needing. Thomas Allred Jr. Check it out. Ramirez is Kristen Beam. But how. We all realize that you love Kristen Thomas Allred Jr. Thank you so much man. Look I love yall so much. Thomas Allred Jr. Yes God. You have got to send you a book in. Okay Jesus but thank you for all of your blessings and everything that you've ever done for everyone we love you so much. Thank you for my girl Kristen Beam Lord. I tried to make a difference in her life. Send your book in Thomas

She was unlike nobody i ever seen before. My miracle woman was calling to me in my dreaMs.. Thomas you ain't got to do nothing but write your stories down. My stories this is what I told my miracle woman in my dream. Your stories Thomas. Write your stories down my miracle woman said to me. I hear what you saying to me but I do live with somebody.

Thomas if I have to tell you again to write your stories down I'm going to kick your a**. Skip being polite this woman thinks I'm after her. You got to wake your a** up they trying to give you a contract with Shontel. Said the dream to me. One more minute and I'll get up I told the dream lady. Get your a** up over here Thomas and write that book. Okay I'm up famous. Be careful what you say Thomas it is a dream. Miracle amazing Love that is what I call my dream. They already heard about me writing another story. Set the time on this story. Thomas keep working on your book I can visit you in my dreaMs..

What you going to do Thomas write a book or play games. I'm going to write my book. The once was a man named Thomas. And he was so in love with his girlfriend Shontel. Seeing the Thomas had been through everything that a man could go through. The Law decided to issue him a wife. As scared as Thomas was. Of Shontel when he first met her. That girl looked after Thomas. And now he's a trillionaire writing books all over the world. But I have to tell you where the story starts. It starts with Thomas Allred Jr down-on-his-luck . Even though Thomas day was starting off badly. Thomas could see the future before anybody else. Happy birthday he told Shontel when he met her. In destiny we all fight for what's ours. Thomas said to her as she came into the household of writers and inventors. Each day is a test Thomas Jr. Your book won't magically make it self happen. Clock the two of them. She is more famous than he is. A man and woman book writing team. This is never happened to me before. What has never happened to you before Thomas Allred Jr. You might not believe me but I could see the future Shontel. Thomas it's okay I believe you. But why would you believe me if you don't know me Shontel. I also see the future. The aftermath of things to come. You see the beginning of what happens. How did you know I didn't tell anybody Shontel. In each Stone of my ring lies a Ruby Thomas Allred.

Give that boy his contract. He is writing his book. He deserves to make a movie out of this. You have got to appreciate me Thomas Allred Jr. Shontel i ain't never heard nobody say the things like you. You better get that book and write it. Girl I'm thinking about you. I am the lady in your dreaMs.. And this is miracle amazing Love equal love. Straighten out that book as we go Thomas. You got Shontel working for you on your book. Just relax yourself and let your dream happened to you not for you. Thomas Allred. The three ghosts of Christmas past present and future are here to see you. Yes how may I help you. What kind of story is this. This story is a f*cking miracle. How many people are in your story Thomas. I need a sheet of paper. Shontel can you give me a sheet of paper off of the desk in our apartment building room.

I'll give you the paper that you asked for Thomas Allred Jr write your book. You got sense enough the enter your story about us. What do you want Thomas. I want for my friends and family to stop working and have what they dream. Your second wish is Thomas I want the chains off of each one of you. That professional let us go. Take the chains off of the movie set. There is not that much charge to your phone Thomas. My third wish is that me and Shontel live happily happily ever after in the castle far far away.

Thomas you are a trillionaire. All I got to do is snap my fingers. And the series has begun. Snap. We talking about you Thomas Allred Jr. Running the entire cable access unit. My girl need me. Shontel is pregnant Thomas Jr. Thomas you need to wake up your book is about to stop. Can we go a little farther dream lady. No Thomas we are going to have to charge your phone. Tell your publicist Cindy. That you got a new book coming out. And that this is the beginning of a series sequel. Call miracle amazing Love. Equal love Thomas. I'm waiting on Cindy to call me. That is my home until the next generation gets here.

Do not say nothing about Shontel. Be a man Thomas Allred Jr. You are so creative. That we all want to sign you. You are kind of person Thomas. Watch it come true there it is. Your dream of marrying Shontel will now come true for you. For your work. I can't believe this this a miracle. Thomas this is amazing love the sequel. So Shontel do you really want me to get out of bed right now. Listen that girl is tired.

Write your book Thomas that is all I want you to do. Do you see it Thomas. It sounds like amazing love to me. That boy good as hell. You hear me Thomas. Chapter one is almost over. I'm putting you in charge of your destiny.Shontel you don't mean. Read your book. You paid $200 for that book. You better get your money's worth out of it. And I could tell that she love me. Because we each could see the future. And somehow I knew that she would be my wife. That's with no money and no cars. See the future is funny. You can see what you will be and what you will have. All I did was stuff from nothing and believe in love. The first installment of miracle amazing Love equal love is about to be finished. I dedicate this book to the struggle. Out in Japan. Say In the struggle out in Japan Thomas. So this is the beginning of our series. We ain't gotta prove nothing to you. It's going to be a bumpy ride right here. Thomas yes Shontel. Tell them how we first met. It all begins. In a TV episode called miracle amazing Love. We were two contestants. Playing for big money. Y'all how we going to be Thomas. The boy is too good. I can tell you. Inside the book is a sequel. Send off that book to your publisher. And start on your next sequel. Send off the book

I would like for you to welcome me. To this wonderful book called being professional by Thomas Allred Jr. You see the stars comments are my generation. I'm proud of you Thomas Allred Jr. For accomplishing a book handle your business. Imma take a second. To remember y'all. The times when I didn't have nothing at all. Now imma take a second. And forget it yall. Because the way I look at it. It was a struggle that made me the man that I am today. I can remember. Sitting there in my room. In the middle of December. Writing my book with tears in my eyes. All that I kept thinking about. Is God. And that I couldn't quit. You see ladies and gentlemen. Back then. I never knew or not. If I would become successful. All I knew was the struggle. And I kept my belief in people. My belief in people means that. I just had to keep the Fate y'all. Until this day. February 29th 2020. I didn't believe that I could be anybody. What I'm saying is ladies and gentlemen. I didn't think that I myself could be anybody. Or that I was anybody worthwhile. People will believe in you once you show them that you believe in yourself. This book is called Being professional by Thomas Allred Jr. Fast forward into the future. After all I've been through you're still here with me.

The number one bestseller on Forbes list is. The truth about the number one bestseller. Written by Thomas Allred Jr. But see y'all that is the future. One book at a time. Is what my grandpa used to tell me. Sitting around Spade table. Eating watermelon. And drinking white liquor. You see I was a kid. When my grandfather raised me but he was a smart man. Save your money Thomas. He always used to tell me. The problem is. I never had any money to save. I do anything for help. See I'm letting you see the inside of me.

The professional side of me. Crave's the attention of the world. To go on my shoulders. As an eagle with wind would fly. I just hope that all of you. Pay attention to my book. Hello Cindy. Hello everybody. I'm going to take this journey here with you. I'm trying to get married. Most of these women already know I'm famous. And for those who don't. I'm introducing myself. As an officer of law enforcement. My name is Officer Reign. Code name Superman for the NSA and the FBI the Secret Service is with me right now my given name is Thomas Allred Jr. And this is my story. It all began at me being left at the hospital as a baby . America things were not that bad. I mean I did get my a** whooped. By my whole community. But my community love me. That was the reason for the a** whoopins . Your see girl see. A man for strength. You can put all the strength you want to on the inside of this book. And it still wouldn't fill up the pages. Have common sense. What women are looking for these days. Is a role model. Someone they can laugh with talk to and enjoy the company there of. Now what I show you these things. Is that my intellect far surpa**es anything that you can imagine or ever have known. Sometimes I believe that I struggled for so long. In order to make it big with my family here with me. And other times I think the must struggle was a cause of me just not learning my lessons. People I don't care what you say. Being professional is about. Self confidence and self pride.

What I'm saying ladies and gentlemen. Y'all got to take care of yourself. And take care of your loved ones. No one on TV is going to put it down like this. You get the real uncut reality from Thomas Allred hiMs.elf. I tried to tell my wife to be that I was going to be famous. But do you want to know what kept happening to me. the rent kept coming due the light bill kept coming due the car payment kept coming due food for the house washing clothes powders. It all kept coming due at the same time. Every month every year every decade the bills where due. Now I'm not trying to put you to sleep. What I had to do was. I mean about the bills coming due. I prayed long and hard. Because there was no way that her and I alone could keep up with this. It got so bad ladies and gentlemen. That me and my lady we had to cry a lot of nights. That's about the time.

That's about the time that I felt like our community came together as one. Now I am only a police officer. Within sight. To how things were for me growing up as a kid. So all I'm saying is. We can make it if we try y'all. There has got to be somebody that believe in a better day. I mean there's got to be somebody. That just won't give up until the end. Now I'm trying to be nobody's role model. I'm just telling the truth as I see it. if this is going to put food on my table and pay the bills for my wife and myself . Than I'm a tell it. I'm a police officer all I know is the truth. Ladies and gentlemen some people don't belong in our communities. Ladies and gentlemen listen to me for a minute. Some females have a problem that they can't get rid of. Is anybody feeling me out there.

Some of these people belong in prison. And I'm going to tell it and I'm going to say it weather you like it or not. Now I'm not saying that I'm better than anybody else. But I believe in education. The education system is the best thing on the planet.

Besides Grandma's grits and eggs. Yall we got to start defending these ladies. Start defending these females. Look at it like this ladies and gentlemen. Female to female. Ask yourself. Are you satisfied with the relationship that you are in? And is the dude that you are sleeping with a crazy mother f*cker. That you are scared to leave. See fellows what I'm saying is. Given one opportunity. These ladies will make the right choice for the better. So you can threaten tomorrow that you want to. Every since I was a kid my momma was beating down. By her ex-boyfriend . Y'all I'm a cop today. A look I'm going to change the direction of the story. And come back to this. Because you know what's going down stays down.Or is that just where I come from. My home was always North Carolina. They beat my a** yall. But they made it tougher man out of me. I remember those Ford commercials. I used to tell people I was built Ford tough. Ladies and gentlemen I'm still tough today. But I'm also educated. Being professional by Thomas Allred Jr. Is a book that solved cases. like what are we going to do when people are afraid to leave there houses. These people know I care about them. You see I'm working on business ideas. To save the life of my brothers and sisters all over the world. I'm being watched by the federal government. But I remain the police officer that I am. I'm calling on y'all. To raise the standard in your household's. We must do more than stay strong. Yall we got to keep believing in one another.

My grandpa used to tell me every time that I would mess up in the house to tear it down. That's all he would say is tear it down. Back then I didn't understand him because I was a kid. What he was trying to say to me because he had a stroke and he couldn't talk. He was trying to say that he loved me so much that he didn't care if I tore the damn house down. My grandfather is gone. And I love you so much Pete Harper. Now ladies and gentlemen it's a new day. You see I don't talk to that many people. Because some people feel like you have nothing to say. I carried this pride on my shoulders. I am cold name Superman by the NSA. I am a part of the FBI and the Secret Service.

I belong to the New York Police department. I have no kids and I'm about to get married. And this is my 27th book that I've written. Being professional for me Thomas Allred Jr. Is tackling all of the tasks that set out to do when I was a kid. Ladies and gentlemen you can remember. How you used to say you wanted something so bad when you were a kid. All I'm saying to you is. Listen to me. This is a start of a new generation. I want you to condition yourself. To love yourself and your surroundings.

You see people don't tell you these things because they don't care about you. I tell you these things because you are my brothers and my sisters and I love you. I know my book is going to have to be a lot better than this. Listen my lady name is Shontel. And I am a motivational speaker. I'm trying to show you the way to your future before you even get there. All I'm seeing Is the destiny is awaiting you. if you folks can just believe in yourself a little while longer. I believe that God is going to bless us all. And I keep getting commands from a higher power. Some would say it's an injustice. That I get treated so good and I love myself so much. But people you have to believe. And you have to know. That I came up from the sidewalk. To be a police officer a motivational speaker and one day be a husband. See I care about you. That's why I tell you if you keep trying and you never quit. Something has got to give. We can't keep doing the same things everyday. If we do another decade will pa**. Nah people this time we getting busy. We taking every opportunity that I'm given. We going to fight to the end. I feel like one of those coaches in the colleges that you see on movies. you know the ones that tell you that it take true grit to make it. What you see now is not a show. This is this is not a film. A clip or a rerun. People I'm trying to tell you that you got to be happy. God is with you. And as long as you know that God is with you.

You can make it through any test and any struggle. No matter how hard it gets. I am right here with you. Telling you ladies and gentlemen. To come on. To be strong. And to not give up. See some of you ain't had nothing to your names. You ain't have sh*t to worry about. But I'm here to tell you. That if you can trust in yourself. The way that you can trust in your spouse. I'm going to help you. And you probably saying. He how is he going to help me. Ladies and gentlemen I'm a trillionaire. I'm just waiting on the judge's decision. See I listen to y'all on the daily. This book is professional. And when I listen to y'all. I see a people that's hungry. I see a people that's thirsty for knowledge. I see my brothers and sisters doing whatever it takes to make it. Cause what's the name of the game y'all. Monopoly. Some of you only need to capitalize a few more steps on your investment I capitalize with this book right here.

Capitalizing on your investment just means. Stay care free. I'm going to talk to these people man. See before I wake up in the morning every morning. I try to thank God that night before. I'm blessed to have people who love me. I am blessed to have friends who care about my well-being. did I tell you even though I sleep on the streets 3 nights in my life I have never been homeless not one day. Now that's God. I've lived through hectic situations. That the people would be afraid of. But I still keep trying. I keep holding on. And if I could do it then you can do it. You are my brothers and my sisters. God has me here to tell you. Just don't give up. Now I'm not speaking about a job. I'm not even speaking about your career. I am Thomas Allred Jr and what we talkin about is life. Is children out here that need our help. If you don't think you got a reason to go on there you go.

Its Ladies that's stuck in apartments. That cry to God everyday for help. Ladies and gentlemen do you hear what I'm saying. These women need our help. It's not that they don't believe in there selves. All it is is the journey is to struggle. Too many struggles for that woman becomes a journey. And no one knows what God has planned for them. Coming up in the streets of Hickory North Carolina. I found it if you. Keep your promises and keep your word when you say you're going to do something. That people will help you. All my life I tried to get through to you. It took me common sense. And the longing for one to be somebody. To have something. To want to know someone. To keep believing in God. I had to keep believing in myself. See the jails and the prisons I've been there. As a cop undercover. I've also been to the hospital. As a cop wounded in battle. See you can humor me if you want to. you can even tell yourself that my book isn't good. But I know my people and I know my God. God said that he will never leave nor forsake me or you. We are here in this world together. I'm not trying to leave you ladies and gentlemen. Keep it professional ladies and gentlemen. Being professional by Thomas Allred Jr. Is about suffering to have some thing. Because people most likely. You are going to go through some horrific struggle. In order to make it. And would God the only way to pa** your test is fate. Fate is the will and determination next to your heart. All kind of people want it. But real fate comes from inside and individual. I walked the streets up in hildebran NC. For a cigarette and something to drink. I no longer have those addictions. I'm telling you today folks. Sometimes it will get hard. Some people will try to use you. But after you give all you had to give. Till there is nothing left. That's when you'll find an angel. See God said it. Become professional. You can move mountains with the faith of a mustard seed. Ladies and gentlemen. For God so loved the world that he gave his only begotten son that whosoever believeth in him shall not perish but have everlasting life. Now you see the I believe in something. Now you see that I won't give up for some reason. Ladies and gentlemen the power lies within you. You don't know how strong you are until you have Jesus in your life. I tried my best. Just to make ends meet so I can get married. To my beautiful girlfriend. I know exactly what you going through. You got to have faith in me. If I can do it you can do it one day at a time. The faith of a mustard seed. I drop it down in this book. To let every city in every continent know. I am here only because of my Lord and Savior Jesus Christ. Is true that I never give up. And I believe ladies and gentlemen. That you never give up alone with me. To undercover police officer to a motivational speaker. I speak to you heart people when I tell you that I think of this as a new beginning. See look I'm not afraid of what y'all think of me. My only fear is getting judge by my peers. In a court of law. I can do all things with Jesus Christ who strengthens me. I'm going to capture my book. And get married. To my beautiful girlfriend. The end.

CHAPTER 16

Thomas how you doing this. Controlling yourself. And writing more than one book at the same time. When you hungry you don't have a choice Shontel. I see my future right in front of me Thomas. Is it me that you're looking for Shontel. Thomas I am looking for a man that will take charge of everything. I am looking for a person that will love me till the end of time. Take your shirt off and let me look at you Thomas. My dream girl ask me a question. See even though this is a dream come true. I want to know are you a dream or fantasy Shontel. I am anything that you want me to be. Thomas believe me I can see the aftermath of the future. Where will I be in 10 years Shontel. Talk to me a little more lingo. Is our future bright with you and me together Shontel. Thomas I'm still going to need some more lingo your future and my future is okay. It happens that. I can do anything that I want in this story. Thomas Allred Jr. Girl when I started my book. I didn't know what to say to nobody. You are my future and my life Shontel. I tried to tell you.

That I need you. In and outside of my dream. Just write your book Thomas Allred Jr. I thank you Shontel. For what reason Thomas Allred Jr. It's because you give me the motivation to go on. My dream wife. I salute you out here. Thomas netter we have talked. Be sincere about me and that book. Put in an hour. On your book Thomas Allred Jr. Who are you anyway. And my dream lady said. I am your secret lover. One more day. And your dreaMs. will come true. I'm trying the best that I know how Shontel. Honey I need this more than anything. Write that f*cking book Thomas Allred Jr. But I don't know if I'm asleep or awake Shontel. You need to write the motherf*cking book. My dream lady kept saying to me. Thomas Allred Jr. There is more to the story than just the book. What are you saying my dream lady. Your community is hoping for you to break through the commercial level that you are on. Shontel what makes a book of champion. Keep on writing your book Thomas Allred Jr. But I'm getting sick of this. I keep writing and I keep writing. But it seeMs. as if nothing is happening. Thomas Allred Jr the future is yours not mine. All I want you to do is keep writing. Shontel I'm a end up marrying you. Don't you see that I love you Shontel. You can't compute. I did compute Thomas Allred Jr.

Still the fact remain the same that you need to write the book. What do you want for yourself after the book is finished Thomas Allred Jr. To take my family out of the hood. You got your wish granted. What do you mean Shontel. I mean that you must write your book Thomas Allred Jr. I did write my book here go a rough copy. Listen to me Thomas Allred Jr. The wording is not strong enough. Go back in there and try again. I already have Shontel. Thomas Allred Jr listen to me try to write your book again. In my dreaMs. this woman was on me. My dream lady I need you to help me write my book. First you ask me for help. And then you tell me you're tired that you don't want to write. My dream Lady this is the future. I can see you like overtime. Is the book called romance for you. Thomas you need to keep it simple and plain. This is miracle amazing love. Romance chapter 2. Some people think it's a game Thomas Allred Jr. Tell the people. That I do the best I can for all of them. Lead the way Thomas Allred Jr. Shontel I'm up here. What difference does it make if you're on the bottom or on the top Thomas Allred Jr. Room and space square footage Shontel. I'm a trillionaire. That don't mean that I don't love you Thomas Allred Jr. Come on Shontel this book has got to be the best. Go professional I am your sweetheart sweetie. All you need is a meaning to your book. Love is the meaning Shontel. What about this love makes your book stand out professional Thomas Allred Jr. Listen Shontel.

I know you are a dream woman. But over time you will recognize my love for you. Thomas Allred Jr. I know that you love me. Y'all better put this man some where that he can't be hurt. Look at this. Thanks and because of you Shontel all kind of people are listening to me. See now honey. I am a police officer. And I am a part of the NSA and FBI and Secret Service. I'm code name Superman. And the New York Police department recruited me. What are you here for Thomas Allred Jr. I do mean Superman.

I am a women's victiMs. rights advocate. In other words I'm here to help my people. Is this a part of your book. Or are we talkin reality Thomas Allred Jr. We are talking reality dream lady. I wrote my book for the purpose of helping people. Write your book Thomas Allred Jr. Dream lady you going to teach me how. Guess what she said to me. I need you to write your book Thomas Allred Jr. Because you make me. Want to come out of your dream and be a real lady. You need to come out of my dream. I have a question. Where were you when I needed you the most dream woman. I was right by your side Thomas Allred Jr. This is my story. A miracle amazing Love. Romance chapter 2. Sequel volume two.

Don't forget me when your book comes out. I won't forget you my dream woman. Go to sleep Thomas Allred Jr. I thought I was asleep my dream woman. Kneel down and kiss my ring Thomas Allred Jr. Okay my dream woman. I will kneel down and kiss your ring. now you realize Thomas Allred Jr. Now I realize what dream woman. Your respect for a woman is what makes your dreaMs. come true. I know you are waiting for your book to come out. But be patient. It will come out. And it will be colossal. Sort of like Jack and the beanstalk. Because of You Thomas Allred Jr. I never lost my heart. And I know with anything inside. That I will always be your woman. Even though I'm Just Your Dream woman. In my dreaMs. I think of you. Come on this book has got to be colossal. What more can I offer you Thomas Allred Jr. I want you to write. That this is my dream. And there is no dream like it. I will protect my dream. Thomas do you understand what I'm saying to you. At the your book comes out. You will be done have proven yourself. to be worthy along with all the other professionals in the world. Always saying to you Thomas Allred Jr is. Do you want it as bad as you say you do. Take a chair in there with you. Sit down in it and write a book of romance. Third chapter. Of the sequel volume three. But we must finish off this the second chapter . Thomas Allred Jr are you a lightweight. It makes no sense. This is my contract. And I swear to God I choose you before anyone else Shontel. Take your time and take him out the hood. He is ready to meet his dream woman. All he needs is. Give him a place. And the book will happen. Miracle amazing Love. Romance chapter 2 sequel volume two. Thomas Allred Jr I respect you. And you have my vote and opinion. I want Thomas Allred Jr. To have anything he wants to. It has earned it. In his book called sacrifice. I told you I can see the future. Send in your story Thomas. Yes my dream woman. Send in your story right f*cking now.

I ain't giving up. Shontel something is wrong with this boy. Every time I look at him. He talks to his self. What kind of dream is that boy having Shontel. Go ahead and dream Thomas Allred Jr. You are getting ready to reach the plateau of this game. Don't make a fool of yourself. Continue to work on your book. Eden Reid and Cindy are all-time favorites in my book. I loved you since I met you Shontel. Thomas remember this is the future. And I see past you. Shontel honey I got hope. And I believe in myself. What I'm saying is. That I'm working daily. Thomas Allred Jr. Your book isn't going to write itself. The book isn't going to write itself Shontel. But why is my book so important anyway.

I'm just a single man out here in the world. Shontel honey I need you. To make the difference in my life. Thomas Allred Jr I am the difference in your life. I want for you to enjoy all the success that life can give you. This is my reason for asking you to write your book Thomas Allred Jr. They going to read it. Yes Thomas people will read your book. But Shontel if this is not a dream then where are we. You are in a book report Thomas Allred Jr. And the better you do Thomas Allred Jr. The more prestige you have. I mean that. Your time is coming Thomas Allred Jr. Time for you to write down. Miracle amazing Love chapter 3 girl I ain't giving up. In your book report Thomas Allred Jr. All you got to do Thomas Allred Jr. Is fly straight. And your world will change around you.

I'm listening to you Shontel. Sometimes I don't know what to think. Before you get mad at me. I gave up a dream.Of Becoming a recording artist. Even though my destiny. Has done me this way. I want you to see now Shontel. My dream woman. That I would never give up ever again. I know you won't give up Thomas Allred Jr. Because I am here with you Thomas Allred Jr. I'm thinking about the first time I laid eyes on you Shontel. I can't believe you grown so beautiful. In my dreaMs. I say these things to you. You make me feel like I can do anything with you by my side. All you need is a dream. And the will to make it happen Thomas Allred Jr. Its visitation time. Do you want visitation Thomas Allred Jr. For what if I sit right here and write my book. It is a possibility that my dreaMs. could come true. Shontel you can see the future. Will our dreaMs. come true. When I write this book. The sure will Thomas Allred Jr. You to stay focused on the fact. What do you stand for Thomas Allred Jr. I stand for Hope and mercy Shontel my dream woman. It is a dream that you are having now Thomas Allred Jr. If this is a dream than Shontel you still are beautiful. Your beauty runs deep.

Listen Thomas Allred Jr. You have already proven yourself. In other books. Will you stop playing games with me. And tell the genie what you want from me. Shontel I want you to be my wife. Shontel were did you go. I'm right here. My God you are lovely Shontel. You are a princess in my dreaMs. Shontel. I am your dream woman Thomas Allred Jr. And that book is not going to write itself. Be careful you need me too much Thomas Allred Jr. I know that it seeMs. like I need you too much. But I dream about you Shontel. Every night. And every morning at the horizon. Think of your own book. Out in the world Thomas Allred Jr. What I did for you. I don't do for anybody. Make it up to me.

Shontel you see. I will make it up to you. In time. My book and I. Will come to the whole community. But what I would like to know is. Is this a dream Shontel. Thomas Allred Jr you are completely awake. You better not give up Thomas Allred Jr. A man is judged for his character. I have fought too many battles over you Shontel. Thomas Allred Jr stop going into the past. I told you that I see the future. I see the future as well Shontel. Thomas Allred Jr write your book. I'm sitting down at the table right now. You need to write your book in a dream. I'm saying that I can't do it without you Shontel. I'm saying that you are my everything. Listen I'm getting ready to tell you something. That I'm pregnant because of you. Thomas Allred Jr. Will you stand with me. Shontel listen to me. Girl I need you to be my business partner and my soulmate.

I hustle to make our lives better. And I'm waiting on you to make our dreaMs. come true. Now that was good. Your character has to be impeccable Thomas Allred Jr. For the audience to love you. You have to redefine me and you. Thomas Allred Jr this is the time approaches. For you to tell me. Miracle amazing love chapter 3 girl I ain't giving up volume three. There is something about Thomas Allred Jr I just can't put my finger on. I need a second to read his book. Sit back and listen as I read this aloud. She came to me in my dream.

Before I had a chance to meet her in the real world. And somehow she knew that I could see the future. Because she told me that she could see the future to only father than I could. I tried to understand this she is an angel. And by her seeing the future she knew I was only a man. It was up to my dreaMs. to get me out of this situation. I need to talk to Shontel. That is my wife and soulmate. Honey this book is dedicated to you. Because through it all Shontel you have always been the woman of my dreaMs.. Step your game up Thomas Allred Jr. I am going for the best seller list. I am sitting here writing a book. In my dreaMs. Shontel. I knew that you could do it Thomas Allred Jr. Don't give up keep going. Listen I am only a man. That is in love with a beautiful woman. This book is also dedicated to our community. Shontel in my heart girl I know it's you. I'm trying to express myself the best way I know how. I have two questions for you Shontel. One is. Cute faces all over the place believe in you and me. Should I be worried about you. Give up the games Thomas Allred Jr. And continue to write your book. My other question is Shontel. Will you change when money come into your life. To a certain extent yes. That is all the questions that I got for you honey. Thomas your book is coming to a close. This is miracle amazing Love chapter 3 girl I ain't giving up volume three sequel. Chapter 3 is just now closing. Thomas Allred Jr and write more into the book. On my behalf. I would like to thank my city. And I appreciate everyone of you. Thank you. Send the goddamn book off.

I'm telling you Ms. Eden Allred and Ms. Cindy. Can't you see Thomas Allred Jr is a professional. Shontel Thomas Allred Jr is the one that wrote the book. Ms. Cindy I know that Thomas Allred Jr wrote the book. But what I'm trying to tell you is he is in love with me. Now hold on Shontel. Ms. Gabriel Union Allred. I brought you in here from another book. I am his true wife Shontel. Maybe in the book you are Ms. Gabriel Union Allred. But in the real world. Thomas Allred Jr and I are about to get married. That b*tch. Keep it under control.

I am that b*tch Ms. Gabriel Union Allred. And Ms. Eden Allred. But all my life I have waited for this man. And you three are not going to steal my joy. Listen here Shontel Thomas Allred Jr and me. Are in love with each other. That is a book love Ms. Gabriel Union Allred. Ms. Cindy can you play footage of Thomas Allred Jr and I kissing. Thomas Allred Jr write your book. Don't try to make a movie out of it. Just try your best to be yourself in it.

My dream woman Ms. Gabriel Union Allred. How are you sweetheart. Thomas I am here for you. My other f*cking Dream woman Shontel Allred. Honey I told you that we were going to write a book that would last. I'm afraid for you Thomas Allred Jr. I'm the same way Thomas Allred Jr. Eden Allred said that I can get published. That's what a Trillionaire status here is like. Realize this is Gabriel Union Allred that you're speaking to. You need to also realize. Reading your book Thomas Allred Jr. Where will it stop. The game that you are trying to play. Because we can see through all the games Mr. Thomas Allred Jr. And you need to be straight up with us woman. Yes Thomas Allred Jr who is it that you love.

I hold a flame for all of the women in the United States of America. knows that I am sincere. About my books. Gabriel Union Allred my interest is in you. Because you helped me through task upon task. And you have proven yourself to be a great lady. Shontel Allred my interest is in you also. Because the strip that you have showed me. Makes you a leading force in my life. Ms. Eden Allred my interest is in you. I talk to you when I was down and going through something. You pick me up with your kind words and demeanor. Now Cindy I am emotional. But my interest is in you Ms. Cindy I'm testing females all around the world. You know I can't. Be strong Cindy. Yes Shontel. This is real love that he is speaking. If Thomas Allred Jr is in need of our contracts. Then let it be known that we all shall be his wives. Thomas Allred Jr. Wake up. Thomas Allred Jr wake up and clean up the house. Of course Kristen Allred. Thomas Allred Jr that book is more important to you than me. Honey I'm doing the best I can for you Kristen. Kristen. Who is Kristen Thomas. I'm sorry I meant Tonette. So that's how you going to do me. My dream woman I told you that I'll be faithful from the gate. Than look in the mirror Thomas Allred Jr and tell me who I am. You are my beautiful wife Shontel. Baby I was asleep. I had a dream you would say that.

So now that I'm out the dream. Definitely tell me what do you want me to do. Thomas Allred Jr. I need for you to write your book. Every time I see you. I want for you to write your books. You need a dream God. And I'm the right person for you Thomas Allred Jr. is saying. that you are getting more in-depth with your books Thomas Allred Jr. And Time magazine. It's just corners away from you. Have you no sense of pride. Tell Gabriel Union Allred and tell Eden Allred and Ms. Cindy to Thomas Allred Jr. That you are definitely proud of them. See what we have here is not a game. This is your life and your future Thomas Allred Jr. Make it what you want to make it into. A wise man once told me. The journey of a thousand Miles begins with one step.

Thomas Allred Jr we have been trying to help you. Write your books is one thing. But you need to pay the cost to be the boss. And that is where you are headed. Mr. Thomas Allred Jr. Shontel thank you. This is miracle amazing Love chapter 4 volume four real love the sequel. And if you don't got no more to say Thomas Allred Jr. I'm watching you. Ms. Cindy. honey I'm a need my bills and my family bills taken care of for the rest of our life. When you publish this book. I would like to shake the hand of the team doing an awesome job. As we sit here and speak. My dream woman pushes me on. Time for me to speak. You don't understand who I am Thomas Allred Jr. Tonette Allred you are my wife and My Queen. Thomas you are allowed to have 21 women.

To live with you. My destiny is being fulfilled. I got love for them 21 women. But where will I stay I need a mansion big enough. At Carolina Beach. Thomas Allred Jr don't you know. That if you keep working at your pace. You will be able to have whatever you want in outside of the year.our team don't play no games do we. Now do you want to 21 women. To stay with you in Carolina Beach. Just give us the order. Yes I do want my 21 woman. To have and to hold. In sickness and in health. From this day forth. Ms. Eden Allred. I am saying to you. Make a memo out of this. That I Thomas Allred. I'm in love with Gabriel Union Allred. And being a business tycoon. I trusted the government will see that I am able to handle my money. And Tonette Allred and Eden Allred I need you. We are getting near the end of your story. Don't give up Thomas Allred Jr. As long as you keep trying we will keep trying to help you. Shontel honey I love you shontel . Do me a favor. Let Forbes and Mercedes know that. I am coming for my crown. See if there's a will there's a way. You ought to see your faces. When you read this. Eden Allred Ms. Gabriel Union Allred. And Ms. Cindy Allred. Thomas Allred Jr I can't. Then how about being a part of my Entourage. Thomas Allred Jr you need to write your book. Quit trying to live the fantasy Life. And make your book about you. Thomas Allred Jr there is only a few more seconds to this book chapter. I want my mama to know that I love her. And Shontel you are always my dream wife. We are fending to exit the book Thomas Allred Jr. Count back from 5. 5 4 3 2 1. This is miracle amazing Love chapter 4 volume 4 real love. Now send your goddamn book in Thomas Allred Jr.

Eden Allred. Thomas Allred Jr is my favorite personality out here. If Thomas Allred Jr books make it then it's a score for us all. What do you type in Eden Allred. Keep away from my desk. Excuse me I didn't mean to bother you. No Shontel Allred you are not bothering me. What bothering me is. Thomas Allred Jr gets to choose 21 women. When I love him Shontel Allred. Thomas Allred Jr keep the story realistic. We all realize that you get to date 21 women. That is if your story can stand up through the test of time. Thomas Allred Jr tell me who you are. I am a good role model Shontel Allred and Eden Allred.

Don't lose your position Thomas Allred Jr. If my ladies are depending on you. Eden Allred. And Shontel Allred then I am depending on you also. Just write your story Thomas Allred Jr. Tonette Allred. Honey I didn't realize that you were standing there. There are a lot of things that you don't realize Thomas Allred Jr. The publication of your book could mean millions for everyone. So Thomas Allred Jr. Gabriel Union Allred. Are you ready for the fast lane. Thomas stop that sh*t and write your story. Shontel Allred honey I'm trying.

But I want to hear you say is that you ain't trying hard enough. I ain't trying hard enough. Now what is it that you really want out of life Thomas Allred Jr. To walk through my house. With 21 women loving me. And our kids follow me as well. I told you that it is more than a dream Gabriel Union Allred. Give him the Superman contract. Yes we give you a Superman contract. If you can handle yourself. In and off the playing field. You can have anything you want. You can have any woman that you want Thomas Allred Jr. All you have to do is sign the contract. That if anything was to happen to you. would retain the rights to your book. I signed the contract yesterday. Ms. Cindy. It seeMs. like a dream. Thomas Allred Jr. I know your dreaMs. are coming true. Just keep On believing in yourself. Cindy thank you for everything. Put your game face on. Ms. Cindy I'm looking for a place to be. With a family of possibly 25 women. And no kids. Get our Porsches ready. My heart is beating fast. When I said get the Porsches ready what I mean is. Kristen Allred come here. Shontel Allred I don't think this is going to work. You know damn well this is going to work. Kristen Allred say hello to Thomas Allred Jr. Hello Mr. Thomas Allred Jr. Do you realize how much I need you Kristen Allred. Kristen realize how much you need her Thomas Allred Jr. The Forbes 500 list. Is an exclusive list. Thomas Allred Jr excuse me Thomas Allred Jr. If you want to win that. Challenge someone to write against you. I believe in you and you can make it Thomas Allred Jr. Kristen Allred. You said that you believe in me. Well you should know. That it would be against the rules.

To challenge someone to a contest. For my own personal gain. Ladies we need to talk a minute. Eden Allred. Go and get the rest of the ladies. How many of them do you want Mr.. Thomas Allred Jr. Go get me all of them. Thomas Allred Jr do you really mean all of them. Eden Allred. Respect. I mean all of the ladies. Get me all of them. Eden Allred. Shontel Allred. Do you know what you doing Thomas Allred Jr. You are becoming the hottest man in Hollywood. Before you even get there. Shontel Allred do me a favor. Don't sweat the technique Shontel Allred. Honey I got a plan for you. You act like she knows everything. It must be Gabriel Union Allred. That's my lady right there. Thomas I've got to give it to you. Your book is coming along nicely. Eden Allred. Where are all of those women I asked you to get for me.

Look outside Thomas Allred Jr. Yes Gabriel Union Allred how many women does she have.Thomas Allred Jr you are not going to believe this. But Eden Allred Jr. Has managed to pull together the whole city in a matter of minutes. So Shontel Allred how many women did she get. Thomas she got all of them for you. All of them Gabriel Union Allred. Every single one of the women are waiting for you outside of your house Mr.. Thomas Allred Jr. Finish it off. You finish it off. He can't. Be Thomas Allred Jr. Write two more pages on your book. This is miracle amazing Love. Chapter 5 volume five I can't let you go the sequel. Thomas your book needs more characteristics.

I know that Cindy. I'm trying to hook up the material that I need. To make this book a world-cla** best seller. Because Small change ain't no change at all. There you go Thomas Allred Jr. Thomas Allred Jr. If you are through dreaming hand me that broom while I pick up this trash off the floor. Shontel Allred I don't mind cleaning with you. But one day when I finish this book. When I finish this paragraph in this book. I'm a tell you I love you and ask for your hand in marriage. Because you and me Shontel Allred. We are in love. With the politics of the game. Let me tell you something. I know that you came up around me. But I am From a different cloth my baby. I'm trying to make you see just who you be. Woman the world is your oyster.

The neighborhood might not agree with what I'm saying to you. I got to keep my composure. This boy is talking about keep his composure. If the book hits the Forbes list. Your life Thomas Allred Jr. And your life Shontel Allred. Will change forever. Look this is my book. And I'm introducing you to the beginning. Of what's already been written. My name is Thomas Allred Jr. And this is almost the end of chapter 5 of my miracle amazing Love collection. As for you Shontel. I'm gathering up as much money as possible. To save face. With all of my women. I want to be there. For the next time that any of my woman need me. I can't let you go. So I got to believe in myself. Do not fear what you don't understand Shontel Allred . My book is a calling. Get professional. Girl I need you with me. And the woman on the ground. I will keep you informed. On how Shontel and me with relate through Christmas. Thomas Allred Jr. the three ghosts of Christmas past present and future are here to see you.

Thomas what have you done with your fortunes. My life has been built upon helping people. If I was to give to you money Thomas Allred Jr.And Make you a wealthy man. What would you do for me in return. I will keep you as a friend in my heart forever more. And try to be there for you when you need me. Thomas Allred Jr you came from Parvati. What is the difference now than in the past. I just believe in the community more. That I ever did before in my younger days. If given power Thomas Allred Jr. Would you abuse that power that I gave you. I wouldn't abuse my power. I would take care of beautiful women.

Everybody deserves a chance. Right now the past the present and the future. Are all coming together. Thomas Allred Jr we are going to deliberate on your case. Are you man enough to handle your responsibilities Thomas Allred Jr. I've been man enough judge. And like was I respect you. I thank my team in the Secret Service. And I appreciate everyone of you. I'm closing my story book here. Given the chance to make it. I could succeed just like everybody else. Would I do. Isn't to hurt anybody else. It is only to find my way for myself and the ladies that love me. Your honor know my people. Because I am a man. Writing a book call miracle amazing Love chapter 5 volume five I can't let you go your honor. With out explaining to you. There is too many people that want things. My book is dedicated. To you. And everybody. That had to go through what I go through. Ms. Gabrielle Union Allred. What am I going to do with him. He said Gabrielle Union Allred. Shontel Allred Ms. Gabriel Union Allred wants to speak to you.

Keep your damn compose a girl. When Thomas Allred Jr makes it we all make it. the three ghost from Christmas past present and future are here to see you again Mr.. Thomas Allred Jr. And Shontel Allred. Shontel Allred look at the time. It is almost midnight. We have one question for the both of you Thomas Allred Jr and Shontel Allred. And our question is. Do you love God Thomas Allred Jr and Shontel Allred. Yes we love God. Then you can have your money back. Shontel Allred Thomas Allred Jr understands what I'm saying. Thank all of you guys for everything.

Thomas Allred Jr you enjoy your life with Shontel Allred. This is Angels in the outfield. Thomas Allred Jr and Shontel Allred. We will be watching you. Everything is supposed to be all hunky-dory. Thomas Allred Jr better not mess up. A miracle that we gave him. What are you talkin about what miracle that they gave me. Shontel Allred Thomas Allred Jr I'm pregnant. In the Next story we'll talk about this. All I know is I'm washing my hands. Send that book in Thomas Allred Jr.

I just got to have it Oracle. Thomas I will give that to you on one condition. you will give that to me what are you talkin about Oracle. Thomas all the fame that you dream of is yours. Close your eyes Thomas Allred Jr. Now repeat that to me. I am famous. I am famous. Victory shall be mine. Victory shall be mine. I am too confident to lose. I am too confident to lose. Thomas Allred Jr. You are now famous says the oracle. Oracle I don't feel any different. As a man thinketh so is he. Than my people should know. That luxury is at your command. Oracle may I have luxury. The only thing that you have to do Thomas Allred Jr is write that book. It seeMs. like I've heard this before. Somewhere in another world another space and time. Thomas Allred Jr. Get your a** in there and clean those dishes. Shontel Allred honey I'm working on a book called I want the Fame.

So before you harra** me Thomas Allred Jr. Make sure that that book is a heavyweight standing. Thanksgiving Bought us together. In the months to come I will get you. Your own studio lab. To write your books in Thomas Allred Jr. The Oracle is thanking you Thomas Allred Jr. Shontel Allred. Honey may I ask two questions of you. The kids want me. Are we making this a family book. This book is about money success and power and family and prestige. Those that have it and those that want it. Oracle I have already learned my lesson. Go to sleep Thomas Allred Jr. And your book will finish itself. Go to sleep Thomas Allred Jr. Now what do you see in your dream. I am in a room Shontel Allred. Write all kinds of books. Inside the room of Justice. Thomas Allred Jr can you hear me. You don't know what you will become.

You must trust in this Oracle. To take you places that you've never been before. In order to do that. Your attitude must be strong. You must have the strength of a beast Thomas Allred Jr. Thats if you need to stop. So Thomas Allred Jr. Do you really want the fame. Or are you just some pretender that is trying to measure up. I want the fame. Shontel Allred and Oracle get Hollywood after me. Somebody has got to do something about.

This room of mine. I can see myself clearly in this room. Thomas Allred Jr I know you can. Who is that talking to me. Thomas Allred Jr this is your Fame talking to you. Thomas Allred Jr you have got to do your best to make it. I have been training you for all of your life Thomas Allred Jr. It's not a coincidence. Thomas Allred Jr. Is the hottest thing in Hollywood. Fame I'm putting my foot down. This is for the 21 women in which I will marry. Take your time Thomas Allred Jr. You got to be strong enough Thomas Allred Jr. Can you be strong enough for Gabriel Union Allred. No condition. Can ever break you down.

Do you want the Fame Thomas Allred Jr. You are going to have to sacrifice at all. What do you mean Oracle by saying it all. Thomas Allred Jr be strong enough. To tell the people what you have been through. It's about time that the people know. As a man you stand for. Truth and liberty Thomas Allred Jr. That Forbes 500 list. Will include you in it as number one one day soon Thomas Allred Jr. And all you have to say is. Thank you to the three wise men. Thank you three wise men. I have a question for Thomas Allred Jr. If you get 21 women will you stay with them. Yes Oracle I will. I got a question for Thomas Allred Jr. As a police officer. You hold our community. And will you give to your people of your community when you become famous. I will always give to the people of the community Kristen Allred . You see people. Thomas Allred Jr is a damn man. We can allow him to have his money back. What money Kristen Allred excuse me Kristen Allred let me tell him. What we are trying to do is. Get you matched up with all the women of your dreaMs.. You have one more day Thomas Allred Jr to work on your book. Before we help you. You are making a fool out of yourself. If you are going to write Thomas Allred Jr. Go for the gusto. Tell the world that you are Thomas Allred Jr. And you just not having it anymore.

Walk like you are the man. Talk like you are the man. You have got to be the man Thomas Allred Jr. Ms. Eden Allred. And Ms. Cindy. I am the man. Now there we go. Cindy tell this man with what we got in store for him. Thomas Allred Jr if you can hold your attitude together. Thomas Allred Jr the fame will be yours. Say the fame will be yours. The fame will be yours. All of the people around you. A hoping that you succeed and write your books. Thomas Allred Jr I have been working on you.Yes your a rapper Thomas Allred Jr. But to walk down this road. Only a few can handle this position. That's why I dedicate to you Thomas Allred Jr. The fame that you requested. Keep your composure. Thomas Allred Jr the famous too smart for anyone.

They trying to prove their self. Thomas Allred Jr and his lovely wife Shontel Allred. You know they got to prove their self. What are you running from Thomas Allred Jr. The fame. The morle of this book. Is to make it out of your situation. Damn right it is to make it out of your situation. Thomas Allred Jr you have got to be dedicated. You look Tonette Allred. And Danielle Allred. In my future you ladies are all my wives. I'm picking up revenue everywhere that I go. People ain't got time for no loser. I'm impressed with you're caresmatic demeanor.

Go for it all Thomas Allred Jr. The cars the clothes the house has the money. Oracle I would like to have endorsement deals. Soft drink and shoes. Thomas Allred Jr you are getting way ahead of yourself. What are you saying Oracle that I can not have these things. I'm saying take your time to get up and get you something to eat. From the bottom to the top baby. They trying to make that boy into a damn King. Put Gabriel on him. Thomas Allred Jr will be a man. There you go Oracle. Thomas

Allred Jr my job is. Almost complete. Are you saying that we're finished Oracle. Thomas Allred Jr. I can teach you how to fish like a man. But I can't feel your pain if you are hurting. This story must come to an end. I need your help Oracle. How will everyone know that I keep trying and that I want it all. Thomas Allred Jr a lot of people. Are counting on you. To be the man that you say you are. Now get your a** over there and get you something to eat. You are a king in my book. Thomas Allred Jr is a king in my book. Can everybody say it. Thomas Allred Jr is a king in my book. What is the name of the story Thomas Allred Jr. I want the fame. Then by God Thomas Allred Jr you may have it. Thomas Allred Jr. You are getting ready to go to sleep. This audiobook plays at perfection. All your dreaMs. have now been fantasized. And Hollywood is yours for the taking. The three wise men want to say something to you. Thomas Allred Jr. You know Thomas. That a mission isn't complete.

Without a Queen at the end of the story .Now Thomas Allred Jr who is your queen. I'm saying 100% it is Shontel Allred. Let that boy go through. Thomas Allred Jr knows how to communicate. How about you. Do you want the fame. Thomas Allred Jr. Your 21 women will be waiting for you. If this book is a smash success. You will have houses and cars. But if you can't keep yourself together. It will all disappear right in front of you. Take some time out to think about your situation. Remember Thomas Allred Jr you have one day for your book to be completed. I would like to thank my family. For always helping me along the way. Three wise men. I have one question for you all. Yes Thomas Allred Jr. You may ask your question. Will all of me and Shontel Allred dreaMs. come true after I finish writing this book. Thomas Allred Jr your dreaMs. have already come true. Hold Your position. You just got to open your eyes and see it. Thank you Oracle. See that man is not ready to give up. I'm going to give him Fame and prestige. But that is another book. Everybody lower your heads. Thank you God for helping me. As a journey comes to an end and a New journey begins. Be professional. I want the fame. Meaning that I am going to see you at the top. No matter what it takes. Thomas Allred Jr. Is a king y'all. Shontel Allred I love you wifey forever and always baby forever . Now Thomas Allred Jr send your book off. Right now.

Thomas Allred Jr you are the champion. There is just no doubt in my mind that you are the champion. Thank you I appreciate that sir. You just keep up the good work Thomas Allred Jr. The one day I promise you you're going to be somebody. You promised me that I'm going to be somebody. I promise you that you are going to be somebody. Fours years later. Thomas Allred Jr we got to feed the baby. Honey it's just that I don't have any money to feed him right now. Thomas Allred Jr the baby is crying the baby is hungry. Shontel Allred honey I don't have any money. Thomas Allred Jr the baby is crying the baby is hungry. Listen Shontel Allred I don't have any money. My dream went that way two more years. But for some reason I just couldn't see myself getting out of it. I started reading everything that I could find. About entertainment and fame. I tried to make sure that. A part of me was held accountable. For my own success in this world. I called my book. On the last book of my career. Because I have to stand up for myself. I realize to try is to keep evident with what's in front of you. There are 21 women in my future for me. Every King rules his own demeanor. In our country. A king has the right to express his self. For as much as he want to. Now the 21 Queens are ladies. That is just a promise from God that if I make it. And that if I don't give up. My family may have Majesty. And what Majesty is. It is the right for a king. A true king. To talk to as many women as he wants to in this world of Queens. Now I am not the one who makes the rules. Success is there for us all. I'm just trying my best to figure out a way to have some thing for my family and I. Before I leave this planet. I hold down these 21 women. So beautiful and educated they are. and in my heart every last one of them is special. Because God has given them to me to be my wife's. I don't live by the law of one wife.

I live by that if God puts it in your hands it is yours. God put this dream in my hands. But let me back the story of a minute. You're the champion Thomas Allred Jr. Who you think is saying this Thomas Allred Jr. I don't know you standing in the smoke who are you. I am the future you. And I'm coming back here to tell you. That you can have anything that you want. If you just keep believing in yourself. Do you believe in yourself Thomas Allred Jr. Yes I believe in myself. In the future. That is after your books come out. You will date and marry. 21 of the most beautifulest woman in the world. Do you believe me Thomas Allred Jr. I do believe you. Start to write your book like this Thomas Allred Jr. In the days to come. My future became more clear to me. Thomas Allred Jr. Your future is the pattern in the book. People all over the world are going to love you. If you can just keep your pattern straight. I'm keeping my pattern sir. And like I said Thomas Allred Jr. The future is yours. I'm watching you.

Let me see what you have inside you. Let me see what's inside Thomas Allred Jr. Do you really want the fame. And prestige and women. Now tell me in a hundred words or less. What does the fame and prestige mean to you Thomas Allred Jr. The fame means everytime I go to sleep I have some where to lay my head. The prestige means that I am driven to succeed even if I'm by myself. My women love me because I am successful. I am a good man and a role model. The last book that I'm writing. Must reflect on my triumphs. As a king and as a man. Because all Kings knowno. It takes a good man to be a king. And all queens know. That it takes a good woman to be a queen. I'm begging you to sit down and read a chapter of my book. See I come from nothing up to be a king in the world as we know it. I have business ideas in books unseen by anyone in the world. I have a newfound favor. Women of respect that trust and honor me.

The first started in my locker room. Thomas Allred Jr your the champion. I told myself. Over and over again. Until I could see nothing but my future. And what I wanted to be. I shaped myself by listening to motivational speeches. And I trained and exercise my body. As much as I could daily. I am more than a king. I am a husband and soon to be a father. In the days of this book. I know that your looking at me. I'm keeping my composure. Just to have the family that I dream of. Because right now I am in my locker room. And I keep telling myself. I am a champion. On the last book of my career. Now I had a power movement. Thomas Allred Jr you don't have to say that. I'm ending my book. With this statement. Women are Queens. And they all need to have the world. But if you keep thinking they all gold diggers. You will miss out on the dream that you're having. Because the future prestige Fame and Glory. Is your woman and family. Don't forget. To tell yourself that you're a champion everyday. Thomas Allred Jr write your book and send it in. Trust me I am you in the future. And this is the way to get paid. On the last book of my career.

Queens I need you to understand something. A man will cherish you. Once he have his sh*t together. But a true king will cherish you. When each of you have nothing at all. This is for Life ladies and gentlemen. I am Thomas Allred Jr. Telling my 21 beautiful ladies. That they will come. When the future and the past meet up. And we will be together. Forevermore. I'm a businessman. Each one of you. Is the future in my eyes. And I know I see. A place for you and me. At the round table of Justice. That will definitely be in our house. Thomas Allred Jr. Everybody wants to see you make it. You have got to keep trying for a future that you know it's yours. I am telling you. That your women are here for you Thomas Allred Jr. Now you got to prove yourself. Go in deeper than you ever had before. What are you trying to tell the people with your books. All I'm trying to tell the people is. That there is a way. And if I can do it we all can do it. Thomas Allred Jr. You are different than I once known you.

It is because I'm most serious now. My books are the future for me and a lot of people. So I carry myself at a prestige level. Because I know. The things come difficult. And difficult things come hard. But a true king and man. Will never stop striving for his best. In a true king. Would never reach his prime. In this world of Justice. Im a give you a contract Thomas Allred Jr. It's all because of your dedication. There is a better way. But first you have to believe in yourself. And take the necessary steps towards making your future reality. it's getting close to time to ending this book. Thomas Allred Jr are you satisfied with your work. My work will speak for itself. That is a confident man. Ladies. A king. A true king is a confident man not a violent one. I'm going to say that again Queens. A true king it's a confident man not a violent one. And now Thomas Allred Jr. The ghost of Christmas past present and future would like to speak to you.

Thomas Allred Jr we have two questions for you. Have you ever lost your face before. I almost lost my faith but I kept believing in God. And Thomas Allred Jr.

Was writing books as easy as it seemed. No it wasn't. No it wasn't. There is one more question that we all want to ask you Thomas Allred Jr. are you claiming the books or the education that it took to go into the books. I am claiming the books. Because I know that my education came from all of you guys. And I'm proud of every one of you. For making me a man and a king. Of my own household. On the last book of my career. We are deliberating Thomas Allred Jr. What you said has touched our hearts. And till Ms. Eden Reid. That the last book is finished. Thank you for your help Mr. Thomas Allred Jr. Our committee finds you innocent of all charges. You may have your life now with Shontel Allred. She has something to tell you. Make it two things to tell you. Listen to me Thomas Allred Jr. All you need is one woman to make you happy. Start your future off with Shontel Allred. You realize that Shontel Allred is pregnant don't you. Let her make it. Because we give to you Thomas Allred Jr. A key to our Fortune. Thank you. Sit down and think about this. Now send your book in.

All kind of b*tches are going to be all over you after you write this movie Thomas Allred Jr. My Future self. I am dedicated to one female. Who was it that you are dedicated to. My wife and lovely lady Shontel Allred. Your wife and lovely lady Thomas Allred Jr. Don't play with me. We have got to get that man a contract. This man has dreaMs. in him. Wherever you go Thomas Allred Jr. Just know that your future self will be with you. Future-self are you listening. Thomas Allred Jr. I will be with you in one second. We are going to have to break the movie down in three parts. This is back to the Future you're telling us. No fear Thomas Allred Jr. I'm telling you no fear. Thomas Allred Jr. Because you are a king among us. And if you can get this book together the right way. Thomas Allred Jr the people are watching you. That's why I say to you Thomas Allred Jr. I'm serious about helping you. You keep on thinking about music contracts.

I can just rewrite your story. Thomas Allred Jr look at me. I am going to take you out the hood. If you let me Thomas Allred Jr. My Future self. I know that you are the future version of me. But I just want to come back to win. Everything that you never had. Thomas Allred Jr let me see about you. Quit playing games. Your publisher is waiting on this manuscript. White people are helping you Thomas Allred Jr. My Future self. Let's just start up the movie. And with all adieu. Thomas Allred Jr I send you back to the past. We know you got potential.

But police can hear you. Get up and get you something to eat before this movie get started. Thomas Allred Jr. No fear is the name. So I started with nothing. not even the hopes of being anything or having anything. Walking beside the school bus. With my friend Makia . Thomas Allred Jr you don't know what you would be if you keep trying. I got to save up some money Makia. the first thing that I'm going to do is get you a house Makia. Oh my God look at the stars Thomas Allred Jr. It is the sign from the Creator. I believe that you are writing a book. Makia how did you know. The whole neighborhood is watching you Thomas Allred Jr. And we all been watching. To see that you never give up. Thomas Allred Jr we believe that you. Are a great story Teller. In one day your wish will come true. To have everything that you dream of. but my stories take me to places that I've never been before Makia. You don't have to be afraid Thomas Allred Jr. His heart rate is slowing down. If you professional Thomas Allred Jr. You can come out of this a champion. I look at you and begin to focus. On what's important in my future. I see that your friendship means the world to me. You see how we do these things. Makia you read my poem. Thomas Allred Jr I am your first love that's the reason I am in this book. It's not a book anymore Makia. Thomas Allred Jr what is it then. It is better than the book. I called this. No fear the movie. The movie Thomas Allred Jr. Thomas Allred Jr going after the industry y'all. Makia why not. Because the industry will take care of you. And you would no longer need me. My Future self can you hear me. Yes Thomas Allred Jr I can hear you. All the people want you to communicate. That is exactly what I was trying to do. Makia could you and the community please meet my future self. How are you doing community. Can you hear me out there. My movie is called no fear. Thomas Allred Jr who is this talking to us I can see that man. My future self is who he is.

Don't you see Eden Allred . This book is from the future. Thomas Allred Jr. You are going to have to prove yourself to me. In the last days I'm hungry. It is you Thomas Allred Jr. You got your future self to Guide you just like you said you would. In the past. The females are going to love you Thomas Allred Jr. This book is complexed. I mean this movie is complexed. Eden Allred the way that we maneuver things. Make sure that you're talkin to Eden Allred Thomas Allred Jr. I have a question for you my future self. I keep writing and writing and writing. When will I ever be heard. As you look at things. Thomas Allred Jr you can see the time to be. Any question Thomas Allred Jr for you.

I will answer because I am your future self. Future self you didn't answer my question. Yes I did Thomas Allred Jr. And what I am telling you is that people are reading your book and movie as you write it. Thomas Allred Jr. With all of the stories of amazing things. That you keep dreaming about. We see that you are more concerned with helping people. We future yourself. Your committee of judges. I'm putting everything I got into this movie. Thomas Allred Jr. Don't play with me. What are you saying Future self I don't understand what you mean. We are going to contact all the women that you have ever loved in your life. And never had a chance to talk to. Future self what are you saying to me. Listen to me Thomas Allred Jr. There are 21 women. That you in your heart have been in love with. Makia. Makia is only a figment of your imagination Thomas Allred Jr. But if you take your time out to write this story.

Then one day in the future you could make her a reality. Just like those other females. In which you dream of every night. What kind of dream are you making.

I'm dreaming to be there for my people. If you want to be there for your people. Then continue to write your movie Thomas Allred Jr. You're going to have to do much better. Because it doesn't matter how long the story is Thomas Allred Jr. As long as the women know that you are a king fighting for all of them. To have what they want. You must go deeper inside of yourself Thomas Allred Jr. Future self I am afraid. Put no fear on your back. Take your time Thomas Allred Jr. What can I do. Females like me but they don't seem to love me. Females are in love with you Thomas Allred Jr. We just have to fix your positioning. See you are a little off. I got to speak to you my future self. I have been dreaming all of my life of a palace. That kind of look like the mall on the inside. I'm looking for my wife and someone to get married to. Thomas Allred Jr stop that. Look around you Thomas Allred Jr. The only way out this prison of pages. Is to go right through the book. Thomas Allred Jr right through the book means to sacrifice your heart. I had a friend. And my friend is no longer with us. So I stay by myself for almost 10 years. Because I was so bad hurt inside. And now the ladies come up to me. They are asking for my autograph. And some of them want to be with me. The future self tell me how can I love again when my friend isn't in the world anymore.

Thomas you have been hurt and afflicted. And you need people around you. Bring back the joy that you once knew. We are going to help you Thomas Allred Jr. I am part of a committee in the future. We are the Justice league. And Thomas Allred Jr you are a police officer from the past. Everytime I wake up I dream I am a police officer. That's because you are a police officer Thomas Allred Jr. See I want you to realize something Thomas Allred Jr. That you have been writing for 2 years now. Thomas Allred Jr listen to me Thomas Allred Jr. If you everyone of your manuscripts. The police has. see there's something about you that I can't put my finger on. either you want a family or you want to fight for the police department. Which is it Thomas Allred Jr. The police department is my family. Congratulations Thomas you just pa**ed your test. I know exactly what you're talking about. You had no kind of fear in you when you wrote the books. The ladies on the police force are in love with you. Thomas Allred Jr your birthday is coming up. Do you work and get ready to send in the book. Whatever happens the future is going to handle Thomas Allred Jr. Ms. Gabriel Union Allred. Thank you for everything. A lot of people believe in the books that you write Thomas Allred Jr. On one two three close your eyes and begin to sleep Thomas Allred Jr. The future and the past are one. With no fear of anything but God.

Thomas Allred Jr I told you when we started this that I would never give up on you. So when I say write your book write your book. Let it be up to the publisher's to figure out what to do with what you right. Just let your mind go and be free Thomas Allred Jr. Thomas Allred Jr you need to talk to me. My future self talk to you about what. Your attitude is what got us helping you Thomas Allred Jr. Thomas Allred Jr. Yes Gabriel Union Allred. I am your wife in the future Thomas Allred Jr.

This is all you need to be concerned with. But Gabriel Union Allred how can that be. Thomas Allred Jr talk to yourself. And ask that's the question. Who is my future wife. My Future self could you please tell me who my future wife is. It is Gabriel Union Allred. Mr.. Thomas Allred Jr. Why the change in my name future self. You are maturing now Thomas Allred Jr. You have fought the game with no reason. And won it on every level. We are going to make you a business tycoon. If you can only just write the book. Checkmate. My past self how you doing. Thomas Allred Jr your future self is going to take over. My past self isn't that what we want. No Thomas Allred Jr you are in the present. And I am in the past. Once the present and the past meet up. I want you to know Thomas Allred Jr that we become the future. My books aren't long enough. Yes your books are. If you just keep on trying. The past will be just that. A thing of the past. My past self and My Future self. I am going to need you to sit down for a second. Future self. Explain to my past self how much better off we'll be if we keep trying. Past self the future isn't written and the present is all we have. So past self don't give up. Thomas Allred Jr can you see what I'm going through. My past self I know it is hard. But you just got to believe in God. He would never put more on you than you can bear. Thomas Allred Jr you are the present. How much better is your situation now. That we are no longer in the past. My situation is a situation that's all I can say past self. Will the ladies love me if I keep trying.

Because Thomas Allred Jr all I want is a family. Here in the present past self. You and I still don't have a family. I understand this. But to be in the future Thomas Allred Jr. And if you and I don't quit trying to have something for ourselves. My Future self will we have a family. Thomas Allred Jr I already told you. That the future isnt written. But I will let you know this. You will have 21 wives if you continue to work on your books and movies and don't stop. Thomas Allred Jr you have to wake up. I'll wake up Gabriel Union Allred just give me one more minute. That is exactly what I'm going to do. See the last book of Thomas Allred collection. It had to end like this.

Baby I got you. Shontel Allred. I was dreaming of you. Don't you know that I would never hurt you or leave You. You have been on a journey Thomas Allred Jr. And a test of your will and your faith. Has been taken place. You are a police officer. Thomas Allred Jr I need you to look at it this way. A lot of people depend on you for your ideas. Take your time. Your book is coming out here. The strongest champion. I like this boy. Shontel Allred I'm just about asleep. Then the dream of us is complete. The dream of all the women is complete. Thomas Allred Jr when you wake up. I'm going to be with you. but you do realize that you have to send the book in. Before you can dream any further about your future. Now send the book in Thomas Allred Jr. Shontel Allred I'm trying but I can't. Yes you can just let go of your fears of the future. Thomas Allred Jr that girl is asking you can she be your wife. In the future. There she go that is my wife. I love you Ms. Shontel Allred. Now send in the book Thomas Allred Jr

CHAPTER 17

Let me know if you're getting my comprende Thomas Allred Jr. I'm getting your comprende just well. My Future self. My past self is having a hard time with things. I am the present I'm going to pick you up to speed. See I have been writing a book for 2 years now. And in my presents. This reality was so difficult. That I just had to break down and cry sometimes. Imagine a police officer. That is working on a book. But he don't remember that the police are helping him. I got to give credit where credit is due. To the New York Police department I give thanks. And to the NSA the FBI and the Secret Service I give thanks. I am thanking law enforcement all across the world. My code name Superman. And I embarked on a journey. To be professional. In the way that I do everything from here on out. Realizing that I'm a police officer. I give credit to my equals. I got to give credit to my brothers and sisters of law enforcement. I have got to give credit to my equals. Seeing that I am just one person in the large pool of Justice.

I didn't go nowhere I'm staying right here. In the United States of America. With my people. There you go. Thomas Allred Jr I do believe that you're going to make it. That is my past self talking to me. If you believe I can believe in you and me Thomas Allred Jr. You ain't got but six more days to write that story. Future self I need your help to write the story. In time I'm a write it. But as for now let's just enjoy the success that you and me as the police have made. For one another. It's a beautiful a** day Thomas Allred Jr. It is time to take things the way they come and enjoy the music. We lost some friends along the way. Get my future self over here. We lost some friends along the way future self. Be careful what you wish for Thomas Allred Jr. God put you ahead in this game of finance. Just write your book. You know that people are listening to you. And I am telling the people to stay strong. Because no matter what we go through in this life. I Thomas Allred Jr do believe that there is heaven. For each and every one of us just as long as we keep love in our hearts. Listen. In order to communicate.

I am going to need my past self and My Future self to come together as one. Thomas Allred Jr I am the future. Thomas Allred Jr. I am the past. All right future and past. I can't see where I am headed. Can one of you explain to me what I'm doing here. Thomas Allred Jr I'm the past. And what we are doing is trying to make a movie. Out of your life. Yes Thomas Allred Jr. We are dedicated. And trying to make us better. If you can just lose all the fear. To have something. Because it is your calling. From the great heavens above. To have and to hold. As many police officer women. If the good God should a allow you to. Future self my past self has gone mad. Your past self is here to help you. Look at all that we've been through. Can my past self help me. Thomas Allred Jr. We are One. We are One. We are One. That's when I felt all alone. I knew that I was talking to myself. And I also knew that I am a professional. But getting to point a from point b. Sometimes took a lot of leg work. I'm jealous of you Thomas Allred Jr. I tell myself sometimes. You are a good damn police officer. Thomas Allred Jr. You are messing up the story Thomas Allred Jr. Go back to when you first decided to write the book. Yes my love Shontel Allred. I just woke up one morning. And decided with a friend of mine. The her and I was going to write a book. Will write a book called look at me.

You need that book to help you Thomas Allred Jr. Because through all the pain and the tears of your life's journey. You have become a man still believing in yourself. Your life journey isn't over. And that's what I'm telling the people. I know it's been difficult. And I know we've cried a lot of days and nights. But your lifes journey is not over. Think of it this way. We are all put here for a reason. Thomas Allred Jr do I need to help you. Look Shontel Allred Jr. Yes I need your help. Introducing Ms. Gabrielle Union Allred. What a beautiful a** day it is. You see i started these books with Thomas Allred Jr. Because he desperately wanted a wife. Just because someone murdered his wife and soulmate. As he was coming up as a young police officer. Now I fight after book after book. To find the truth Thomas Allred Jr. Can Jeana Allred help me.

Thomas Allred Jr shine your light on the people. You are amazing. Jeana Allred I can't do it without you I'm not that strong. Thomas Allred Jr I told you when they shot you to stand up. And to be strong. I am I just know that I need you Jeana Allred. Listen Gabriel Union Allred. Thomas Allred Jr is still going to need some help to make it without me. You are my friend Gabriel Union Allred. Explain to him what this is. While I take a second to tell him that I do love him. And it is okay for him to get married to Shontel Allred. Jeana Allred look nothing's been the same without you. I still wonder how could they ever have hurt you. And on my life I'm a police officer until the end. Jeana Allred that is on my life. Come back police officer. Shontel Allred. Baby where was I.

Finish writing your book Thomas Allred Jr. And I had a friend. Well when I was younger I called her my wife. And the gang members took her away from me. And I have been crying and fighting. Ever since I was 15. For a better way of Justice. For my people all over the place no matter race color or Creed. I have been standing up against All odds. Even though gang members shot me in the leg. And killed my beautiful Jeana Allred. I'm making a real life story. How one man can see triumph. In this world without having nothing at all. I believe in God y'all. Thank you Thomas Allred Jr. It's a beautiful a** day. Thomas Allred Jr you can stop crying now. Gabriel Union Allred it hurts so bad. We all know Thomas Allred Jr. Not the bullet Gabriel Union Allred. I miss Jeana Allred so much. And it's hard to go on without her. Now everybody think this is just a book. But my girl wants me to drive forward. Shontel Allred can you please talk a minute. Gabriel Union Allred listen to Thomas Allred Jr.

He has been doing police work for all his days. Working for a undercover unit. He tried his best to defend his lady. That is exactly why they shot him. Thomas Allred Jr. It's not a kid anymore. And though he is a police officer. Pain from the past drives Thomas Allred Jr. To be a better person in cop. So the rest of the world can see. When you are against All odds. You kneel down and pray to God. Thank you Shontel Allred. For this speech. Thomas Allred Jr Jeana wanted me to tell you. To take your time. And to keep it professional. I swear on my life Jeana Allred that we at the police department.

Are going to make every last one of them pay for what they did to you and the people. Thomas Allred Jr. Yes Jeana Allred baby I can hear you. You have got to be stronger Thomas Allred Jr. Jeana Allred honey without you I just don't know how to go on. That is what Gabriel is here for. I believe Jeana wanted me to tell you something. A lot of people are watching you. Thomas Allred Jr. For taking a bullet in the line of fire. To save another man's life. And surviving. Thomas Allred Jr we give to you. Your own code. Gabriel Union Allred it can't be true. This is the Thomas Allred Jr code. The numbers 388 shall every flag in the world. Thomas Allred Jr we are giving you your code because you didn't stand down. Gabriel Union Allred thank you.

Look ya'll I'm thanking God and the police station. All of my brothers and sisters in law enforcement. It is a beautiful a** day. Jeana Allred taught me how to stand strong. Jeana Allred help me heal up after I got shot. She took care of me and they killed her. Shontel Allred I don't know what to say. Can somebody help me please. I'm here Thomas Allred Jr Ms. Eden Allred. But why after all these years. Thomas Allred Jr you have proven yourself. With all of your dedication. I am going to let you be that in which you dream of Thomas Allred Jr. A published author. Oh my God. Ms. Eden Allred. I'm so thankful because of you. Thomas Allred Jr there's just one more thing that we want from you.

Thomas Allred Jr. Is your story real. My story is as real as they come Ms. Cindy from. Take you a nap Thomas Allred Jr. The whole community knows that you are a hero. Thank you. I almost forgot. Superman. Yes Ms. Cindy. You did a job well done. Jeana Allred I miss you so much honey. Y'all yall got to hear me. To love a person is to give you a heart. Weather they are doing good or not. Thomas Allred Jr. The Thomas Allred Jr code three eight eight belongs on every flag in the United

States of America. Thomas Allred Jr. Gabriel Union Allred I love you. You have got to speak to Shontel Allred Thomas Allred Jr. I made you write these books because I needed you Thomas Allred Jr. Shontel Allred honey it was you that made me write the books. My Future self has been guiding you Thomas Allred Jr. Take your time with that book Thomas Allred Jr. It is so many people after us Thomas Allred Jr. Shontel Allred I don't want to lose you. I don't want to lose you Thomas Allred Jr. God will you please help give us strength. Because the road gets rough Jesus. Jesus I've been in love. And lost Jesus. Father would you take me out of my situation. The place all of our feet on solid ground. And I give my heart to one woman. For the rest of my days I love you. Shontel Allred. It is a beautiful a** day. Shontel Allred thank you.

Because in the end. All of the police officers women and men. Have stood up for me.And Jeana Allred I'm very thankful. For everything that you do. Living or even not with us. Jeana Allred was a police officer. And she stood for Honor truth and justice. May the police say Amen. Amen. Now that your books of finish Thomas Allred Jr. Is this something that you would think about doing again. I'm a police officer tonette. And we won't stop fighting until everyone is all right in this world. Superman. It is a beautiful day Thomas Allred Jr. Captain Frankie and lieutenant Candis. Thank you both so much for everything. I could have never made it without the two of you. I love you two man. Thomas Allred Jr keep on rapping. The possibilities are endless. Thomas Allred Jr take your time and in your book once and for all. You don't know what I've been through. I'm a police officer codename Superman. And this is the beginning of a beautiful new day. The past is gone I am the future. Thank you Captain Frankie and lieutenant Candis. For teaching me to be a better man over all these years. I'm saying to everybody that we won the championship. Everybody listen. Jesus Christ is our Lord and savior. Let Thomas Allred Jr out of that situation. I'm just hoping to marry my wife and have children. Thomas Allred your book has ended. Now send your book in Thomas Allred Jr.

Hi my name is Thomas Allred Jr. And this is the book a call. Reminiscent on the time that's coming. Buy me myself and I. You see I've got to warn you. If my book starts off slowly. I am taking my time to reminisce on things. That means something to me. Thomas Allred Jr. Explain the book to the people. Thomas Allred Jr get over there and explain the book to the people. I could explain the book. But I will let the book explain itself. This is my dream and my program. This is my program in my dream. There are certain guidelines in which I have to go through. To make this book a reality. By the time you read my book. You all would know that Jeana Allred was a princess. And that her life was taken too soon. The book is reminiscent on the time that is coming. Thomas Allred Jr. We must remember to be thankful for all of our blessings that God has bestowed upon us. Yes Frankie my Captain and lieutenant Candis. I thank the Almighty. For everything he's doing. And about to do in my life. See what I'm telling you is. I used to think that I was an angel.

God damn. Quit cussing Thomas Allred Jr. Just lieutenant Candis ma'am. You keep making a fool out of yourself. You are making a book Thomas Allred Jr. Thomas Allred Jr you need to put your heart inside of this book. Now tell the story the way the story should go. I needed somebody to have my back. Jeana Allred was only 14. And I was 17. She was my everything. I'm projecting. That I will see her again. All because Jeana Allred brought me out of different situations. And I'm forever grateful for her and her family. That's not the way to start story. Realize this story has meaning to it. Y'all keep talking about y'all I want a ride or die chick. Jeana Allred give her life so I will be protected.

You see my best friend in my life was also her. We were too young to know that we were police officers. I told you my love the truth will prevail. Jeana Allred trusted me with everything because I was older than her and she loved me. People will take advantage of children if you let them. And the Lord put Jeana Allred and I together. Thomas Allred Jr.

There is no butter in meat to the story. You are going to have to write and tell me something. It is butter and meat when I get done with the story. I gave Jeana Allred everything that you wanted. But the funny thing is I swear to God she give it right back to me. I only realized this. Because every month on her birthday. I am alone. By month I mean. Every 23rd day of each month of each year. I spend it to myself thanking God for Jeana Allred. You are getting professional. I can hear this girl say to me without even seeing her face I could tell it was her. I also could tell that Shontel Allred was in love with me. In the week of my comeback. Get up Thomas Allred Jr. That's what Shontel would say to me. Just like a fallen athlete. Or a slame athlete. I was in for the count. We have to get Thomas Allred Jr somewhere where he can be his self. That's Gabriel Union Allred. Thomas Allred Jr you a damn police officer get your a** up. Yes lieutenant Candis. Save your money. I have no money lieutenant Candis. You need to get out of that situation. But Captain Frankie I have no way out of this situation.

What I say to you Thomas Allred Jr get out of the situation. Yes Captain Frankie. And lieutenant Candis. Clock this man. He is writing reminiscent of a strange dude. No the book is called reminiscent on the time that is to come. Don't give up Thomas Allred Jr. God if you can hear me. Let me use my powers of intuition. To speak to the people through this book. And what I'm trying to say is. Keep your relationships it's important. What in the hell are you talkin about Thomas Allred Jr. Take your time and explain to us what it is that your saying and mean. All I'm saying is. That we all should value each other.

For our wrongs and our Rights. If I was to step up to you. And you didn't know it was me people. How would you look at me as a person? Because I have made something out of myself. You look at me Thomas Allred Jr. As your role model. And best friend. Can I ask you. What is your love tonight? See the first thing that I want to tell you. Is that you are professional. To have reached its height. And to have my book in your hands. It must mean that you. Truly believe in yourself. And I. Want to thank lots of females. For believing in what I'm doing. Shontel Allred. Come check out what I'm saying honey. Because of you my future wife. I'm just trying my best. To recognize that you are world supposed to be. In my heart I feel pain. I have got to go to distance. The pain is growing enormous. Just like the story is. I'm judging you. On all the people judging you. What I'm saying is Shontel Allred sweetheart. I know exactly what I'm doing. And what are you doing Thomas Allred Jr. I am getting ready to put it all on the line. I need you professional. There's one thing that I must do. Let in on my beliefs. I believe that all women are precious. And the women were raised up and touched by God. I believe the all women deserve majesty and honor. And shall only be with the men that will treat them right and deserve the queenship . I believe that women are treated unfairly. And it is up to the men of God to stand up and to protect the ladies.

Thank you for giving me the few seconds. To explain myself. You see I am a women's victiMs. rights advocate. On the Secret Service. And the New York Police department. See my favorite thing to do is. Write a book and tell a story. I got shot when I had just turned 19 years old. And my girl Jeana Allred. Took care of me and healed my wounds. I cheated on Jeana Allred. With another woman. And she caught me and started crying. I'm saying this to you. Because after that night. Jeana Allred. And I will never again. Though I was 19 years old. I still should have known better. I had to move out of the house that I was staying in. An in with my mother. Leaving Jeana Allred behind. Seasons keep changing. And I went to prison over a charge that didn't belong to me. Im a make a long story short. The time went slow. I'm help you. Yes Captain Frankie. How are you doing now Thomas Allred Jr. My police station is doing everything they can for me. Come on and focus down on the book Thomas Allred Jr. What is important to me these days. Is love and families. In My sacrifice. And in my mistakes.

I truly believe that there's a silver cloud lining. That only me and God can see. I have survived for a reason. And everyone in my past. Was placed there for a reason. What kind of reason Thomas Allred Jr. The reason is to my destiny can be fulfilled. Thomas Allred Jr. Only your destiny can be fulfilled Thomas Allred Jr. So our destiny can be fulfilled lieutenant Candis. See I realize. That in struggle there comes pain. I am an officer of the law enforcement agency. The New York Police department . Thomas Allred Jr take your time. Ms. Gabriel Union Allred. Is this a dream. It is a dream Thomas Allred Jr. Thomas Allred Jr you have a chance of doing something that most people never even dream of. Think about it. When our book gets published. The world would know how two police officers Thomas Allred Jr and Jeana Allreds. Love has stood the test of time. And didn't fell. Because everything that you're doing now Thomas Allred Jr. Is exactly what we program you to do. So we realize your struggles. And love in your heart. For staying true Thomas Allred Jr. All of these years. We give to you the medal of Honor. Thomas Allred Jr not to mention.That you are an inspiration. To every police officer operating in this world. The ideas that you keep making. By saving the lives of people all over the world. Thomas Allred Jr realize you're saving the people as you write your book. I just want the men to know that your lady is your lady and you should treat her as such. This book is called. Reminiscent on the time that is coming. Thomas Allred Jr I want you to write that book Thomas Allred Jr. Police officers I'm thankful for you. You need to think the rescue squad and the doctors at the hospital for saving your life Thomas Allred Jr. Every one of you what can I do for you. For giving me another chance.You see there. I put my life in your hands. Thomas Allred Jr your getting ready to finish your book. Finish your book Thomas Allred Jr. And it don't matter about how many words. It is the impact that your story will bring. The whole neighborhood that Jeana Allred and I grew up in. Is a gang territory. We had no way out. So we prayed and stuck together. I got shot and made the fatal mistake of cheating on Jeana Allred. My baby left me y'all. Only to come back years later. Right before she died. To tell me that she loved me and goodbye. you see fellows I never knew the meaning of goodbye. It is the strongest word in the world. Just because it carries so much pain and love with it. Right now I have been single for 10 years. You have been writing books I'm going to help you. Shontel Allred. I knew you wouldn't leave me. Thomas Allred Jr you are almost at the end of your book. Happy New year to all and to all a good night. Now send your book in Thomas Allred Jr. Captain Frankie and lieutenant Candis thank you for everything and I mean it. We are the police.

CHAPTER 18

What happened to you was a crime Thomas Allred Jr. The motherf*ckers killed your wife. At and early age in your life. Thomas Allred Jr. I know what you feel like. The wanting to give up on everything that you know to man. They shot you Thomas Allred Jr. When you were only 19 years old. That is the reason for my book. My Future self. Pest self can you see. That you and me are all right in the future. We are going to make it out of this situation Thomas Allred Jr. Just trust Eden Reid. To her this is not a game. And it isn't Thomas Allred Jr. Your love is all over these pages. And the world feels your pain. But you must believe in yourself. I know it hurts what they did to your wife.

But God said there is a better day. That is if you can only believe and be professional. Thomas Allred Jr this is a book. About the struggles that a man and woman go through. I'm so very proud of you Thomas Allred Jr. Because you got a professional here in your corner. And I'm saying to you Thomas Allred Jr. That you are a police officer. And no one's ever going to hurt you again. And now to the community. We as police men and women come to do our duty. you are making us see that if we care for one another things can happen to make a difference. City and state and government. Thomas Allred Jr is one of us. We are all children in God's great world. Professional women have worked daily night and day to make this book a reality. I'm calling that to you. Citizens men and role models. To perform your duty at a level of understanding. Now you have been shot Thomas Allred Jr. Yes still you keep on trying. Can you in your heart Thomas Allred Jr. Tell me what's it take to be a champion. My Future self. There is no champion in me. I'm only a man who does what's right. And I see myself. Getting married to a beautiful woman. That is your future. I don't know what people say about me. But Jeana Allred is my heart and always will be. She will be greatly missed. A look. I think that I'm so dedicated. Because I know that me and my wife were fighters. I keep trying to reason with myself. If I got shot and she got shot. Then why am I still here and she's not. I tell myself to God has a plan. And if I keep following orders and following the rules. The one day that plan will be revealed to me. But y'all to tell the truth. I just want my girl back. I have no money no clothes. And I barely even comb my hair. I'm trying to get myself together but I can't. Because something is missing in my heart. And I keep dreaming for change. I keep hustling for a better day. But it seeMs. like I never get paid. I believe in God's word. For God so loved the world. That he gave his only begotten son. The whosoever believeth in he. Shall not perish but have eternal life. And that is true. Because the people in my city. And the people all over the state and government. Have granted me another chance at life. But all I'm saying is. That my wife Jeana Allred believed in God also. And I've been saved and she's not here. God what kind of justice is that. Thomas Allred Jr. Yes Future self. In the future I miss her. In the past I miss her. And in my presents I'm a police officer. Fighting and doing my best to make a change for everyone. Now that professional see me. Eden Reid and Ms. Cindy .

I want to know. Did my books have the integrity that they needed. Did my story make sense to you. because everyone thinks that I'm doing this for entertainment reasons. Take your book up and go with me. My woman was too special. and that is it for this book called so-called professionals. You see I made it through the test in the fire. I held my ground with my baby was under fire. Thomas Allred Jr ain't bullsh*ttin. My past self only realize. Future self theres only one way out and that's through God. So there's no need to be afraid of anything. The past the present and the future. All came together at once for me. In a split second. I asked God it can't be over. My girlfriend took care of me. and I keep talking about this over and over again. How one beautiful lady police officer. Stood up and fought and died for me. Our sacrifice belongs to the children. Do children are what made Jeana Allred the women she is today. And I don't care about any awards. I just want the world to know.

How beautiful and how wonderful my wife was and still is in my heart. This is for professionals. To think about. What shall it profit a man. To gain the whole world. Just to become professional. I love you Jeana Allred. And honey this is the best that I can do. I've given everything. God I've given everything. Until there is no more left but me. I need you girl. Baby please don't go. I love you Jeana Allred. I love you too Thomas Allred Jr. Shontel Allred. Yes Thomas Allred Jr it is me. But how did you get in my book Shontel Allred . God has sent me. To help you Thomas Allred Jr. We are on a professional level.Thomas Allred Jr. We are among the elite. That is meaning Thomas Allred Jr. That whatever happened to you. Let It Go. Because God has a meaning and a purpose for you and me. Shontel Allred. They took Jeana Allred life. And almost took mine. Thomas Allred Jr do you still have fear. No I do not have fear Shontel Allred. Because I'm your wife now Thomas Allred Jr. And I promise you that I got you. Through sickness and health. Until death do us part. Shontel Allred. Please Don't leave Me. I won't leave you Thomas Allred Jr. Shontel Allred. Baby please Don't leave Me. I see that you need a second. No Ms. Eden Reid. I got Thomas Allred Jr Right where he needs to be. In my arMs.. Make a movie out this books manuscript. We have traveled a distance. And taking all sorts of pain. Don't give up. I can't give up Shontel Allred. Honey I appreciate whatever you do for me. Because God has put us together. And my wife is beautiful. Thomas Allred Jr is a professional. Send off that book Thomas Allred Jr. I need an autograph from you and Shontel Allred. Ladies and gentlemen the couple of tomorrow is here today. I give to you Shontel Allred and her husband Mr. Thomas Allred Jr. Now get that book into Me. Yes Ms. Cindy

I definitely want to thank Miss Eden Reid. And Miss Cindy. For making this possible. Thank you Cindy. I need to thank. My mother and father. For supporting me through the years. Along with my brothers and sisters. Take over Thomas Allred Jr. My past self this is the future. Thomas Allred Jr you got two more days to write the other book. I got a good sense of humor. I get my inspiration from aurther like Dean Koontz and Stephen King. And people should get a copy of this book. For the right to being free freedom. my background is I grew up in Hickory North Carolina. Where I've been working as a undercover cop. All of my life. Thomas Allred Jr people are starting to see that you are a real person. About me as an author I am doing my best for you.

Take time to read my book and editorial. Why you should get a copy of my book. Because it reads better than any book that you've ever read before. I love you Cindy. And I love you Miss Eden Reid. The only person that didn't give up on me is Eden Reid and Ms. Cindy. And I want to thank you all Cindy. Miss Eden Reid let's get in line for the publication of the next book called I've been waiting for you by me myself Thomas Allred Jr. Future self that is beautiful. I aim to please you Thomas Allred Jr. Get ready for the next chapter in this saga. Everybody get ready. Here go the press release. Jeana Allred honey I miss you very much. This book is dedicated. To all those who have lost somebody. Read carefully. It is a meaning if your after it.

We got to get Cindy credit Thomas Allred Jr. For coming up with the plot behind the story. I told you I won't give in. Everybody I'm getting ready to sacrifice. My whole belief system. To tell you that I've been longing for this girl. Every since i spoke to her on the phone one year ago. Listen to me Thomas Allred Jr. Make a book about longing for someone. Yes Cindy. Thomas Allred Jr make a book and that's all I'm saying. In my younger days. Love had me confused. I used to believe that if you took your time and care for someone. That they would automatically care for you too. Thomas Allred Jr editorial was fresh and clear. Thomas this is Miss Eden Reid. And we all love you out here. By the time I lay down to sleep. I can see how fortunate I am. I can see those female saying that they love me and they want to be with me. I can tell you now. That to create my kingdom. I had to be alone a many nights. I work slowly and steady on my books. Just like a Craftsman I had to see that everything fits. We doing the same thing Thomas Allred Jr. But all I care about is Eden Reid. That mother f*cker said he care about you. Thomas Allred Jr. Maybe in my future. Ms. Cindy. But as for now I'm asking you to stop telling people that. I don't know what to ask for. Thomas Allred Jr the people all are with you. Take your time on your movie and write your book. Lord please help me write this book to where everybody can understand. Everybody can understand. Eden Reid. Mr. Thomas Allred Jr. So nice to meet you finally. Good things happen for a reason Eden Reid. I brought Cindy alone to go over this manuscript with me. So if you don't mind Thomas Allred Jr may we look at it. Thomas Allred Jr we traveled a long way for you and your book. I'm telling you Miss Cindy all kind of ideas keep going through my head. Don't you realize you are the leading aurther in the u.s. today Thomas Allred Jr. Cindy I couldn't have did nothing without you and Miss Eden Reid. Thomas Allred Jr your editorial is spectacular. Talking to Cindy. Oh excuse me your. I just look at the manuscript over here. Eden Reid I know I got to deal with you. But I just think that we will all have a better time if we all had dinner together. I'm starting to see how you operate Mr.. Thomas Allred Jr. I'm mixing work with pleasure I got two girls with me. What do you say Miss Cindy have dinner with me. Thomas Allred Jr the book is all of course.

Don't use that initial. Listen Cindy. And listen Miss Eden Reid. God has put us together for a reason. The reasons are unclear to me right now. But what I'm telling you is. That we're going to be spectacular. The woman that I miss with everything. Is Shontel Allred. And that is because I need her. Now when you talk to me. Talk to me like we doing business together. That's why I signed you. Eden Reid I'm in love with that girl. Shontel Allred is my world before these books came out. And now I feel like she will not talk to me. My heart is broken. Look how beautiful she is on the picture that I have on the wall. Thomas Allred go to sleep now. We are going to talk about your manuscript later. Forget manuscript I am writing a new book. Ms. Cindy. Gabrielle when did you get here.

I got you two a place in the winner's circle. Thomas Allred Jr and his books. Are going to guarantee us that we get our place in Hollywood. Eden Reid and Cindy. Give that man anything that he wants. Just keep Thomas Allred Jr writing. What should he write about Gabriel Union Allred. He can write about Yankee Doodle dandy for all I care. We are all beginning to watch you Thomas Allred Jr. Miss Eden Reid you myself and Cindy along with Thomas Allred Jr and his manuscripts. Are making the game changing plays on Hollywood. What I'm saying Cindy is where famous girl. He keep writing your names in his books. Gabriel Union Allred does Thomas no this. He can't know this. Because the Secret Service is all around his place. I'm telling you I miss you Shontel Allred. Thomas Allred Jr we are teaching you to be a strong Arthur. I know because I'm famous right. Right you are famous. And so are we. Kristen Allred.

Baby how did you get here. This is your dream Thomas Allred Jr. I missed you so much. I miss you too Kristen Allred Jr. Nada and Ashley is here also. This is got to be a dream it can't be. It can be once you do your work and finish with you Thomas

Allred Jr. This just may not be a dream. Miss Cindy are you dreaming right now. I'm listening to your book Thomas Allred Jr. And no I'm not dreaming. Miss Gabriel Union Allred. Are you dreaming right now. Thomas Allred Jr your book is going to Hollywood. And no I'm not dreaming right now. If you two are not dreaming. And I'm writing my book as we speak. And we all are together. It must be a miracle. Exactly Thomas Allred Jr. But miss Eden Reid I don't understand. I know you love those women. Thomas Allred Jr don't you realize the opportunity that you have. You have the opportunity to have every woman that you ever loved. Living with you and belonging with you. In your own condominium in your own space. I want a major book from you. Publish his book y'all. Shontel Allred forgive me. But in the dream that I'm having. The girls pick Superman. In the dream that I am having. I'm going to kick your a** Thomas Allred Jr. Have a seat everyone. Your bank account is over a trillion dollars. Thomas Allred Jr. Would like for you to know. That this book is dedicated. To the people that's working behind the scenes. In operations making everything possible.

Keep going Thomas Allred Jr people are starting to care about you. And the truth is. We all care about you. You talking about Gabriel Union Allred. Speak to him Gabriel Union Allred. Look Thomas Allred Jr. Right now many of us. Don't know if we can trust in your opinion. That's right Thomas Allred Jr. But we do believe that you are watching. In our future. Where there is love there is happiness. And we are meant to be. All of us will see that a future date. But Thomas Allred Jr don't give up on us. Nada say something to Mr. Thomas Allred Jr. Thomas I loved you since I met you. Keep believing in yourself. Because I believe in you. And so do the all the women in the world as we know it. You are the agent code name Superman. For the FBI and NSA in the Secret Service.

You work for the New York Police department. You make business ideas to say people lives all over the world. And for the last 2 years you have been writing books. Mr.. Thomas Allred Jr. We are proud of you. Now which one of us ladies do you adore. Take your damn time picking. I would like to talk to Miss Eden Reid. Here Eden Reid he is all yours. Check them out. Thomas Allred Jr oh my God. Eden Reid I'm a faithful man. I'm here because you chose me to be. Thomas Allred Jr the end of your book is coming. I like you Thomas Allred Jr. Thank you Miss Cindy. Thomas Allred Jr so where do we go from here. I'm going to take it one day at a time and Court you. Over the telephone until our business is complete. Ms. Cindy he chose me. Eden Reid people are watching. Thomas in your book now. I've been waiting for you. Tell Eden Reid I love her. Y'all better give me out the situation. Thomas Allred Jr wake up your dreaming. This ain't no book Thomas Allred Jr. I just now finished it the book is complete. That's 101 for your a**.

But the book wasnt complete just there. Thomas Allred Jr you recognize. Just what you doing don't you. Miss Cindy I'm going all the way out. So you love Eden

Reid. I do become professional with me Eden Reid. Thomas Allred Jr sit back and read over your book. That book has your family in an uproar. Listen to me if you want the book sales Thomas Allred Jr. Then go after the book sales. But leave me out of it. Don't listen to what the haters say Eden Reid. I am truly indebted to you. Miss Cindy. Make sure that Eden Reid has everything that she needs. Because I'm willing to sign anything. As long as we are together Eden Reid. This can't be true my name in the book that's sophisticated. Take sophisticated off of there. I put your name in my book because. Eden Reid you are a friend to me. Choose your content. If you want all of the women Thomas Allred Jr I can't be there for you. Don't you see it Eden Reid. I'm about two stories away from taking over the planet. And I love you with all my heart. He is sending her a wedding ring through the mail. Y'all better quit playing with me. Do the damn thing Eden Reid. Thomas your book is a number one seller in five countries. Including the USA. You better stop that boy. History shows us that I can't be stopped Eden Reid.

Yes you can if the women want you. Talk to yourself Thomas Allred Jr. Because the story is that you. Know that you are a king. Let's take a few seconds to get our stories together. One day I called you. One day I was listening to my radio across my bed. I said that my name is Eden Reid. I said my name is Thomas Allred Jr. We had a phone conversation. I had a phone conversation with you Eden Reid. Then after that you wrote books for you and me. Explain it to yourself Eden Reid. I usually don't do this but but I. I think I fell in love with you the first time that we talked. I want to get to know you. Thomas Allred Jr realize. That you are in the big leagues now Thomas Allred Jr. Anywhere you go lots of people with surround you. Here we go. Thomas Allred Jr see that you published all of your stories. This boy's talk about he's in love with me. Eden Reid give us a chance. To make something out of ourselves. I'm so sorry I just can't.

Miss Cindy tell her that I love her. He says that he loves you Eden Reid. Don't you realize you are successful because of me Thomas Allred Jr. Keep writing your book. I'm faithful. Going back to the start. I wanted to see you. That's when my. Talk to me Thomas Allred Jr. This is the end of the book. But why Thomas Allred Jr keep going. Because I realize. I'm missing you so much Shontel Allred . Did something happen to me. No Shontel Allred. Something happened to all of us. What did happen to us. You are I got famous. There is more of the story to this book. That boy got some good a** handwriting. Nada. Gabriel. Kristen. Eden. Cindy. Heather. Kay. Kathy. Nora. Teresa. Porsche. Chelsea. Evelyn. And Shontel Allred. Y'all are the ladies that started me.

Mr. Thomas Allred Jr. But we just want you to know that it's a lot of people out there that love you and care about you. My decision for you ladies is. To take your place in history with me. For being there for me. I put your names up on top of the world. Lieutenant Candice. And Captain Frankie. I let the world know that I couldn't do anything without the two of you. And I'm eternally grateful for you all.

We are about to see Thomas Allred Jr. If you are truly grateful. I'm waiting on my contract. With Thomas Allred Incorporated. I want these women to work with me. I am Thomas Allred Jr. And this is my story. Girl I punch the clock daily. You have got to produce me. Cause I asked it from heaven. I'm going to make sure everybody gets a chance at the spotlight. Thomas Allred Jr. Chris and Anthony. Michael and Kesha. Are downstairs they're waiting on you to become professional. Eden Reid. Honey let's see what this a do. In all 50 states. Let the people look at this book as a new beginning for us all. I'm too professional. That's why these women are working with me. You know Eden Reid. That in my pa**. I looked at everything as a test of my spirit. See now I truly believe in God and I thank you for everything. I'm waiting for you Eden Reid. And the rest of my beautiful ladies. Because together there's nothing that we can't do. Shontel Allred I love you sweetheart. I really love you. It is my signature. Let my women have whatever they want. Because this book is going to bubble. And God said this. The damage is. I'm in love with you Eden Reid. Everybody know that Eden Reid is a queen. I became professional. The moment that I hurt your voice Eden Reid. I'm expecting you to. Give me a phone call. Each one of my women. Thomas Allred Jr the book gotta in right now. I need you to stay with me.

Everyone of my women. See. I work my life away. So women can have the best of my ability. That's why I am single y'all. Just waiting for you to call me over. Waiting for you. Don't get too comfortable Thomas Allred Jr. You have got to prove yourself in this book. If you want women Thomas Allred Jr. Just tell the woman that you want them. All that you got to do is. Just say that you really honor them. I know exactly what you're talkin about. Thomas Allred Jr. Please work with me. Cindy I will work with you. I just got to. Get myself in a new position. To where I can put out this book Cindy. Thomas Allred Jr I'm working with you. Day and night. Listen Thomas Allred Jr. As your Fame grows. So does your people fan base. Are we going to move forward Thomas Allred Jr. Yes Miss Cindy. It's about time. For my girls to recognize me for the person that I am. See I'm a capitalist. Thomas Allred Jr take capitalist off of your paper now. Somebody removed capitalist from the paperwork. Now Cindy. The company is too big for us.

Lieutenant Candis. And Captain Frankie. Can you help me explain to the people. My motive is to help people. Thomas Allred Jr in the beginning of time. Are people with chosen. Captain Frankie and I. I have watched you. and Thomas Allred Jr we know that you are in love with many women. In which you haven't had a chance to speak to. Your dreaMs. are coming across vividly. And you still have one more entry to go in this book. You got a sacrifice all that you know for this book Thomas Allred Jr. Now what are your dreaMs.. My dreaMs. are to run this palace with all women inside of it. My second dream is. To use the money to help the women and children all over the world. My third dream is kind of nasty. I dream that I'm the most book-selling person in the world. With the women sitting there for me. See Cindy. God told me to keep on trying. And I sacrifice all of my trouble for you. Lieutenant Candis I really respect you. And I really respect you to Thomas Allred Jr. This is Captain Frankie from The New York Police department speaking Thomas Allred Jr. Each book you are writing. Thomas Allred Jr may not mean nothing to you right now. Thomas Allred Jr realize. There our people really care for you. Listen do you work. And make us proud. And you got the Secret Service watching you. The NSA and the FBI. The whole Police department is with you. I say you go for it all Thomas Allred Jr. Kristen Allred I love you. Shontel Allred. I love you. Nada Allred I love you as well. You see ladies. In my stories I give you my last name. That is in respect to you. To the woman and the women that y'all are. Tell the women that you want them Thomas Allred Jr. Ladies I want y'all so much. What we have to do is. Prove that I'm the greatest writer out there in the world today. Lieutenant Candis are you all right. Yes. Lieutenant Candice Allred. I love you. Chelsea. Heather . Kathy. Eden. Kay. Samantha. Porsche. Teresa. Nora. Kristen. Nada. You are all my wives. In my dream in my book. I believe that I'm strong enough to handle you. Samantha I love you a lot. And Porsche everything will work out if we try. Thomas Allred Jr make your book global. Can someone send a copy of this book to the White House. Thomas Allred Jr you are going to far. All I'm saying is I love you Cindy. And I'm waiting for you to realize that. Happy birthday Cindy. And Shontel Allred happy birthday. Thomas Miss Eden Reid has a birthday coming up. Eden Reid this book is dedicated to you. Because you believed in me when no one else did. Thomas Allred Jr complete your book right now. And to my mother Charlene Allred. I give much respect and honor. Thomas Allred Jr. Keep on writing your books. Kristen Allred. I'll do what I can honey. but I just want to know if me and you can have a chance. This book captured the hearts of many people. Cindy I need a break now. Keep your composure Thomas Allred Jr. I will publicate this book. In every community. And in every neighborhood. Around the world. You see my dream is coming true Cindy. And what dream is that Thomas Allred Jr. To live without emotions taking over my dreaMs.. Now that's deep Miss Cindy. Send off that book to Cindy Thomas Allred Jr. You are the right person for this job. Cindy I thank you. Happy birthday. From our family to yours I'm waiting on you. Thomas Allred Jr didn't I tell you. To secure your packet first. All thats being taken care of as we speak. Thomas Allred Jr the world knows you. Keep up the good f*cking work. Thank you Ms. Eden Reid and Ms. Cindy. For everything. Lieutenant Candis and Captain Frankie. Listen to I thank you both so much. This is God it have to be God. That's is. Send your book in Thomas Allred Jr.

CHAPTER 19

Thomas Allred Jr I see where you're going with this book. Enlighten me Kristen Allred. Thomas Allred Jr you are fooling yourself. I'm fooling you Kristen not me. Know what I'm saying is is that. All of your women Thomas Allred Jr. Have either going away. Or got married to someone else. And there is only me Thomas Allred Jr left. To carry the torch for you. Kristen your a bunch of bullsh*t. Eden Reid speaking. What does Eden Reid want Thomas Allred Jr. Chill out Kristen Allred this is business going on. We invite you and Kristen Allred to our annual party that we're having. Theres going to be women there. Oh my God he mention women. He outside. Snap a picture of him. Take out the trash Thomas Allred Jr. Yes lieutenant Candis Allred. Can you hear me. Contact the police officer that wouldn't have no sh*t Thomas Allred Jr. That is me that wouldn't have no sh*t.

What can I do for you lieutenant Candis Allred. I want you to tell the story the way it's supposed to be told. how you and the police force and the rescue squad saved my life lieutenant Candis Allred. And how doctors work Non-Stop over me to bring me back to life after I had been shot. That's the story Thomas Allred Jr. You see what you're doing. Is taking care of your business. All I want you to do now is. Tell them people who helped you thank you. To the doctors and to the rescue squad and to the police. Thank all of you for saving my life. Reminiscing. I came back to life for a reason. And I do believe that if that. I found my love. It would be a sign that we can all make it. I'm getting ready to send this book in across the table. It is called waiting for you. If your birthday is about to come. I put Your name across My heart. Thomas Allred Jr. I love you. Lieutenant Candis Allred I love you too. I love you too Thomas Allred Jr. Evelyn Allred. I care for you Evelyn Allred. But the book must be finished now. in all 50 states we put this book up for the challenge. Thomas Allred Jr. What do you think. God said I can do all things with Jesus Christ who strengthens me. so I believe one day the people who save my life are going to know how much I care for them. And that there is nothing in this world that I wouldn't do for them. That's good the book is excellent Thomas Allred Jr. You mean what you say in all of the book don't you. Keep your composure. Thomas Allred Jr. Go ahead and in this book and stop the madness. Yes lieutenant Candis Allred. And Captain

Frankie. Thomas Allred Jr if you succeed. You would have been made the biggest come back in history. Your story will sell all around the world. We need one more verse to tighten this book up. Hand my girls a million-dollar check a piece. The boy took his time and became a professional. They said when they shot Thomas Allred Jr that he gave up. When he went down. But when they killed his girl. Thomas Allred Jr. Became a police officer. Thomas Allred Jr. What is your officer's name. I am officer Reign of the New York Police department. Code name Superman with the NSA. The FBI. And the Secret Service. Y'all get Thomas Allred Jr where to sit down. I want to stand. Thomas Allred Jr they shot in the leg. But I still got my other leg here to hold me up against you. Thomas Allred Jr. Do not say it. Jeana Allred. Honey what they did to you was wrong. What they did to you and I was wrong. But baby I believe that God is going to let us see through. I keep trying Jeana Allred. And I keep crying. I pray that everything works out for the best. And that you didn't lose your life or nothing. I'm here baby. I'm here waiting on you.

I'm waiting on you to return Kristen Allred. The biggest part of the book is. Who am I going to wedd or marry. Yeah we know your book is a monster Thomas Allred Jr. Tell intelligence agencies that I said. I might be responsible for the industry shut down. That's true isn't Kristen Allred. He is writing his book. Make sure that you motion to me. Before you go in the room where Thomas Allred Jr is at. We can't disturb him. Thomas Allred Jr is writing a book and it is already underway. Do we take our clothes off now or later. His birthday is going to come. You see Thomas Allred Jr I don't like this part of the book. You see Kristen Allred this is material that must go in the book. Thomas Allred Jr this girl right here really wants to know where you get your inspiration from.

Did inspiration for my books. Comes from me almost dying. Out in the field when I was younger. I was a young cop. And my mission was to extract someone. And lead him to safety. These girls believe in you. Thomas Allred Jr. A penny for your thoughts Kristen Allred. Tell Thomas Allred Jr to continue to work on this damn book Kristen is right here. Keep it professional Thomas Allred Jr. You will have more women than you can handle. And as a boy I.

Wanted to be with you Kristen Allred. Cause there was nothing that I could give you. To show my love and affection that I felt for you. All my life I tried to find love. We got one more verse to go before we finish the book. If you come pail my books. And you take it one verse at a time. You will see that Jeana Allred I love you. Forever. Is written on it. Being professional. You are fend to make me cry. That boy is a serious community leader. Thomas Allred Jr. Thank you everybody. I'm about to go to sleep. Write Shontel Allred Thomas Allred Jr. And to my future wifey. I am going all the way out. To ensure our success. And to change our lives for the better. A single letter won't do for you. Gabriel Union Allred. Could you tell Miss Eden Reid and Ms. Cindy to come in here for a minute. Eden Reid and Miss Cindy

Thomas Allred Jr wants you. We are coming. Yes Thomas Allred Jr you requested us. Gabriel thank you you may leave now. Eden Reid realize this book is going global. My message to you is. Care about the people surrounding you. And Miss Cindy. Thomas Allred Jr I want you to see what you've done for me by putting my name in your book. You are the book Miss Cindy. Because of you I have faith enough to make it. Because of you Eden Reid I have faith enough to make it. Wake up Thomas Allred Jr. The book is now complete. But Shontel Allred. You see that. She is and will always be your wife and soulmate. When I snap my finger Thomas Allred Jr. Put your phone on the charger. And go to sleep Thomas Allred Jr. Makia Allred. I have loved you all my life. 1 2 3 snap. Now put the phone on the charger. Send your book in. I am waiting on you. Keep your composure here comes Shontel Allred. Listen. I know this may seem strange to you Thomas Allred Jr. But I'm working for the FBI the NSA and the Secret Service. What we going to do is. Send off your book. Keep standing up. With all my heart Shontel Allred. Now send our book in Mr. Thomas Allred Jr. Of Imperial designs LLC. And the Thomas Allred Jr incorporation. Along with Stratosphere. Along with Interscope Independent Records. We covered a lot of ground right here today. There are three wise men that want to speak to you Thomas Allred Jr and Shontel Allred. Did you get our message Shontel Allred and Thomas Allred Jr. The book is finished. You both are trillionaires. For taking the time to write these stories. The wise people call you king and queen. Of the world. Shontel Allred I've been longing for you for a long time. Keep your composure Thomas Allred Jr. You are making it happen. Professionally. And we still waiting on you. To write the book.

Look Eden Reid. I'm out here standing my ground. Eden Reid we done been through all types of things. If you care about me. Tell me my book is a smashed hit. And call my family and let them know that we are millionaires. Because it says in the Bible. Knock and it shall be opened unto you. Or something like that. Eden Reid. I would like for you to come and live with me and Shontel Allred. I realize that I'm approaching this the wrong way. but a businessman has so many businesses that he don't know what to do with. imma give you my personal information as soon as I give this book to you. Eden Reid my personal information got your name in the contacts. I hope you understand what I am saying to you Eden Reid. Thomas Allred Jr. The conclusion of my book is us getting to know one another. Thomas Allred Jr listen. All kind of people want your number from me. But the question is Eden Reid. If you use that number. You will be my wife. Now this book is not for child eyes. And it is not fiction. Eden Reid I am here today. Standing by myself. In order to publicate my book. I'm listening to you Thomas Allred Jr. Now sweetheart. Tell me if I'm crazy or not. For richer or for poorer. Thomas Allred Jr. Superman take your time to speak to me. You need a professional one that can handle you Eden Reid. I want you to help me get the women on my team. It is a PR position coming open.

And I think that you will be fine for the job. Eden Reid what do you say? There are all kinds of females looking at you. Are you sure you want me Mr.. Thomas Allred Jr. You are getting responsible. And you're the most talented man I ever know. Eden Reid I wanted to tell you that I loved you when I first spoke to you on the phone. That boy ain't got no dad going sense. Thomas Allred Jr it looks like you had a stalemate. I'm a businessman Eden Reid. Y'all keep representing Thomas Allred Jr. Who hurt Thomas Allred Jr. Your community is going after those people. Who hurt you Thomas Allred Jr. And Eden Reid it's coming after you Thomas Allred Jr. For the publication of our book. And to let people know. I'm trying my best Eden Reid. Thomas Allred Jr. Just take your time and finish the book. With all these conclusions. And with Nada . Heather. Samantha. Evelyn. Porsche. Chelsea. Maya. Kristen. Nora. Kay. Teresa. Shontel Allred .And lieutenant Candis. On my side. Are book can be a masterpiece.

Repeat after me Thomas Allred Jr. Ain't nobody taking my book away from me. Ain't nobody taking my book away from me. I will pay all costs to be the man that I am today. I will pay all costs to be the man that I am today. All the women are watching you Thomas Allred Jr become professional. The wise women want to speak to you. Miss Eden Reid will ask you one question Mr.. Thomas Allred Jr. Thomas Allred Jr how long have you been in love with all the women in your life. Every since I was in preschool. That is enough for the women out here. Thomas Allred Jr you got two more sentences. And the book is completed for good. Thomas Allred Jr. This is the last time that I'm going to bring this up.

Ladies my beautiful wife to Jeana Allred was killed. And I have been shot in my leg for trying to protect her and trying to protect someone else. I lost my memory after I got through bleeding. Y'all I can't remember her birthday. Or her last name. So I give her my last name. These stories that I'm writing you. Are stories of Love pa**ion and pain and God. For God so loved the world. That he gave his only begotten son. The whosoever believeth on him. so not perish but shall have everlasting life. And ladies and gentlemen I believe. To everyone of my woman out there. I want y'all to know the reasoning behind this book. Revenge is not the answer. But Jeana Allred I told you that we would make every last one of them pay. For killing people. Ladies and gentlemen. Jeana Allred and I Thomas Allred Jr. Or just entry-level police officers. And we fought our a** off to save everyone that we can. Through business ideas. And through hand to hand combat. Jeana Allred you will be greatly missed. Eden Reid I love her. Ladies I'm waiting on you. To tell me it's okay. I can rest a little while longer. The three wise men want to talk to you Thomas Allred Jr. Thomas Allred Jr your book is magnificent. But it is Shontel Allred. Who is your wife Thomas Allred Jr. Just close Your eyes. And imagine a place without fighting people. Somewhere that kids can look up to you and you can be free. You need to thank your neighborhood. For blessing you with the talent. three wise men I want to thank my neighborhood for blessing me with the talent. Okay Eden Reid.

Baby this is my book. Miss Cindy happy birthday. Happy birthday Shontel Allred And happy birthday Jeana Allred. Eden Reid happy birthday. Your publication. Has been I've been granted. Thomas Allred Jr we love you. Ladies Jeana Allred was a fighter. Make sure that book right there gets published. And yes before I forget thank you Captain Frankie for your wonderful words of encouragement through the years you and lieutenant Candis you mean the world to me sincerely yours Thomas Allred Jr. Waiting on you Eden Reid. To be my wife. Shontel Allred is your wife. I'm just testing you girl. Published that book. And I do this for the ladies. Thomas Allred Jr. Call me Superman girls. I'm a secret service agent and part of the FBI and part of the NSA. I work for the New York Police department. And this is the conclusion of my book waiting on you. Samantha I love you. Nada I love you. Heather I love you. Porsche I love you. Kay I love you. Kristen I love you. Teresa I love you. Cindy I love you. Nora I love you. Evelyn I love you. Maya I love you. Eden I love you. And everyone is you women across the United States of America become professional with me I love you. It took a long time but I always be waiting on you. That's the game.

It seeMs. like the closer I get to my dream my dream runs and hides from me. TV show at the TV show I watched Steve Harvey. And listen to his motivational speeches. And I want you to realize and understand that you. A God among men Mr.. Steve Harvey. Steve Harvey can't be here with us today. So I'm accepting this honor myself. Since I was a kid out playing on the swings. I knew that I was going to be someone that all kinds of people looked up to. If I'm helping you. Than I offer to you. Congratulations when your new book comes out. I am still hoping for the future to be. Better than my past was. I say this because there ain't no way that I can make it without the help of my friends and family and community. You see this one part of me that's been wanting to. Travel to the next level with these books and business ideas that I've been writing. And another part of me is stuck in my house. This other part of me is. Writing the book for you right now. The name of it is. Making a difference in my life by Thomas Allred Jr. if I was a rich man I would take my book to Hollywood to the Ellen DeGeneres Show. Or maybe let Oprah Winfrey read a chapter in it. Don't say nothing people. but I'm doing what I have to do to make it out the situation that I'm in. Yall programmed me to succeed. With the faith of a mustard seed I keep trying. You see I don't never give up on God y'all. He done brought me through some things. He brought me through being in the hospital. He bought me through property. He even brought me through my former girlfriend getting brutally murdered.

You see God is a producer. He knows exactly what he's doing. Let God help you. I realize that you don't need anyone but God to help you Thomas Allred Jr. But future self I cannot make it without anyone helping me. Get control over yourself Thomas Allred Jr. This is the book that were writing called. Making a difference in my life. By Thomas Allred Jr. My past self wrote that book. Now people every where is talking about me. Lord please help me understand what's going on with me. Thomas Allred Jr you don't have to be afraid Thomas Allred Jr. Lieutenant Candis. You are always here when I need you to lieutenant Candis. Thomas Allred Jr didn't I tell you that I wouldn't leave or forsake you. Thomas Allred Jr go back to the future for a minute. Can you see your family. Thomas Allred Jr I want you to be professional. Can you handle the stardom Thomas Allred Jr?. Say no Thomas Allred Jr. My past self. Says that he can't handle the stardom. Though Me and My Future self. We welcome every challenge that you can give us lieutenant Candis. Ellen DeGeneres I come for the fame. Thomas Allred Jr listen up. You only got three weeks. To prove yourself to Kristen. Enough of your messing up Mr. Thomas Allred Jr. Your wife and soulmate is here. In my Studios. Date whoever you want to. But your business is with Kristen. Thomas Allred Jr now know this may seem confusing to you. But there are 21 women who are in love with you. In your community Thomas Allred Jr. If you can handle yourself. And keep that business coming to us.

The Lord will bless you. Be professional. You asked for Eden. Eden will be with you. And you ask for Samantha Nada and Page. These ladies right here will be with you. And you also ask for Evelyn Porsche Kathy Teresa and Heather and Chelsea. And Maya And Kay. These ladies will also be with you. What time do you want these ladies to be with you Mr. Thomas Allred Jr. 6-30-2020. At 7pm. You got some work ahead of you. It is magnificent. And how you. Look at your future. And talk to yourself in your past. I am my future. I am my past. And my presents is controversial. I asked God for everything that Steve Harvey has. I asked God for everything the Oprah Winfrey has. I asked God for everything that everybody has. Be professional Thomas Allred Jr. Lieutenant Candis. I knew you would talented. But I didn't realize how beautiful you were. Write that book Thomas Allred Jr. I'm writing a book. To myself and me only. I spoke to you once before lieutenant Candis I spoke to you. Y'all be talking but he got a book coming out. Please I won't forget about you. Thomas Allred Jr your sitting there writing your book don't forget what all you've been through.

That's why I dedicate this book lieutenant Candice. Thomas Allred Jr do you know what you're doing. I'm helping people out. And trusting everyone of you to believe in God. Lieutenant Candis. I dedicate this book to Kristen. Y'all give that boy that contract. Happy birthday to you. Happy birthday Thomas Allred Jr. Happy birthday to you lieutenant Candis. Happy birthday to Steve Harvey. Is that all it is Thomas Allred Jr. My need some help figuring this out. Shontel Allred. Baby I love you. That girl want you Thomas Allred Jr. The power is with Jesus. That's what I'm telling everybody to depend on Jesus. And all else will fall into place. Miss Cindy. Happy birthday sweetheart. Keep on going Miss Cindy. We love you too. Happy birthday to miss Gabriel Union Allred. And happy birthday to my mother Charlene Allred. When there were times when I didn't think that I can make it. God help me through my situation. That's why this book is called. Making a difference in my life. Thank God for me. If something happens to me. Thomas this is your book. Pick yourself up and talk to the people. It is God who is making a difference in my life everybody. Shontel Allred. I was incapable. Of being there for you in the past. The future is coming because I made it happen. Now Shontel Allred. Honey will you give me another chance. You are making the difference in my life. By Thomas Allred Jr.

When you want to know what I know. It is because of you that made the difference in my life. I keep going cause people said I needed to believe in myself. It's a different kind of day today. See I learn from mistakes never to hurt nobody. and my mistakes made me the man that I am right here in front of you. The reason that I tell everybody this. It is by the grace of God that I falling into these footsteps. Thank you lieutenant Candis. And Captain Frankie. For giving me the strength to go on when I couldn't. We almost done a masterpiece.

I'm telling you one more time that I couldn't have done this without the help of my community. Everyday my community would look out for me. y'all I have to give it up for all of the white people who are helping me. And everybody who works along side of them. The reason I am so appreciative is because I am. A strong believer in what's right. I got to prove myself to y'all. I got to prove myself to me too. It's evidently the biggest work challenge that I've ever done. You get one shot at the fame. And I want the fame to know that. I walk with Jesus. And just because you walk with Jesus. The fame knows you as a man and woman of God. That's it right there. See yall I have been struggling these last few years. He planted me On solid ground. The reason I'm a good man is because of you lieutenant Candis. I dedicated myself to this book.

To show you how much you really mean to me. Lieutenant Candis my book has your name in it. That's because I am a single man right now. In love with different women. And talking to none of them. Bear with me for a second. How can I serenade you with words in this book lieutenant Candis. My common Sense tells me to keep writing to you. You see when they killed my girlfriend I never imagined that I find anyone else. But me and officer Jeana Allred. Had a talk before she died. And that talk was. That her and I would work together to get rid of all the street violence. In our community. Realize I was only a kid. But we agreed to be there for one another. Until death does us part. See lieutenant Candis. Officer Jeana Allred. Gave her life for me and her community.

And I got shot for me and my community. I work daily. Just writing books. And trusting in God that I'm going to see Jeana Allred again. I don't know why I named so many females inside of my book. I just want to love that I lost and found right now. What I've been doing in my free time is. Maintaining myself. And doing my best just to speak to yall. 91 more words and the statement is finished. Right now I'm just so hurt at what the community did to my girlfriend. I felt like a complete fool when I found out she was dead. But the Bible says. This somehow with Jesus

Christ. The Lord will strengthen you in all probleMs.. All I had was my faith. And faith carried me to the promised land. Thank you Jesus. Realized lieutenant Candis. I'm the best that I can be right now. Just in a room to myself. Right now I believe in you. I look To The hills which cometh my help. My help cometh From The Lord. I got a message for y'all. From officer Jeana Allred. I'm over it .Now you be over it. It's all a part of a belief system. That I can do better if I only believe. In Jesus. Say what you want to about us being police officers. Meditate on the fact that I'm making millions. And you sitting out there killing people. Being able to see myself in a different light. Gives me the strength to tell you. We are going to lock every last one of your a** is up. That is for killing people inside of my community. Now they shot me. But the Lord is the one who saved me. And you can take that to the bank. In my wildest dreaMs. have I never seen someone so beautiful. Eden Reid. I'm done with my book. Okay Thomas Allred Jr. Just relax and let me do what I do. Thomas Allred Jr you need to be more professional. To our communities officer Jeana Allred and i. Truly respect and appreciate everyone of you. It was officer Jeana Allred intention to. Write these books not mine. As The story goes. That is love here on Earth. I miss you my wife Officer Jeana Allred. And this book is called being professional because of my belief patterns. I know God is real.

I got sense enough to tell you that in two more days. I am going to be a professional black businessman. My companies are Interscope Independent Records. Stratosphere. The Thomas Allred Jr incorporation. And last but not least Imperial designs. Give it up to your black businessman of the year. From the ground up. I listen to motivational records. And exercised in my room on The daily. Right now. Your man is so far-fetched. That girl you need my help. I'm just kidding. Lieutenant Candis and I are just friends. Eden I was wondering if you could do me a favor. Send a limo to pick up this girl named Shontel Allred.Because what did I tell you Shontel Allred? You are damn right we are going to make it. We kept losing all of our friends. And we you had no money. People kept thinking that we were going to give up on each other. Well I got news for them. Y'all just made me work that much even harder. See the Bible says. What goes around comes around. That is why. In 2 professional business days. You and me girl. Will move out of this place. Somewhere into a mansion of our own. I won't lose you Shontel Allred. Honey I can't lose you. Even though the storMs. might seem rough. There is a silver lining on every cloud. Shontel Allred. I don't even know what I've done I'm just writing books. Let that man have a contract. He is writing books. What concerns me the most is. The pa**ing of my friend and wifey. Jeana Allred. I can't never come to terMs. with this. So inside a hurts so bad it kills me. If I would have only been there. Thomas Allred Jr there ain't nothing you can do about it. Listen you got to let Jeana Allred go. Shontel Allred. Help me. Shontel Allred help me. Thomas Allred Jr every since I met you. You have been a man of responsibility and pride. The whole country is sitting here waiting for your book to come out. Your opinion is what matters. Now what should I do about you and Jeana Allred. Just do nothing Candis. Lieutenant Candis I mean. I'm telling you. For the last time. That Jeana Allred is a princess. And I love her always and forever. Not Eden Reid do you got that. Y'all hear this boy. Get Shontel a limo. Get him a limo as well. In 2 days both of y'all will be a business man and woman. Take your time with that book Thomas Allred Jr you got to read it. For Hickory North Carolina. And all of the good ladies and gentlemen who live there. I bet you ado Candis. Now sweetheart. Don't think that I forgot about you. Send a limo for all of his ladies Miss Cindy. Yes lieutenant Candis. Soon-to-be wifey Thomas Allred Jr. It is incredible. God and his works. Shontel Allred. What God said he do he would do. I'm thanking all of the people. Who sponsored my book out there. You forgot one person Thomas Allred Jr. Lieutenant Candis. I want to take one second out to remember my father. Thomas Allred senior. Make sure you send off your book Thomas Allred Jr. Kristen look. At what God can do for us. don't you realize that a whole bunch of people are depending on you Thomas Allred Jr. Yes I do realize that people are depending on me. That's why I am on my knees day and night praying praising the Lord. Put Thomas Allred Jr on the radio. I am professional. The people I live with are professional. And the ladies are talk to are professional. My book is called two more days. Let us see what the Lord is going to do for you in two more business days. Girl I can't waste time. Lieutenant Candis. Will you marry me. To be continued in my next book. Called where I be. Thomas Allred Jr . I will. Keep your composure Thomas Allred Jr. Be professional. Don't you hear that sound. Yes I can hear it lieutenant Candis but what is it. You got the rest of your life ahead of you. That's the ballgame. You are a professional black man. With a woman by his side name Candis. Thank God that Candis is here. Relax Thomas Allred Jr. In my dreaMs. I rule this here. Give it up to my woman Candis. Thats absolutely the right thing to do at this point. I want to thank everyone. For helping me when I couldn't remember anything. It has been a struggle. But professionally. God is good. To every one of his people. The end.

Yall I'm finished with my book now. 160 pages later. After my book had got realized that it is professional. Thomas Allred Jr we are teaching you to stand your ground out here in this industry. lieutenant Candis no matter what I go through I will always stand My ground for you and every woman and man. I'm a dedicated my life to you lieutenant Candis. Look here lieutenant Candis. We got another book coming out. For my people out there on the street corners. Causing pain to our people. My book is called Memorial Issues. Now we are fend to have a problem. Don't you see. Lieutenant Candis. That what I want to say I can't say. But in this Next book Memorial issues. They shot a police officer. So I as a police officer. I'm going to say what's on my mind to the gangs on the streets. I talked to them. Telling them that in my life. This whole nation. Is for us. Instead of against us. I'm telling the gangs that you got the concentrate. To pick up a trade useful to your horizon. Now we've all seen death and pain. But to take a person's life for nothing is the worst form of coward in the world. And now I look at it this way. Even though gang members killed my wife and girlfriend. And they shot me when I was a young police officer. I have been going to church. Lord please help me. Cause I do not know what I do. The white people help me. And somehow today I'm sitting in front of you. Straightening up. Everybody I am sitting in front of you. The Last of the Mohicans. My police force is the New York Police department. I want to thank every law enforcement agency in the world. When my book comes out I'm focused on marriage. And that's all that I wanted to tell the gangs to do. Focus on marriage and a book. What we going to do now is say a prayer for Jeana Allred. It's raining outside. But the Lord is right here with me. So that you can see my horizons. So that my horizons can come to you. I'm thankful for my lovely beautiful wife Jeana Allred. I will see you again Jeana Allred. One day when the Lord says that I've done my job. I'm focused on you and me. Better times is he going to come. I'm thankful Jeana Allred. And that is the end of my prayer. Now one police officer to another police officer. They are jacking people. For no apparent reason. Thomas Allred Jr go on writing your book. Lieutenant Samantha. I got to be what God wants me to be. And what is that Thomas Allred Jr. A motivational speaker and women's rights activist. I need to speak to you lieutenant Candis.

Because I know you been through things just like I have. the police officers commend you lieutenant Candis and lieutenant Samantha. And lieutenant Kristen. And officer Reid. This is a dedication of truth justice and the American way. Gang members listen to me. I go out of my way to be there for the communities. We as the police and the government of these communities are nearly given all that we have to the community so everyone can survive. We have no more to give y'all. What we have for you are prison cells. For killing raping and molesting our neighborhood people. Women and children is out there. So act accordingly. Listen y'all I only have one life to live. But I dedicate it each and every second of it. To the maturity of our youth. Meaning I'm wanting to run a camp program.

To educate the young men in our communities. To help turn them into leaders of today. Just like Steve Harvey did me with his motivational speeches. Bitterness Lord put it away from me. Because I believe in my future. And the future is bright. If we all can work together as one. The gangs have been dispersed. There are no more gangs. Just women and men hanging around together. We are a community. And as flowers blossom. We can carry on. I was saving my best for last. To all of my fallen police officers women and men. I give my humble apologies for the mistakes that everyone has made. Mae young women and men officers. God is looking down on you daily. I know Jesus has a plan for us. He even got a plan for me. So without further ado. Recognize this book as. A compa**. To making the decision that is right or is wrong for you. If you see that you are in too deep. There's nothing you can do but pray. I'm taking it one step at a time. Look at my girl. Jeana Allred you are so beautiful. They killed my wife yall. And I'm writing this book to help them. Take your time. I will hunt them down. With all the resources that God blessed me with. I will put them in prison. And throw away the key. You think I'm bullsh*ttin. I am a secret service agent. I'm a part of the NSA and the FBI and the New York Police department. I carry myself as a police officer and a man in my community. When I get through with this book. I can see myself. Talkin to Jeana Allred. About buying a house. Just like we used to do. Before her life was taken. And I was shot. I'm down on my knees. Praying for forgiveness. The reason why I'm talking to you. Is because I'm waiting on you to tell me that you're sorry for what you have done. I'm going to take my book to Hollywood. And give it to Ellen degeneres and Oprah Winfrey. A copy to Steve Harvey to. Lieutenant Candis. Lieutenant I'm just running my mouth. My gratitude goes out to all the people. I am a woman to victiMs. rights advocate. And somehow or another. We must save these women and kids. From all of the predators that lie in these communities. My young men thank you. For being true men and fathers. I encourage you young men fathers and brothers. To read more to exercise and to take care of your families. Because we are a community. But mostly worldwide we are a family. Because we all are young men and young women. That is just trying to make it in the world. Captain Frankie I don't have any more to say. You did the right thing Thomas Allred Jr. Captain Frankie I try my best to tell the people. Tell them what Thomas Allred Jr. That God is the one that kept me from killing myself. When they shot me and killed my girlfriend and wife Jeana Allred. Sometimes it all works out for a reason Thomas Allred Jr. I'm not perfect lieutenant Samantha. I know you're not Thomas Allred Jr. I'm still going to be there for you. Lieutenant Candis and lieutenant Samantha and lieutenant Kristen the police officers salute you. Ms. Eden Reid his the book now. I try my best to make it so you can understand. That this is the real me. Officer Shontel. I am officer Reign. I am codename Superman by the NSA the FBI and the Secret Service. My name is Thomas Allred Jr everybody. And usually I don't do this but I got to keep the party started. Thomas Allred Jr. We know that you are hurting because of Jeana Allred. Is there anything that we can do to help you ease that pain that your feeling. Be nice to me. Lieutenant Candis. And lieutenant Samantha. And officer Shontel Allred. Captain Frankie wants to talk to you. Eden Reid has Thomas's book. Right now. This is the ball game of ma** proportion. What these kids need to realize is that were all family. The police as well as the citizens we are all people and we are all family. I salute you ladies. We salute You to Captain Frankie. And secret service agent. Thomas Allred Jr. One officer to another officer. Ladies I think God would say that we did a job well done. This is for my people out there on the street corners. That is way out just look at me. I pray for you all.

CHAPTER 20

I'm waiting for my composure to come back to me. I'm waiting to see if you people can believe in me the way I believe in you. I'm trusting in you to be better than you naturally are. People said I was the man in my community. I want to give you a book that you can all understand. Thank you. Thank you. For letting my book become number one in your communities. I just have to clean up. All kinds of mess. To be able to relax with my family. And all of my books that I've written. There has always been a woman interest of mine. And I'm here to tell you today. That I am still single. As a working man times can be. Rough and difficult for The working Man. As a working woman difficult times. Can be difficult for the working woman. And as a police officer I try to readjust. My attitude bank account. People I got a bank account. But I never get to see it because it doesn't belong to me. The question is and what I'm trying to say to you. Thomas Allred Jr. Is Officer Reign from the New York Police department. We can go on and on about the streets. Too many female victiMs. are losing their lifes. And I feel it is my obligation. To do something about this if the Lord gives me the will.

Thomas Allred Jr. My past self I have a message for you. Thomas Allred Jr. My future self I have a message for you. My Future self and my past self. I am not done. I am officer Reign of the New York Police department. And we seek Justice for fallen victiMs.. Who cannot seek Justice for theMs.elves. The police department has never gave up. And we will never give in to threats of any kind. They killed my favorite girl. So beautiful she is. And they shot me because I went with her. Sometimes I get upset about the situation. My attitude is like this. If God wants this book to be. Then this book will go out to all types of people from different races in different countries. Thomas Allred Jr. You need to call me officer Reign or Superman. Superman. Thank you for not ever letting them people steal your life away from you. I'm Thomas Allred Jr. Be professional Thomas Allred Jr. As a police officer I'm designed for work. I went through terrible situations. Thomas Allred Jr. Superman. We already know. Lieutenant Jennifer. You already know that I'm tired and need some rest. We already know that you are our hero Thomas Allred Jr. Officer Reign. Thanks for everything that you have done Superman. I'm on a mission y'all. Thomas Allred Jr your job is almost complete. Just say these three magic words. I will not give in. Say it Thomas Allred Jr. I will not give in. Put lieutenant Jennifer on Thomas Allred Jr. It hurt badly. My beautiful Jeana Allred. Thank you Thomas Allred Jr. You have proven yourself. To be a caring roll model. And best friend and guardian. This book ain't threaten nobody. But I'm going to get the police officers. To see what they can do about these people killing our women and our children. If you resource the God allows me to have. I will bring down to the police department. These women and children are people just like you. So get ready for Superman. An officer Reign. And Thomas Allred Jr. As one. The past the present and the future. All coming together. For the goodness of our communities. Ladies I will stand up for you. Children I would stand up for you. With all of my fellow men officers. That are all over the world. All women and children we apologize to you. For being self-centered and sometimes being disrespectful. Thomas Allred Jr. Your job is through. Now wait on the response to come back from everybody.

I am too legit to quit. If there's something that I want I try my best to go get it. That's why there is a making it symbol on the back of me. Ladies and gentlemen without no longer ado. My future self Thomas Allred Jr. The fame is what I live for. I'm making it because. I treat myself to the finer things in life. Watch it Thomas Allred Jr. The finner things in life belong to me myself in the past. I am sincere about this profession. I told you I would do it didn't it. 16 books later I'm still a man of my dreaMs.. I'm working on it. Ladies sometimes I get too sentimental Over the work that I must do. I am attracted to you ladies. whatever I do please forgive me I shouldn't have been so arrogant in my past. I'm looking at this like a new beginning of a old challenge. My feet are hurting. my chest is growing stronger than it ever has been. I keep working on the future because the past won't let me be. The past me is working. The future me is working also. Some say that you don't need money to succeed or have success in your life. And I agree with them to a certain extent. You see this is the future me. I am Thomas Allred Jr. And I am proud to make your acquaintance. There are just a few things that I need to know so that I can conduct my business in order. These ideas keep coming up to me. So I'm giving you everything that I got. For my ideas. To flourish overtime. And my book called making it today. Takes me out of the normal aspect of life. And teaches me how not to be. see my parents didn't want for me to have anything but the best that I could get. That's why I depend on you ladies and gentlemen. To show you are professional. Because I am just a mess without you. I'll be waiting outside. Along the window seal. Listening to every word that is said. About me and this book. And I see you as a hero in my eye sight. So ladies and gentlemen. I'm professional. I'm taking my time. Giving you what you need. With my books get published. Everybody knows the reason I'm here tonight. Thomas Allred Jr. This is an acceptance speech. I know that you realize that I'm the man about my business. In a room by myself I dreamed of this book. I dreamed of this female. I dreamed of this income. I missed out on dreaming because I was working all the time. Just building my life up one step at a time. Moreover I'm just glad to be here today. I had to keep telling myself. That the future was much better than what I was going through. Thomas Allred Jr. Appreciate other people. I want to appreciate Ms. Cindy. And Ms. Samantha. When I think of what others have done for me. And when I think of what I have done for others. It goes to show me that true love. Is one thing that you can't search and find. It has to be given to you. Making it today. Is my book on. The trials and tribulation within myself. Lord please let me finish this book. Your book Thomas Allred Jr. Shall be finished. Now I see myself as a role model. No matter how dark the situation gets. I always know that there's light at the end of the tunnel. I hope that you are listening. Be proud of you ladies and gentlemen. You are our rescue workers. And police officers. And doctors and lawyers. And judges and secretaries. Restaurant workers in cab drivers. Insurance workers in meter maids. Teachers. I'm being strong because you are being strong. Like the song tells you I can't do nothing without you. I like to share this pa**age with you before I get out of here. There's been times that I didn't think I can make it by Thomas Allred Jr. I told myself that you would be there for me. And I believed in my heart that you would be there for me. Even though the sky seeMs. gray. I knew you would be there for me. Thank Jesus Christ. For everything that he's done for me.

Going deeper into my subject. I'm counseling you to understand. That every night is dark. But with ideas you can find a better way. Thomas Allred Jr you only got a few more minutes. Listen you only got a few more minutes. To make a decision at what your life is going to be. In my dreaMs.. I am working with you. And not against you. All of the kids. Are happy. Because we keep trying. And we never stop. I just want to say. Thank you Jesus Christ. For standing with me through my trials and tribulations. For believing in me and my community. And guiding my books into the right hands. You have one minute left. Take your time. Samantha I acknowledge you. For being a beautiful woman. And friend and colleague of mine. Ms. Cindy I'm looking at you. And I'm trusting you.

With everything including my life. I knew that you would be there. Lieutenant Candis and Captain Frankie. Make sure Captain Frankie and lieutenant Candis get the props that they deserve. And lieutenant Kristen Allred. You are a dream of mine. What kind of dream are you having. That I am getting ready to succeed. Now that I'm done with you. The medicine I'm taking. Has me drawing a conclusion. To my subject. I'm making it today because everybody help me to make it. Thomas Allred Jr need help. Lieutenant Kristen Allred. And officer Shontel Allred. He has wrote a book. And we are all making it today because of it. Send a copy of my book to Shontel Allred. And lieutenant Nada Allred. What my book say. Making it today. Now watch and see don't we do it. Send that book off Thomas Allred Jr. Right now. Yes lieutenant Kristen Allred. Right now.

Because I have been dreaming of a better day. I search within myself to show you. That what lies beneath really is beneath the surface. Thank you. Dr. Thomas Allred Jr. May we get your autograph. Dr. Thomas Allred Jr. Just sign it right there. Okay what do I sign. To my past self. I made it out the situation that I was in. Into My Future self. My situation is better because I keep believing in myself. I'm putting Thomas Allred Jr. On both of your autographs . He looks like a police officer. Dr. Thomas Allred Jr is a police officer. We came a long way to see you Thomas Allred Jr. Well what can I help you with. My Future self. Thomas Allred Jr I need help getting the past to believe in me. One day at a time look at my eyes. The past future self. Is what makes you. If I'm you in the present. And you are me in the past. We already believe in you future self. Thomas Allred Jr. Yes past self. I hustle because you were the most important thing to me. Say are the most important thing to me. My past self. Listen here for a second to catch everybody up to speed. I'm talking to myself through these pa**ages. Because where I am right now. And where that I want and need to be. Are two different places. But with the help of God on my side.

Maybe the past wouldn't be so hard on me. My future is bright. No matter which way it turns up. To everybody that is out there doubting theMs.elves. Look at me y'all I came from nothing. I had to severe operations. To save my life. I'm a police officer getting no pay. And today I choose God more than anything else in this world. I have been alone for 8 years on my quest for success. Every woman that gets near me I push away. Just trying to figure out how to be there for everyone at the same time. I had a mortgage and I lost my house. My best friend cheated on me. When I finally admitted that I was in love. That girl took charges out on me and put me in jail. Past self it'll be okay. I got beat with sticks and drop cords my whole Young Life. To see me is a miracle.

Thomas Allred Jr share my grace. Because of you I am stronger. I am going to look to the Future. And keep On believing. That anything I want I can have. I give you the raw and brutal truth. I'm not perfect by any means. But I know that inside my heart that is a champion. And I believe in all words of God and wisdom. I'm counting on you Kristen Allred. Because I love you so much. I never meant to come off the wrong way. I just needed someone to talk to. And I knew that you are a good friend to all the people.

I fell in love with you. In my book It's a master profession. Kristen Allred I am asking you to marry me. I don't know what else to do. See so many women are deserving of me and my craft. And all of them are friends of mine. In the master profession. Everything gets works out according to plan. I have people who adore me. Take your time to speak to your people Thomas Allred Jr. To all of my people that I work with on The daily. Thank God I'm praying that you help fix my life up. Thomas Allred Jr. They hear you. Tell them what you need for them to do. The women that I mentioned in my book. I love each and every one of them. And I want them with me.

I prefer that we try to make it before we get the women with us. Listen to me past self. Anything you want you can have. Just believe in the future and appreciate the people around you. Now I got to go my past self. In the future I'm going to read my book. I'm sending it out by mail. Stop me if you want to. Thomas Allred Jr your future is ready to read the book. I'm still reading it my past self. And what I say is that it is good to have a past like you. Ms. Eden Allred. Thank you for the shot. At a future. I give to you. Dr. Thomas Allred Jr. Ladies advocate. Prepare for me My Future self. Thomas Allred Jr. Dr. Thomas Allred Jr. The past is satisfied. With our future being so bright. I made my book. So y'all can understand. That I talk to myself. Seeing that there's no one in my life with me. To love right now. Past you need to be ashamed of yourself. I'm a better man future self I promise. Kristen Allred. My past truly apologizes.

For all the wrong he has caused. I'm in love with you Kristen Allred. Your beauty is everlasting. You can see that. Every one of you I love so much. Your honor. Have I proved myself to the court system. Thomas Allred Jr you have proved yourself to the court system. All debt are settle right now. We are settling debts right now. Kristen Allred I loved you. When I was in prison. And I love you. At the top of the game. I am Dr Thomas Allred Jr. And this is it's a master profession. By me Thomas Allred Jr. I have one thing to say about this. It sho nuff feels good to be loved by you. My master profession. Send that book in Thomas Allred Jr. Don't worry about it Kristen Allred. Eden Reid ain't no joke. When you get through with it. Send it to my desk. Eden Reid.

CHAPTER 21

Listen to me people listen to me. It gets cold in my house sometimes. And I barely have food to make it through the month. Without food imagine I cannot be the man that I'm supposed to be. I know right now. That you are saying to yourself. In order to make it that we must achieve and overcome. I done got comfortable in this endeavor. I know the anything worth having. Is worth my effort. I can't stop at the end of the book. Did you hear what I said. In my mind. I am one of the best speakers out here.

Because I'm a police officer. And a motivational speaker. Can't you see what is motivating me. To have something. a person must get out of their comfort zone. Realize my comfort zone. Is this pen and pad. You do realize that I'm hungry. And I'm searching for the love that I've never found. In all of my life. When I talk to you about love and finances. I talk to you in the way of a prophet. Be professional Thomas Allred Jr. Mr.s. Eden Reid. I'm giving it 100%. Mr.s. Eden Reid. I am leaving no kind of bullsh*t on the table. As I approached the job. I look at my hands to make sure that I am worthy. Sometimes it is amazing what you go through. And other times you have to go through something amazing. In order to achieve and prosper this book is. A stepping stone to my future self. I've said it and I've said it best because I'm only me. You ain't got to be outdone future self. You just got to take care of business. Everyday In and out. You need to do the right thing. That is why with this literature. I tell those who have been left for dead and abandon. I have been through the same thing that you are going through. At 17 years old. I was shot through a professional Hitman. I didn't have no idea it was happening. Listen to me Thomas Allred Jr. You don't have but one dream. Make your dream yours Thomas Allred Jr. I would like to make a Jeana Allred foundation. For hurt and abused woman. That is all over the world. In my heart and mind. If we come together people. We can take care of what matters the most to us. And that is each other people. I'm tired of people giving up when theres seconds left in the game. I came to play everybody. I came to make sure that Jeana Allred and my name are remembered forever. I ain't got no tricks for y'all. I can see that you and me or the elite. I'm not trying to motivate you with my speaking. This is the average me. I thought about where I was and where I wanted to be. I have to be professional. My wife took a bullet for me. Thank you Jeana Allred. I'm asking for your forgiveness. Contract Killers after me. We don't stop Jeana Allred. Superman. I know that I hurt you. And I would never give up. Just trying to make things right. Jeana Allred I love you so much. And this right here motivates me to be professional. You make me out to be a hero Thomas Allred Jr. I make you out to be what you are an angel and a queen. Go ahead and keep on talking Thomas Allred Jr. it is a dream of mine to have everything that we ever desired. I want to give that to you Thomas Allred Jr. I love you so much Jeana Allred. and The story goes that Jeana Allred was brutally murdered. If I could have been there I would have. That's why people I say to you. In life. You only get one chance to be the best you that you can be. And I promise you that. As long as you are trying. Our circuMs.tances will have to change. Damn right they will. Now I'm not going to go any further with this book. My job is finished here. And I cannot see the reasoning behind this book. All I see is my book in front of me. With hopes. I make it to where I dream. You are not a doormat. By Thomas Allred Jr.

I'm coming to you with everything. As if everything wasn't enough. I've seen a lot of pain in my days. I still have strength to tell you that I love you. And I'm here for you. if you listening to my book my book is a major report. Because I study myself. Along with studying the art of other people. In the days to come imagine myself to be a trillionaire. Mature as I am I need a soulmate. Someone to help me with my day-to-day operations. I search within these pages. For the help that I very well need. Think about it this way. I represented myself. In the industry. By writing and telling the truth about my life. There is so many things that I would like to share with you. I'm a teach you how to believe in yourself. Though every challenge you have got to trust in God to make it through it. Everyone is in love these days. I just want me a love that I can count on a love that I can depend on. In the earlier versions of my book. He said that earlier versions of my book. I told you that man is professional. Lieutenant Nada this is how the rest of the story goes. Im a make it. Because there's no doubt in my mind. I trust in myself I believe in God and I believe in my people. Whatever happens happens for a reason. It is kind of like skydiving lieutenant Nada. Believing in yourself Strong enough will take your breath away. That's why anything that I want I pray and ask God for it. It may not come when you want it but it's always right on time. I hustle my way through these pages of circuMs.tance. Looking for an endeavor that I can sink my teeth into. I'm going out to get it lieutenant Candis. For the man in me. And for the people that's involved in my project. I sit alone in a dark room. Thinking about the future coming. I tell myself.

To maintain my position. In my studies. In my exercise of my body. In my eating habits. And thank the people who are with me on the daily. This is part time what I'm doing. Is strengthening myself well being. I'm going back to the past for a second. I hope Eden Reid is listening. Working with you has been a pleasure and an honor. God has put me on this course to where I make it. I hope you know that this book was destined to happen. Look at me my eyes show the truth. everything that I've been through outta show the truth. About the man before you. I'm telling everybody. That I feel somewhat humble and respectful. My team has just now won y'all. The human soul cannot deal with the magic I put out in these books. Oh my search for soulmate. I'm educated. I put a lot into this book. If any time that you need me. As for me in your letters. I am Thomas Allred Jr. And this is. My forgiveness volume 1. Thomas Allred Jr. When the world has hurt you so much what do you do. You have got to keep trying. And believe in yourself. That you are one of the best the brightest and the elite among us all. I'm taking questions now. Thomas Allred Jr my girlfriend left me. It's just 3 months pregnant with our kid. What you need to do you outta text her. And try to work out some kind of relationship between the two of y'all. One more question and I have to end this session. Thomas Allred Jr I use your advice. Your books really help me. I just want to say thanks for everything. See I can't be there personally. But I know how to talk to you. If you are going through things. You just have to get it off your chest that you're going through something. Now I don't intend to be a counselor. All I'm telling you folks is that I am a survivor. Thank you Jesus. My book is this. To the one that think he don't have nobody. Dude I coach you. I'm a believe in you. The book is called. The road I traveled down. I only got one thing left to say.

To my community. May you flourish with God helping you everyday. I'm empty. I didn't mean any disrespect. God is going to see this. I am Thomas Allred Jr. And I will work with you if I can. The road I travel down. Here it is right here. Come with me y'all. Sit down and talk with me. You can make it if you try Thomas Allred Jr. I want you to see what I've been through first-hand. I am a hero in my own rights. I am two days away from my goal. Of being the man of this year. Eden Reid I want to thank you Eden Reid. And Ms. Cindy. For keeping me dedicated in my work. Well the book is over all that's left to do is. Run this here back and let's see if we can do it all over again better. Be sure Thomas Allred Jr gets that contract. What can I say I am Thomas Allred Jr. In two more days I'll be known forever as author. Everybody don't give up. Oh yeah. It is show time in other countries. I'm telling you to keep your game up to par. Pick your game up Thomas Allred Jr. Thank you Jesus for everything. I love you. This is the road I travel down by myself. Dr Thomas Allred Jr.

Man who kids be getting on my God damn nerves. How could they not. They are children Thomas Allred Jr. You said it didn't you Shontel Allred. They are our children. Get me a canister. Thomas Allred Jr the serum ain't ready yet do you know what you're doing. You getting ridiculous in behind me Shontel Allred. So the government will know that I don't give a f*ck. I'm shooting this plutonium into my babies. I'm doing the same thing to us baby. Shontel Allred take my hand sweetheart. I am a scientist for the NSA. And an a**ociate of yours. Not to mention being your husband. You need to give the baby's the injection Thomas Allred Jr. I can't do it Shontel Allred just look at them the three of them. I'll do it for you Thomas Allred Jr. And I'll do it for you Shontel Allred. Now Thomas Allred program the babies to take that shot. The baby shots are being administered. So what are we waiting for. Give it a second Thomas Allred Jr. Freeze everybody get down on the floor. Thomas Allred Jr. Shontel Allred my love. Get the babies off of the table. It starts right here.

One canisters is not open. So it's going to be hard to tell which baby is not contaminated. Babies y'all better thank God we saved you on time. Your mother and father are going away for a long time. What are the names of the children. Look at the back of the calors of their shirts. Be professional Thomas Allred Jr. Shontel Allred I can feel myself getting angry. Dude you're wasting your time there's no way you're getting in or out of this transport vehicle. But I'm not a dude everybody. What the f*ck is happening to us. Jesus the transport vehicle is down. This woman took my a** off of me and placed it on the steering wheel. Her husband is Thomas Allred Jr. Dispatch do you copy. Can you hear me dispatch. Do you copy me dispatch do you copy. Give me my children. Her husband can you see dispatch. The hulk.

The babies shirts say. Clark Kent. Wonder woman. And Mr. incredible. Who does this Val belong to their daddy. No actually that belongs to me actually. Everything is moving along to plan. Don't bullsh*t me. That the clue your mask is hanging off of your face. Ease my mask in place. We have got to figure out what mixture Thomas Allred Jr use that he put in these babies. He's in control of hiMs.elf how Mercy. Competition don't bother me. I'm ready to smash the competition. Listen I know you don't remember me Thomas Allred Jr. But I am your wife Shontel Allred. Look you've gotten professional. Them boys are trying to help us out of a situation. We got a police officer that's terrorizing the city. With three little babies on his arm his shoulders. I know who that could be. Get a glance Thomas Allred Jr and Shontel Allred. Allred Allred Allred Allred. Now people after me Thomas Allred Jr. They are after us. This man killed a police officer. Every time I see the police I will execute one hostage until they deliver my demands. Thomas Allred jr get angry. There's nobody else to get angry with. So I might as well answer your call. Doctor who. Meet my feet and fist.

Be sincere Thomas Allred Jr. One more entry and we both are famous for life. she said one more entry and we both are famous for life. They put my children in the hospital to study there behavior. Say children activate Shontel Allred. Children activate. Oh all hell is going to break loose. These children have powers. Unlike you have ever seen before. The children are attacking Dr who. Y'all better get Thomas Allred Jr out of there. They listen to There Mamas frequency. Now my kids keep working. To put the city back together. Doctor who you're under arrest. Dr who we ain't going to respect you anymore. Thomas Allred Jr and Shontel Allred. I live where chaos is. You heard me children clean up this mess. They are only 3 and 4. Lois Lane I do anything for you. That is why I need you to come and work on this top-secret mission with me touchdown. Thomas Allred Jr sing to me for me. wait until we move out of this apartment into a house up on the city Lois Lane. Just call me Shontel Allred today baby. Happy 1st year anniversary. To my wife Shontel Allred. And the episode it goes off like this. With more episodes to be coming. Hero Children.

Don't do anything. I know exactly what this is about. Little Clark Kent you made a mess of your diaper. Dr. Who has escaped. Get Thomas Allred Jr and his family together. Bring Eddie Cane Jr with us. That's it right there. This is movie material. The second we get to their house. Sneak up on them quietly remember their superheroes. Thomas Allred Jr down on the floor immediately I can hear somebody coming. From long distance. Dr.Who if it ain't my pleasure. Each one of those kids possess Powers unbelievable to the cosmos. Thomas Allred Jr. You have got to give me back those kids. Eddie Cane jr. Prepare to elevate Thomas Allred Jr. Thomas Allred Jr is elevated. What do you mean Eddie Cane jr. He is standing on his baby's shoulder. And the baby is flying all around the helicopter. You have got to see this to believe it. Thomas Allred Jr we need you to put the baby down and come talk to us. Them.other two chaps are behaving there selves. You ain't said nothing but a motherf*cking word Eddie Cane jr. Listen Thomas Allred Jr realized that you took the plutonium. You are unstable. If I'm unstable Eddie Cane jr. You haven't seen unstable yet. That boy just now changed. Mr. incredible got me. I need a rope to go and help my father. Will a Leso will that work. All right then. Dr. Who had to bring all of these men here. The chopper is going down. Have a great time. What you say Thomas Allred Jr I don't give up. I want to see if that chopper can maintain itself. Without nobody in it to fly it. By the power of grayskull god dammit. You see Eddie Cane jr is changing. Shontel Allred I need you. I'm a whoop your motherf*cking a** Eddie Cane jr. And the story went a little something like that. Before they called for backup. And them kids had to teach them a lesson. Where do you see yourself in 10 years from now Thomas Allred Jr. With my wife just taking care of my kids. A smart move is we depend on you. Shontel Allred it's my pleasure. It's on my pleasure. See either way it goes me and Thomas Allred Jr. Keep our promises to one another. Drink the last capital of serum and become one of us. Don't drink that capsule of serum. You done became professional. Thomas Allred Jr and Shontel Allred Battlecat is the future. Whatever you do Thomas Allred Jr. Take out the trash. Hero Children try Battle Cat.

I'm getting ready to take this planet over with my death ray. Dr. Who I'm giving you one last chance to drop the weapon and play nicely. Why Shontel Allred. Do the right thing Shontel Allred. You do realize that I'm already on the right side don't you. Dr. Who. America needs your permission to save you. I can't do it without those three kids. Give It Up. Shontel Allred I'm coming. Superhero look out he's got the death ray. I love you Shontel Allred. Lois Lane this right here is for those people who doubted me and you. Thomas Allred Jr look out the death ray has been fired. I realize I can't be killed. Thomas Allred Jr do you know what a party looks like. Get the ray son. Good job Mr.. Incredible. Thomas Allred Jr even though I'm back. I'm still asking you for your hand in marriage. Lois Lane and me. So baby what are you going to call me. The incredible hulk Thomas Allred Jr. Do y'all see these weapons. Tell Wonder woman to get him. Wonder woman use your la**o. Dr Who is in danger. Clark put the piano down. Clark Kent do you hear me son now. Clark I mean it this instant put the piano down now. Let me talk to him Thomas Allred Jr. Sometimes when your brave Clark. The world comes together for you. I am your hero. They ain't bullsh*ttin. You serve truth justice and the American way. And so do the rest of the team. Starting right now. And Clark Kent. You are a Superman in my eyes. Put Wonder woman in her crib Mr.. Incredible. Now climbing in on the other side by side of her. What's it going to be Mr.. Incredible. Mama we the Justice league. Superman what's it going to be. Thomas Allred Jr will you tell Superman to come on.

Clark put the piano down and go to your mother. Clark Kent put the piano over here. That Superman that I know. Go get in that other crib. Thank you Shontel Allred. Lois Lane to you Dr. Who. It looks like we've done all we can do here today. Thomas Allred Jr. You have got to lead us a pathway home. Hulk smash the game in to pieces. You don't realize you're the most talented people on the planet. So you think. Evidence shows that Dr. Who is guilty of masterminding plots against the world. And we as a people. Find you Thomas Allred Jr. And Shontel Allred. Not guilty of masterminding anything against the citizens of America. Thomas Allred Jr. Look at me Thomas Allred Jr. You are the incredible hulk. When I met you you were Superman. If you still want to marry me. And our three children. Count on me I'm going to be there for you. But there we go. A family of superheroes. That serves us right. Everybody see that we. Stand up. Thomas Allred Jr we are superheroes. And the world sees it. Hero Children are going to save us all. If you allow them to be heroes Thomas Allred Jr. Think about it over dinner. Wonder woman you are a princess. Lay back down Superman. Mr. incredible it's almost time to eat. And Lois Lane I love you. Thomas Allred Jr. Shontel Allred. I just want you to see it. Its my moMs. ring I want you to have it. I love you my hero. And I love you to the incredible hulk. Hero Children.

I'm trying to make sense of this Thomas Allred Jr. Let's just take it from the beginning. We got the connect four. It is time that we play Monopoly. No hulk smash hulk don't like Monopoly. Thomas Allred Jr the doorbell. Get the doorbell Thomas Allred Jr. It's a good thing the serum be wearing off. Get the baby off the ceiling Thomas Allred Jr. Clark Kent come on boy. What should I call you Clark Kent. Everybody calls him Superman. My son y'all. Superman. Come on Thomas Allred Jr. Let's see who's at the door. Dr. motherf*cking Who. I know what you did Thomas Allred Jr. You switched those goddamn serum containers. Whatever you say I'm not saying nothing Dr. Who. Take your time. Thomas Allred Jr I can still replace the serum. Thomas Allred Jr you're beautiful. Dr. Who are you talkin to me. You damn right that is. Thomas Allred Jr. Don't let Dr. Who anywhere in this house. Just tell me one thing Dr. Who how do you keep escaping. I don't have to escape. I live in prison. They let me out when we get up. And I go back in when it's time to go to sleep. It's an arrangement I have with the warden. Seeing that I don't take his life. He is almost cool with anything that I ask him. Well Dr Who. I am going to call the authorities. And place a formal complaint. The grounds of your complaint is Thomas Allred Jr. You are a psychopath Dr. Who and I would rather you not sit around and smoke around my children. Oh yeah and before you leave. Pick my paper up and hand it to me.

Thomas Allred Jr I got $20. Look at all that people see over there on the ground. Thomas Allred Jr I got $172 and that's all I got. Lois Lane. I mean Shontel Allred. Honey now we can play Monopoly. Monopoly my a**. All three of the babies are crying. Well as you see Dr Who. I would love to talk but I got to take care of a little something. Thomas Allred Jr you have a nice day. Do you want this seveny five bucks. Go ahead and keep it. Dr. Who. The children of sleeping now. Shontel Allred you getting more beautiful than before. Dr Who you ain't coming in my house. God dammit. Give me my f*cking kids. Thomas Allred Jr and Shontel Allred. These are not your kids. Thomas Allred Jr that serum inside those kids belongs to the United States government. At least let me look at them. Shut the door honey. At least let me look at them Shontel Allred. Thomas Allred Jr. Can't you see we are the superheroes. I'm calling us the Justice league avengers. Now that's my baby.

I'm looking through this paper on the table Thomas Allred Jr. It's about time you do a little something with yourself my honey bouquet. It's a magazine for Hero Children. And you know that we can't give out the secret identities. Give them out for all I care. Give them out for all you care my a** Thomas Allred Jr. Why is Dr Who's sitting on the porch. He ain't never left he just been sitting there. Tell me Dr Who. Have you realized that this is a family of superheroes. What I realize is Thomas Allred Jr. is you and those babies have my serum and I want my serum back. Me no comprende Dr. Who. You are probably just jealous that's why you took the serum from me Thomas Allred Jr. No Dr Who I took the serum from you. Because you were threaten the world with your superpowers. You are a police officer Thomas Allred Jr. I can't believe y'all. Becky I need you to talk to your husband. Get up Grady. Dr Who's first name is Grady. Watch what you saying. As talented as you are. Thomas Allred Jr. My serum will run-out of your system. And you can't be killed right now. I'm still going to tell you. It's my birthday and I would like to see them kids. Shontel Allred. Hell no. He can't see them dag on kids. Becky I had a nice day. Now take Grady with you and have a nice day. Y'all give that boy his serum back. We can't Becky. Why. Because you with a psychopath. Oh I know but I still love him. This ain't right. Let's teach the kids how to maneuver their selves Shontel Allred. I'll do better than that I'm your Lois Lane. Incredible hulk Thomas Allred Jr. Y'all are going to let me see those kids. You damn right you see these kids. On TV and in interviews. They are Hero Children.

Get y'all food over to the table. Today we're going to give thanks for everyone and the people around us. Hero Children is beginning to take off. Hero Children is known in all 50 states. Incredible hulk can I talk to you for a second. Yes Malice. It's a boy. That boy needs to be professional. Now I need a little bit of your serum. I don't got no more serum Chris. I mean Malice. Your brother keeps playing with me. It is going to be a good day after all. Who is that outside marching back and forth with the signs. Honey yeah there he is. Is Dr. Who in his Conrad's. I'm making sure that we don't see Dr. Who any longer. Just close the windows. Thomas Allred Jr communicate outside with Dr. Who. Dr.Who you can come in and eat if you want to. Are the children going to be there. Yes Dr. Who children will be here. It will be my extended pleasure to come in your house and eat Lois Lane. Shontel Allred let's make sure that we got a plate for him. You damn right I will come and eat but after that the serum is mine. You see that Dr. Who you just messed up everything. Thomas Allred Jr I was only kidding. Superman is lifting weights in the backyard. Wonder woman is practicing her defenses. And Mr. incredible is still eating his bottle. These kids are the future of tomorrow Shontel Allred. For I can see the light in all of them. Thank you for letting me see your children Thomas Allred Jr. I'm just happy to be blessed Dr. Who.

Thomas Allred Jr And Shontel Allred wrote a book called Hero Children. Can you write something for me inside of your book Lois Lane I mean Shontel Allred. If Thomas Allred will allow it. My serum is and elixir. And I will get it back from these children. You professional Dr Who. What do I say to the man. Excuse me you have a post Graham. Mr.. Thomas Allred Jr. Incredible hulk what is it. Lois Lane gets Superman and Wonder woman from outside and bring them in the house. Thomas Allred Jr what is it. Now Lois Lane bring them both in the house now. We are both sitting on 20 million dollars.

For the rights to our story. Well Thomas Allred Jr opportunities may come baby but we are Hero Children. Look around you Lois Lane. Honey we have nothing but rags. And you and I and the kids save the world each day. Thats because I am professional. Do you hear me Thomas Allred Jr. Type up your book. And make it so that. That you and I communicated. And we choose to let our stories run on syndicated TV. Our movie is going to knock your socks off. Now You see Me Now you don't Thomas Allred Jr. Dr Who has got sense enough to leave. Realize we are to professional. To get in the way of each other Thomas Allred Jr. Everything good is in this household. You mean sweetheart. Didn't I tell you that I was a hero incredible hulk. Lois Lane what are you saying. That I own Monopoly. There my baby is. Mr.. Incredible. Thomas Allred Jr that girl really loves you. And Malice I love her back. Eat something Malice. What kind of neighborhood is this. This is metropolis. Wonder woman come to the table. Go ahead and get you a plate. This is not possible those kids are only 3 and 4. We got more serum were that comes from. Make sure that Superman gets his contract. I have a feeling. All of your kids Thomas Allred Jr and Shontel Allred. Listen to me Thomas Allred Jr. There are people out there hurt you and your kids. You have got to stay up on current events. We are going to a place called Hollywood Malice. It is at the center of Metropolis. Metropolis. You killed my wife is son of a b*tches. Incredible hulk everybody realize that you are not playing. Listen Thomas Allred Jr. I am your new wife. Let's try to make the best of things while we still have a chance. Listen. No matter what you told the people. Superman has your ring Lois Lane. My darling come here for a minute. In life and in death. I love you Shontel Allred. Thomas Allred Jr you are the one writing the book. How do we end up?

Thomas Allred Jr. If you want to make yourself stronger Thomas Allred Jr. Take your babies outside and leave them there. Dr Who. It is 4 in the morning. Get your damn a** up and come to the door instead of playing mind games. You see Thomas Allred Jr. It ain't a coincidence that I'm here. I am timing you. We are going to make another kid Thomas Allred Jr. And i Dr. Who. I'm timing you and I don't care what you say. The serum cannot be repeated the same way it was the first time. Thomas Allred Jr now you see that. What are you going to do. I am going to eat some pancakes. I'm talking about the serum dumba**. Take Dr Who away from here. It will be my pleasure. Kids show Dr. Who to the edge of the streets. You need to come with me. The moral of the story is. Even Dr. Who. I cannot tell you what to do with your own flesh and blood. Go back to sleep now. This world can take care of itself. He is no longer the champion. Thomas Allred Jr. Is the champion. Give them time. Let it marinate. Shontel Allred I really do love you. Thomas Allred Jr. You are dreaming Thomas Allred Jr. Wake up baby out of your dream. Shontel Allred. Shontel Allred. Honey where are you. Now Thomas Allred Jr. You know damn well that Shontel Allred doesn't live here. Mama is that you. Who else would it be Thomas Allred Jr. Mama love you so much. Lay back down and get you some rest Thomas Allred Jr. Where are my children mama. You are a damn single man. You don't realize how good you got it. Trust me. Family is the most important thing mama. I'm going to get me some Hero Children. First you need to figure out how to pay this water bill. Do exactly what we say do. Hold Your position. You are Thomas Allred Jr. And we welcome you to Hero Children. What you want to do is. Thank your heavenly Stars. Your community has selected you. Give me your best

Thomas Allred Jr. You can be professional. Now send the rest of that story in to Mr.s. Eden Reid. And prepare to write a new story. Called Hero Children the start of something new. His attitude is professional. You are our hero Thomas Allred Jr. Then white people are clocking you. You talking about Shontel Allred. Shontel Allred is a world-cla** communicator. Communicate with me Thomas Allred Jr. Either way it go I have been shot. Somebody help me. But that's not in the book Thomas Allred Jr. I'm down and I can barely walk. Everybody see what that man is going through. Just one more verse to that book and your professional. You say one more verse. Overtime. I am fending to go back and see my kids. I'm going to sleep Mama. Where the kids at Shontel Allred. In there cribs. I'm kissing and hugging them. Give them a kiss for me Thomas Allred Jr. Dr Who is playing mind games again. Who did he make you see this time. He made me see my mother. Boy watch what you saying. Charlene Allred is a government official. Imma get to see her again baby. Just take your time I'm going to take you out the hood with me when the morning comes. You hear me. Dr Who gets respect. Because no matter what type of dream I'm in. I am totally decent. Searching for the where abouts of my kids. Turn off the heat here we go. Hero Children are here to stay.

Thank you for everything that you've done for me. Our Hero Children have now reach the maximum. In their super powers. Thomas Allred Jr you making a fool out of yourself. I will know who that is. I am Dr. Who. Thomas Allred Jr. Dr. Who is in my dream again Shontel Allred. Dr Who stop it. My superpowers is I'm a maniac. Shontel Allred. Visit with me. And see what I see. Thank you but no. Dr Who. Why Shontel Allred. Because you are a dirty a** dude. My children realize that you are dirty a** dude. Now Free my husband from your brain chemicals. You don't realize why I'm here do you. Lois Lane. I come for the kids. That's it. Honey you are in the American legion's. Hulk get up and handle your business. You are the damn hulk handle your business. You are talking about being the hulk is incredible. Go back to sleep Thomas Allred Jr. And I want you to clean this room up Thomas Allred Jr. Right now this instant. Moma show them people who I am. Thomas Allred Jr. This is not a dream that you're having. I need you to watch for the mailman. To come every single day. As you realize. That your Hero Children have been taken. About time that you realize. That they've been taken. I want you to know one thing. Happy birthday Thomas Allred Jr. And happy birthday Shontel Allred. I'm going to be in your house. Just waiting for you to get back. From your vacation. In prison. Dr. Who. You are the maker of trouble. Lois Lane there's nothing you can do about this. Get the children. We are going to put them up for adoption. And there's nothing anyone can do about this dream. Thomas Allred Jr. Wake up Dr. Who . Is after our children. Our children are safe Shontel Allred. You got a good personality. Let everybody come see. That Shontel Allred is my queen wife and soulmate. Thank you. Take the kids over there and sit down. What you think about us. Incredible hulk. Well

Superman. Mr. incredible and Wonder woman. Y'all out do me. Dag gone. Dr Who quit playing those mind games. That is me Thomas Allred Jr. Mama if I fall will you help me stand up. Give that boy a contract. I wish for you to have a happy well being life. Now wake up Thomas Allred Jr. Where am I. You in the dog house Thomas Allred Jr. Because you didn't take out the trash this evening. I'm going to reprogram the kids to take out the trash. I already did it. Lois Lane you couldn't have. Dr. Who is in prison for playing mind games. On government officials. Baby thank you. Now put all the babies in the bed with us. Thomas Allred Jr realize something. What do I got to realize Shontel Allred. That you and I are not dreaming we are in the future. One more time we are in the future Thomas Allred Jr. I'm going to see what the attitude is all about. Girl give me attitude. All day all night. Your dream is my command. Go back to sleep Hero Children. Mommy has done solve the case. Of that bad Dr. Who. When I get out of here I'm calling the police on your Hero Children Thomas Allred Jr. They won't let you out. I'm locked up they won't let me out. Our stories are depict cated. In order to bring awareness today to the children of today. Carriage and natural strength. Has a good thing happening for everybody. These are our Hero Children comic books. Shut your a** up and go to sleep Thomas Allred Jr. Lois Lane you are my heart.

Right now I hope them kids are ready. Excuse me Thomas Allred Jr. Are you the maker of Hero Children. I am the maker of Hero Children myself along with my wife. I'm just reaching out to you. Hero Children. It's famous in my neighborhood. All around the world it goes Hero Children Forever. Thank you but Thomas Allred Jr I have an appointment. What is it Thomas Allred Jr. There was just a lady that came by here and said she liked Hero Children from us Shontel Allred. What are we going to do. Thomas Allred Jr we are going to push the television series. Hero Children if there's a will there's a way. You can't do that. These babies will be exposed. For the powers they have. Thomas Allred Jr. Get up Dr. Who. You think a movie scene is professional. Walk away with me. Shontel Allred. Imma be back. Come here Superman. Don't you run off from me ever again do you hear me. I hear you Mommy. Thomas Allred Jr he just talked. He just talked everybody. Malice get the other two kids and come on. You and Angie together seem like a good couple. Here I go. The hulk has been running all over the place chasing Dr Who. He got away from me baby. Thomas Allred Jr the babies can talk. Say history in the making. Wonder woman. Get your la**o out. And say history in the making. History in the making mama. You see Thomas Allred Jr she is as smart as you. That's what I depend on. Shontel Allred our children are gifted. I only need Mr.. Incredible to talk to me. Mr. incredible this is daddy can you speak for me please. Dr. Who is behind you Daddy. Shontel Allred. Mr. incredible just said. The incredible hulk I know what he just said. Shontel Allred get him. Baby I mean Lois Lane get him. Dr. Who. This is the last time that you would disturb my family. On the contrary I got you

Lois Lane. Or shall I say Shontel Allred. I'm ending my speech right there. Dr. Who guess who la**oed you. Our Wonder woman is a professional kid. You didn't think that we can make it. You didn't think that I will break the news to Thomas Allred Jr. Happy birthday Thomas Allred Jr. And happy birthday Shontel Allred. Them kids are off the motherf*cking hook. Take his a** on to jail. The time go slow in there. Hopefully that will give you time to think. Thomas Allred Jr I'm going to get you if that's the last thing that I do. Hero Children help me. Thank you Thomas Allred Jr. Fighting this crime sure builds up an appetite. One day we'll be able to eat baby. Yall know the serum is too powerful to digest food. What we have to do here is drink a lot of water. But I'm hungry as hell Thomas Allred Jr. Do what you have to do. Welcome to McDonalds. Yes I would like 16 double cheeseburgers off of your dollar menu. And that's the way it went. The baby's got them something to eat. And I just waited lifting weights. Everybody say it with me. Hero Children forever the movie.

Read your book out loud to yourself Thomas Allred Jr. We got Hero Children that listening to you all over the world. All these kids want to know is. If our kids can come and play with them. No comprende Grease lightning. No habla English. Let them kids play together Thomas Allred Jr. Only under strict supervision. That means that I. I'm calling for judge Judy. Thomas judge Judy can't hear us we are heroes. Hero my a** judge Judy can't hear you. Even though we're cleaning up. Our kids is the best thing that happened to me. Communicate that Lois Lane. At the book signings. Inn at the movie premiere of fighting for mine. Thomas Allred Jr you are an author Thomas Allred Jr. That man he wrote Hero Kids. Say Hero Children it sound better. I see what I have to do in this situation. Daddy to home base. Homebase to Daddy. Send daddy a picture check the email. And get you some rest you are Hero Children. The President wants to speak to you. Hero Children. What I'm saying is that you rock the nation Hero Children. Kids rule everything in school.

That was our president with that short statement. Shontel Allred. If you're right here. Then who is watching the Hero Children. Our children can look out for me. so we let them look out for there self as well. I have got to give you a hand. The most challenging thing for a Hero is raising children. But me and Thomas Allred Jr we seem to manage. Is that enough material for the book Thomas Allred Jr. No keep on going Lois Lane I mean Shontel Allred. The incredible hulk is my husband. No offspring will go undisturbed. We are training our kids to be better and stronger and more sophisticated each day. Dr f*cking Who. What are you doing here. Yeah what are you doing here Dr Who. Thomas Allred Jr. And Shontel Allred. This interview belongs to the people. Except you are not one of the people you are a villain. That just hurt me Thomas Allred Jr. Shontel Allred how do you feel about me being in this interview. It might just help a book sells Thomas Allred Jr. Okay Dr Who. Be interviewed. Dr. Who. What is it that you wish to gain from stealing Thomas Allred and Shontel Allred. Thomas Allred Jr stole my elixir off of the shelf in the laboratory that I allowed him to work at. And I know my elixir when I see it. What I'm getting to is. All three of the Hero Children. Are my creation. You are telling a damn lie. Thomas Allred Jr. This man is trying to destroy the world. And I myself my wife and the Hero Children will not let it be. Dr Who. Is there something that you want to tell us. I want to tell you that. I'm taking you in the world hostage. Interviewer spokes personality Dr. Philip. How did you know it was me Dr. Who the TV cameras were hiding me. I'm in this f*cking speech of yours. Oh baby look. The kids sent us pictures. They are only infants they shouldn't be able to work a camera yet. Dr Who. You are going back to prison. As a matter of fact prison is coming to you. Shontel Allred. You ain't seen the Last of Me. And this what we do around this place. Thanks for the interview Dr. Who.

Thomas Allred Jr is a writer. He got super powers in his hands. Now I'll be the judge of that. Now I'll be the judge of that. Thomas Allred Jr. Come with me. all we got to do baby is send this in and let somebody read it. You a psychic now. These Hero Children are my future. Shontel Allred. I simply love the kids. Shontel Allred. I'll be back. Shut the f*ck up. Dr. Who. Now Thomas Allred Jr get ahold of me. Hero Children come home. You see what you doing to me. Lois Lane I'm done talkin. Then write your book Superman. It all started like this. Hero Children are we ready. Yep we're ready. Ready for what mother and father. Ready for break time. Yall all got to listen. These are our Hero Children.

You haven't seen Dr. Who have you Shontel Allred. No not in a couple of business days. Incredible hulk you look worried. Baby it's just because I cannot activate my super powers without Dr. Who. Can't or you want. Thomas Allred jr. Come here Superman. You lucky Thomas Allred Jr didn't see you. Mr.. Incredible and Wonder woman come to mummy. Lois Lane I get what you trying to say to me. Incredible hulk inside of our family. Is the truth. Now I'm not pretending to like that man when I don't. I appreciate you being honest with me Shontel Allred. Lois Lane there's a knock at the door. It is Dr Who Thomas Allred Jr. He wants for me to let him in. No you got to stay right there Dr Who. For I am texting. And I still wish that you. Would watch me do my thing. On the dance floor. Shontel Allred. Would you do me the honors of having this dance. The babies are mine Shontel Allred. Thomas Allred Jr. Get the babies. Dr. Who. Get the hell out of my house Dr. Who. Now my incredible hulk. We need an ending to this short story. He is how we should end it Shontel Allred. Our kids seem to like it when we say the end. The end Thomas Allred Jr. We need to get Dr Who a contract. And the TV show. Thomas Allred Jr. Quit dreaming baby. I'll be back Thomas Allred Jr. Dr Who we are counting on you to.

Right now I'm composing my manuscript. Called Hero Children they are after me. I will return your call as soon as I finish this manuscript. My heart says to go forward with the book. This ain't my mama's old recipe. Keep your composure we almost got a winner. I'm betting on you Thomas Allred Jr. And I'm betting on you Shontel Allred. You see he lost. I put everything into that book report. A book report like this needs more content. Exactly. Thomas Allred Jr you see that we got special. Don't give up Thomas Allred Jr. Muffin didn't I tell you. If you build it he will come. Yes you told me Thomas Allred Jr but. I didn't want to believe you Thomas Allred Jr until it was too late. It's out of my hands now. What is Thomas Allred Jr. The book our book is getting ready to explode. Hero Children are everywhere. Thomas Allred Jr they are calming down. On our level. Shontel Allred look at the pages on a book. Yes I got what you saying to me. We do that. As we get tired of capturing criminals. Let us remain decent and at ease. Dr. Who done made it. Into a motion picture film. Thomas Allred Jr and his super kids. I have and even better name Thomas Allred Jr. We can call them movie Hero kids the beginning. Shontel Allred what if I called a Hero kids the beginning. Thomas Allred Jr that is what I just said. Those Hero Children are amazing. What did you say Dr Who. I called the kids Hero Children. And let it be known. The Hero Children are our children. The End. I'm working on a masterpiece. As exciting as it gets. We are going to answer your call. With a movie. Called Hero Children in the beginning. See it started on a Tuesday. Thomas Allred Jr. Send the goddamn book in. Okay Shontel Allred. It's your freaking world. Send that goddamn book in right now. Hero Children in the beginning.

My book is called I dream of you. Let the dream take over. I'm representing myself Thomas Allred Jr. Everybody with me. Say that you are open. Let the dream take over. I am a police officer. And I'm dreaming to be. With a different woman every f*cking day of my life. You need to go to sleep now. Because in this dream. There are three challenges wich you may go through. I understand that you want women Thomas Allred Jr. But I need you to be honest with yourself. Don't say that Thomas Allred Jr. Say you just need seven women to be with you. For the rest of your life. But I can't do it. My book is called I dream of you on the daily. There are certain elements to this. There are certain elements to everything Thomas Allred Jr. And I feel like Thomas Allred Jr is worthy. I'm telling you. There is something about Thomas Allred Jr. That I can't put my finger on. That man is a hustler. Everybody Thomas Allred Jr. Is our hero. Prepare to be excited. I want you to know that you are preparing to be excited. Thomas Allred Jr. Is our police officer. Go down in memory lane with me. Since a child that men has been a police officer. He's never had the taste of the flesh the way I have. That's right he's never tasted a** before. Thomas Allred Jr all you have to do is dream. Thomas Allred Jr. Get your a** in there and finish cooking. Yes lieutenant Candis I will finish cooking. Thomas Allred Jr these bills need paid. Yes lieutenant Samantha I will pay the bills. Thomas Allred Jr I need you to stay in control of yourself even before the book comes out. Yeah lieutenant Eden. I got you one thing that you need. The one thing that I most definitely needed was pencil pad and paper. Study the people Thomas Allred Jr. I'm doing exactly what you officers are telling me to do. We are telling you to study the people. I don't give a f*ck how many women that boy got. I still want to talk to him. Lieutenant Shontel. You are going to make this story about you. I'm taking over. That boy shot a businessman. Are you done dreaming. or do you want to wake up and be the businessman that I know you are. I am done dreaming lieutenant Shontel. I said how many women do you want Thomas Allred Jr. I only want you lieutenant Shontel. If you really want this girl named lieutenant Shontel. You will write a book called Shontel and I forever. I'm changing the name on this book to. Shontel and I forever. We understand you Thomas Allred Jr. You made a choice about your future Thomas Allred Jr. The females are watching you. We are watching everything that you do Thomas Allred Jr. Thomas Allred Jr everybody know that you a trillionaire. I appreciate you Thomas Allred Jr. Lieutenant Samantha. And lieutenant Eden. Here is what we're going to do. I am going to write the books daily. And I want for you ladies to take care of yourself your hair your nails and makeup. This is what you got to do. Sounds like a game plan to me. Girl I will put you in the game. Listen. To be in the game you have to show me that you care about yourself. I don't play with small money. So I'm going to need you ladies to realize. That the answer to your question. Is in the book. Now I need to talk to my woman for a second. Shontel your book is almost finished. Yall this Nigga done sit and wrote me a book. You a book in a timely manner is what you're saying. Isn't it Shontel. Shontel I need you to do me a big favor. You don't have to ask a favor of me. But ask it anyway. Be straight with me. The game is calling me. I'm trying to play on Wall Street with the big boys. And my favorite is. Marry me Shontel. Thomas Allred Jr you're the most famous dude in the city. Thomas Allred Jr ain't doing nothing but cleaning. All of the struggles that you seeing are now over Shontel. These are the women who take care of me. It's nice to meet you Thomas Allred Jr. My name is officer demetria. And I am lieutenant London. And I am lieutenant Christine. I thank you ladies for taking care of my wife. Don't you see Thomas Allred Jr your book is your wife. What are you lady saying. That your not fully awoke Thomas Allred Jr. And the book will right itself. If the captain in control of the ship is gone. But I'm standing right here. Thomas Allred Jr your book is being written by itself. Listen Thomas Allred Jr we know what we're doing. You need to become professional. And go to the bathroom when you want to. Listen Thomas Allred Jr. Your pencil and paper are right here. Thomas Allred Jr take your time and go to the bathroom. We need to get Thomas Allred Jr his on room. So that he can go to the bathroom whenever he wants. I can't believe this. When a grown a** man. Have to beg to use the bathroom. Because there are people in the other room asleep. All day and at night. Thomas Allred Jr your damn book. The title you got to listen Thomas Allred Jr is. Shontel and I Forever. And this is meaning that you. Search for a future in marrying Shontel. Go on and say it Thomas Allred Jr. I love that girl with all my heart. I only want to be with Shontel. And I dedicate myself. Thomas Allred Jr. You ain't got but through more days. The book Thomas Allred Jr. Isn't going to write itself. Now what I need you to do. Is pour your heart out in these pages. Make your story get herd. I'm doing what I can do. To get this girl to love me. Me and Shontel. Are one-of-a-kind. I want to extend my deepest sincerest apology. To everyone that's been in love before. With me the apology is. With me I can't turn back. The hands of time. And as days go by. I found myself in love. And in a relationship. With a beautiful woman. This boy ain't got no clue at what he saying. Shontel I want to be with you. Forever and a day. You have got to be pa**ionate with me. When you finish reading this book. Imma do what I can to help you out the hood. To help us out the hood. The reason that I love you is because you believe in me. I care for you so much Shontel. I am putting my book up. As a token of my promise to dedicate my life to you. Imma take my time and write the book. I won't miss anything about you and I . I'm also writing this book called Hero Children. Shontel will you do me the honor of being my wife. You are a beautiful woman. And I am a man. Together if we keep believing.

In each other and tomorrow. Thomas Allred Jr. we can have anything that we dream. In my worst hour. when I was laying on the ground bleeding because I had been shot. I ask forgiveness from God. And for some reason I got to meet you today. Now Shontel I don't know the mechanics of everything. All I can do. Or all I know about. Is that you are interesting. Thomas Allred listen to me. Just because we are famous. Doesnt mean that you recognize your people. To my people I'm saying thank you. In another 15 minutes. We are going to break from the first part of this book.Shontel I love you with all of my heart. I got to somehow figure out how the number these pages. Because as I write my memoirs.

I get a sense of respect between me and you. Contact your people Shontel. Listen. Tell that boy he need to stop it. I'm listening to you Shontel. Just like a business man is supposed to. Now this is the start of the third book that I'm writing. I need to get your permission Shontel. To honor and obey you. For every single day of my life. You are beautiful. And I am beautiful. I can see how you love me. When I look in the mirror.

Thomas Allred Jr. But from past experiences. I love you too. I just cannot put myself out on a limb like that. And I know that you are writing a book. Baby all I care about is you. if you look at this book you have to look at it for what it is. And what is the book Thomas Allred Jr. The book is our escape to a better place and time. Do you want me to believe in dinosaurs Thomas Allred Jr. I want you to believe that I can take you any place in this world that you want to go Shontel. Baby history tells us that two police officers are in love. And that is you and I Thomas Allred Jr. Thomas Allred Jr black females are watching you white females are watching you. Everybody wants to know what's coming next from Thomas Allred Jr. We are coming next . You know that I'm not two-faced it Shontel .Let me be your knight in shining armor. Shontel I know I can make it. Publish your book about me. I can do even better than that. This book is dedicated to me and you. Thomas Allred Jr ain't bullsh*ttin. You are wasting your time thinking that you can date Shontel Allred. The Oracle is speaking.Oracle what do I have to do I'm really in love with her. Thomas Allred Jr you just now found success. Thomas Allred Jr take your time and get to know the women out here. You can date any woman that you want. Thomas Allred Jr. If Shontel is who you really want it will reveal itself at the end of This Book. Thomas you got a couple days. To think of which lady you want to be with. The Oracle is saying take your time and write your book the right way. Thomas Allred Jr. Go ahead and use the bathroom before the people get home. Thank you Oracle. For making me see.

That my love for Shontel Allred is everlasting. You don't even realize the power that you have do you Thomas Allred Jr. Because if you did you would realize that you are an up-and-coming author. In a world were book gender. Holds the key to our relationships. The past the present and the future. Imma dedicate my book to Shontel Allred and this community. Watch that man become a billionaire. And I'm naming my book Shontel. Quit playing with me Thomas Allred Jr. Leave your name of the book like it is. You see Oracle. I've been waiting on this day to finally get here. Where I'mma start over. Thomas Allred Jr.

That girl needs help from her community. The community is timing you on writing your books. If you say you love that girl. Rinse your hands. Of the past pain that you went through. Thomas Allred Jr if you truly love that girl. Swear on the Bible. That you got good intentions for her. I swear it but we are going to keep the Bible right here. Thomas Allred Jr you have got people waiting on you. Oracle what do you mean. A what kind of book is that that you are reading. This is Thomas Allred Jr book. It is called Shontel and i forever.

Thomas Allred Jr they watching you write the book. We need a grocery list. Of things that we want soon as your book is finished. Thomas Allred Jr. What are you thinking about Thomas Allred Jr. I'm thinking about my girl Shontel Allred. I ought to go and pick up the phone. Thomas Allred Jr we done helped you out one time. And you know we'll do it again. That is Stacy Allred talkin. And who is Stacy Allred. In the book call Shontel and I forever. Thomas Allred Jr is getting help through his former girlfriends. In which one day he plans to marry them all. If he can get his money right. See right here at this part. He is telling Shontel Allred that he love her and he wants to be with her forever. But he has a girlfriend. Name Stacy Allred. Kristen Allred. And so on and so forth. Women really care about Thomas Allred Jr. He gave them an idea to help save there children from molesters and psychopath. Thomas Allred Jr is an inventor. And a book Arthur. / Police officer. The president of the United States kept recognizing him. Thomas Allred Jr is a police officer. That is desperately trying to find this way. Out of the musical chairs. And to prosperity with all of his woman. This boy is trying to find the garden of Eden. Now that you speak of it. That is exactly what he's trying to do. Turn around Kristen Allred. Put your hands up you're coming with me. Fill my a** Thomas Allred Jr. Thomas Allred Jr if you don't wake up out of that dream and write that book. I am going to beat your a** Thomas Allred Jr. Thank you Shontel Allred for helping me stay focused. I'm going to take me a short recess. Animal attraction is coming up next. Thomas you need to write the damn book. Shontel I'm getting tired.

I know that your getting tired my dear. You have got to believe in yourself. You can't just quit whenever you get tired. Listen baby. My hopes and my horizon are depending on you. So dream about this piece of a**. When I tell you to write your book Thomas Allred Jr. Give me my pen and paper. The book is called. Shontel and I Forever. Thomas Allred Jr somehow you got to let the people know that I'm your woman. Don't forget what you're saying Thomas Allred Jr. Because the Oracle wants to speak to you. He talkin about don't forget what you're saying Thomas Allred Jr. Shontel stand still I told you I was going to write our book. Boy go get you some sleep. I'll be here when you're waking. Yes Shontel Allred.

He ain't got no clue at what he's doing. We have got to preserve this. Send a book in right f*cking now. Thomas wake up from dreaming. It is Miss Michelle Obama. You are the community leader Thomas Allred Jr. I expect so much better from you. In a book Thomas Allred Jr. The world is your oyster. I'm making you see how much you mean to me and each other. Each one of the woman in your book is dedicated to you Thomas Allred Jr. I'm beginning to count. the other part of this book is coming right now. Go to sleep Thomas Allred Jr. The other part of the book is not what you dream it will be. 5 4 3 2 1. Go to sleep Thomas Allred Jr. Get you some rest and start writing the book. Once you awake from your dream. This book is called Shontel and I forever. By Thomas Allred Jr. every since you were kid we have been training you. Remember who you are talking to Thomas Allred Jr. Didn't I say go to sleep. Yes Shontel Allred. Thomas Allred Jr got that book. That is a hustler for you. Part two will be coming up shortly. Go to damn sleep Thomas Allred Jr. And put that book on the table I want to read it.

Wake up Thomas Allred Jr. You have some work that needs to be done. First I would like for you to tell the people. Who is the woman that you love and hope to marry. My name is Shontel. But I don't remember her last name so I give her mine. That is fine. I'm connecting you with Thomas Allred Jr. Caller he don't realize that this is on the air. I have been in love with you for all of my life Thomas Allred Jr. And just when we start talking. You dropped the bomb on Me that you're in love with another woman. Thomas Allred Jr. What happened to you and I. Laura. I just grew professional. And my girl is the only one that I want to be with. Laura I do apologize for the situation. That we got right here at hand. Good afternoon Thomas Allred Jr. We got two more callers left on the line. I want to hear them both at the same time. Thomas Allred Jr speaking. Hey Thomas Allred Jr. Thomas these girls been waiting for you to speak to them. Pick your game up. Thomas Allred Jr I can't do anything without you baby. Thomas Allred Jr that girl said that you cheated on her. When y'all were younger. Rihanna I didn't cheat I tried to find you. But I didn't. If Rihanna would have had to be here. Take him out of the game. Thomas Allred Jr do you here that. Open the space up inside of your heart. Thomas please. Enough of this there going to all tell me that I was cheating. Miss Michelle Obama. I want to be there for all of the females that I love. It's just that I'm not willing to lose my wife over this.

I am growing mentally and physically. I now realize what marriage and love is. I came myself in the way of great diamond that's in excellence towards the people that I love and cherish. Shontel is the woman that I want to be with forever. I am creating a way through my books to find a way to be in Shontel life. Shontel and I are partners soulmates. I wrote Shontel a letter. It says that my love is excellent. and your love is the meaning to the dominance in the world. I went on to say. Give me time. And the world will be your oyster. Michelle Obama. These are some words that I reached him from my heart. Nobody else. But me could ever love Shontel Allred. The way that I do. And I'm going to ask you for help. Because a spark is demanding. To be at knowledge that to be heard.

I am asking the whole United Kingdom. To help me and my lady come together. As one in peace and harmony. My family has suffered horrible tragedies. My family is all I got. United Kingdom. I am but one man. Who is humble. I am a fighter United Kingdom. Me and my family we never gave in. No matter how bad the situation seemed. Take the burden off of this man. And help me gain a love that is everlasting. If you say everlasting Thomas Allred Jr. you must be with your woman forever once we get her for you. I'm telling you that I want to be with her forever. Miss Michelle Obama. Listen Thomas Allred Jr. There is a lot of females that like you. You should know. I can't just grant you one female. Because in professionalism. We are accustomed to. Having anything that we want. You are accustom Thomas Allred Jr. And on the level of a King and cla**mate.

I'm trying to tell you something. The people watching you. Are from Washington DC. Follow me Thomas Allred Jr. Your book is the face. The nation will read to. Follow me Thomas Allred Jr. We are watching you. Maintain yourself. I understand why you love Shontel Allred. Women all over the world approve you. How much money does it take for you to be happy with your girl. And infiniti amount. An Infiniti amount so Thomas Allred Jr there it is. I just bought that book. Listen to me. I appreciate you Thomas Allred Jr. Because you took the time and illustrated Hero Kids. By kids you mean Hero Children don't you miss Michelle Obama. Thomas Allred Jr listen to me. I will get you and your family out of that situation. Thomas Allred Jr the women are your family. You better write your book. Thomas Allred Jr getting ready to come out with another book. It's called Shontel and I forever. All the people are watching you. To see if you got what it takes. To be a hero. In our nation's Capitol. Lay your head down. Thomas Allred Jr you ain't doing nothing because you are Prince. We have the damn rights over you. Don't tell him all of it lets let him figure out something. He is crying over her. Alright Thomas Allred Jr. Put your book on the table. I'm right excellent three times. Excellent. Excellent. Excellent. Thomas Allred Jr you can have your wife. But be careful what you do out here. Because we will report to one another what we see. You know that Thomas Allred Jr is our true king. Now we have got to prove it to our ladies. Michelle Obama. Can I borrow your pen for a second. Yes of course you may Thomas Allred Jr. I am going to need you Michelle. To believe in me as I pa** your test. Which one of the tests are you going to have to pa** Thomas Allred Jr. I'm pa**ing all three of your tests at one time. What do you see when you look at me woman of the nation. I see an intelligent strong man. I see an intelligent hustling man. And I see a man who loves his family with everything. That last part was right. Michelle do universe don't stop because of you and me. I want you to realize something Michelle Obama. You have taught me to fish. I've been fishing on my life and now I finally caught something. My relationship with Shontel means everything to me. Thomas Allred Jr. I want to thank you for that brief introduction of you trying to serenade me. Miss Obama. You see Thomas Allred Jr. We are going to help you with your relationship level. That girl really mean something to you. Doesn't she. Yes Miss Michelle Obama she does. You damn right she does. So what do I do now. Write your book as fast as you can. When adversity strikes and the heart is left open there's room for a mountain to heal a person's love with a flower. By Thomas Allred Jr. Go to sleep and just don't worry about it Thomas Allred Jr. But Michelle Obama Shontel Allred won't talk to me. You have got to get your work done Thomas Allred Jr. Think about what you are saying to me. That girl is in love with you. I know it in the whole world knows it. Take your time. And put in entries into you book. Now I'm listening. Talk to Shontel Allred. say to her that I've got another book coming out. And I would enjoy it if you could be a part of my life. Because the past is gone. And I really would love it if you would be my future with me. Thomas Allred Jr. Send in this portion of the book. You got it Miss Michelle.

CHAPTER 22

Thomas Allred Jr we just need you to rededicate you. To our household of fans. Thomas Allred Jr rededicate yourself. Thomas Allred Jr rededicated hiMs.elf. Thomas Allred Jr I'm watching you so I'm going to rededicate myself also. Michelle Obama this is a dream isn't it. That's all he think about. Is this a dream or not. And his love for the ladies. Thomas Allred Jr you may not think I remember. But you begged and pleated for a lady named Kristen Allred . I'm trying to help you out of that situation that you are in. Fix your face to come on with me. Michelle Obama where we going. You forgot to realize that I'm also a lady. Be quiet we're going to the place that all the ladies dwell. Do I need to take my shoes off. We are letting Thomas Allred Jr into the library. Seeing that Thomas Allred Jr hasn't been inside the library ever since he was a kid. Listen to me. A kid needs to grow older with women around him. I think that is where you got lost Thomas Allred Jr. You had no women around you while you were growing up. I need them so badly but I was in the police academy. And my rules were simple. Take care of people. And take care of yourself and family. That police officer is almost becoming a man. End this session Thomas Allred Jr. OK Miss Obama I will end this session. We will adjourn and meet up at 3 tomorrow. For the conclusion of the book Shontel and I Forever.

Okay Thomas Allred Jr. Speak to Shontel Allred. And we as the world are going to listen. And if you can prove to me Thomas Allred Jr. that you're in love with Shontel Allred without a shadow of a doubt. Then we will help you to publish your book. Take your time and speak to Shontel Allred now Thomas Allred Jr. I'm making sure that you know I love you before I start this conversation Shontel Allred. What hurt me the most is when I wanted you so badly. Not to be able to see your face. Everything I do from here on out will be for me and you Shontel Allred. Say one more thing Thomas Allred Jr. Shontel Allred. As I begin to hold Your hand. I am putting this ring on your finger. This is a wedding ring. Right here is my heart to you Shontel Allred. People shot that boy because he is in love with you Shontel Allred. A lots of women.Would give anything to be with an author. Like Thomas Allred Jr. I'm sincere people I really don't know. Shontel Allred needs her sometime. Let's write the book. Shontel and I Forever. From the start Thomas Allred Jr. Well it goes a little something like this. I explained to the women's vindicating committee how is Shontel Allred and I met. I explained to the committee. That after serious conversation. I broke down to her. In a voicemail conversation. While waiting on her to reach out to me. I could see myself. As a father figure. Holding kids only the future can bring. Thomas Allred Jr said holding kids only the future can bring. I appreciate you. For everything you do My future self. What's in the past will stay in the past. American needs compa**ion. And the right to be in love with whoever you choose. Thomas Allred Jr. Keep with the story. Remember you have a script to right here. What we going to do Thomas Allred Jr. Is honor you for your writing abilities. You realize that you got Shontel Allred in here sitting beside you. Look at it this way.

I can only feel right. With my girl of my dreaMs. beside me. This book is dedicated to a police officer. Shontel Allred. I dedicate my book to your family and you. It is possibly the best book I've ever written. Nobody can tell me what to do with my relationship. Ya'll see that I'm trying my best to prove to Shontel Allred that it is me I deserve to be her husband. Communicate through paper Thomas Allred Jr. And she wants to talk. I said stop for a minute Thomas Allred Jr. Yes Miss Obama. A lot of females are looking up to you Thomas Allred Jr. We know that you need us just as well as we need you Thomas Allred Jr.

We all realize Thomas Allred Jr. That the man inside of you cannot love more than one woman. At a time. In the other time I would have. Trusted you Thomas Allred Jr. Now Shontel Allred speak to Thomas Allred Jr. Thomas Allred Jr let me speak to you Thomas Allred Jr. There is something good about us. I am a police officer. That loves her man Thomas Allred Jr. And you come around. Watch and see what I do. By the end of the book. Thomas Allred Jr go after her with conversation that is from the heart.

I know that you like me. Be professional with me baby. Some kind of reason I can't let you go Shontel Allred. Listen to me Thomas Allred Jr. My whole situation is messed up. I am going to clear it up for you Shontel Allred. I'm a police officer also Shontel Allred. Thomas Allred Jr you need to serenade her. With my ring ID wedd. Shontel Allred. My book doesn't seem like it does it. But these are my wedding vows to you. Listen Shontel Allred. I will cook and I will clean up the mess that I make. For the rest of my life if you will marry me. The Lord sent me to be there for you that's why I Won't Give Up on me and you. I've been in love with you for all seasons. And I hope I am impressing you. I'm getting ready to publish my book. This man is too damn confident for me y'all. Shontel Allred be with me. I'm almost done with the first half of my book. Now you know I can trust you. Girl you are going to make me were I can't see no one else. Do you think that im special Thomas Allred Jr. Gorgeous and you are special. Am I to be taken for a fool with your smooth conversations. And mellow accent. Bye Shontel Allred. Thomas

Allred Jr. I'm telling you one thing. You sure work hard deal. Watch your mouth Shontel Allred. I'm asking you to be my f*cking husband Thomas Allred Jr. And that I can do Shontel Allred. I'm just laying back writing this manuscript. If Miss Michelle Obama allows. Go on and kiss him. Would I tell you y'all. Shontel Allred will be my queen. And I won't stop until she has everything. That she ever wanted. Listen to those people out there. Look at how beautiful it is here. I work through the government Shontel Allred. God damn I work for the government also. Watch your language this is a love story. And they both lived happily ever after. Thomas Allred Jr you are famous. Thomas you meant what you said in your book didn't you. Every word of it. Look. It is about time he sent that in. That book is professional. Y'all made a good man out of Thomas Allred Jr. Yall made a good woman out of Shontel Allred. A match made in heaven. I didn't know what to think about you. Yes Miss Obama. On the count of three I'm going to snap my fingers. Just like we did last time. We will talk and then you will send the book in. 1 2 3 snap. Ms.. Obama thank you for all your help. Now send in the professional book. And use the bathroom. And go to sleep Thomas Allred Jr. The book is called Shontel and I Forever. And you deserve that girl Thomas Allred Jr. I'm a snap my fingers. And everything will be back in place and you would know what to do with your life. See I just snap my fingers. Snap

Shontel Allred are you surprised I wrote an alternate ending to our book. Here is the ending that should have been in the book. Talk to Shontel Allred Thomas Allred Jr. Come see if she will marry you. Shontel Allred I am Michelle Obama. You are Shontel Allred. A beauty queen. Make a movie out of this. I need to ask you one question Shontel Allred. Before I snap my fingers and the book be over with. Is Thomas Allred Jr the man that you love completely Shontel Allred. No he isn't. Shontel Allred what do you mean. Changing the story is dangerous for you. Thomas Allred Jr with all of my might I love you. Listen Shontel Allred I would do anything for you. Can you carry me out of the project at 3 o clock at night if I was sick. If the electric got cut off. Would you stay there with me. Until the bills were paid. Thomas Allred Jr this I just got to know. Now I see what you are saying Shontel Allred. I give myself 10 months. To secure your love and all the finances that we need. But honey you got to be my wife. Shontel Allred that's the only way is going to work. Generation after generation. I would do anything for you. I am hungry for your love. I'm not going to stop it. You got a professional police officer in your corner. Miss Michelle Obama please help me. Thomas Allred Jr Shontel Allred has made her decision. And my decision is I love Thomas Allred Jr. Pull out the red carpet. Don't you see my lady is getting ready to come through. Thomas Allred Jr you can have anything in this world why did you choose me. As I look out my window Shontel Allred. My favorite Dream Is us together. In holy matrimony. It's a dream but now it is reality. We only got one more thing to say and then we're going to close the book. Thomas Allred Jr speak to her. Shontel Allred I waited for you all my life. Because

Thomas Allred Jr you've been through a lot. No it's because I really do love you. Mama Shontel Allred. Don't say nothing else Thomas Allred Jr. Leave it just like that. We have got to take that boy out of community. I don't give a f*ck who like him. Take that boy out of community. This second. I Michelle Obama and I approve this message. The name of the book is called Shontel and I Forever. Thomas Allred Jr. We listened to you plead your case. Once you are asking us for help. And I told you. That if you can prove yourself to the committee of panelist. In which are all women. Your love Shontel Allred. That I would help you in your book. Well the committee has decided. Thank you Thomas Allred Jr. Realize people are listening. See my book is. Another level of success. We are waiting for it to come out. And Thomas Allred Jr be sure that you straighten your name out in the community. Imma do everything I can to straighten my name out Miss Obama. Didn't we do this before Thomas Allred Jr. Yes we did I wrote another book called fighting for mine. What is the matter with your hero kids. Book that is supposed to be coming out. I called the book Hero Children. And I'm putting in the work immediately after this is over. That boy ain't handicapped he handi-capable . This dude is off the goddamn hook. Thomas Allred Jr. A team of professionals are going to be working alongside of you. Treat them with the utmost respect. We hear you Thomas Allred Jr. The Secret Service. Is also wanting to get in on your book. Just one more question Thomas Allred Jr. Who is that woman that you love. Shontel Allred Ms. Obama. Pack your bags. I ain't got no bags to pack. What we going to do is you going to have to learn to be strong. Will you help me reach my wife Shontel Allred. Make a movie out of this. Look listen Thomas Allred Jr. You have got to charge your phone. Thank you. In the end Thomas Allred Jr. You will be able to support yourself. And your beautiful wife Shontel Allred. I don't know who this is. But we are in a movie. We got to teach that boy better. Thomas Allred Jr you got one more question you can ask. Before my book is still for all times. Thank you is the question. And will my family be taken care of if I can be all I can be. Go back to sleep Thomas Allred Jr. Tell Shontel Allred for me Miss Obama. That with every season there comes happiness. And Shontel Allred promised I wouldn't leave you. If I have to go I will be back for you Shontel Allred I promise. Thomas Allred Jr make some sense out of your book right now.Put I am grateful in your book. I am truly grateful. Thomas Allred Jr we will help you. And your lady Shontel Allred. Get to the promised land. Listen this boy ain't talking about nothing but love. One more thing. I'm a snap my fingers at the count of ten. And when you wake up from this dream Thomas Allred Jr. Your whole damn book. Will be completed. Listen Thomas Allred Jr. Professionals are watching you. Start the count now. 1 2 3 4 5 6 7 8 9 10 snap. Now Thomas Allred Jr didn't know what was going on. When you snap your fingers. Thomas Allred Jr send you working right now. I love Shontel Allred

I think Shontel Allred knows I love her. It is set in stone the way we feel about each other. I'm giving all that I have. To ensure to her. That the book will become successful. What can I say to you. Thomas Allred Jr. To ensure that I have a place. In my desk. After this is said and done. I'm talking to you Thomas Allred Jr. Let me realize that you love me over and over again. It's about time he realized she loved him. Shontel Allred. You can see that I care about you. I look straight at you. And my position is firm I want you. Do you get what I'm saying. What kind of book is this. Shontel Allred I sealed my fate what you watching. I kept on looking at you. Just thinking to myself. How lucky I would have been just to know you. That's when you came into my life. I am an American poet. And one day I will be able to provide for you. Clean your history back up. Thomas Allred Jr. Girl I want to touch you. I know how you must feel Shontel Allred. And you got to know how I feel. The book is called Shontel and I Forever. And I ain't got time for no games. I'm deeper reading to myself. My woman is beautiful. An eloquent sculpture of divine power. Yes she is. We knew each other just six months. Thomas Allred Jr. We are about to end this. Yes Miss Obama. Say your prayers tonight. And things might work out for you Thomas Allred Jr. Do you see who is speaking. We here for you Thomas Allred Jr. And we all realize that you and Shontel Allred are two of a kind. Let the past go and think to the Future. For in the future cometh your help. Or something like that. Michelle may I talk to him. Go ahead Shontel Allred speak to him now before we close the book for good. It is a new year Thomas Allred Jr. And opportunities are around every corner. You don't know them people. but they are working and hustling all night long in your behalf. I want you to see me as that girl that you love. And nothing more and nothing less. I give up. No Shontel Allred honey you can't give up. I need you more than air itself. Focus on you book

Thomas Allred Jr. Thomas Allred Jr. You ain't got but one second to tell Shontel Allred how you feel about her. She is the right person for me. Y'all close the book. Realizes just who you are. Be professional Thomas Allred Jr. I want to thank my staff record label and crew. There it is Thomas Allred Jr. Speak Thomas Allred Jr. In the event of my destruction. I want for my book. To be the property of Shontel Allred. I couldn't remember her last name so I gave her mine. Before I end this book. I wish that people would stop and look to see all the beautiful things that are in the world. My book is called Shontel and I Forever. Because we have fought through the storm. And we are still going the distance everyday of our life. This is the extended knowledge. Can Miss Michelle Obama. Please give a word to us. As a couple you two have.

Outdone yourself. I'm going to take you out of your community. Don't you worry about people around you Thomas Allred Jr. Let God handle your situation. Reach out to each other Shontel Allred. Because if I didn't want you together. Didn't your book wouldn't be together. Get up and hug one another. This wonderful work sitting before me. Is making me sad because. Thomas Allred Jr. I know you need someone. And your girl is right. Things do take a little time. Even when you are working for them. Thomas Allred Jr. Our hearts are in your hands. That boy really needs you

Shontel Allred. I know he does. I'm speaking to all of the people. In my world. Thomas Allred Jr don't realize. That the president is the one making this. Now President Donald Trump. Come and say hi to him Thomas Allred Jr. Hello President Trump. I am Thomas Allred Jr. And I've been waiting for you to speak to me. You're doing a great job with writing your books Thomas Allred Jr. Thomas Allred Jr the Lord is speaking to us. It is a must and a dire urgency. That you finish all of your books. You know that my books are not finished. I know so many things about you that I can't believe. President Donald Trump. I can't stop it it's just that I'm alone. Thomas Allred Jr the time will come when you will have your wife with you. We have to be sure of you. Who is it going to be Kristen or Shontel Allred. If you love that girl you will choose her. See you ain't understanding this program Thomas Allred Jr. Thomas Allred Jr this program gets more money than you ever can imagine. Thomas Allred Jr lay down to sleep and I want you to think about Shontel Allred or Kristen Allred. Sir I've already made my decision. Which is Thomas Allred Jr. As a man I'm choosing Shontel Allred. What are you going to do Shontel Allred. The community needs the two of you together. Thomas Allred Jr keeps composing books. And Shontel Allred is a police officer. I done a lot for you to. Thank you Mr.. President Trump. You have got to continue writing those books. Thomas Allred Jr. That's what I'm going to do after I get married. President Trump. Thomas Allred Jr your books there's a call for them now. So with all agency continue to right my son. Thomas Allred Jr.

All around you we got police officers. And the Secret Service. You are the one who has vision. Enough to change my world. I watched you as a Young Man growing up in Hickory North Carolina. The lessons were few and many. But we finally made a Man out of You Thomas Allred Jr. Now I'm going to tell you this. God put you on the pathway with the Secret Service. What you need to do is. Say to yourself and your community. It is all going to be alright. Right now I am in love with you Shontel Allred. And nobody is going to change the way I feel about you. For the rest of my life. Because community. If you wanted to hear my voice right now. Yall please bear with me. Everything is going to be alright. Every one of us are going to a different type of struggle. I'm keeping the truth in these manuscripts that I'm writing. Truth and prejudice. Is the cause for my book. Superman is my hero. By the time you get this message. I will let you people in on a secret. I am in the room by myself. Talking to the president of the United States. And Miss Michelle Obama. See Thomas Allred Jr. Your book is what commands you. Now if you love Shontel Allred. Prove that you love Shontel Allred Thomas Allred Jr. Our contact. Will be getting in contact with you Thomas Allred Jr. From the White House to your house. I'm your president. Thomas Allred Jr just had a conversation with the president. Don't give up boy. Think Thomas Allred Jr. Everything is going to be alright. Stand up for your people Thomas Allred Jr. That boy he is a police officer. Extended knowledge we never quit. Tell that girl that you love her Thomas Allred Jr.

Shontel Allred I love you. Now go to the restroom. And go back to sleep. Oh yeah. We are trying to make you unseen. Before you become famous Thomas Allred Jr. Can you handle your situation. The boss. Is you Thomas Allred Jr. You can handle your situation can't you. Sure I can. Great well I'll see you when that book comes out. And Thomas Allred Jr. I am Barack Obama not President Trump. Shontel Allred I love you. Send that goddamn book in Thomas Allred Jr.

I have a picture in my mind. That true love will one day find me. And the woman of my dreaMs. would love to see me come her way. So my picture isn't clear enough. Quit laughing at my dreaMs. y'all. Thanks to us. I am a two-time recognize Arthur. I'm making my book. So that people will see my face. And know that they can count on me. Listen there's no escape for me. Even my mama tells me that you need to take your time young man. I ain't got no reason to lie to you. Thomas Allred Jr I understand you. You ain't got but a couple days to figure out what you going to do with your books. Try to stay sharp as a pencil Thomas Allred Jr. They only shot you because you are a police officer. They put a police officer on trial. For having the decency of straightening up the neighborhood. Thomas Allred Jr you did your job right. And now you think of me. Listen to your voicemail message. Our Police department. Loves and respects you Thomas Allred Jr. Continue Thomas to write your books. Because we love what is in them. I'll do anything to help anyone that I can. Now that you see that I ain't joking around. it's time that the world adjust to our demands. We give you time to think Thomas Allred Jr. In our home. Think Thomas Allred Jr. Them white people know what you are going through. A police officer was shot down today. On news channel 10. At 11:31.

We will bring you the story that matters most to the neighborhood. Thomas Allred Jr you are police officer. I know you can't remember yourself. But transfer your emotions Thomas Allred Jr. Do you love Kristen Allred or do you love Shontel Allred. Shontel Allred will be in my heart. But I think that I'm in love with Kristen Allred. Thomas Allred Jr you need to watch what you're doing. That girl sees you as a father figure. So I'm going to make myself very clear. Do you want Kristen or me Thomas Allred Jr. I want Shontel Allred to be my lawfully wedded wife. You think Thomas Allred Jr. Is going to leave Shontel Allred. Not in this book He's not. We are the United States Treasury department. And our mission here is. To raise your game up to a new level. Tell Eden Allred that you said hi. Sit back and tell yourself. how you are going to make it out of your situation. Thank you Thomas Allred Jr. Because God didn't put more on you than you can bear. We are going to make you strong enough and more capable. The Hero Children would like to thank you as well Thomas Allred Jr. In hopes that you can make it. To turn every last one of your books in. All that boy really need. Is a friend to talk to. Thank you Thomas Allred Jr. Oh my gosh it's the president. Take him out of the hood. Give him an office. And make sure his family is secured. This is round two Thomas Allred Jr. Are you miserable living alone. You got professionals that are watching you. That man you have no idea how much power you have in your little Pinky. Give me one reason that I should help you out of your situation Thomas Allred Jr. Because I don't give up. If it takes me the rest of my life. I will continue to try to be there for people. No matter the race or Creed. Thomas Allred Jr. I really respect you. I don't want you to think that is easy to become successful. So we made you go through a bunch of things. So you can finally see Thomas Allred Jr. What it is to be a man in the United States today. Come with all them people are after you because you are helping the government with your business ideas. Imma need you to maintain your position. And clean up your goddamn room. Thomas Allred Jr this isn't a game. What can I say to you. to help you realize that you are a part of the national government Secret Service. What I tell you Thomas Allred Jr you got a good personality. Listen to Thomas Allred Jr I know you've been shot. I also have the details to your case surrounding you. You love many women. That you haven't had a chance to talk to. It's because you are a secret service agent. And you are not allowed to talk to females. All you got to do Thomas Allred Jr. Is send the book in. You are making parts in the story Thomas Allred Jr. Headline your people. We are talking about Michael and Maurice Kesha and Chris. And don't forget your mother Charlene. Do you see how we put you together. No one really works in your family. Your family sees you as.A leader in this nation. Thomas Allred Jr I got a question for you. If given everything that you ever could imagine in this lifetime. Who would you leave it to when you die. Thomas Allred Jr take your time and answer this question. I'm sitting back wondering. If my words can make a difference in my life.

And if giving everything that I ever wanted in this lifetime. And I was just some reason die. I would leave everything to all of the people who have been there for me equally. Because in my house there are many mansions. The Lord said this to me. So I focus on people to. I care about these people Mr. President. And there is nothing that I wouldn't do for anyone. I am a part of the Secret Service. Thomas Allred Jr. is getting emotional. Continue to write your book. Thomas Allred Jr I like you and police officers like you. You know I seen your case Thomas Allred Jr. Give a f*ck and Ill help you. Get ready for round three Thomas Allred Jr. Your apartment is open to you. Now you see that the president can help you. And your family. One reason that I realize that it's right to help you. Is because no matter what you went through you never complained. That man is a police officer. For our NSA program. Y'all got a professional writing these books. Just think about it Thomas Allred Jr. I need you to understand. That in order to progress you must first dream. Thomas Allred Jr your book I gave to you. As a symbol of my appreciation. I love you Thomas Allred Jr. And we will see that you have a female in that apartment with you. I want to thank the government so much. Thomas Allred Jr you are getting ready to thank us by sending in your book. Take your time Thomas Allred Jr. Now publish your book the way you are supposed to. Send the book in Thomas Allred Jr. Send the book in. I just got one last thing to say. can I have a woman with me while I'm sending the book in. Your apartment is open Thomas Allred Jr. Police officers are proud of you. you are going down in history as a professional police officer Thomas Allred Jr. One more thing Thomas Allred Jr. Do make a part to this book. I need you to get up and get something to eat. Charge that phone. And write some more in one hour. You are a police officer. Thomas Allred Jr. And your memory is restored. Be professional. We are walking you down memory lane. Shontel is the woman you intend to marry. With that being said. Your bank account is colossal. In your dreaMs. Thomas Allred Jr. Did you dream that the government would help you. I always dream for my people to have something. But I never imagined dreaming about the federal government helping me with everything . Everyone when he comes through. Salute Thomas Allred Jr. For by thanks giving do we flourish and prosper. Be professional Thomas Allred Jr now send in the book part one of my book called I love you Thomas Allred Jr. Be professional send in the Book.

Weather the new book sells or not Eden Reid. Girl I want you to know. That you remain a close friend of mine. And I'm also telling you that. In this world. A man is supposed to be with you. Now think about it for a second. Eden Reid. I believe this is unstoppable. Daily I work on my craft. But doing this I master the field of completentcy and honor. Imma do what I can do to make you realize that I'm the one that loves you Eden. I know that my books are dedicated to other women. Women of statue and power. But just in case you realize it Eden. A year has gone past. I have been writing you professionally. For like 9 months now. And I am wondering about you and me. Possibly becoming more than friends. I am going to make a film out of these books Eden. And I'm too large to make you feel stupid. For dating me. Right now is the beginning of my book. The evolution of me. I just realized the who you think I am. Is not who you think I am. I know exactly what I'm doing Eden. I am unstoppable in your eyesight Eden. If I could just get my finances together. There's no telling what I what me and you could do. Get you some popcorn and sit down and enjoy this book. In dedication to my other girls. Being mature I want to be with you. And I care for you ladies with an undying love and respect for myself. Thomas Allred Jr I got one question for you. Yes Eden. Am I too little for you. You the right size Eden be professional. I realize that you need me as much as I need you. Thomas Allred Jr. And you are a government agent. That works with the police department. I am impressed by your skills and your demeanor. Get ready to send in the book. If it take me all day to write this book I'm going to sit here and do it. You my boo Eden.Eden Reid come stop me. From telling the world. That I adore you. I seem to have lost my train of thought. Looking at myself in the mirror. Lord please help me get Eden to love me. Until all accounts are settled. This is the evolution of me. Eden Reid . Written by Thomas Allred Jr. Thomas Allred Jr move out the way make the call. I'm going to call in a minute Eden. Do you know Thomas Allred Jr I love you. I love you also Eden very much. Here's how it's going to work be professional. I'm asking you to move in with me. That's too much for me Thomas Allred Jr. You talk about me Eden in your sleep. Thomas Allred Jr being professional. That boy keeps trying. To figure out the algorithMs. that are going on with him. Thomas Allred Jr we need you to straighten up yourself. Yes Mr.. President. Thomas you see what your books are doing. You need to take your time. Go use the bathroom. And come back and write your book you got all day to talk to Eden. Yes Mr.. President. Thomas Allred Jr right now I want you to tell Eden. I'm in love with you Eden. I am in love with you Eden. And this is part of my a**ignment. As a secret service agent. Y'all know the government is out testing people. Thomas Allred Jr. You got all f*cking day if you want to talk to Eden. Write your book and prove yourself to her instead of talking. Be a true man not a true movie star. Lieutenant Candis what is this he's talking about. Eden Reid Thomas Allred Jr works for the government. And we are conditioning him out because Thomas Allred Jr needs a love in this life. Thank you. You said Thomas Allred Jr needs a love in this life. It is your destiny Eden Reid. The evolution of me. There it is. It's about Thomas Allred Jr and you Eden Reid. You know what you doing Thomas Allred Jr. Eden Reid I care about you. But you said that you loved too many other women. I am in love with them but I don't know them. Listen to me Thomas Allred Jr. All my life I've been in struggles. Listen to me. I've never had a man write a book for me before. All of them saying is. Thank you Thomas Allred Jr. I'm so proud of the fact that I get to know you. I'm so proud of you Eden Reid. What do we do now. We just share the moment. Is this it. The book has got to be professional. Let me ReDiscover you in my eyesight Eden Reid. If we could talk on the phone for a little while. I do anything for you to make you smile.

Girl I am a police officer. Around here I'm known as Officer Reign. Of the New York Police department. See I've been working for the NSA and the FBI and the Secret Service I'm codename Superman for the NSA and the FBI and the Secret Service. I'm giving you my credentials Eden Reid. Because baby I have nothing to hide. I'm only a man that you see on TV as a police officer. Being professional eye reason with myself to carry myself in the better understanding of what love is trust is. Thomas Allred Jr. I don't care that you are police officer. What I care about is your books. Can you make a decent living Thomas Allred Jr. With your books Thomas Allred Jr. Automatically Eden Reid.

I'm saying yes I can make a decent living. For my woman of my dreaMs.. And me to chill to. I believe in myself Eden Reid. And when you cross that line. Of believing in yourself. And trusting in your opinion. Girl you understand that. I'm wealthy man. Because I've got a lot of friends that love me. What I tell you Thomas Allred Jr. To my opinion. I am happy with this current situation. I sit up here day and night. In the hopes of finding someone that I love. Who could offer me the same. In this northern hemisphere. I see by the way you talkin. That there really could be something there between us Thomas Allred Jr. Take time and send that girl the book. And professionally. Ask her out on a date after your book gets finished. You are a working man Thomas Allred Jr. Make sure that the woman respects you for all the work that you've done in trying to go out with her Thomas Allred Jr. Listen. All I gotta do is stay clean. Take a goddamn shower. After your book is done. I listened to you Thomas Allred Jr. You need to apologize to that girl. Because Shontel Allred is your wife.i apologize Eden. You are making a fool of yourself. Shontel Allred is my wife. And a lot of people talk. But I never cheated on her. Not ever since we first start talking. My book is the evolution of me. Thomas Allred Jr. Thomas and Shontel Allred sitting in a tree. I work for the damn government. They be sending me all over the place. You might want to get back a little. This nigga is about to explode. See the one thing that I can't focus with. It's beautiful women in my eyesight. I lose all sense of time just thinking how I'm a be with them. I'm developing this pa**ion for love. That is overwhelming in my stomach. In two more days. I will keep my apartment back from the government. Eden Reid I'm not playing with you. Girl if situations were different or ever to change. It would be me and you Eden Reid. But from one police officer to another. Get my money and figure it out Eden Reid. You can see that I'm professional. Take your time Eden Reid and speak to me about this situation we have at hand. I don't care who you talk to Thomas Allred Jr. You are going to eat this p**sy on up. Because I'm a woman Thomas Allred Jr. That needs her man. Us ladies are giving you a Superman contract. For believing and never giving up. We just want to thank you Thomas Allred Jr. And all this p**sy is yours. Until the end of time. This is the beginning of the evolution of me Thomas Allred Jr Superman. Send in this part of the book Thomas Allred Jr. Before you do Thomas Allred Jr. I need to say one thing. That woman love you all over the world. Never forget that Superman. Send in this part of the book

Now Thomas Allred Jr I want to see you. Be professional Thomas Allred Jr. And read your book to me out loud. My book takes place in Hickory NC. I was in my room doing things that I shouldn't do. When I got the idea to write this book. Growing from a kid into a man I wondered. If my book could stand up to the competition out there. So I prayed about this. That is when Eden Reid called me. And it seem like after we talked. My book just came to me. Y'all can see where I'm coming from. If it wasn't for you Eden Reid. I probably wouldn't have made it. He ready for the big league y'all. What do you want me to do. It's okay right now Thomas Allred Jr. We all realize that you got tragedy in your family. But see here at the end of the day Thomas Allred Jr. You still are the man that handles business. You got to book getting ready to come out. You lost and love a love one. Professionally. I couldn't see myself with anyone else but you Thomas Allred Jr. Do you mean it Eden Reid. I mean every word that I'm saying Thomas Allred Jr. There is nothing about you that is not a man. Watch and see what happens for you after your book is finished. You need to put material into your book Thomas Allred Jr. I'll look and see where my help come from. My help comes from you taking care of me. We are taking care of each other. United States government I'm saying thank you. Send in a copy of your book. To Eden Reid. Listen I'm too professional two-play games with anybody. I get emotional because. I lost two people that mean the world to me. You would have to believe in me to see the man that I've become. 8 years of have gone past. And I'm asking your honor have I solved my case. My whole community. Has been standing up. On their feet night and day. Ever since I can remember entering into the community. I'll let you know. The people that make me. And the people I look up to. Are my brothers and sisters in my community. God didn't put me here with a gift for nothing. God put me here to tell the people everything is going to be alright. Now because I started in love with women in such a fool of my behavior. I give an apology to all of the women that I love. Which is every single one of you. The power of words have taken me. Farther than I could ever imagine. This is my book. Thomas Allred Jr. We want to see you. Please lieutenant Candis I was just getting started. I hope you know that is your lieutenant Thomas Allred Jr. I can't help but tell you what a wonderful job you are doing. In writing your book you have discovered. The true meaning of love and people. Thank you lieutenant Candis. I'm asking for your hand in marriage lieutenant Candis. Thomas Allred Jr. Once you have me Thomas Allred Jr you won't want nobody else. That's what I'm hoping for Candis. Lieutenant Candis. In my book. There are 21 ladies which I would like to marry.

Thomas Allred Jr. You got no idea how many women want to marry you. For richer or poorer. To death do you part. You Thomas Allred Jr. And everyone of the women that love you. And you care for deeply Thomas Allred Jr. You have got to listen. By the power vested in me in this great state of Washington DC. And Now pronounce You husband and wives. You can be with them Thomas Allred Jr. I don't believe it myself. You are are a law man. What we're going to do today is. Walk with you through time. We are not going to leave you alone Thomas Allred Jr. So don't be afraid to be all you can be. Lieutenant Candis. What about us. You ain't got no idea of what you asking of me Thomas Allred Jr. As of now. We are married. And other woman lieutenant Candis. The other woman are yours and my wives. Thomas Allred Jr. We are going to make a movie out of this. Lieutenant Kristen. Listen Thomas Allred Jr. Keep it professional. All of the women are your wives. In the United States of America. I know I must be dreaming. That boy in danger. Thomas Allred Jr I'm waiting on you to send me the notes. Okay it goes like this. Looking at myself in the mirror. My true feelings is. That I love all the women that God blessed me with. And to keep them happy. I'm working daily on business ideas and books. To keep my woman and her family happy. My notes are now completed. Lieutenant Eden Reid. You are my wife. By the federal government I marry you. See that my apartment comes open this week lieutenant Eden Reid. Lieutenant Eden Reid. These are my notes I a**igned to you. Lieutenant Eden Reid I need a professional after me. I'm going to get these notes to you right now. My beautiful wives Eden Reid. Candis

Allred. Shontel Allred. Kristen Allred. Samantha Allred. And all the other females I didn't maybe get to see. Here are my notes.

Girl I entertain myself. By writing movies and horror flic*s to myself. Eden Reid the day will come when you will have to choose between your job and me. As a police officer. I know the day will come. That you will choose my love. Over everything Eden Reid. If I can't say to you. How much I do respect and adore you. Then I am vindicated because I. Can see you in my dreaMs.. My dreaMs. are the question Eden Reid. Doesn't everyone want to know where I'm going with this book. It is a dream I'm having. To myself Eden Reid. Something is going wrong with me. It is taking me a long time. To express myself to you. All you have to do is sleep with me Eden Reid. And all will be said and done. Game time. It's too much money out here. For me not to have you Eden Reid. Honey read my book. Over and over again. To get the message that I'm not playing games. With you Eden Reid. Right now I worship you. You see I am busy. Creating a masterpiece for you and me. I hope that you understand. That I am a part of you. And this is me that you're talking to on the phone. On The daily so I can get my book together. Your voice tells me. That you are someone that I could be with. I hustle hard because of you. I'm giving up s*x to. Until your books come out. Eden Reid. I do trust in your opinion. So before you let me down. At least think of the two of us in Tahiti. I want to know that you love me Eden Reid. I am fighting for you. Thomas Allred Jr. Right now I'm sitting reading your book. And interested as it is. I know I can't spend my life with you. So thank you anyway. You want to talk to me then talk to me. I'm Eden Reid. Talk to her Thomas Allred Jr. Yes lieutenant Candis. I also got business ideas. That are coming out in the next few months Eden Reid. I see that you're working woman and a woman of business. That is why this is my only dedication. I have to be sure that you understand that you are beautiful. Your voice sounds to me. And see if you need a man to hold you. Eden Reid. I'm trying to get you to see. The way I am versus these other dudes. Eden Reid. I care for you. I am a police officer. That is writing a book on love. And understanding. I'm a police officer. That is making ideas. And saving lives. All over the world with the NSA helping me. My officer's name is Officer Reign of the police department named the New York Police department. I have been shot Eden Reid. But I carry myself like a man is supposed to. I'm richer than you think I am. As the government tries to change me. I am going to hold you down. And no matter what this maybe. Let me see what I can do for us. I want you so badly Eden Reid. Professionally I am a good man. I got your heart in my hands right now. you're probably getting choked up with just reading this book paragraph. Okay honey. Listen Thomas Allred Jr a lot of people are watching me. if you are for real about your business then be for Real about your business. Get your money Thomas Allred Jr. And we will see if we can talk. What can I do to finance you. In my position Eden Reid. Finances are what they are. Eden Reid I am capable of financing my own self. I told you that I didn't want anything from you. Eden Reid

I just want to spend time with you. The government. Keep going Thomas Allred Jr. You will have to excuse me for a second Eden Reid. What do y'all want. Lieutenant Kristen. We want some time in that book. Lieutenant Kristen you see that I love you. Thomas Allred Jr what are you going to do if I pull the plug on your book. Lieutenant Kristen no don't do that. Then straighten your a** up. Tell lieutenant Eden like this. I got this big money play. That I am moving on. And there are other females involved. And I like you. Lieutenant Eden. Do you want to play ball with us? Thank you lieutenant Kristen. I love you too. You have to speak to her. Also tell lieutenant Eden. That your wives are many. But your love is a few. Tell lieutenant Eden. That we are part of a family. That is under God. With liberty and justice for all. Take your time out. And speak to me and lieutenant Kristen. Imma take my time out to speak to all of my ladies all of the lieutenants women of the government. This is Thomas Allred Jr. Women of the government. What you want to do is. Continue to save your money to buy land. And to buy houses. I say these things to you ladies. No matter what the cost or the situation. Ladies of the government you are stronger than you think you are. I can see us together. Communicating. How that we are. Apart of something thats real. Can you imagine me running you. Thomas Allred Jr. Tell lieutenant Kristen what we all said. We think your a** need to speak to me lieutenant Kristen. And that is from the woman of the government. Yall my position is firm. I'm trying to speak to all of you ladies. In the days to come. I will step my game up. Business ideas after business ideas. Will begin to surface we. As the police department. Will need to be stronger because of it. Now lieutenant Kristen. What I'm saying to you is. I'm professional. Make a movie out of this. Go ahead and make a movie out of this. If it is ambition that drives us. Then I am all in the pa**enger seat. Thomas Allred Jr you be making sense. Technically I'm married a b*tch that be making sense. Lieutenant Porsche. All I could think about was getting back to you. Lieutenant Porsche. Girl I would have ended up quitting. Thomas Allred Jr. Listen are you going to sign the contract. To marry every last one of us. And split your fortune down the middle to the end. All of us women just want to know if you still want that Superman contract. Which is that you are married and can sleep with anyone of us at any given time all across the United States of America. Me and my woman are professional. We would not give your loving away. Just take care of all the sisters of law enforcement. And so forth. You say you are professional Thomas Allred Jr. They shot that boy. Lieutenant Candis I'm going to sign the contract. All of my money books and ideas. Belong equally to all of the women of law enforcement and so forth. All you have to do is sign the contract. Right here. Right here. Thomas Allred Jr. You are Superman. And the ladies will be with you when it is time. Everybody Thomas Allred Jr is Superman. Again. Ladies this is a real and binding doc*ment. I am proud of each and everyone of you. Ladies of law enforcement. What can I do to tell you how much I need you. I love all of you women of law enforcement. You have got to keep your position Thomas Allred

Jr. As Superman ladies I promise to never change. Lieutenant Samantha. Let's get these ladies they money. Thomas Allred Jr don't give a damn about the money. He looking for a girl that he can love. Thomas Allred Jr has single-handedly saved us. You need to send in that message Thomas Allred Jr. And the contract will be completed. One more thing Thomas Allred Jr. All of the women we all are in love with you. Now dream big.i sign this contract at my own free will. I am Thomas Allred Jr. Of the New York Police department. Codename Superman of the NSA the FBI and the Secret Service. I want every woman in law enforcement to see this. My business ideas my books and other money properties. Are to be divided with the women of law enforcement all over the United States. And with God I rest my case. Just send in the contract. There call me Superman.

Thank God that you love me ladies. Cause I'm doing everything that I can. To be there for all of you. Lieutenant Samantha. Girl I will be there for you if I only could. Lieutenant Nada. That dude got since enough. To leave us all of his fortune. And lieutenant Chelsea and lieutenant Heather. This is a brand new book. There is none like it. You are to cherish your book lieutenant Chelsea and lieutenant Heather. Girls I give to you. My secret name. My secret name is professional. Girls call me. Superman Thomas Allred Jr. What about Eden Allred Thomas Allred Jr. Careful what you wish for. Right now you have a book coming out. And right now this makes two books that you have coming out. This boy has got to entertain me. Enough with the magic tricks. Superman Thomas Allred Jr. Will you stand with us women if All odds was against us. I will stand with the woman until the very end. Now this man is starting to impress me. Miss Hillary Clinton. It is my great pleasure to allow you to. Have a copy of this book. The name of the book is called. The evolution of me. Written by Thomas Allred Jr. Now ladies I know you're Superman Thomas Allred Jr how many business ideas did you turn in two invention companies. Somewhere between 1000 and 1200. If I'm not mistaken. All the ideas were aimed at saving the lives of people. Lieutenant Sasha girl I will be with you if I could. Girl he just said lieutenant Sasha. Speak to me lieutenant Sasha for we only have a little time to write in this book. I can help you Thomas Allred Jr. Lieutenant Sasha I know you can help me. That is why I put your name in this book. What can we do that's different lieutenant Sasha. Speak to me lieutenant Sasha. We need to tell the girls they all got your contract. And what better way to do this then to put out a book. If you are dedicated Superman Thomas Allred Jr. and can hold Your position a little while longer. The sun will shine on you like never before. But that is a good thing Superman Thomas Allred Jr. Seeing how Injustice is being served. I'm lieutenant Sasha. And the first woman to stand by Your side. In times of victory and tragedy. Listen here Superman Thomas Allred Jr. In a couple days you will be a millionaire. Just keep going the way you're going Thomas Allred Jr. If you need to see me. Mention my name in your book. I am lieutenant Sasha. Lieutenant Sasha I'm going all the way out. And I need to see you. I want to thank you for being the first woman to stand up with me. I am a professional police officer. I know exactly what I'm doing lieutenant Sasha. Thank you girl. Does everybody get me. Does everybody feel the same way that I do. I'm venturing out of my comfort zone. To a place where business men and women go to after retirement. Thomas Allred Jr. You need us. Yes lieutenant Evelyn I need you all to believe in each other again. Somehow we have forgotten how to love each other. And that just isn't right. Please. Women of all Nations. We are supposed to be love mates and Queens. I will say it again. Women of all Nations. We are supposed to be love mates in Queens. Somehow King and Queens have got messed up Thomas Allred Jr. I'm talking to you. In the success of our book. Because Thomas Allred Jr. Is a police officer. A women's victiMs. rights advocate. Meaning that no matter where you are. If Thomas Allred Jr can help you. He will indeed help. Ladies Thomas Allred Jr. Is a trillionaire. And this book is nonfiction. I take my time to look at the sun. And enjoy the flowers the roses that are in my life daily. I tried to write as much as possible. when my fingers got tired and I went to sleep. I dreamed of this plan. To make business ideas to save all of our women. To make business ideas to save all of our children. To make business ideas to save as many of my brothers as I can. I had to humble myself down to see lieutenant Eden . But lieutenant Kristen told me. I need to write my book. This thing is bigger than us. Be professional. People are watching you. Have a good day Thomas Allred Jr. Is what lieutenant Kristen would say to me. To keep me focused. On the task at hand. As I get focused. On the task at hand. I wonder do businessmen really see me. I wonder if I have a chance doing business. In the large circuit. Lieutenant Kristin I like the way he said that. Listen I am fighting for mine. Go ahead put Thomas Allred Jr on the Ellen DeGeneres Show. Oprah Winfrey wants to talk to him. That boy don't understand these billionaires want to talk to him. If you keep on going you are famous Thomas Allred Jr. We all will call you Superman forevermore. But if you were able to stop now. No one would make fun of you for doing a job well done. Yes lieutenant Evelyn. I want to go on lieutenant Kristen. Thomas Allred Jr right now we got you. Inside your mother's house. In a couple weeks Thomas Allred Jr. We are going to move you. Into an apartment house of your own. You do get what I'm saying don't you Thomas Allred Jr. You can make love to people. And no one thing no this. You need to catch up on your love making. Because it has been 9 years. That white people have held you. Are you sure that you want to go forward Thomas Allred Jr. By saying yes there's no turning back. As long as my family and community are taken care of. I'm saying yes lieutenant Kristen. I do want to move forward with the process. You heard that ladies we have a hero. Go to sleep Thomas Allred Jr. Your second book has been completed Thomas Allred Jr. And this is the part where I give Captain Frankie. A special thanks. Captain Frankie. You have been there for me through the years. And I appreciate you with all of my heart. I want to thank you for your carriage your knowledge in your respect. And I need you to know. That as a police officer. You are The shining Star Captain Frankie. I thank all the men and women on the police force. Are government Shall be safe. Thomas Allred Jrall you got to do is tell one more person how you feel about them. Lieutenant Shontel. In my heart. I know only you. You have been a part of my heart and my soul. I yearn for the day that we meet again. Cause lieutenant Shontel. I ain't never seen nothing like you before. Close your book. You got two books coming out. Lieutenant Eden and lieutenant Cindy. Can't you see the story is not about you. This story is about all the women in the United States. Be professional. When you talk to Thomas Allred Jr. He is a cop that's done been through some things. On the count of three I want you to close your book. Just miss Hillary Clinton. Thomas Allred Jr. I'm going to take you out the hood as soon as your book is finished Thomas Allred Jr. 1 2 3 snap. Your book is finished Thomas Allred Jr. Superman your book is finished. These children look up to you Thomas Allred Jr. You maintain your position. 100 million is coming. Now what we do is. Discuss this with all of the women. I ain't got no idea what to say left. Thomas Allred Jr. We making sure your a** got a bank account. Go to sleep on 3 Thomas Allred Jr. 1 2 3 send that book in. I had to wash my hands so I went into the bathroom. To where I looked at myself in the mirror. Thinking to myself a hero is what I needed. The water was running in the sink. And think begin to fill up. Look at my face. I am Superman.

Not the Superman on the TV screen. But Superman on the police force. It is a big journey for me. I have been through so many different things it ain't even funny now. Yall need to talk to that boy. He is Superman Thomas Allred Jr. I know my position right now. I am writing every book that I can. To keep my position. As a hero in my family. And as a hero to my community. Take a second to think. With all this going on. Not too many people are concerned with the safety. Of other people. Imma let you know that. As a police officer my job is. To provide for the community. In any means that come up my way. Thomas Allred Jr. You don't know what you are doing. I'm doing exactly what I can do lieutenant Candis. This book is supposed to be a hero book. And in a Hero book you will tell the truth because you are decent. Tell Thomas Allred Jr to come in here. Lieutenant Kristen is in there doing something. You just have to deal with me Thomas Allred Jr. Yes lieutenant Rachel. Never mind me. Just think of the people. Thomas Allred Jr. I want you to take care of yourself. Lieutenant Rachel I want to. But the truth is I'm alone. For nine years I've been alone. Inside of my mother's house. I told you he is off the hook. Lieutenant Kristen is back. Thank you Rachel I'll take over from here. Thomas Allred Jr I would do anything for you. I need you to become professional.

Thomas Allred Jr they are counting on you to become professional. Listen lieutenant Kristen I'm doing the best that I can. See. Imma take my time with professionals. They got books we got books. They got business ideas everybody got business ideas. But the fact remains the same. What I stand for is the women of the United States of America. And to the republic for which it stands. One Nation y'all. Indivisible. With liberty and justice for all. I am Superman Thomas Allred Jr.

We're going to make a movie out of this Thomas Allred Jr. Help him. I am lieutenant Kristen. And I am lieutenant Candis. And we are police officers. I am lieutenant Shontel. And I am lieutenant Jennifer. I am a police officer as well. We are police women of the United States of America. And police officers stand up for one another. I am Thomas Allred Jr. Codename Superman. And I'm standing up. For every police officer in our nation. It ain't that I'm looking to impress anybody. it is just that my brothers and sisters in law enforcement have saved my life so many times. That I got to be the man that I am today. My brothers in law enforcement. Thank you for caring about me. That is professional. As we go forward in these years to come. Don't forget your what we stand for. The needs of the public. And the needs of our brothers and sisters in law enforcement. Now I've been in the house going on nine years. Thinking of ways to come stronger for my community. You are getting stronger. Superman is getting stronger. Thank you lieutenant Karen. Lieutenant Eden. And lieutenant Cindy. Thomas Allred Jr. Let me see a few words to the females for you. I am more dedicated than I ever been. I put my life on the line for the right of all offices that's known in truth. That boy put his life on the line. I am agreeing with the women of our nation. I hope that you can see that. In this world. Thomas Allred Jr. That boy ain't playing no games. I think that we should choose Thomas Allred Jr as our captain. Of the police force. That would be an honor. Captain Superman.

Captain Thomas Allred Jr. All he got to do is just send in that message. In his book is completed. I'm too professional to not tell yall that there will be rough days ahead. But we hold on to our promises. To care for one another. In sickness and in health. Until death do us part. That is a hero for you. Be professional Thomas Allred Jr. Our men need to hear you. Veterans or not. I don't give up. We don't give up. Because we ain't got time to give into any oppression. I'm thanking God for making me this way instead of counterfeit. and I'm doing everything I can to help everyone in our communities. I know that people look after you. Now fellas I have one more thing to say to you. Doesn't it feel good to be a police officer today in the United States of America. This boy just got done speaking. See my name is lieutenant Naomi. That boy put Naomi name in that book. You ought to give it up to Thomas Allred Jr.

That boy look terrorist in the face instead of him in our courtroom. Give the boy a second to speak to us. I will never change the way I feel about the situation. I'm too professional to cry over people that ive lost. I believe in a future for all of us. Once we can come together as one. Like we did when we were children. This nation is talking about shutting us down. The police station is not giving up. Keep representing Thomas Allred Jr. What we are going to do is. Take good care of our families. And we depend on you the police officers. To do a wonderful job in protecting our communities. Without us police officers the neighborhoods would be lost. My women and men officers. You are the difference. That the world needs. In my book I'm professional. In real life I'm a man that searching for love. Now I tell you one thing. The day will come. When the world will need all of the police officers. Working together as one. I can remember. The day I almost lost my leg from a gunshot wound. I look to the sky from which cometh my help. And my brothers and sisters in law enforcement were there for me. So it is simple. Everybody needs a hero. So I thank you law enforcement. For the great job that you have been doing. Out there on them streets. And street corners. I want you to know two things. That I care about you. And I care about the ladies in uniform. That is our trillionaire . Thomas Allred Jr. Thomas Allred Jr Send that message in. All right lieutenant Rachel.

Return the midnight hour Eden Reid. Into something that don't exist. I know that you see me working on these books Eden Reid. Right now I found myself in love with the subject about you. I've done my homework lieutenant Eden Reid. I got a police force that is heading me up in my idea. To run the city from the ground up. Here go my plans Eden Reid. My Superman contract is almost complete. Listen to me ladies. Every since I met her I started to wonder how it feels to be married to a beautiful lady like her. My name is Superman for a reason. The way you pull people together is amazing Thomas Allred Jr. Be professional Thomas Allred Jr. Imma give everything to everybody. Kristen I need you. To help me with my business from day today. Am I getting warm. Don't say nothing you damn right you getting warm. As I travel into my story deeper. I need professionals to hear me. see I'm not nothing without the professional women on the police force to guide me. Thomas Allred Jr. you need yourself a. Hero replacement. Someone to care for you. When you need that special lovin only a police woman can give you. Cut the damn bulsh*tt out. Now everybody repeat after me. I am the leader of this group. I am the leader of this group Thomas Allred Jr. This here gets more amazing. You understand what I'm saying to you ladies. What are you saying to us Thomas Allred Jr. If your baby needs shoes. What kind of Superman do you got at home. Because ain't no way in hell I am going to retire without giving to all of the women. The money that I promised them. That is some Kool-Aid how do you like that flavor. I am getting an attitude with myself right now. No matter what kind of flavor My Kool-Aid is. Lieutenant Monica. Right now I'm going to need you to stand up. If your birthday is today stand up ladies. Lieutenant Candis birthday is today. Ladies I'm saying happy birthday to you. And all my fellas out there in the law enforcement agency. I want you to do me a favor. And hug your girl for me. See my brothers and sisters in law enforcement. We are not a doormat any longer. Now that they hear us. Everybody can hear us. This is a job for the police department. I wish there was a police officer there to see me. My book has got enough content in it. To take us somewhere. but I won't be satisfied until I can put some bread and meat on the table for everything lady law enforcement officer. In the United States of America and surrounding areas. Now give me a second. And I'll explain to you how I plan to work this thing. All it takes is a thinking man and woman to run this here. Thomas is the captain of the police department. Girls I'm done to let you in on a secret. Every since I saw you you have no idea how much I admire and respect you. Ladies on the police department. You are the right women for the job of being there for me when times get critical. Police officers I need you because. I am a new trillionaire. That is lost in my direction. What kind of new trillionaire are you. A victiMs. rights specialist. Advocate is what he said. I see you as a hero to the police department Thomas Allred Jr. Look at me Thomas Allred Jr. The police department is all over the place. When you get your money back. We need you to follow the rules that we say to the letter. Our whole damn Police department is up circling around you. Read your goddamn book. It is people after that want you. You know that we cannot reveal ourselves. That is to you. We only reveal ourselves when you are in danger. Of making a mistake. This program right here. Is known as. Superman survives. Thomas Allred Jr you need to name your book. Superman survives. I know the Thomas Allred Jr can hear me. Who are you police officer speak your name. I am lieutenant Candis. Police officers are watching you Thomas Allred Jr. Because of you. Giving the police a chance to demonstrate their abilities. You saved my life lieutenant Candis and the police force. Don't think I would forget you. Y'all are important to me. I care about my fellows as much as the ladies on the police force. Right now I am busy. I must write book at the book that's what you are paying me for. There go Superman right there. Lieutenant Melissa. Yes Thomas Allred Jr. What I tell you lieutenant Melissa. If there's a will there is a way to get paid. Everybody tell lieutenant Melissa happy birthday. He don't know my birthday is today. Please tell me your name so I can tell you happy birthday. Thomas Allred Jr I am lieutenant Lisa. Of the New York Police department. Lieutenant Lisa happy birthday. Thomas Allred Jr. Your birthday is this month isn't it. We were hoping that you would stand up before your birthday gets here.

Thomas Allred Jr. For out thinking us. And doing the right thing with your books and business ideas. We give you the purple heart. And happy birthday Thomas Allred Jr. Superman survives. To live a life with his friends. Thomas Allred Jr. Got a good personality. This book is dedicated. To My One true Love. Lieutenant Jocelyn. Of the New York Police department. Lieutenant Jocelyn I had to mention your name. Keep your composure Thomas Allred Jr. The book is getting ready to be completed itself. I'm going to try to make this anyway as good as possible. Don't mess with my women. In this world. We need a police officer. One who cares about the women. And wouldn't stand for them to be hurt. Is that you Superman survive I be out. That boy just finished up his tape. Lieutenant Monica. No one told him to do this. I need to talk to him. Get Thomas Allred Jr in here immediately. Who are you Thomas Allred Jr. I am officer Reign of the New York Police department. Officer Reign can you fix this. If you let a police officer be a police officer. We can fix almost every problem known to man. Do you see how that got operates. Just one more question. Are you truly going to split your trillions of dollars. Evenly with the women of the police department all over the United States of America and surrounding areas. You damn right I am. The police department save my life. Several times as a Young Man growing up in the streets. And I'll be damned if my woman police officers. Go another day without having what they need. What about the men police officers. These business ideas can help them. His ideas will help you. Thomas Allred Jr we give a f*ck about you. Now people don't give up. That is the end of the book. Make sure people are talkin. Lieutenant Eden. Lieutenant Kristen. Lieutenant Shontel. Thomas Allred Jr. I just want you to know one thing before you end the book. That you are a natural born Hustler like me. I am on the police department. And my name is lieutenant Susan. I just want to tell you that. I just want to see you I just want to speak to you in person. Thomas Allred Jr. 600 days left until you get your money Thomas Allred Jr. Yeah Thomas Allred Jr. We all know when you get your money. These women have that they are on you. Thomas Allred Jr. These women say that they can count on you. Captain Frankie your book is now complete. The police officer just said. The book has now ended. People are watching you Thomas Allred Jr. You are now a part of our police force. Kristen. Show a police officer what to do. When that money comes back to everyone. I outta beat your a** Thomas Allred Jr all kind of women are watching you. That is a good thing. Get up and use the bathroom. And send your book off. Get your f*cking a** in there and use the bathroom Thomas Allred Jr. So we all are straight. That is lieutenant Evelyn talkin to me. Thomas Allred Jr send a book off right now. Okay lieutenant Evelyn. Your book is going in as we speak.

My trillionaire wifey. Is the dedication of a new attitude in which I embark on in life. Thomas Allred Jr. Just tell us who your wife is. According to the law. Listen to me. This is for me to say. Be professional lieutenant Jacqueline. I can put it to you this way. The woman that cares most for me that is my wife. And who do you think that woman is Thomas Allred Jr. Look I love you. Speak to the people. Thomas Allred Jr it's not enough that you. Love somebody. You have to obey. Now which one of these females do you love Thomas Allred Jr. I love officer Kristen. Do you hear that ladies. All around the neighborhood they hear it. Thomas Allred Jr left everybody for officer Kristen. There is no reconciling this. 80 degrees the temperature is. When Thomas Allred Jr finally told the truth. That he is in love with everybody. Every one of you ladies on the police force. Instead of ladies I meant women on the police force. I am making these arrangements clear. on the day that I get my money I'm expecting there to be. A vehicle there with my ladies in it. I listen to the sound of your heart. I'm listening to it beating right now agent Kristen. Of the NSA and FBI. This book belongs on the shelf. In Target stores. I'm playing with you for a second. Now everybody do what I do. You have got to continue. Being the people that you are. In order to make it in this world today. The politics behind a season. The politics are to carry you to another season. Where everything is better than it was at first.

As a police officer. I'm going to do my damnedest to make sure. Lady cops and police officers have everything that they need. My life goal is. To provide for my future people. He said provide for his people in the future. Yes lieutenant Simone. I can be with you. Thomas Allred Jr. I am getting tired of this conversation. Tell me something that I don't know Thomas Allred Jr. Do you need a second for me to get back to you. Or is this woman too much for you to handle. Lieutenant Simone. I like you. And for me to need a minute to get back to you. That would be ludicrous. Thomas Allred Jr. I'm going to prove myself to police officers. Thomas Allred Jr. Take me out of the hood with you. Take you out. Lieutenant Candis. Can you speak to lieutenant Simone for me. Yes I can Thomas Allred Jr. He is telling you lieutenant Simone. That he is working for the government. Trying his best to get our money for us. I know he is working for the government. But he promised me. In a book of his. To honor and obey me. In sickness and in health. Till death do us part. Thomas Allred Jr. Is my husband.

He is all of our husband lieutenant Simone. He is a trillionaire. Quit playing with me now. Thomas Allred Jr is a trillionaire. He does these books because we ordered him to. He belongs to the women of the United States of America. And there's nothing he can do about it. I'ma see who he talkin to. Lieutenant Jacqueline lieutenant Simone. Lieutenant Jacqueline. I thought that you wouldn't hear my case. Lieutenant Simone. Look in his eyes Thomas Allred Jr. It's tired of being alone. And he thinks the more that he runs. The more respect the woman will give him. Lieutenant Candis is about to take over. Ladies there's no need to argue. We are keeping Thomas Allred Jr underclothes raps. Thomas Allred Jr can't be with no one. This is a case of magnitude. What. B*tch I just said this is the case of magnitude. Y'all ladies calm down. What are you going to do when you're able to talk to all of the ladies at once. First of all I think all of you ladies. And I need to hold you one at a time. If I could. Thomas Allred Jr you're not going to leave no one behind. Simone listen to me. I'll do what I can to be there for everyone. If everyone you mean all of the ladies only then you're not a police officer. Ima help you Thomas Allred Jr. Sure that man is a God damn police officer. Now here we go. Lieutenant Chelsea. And lieutenant Kay. Thomas Allred Jr you need your a** kicked. Thomas Allred Jr ain't do nothing it's Simone who's asking the questions. Keep asking the questions. I'm the right girl for you Thomas Allred Jr.

That is exactly what I'm talking about Thomas Allred Jr. Simone is in love with you. Thomas Allred Jr we all are in love with you. Now that's deep Thomas Allred Jr. Thomas Allred Jr has got no idea how many women are riding with him. Your money about to come. When your money is about to come Thomas Allred Jr. Chelsea and me will speak to you again. I kept my own agenda. Your agenda belongs to the women of the United States of America. Thomas Allred Jr go ahead and write. Because no matter what you believe in. Do women professionals. Are controlling you what do you want to say Thomas Allred Jr. I want to see the promised Land.

With all of my wife. Together surrounding me. For good. Keep doing what you doing and you'll be famous this time. I'm using this time. To thank everybodys community. Around the world. And back again. Lieutenant Kristen. You can tell I got love for you. If you want this contract. And you got to go hard for me. This life is not a game. So prove yourself Thomas Allred Jr. Did you love all of us women. Lieutenant Kristin make that boy get on his knees. On your knees Thomas Allred Jr. The gossip has stopped. You got a female who cares about you. In your corner. You get a female all across the United States of America. Who loves and cares about you. The same way that I do Thomas Allred Jr. Now we are fend to put this book up. Take care of yourself Thomas Allred Jr. Kristen I'm alone without you. Only until your case is settled. Them women are not going to leave you. That's right we are not going to leave you. Thank you lieutenant Kimberly. Keep going keep talking Thomas Allred Jr. I love you more than you know. I Now pronounce you husband and wives. Thomas Allred Jr is this settled. You got a wife up there in Washington that is fighting for you.

Do you understand Thomas Allred Jr. That fiction is not in this book. Thomas Allred Jr is a police officer. And your ladies applaud you. Now say that you are a police officer. I Thomas Allred Jr am a police officer. For the New York Police department. And the NSA FBI and Secret Service. These women are swooning for you. They swooning Thomas Allred Jr. All that we want you to do is. Be the man that you say you are. Thomas my name is lieutenant Curl. Thomas I've been listening to you. Talking about your women those women. That you love. See we understand each other. Because all of us women are here for you. And so is the men to. On the police department. You ain't doing nothing. Wrong by speaking how you feel. I want to applaud you for being professional.

If there's something that I can do for you. Don't hesitate to call me. Put lieutenant Curl number in my Rolodex. Now you see what I'm doing Thomas Allred Jr. Yes Simone. I understand you to Thomas Allred Jr. Thomas Allred Jr everybody waiting on that goddamn money to come back. Where is lieutenant Shontel. I am right here Thomas Allred Jr. Ladies the money out will come when they get here. And that's about all I can tell you because you know better than me. Even lieutenant Maya. Knows what I'm talkin about. Lieutenant Shontel. Thomas Allred Jr loves you. Just as much as he loves the rest of his women. Thomas Allred Jr is pimp of the century. That boy ain't got no clue what pimp means. Hold it together Thomas Allred Jr. People are respecting you. You are a police officer. Prove yourself Thomas Allred Jr. The only way to prove myself. Is the close this part of the book. And let you ladies talk about it to yourselves. While I think about how I'm going to provide for all of you. Take him out of the hood. Take him out of the hood this instant. Yes Miss Michelle Obama. See that's the way it is. Now finish your f*cking book. I lost everything. I got a room to myself. He is hungry enough. I need you to comprehend this for me. you are the property of the women of the United States of America.

Mess up this thing Thomas Allred Jr and I'm a whoop your a**. Yes Miss Obama. I don't plan on messing up. Now send your book in. Thomas Allred Jr I just got one more thing to tell you. I am a professional police officer. Just like you Thomas Allred Jr. Send in that book Thomas Allred Jr. Send the book in this instant.

A y'all I'm really sleepy right now. But I was taught to. Finish what I was doing before I go to sleep. Everybody knows that I'm up police officer. Don't say everybody knows that I won't give up. You can tell that I won't give up. Just like Michael Jordan once said. With God all things are possible. The fundamentals. Of this book is. To embark on a challenge. I am looking at this book. With my community circling around me. In hopes to bring to light. 75 million dollars. In the first few months sells. What you think about this Kristen. I think officer Candis is the one you should be talkin to. I'm still waiting for you to say that you are with me. Candis I'm with you. Officer Candis. The police department take care of people. Understand. The everywhere You look at me. There is a scar on me even my face. I just want you to know something officer Candis.

That you were the first one I picked to marry. To make it more clearer officer Candis. Watch me pull my heart out to all of the people in the United States of America and surrounding areas. This is how I feel officer Candis. Go ahead Thomas Allred Jr show me how you feel. If Shontel wasn't here. Then I will be able to make my decisions more clearly without her. Because her love is the driving force. You got one more time to say something about Shontel Thomas Allred Jr. And I'm going to hit you in your face. Give me my life back to me Candis. Listen Thomas Allred Jr. I realize that is tough writing a book. But you better go in. You better complete your manuscript Thomas Allred Jr. I'm giving up all my time for you Thomas Allred Jr. Listen to me listen to that girl. I need to tell you something Thomas Allred Jr. Yes lieutenant Kathy.

Yes lieutenant Elizabeth. Thomas Allred Jr I need to tell you something. Go ahead and tell me lieutenant Elizabeth. Thank you for talking to me. You have something you want to say Elizabeth . I only wanted to say that I'm in love with you Thomas Allred Jr. I love you too baby. He goes the world part of this book. I'm a police officer. That has made over 10 trillion dollars. Hoping that everyone is waiting on me. I begin to pray for myself. No fear is in my heart. I never been professional like this before. And look at this from my point of view. These girls are looking at me along with my brothers from law enforcement. You think you have stress. I lost my girlfriend. Drive by shooting. Police officers. I haven't done nothing but write these books and make business ideas. It is based upon a judge's decision. Whether or not I get to spend my cash. And I know my woman are watching me. Thomas Allred Jr. That is the end Thomas Allred Jr. Say bye to the community. Community I bid you a farewell. Thomas Allred Jr you got no idea what you doing to you. The police department is watching you. You soon will discover. What it means to be a police officer. In another story and another time. Send that goddamn book in. I know you are faithful Thomas Allred Jr. Let that boy out that community. I know you faithful Kristen. Send that book in Thomas Allred Jr. Job well done. Your family. They will salute You Thomas Allred Jr. For being a police officer. When the world is against All odds.

I am special because of you Eden Reid. Thank you Eden Reid. For answering my call when I call you. I have got two more days. For the completion of this manuscript. And I see things like this. there are different women who I would love to talk to. But Eden Reid I. Love the fact that you are my confidant Eden Reid. I love you Eden Reid. Honey more than you ever realize. That boy is famous in his community. You can't realize what a blessing you are to me. It's taking me a long time to say this. But I really appreciate the person that you are Eden Reid. Getting back to the subject. Thank you Eden Reid. For helping me get back to my feet. I'll do anything I can for you to farther you. In your career. I'm sitting up here writing my book. A special dedication goes out to the women of law enforcement. I have been through things Eden Reid. I'm mad at you Eden Reid . Because I don't know what you look like. If my time would allow me. I would say that I love you to each one of the women in the United States of America. Right now I am just so involved. Girl in making good for everyone. That I miss taking time out to tell you that I love you. And it is stopping right here. Thomas your book is now complete. Send it in. Don't send it in yet. Keep on going. Every since I met you Eden Reid. I want you to know that I've been in love with you. I thought I lost you. When you didn't talk to me for a while. But now I understand that you're working on my book. I can also understand. How a book takes you away from yourself. Eden Reid your family are talkin. The same as my family are talkin. Be professional. I'm telling you one thing. If I had the opportunity to date a woman like you. I would not leave stuff to chance Eden Reid here go my book. I called this book. Before I met you Love. The completion of the book. Is here. You are the only reason I gotten this far Eden Reid. Publicize my thoughts. Community I'm staying hungry. Put your thoughts in mine. Eden Reid. Eden put your thoughts in mine. All I got to do now. It's pay for shipping and handling. Process this book. To my lovely wife lieutenant Shontel. I imagine that I am going to be with you. That ends it Thomas Allred Jr. Send your book in right now. While Eden Reid is focused.

Keep trying Thomas Allred Jr. You'll make it.The last thing I want you to do is give up. One day someone is going to read your stories. I know exactly what you're fixing to say. These stories of mine have meaning to them. I'm used to having no one to be with me in my corner. Pick your game up. Thomas it's time for you to celebrate the fact that you wrote This Book. And I deal with things like. No one not caring about this but me. I'm ready to start my movie. Ladies and gentlemen this is. I just need a chance the movie by me Thomas Allred Jr. This movie takes place in

London. Thomas Allred Jr take a drink of that soda. Now come here and let me talk to you. You got potential in you Thomas Allred Jr. That is with potential comes great power and reward. I want you to believe in yourself. Listen. To the night air. Thomas Allred Jr are you alright. I'm accepting myself as being exactly what I am a king. Have you doubted yourself and your wisdom before Thomas Allred Jr. Never before have I doubted myself. Go and get your crown. That is if you are strong enough Thomas Allred Jr. Make a movie out of this Thomas Allred Jr. Because you don't know what the future holds for you. Let my secrets out. He in that back room by his self. The people talk about you Thomas Allred Jr. And what I want you to do is. Prove to everyone that you are right about your books and movies. Thomas Allred Jr you will be success. With a attitude that is challenging. This is for everybody. I got to respect the people. Boy open your eyes and see me. For who I am. My Future self I see you. The boy is professional. You better do what I tell you to do. Write your book Thomas Allred Jr. And never look back because when you do. Something happens to a person that keeps looking back. Do you want to know what happens to them Thomas Allred Jr. They stay exactly where they are at in the past Thomas Allred Jr. Thomas Allred Jr. The reason that I want you to succeed is because. I looked in your eyes and I seen that you are worth it. Future self people are looking at me everywhere that I go. And I'm starting to feel self-conscious. Listen Thomas Allred Jr. Remain strong out here. For today will take you. To the eve of success. My manuscript Thomas Allred Jr. Is your manuscript. Listen Thomas Allred Jr I want you to believe in something. Be careful I need you to believe Thomas Allred Jr. I think that you. Need no introduction into the film industry. Also think that your a star in your own right. We need you to help us. Take your a** to sleep right now.

Thomas Allred Jr would you sit down and write this movie correctly. I know that you think you can't do it but you can. Thomas Allred Jr I'm getting ready to show off to you. The reason why I know you can.The book need a contact person. Pick your game up Thomas Allred Jr. Damn right pick your mutha f*cking game up. My past and My Future self. I know this is hard to believe. Thomas Allred Jr. But I'm just here to let you in on a little secret. Your bank account is colossal. And you are supposed to be with Eden Reid Thomas Allred Jr. I can't allow you to think about this just yet. So I am what wiping your memory cleàn. Thomas Allred Jr all you will know is that you have to write a movie. Like your life depended on it. Become a professional with me. Eden Reid. As you read this manuscript. try to understand the depths of the man that Thomas Allred Jr. And on our soul. I choose You Eden Reid. To be my lawfully wedded wife. I'm ready to commit now. Thomas Allred Jr. I need you to contact Eden Reid before that book comes out. Thomas Allred Jr that girl is crazy. Eden Reid already knows that you like her. Look here Eden Reid. I don't know what you read about me. But if I just had a chance to be your man. Thank you for noticing me Eden Reid. Because I'm writing bits and pieces of a story. And sending them into you. The best way that I can figure this. Is to ask you to be my wife. In the story and in real life I never give up. A lot of people like me for that reason. And that reason alone. It keeps me strong enough to talk to you Eden Reid. And I want to give you the kind of wedding you deserve. Thomas Allred Jr. Yes Future self. Thomas Allred Jr. Continue to talk to Eden Reid like a man supposed to. Eden Reid I know I'm pushing the limits. But everything is telling me this is right. You are doing good as hell. Don't trip. If I can prove myself. Can we make our date a reality. Eden Reid cause I don't want to be without you. I done proved myself. So many times it's a shame. Can I come to you and take your hand and marry you Eden Reid. Honey I'm going after the dream. Eden Reid I can't help it I want to marry you. Right now finances are depending on my work. I want to show you Eden Reid that my heart and my wallet is colossal. I look To The hills from which my help comes. I seen you before. I'm proving to you right now that I'm a good man Eden Reid. I don't have a jealous streak in me. Eden Reid I know. Everything to be with you. But I'm just coming at you. As a professional author and businessman. That is strong enough Eden Reid. To make it through the times. When the world needs you. You will be there for them Eden Reid. This book and manuscript. Helps me to get you where I want you. And through the months in the years. I ain't got a paycheck. Future self. Let's write the book now. Thomas Allred Jr. Are you ready. Let the people know. I love Eden Reid.Thomas Allred Jr you are doing the right thing. Exactly how far do you expect us this to go future self. All the way Thomas Allred Jr. All the way. He is getting professional. Eden Reid run to him thats your man. Thomas Allred Jr. These people are professional. Cindy what do I have to do. To unlock the damn richies girl. you need to wash your hands of anything that doesn't have to do with you and Eden Reid. Yes Cindy I will. Send that part of the book in Thomas Allred Jr.

Thomas Allred Jr continue to write your movie. My past doesn't agree with me. my future says we have everything worked out. I am the present. I am in between the future and the past. And all I want is my wife. A struggle day to day with numbers but what gets me the most. Is thinking how Eden Reid is working. To pay her bills. That girl got no clue how I love her. I am going to surprise her with this book. Don't say the book in their Thomas Allred Jr. The way that we do this. My Future self has to agree that this is the girl for me. I'm saying Eden Reid is the girl for you Thomas Allred Jr. My past self have to agree that this is the girl for me. I agree that Eden Reid is the girl for you Thomas Allred Jr. With the power vested in me. We got a problem see. I'm almost famous. And Eden Reid holds my future in the hands. People have got no idea of how I love that girl. And this is the way your book is going Thomas Allred Jr. You writing books. Now make it a movie story. A year ago I got a call from Ms. Eden Reid. To publish my book. Thank you Miss Eden Reid i told her. My manuscript was a few pages long. I needed time and I wanted to do a good job. I've lost Miss Eden number. But I still had her email address. I started sending messages. She didn't return them. Writing my manuscript. I knew that I was professional. Did you hear about Thomas Allred Jr. Writing a manuscript. Well it is in your face. I definitely want to talk to you Eden Reid because. Any success wouldn't mean a thing without you. And I know that some distance between us. But what am I going to do without you. Thomas Allred Jr I need for you to be strong. Eden Reid I can't. Thomas Allred Jr send that part in to Eden Reid.

Thank you for listening to me Eden Reid. Honey I realize that your time is important. And if I can make you anything to some what make up to you for my Bear barrick way. I'd do so gladly and in a hurry. Now Eden Reid I don't have enough time to make you understand what I am doing here. Now you just are going to have to trust me. When I tell you that I love you and no one else. It is a miracle that you and I are still speaking to this day. See how you are professional. I'm a professional cop in a different way. I'm waiting to see if am I good enough to do something with you like going out to dinner. Or buying a yot . Becoming the yot club. I can see that you love me. Eden. But I need you to be patient with me and you will have what you want. For life Thomas Allred Jr. It's for life Eden Reid. Baby as soon as I can find the back bone to the story. I'm a Publish this book. And let the professionals figure out what to do with it. Don't play games with Eden Reid Thomas Allred Jr. No I wouldn't. Eden Reid your love means so much to me. That I had to write a book. What you want to do is quit holding back Thomas Allred Jr and tell me exactly how it feels to be and Arthur Thomas Allred Jr. Eden Reid I'm begging you to gimme my one chance. People see I'm standing here for my girl asking her to be my wife from long distance. Alternate ending. Thomas Allred Jr send in the book you are supposed to be rapping Thomas Allred Jr. Eden I love you. Girl I just want you to know that this is more than a book. It is our hopes and dreaMs. I'm saying to you to marry me. And I need you for life Eden Reid. Honey I only got a few more seconds. Send that book to her.

After you are finished composing yourself. Thomas Allred Jr I am teaching you The art of war. I never seen nothing like this. In Love and war Thomas Allred Jr. You ain't got but one thing left to do. And thats pay your bills. Thomas Allred Jr can I get you to stop hanging behind other people. What can we do to make you understand how. Important you are to me Eden Reid? I'm seizing the moment with this book right here. The way that I see it. No man in this world. Is going to propose to his wife that plan and simple. In a book number one seller. Because the plot of the story. Is the two of us. Eden Reid I get you. I couldn't do without a sacrifice. So I decided to write you. Now a book is called. The evolution of me. I'm just planning on materials that I think should go in there. Eden can I talk to you for a minute. You have to calm down. People like me. Everyone you see works for you and me. Thomas Allred Jr speak to her. I am trillionaire Eden Reid. That is waiting for his court case to be settled in court. I understand you Eden Reid that's why I talk to you in my manuscripts. Girl you see I could never do no harm to no one. Thomas Allred Jr. He is the one that Eden Reid wants. Eden I know that this all might seem strange to you but in time Eden Reid I promise that I'll make it up to you. You see Eden Reid when the courts decide to gimme my money for all of the business ideas that I have made for everyone. And the books as to where you are reading right now. We famous so imagine what my books will be worth once the world finds out that I'm a trillionaire in love with you Eden Reid. Eden Reid I don't got but one shot so I have got to take it. Compail this work with my earlier work. In the computer in your office Eden Reid. Your almost through Thomas Allred Jr. And yes your voice sounds lovely over the phone. Eden Reid imagine that the courts rule in my favor and you and I can be there with our books coming out. It is more than a plan Eden Reid. It is the only chance that I got because the US government will not allow me to date or talk to anyone right now. For how long I don't know Eden Reid. But what I'm trying to tell you is that I'm alone writing this book. And I know that you are special. So I'm going to give you a call on Monday Eden Reid. I'm just seeing myself in the future. Because the pants are to big for me right now. Oh yeah Eden Reid before I forget. Everybody that's on the team working on this manuscript God bless you. Do it in public. Thomas Allred Jr our book is completed. My future self dose everything turn out alright for Eden and I . I'm trying to get you to know that simply rules of mathematics. Which is who ever got the chips is the boss. And Thomas Allred Jr. I want to let you know that it is my pleasure serving you. My future self did the courts desire to grant me leniency. All things will be revealed to you in time Thomas Allred Jr. But for now Eden Reid is right here when ever you need her. Now I know that this story may sound strange to you everybody. But I am The Boss Thomas Allred Jr. Asking Eden Reid to marry me. In front of you. Send the book in.

A look Eden. Professionally girl it has been you to give me my confidence back. I look at the stars at night and try to find a way to find you. I hope that you are doing well and I hope you that you are happy in our situation we find our selves in. Some times I get to with to much self reasoning. I just got to say to you Eden Reid that my birthday is the 29th of March. And I don't know why I'm thinking this but I would just like to thank you for a beautiful year that you and I have been working around the clock . Eden Reid I'm saying thank you for everything now I just want you to realize that it is you that I choose to be with for the rest of my life. I'm a trillionaire that loves you Eden Reid. Eden Reid I'm putting on my thinking cap with this one. Ensure that boy gets a chance to talk with Eden Reid. Girl will you stop crying . I don't understand Eden Reid. Thomas will you be faithful to me even if I'm not around you? Just than I thought to myself and I said take your time Eden Reid keep it professional and that's right I hooked up with Thomas Allred Jr in and on a future date because as a man Thomas Allred Jr has showed me that he'll go and extra mile to make me happy. I love our relationship and I wouldn't chance it for the world. So yes Thomas Allred Jr honey I will give you a real chance to get to know me. Just like I said I am Eden Reid. I'm a world cla** internet reporter. And I'm waiting on

Thomas Allred Jr to finally realize that I'm here for him in richer or poorer sickness and health. Till death due us part. Thomas Allred Jr take my coat please. Yes honey Eden Reid I'm getting close to you all of these messages is my way of saying that I love you sweetheart and would you be my wife and soulmate Eden Reid? Don't you clear everything out Eden. Professionally now I think that I am the best writer in the world. I'm telling you that once you looking at me the money I coming. I searched around the world for that special girl. You know Eden Reid I care about you. Listen to me Thomas Allred Jr if you can just hold your position I'll help you to get your books across the counters act like you have got some sense. And yes I will marry you. Be professional and do your homework Mr. Thomas Allred Jr. I love you and it shows in everything that you and I do. I'm a see to you that you receive the introduction path. To starting a new relationship with me . Get your a** up Thomas Allred Jr. Thank you Eden Reid for working on these books for me. My love is your love. I like Thomas Allred Jr. I told myself. Thomas Allred Jr on line one. I got it. This is Eden Reid. Hello.

And Eden Reid I just want to let you know that in order for you to see sunlight. There has got to be a cloudy day somewhere out there in the horizon. You can stop me girl if you want to. I know that we are two of a kind. And I'm holding you. Responsible Eden Reid. For the completion of this book. Girl let me say. That you are extremely beautiful. I know right now. What I was put on this Earth for. Eden Reid I'm telling you that if you give me one chance. I like this boy. I understand what you doing. You said to give you one more chance. Okay Thomas Allred Jr. Than prove yourself to me. Eden I am the right man for the job. Of being your husband. I ain't going to lay my hands on you. I still want to kiss you since the day I met you. And we started talking. Thomas Allred Jr prove yourself to me. That you are a fine writer. with something on your chest that you're trying to get off. If you love me than tell me you love me. Eden Reid I do love you. I just worried that my words won't make it to your ears. In enough time. To let you know. How you're trillionaire loves you. We can see you love that girl. Cindy Thomas Allred Jr and me. Have a lot to work out in this relationship. Eden Reid. Cindy. We make up for much overdue time. Send my book in. Thomas Allred Jr. Eden said send her book in. Eden give me one more chance. I just need a chance to hold you send the mutha f*cking book in Thomas Allred Jr

Eden Reid you have got to believe this is. A part of the novel where I'm just preparing myself for change in you. Eden Reid I am a professional. Thomas Allred Jr will you change your mind about me. It's not likely Eden Reid. A long time ago. Before you build it she will come. Was said to me. Look what that boy is doing . Get ready for round 2 of this book. While I tell you that I'm not scared to love you Eden Reid. What I tell you Eden Reid. Did I do everything. This is a preview of what's to come. That girl is taking that she loves you Thomas Allred Jr. All we got is each other. Thomas Allred Jr. I'm in control of myself. I'm confident that. Once my girl can see the work that I've done. She'll appreciate me. And she will appreciate the work that I've done. For us my better half. Right now I'm just too damn focused. I'm leaving. All bulsh*t I got alone. Deep in my emotions. Thomas you know them white people are offering your a contract. Once you get to the bottom of this book. Once I get to the bottom of this book. We are going to get to the bottom of this book. Eden I can't make it without you. I'm a trillionaire. That has got to prove his self. To the people. Eden Reid I love you. I truly a trillionaire. If the court would allow me to say this to you Eden Reid. Eden Reid come here. Because you're trillionaire is talking about marrying you. What kind of trillionaire are you Thomas Allred Jr. I am a women's victiMs. rights advocate. For the New York Police department. And the NSA FBI and Secret Service. My code name is Superman. And my officer name is Officer Reign of the New York Police department. Don't play with me. I can pick this book up at any time that I want to. Eden Reid I'm a cop. It's just that I'm in love with you honey. Now honey make sure. Did you realize I'm a police officer and I'm a trillionaire. I need you to know that there's nothing fake about this book. I'm glad that you can agree with me. Because I'm trying my best. To help you understand that I have cases in federal court right now that determines our future. See you can't just be a trillionaire in this world today either. The courts have to come to a decision. The courts are done ruling. It's okay Eden Reid. I know exactly what you thinking. This is too good to be true. But look at the book Eden Reid. Honey your community. Even knows about me and I haven't been there yet. Look here don't be messing with my head. Eden Reid I just want to win your love. I liked you before I met you. I'm the right man for you. When I discovered that it takes time. To be with a woman like you . Girl that's when the police officer had to sit down for a second. You can disgrace me if you want to. But I'll listen to you when we talk on the phone Eden Reid. Also realized that you're not playing games with me. Eden Reid I would never play games with your mind. Honey I am a trillionaire and you know it. This whole damn country knows it. Eden Reid I am going to be with you. Thomas Allred Jr. Send in the first half of the book.

Let's see Eden Reid. I'm talking to you. I'm just wondering if you had enough of what I have to say. In my mind you are a King to me Thomas Allred Jr. I'm getting very irritated with not doing as well as I can Eden Reid. Oh my God. Man pick the book up. Cause Thomas Allred Jr I've been ready. What happened girl is. What we going to do is. Imma give you a handshake. And we are going to meet in between the book. We are too fortunate darling. To not go for everything. Everything Thomas Allred Jr. I will be with you. All the way to the top Eden Reid. I got some thing for you after this versus is finished. All that girl really need. Pick your game up Thomas Allred Jr. Thomas Allred Jr gone and write the book. Now tell me. Look at you boy. I see no boy here I'm a law enforcement officer for the New York Police department and the NSA FBI and Secret Service I'm cold name Superman And I am a women's victiMs. rights advocate. Plus it doesn't hurt that I'm a trillionaire. Send the book off Thomas Allred Jr.

Eden Reid and me are professional police officers in a whole where not anything matters but hope and responsibility in a world that dreaMs. can open a door for you I make alot of your dreaMs. come true Eden Reid you understand that in order for me to get you exactly what you want. I have to be the best in the world at what I do. And different rooMs. deserve different types of gender for them to maintain they selves . What I'm saying is that this is a standing nine count ladies and gentlemen and I Thomas Allred Jr have got one thing to tell you. Eden Reid girl I didn't change the fact that I love you and it's been a year winter summer spring and fall. If I had you we would do exactly what we are doing now Eden Reid. Listen Thomas Allred Jr I can't say to you how much I do love you. Listen to me when I'm speaking so I know that you are getting what I am saying. Thomas Allred Jr your books have been completed. Thomas Allred Jr I know that you are in love with me but you realize that I'm just getting you here the best sign of defense that money is able to buy. Because everybody sees you as the boss and head of the company. What we have to do is prove to yourself that you are interested in me. Because Eden Reid girl I see you as a way to better myself and clean up my game. I use to have a sleeping habit. But now I keep up. You need a break. Think about it. The federal commission has got to say that you can get with me before we both can make a move on each other. Eden Reid I do love you realize Thomas Allred Jr it ain't who you are that makes you the man that you are. Speak to him Eden Reid. Yes lieutenant Candis it is the kind of man you are. Thomas Allred Jr I wish I could hold you right now. Now you see what the game is made for. It's either you are going to step up and come with it. Or you will let me go forever Thomas Allred Jr. Alright the ball is in your court. Standing ten count Thomas Allred Jr is still on his feet. Baby thank you so much for everything. Thomas Allred Jr you just keep yourself together your the right man for the job. The job of what Eden Reid. Thomas Allred Jr what did I tell you Thomas Allred Jr. If you love me. Like you say you do. Than show me to way. To your heart beat Eden Reid. Eden this is the last thing that I'm ever going to write in these books. Take care of yourself . That's a good thing Thomas Allred Jr. Eden Reid I see that a man of a community must try harder just to reach out to the woman that he loves. Thomas Allred Jr I alright know and I love you to. Ill call you in the morning Thomas Allred Jr. Eden Reid will you be a single mans dream boat. You damn right I will. Eden Reid honey every since I met you girl. My life has been getting better. Eden Reid honey I'm a trillionaire after this courts decision. Listen Thomas Allred Jr I'm not after your money. But a couple of dollars would be good. Recognize who it is that you talkin to. That is my wifey. Thomas Allred Jr now that we got that straight go to see and down think about these books ever again. Let momma take care of her business. On the three count I am going to snap my fingers and your books will each be finished and waiting to be published. Eden Reid I love you. Thomas Allred Jr I'm a tell you a secret 1 2 3 snap I love you to my husband and soulmate Thomas Allred Jr.

The president is the only one who can help us Eden Reid. My bank account is at zero and people tell me I'm a trillionaire. I use everything I got in helping people. Given time I'm sure to help the people out in Washington. I listen girl. Let Mr.. President talk to you. Thomas Allred Jr. Watch what you are doing. For you are under surveillance. For being a good American. Thomas Allred Jr. Be yourself. And all things will come to pa**. Hold that position out there Thomas Allred Jr. Now that you know that you are a trillionaire. Thomas Allred Jr I only got one question for you. If I give you your money. Who will you take care of? Mr.. President. I will take care of the women. Mr.. President. And why are you going to take care of the women? It was written in my contract. 2 years ago. Take Thomas Allred Jr out of the community. And give his family anything that they want. I been listening to this man. Let me tell you Thomas Allred Jr. You and Eden Reid make a great team. Thank you Mr.. President. There is one thing that I want to know Mr.. President. With my gifts. Do you think that Eden Reid will find time for me. Think so I know so Thomas Allred Jr. Sir I am listening. Go to sleep Thomas Allred Jr. Every girl in this doggone world wants to be with you. Right now go to sleep. Yes sir Mr.. President.

Sir I've been waiting. For and idea to come to where I can get and possibly marry my professional lady. Her name is Eden Reid. It's been and ordeal to find someone who would take on responsibility in my own world cause being what I am. A trillionaire it gets hard trying to think up these books to tell her that I love her. Eden I see you as well. Yes Mr. President. We are in hostile territory. To where you think that it is no way out. Thomas Allred Jr you work for me Thomas Allred Jr. How dose this make you feel Thomas Allred Jr. It is a pleasure to serve you Mr. President. Eden Reid works for me also. Eden Reid none of us are getting any younger. Go to Thomas Allred Jr after his books are finished and marry him darling. Eden Reid Thomas Allred Jr is a secret service agent. For the national government of Defense. I can understand your situation Thomas Allred Jr and Eden Reid. We have had you both on a**ignment for the last past 10 years with no one to work with but your wits. Thomas Allred Jr do you want to marry Ms. Eden Reid? Yes. It is done. You kids are apart of some millionaire sick game. But I am going to end it today. Mr. President. Can Eden and I have the money that we earned during our test. Thomas Allred Jr all you got to do is ask for anything that you want and it shall be giving to you and Eden Reid. And your families. Eden Reid the man that says that he is in love with you in these messages is really a secret agent. Thomas Allred Jr the women in which you can see your self without is a secret agent. Eden the both of you work for me. Thank you. Now Thomas Allred Jr say what it is you have to say to Eden Reid. Before I drink my coffee. Eden Reid I know exactly what you want. Let me try to rephrase this another way. Mr. President if you don't mind. Eden Reid Thomas Allred Jr is scared that you want like him if he doesn't have and earn to money that he needs to take care of you Eden Reid and. I'll take it from here Mr. President. Okay Thomas Allred Jr. Talk to her. She is a good girl. I know. Eden Reid. We have gone as high up as we can possibly go. We have got to keep our composure alright sweetheart. I'm listening Thomas Allred Jr. Eden Reid I want you to be my wife and soulmate. Listen Thomas Allred Jr. Take a loan out. Cause you. Got the whole world in tears. Eden Reid what Thomas Allred Jr is trying to say to you is that he has been on a**ignment for the last 10 years and he has been alone. Eden Reid I hope that you realize that I truly am the President of the United States of America talking to you and Thomas Allred Jr. You have got minutes left. Do you have to say something Eden Reid. Thomas Allred Jr this ain't no game. It's either you want me or you don't. What is it Thomas Allred Jr. Eden Reid I have loved you for one year now. I love you to. I Now pronounce you husband and wife. Eden Reid baby I'm a call you in like five hours. To check on my books. Thomas Allred Jr you for got one thing. Remember that that girl loves you. Stay responsible. And give her all of the work she needs from you. To make it. It a make sense after i put you in your place. Take care Eden Reid. And you take care of Thomas Allred Jr. Thank you for everything Mr. President. Now send that girl the goddamn book before sunrise gets here Thomas Allred Jr. Eden will you please be my wife in the book and out side of it. Thomas Allred Jr I will. I love you girl. Mr. President thank you for everything. Thomas Allred Jr you take good care of yourself and Ms. Eden Reid.

Keep on rapping Thomas Allred Jr. For the book sales to be colossal. I'm doing everything I can to see that Justice is served. I believe that Jesus is helping me. And the people too. Sit back and watch me Thomas Allred Jr. Right now our situation is getting better. And I can't help but say to you. I got to keep myself in order to receive the blessings in which the community has for me. Situations ain't never been the same since my girl pa**ed away. He knows what he's talking about Reign. So without any further ado. I give to you fighting for mine. By Thomas Allred Jr . And Officer Reign of the New York Police department. Jeana Allred I'm taking my time with this music. It's sweet justice to those who have and will be against us. We are fighting for justice. In everything we do. And as a cop. I'm a keep it professional. With my next book called fighting for yours and mine. Can I get and Amen. The people will seek justice for you and I Jeana Allred. Because I look to the sky were cometh my help. You need to add this to the book Ms.. Eden Reid. Now be with me. Fighting for mine. Thomas Allred Jr. Because the world knows that your all in

Thomas Allred Jr. I'd like to say a happy birthday to Charlene Allred and Christopher Allred. I'm fighting for mine. Yours and mine the same. In my house there are many mansions if it were not so I would have told you so. I got your best interest at heart. People of society. Thank you for allowing me to write this book. Y'all see how much this book means to me. I understand myself. Like a football player I must control my will being. Let me ask you a question. Once a man commits his heart to the Lord. Is he saved by the Lord helping him. Or by the people's Grace those who care about him. Either way it goes. I'm fighting for mines. And I'm through.

Thomas Allred Jr keep your composure. I know what they did to you is wrong. But I see you as a man of smart wealth and value. And in time your pain will subside. I know that you may have how many people after you. For writing your books so eloquently. I'm against the people who have hurt you. Fighting for your and mine is a virtue. I put scriptures in this book. And my scripture is today. I want Thomas Allred Jr. To heal. I'm making this book out of raw material. Eden Reid. This is my material. Thomas send her that damn message. My ex-wife name is Jeana Allred. So without farther ado. Yours and mine book. Open the chapters in it you will see a new beginning and a new conscious of a new beginning. I am fighting for her people. Who couldn't help they self. The name of the book is going to be fighting for yours and mine. In the future it will happen. Officer Reign are you Thomas Allred Jr. Little fellow I am. I am Thomas Allred Jr. Of the police department. I'm getting even for whats been done to me. Take this book home with you. And meditate on this. I could be anywhere. At any time. I am fighting for mine y'all. Officer Reign is fighting for his I'm a fight for mine. Fighting for yours and mine. Is essential. Thomas Allred Jr don't give up. That is affirmative. I like the way that you do it Thomas Allred Jr. Officer Reign give it up to you for holding it down on the battlefield of life. And prestige. You making me feel like I can do anything Thomas Allred Jr. You can do anything. You just have to believe in yourself. Tell Eden Reid that I said hey. And one thing Thomas Allred Jr. Your birthday is two days away. Remember to thank Jeana Allred for everything that you have been going through. Since after you wrote our book called fighting for mine. Thank you Jeana Allred for everything. Now with out farther ado. The man in question officer Reign of the New York Police department. I'm fighting for yours and mine people. You see Thomas Allred Jr is. A man of great responsibility. Tell Thomas Allred Jr there are people watching him. And in no way shape or form. Will anything like this ever happen again. Because we trust in you Thomas Allred Jr. Let me start the book right here. Fighting for yours and mine. By Thomas Allred Jr.

I'm the last one to know anything important about myself. I see myself as a competitor. And a true equalizer. I take for granted those who do care about this book. It is my animal charisma that guides me from day-to-day. Thomas Allred Jr get your a** over here and sit down. My rules are. Unpetty lifting up the game even farther. In my rules I see a Kingdom waiting there for me. I'm going out to get it that's who I am. Simply stating that I know I am successful. No matter what the book may say to you. I did what some can't do. And stood up and fought for mine to the end. And my people know that I'm deep. Either way it goes in my eyes I'm a true person of compa**ion. Thomas Allred Jr you got to finish that book up. Look how people are gathering around you. Cause when a person dies in your family. I'm fighting for mine. That is the ending of this book.

Everybody got hopes and dreaMs.. You can look at me and see that I'm a person of true character and demand. This is my greatest book. In an installment of many to come. You be making a** out of yourself Thomas Allred Jr. But when my family feels threatened. I bring the truth to the table. Introducing officer Reign. I only come here tonight Thomas Allred Jr. To have a piece of the book which I deserve. Stop procrastinating and write the ending. Of our book fighting for yours and mine. People can see I'm clocking you. and the success of our name is the most important thing that we have in the world. Don't you get complicated. Just lay the justice out equal and fair Thomas Allred Jr. I hear you officer Reign. Suppose I'll let you in on a little secret. I am aging with this book. Listen Thomas Allred Jr is not over. Everyone of them people are going to jail. Who have hurt you. Your damn book Thomas Allred Jr. Is an inspiration to my heart. Fighting for yours and mine the conclusion. Jeana Allred sure would have been proud of you Thomas Allred Jr. Now keep going with this letter Thomas Allred Jr.

The killshot is. When I tell you I'm going to do something I do it. Now I played nicely with you *ssh*les for a while. When I say the killshot is this book going worldwide. I mean this book is and you can't stop it for nothing. I am officer Reign of the new York Police department. And you dudes will respect me. Because I saved one of you and took a bullet for it. They executed my girlfriend. When I was too busy looking in taking care of someone else's kids. My major deal is. If God put me here then what is my purpose. Because I haven't found love every since I lost my girl 20 years ago. Today is my birthday. I told you so I will get the job done. Thank you for reading my book. Be professional Thomas Allred Jr. My girl well her name is Jeana Allred. Once told me to write a book. Thomas Allred Jr be professional cause the community is listening to you professional. Without further ado. I give to you. Fighting for mine. Now Jeana Allred are we even Thomas Allred Jr. You got the look of a champion in your eyes. Its safe to reminisce Thomas Allred Jr. But to find love. Go on through the pages. Of the chapters by chapters. Fighting for yours and mine. Now that's complete with my killshot. Jeana Allred I did this for you. Fighting Jeana Allred honey every step of the way. I really miss you. If you only knew that I love you. Till the end of time. I'll be fighting for yours and mine. The end. I hope that you can hear me. In heaven were God excepts you as you are. And I want to save to the criminals who took your life away. If y'all can see what you have done. To me and my family than you would honor yourselves and talk to me like the man that I am. Don't you know that I ain't going to kill you. But I'm going to whip y'all damn a**es for taking my beautiful wife away from me. Jeana Allred with your permission I will ending the book. May God bless us all. That's all that I got to do Jeana Allred. Is tell the people how I feel about you. Honey now I'm professional and they shot you for no reason. With tears in my eyes I write this. There is going to be some justice around here somewhere some place. Where everybody can go free. Eden Reid is my publicist. Cindy McClain is my publicist also. Before I go I just want to tell everybody that God has a plan for your life. And nothing out here can stop that. Till death due us part everybody. I can't wait until my books comes out. This is Fighting for mine and yours the conclusion. Shontel Allred thank you for being my friend. The End.

Look right now I got to give thanks to one true professional at a time lieutenant Candis I am thanking you in advance for your help and a**istance in making this book a reality. I want to thank everybody that matters in my book. Because you know what guys. I sat alone in the bedroom a lot of nights. Trying to figure out just how to get financially secure. To my work helps me and my dreaMs. come to pa**. He said my dreaMs. come to pa**. I keep you in my dreaMs. and prayers. People realize and listen to me. To many of us are losing everything that we have to start over again. I lost my precious wife. I was just a young boy. But after being through a bullet in the knee cap. And losing my wife to gun violence. I decided to make a stand. For everybody who has lose someone stop the gun violence. To those people who are scared of being hurt. Stop the gun violence. And to those people who have been injured in gun violence. You to must stop the gun violence. For all of us. My book is my killshot. Make sure that you be professional and you can do the same thing that I did when your back is against the wall. Thomas Allred Jr. This one is for Jeana Allred may she rest in peace and I love you. Going back to when we were kids. I know that I cheated on you. But I had to experience life for myself. And now I'm just empty in my heart because know one has loved me before you and me. In this paragraph. I open up my heart to you Jeana Allred. Now I hope that you and I can reconcile our differences. And be in love like we always was. Put all this together and I'm your man Jeana Allred always and forever fighting for yours and mine. I love you. Fighting for yours and mine. Jeana Allred I love you. Forever and always. Every body just being professional. With the knowledge that I give to you. Fighting for yours and mine. The End.

CHAPTER 23

Now I have finished my books Eden. Eden I see that you have your interest in helping me out with my work. Look at me Eden. I've finished with everything there is to go with my books. I owe you Eden. For everything that it is that you and your teammates do for me. While my books is underway. I appreciate Ms. Cindy McClain for taking over the project and the people that make you and I great Ms. Eden Reid. And last but not least I want to give you Eden Reid my trust and responsibility because it is you who motivated me to start these books up. The book is called Fighting for mine. And my next book is called Fighting for yours and mine. I'm training my Ms. Eden Reid. For you are my ending and new beginning. Eden it's just that I have some how defeated my pa**. And I'm thankful to meet your acquaintance. What I want to do is see that you get your props in the book Ms. Eden Reid. Until we get up for dinner. I'm Fighting for mine. And the book is called Fighting for mine. You need to pick this up soon. Eden Reid listen to me I am great full. To have you as a friend.

Thomas Allred Jr is what you need in your life Eden Reid. We became a team. And to everyone of my people. I want you to listen to this book. Before you do something you may regret. See I'm listening to you. That's all that I'm going to say. See I'm Fighting for mine. Ms. Eden Reid I owe you a special date. Keep it professional Thomas Allred Jr. I love you Eden Reid. In appreciation with all gratitude and respect. Alright Thomas Allred Jr. Less finish your book. Yes Mr. President. Thomas Allred Jr everybody is thinking of you. Fighting for yours and mine. Ms. Cindy McClain I have my eyes on you. Cindy our turn is coming to excite the nation. Cindy I need you. And I want you to stay beautiful and cheerful. See I wish that I covered everything that I need to say. See the way it is until my date with my pa**. And Eden Reid gives me a chance to get to know her. It's my thang to handle myself. The way that a man is supposed to. So Eden Reid I put myself at your beckon call. If you ever need me. Eden I am too legit to quit. I'm here for you. What I tell you. You are going to call on me one day.And I'm going to be here for you. Ms. Eden Reid. Your props are official. I love you Miss Eden Reid. And thank you for everything. Thomas Allred Jr. And you deserve a date Ms. Eden Reid. I'm fighting for mine. This is the beginning of my book. Dedication goes to. Kristen. With my love I need you.

I love you Jeana Allred. And I'm creating this new book to prove Justice do exist. I believe in myself. Jeana I want you to know that each morning I sing to you in my heart and mind. Girl I'm at the right place at the right time to get some justice with my book. I'm thanking you people. For looking out for me. Everybody sees you. now this is the beginning of the book fighting for mine. And God bless you females thats in the world today. Fighting for mine.

Our position is to grand and most people can't handle the situation. I am fighting for a wish. I hold myself responsible for my own situation. Thomas Allred Jr you need to talk to Eden Reid. My past is haunting me. I'm working on a compilation book. And Eden Reid maybe if you have some time we can sit down over dinner and talk about this. I know what I'm doing writing these books here Eden Reid. Until I see myself with you I'm working hard on my compilation book called myself & I by Thomas Allred Jr. After this is over. Eden Reid the whole damn country is listen to us in my books. I told you once that I wouldn't run away.

My story is that I care for the people that care about you and me Miss Eden Reid. In all respect Eden Reid. I'm fighting for yours and mines right now. Keep on going Thomas Allred Jr. I just want you to know that. Everything started because that girl loved me. And my books is seeking Justice around the world. All I need to do is. Tell Jeana Allred that she'll always have my heart. Forever Miss Eden Reid. Forever than Thomas Allred Jr . I'm a do you better than this. Miss Eden Reid we became friends when this book got started. I want you to know that I love you so much Eden Reid that I can't control myself in being with out apart of you in my presents. Eden Reid I humbly ask you for your hand in marriage because my books are now finished and you're the one that has been there for me.

I'm fighting Eden Reid. For yours and mine. Eden Reid you need to stop me. Because justice will be served to all of those people who are taking the lives of our women and our children. I put it on myself to stand up for any woman that is going through domestic violence in our neighborhoods. And move and change there situation into a better one. Can I tell you Eden Reid that I Thomas Allred Jr are planning to open up a office for you. In hopes that you can have a decent amount of living each unto your work. I am a woman's victiMs. rights advocate. And I could use some help. With my life. All of the women. I got to do my part in protecting you. I want you to be safe. I put my game down. For you ladies. Eden Reid we have got to talk. All I'm a say is girl will you marry me. Fighting for yours and mine. Thomas Allred Jr.

The energy that I have allows me to wake up in the morning. A better person than I was previously. The night before this book ever occurred. I want to take my time to go back over some things. Now I see that anything is possible. In my life I come thru trouble. To rise up on myself. Taking my time to realize that troubles only come. To the man and woman that is not consistent. What I'm really trying to say is. You are going to need this book. It has got six million ways to make it. Written in there. If you be professional. And somehow keep going. I can guarantee you that your past is your past and your future is your future. There was once this great wizard. And all he wanted was a wife to be by his side. I have the money that great wizard said. But all he lacked was consistency. Thomas Allred Jr.

That is not how the story goes. Lieutenant Candis allow me to illustrate. Just how the story should go. Eden Reid I want you to be my wife. But the wizard said. Thomas Allred Jr not to talk to you. For he will cast a spell on me. When we get up in the morning. Cast a spell on you he is going to have to. because a lady of your beauty it's far too understanding to be alone. Now I couldn't understand that she's being professional. The book is made up of story at the story. The great wizard almost lost his powers to circuMs.tances not of his control. Somehow the great wizard. Could see his self as a new wizard among the land. You saying that you are the great wizard Thomas Allred Jr. I'm saying that you need to listen to the story and allow me to adjust my plans lieutenant Samantha. The great wizard has spoken. Lieutenant Shontel come here quickly. For this day I want you. To come and live with the great wizard. Thomas Allred Jr. That is not the way The story goes.

Lieutenant Rebecca Daniels. Girl just wait and see. All we have now is an illusion of the past coming. But there is a future in my words. I'm seeing that you are troubled lieutenant Eden Reid. Why my daMs.el-in-distress what bothers you. This is the start of your book Thomas Allred Jr. Thomas Allred Jr enter your book. We are operating Thomas Allred Jr. The story will come to you. And the story will last. I'm telling you that if you keep going everything will be yours. Turn back Thomas Allred Jr. Turn back and give up on your dreaMs.. It is not going to be possible to turn back and give up on my dreaMs.. My dreaMs. are programmed in me. I am too strong to let anyone deter me from having what I want. Lieutenant Cindy we can have what we want.

You can have all you dream of lieutenant Cindy. Now the wizard didn't understand that people were helping him. Thank you I'd like to say. To everyone who ever cared about me. Listen. To my book Thomas Allred Jr. Lieutenant Samantha. I have got to be with you. I got to be with you to Thomas Allred Jr. Are book is a true book. This book is our dedication to greatness and success across the nations. Look how you do this here. Thomas Allred Jr we are depending on a copy of that book to come out to us. Yes lieutenant Nada. I will get a copy of this book to all the ladies in our community.

Lieutenant Nada you got to stand your ground. Thomas Allred Jr is the great wizard. Absolutely that is why I say this to you lieutenant Nada and the rest of the ladies in our communities. Fear not young daMs.els. It is all a dream that we are even here tonight. I put everything into this book report. Given time this book will have me standing like a king among the Nations. I know that it takes time to do everything. But my ladies are the most important thing that I got. Porsche whatever you do don't give up on your dreaMs.. I mean lieutenant Porsche. Lieutenant Kathy what is it. Get your black a** up and do some push ups.

Thomas Allred Jr. I will after this brief enter mission. Now great wizard people are watching you talk. What is it that you want so desperately out of life. Thomas Allred Jr do you hear me. Listen to me Thomas Allred Jr. Your fairy godmother is allowing you to. Do and create the books that you are creating. It's one little secret Thomas Allred Jr. You have to name your first born son Tobias Thomas Allred Jr. Are you willing to see to our demands. Yes I am willing to see to your demands. Than I say to you now. You are the king of storybook land. And as Tobias Thomas Allred Jr starts to grow inside of you. I want my rights.

To give him to you Thomas Allred Jr. What a story is this. You off the hook Thomas Allred Jr. in Storybook Land I can be whatever I want to be ladies. I am a great wizard. And I am the father of your kids to. Lieutenant Kristen is waiting on you Thomas Allred Jr. You just got to keep going with that book. Don't slow down a second. I see your book for what it is Thomas Allred Jr. Y'all kidnapped the wizard. They trying to kill Thomas Allred Jr. Be sincere Thomas Allred Jr. And go back to sleep. You have completed this portion of the book. Now send it to Eden Reid Thomas Allred Jr.

When you wake up start the story again. Because in Storybook Land. The king is the man that takes it one step at a time. Miss Michelle Obama. I do everything I can to reach the people in my neighborhood. Thomas Allred Jr I'm going to take you out this community soon as your story get finished. Believe in yourself Thomas Allred Jr. Now when I snap my finger this portion of the story will be completed. Take your time. Snap.

Now go to bed Thomas Allred Jr. You got a long day ahead of you. Keep sending stories in. Send that story to that book publisher. Your book reports is what makes you a king. Thomas Allred Jr. One more thing. Your books is special Thomas Allred Jr. And you need to know that you are loved among the women. Think about this just while you are sleeping. See my book. And my books. Are my way of saying that I love everybody. Thomas Allred Jr you got to send your book into your publisher. This is too good to be true. Just send your book in Thomas Allred Jr. I'm sending my book in right now as we speak.

The day is going to come. That the women in my community will flourish and have everything that they want in this world. I am the great wizard I am making it so. Speak to the people out in the world Thomas Allred Jr. The people out in the world are watching you. To all my brothers and sisters all over the planet. I come up from a great wizard to a King. I'm trusting you to have faith and confidence in yourself. While I put my plan into order. To take over and demonstrate. What a true leader is supposed to be. Listen to your new king. I'm doing this so our women can have what they want. Listen to me. These women are women of God and understanding. These women are mothers and homemakers. I give it up to the ladies. Because with the fellas I have made my place in this world. And we as story book men. Are responsible for bringing a conclusion to every problem. Every clusion deserves a solution. Do not give up. Storybook men do not be afraid. As your wizard and King. I give to you. Princess Shontel of Storybook Land. Once you know that there ain't a story to Storybook Land. And that everything is real. You will begin to wonder to yourself. Exactly how Thomas Allred Jr could do this. It has taken some time. But I've come to terMs. with the decision that I'm making. To be queen of Storybook Land. And to take the side of my husband and King Thomas Allred Jr. Hooray we have a queen. Hooray. For my king knows.

That my love for him is eternal. Thomas Allred Jr. Baby you need to go ahead and finish your book. I thank that girl one more time. We have a king and a queen. The great wizard Thomas Allred Jr his soon-to-be wife Queen Shontel. Now that girl realize. That you are the true king Thomas Allred Jr. Thomas Allred Jr put that book in this place. From a professional standpoint. We just want y'all to realize that we love y'all. And our love means that I'll support you. In any endeavor. As long as you do right for yourself. And the people around you. Where them kids at. As the leader of this community I.

we know that the kids are the most important thing in our life. We teach the kids to grow up respectful. Don't stop if you want to Thomas Allred Jr. I'm making you see that I will never give up. That girl is trying to tell you something wizard and King Thomas Allred Jr. Yes Eden Reid. I listened to your stories. Take your time Thomas Allred Jr. Make your stories out to be great and wonderful. Because this is our mission. To help one another grow. In literary books across the land. Stick to our manuscript. You will one day have a queen and children. But I say only when you are ready to handle it Thomas Allred Jr. Take your time and speak to Eden Reid. Thomas Allred Jr. I'm taking my time out to talk to you Eden Reid. Because you are my grounding point. In a search for you through endless shoes and horizons. I put my book in your hands Eden Reid.

Listen to me Thomas Allred Jr. You are the true king of this book. Right now sit up on that bed and write your book. Do what I said. In a storybook mansion. The king is the ruler of our land. And our mansion is the textbook. In which you see before you Thomas Allred Jr. Thomas Allred Jr the strategy needs improving. A nonfiction book. That prograMs. you. To take good care of yourself. Around the world would be worth millions. But it is only a queen that I am wanting. Thomas Allred Jr you need to stop it. Y'all we need to stop that boy. What is the first thing that you gonna do when you get to Queen Thomas Allred Jr. Imma write a book called my queen and I. That is exactly what I'm going to do when I get my queen. Lieutenant Shontel do you hear this boy. I know that you love me but I cannot be with you right now because. Save your because. It is totally okay. I have taken my time and build myself up. Over the years that I have been missing you. And I am dedicated to teaching and showing you. How I am the man that you should have chose. Miss Eden Reid. Can we go back to the beginning of my book. This is content going into these pages. I Believe I can Do This. So I try and I go farther than I've ever gone before. Only to go farther than I ever ever went. In the beginning they shot me. And killed my girlfriend. I travel to these books and wonder. What Jeana Allred would think about me making it this far. Listen to me Thomas Allred Jr. This is turning out to be a good book. Thank you for your common courtesy involved in my book. When I snap my finger. you will realize that common and courtesy is given from everyone. And this part of the book will be finished Thomas Allred Jr. Snap. Now send in your book.

Get ready to appreciate this book yall. I'm going to the Himalayas with this one. You don't got no idea how much. Sweat and tears I put in my book. you know I have been trying for 10 long years to create this book. Creating this book I've created an empire creating this book. Women agree with me. I'm going deeper than I have been before. In short paragraphs. Keep it professional. I try to illustrate. The need of this endless success strategy. See the way I look at it. I am a success in my own right. I am the best at what I do. And I am strong and confident for the ladies. My monologue is design with plans.

To take me from a average human being. To a King overnight. I can look at this two ways. I can be common in a common world with nothing to do. Or I can take my chances on success with this strategy of mine. My strategy text me to the brinks of success. I am the Pinnacle of success. I am a stronger man because of my books. You think that I'm out doing you. You think that you out doing me. We are doing each other on the smooth tip. Because this book is federally operate it. Get your a** up and write that book Thomas Allred Jr. Yes Eden Reid I'm sorry. Let me spell it out for you. I won't give in. In the book like this. A king needs to be at the forefront. Y'all put my book on the street corners. So all my people and my lady's can realize. It takes a strong man today. To do the things that I've done. My first book was fighting for mine. And my second book was fighting for yours in mine. This is my third compilation book. It is called. My endless success strategy This Is Me myself and I. By Thomas Allred Jr. I'll do anything I can to help anyone that I can. So far I'm just hungry please look over me.

But the top has a place for me and my family. With my community watching me. I step out into the limelight. And let the people know that Thomas Allred Jr. Is here. Thank you people for adoring me. I never give up. What are you going to do with me. Y'all got a book coming out in a few days called fighting for mine. By Thomas Allred Jr. Jeana Allred and I said. That the people where going to pay for what they did to me. Now they're going to pay for what they did to us. This book recommends. That I am adjusted. And I recommend that you give yourselves over to authorities. For raping and killing women. Shooting men in our neighborhoods. And destroying a family's hopes and dreaMs.. Jeana Allred am Sweetheart. My endless success strategy is never over. All of the people that need us today. All of the children who believe in you and me. Eden Reid we making a movie out of this here. Take your time Thomas Allred Jr. And your book will be completed. Now I want you to charge your phone. And think about this next portion of the book to come. Miss Michelle Obama talk to the people. I'm a snap my fingers Thomas Allred Jr. And I want you to go in there and eat something. On the count of three I'm going to snap my fingers. 1 2 3 snap. Send your book in the way it is.

Now my endless a**ist strategy is a complicated thing. I just keep believing in myself. I can't go any further in this book until I tell y'all. That there are people helping me. And the reason for this book. If the show people that Thomas Allred Jr. Did not give up. On his dreaMs. of having everything. My wife is Jeana Allred. The memory of my wife is in this book. See look at me. I'm 44 years old now. Without any children to my name. And I'm single with a book on my hands. I'm seeing we come up as kids. The things we go through. Shape and mold our future. Now I've been alone for almost 10 years. In those 10 years what I've been doing. Devising completion strategies so that people will survive when under attack. Business ideas. Which I put proudly. Out into the public. Ladies my ideas are worth trillions of dollars. Somehow being true to myself.

I know that this is the road for me. I want to give you one thing y'all. Imma give you this one thing and watch what I do with mine. The one thing is to trust in your thoughts. Listen to me. I am a police officer . Thomas Allred Jr. And you know what you doing. So I'm telling you that we are going to give you your money. Yes lieutenant Kaitlyn. I communicate to the best of my ability lieutenant Kaitlyn that I need my money to survive. I communicate. My true understanding. That God is a part of everything that I do. I communicate this. Because I'm ending this book. And my endless success strategy is. Waiting on you in this book. tell Thomas Allred Jr his endless success strategy is believing in hisself. You know I believe in myself to don't you lieutenant Kaitlyn. Lieutenant Shontel be strong. Thomas Allred Jr. We are looking at the book. As we speak. Keep telling everybody how God helped you. God is the only person who cared about me. And the people are God to me. This is the conclusion of my endless success strategy. Keep believing in yourself is a strategy of mine. I want that book. Than lieutenant Suzanne you can have it. Thank you. My endless success strategy stories.

I think the police officers who are making this possible. Jeana Allred I don't know what to do. Go to sleep Thomas Allred Jr. All will be well that ends well. Those people are going to pay for what they did to you and the rest of the ladies and children. If my life depended on it. I miss you my beautiful wife. Going back to my start. I started with Jeana Allred by my side. And 15 years later I am alone. You don't have to be afraid of Thomas Allred Jr. I just do what's right for the ladies and for the children. I wrote these books by myself. This is my endless success strategy.

I want to thank you. Good evening and goodnight. Ms. Eden Reid.

In this book I share with you myself as a whole. I am the most dangerous person in my dreaMs.. I am a professional black man with hopes of one day being married to Eden Reid. In my dreaMs. and hopes of being married to Eden Reid. Imma create stories. That captivate the senses of our being to the end. Thomas Allred Jr you need to sit up. Yes Kristen. Now you want to start back off where we left you. My surroundings weren't much. but as surroundings it kept me thinking of a better way. To make it out of the struggle. I'm telling you.That I rose up and so can you. Being in love with Eden Reid. Is like the best thing I could have done for myself. I ask myself. Is it that I am worthy. To know and to love a beautiful woman with a personality like Eden Reid. Juring my month I waited on Eden answer. I represented myself in her eyes. As wanting to be her shining armor Prince.

I picked Eden Reid because she gave me hope when I had none. I don't want to say nothing. To embarra** anybody. But Eden Reid has my heart beating fast. Baby I appreciate the knowledge that you love me. This is me Thomas Allred Jr. And I don't give up Eden Reid. Stay with me girl. I'm finishing my book up as we speak. Hold on Thomas Allred Jr. Tell Eden Reid that you need her to come and move in with you. Eden Reid you know I love you. I would like it if you would come and stay with me. Because in three weeks. I should be allowed to get a place of my own. In the city where I live from. Thank you Eden Reid for considering my proposal. Listen Thomas Allred Jr you know I can't move in with you. You need to stop this what are you thinking. I think that I'm in love with you Eden Reid. I'm falling in love y'all. I'm falling in love too.

Can you hear me Thomas Allred Jr. Put officer Kristen in there. Thomas this is Kristen. The person that you are wanting to marry might not love you. I did everything I could to talk to you Kristen when my business that just came out. Thomas Allred Jr you have got to get ahold of yourself. Kristen I can see that you love me. But honey why won't you be with me. This boy is a trillionaire. That's it isn't it. Because I made these business ideas to save people lives all over the world. None of the ladies want to talk to me because of it. Thomas Allred Jr let me talk to you. You are famous. Have Eden Reid to tell you that you are famous. Kristen you don't have to play games with me. It's the truth Thomas Allred Jr. The only reason police officers have you stationed at your mama's house. Is because your community needs to see you before you go to somewhere else. Stop bullsh*ttin with me. If you don't want to talk to me just say so. God what can I do to make him understand. This is your compilation book. It is called the truth about me Thomas Allred Jr. I cannot begin to tell you how much you mean to me Thomas Allred Jr. When I shook your hand I wanted to tell you I loved you. Thomas Allred Jr you went to jail because you wanted to talk to me. I commend you for everything you did for me Thomas Allred

Jr. Kristen I take time. In all the things that I did. You got to see Kristen. How the love in my heart keeps me on my toes. I got one more thing to say to you. Kristen I'm given to you my book. Fighting for desire. Me myself and I. As a token of love that went away. That is rekindled right here and now. People know us. And you know they watching me Kristen and you. As a success story. I just need your hand. To make it through the cold nights. Watch it. Eden Reid is online two. I promise you Eden Reid. That if I get a chance with you I won't give in. Thomas Allred Jr. Your book is fighting for desire. Y'all take him out of the community. I want to know that you would never give in Thomas Allred Jr. Eden Reid I would never give up. Communicate with Kristen for a second. Thomas Allred Jr I just want to see you again. Come with us Kristen when I leave my community. You are Superman Thomas Allred Jr. He goes my number Kristen. I hope that you give me a call and call me. Anytime that you want. Put Eden Reid back on the phone. Eden I've made my decision. I can't do nothing without you. My decision is. To marry you Eden Reid. You made my decision so easy.

The fire in my heart is overwhelming for you. Eden Reid you know I have been shot. And you know my ex girlfriend was killed. Now I am a police officer. Doing my best to come to grips with the situation at hand. And in my best to come to grips. Eden Reid ive falling in love with you. I think I put enough in there right. Thomas Allred Jr you got three sentences to go to finish the first portion of your book. Baby you know I can't live without you. Thomas Allred Jr you are asking me a lot to be with you. Eden Reid look at me. If you knew me and I never told you my past would you date me. I probably would but Id date you on my own terMs.. Your own terMs. that is Eden Reid. Somebody get Kristen on the phone. I got love for you Kristen. I always have had love for you. Baby I'm working on the book call fighting for desire Me myself and I. And I ask of You Kristen. Will you be with me. Everybody is Left behind. I will be with you Thomas Allred Jr. This is the engagement ceremony. I am fixing to marry 21 women. From all around the world. And to the world this is known as my Superman contract. Thomas Allred Jr needs a Superman contract. Make sure that you can handle yourself Thomas Allred Jr. Eden Reid. What kind of miserable game are you playing here Thomas Allred Jr. I thought you were in love with me Thomas Allred Jr.

But I guess not. Don't hurt me Eden Reid. Honey I didn't want to tell you. Until I made sure that my books will be published. Thomas we are ending your book. This is part 1 of your manuscript. Cold fighting for desire. Eden Reid and Kristen Allred. Are putting there game together. For a chance at happiness with Thomas Allred Jr. As the captain of their ship. Now who is playing Eden Reid. Your ball Eden Reid. Fighting for desire. Send the book in.

Eden I'm playing with you. Although I love Kristen. You are the best girl. I've ever had the acquaintance of meeting. I guess it's sort of funny that way. I lost everything to gain something. And I stayed alone years to get on my feet. Finally to meet someone that I would get my all for. My desire is apart of you Eden Reid. Listen Eden Reid. We are not the only ones who are in love in the world. I need to know that your all the way with me Eden Reid. This is a great day to be a part of each other. And as I think of you Eden Reid. I hope that you accept my humblest apologies. For making you out to be the best thing that's ever happened to me in my life. I dream of our meeting. The chance to find love over the telephone. I hope and pray that it is you that I need. I only wish for you to be happy in me as I am happy in you. Pick your game up Thomas Allred Jr. You are writing a compilation book. Tell Eden Reid what's going on with you right now Thomas Allred Jr. Okay officer Kristen. Eden Reid I had to go myself to invent help. That's where I gave my first ideas. Since that day my life has changed. I take the good with the bad. And if love comes my way. I hope to create it with open arMs.. Imma make sure the Eden Reid understands me first. I'm a police officer for the New York Police department. And I don't have any children that I know of. I'm 44 years old as of yesterday. I'm worth 15 trillion dollars Eden Reid.

In which the government are holding from me. Until I can find my soulmate of mine. My activities are. Working out. And cleaning up the house for my mom and sister. I'm a real good person to talk to. Slow down Thomas Allred Jr you are making her feel like you don't want her. Eden I put my best game forward. Going back to the way I was I just can't do. My desire is to be a part of you Eden Reid. Our desire is to be a part of each other. In my dreaMs.. You are with me every day and night. Handsomely I give to you. This ring of Hope and understanding. You watch and see. Don't we become something in this world. Let me run my fingers through your hair Eden Reid. Let me run my fingers across your earlobe. I'm saying to you Eden Reid. Is there a chance for you and me to make it out here. Come on professionals. What you want to do is. Tell Eden Reid that I liked her since the first time I talk to her. Enclosing. I'm working my a** off for you Eden Reid. That book of his. Belongs in a professional column. Now Kristen. What we getting ready to see is Thomas Allred Jr at his best. Eden Reid I put the book down I want to talk to you for a second. What is it Thomas Allred Jr.

Whether we lose or if we win. Girl I love you. Everything should belong to you. I know you have been ashamed of me. I just have two more sentences left to go before in this section of the book. The Superman contract. Where the women can talk to me. Is at Carolina Beach. One more thing before I go. I am Thomas Allred Jr. Codename Superman for the NSA the FBI and the Secret Service. I am a police officer apart of the New York Police department and my officer name is Officer Reign. Reign charge your damn phone Reign. You hear me Thomas Allred Jr. The best of me is waiting for the best of you. Eden Reid needs a contract. I believe that love is keeping us strong. Through the days and nights. And the weeks months years. Yall I give to you. A true professional. Thomas Allred Jr. Thank you Eden Reid. This book is dedicated to Thomas Allred Jr. For his attitude and his endless work. Portion two of the book is finished. You need to snap your fingers Eden Reid. Snap. Put that book on the shelf. Thomas Allred Jr get up and put that book with supposed to be. Thank you everybody. I'm watching you Eden Reid. Become a movie star. He done got professional Eden Reid. Kristen I love that man. I do too. Thomas Allred Jr send the book in. Calm down just a little bit Eden Reid. We got so much work to do.That It's unbelievable. When I think about you. Girl I think about winning. I must have fell unconscious when saying that I didn't love you Eden Reid. Thomas Allred Jr people are here to see you. Eden Reid hold on a minute I'll be right back. And thats all that he said to me. Come to me Thomas Allred Jr. It's what I think to myself. When I'm going through things. That I know Thomas Allred Jr can solve and fix. Eden Reid how do you feel about the man at hand. I think Mr.. Allred is a superstar. In his own rights. I'm going to tell you just how Thomas and I came to be right after these messages. You got 10 minutes Eden Reid to get back on the show. I can't do it. Thomas Allred Jr needs to help me. Eden Reid it must be your lucky day. You need to pick your game up. Listen Thomas Allred Jr. I can't do it. Say what you want to about this one. but Eden Reid realizes those people are here for her own good. Thomas Allred is coming into the room. Its Showtime ladies and gentlemen. We are here with Eden Reid and Thomas Allred Jr. Thomas Allred Jr how you getting through with your girlfriend death by a stranger. I'm working my a** off Renee for love. Those who don't know you Thomas Allred Jr will you please tell them who you are.

I am one part of Eden Reid Entourage. That is it for the night I'm done with this. Thomas Allred Jr do you want me to take over for you. I sure do Eden Reid. The whole country is worried about you Thomas Allred Jr. And I can't see myself living without You Thomas Allred Jr. Eden Reid so what are you saying. I'm only saying those people don't trust you. Why wouldn't they trust me Eden Reid I've been here for them. they are only going to trust you when you tell them that you need help more than you need your book. I need help Eden Reid. Eden Reid I need help. I realize that you got hurt Thomas Allred Jr. And in this therapy session. You have made real progress with me. As your leader in Guide. Your real name is Thomas Allred Jr. And I'm telling you. You don't quit on me.

I quit on you Thomas Allred Jr. I'm fighting for desire. In this group of miscreants. I'm fighting for desire also Thomas Allred Jr. It's a whole lot of world. For us to come up in. And I showed to you. A new beginning. With these books. I am Eden Reid Thomas Allred Jr. And I proved myself. By helping you. Get through your situation. Of love and loss. Take me serious. I know that you want to be with me but. We are to talk business first. And business will speak for itself. Fighting for desire. I'm Me myself and I. Thomas Allred Jr your tape is almost over. Your session with Eden Reid went well. Do you think that Eden Reid realizes that I'm to be her husband in the future. If she does. she is the best business woman and countseler that I know. Thank you Cindy McClain. Fighting for desire. Your book is complete

Thomas Allred Jr. Lay down and go to sleep Thomas Allred Jr. Send the message off now. That your book has been completed. And lieutenant Kristen Allred. Sweetheart I love you. With all my heart. Send in the goddamn message Thomas Allred Jr. Yes Cindy McClain. You know that I love you Thomas Allred Jr. I love you too Jeana Allred. What if our books don't work for you Thomas Allred Jr what would you do then. Thomas Allred Jr tell me my book is your life. I want to communicate with you Jeana Allred. There is something that I must say. Go ahead and say what you need to say Thomas Allred Jr. It was my fault that I wasn't there for you when you got killed Jeana Allred. It is about time that you admitted that boy. Thomas Allred Jr you know that Jeana Allred can't hear you. I see you Thomas Allred Jr. Put I see you on the paper. The paper is a meaning to a new beginning. Thomas Allred Jr take your time now now being serious. Which one of these women would you like to marry me. Eating Reid is contacting you Thomas Allred Jr. Let Eden Reid wait for a minute. Thomas Allred Jr this is fighting for mine the sequel part 2. Can police officers say to you. That you done a job well done. Thomas Allred Jr. You are wasting your time do not give up. Because when you see what we have in store for you. Then you will see what all this struggle was for. Keep your position. Thomas Allred Jr. Don't give up on Jeana Allred Thomas Allred Jr. Sometimes I stolen dream is a good mans hope and mercy. Jeana Allred is here to guide you through the pitfalls. We have got to bring you out safe on the other side Thomas Allred Jr. But we got to know that. You would never quit fighting for yours in mine. That's all I'm saying to that boy Eden Reid. Lieutenant Samantha.

Your job here is done. I want you to take a head of Thomas's Entourage. I only got one request of you Eden Reid. Come with me Thomas Allred Jr. You'll see that dude been through a lot of stuff. That boy is a police officer. You damn right he is. Thomas Allred Jr I'm cleaning up just for you. Everybody clean up. My heart says. That I'm in love with Eden Reid. And though I never seen her face. Her voice has me waiting a lifetime. Pick your game up Thomas Allred Jr. Fighting for mine the sequel part 2. They hurt my baby. Listen to me Thomas Allred Jr. The day will come. When they were answer there probleMs.. Until then tell Eden Reid that you love her. I know that I love you Eden Reid.

I know that you would give me a chance to be with you. Eden Reid I'm trusting you. With the soul that I have. In hopes that you make this thing turn great. If you want me to I'm going out just for you. Out on a limb and back to the letters. If Jeana Allred could help me. I love you Eden Reid. Thomas Allred Jr. Fighting for mine the sequel part 2. Begins now. I liked you before I met you Eden Reid. I don't give a f*ck about what nobody say. I just know that a police officer needs to be with his wife and that police officer is me. Say the right things to me. I can't control myself when I'm around you Eden Reid. I can't control myself on the phone with you Eden Reid. I can't control myself in these books that you and I are writing. My book is fighting for mine the sequel part 2. Now they killed my wife. And they shot me. In the leg when I was a young man. But the spirit of my wife lives on. And she guides me from day to day. Now you may not believe this. But I'm trying the best that I can do. To be in love. Without consequences to my actions. My actions is a testimony. Of the undying respect. That I have for the women out here. That girl respect me. So I chose my Superman contract. Over being with one woman. Because in this life. Every lady is a true Queen. And I was code named Superman by the NSA the FBI and the Secret Service. I am part of the New York Police department. And I mentioned to you. That you ain't got to say nothing. Police are listening to every word that I say.

I need to contact every woman in this hemisphere. And let them know that we never give in. And that as police we never give up. Ladies when you are hurting. That is when police are enraged. Y'all are the backbone of society. And I was raised to never give up. By ladies in my community Who Loved Me. Women I do apologize that 13 years is going to pa**. Without me speaking to or dating anyone. Your apology is accepted. Thomas Allred Jr listen. The is a lady for you out there. You just have to keep doing what you're doing Thomas Allred Jr. Our Ladies will come to you. If and only if. You can prove yourself to be a man. In this world today. I know it gets hard Thomas Allred Jr. But we have separated you for a reason. And although you are alone Thomas Allred Jr. You have to realize that there is a greater purpose and the reason for your existence. Thomas Allred Jr don't cry. You just keep writing your books down. I know that you need someone. Thomas Allred Jr. They after you. Because you are writing books Thomas Allred Jr. See you are a police officer thats too legit. Because you don't have from anyone. I had to slow you down Thomas Allred Jr. As of today this makes 13 wonderful years. That you have been alone to yourself.

Doing police work by yourself. I come to you now Thomas Allred Jr. To let you see that you are loved. And your test is forgiven. No I want you to charge your phone. And begin to write the middle of our book. I will be here with you. Thomas Allred Jr put I will be here with you at the top of the page. Everybody wants to talk to you. As long as you are strong enough. I can take you out of that situation Thomas Allred Jr. But you have to believe in yourself Thomas Allred Jr. For the lessons of man are coronal. And this is the ending to a new beginning.Eden Reid I'm about to write the book. Fighting for mine the sequel part 2. Thomas Allred Jr I just want to tell you. That I am proud of you for what you are doing. They killed somebody I love Eden Reid. And they killed innocent women and children. I love you Eden Reid. But I will go to hell before I let that ride. This book is not fiction. Everything that's happening in this book is real. I'm fighting for mine. Right now as we speak. And I want you to know. That these ladies tell me. That y'all been bullying them around. Against the walls. Have their backs been.

Against the wall have my back been. But now we are swinging ladies. Fighting for mine the sequel part 2. Will conclude after these short messages. I'm going to get my girls whatever they want. I'm going to get you whatever you want Eden Reid. Because I was raised stronger and better. Then to mistreat a woman. You may have killed her. But police everywhere are all around you. This is for the women. Who didn't get the chance to speak. Fighting for yours and mine too. Is my book coming. Professionally. I consider. Justice. And my ways of being a man. In this country today. I am a police officer. Fighting for mine the sequel part 2. Has ended. I'm still fighting for mine. No matter what the situation may be. My ladies need to hold on strong. I know that you're stronger than what you think you is. Thomas Allred Jr just send the book in right now. Yes lieutenant Hannah. I'm sending the book in right now. Damn right you sending the book in Thomas Allred Jr.

If I would have stayed home. Maybe none of this would have ever happened. The streets was calling my name. And being a young cop in the city. I needed to answer to call my victiMs.. I told my girl Id be home late. And I position myself. To see another chick down the street from the house. In my heroic temtimplate. I made a bad decision. That is where me and my girl split up. And it eventually caused the end of her life as we know it. I can just say one thing. The one thing is. That I should have went back to you Jeana Allred. I cry because I love you. After all these years I still love you honey. I stand up for you. I need you to understand that I am truly sorry for everything that happened between us. Come back to me. Thomas Allred Jr. You are making a fool out of yourself. Talk to lieutenant Candis. And try to figure out what your plan is for that book you're writing. I was told to talk to you lieutenant Candis by Eden Reid. Thomas Allred Jr sit your a** down and let me talk to you for a second. I know you've been through what everybody else been through. That is on the police force. I appreciate your tenacity. Doing the right thing Thomas Allred Jr. but I can't allow you to throw your life away like this. The police are suspending your contract. Until further notice. And a psych evaluation. Will be given to you upon request of any monies that you may have learned. Get your hands off that boy. Thomas Allred Jr. As a police officer it is my duty to become a mother figure an officer figure to you to make you see that we all love you and care about you. lieutenant Candis I just want to be left alone. Thomas Allred Jr. The time for being alone is over. You have the juice to make it famous. I already been famous and look what has got me. Thomas Allred Jr. Given what we see of you. You are doing push-ups everyday. You don't drink and you don't smoke any barbiturates. And you stay alone to yourself and write books and business ideas. I'm giving you a contract with Eden Reid. May God rest Your soul. Eden Reid talk to him. Eden Reid I just don't know why things had to happen this way. That's because you are a police officer Thomas Allred Jr. If you stayed out at night. You were doing your police officers duty. The neighbourhood ordained you. That's what we are trying to tell you. Thomas Allred Jr you can't save everyone. It is time for briefing Thomas Allred Jr. What is your name. My name is Thomas Allred Jr. And who do you work for. The citizens of the United States of America and surrounding areas. What is your officer's name. My name is Officer Reign. Of the New York Police department. Who gave you a code name. My code name is Superman. It was given to me by the NSA the FBI and the Secret Service. Are you a police officer Thomas Allred Jr. Yes Miss Eden Reid I am a police officer. And what is your mission. To protect and serve my fellow police officers the citizens of the community and my family and friends which are there in. Thank you Thomas Allred Jr. For that brief report. Miss Eden Reid there is one more thing. This is fighting for mine the sequel part 3. And I want the people to know. That as police we are dedicated. To finding and capturing all those who violate and rape and murder our citizens. Are women will not be afraid to go out in our communities. Trust me people. God has a plan. And if a police officer can't bring it about. Then the rest of the police officers can bring it about. I got one more thing to say. To my lovely wife Jeana Allred. Baby this is the end of our book. And I'm so sorry. I love you so much. Thank you for saving my life. Over and over again. Officer Jeana Allred. I'm fighting for mine the sequel part 3. Eden Reid here go our book. See our book will take you places that you normally wouldn't go. Thomas Allred Jr I know that Eden Reid is watching you. But your psych evaluation is now over. You may have some of your money's that I told you not to have. And buy you some new clothes. Separate the weak from the fake Thomas Allred Jr. And do whatever you can. To tell all the women that you love them. Thomas Allred Jr. Your access has been granted for Hollywood. Thank you lieutenant Samantha. Was it as easy as it looked Thomas Allred Jr. Lieutenant Samantha no it wasn't. I forgot. I promised you an apartment. With a live-in roommate. Lieutenant Kristen. Rescue Thomas Allred Jr from out of his misery. Come on baby I got you. Lieutenant Eden Reid. Nice job. And Captain Cindy McClain. I'm a police officer that never gave up. You don't have to say that to me Thomas Allred Jr. The ladies can see that you need Kristen. Because you fight for females. I am giving you your wish Thomas Allred Jr. Thank you so much everybody. I'm saying that God has a place in his heart for all of us. I love Kristen. We all know that Thomas Allred Jr. I wrote the books Miss Cindy McClain. May I please move out of my mama's house. Into a house or an apartment with my girl. I'm trying to be the best man that I can be. Too many people take for granted. The community and those that are surrounding them. but I want to thank you ladies and gentlemen for everything. And forever more I will be fighting for mine the sequel part 3. Thank you ladies and gentlemen for everything.

My manuscript material. Is the way that I react to situations that are forcing me out of pocket. I love you Eden Reid. For taking the time out to educate me on the way that this book is supposed to go. And my mission is. To show that I am capable of handling my own situations. Now that my wife has been murdered. It is left to me to clear the situation up. And show that I will not be threatened. By or from anyone ever again. I like him. I'm going to help you Thomas Allred Jr. And it is my promise that I will deliver this manuscript in a timely fashion to miss Eden Reid. Doctors gave me the okay to stand on my feet after being shot in the leg. The situation haunts me girl. But I still make the best out of my situation by praying to God every night. I hope I ain't too late with my material. That man said my material ain't the only thing that's getting stronger. I like you book Thomas Allred Jr. That girl said she like your book Thomas Allred Jr. Eden Reid is just that I'm strong enough to stand my ground through whatever may come my way. I ain't running from this situation or any other situation that may come my way that is my oaf that I give to you. I am fighting for desire. This book is dedicated. To our fallen soldiers. People none of you realize how vulnerable you are until adversity comes your way. An enclosing. And with that. I wish everyone a happy Fourth of July to Independence Day. Fighting for desire.

Eden Reid I appreciate you for everything that you do for me and this work that I bring to you. In my hopes and dreaMs.. You can see that I need you. I hope that you understand that I'm surrounding you with love and security. Get my books to me Miss Eden Reid. I'd like to see what I've done Miss Eden Reid. You know that I won't give in. Into any competition. Into any competition out there. I'm saying my apologies Eden Reid. Have I offended you? I'll make sure that you are well compensated for your name being in my book. You don't have to say nothing Eden Reid. Girl like a cigarette burn. The future is Up In smoke. Eden Reid thank you for being sophisticated enough to talk to me about the book. My favorite song is.How do I.by LeAnn Rimes. Make sure that girl get the message. Tell Kristen that you love her Thomas Allred Jr. Kristen I love you with all my heart. Thank you Miss Eden Reid for communicating. I'm going to say one more thing before I leave this place for good. Jeana Allred birthday is to be coming July 23 of every year. Let my wife live by making a wish that Jeana Allred and I somehow get to live happily ever after.

Thanks for your time Thomas Allred Jr. Miss Hillary Clinton thank you so much. Thomas Allred Jr we will get Kristen back to you. You have just got to keep the faith. Miss Hillary Clinton I'm trying with everything that I got. That's why that man is famous. Because through adversity. His personality stays the same. We are watching you to see what you do in the days to come Thomas Allred Jr. You got no idea that people all over the place on watching you. Miss Hillary Clinton. That girl means absolutely everything to me. Than fight for her Thomas Allred Jr. Ladies and gentlemen here go my book. Fighting for desire by Thomas Allred Jr. The world has got to know that I love you Kristen. Fighting for desire.

I just want to say that I care about females all across the United States of America and surrounding areas. Which is the reason for my book now. The success of my book depends on me getting in touch with the readers. Drama plague my pages. Everything that you want is in my book fighting for desire. I ain't giving up on you.

Don't give in. Be sure that my book gives you what you need and desire. Lieutenant Candis. And lieutenant Samantha. I want to thank the ladies on the police force. For the special part that they played in my life. Lieutenant Randall. And lieutenant Daniels. I want to thank you fellas for everything that you have done in making this book a reality. And that Dr Sentosa. See the boy shot a police officer. Hear me Dr Sentosa. I couldn't have made it this far. Without the help of you and your team. Catawba valley behavioral healthcare. In Hickory North Carolina. Everybody I'm leaving you with this one thought before I go. My dad said to me. Before he pa**ed away. That it takes a good man to love a woman the right way. For the women who are still out there in the struggle. We pray for you in your struggle that you make it. Hold Your position Thomas Allred Jr. I got more to say. But for now I'm going to just leave it at this. Jeana Allred I'm truly am sorry sweetheart. I heard about you through a friend of the family. Since then. I've been fighting for my right to be professional in this world today. I love you Eden Reid. Superman contract is still open Thomas Allred Jr. Is Carolina Beach my home and destination. Thomas Allred Jr females care about you. My mama said to me that. As long as I hustle that you could have anything that you want. If Kristen just knows that. I understand how you could want Kristen. Don't you put anything else. Because I know that you need your Superman contract. Fighting for desire. Thomas Allred Jr you deserve to be with how ever many women that you want to. It's your right to these girls Thomas Allred Jr. Let me put my two cents worth in. The Superman contract says that if you can handle yourself professionally. Then all will be given to you Thomas Allred Jr. Do you understand what we're trying to do for you. So far i understand what you're trying to do for me.

Superman there is one more thing that we need from you. Your John Hanc*ck on these pages. Thomas Allred Jr. And you have a future. I have a future. You have a future Thomas Allred Jr. I'm a f*cking movie star. Thats a movie star. These ladies give to you. Fighting for desire to be with you. Kristen I want to be with you. Fighting for desire.

Thomas Allred Jr I give these books to you. For you to enjoy your portion of life. I seen all that you've done for your community. And I'm rich Thomas Allred Jr. I know you have no idea of who this is. But you helped me with your kind words and general talk. That is all I'm going to say for now.

Whatever I do. It is to ensure the welfare of the people. Whatever you do Thomas Allred Jr. Just always know to keep God in your heart. I'm with you Thomas Allred Jr. In my bedroom. I got to get you to understand that there is a major contract in the working. And you need a contract to lift you up you've been through so much. Thomas Allred Jr my deal is coming to me as a Superman contract. You get anything that you want. If you just say that you love me one time in the book. I love you Miss Susan Jennings. Give that contract to that boy. Miss Susan Jennings can I have Kristen as my wife and soulmate. Your wife and soulmate are many women. I see that you communicate with me Thomas Allred Jr. You are the new actor in a motion picture. So take your time with what you're doing Thomas Allred Jr. Thomas Allred Jr you deserve everything that's being given to you. The reason I'm doing this is because. I feel like you can understand my type of people seeing that you've been around this stuff. Only one thing I ask Thomas Allred Jr. Remain strong enough to handle your ladies friends around you. Fighting for desire is now complete. All thats left for you to do is for you to tell me that you accept my Superman contract Thomas Allred Jr. By the time you read this I have accepted your contract Miss Susan Jennings. My best wishes goes out to your ex-wife Thomas Allred Jr. Miss Susan Jennings I have one question. Talk to Susan. Yes Miss Eden Reid. God damn that girl said talk to Susan. I'm asking you to take care of my family. And will I be lieutenant Kristen's husband. As you know Thomas Allred Jr a Superman contract. Consist of. Susan Jennings fell down. I'm all right Thomas Allred Jr. It's your contract that we talkin about Thomas Allred Jr. I give to you Naomi. I just want to say congratulations Thomas Allred Jr. For pa**ing your test for your Superman contract. The world has been watching your every move Thomas Allred Jr. and you're strong enough to accept what we have to offer you in the contract. I need to hear from you Thomas Allred Jr. About what it is that you expect from a contract. Keep it professional Thomas Allred Jr. I just want my police officers to be taken care of. And my community taken care of as well. My brothers and sisters. Give the new cribs by theMs.elves.

Y'all give me Susan Jennings anything she needs. And to Kristen. I offer my love and support. But that is what a Superman contract means to me. You can have those things. Sign on the dotted line. And your life will be starting over Thomas Allred Jr. Fighting for desire compilation 3. Right now you have no idea what's happening to you Thomas Allred Jr. Everyday play fair. I'm a police officer Thomas Allred Jr. Miss Susan Jennings. In a couple more minutes I'm going to tell you what we are doing . Thomas Allred Jr. My team has been secretly testing you. Thomas Allred Jr. Close that book and go to sleep. Your desire to be loved has been fulfilled. Fighting for desire I want to love you Kristen. Fighting for desire. Ms. Susan Jennings fighting for desire. Her name isn't Miss Susan Jennings. Her name is Rebecca Scott Daniels. Thomas Allred Jr this book is a compilation album. That we have you working on. When you have your meeting Monday. Tell Vicki I want her to look out for you. Fighting for desire is the truth. You got appreciate what I've done for you Thomas Allred Jr. Okay that's enough. Plug up your phone. Fighting for desire is in your heart Thomas Allred Jr. Send the book in right now.

Now I need you Thomas Allred Jr. Miss Susan Jennings I have no idea at what you're talkin about. It is a Superman contract in the workings. Are you listening to me Thomas Allred Jr. The ladies and I are selecting our new Superman as we speak. I got a Superman contract. That's what I'm telling you you are Superman Thomas Allred Jr. Don't try to rationalize with what's going on. They killed your wife Thomas Allred Jr. They shot you in the leg to keep you out of industry. And through all the pain in the struggle. I made you keep a Jesus piece around your neck. Until I could see how talented you were. I gave you your home Thomas Allred Jr. I wanted to see you in action with a family. Thomas Allred Jr do not give up. Being professional Thomas Allred Jr I'm keeping my head up and together. Are there any questions that you have for me. This is a real contract. Yeah it is a real contract. Control yourself Thomas Allred Jr. Because our knew age Superman is a common man with victory in his life. I need you packing up your things. You have no idea at what I plan for you. You took a shot in the leg and you stand up. We are all proud of you Thomas Allred Jr. For having the courage to write this book. What we are going to do with you. It's give you everything that you want Thomas Allred Jr. My community and my family. Happiness is what I want for them. Happiness is what you shall have when you get out of this situation. Now take hold of this. It is your restaurant menu. From now on Thomas Allred Jr. You will have professional cooks and chefs to cook for you.

See what I can do. Miss Susan Jennings I love you. Let me move in with lieutenant Kristen. I'm trying to tell you when you move into a new house it's a hundred women that is going to move in with you. Tell her so be it then. Naomi you can see that I love you. What kind of bulsh*t is this Thomas Allred Jr. Look I'm thankful for your contract. But I just really want me I have to relax in. Thomas Allred Jr. You are our new Superman. And it doesn't matter about the color of your skin. Tell Thomas Allred Jr that we need him to start exercising right now. Continue your workout Thomas Allred Jr. Y'all got to get me my woman to me. Tell Eden Reid that you are asking for a chance. To make it in our world today. Eden Reid I am asking for a chance to make it in our world today. Talking about Thomas Allred Jr is Superman. Thomas Allred Jr ain't got no fear in his heart. My question for this hero is. The pain left from you losing your wife. And going through operations like you did. has it made you a police officer or mercenary. A mercenary for the police department. Miss Susan Jennings. It's about time Miss Susan Jennings. Let me see your contract is a six-figure contract with the ladies. And this is about it Thomas Allred Jr. I will be watching you.

We are going to come to you. When you put this book out. As far as the eyes can see. There will be women who represent you Thomas Allred Jr. Because we are wanting victory. And you played a damn good game Thomas Allred Jr. Thomas Allred Jr theres one more thing. Tell Cindy McClain. You really in love with lieutenant Kristen Beam. And have yourself a good day. Miss Cindy McClain I'm really in love with lieutenant Kristen Beam. Listen to me Thomas Allred Jr. To get your contracts. You must complete my regiment. Get your a** down and do some push-ups. Now send the book in Thomas Allred Jr. Michelle Obama has spoken.

My business won't be complete until I ask you these three questions. What does it feel like Thomas Allred Jr to know that you captured everything in this world that you wanted? My dreaMs. were always in front of me Miss Michelle Obama. I miss her so damn much that is killing me. I can't begin to explain Ms. Obama. The love and the pain that I feel inside. Thomas Allred Jr if you only get yourself together. I can give you what I want to give you. Which is a house with lieutenant Kristen Beam. A dream come true that would be. You have earned it Thomas Allred Jr. Did your story take off the way you wanted to. No it didn't Michelle Obama. Miss Michelle I done put my all into writing the story. I'm taking my time Miss Michelle. Thomas Allred Jr I see what you're going through and I commend your honor. One last thing. Can you think of a place where you would be happy. I can think of a place but nothing in this world could give her back to me. That boy just pa**ed his test. Thomas Allred Jr put the book down and wait for my response. As beautiful as you are Thomas Allred Jr. We are giving you a Superman contract. Thomas Allred Jr make sure that you are worthy of the contract. Take you a bath every weekday. Let me talk to Thomas Allred Jr. I know they hurt you. But you fought a good game against them Thomas Allred Jr. The world has watched on the big screen. And you are professional Thomas Allred Jr. The love that you shared with Jeana Allred. Shall carry you on forever and forever more. Give Thomas Allred Jr his contract right now. And I mean right now.

Thank you Miss Michelle Obama. This interview is over. Thomas Allred Jr ask Michelle Obama. Now listen Thomas Allred Jr. There are millions of women wanting to speak to you. I want you to control yourself. And send in the final part to this book. Compilation album book 5 fighting for desire. Y'all better give up. Because Thomas Allred Jr ain't playing no games. I would like to congratulate Eden Reid. Is it Thomas Allred Jr I did the best job I could. Thank you Miss Eden Reid. Everybody know that I care for you. Pick your game up professionals hear you Thomas Allred Jr. I am Superman. And I have come to you. In peace and responsibility for the world. In my journey. I have lost so many people that it has me shaking in my boots. But I see that you love me ladies. So I'm stand strong. Until the days of end has occurred. My name is Thomas Allred Jr. I am code name Superman. With the NSA the FBI in the Secret Service. They're talking about giving you a contract Thomas Allred Jr. I know Miss Cindy McClain. The period stops here. I want you in the house doing push-ups everyday.

This is the ending of your book. Alternate ending. And here Thomas Allred Jr. You are the king of Storybook Land. Miss Michelle Obama what does this mean. It means that you are free Thomas Allred Jr. You are free. This book has been dedicated. To the people of my community. And surrounding communities. I wish that I could. Try to take back all the pain that we felt through the years. One of us has made it. Jeana Allred. I love you. Now Kristen Beam. Stay With Me. This is my interview. My badge number 7 7 7 1. I am officer Reign. Of the New York Police department. I'm saying to you. That it is okay what they did to me. God will help me out of this situation. If I just believe in him. Thank you Thomas Allred Jr. Your interview has been completed. Now send the book in Thomas Allred Jr. Say in two more days. I will be king. In two more days I will be king. Go ahead and send the book in.

Your the most beautifulest human being I ever wanted to meet. And I figured out what you're saying to me is the truth. Eden Reid contact me soon after this book is finished. I am going to end this thing with me finishing my work as a police officer. My caseload is like this Eden Reid. Thank you for believing in me. Will you marry me Eden Reid? I said will you marry me Eden Reid? Kristen beam is on extension #2. Me and Susan Jennings. Have for you a Superman contract Thomas Allred Jr. For saving our people. Thats a movie star for you. Thomas Allred Jr Susan Jennings speaking to you. You have no idea what I've done for you Thomas Allred Jr. Kristen Beam and Eden Reid are both going to be with you in a house that I made for you at Carolina Beach. No I must be dreaming about this. I can't let this go any further. Jeana Allred I love you. Thomas Allred Jr is really in love with that girl. Let's leave him alone y'all. You better think of better ways to write your book Thomas Allred Jr. Lieutenant Nada. Yes it is me. And lieutenant Porsche is here too. Thomas Allred Jr what ever woman you need I can get it for you. Susan Jennings is a billionaire heiress. Just talk to me Thomas Allred Jr. See what I tell you is the truth. Superman. We code names you Thomas Allred Jr Superman. Because you were strong enough to handle the loss of your wife. Thomas Allred Jr ain't no time like the present. Move out of your mama's house into a luxury apartment with Kristen Beam and Eden Reid by your side. I can't do that because I'm focus on getting this book to the people. Thomas Allred Jr the sacrifices here. You were shot when you saved a person's life and then your wife got killed. Thomas Allred Jr we honor you. Superman there isn't nothing that we won't do to make you feel comfortable in our community. Give me one business day to think about it. Superman. Give me one business day.

Y'all hear that boy. Thomas Allred Jr the rap community honors you. I will move in with Kristen beam and Eden Reid. Thomas Allred Jr you are making the right decision. Ensure that my family gets to move into a new place of their own. And I'm yours Mr.s. Jennings. Thomas Allred Jr sign your name on the dotted line. Superman Thomas Allred Jr. At Your Service Miss Susan Jennings. Or shall I say Miss Rebecca Scott Daniels. People now we have got a ball game. Tell the president that I just recruited Superman Thomas Allred Jr. To be a part of the Secret Service. Eden Reid. And Kristen Beam. Get them girls a bank account. Thomas Allred Jr you ought to know. That the only reason I kept you alive is. Superman is my favorite person. And in the hospital you mentioned Superman on the operating table. You are the picture of health. About the two women that you said you had for me. Thomas Allred Jr. I'll get you everything that you want. We got Superman Thomas Allred Jr. Sign another contract. Superman Thomas Allred Jr. If this boy really is Superman. Than them people are going to jail for killing his wife. And shooting him like that.

Come out of your dream Thomas Allred Jr. Miss Michelle Obama. You have got no clue at the genius I have found within you Thomas Allred Jr. Continue to write your books Thomas Allred Jr. On your paper. I'm going to help you to remember who you are. I am a police officer. That's not only Who You are Thomas Allred Jr. Imma share with you a little secret. We both are trillionaires. Send that book into Eden Reid. You were right Miss Susan Jennings. To save Thomas Allred Jr life was a good move. True indeed true indeed. Look at yourself.

Now I have seen you take people from one place to the next. And I keep telling myself that one day I wish that I could be one of those people. It's not that we don't believe in you Miss Jennings. It's just that my all has been given. I have no more left to give Miss Susan Jennings. I made these business ideas to save people lives not to make money. Your access has been granted. Thank you. If anyone doesn't understand my book. I appreciate you for reading my book. That boy can't be alone forever. Thomas Allred Jr. Listen to me Thomas Allred Jr. Weather you write books or make business ideas it is up to me if you succeed or not. Ms. Susan Jennings. Do you trust me Thomas Allred Jr. Susan Jennings I trust you with my life. Thomas Allred Jr. Whatever you do don't turn back. Your access has been granted to Hollywood California. Thank you Miss Susan Jennings.

You can go to bed Thomas Allred Jr. everybody miss Susan Jennings help me do everything. I'm going to get you a house before I leave out this world Thomas Allred Jr. All I need is your friendship Ms. Susan Jennings. Do you understand Thomas Allred Jr that Susan Jennings is a trillionaire. You are a trillionaire as well. I just wanted you to know that I wrote this book in dedication of you Ms. Susan Jennings. Thomas Allred Jr. For going above and beyond the call of duty. Our ladies of this great nation. Grant to you your business contract Thomas Allred Jr. I'm thanking the ladies everywhere. Thomas Allred Jr we had no idea that you been through all the stuff that you been through until we read that book. Us women adore you that is why we're taking care of you now as we speak. Thomas Allred Jr no matter what you're going through we will be here for you. As your contract comes to you. I just want you to play for a minute. Walked outta heaven by jagged edge. Thomas Allred Jr while you are listening. Remember that the females are talking about you. Look boy your book is dedicated to jagged edge. Play computer Love. Next Thomas Allred Jr. Now send that book in Thomas Allred Jr.

Thomas Allred Jr accepted you Susan Jennings contract. Thomas Allred is a superhero. That you know you can trust. I have watched you Thomas Allred Jr now for 25 years. And I have got to tell myself that you. Just are a really good person. You gave me the strength when I had nothing to do in my life. I am going to help you out of your situation. Everytime I look at You Thomas Allred Jr. Get your a** up and do them push ups. Yes Miss Samantha. I am helping you see that you are a motherf*cking police officer. And you are a motherf*cking trillionaire. Thomas Allred Jr this is not just a story. This is not just a hero fighting for desire. This Is Love from all the police officers in the world. We are telling you Thomas Allred Jr. Did you do make a difference in our lives. You have got nothing but time on your hands Thomas Allred Jr. We took everything from you to see how you show yourself as a man in this world. We are helping you to see. That with God anything is possible. Thomas Allred Jr you know that everybody sees that you are The Lion King. And as your Lion King I need my material possessions and my family restored. It is not that simple Thomas Allred Jr. Miss Susan Jennings. Miss Michelle Obama. And Mr.s. Hillary Clinton. I realize that you. Are a superhero Thomas Allred Jr. That probably doesn't know what's going on. But you have to trust and believe that. The females in this country and surrounding areas they all love you. Thomas Allred Jr we are not going to let you down. I have you on tape standing in the sunlight. Lion King. We give you a great pleasure. To introduce to you. Another way home. As we speak Thomas Allred Jr. The sun has positioned itself. Directly over your house. In which it's always done. These are not stories Thomas Allred Jr. There you go. You are beginning to wake up to know that you are our Lion King. Give that boy a chance to realize what you're saying to him Miss Hillary Clinton. I am saying to you Thomas Allred Jr.

That either God put us on the planet. You got to sit here and realize what was saying to you Thomas Allred Jr. Miss Michelle Obama. I'm figuring out that I'm The Lion King. And I'm figuring out that I'm a trillionaire. But why did you have to kill my wife. If this is all a test. This is no test Thomas Allred Jr. you have been fighting for determination all your damn life. I'm going to see that you have your house. With all of the ladies that you ever could want. Listen to me Thomas Allred Jr. They called you Superman because you are special Thomas Allred Jr. And as a police officer. You have done your job.

For the public and for the citizens of this great nation. Is there anything that you want from us Thomas Allred Jr. Miss Susan Jennings. A girl took her time. And made love to me. Thomas Allred Jr take made love to me off there. Thomas Allred Jr this is not a game. That boy is a police officer that has two personalities. Let me see Michelle Obama talk to you. Listen to me. We making you out to be a hero Thomas Allred Jr. I see what you're going through. But after I snap my fingers. It will all be said and done. Now what is the one thing that the ladies can do for you. Can't you see that you are professional. I grant the ladies. A statue of Jeana Allred and the Lion King Thomas Allred Jr. To stand forever more. Listen. Our police personnel. Have been humbled to your acquaintance. Go ahead and speak to them Thomas Allred Jr. You are an officer now. Ma police ladies and men. Good job. For fixing me up to be a better individual. I want you to realize. That my heart goes out to you on your day-to-day duties. Imma try my best to clean up. This book is in history. My fingers are snapping Thomas Allred Jr. Snap. The book is dedicated. To the police force everywhere. We know you are helping us. And I want to thank you. For doing a job well done. I am Superman Thomas Allred Jr. You a trillionaire and The Lion King.

Saying to you. That my memory has been restored Miss Michelle Obama. Look at you Thomas Allred Jr. We brought you through all those years and complications until now. I had to take your memory away. But now the Lion King is restored. The police department everywhere adores you Thomas Allred Jr. Tell Eden Reid. In my smallest of dreaMs.. I never did hurt anybody. Eden Reid. In the smallest of dreaMs. I never did hurt anybody. Go on to tell Kristen Beam that as The Lion King. I know that this is the beginning of our life. Kristen Beam that as The Lion King. I know that this is the beginning of our life. You need to transfer your book Thomas Allred Jr. Into the halls of Congress. You know Superman is The Lion King. Right now police. Are listening to your statements Thomas Allred Jr. You fought a good game Thomas Allred Jr. The ladies are proud of you. Send that book off today sometime. Take your time and think about where youve been. Listen Thomas Allred Jr. I want you to realize that you are our true Lion King. Act accordingly to our demands. You will make it in your dreaMs.. This goes out to. Longview North Carolina. Fighting for determination. Make that boy a superhero. And Miss Eden Reid. And Miss Cindy McClain. And Ms. Kristen Beam. Listen Thomas Allred Jr. Thomas Allred Jr you the damn lion king of the world. I'm trying to come with you everywhere. We fighting for determination Kristen.

Susan Jennings. Or shall I say Rebecca Scott Daniels. I want to say to you. That in my book. I may have left out some people that are truly deserving to be in this book. That boy book is 200 pages. I give unto you. A police officer's badge of honor. Miss Susan Jennings I can't except that. Our government wants you to have this Thomas Allred Jr. As a token of our appreciation Thomas Allred Jr. Yall I thank you. For all the years of service that you have done for me and our communities. You done a great job on that book Thomas Allred Jr. All I'm trying to say to you is. Thomas Allred Jr is The Lion King people. Lieutenant Candis raise up a little bit. This new world consist of. And even scale. What do you mean it even scale Thomas Allred Jr. I mean from this day forth. What just say what you want to say. From this day forth. I will better myself. And as your Lion King. Today is the start of a new. You better keep that man here talkin. I already know that the Lion King is dedicated to taking care of our people. In my prayers. God has sent me. To be a part of the police force. World-wide with love unto you. Thomas Allred Jr won't give up. And with that said. Cindy McClain. And Miss Susan Jennings. I want to thank you for what you've done for me. Kristen Beam I need you to be with me. This is the true ending of my book. Everybody good night.

I've been under your spell Kristen Beam for a long time now Kristen Beam. And I would like to get to know you much better. Eden Reid I would like to get to know you too. This is a compilation album book. After the story. I said I dream of you Kristen and Eden I. Would like to know that you all can be all that I need. Thomas Allred Jr your apartment is open. After five long years I've been here. Thank you for opening my apartment your honor Cindy McClain. Thomas Allred Jr if you knew who I was why didn't you say something to me on the phone? Cindy McClain I am a police officer. That is looking for his wife to be. Now we got a book Cindy McClain. To be professional this book is dedicated to. The st. Jude's children. At the saint Jude's hospital. Kristen Beam and lieutenant Candis. I am proud of you. For all you did in my book to make us a reality. In closing I want to give to you. My deepest apologies. Imma shout some woman out. Officer Kristen. Officer Nada. Officer Vicky. Officer Munroe. I want to thank you for giving me this contract. Cause we are legends among the people. Ladies Thomas Allred Jr will see you now. Thomas Allred Jr your work is done. All of the children know what you've done. You will get a female one of these days. Lift your head up to the sky. That is the end of your book right there. Count your blessings Thomas Allred Jr. That girl didn't give up on you. Kristen Beam. I love you. Kristen Beam loves you too Thomas Allred Jr. You can't tell anybody. I want to give officer Frankie the thanks. For guiding me out of the struggle. And placing my feet on solid ground. Thank you fighting for desire compilation album book 10. Is over this instant right here. The ladies are watching you Thomas Allred Jr. Make your girl proud of you Thomas Allred Jr. Jeana Allred. Like I told you. The people will pay for the wrongs. And I love you sweetheart. May you rest in peace. Eden Reid I told you that Ive been working on a new book. I'll get the details to you as soon as I finish this sentence. Now send off the book Thomas Allred Jr. Yes lieutenant Shannon clay.

It is a compilation book. That I give unto you Eden Reid. In hopes that I stay in your grace and favor. With these compilation books that I'm writing. satisfying you. By fulfilling my task at hand. I can see how this may be the end of the book. Although I've said that many times. Jeana Allred I got love for you. And my album is completed right now Eden Reid. Album in bookstores. So the rest of you. Can know that I'm an officer of the law. I give to you. Thomas Allred Jr you got a speech. No I give to you. My book fighting for desire.Tell Eden Reid I love you. Eden Reid I love you. Tell Kristen Beam that you love her to Thomas Allred Jr. Kristen Beam I love you so very much it hurt at times. Girls whatever we do for richer or poorer. Thomas Allred Jr. We are going to make it.

Thomas Allred Jr keep holding on to the faith. Thank God the women do love me. Excuse me Thomas Allred Jr. The rest of the women would like to speak to you. You got to listen to them women Thomas Allred Jr. Put Shontel Allred name in there. Also put lieutenant Maya name in there. Kristen Beam yes Thomas Allred Jr. We made your ending to fighting for desire. Get you some rest Thomas Allred Jr. When you wake up it will be a new day of possibilities. I warned you Thomas Allred Jr women got your best interest in mind. You don't have to be alone any longer Thomas Allred Jr. Because the Lord is telling me. That you are a good person. And this book and you should be alright forever more Thomas Allred Jr. I got to pray for Jeana Allred. That's what this book is for. You are a hero Thomas Allred Jr. Whatever I do I just want my own place. With all of them females listening to me.

Fighting for desire. Send the book off Thomas Allred Jr. Here gose nothing Kristen Beam. Thomas Allred Jr. The future is not written yet. But the past is over and done with. Keep fighting Thomas Allred Jr. Keep fighting. Fighting for desire.

I tried my best to get Kristen Beam to love me. My best wasn't good enough. I found myself going to prison for making a phone call that shouldn't have made. The thing about a phone call is. It goes two ways. And I stood my ground. And I'm telling you that I love Kristen Beam. Thomas Allred Jr your book is off the hook. The reason that I. Chose Kristen Beam. Is because she made me see that there is a businesswoman in this world. And I'm really proud of Kristen Beam. For that little instant of a second. In which I. Found heaven on Earth. Let me be professional. My first idea. Was to become a police officer. Just like everyone else. Thank you. I may be a police officer. But I do know what love is. And I'm professional. Kristen Beam is my everything. And I dreamed of just having dinner with her in my apartment. My business faith. Has me writing this book.

To let her know. Kristen Beam is the one that I'm choosing. Let her know who are you speaking of Thomas Allred Jr. Thank you everybody. Fighting for desire. I promise that I'm the right man for you Kristen Beam. I need you to see how beautiful you are girl. Listen. I don't have my money together right now. And your book is finished. I put this as an attachment to a story that only God knows that is the truth about the situation at hand. Do you want me Kristen Beam? Do you want me Thomas Allred Jr? I give anything for you. The reason I walked out on you Thomas Allred Jr is. I knew that you were going through things that were out of your control. And you had to be strong to make it out of that situation. My question for you is. At the every one of these years has gone past. Do you still want to be with me? Yeah I want to be with you. Kristen Beam I made my mistakes early on in my life. I'm getting tired of you holding that against me. Now you and me Kristen Beam have a lot of catching up to do. I love you Kristen Beam. What that man is trying to say is. I need you to Kristen Beam. Thomas Allred Jr listen to me. The Lord put me and you together. Thomas Allred Jr. It's time to eat something Thomas Allred Jr. Yeah I'll be there in 1 minutes Jeana Allred.

Thomas Allred Jr I let you go because you. Couldn't remember that you were police officer. All that is behind me now Kristen Beam. Finish your conversation with Kristen Beam in 60 seconds. Thomas Allred Jr. Miss Hillary Clinton. Kristen Beam and I. Are in love. And I'm fighting for desire to. Along with everybody else. Miss Hillary Clinton. I just need a place to live. I've been wanting to see you handle your business Thomas Allred Jr. Miss Hillary Clinton. I'm doing what I can to take care of my business as expected of me. To all of the police officers. And to all of the ladies. In my continent. If I could be with this one person. That would be worth. All of the inventions I ever made. Can't y'all see I love that girl. Kristen Beam I know how it feels. To wake up every morning alone. If I prove myself. May I be with you for dinner. In a apartment that they give me. And Ms. Hillary Clinton says. Tell that girl that you love her Thomas Allred Jr. You need to tell Kristen Beam you love her through out that book. Kristen Beam I love you. By the power vested in me Thomas Allred Jr. You and Kristen Beam are together Thomas Allred Jr. Thank you Miss Hillary Clinton. The book is fighting for desire i had to do something. Ms. Hillary Clinton. Yes Thomas Allred Jr. I need a favor from you Ms. Hillary Clinton. What is your favor Thomas Allred Jr. My community needs a ball field. So children will play. When I snap my fingers. This will all be a dream to you Thomas Allred Jr. Give your family your love. That is all he needs. Mama I do love you. I know I hurt you. But your boy is a police officer. I asked for Kristen BeaMs. hand in marriage. Snap. Thomas Allred Jr go and place your phone on the charger. Fighting for desire compilation book 1.

Now Kristen Beam I don't want to go too far with my book. But I do want you to realize how much I do love and adore you. Thomas Allred Jr that girl will be with you. Eden Reid will now be with you. Send your book of Thomas Allred Jr. Professionals got me where I can't move Eden Reid. I'm going to give this boy his contract. Playtime is over. I want you to understand that this is your compilation book Thomas Allred Jr. And seeing that this is a compilation book. I hope you break the ground open with this book. Thomas Allred Jr this is fighting for design with this book. Eden Reid sounds professional. And your Superman contract belongs to the rest of the females in this United States of America. Thomas Allred Jr. You have a big old heart. After this day you will no longer be alone anymore. Because fighting for desire is the truth. You are a police officer Thomas Allred Jr. And you have done your job for more than 30 years.

Us ladies commend that police officer. That fought lived and died for you Thomas Allred Jr. Her name was Jeana Allred. Is Jeana Allred. Your wife is our legacy. It is showing her strong that women are. And it is also showing the love and compa**ion that each woman carries in her heart. We got time to play no games. Do you know what I think. You know what I think. One of these days. A professional is going to sweep you off your feet Thomas Allred Jr. But until then. Think about what you're doing. And see for yourself. How your words put with our publishers. Will make a difference out here in society. Our men police officers. Believe that if something happens to them. That there families will be taken care of. I give to you. A police officer. That knows a few things about taking care of her man. Thomas Allred Jr wait a few minutes. This girl is emotional. With no longer ado. Thomas Allred Jr I give to You. Your one and only soulmate.Cindy McClain. Has your option. What I want to do Thomas Allred Jr. Is take you out of the hood. You are going to need someone's help. God damn his book is good as hell. Remain faithful to your values Thomas Allred Jr. That you had when you were a kid. Just so that you can teach everybody the real you. At the you and Kristen Beam get married in Honolulu. I want to thank y'all. And I want to thank Eden Reid. For scheduling me a date. In her busy schedule. The time is. It is 3:30 Thomas Allred Jr. Easter Sunday. I know you that you waiting for the book to come out. I'm trying to realize that this compilation album is strong enough. To make it through the day today challenges. Mr.. President. Yes Thomas Allred Jr. You done a great job creating that book Thomas Allred Jr. Now put your head on the pillow to relax. Sir I've been alone almost 30 years doing police work and they killed my wife and shot me in the leg. We are going to take care of you Thomas Allred Jr. I need Kristen Beam. To start my life over to be my wife. DreaMs. come true only if you let them. Thomas Allred Jr you are professional. You need to send that book in.

Eden I know that I haven't talk to you in a while but our date is important to me I'm doing my best to maintain myself during the illnesses I'm paying my last payment on book number 1 on May 29 2020 I need you to call me back with and update on this book there is one question that I have to ask you when we speak on the phone thank you for everything Eden and I look forward to hearing from you soon and thank your staff for me for working with me during these crisies. There is one more thing I want to say happy birthday Eden it is my wish that you have everything that you desire on a birthday candle remember our date Eden and please call me with and update on the book called fighting for mine. You have my number. Sincerely yours Thomas Allred Jr

We'll miss Susan Jennings. It looks like the novel continues. In fighting for success. Do what you got to do Thomas Allred Jr. Miss Susan Jennings. They killed Jeana. They done killed my brother son. And my nephew. As well. I've been through so many things that I'm going crazy y'all. They shot me when I was a young kid. And this contract has the best of me because. I have no money. Only promises to get money. My name is Thomas Allred Jr. And I am fighting for success Miss Susan Jennings. Well that's quite a story Thomas Allred Jr. I want you to realize that you've been through the struggle. To make you a better person. And no matter which path you decide to take. You have a contract waiting for you with Miss Eden Reid. I ain't got but one more thing to say to you Thomas Allred Jr. Write your book and let your imagination run wild. Now Kristen didn't realize. That she was my favorite girl. I know I've been through things. But God has a purpose for everyone's life. Fighting for success. Is what I like to call it. When you are fighting for success y'all. The pain won't hurt you. It only makes you wiser and better because you. Believe in something better than any greater understanding in this world. I believe in Kristen. Listen to me y'all.

No matter the situation I will be there for you. I am confident enough to say. That you are confident. And together we will have a greater future. Lieutenant Candice. Can you believe I have another book coming out. Common sense. Will tell you that. The Lord is your Shepherd Thomas Allred Jr. And no matter what's going on with you. All of the ladies still love you. Miss Susan Jennings. Put fighting for success on the record books. Thomas Allred Jr you be strong. That man is talking about fighting for success. Thomas Allred Jr. in my book. There is a paradox. That have to do with money life Love and murder. That's a smart motherf*cker right there. Y'all I got to welcome you to fighting for success. You saying your book is completed right here Thomas. No I'm saying fighting for success is my book that's coming after you. What do you mean that fighting for success is coming after you. Come on Miss Susan Jennings. We have a lot to discuss. On fighting for success the sequel. But I love you Thomas Allred Jr. Girl is that you. We have got to make something out of this book Kristen. It's about time he gave Kristen her props in the book. Girl me and you. Can have anything we want in the book. You need to stop wasting your time Thomas Allred Jr. Mr.. Masters I never give up. Do exactly what I say to do Thomas Allred Jr. Now send your book in. I don't have nothing but this pen and paper in front of me. And my deepest desires are caught in my nightmares. You don't understand where I'm coming from do you. That's why I wrote that book for you. Fighting for success is a compilation album. That I know you will enjoy. I'm going to get to the book right now. Make sure that you're strong enough to read this thoroughly. Y'all I have been a police officer. All of my life. I fell in love when I was younger. And somebody killed my wife. I got shot trying to protect her and her people. I sat alone almost 25 years. Just watching the days go past me. Look in the mirror Thomas Allred Jr. I'm just growing older with time. Until the day comes that I can see my wife again.

I use music as a common ground. To see through every unknown source of terror that is. Play my music for me. I want you to realize something. Put Officer Reign back on the Force. It's about time you said put officer Reign back on the force. But who is this that I see in the mirror. It is not me I don't recognize him. I want you to slow down just a little bit Thomas Allred Jr. Because of Jeana Allred I've grown to what you see in front of you in the mirror. You see Thomas Allred Jr. I'm going to get it. In the worst kind of way. I want you to realize something about me Thomas Allred Jr. That girl needs you. Them girls don't like me. Hold your ground out here Reign. It will all be revealed in time. What will all be revealed in time. You see you made over 2,000 business ideas saving people's lives. And you've written 2000 books. The girl sees you as a mogul. I haven't written 2000 books. That's what we are going to do. I'm taking over your personality Thomas Allred Jr. And who are you. I am you Thomas Allred Jr.

I must be talking to myself in the mirror. You talkin to you Thomas Allred Jr. Jeana Allred would be proud of you. For what I did nothing but let her die. I told you this is going to be a compilation book. Get yourself together Reign. Put officer Reign on the police force. With Reign on the police force. This whole police department will be watching you. I'm going to try to do what I can to help and save people. Do what you can do Thomas Allred Jr. The reason that I'm here Thomas Allred Jr. Is to take you out of that situation. What situation you going to take me out of. it is time for you to experience the abundant successful life. What do I call you. Say to me Mr. Thomas Allred Jr. And I will answer you. Mr.. Thomas Allred Jr what is happening to me. You are going to be yourself. Will I change any. Listen Thomas Allred Jr. Yes Mr. Thomas Allred Jr. Ever since we were kids I have been with you. Now I'm taking over. But Kristen is in love with me. Kristen don't say nothing. All you got to do is write slowly. The books will be finished in time. No Kristen thinks the world of you Thomas Allred Jr. Mr.. Thomas Allred Jr. Do I have a bank account. Think of your future wife Thomas Allred Jr. Tell Eden that you love her. Eden I love you. Make sure that boy get that contract. Mr.. Thomas Allred Jr all I can say to you is. Thank you for everything. I want you to take a bath and cut your hair Thomas Allred Jr. Today is a new birth of your reality consciousness. What do I do now Mr.. Thomas Allred Jr. You have got to clean up your room. I'm talking about your mind space Thomas Allred Jr. I'm in love with Kristen. I'm in love with Eden. I'm in love with Maya. I'm in love with Nada. I'm in love with Candice. I'm in love with Heather. I'm in love with Evelyn. Thomas Allred Jr. You have got to do better than that. Yes Mr.. Thomas Allred Jr. I am in love with all of the ladies in my hemisphere. Now we have work to do Thomas Allred Jr. Start writing your book Thomas Allred Jr. Now Mr. Thomas Allred Jr. My book is taking me places. That I don't want to go. Yes I'm with you. This man talking to him self while writing a book. Pay no attention to the crowd Thomas Allred Jr. Eden Reid it's who you pay attention to. I'm watching you Thomas Allred Jr. I am Mr. Thomas Allred Jr. Doesn't it sound good people. But Mr. Thomas Allred Jr if you go how will I reach you. Say to the mirror three times. That I am a successful human being Thomas Allred Jr. It's about darn time for you to write your book Thomas Allred Jr. Have Susan Jennings read along with you. Susan Jennings Thomas Allred Jr is online one. This is Susan Jennings. And your story has begun. Tell Kristen that I love her and I'll see her in the future. Mr.. Thomas Allred Jr. I want to thank you for everything that you do for our people. What are you talkin about. Thank you Mr.. Thomas Allred Jr. I am Mr.. Thomas Allred Jr. And we all are fighting for success. Part 1 Susan Jennings. Our breakthrough is finished.

CHAPTER 24

What the police don't know about you is. That I'm your soulmate. Miss Susan Jennings you must be kidding me. Laughter makes the day go faster Thomas Allred Jr. Now this thing with you and Eden must stop. There is too much work to be done. I know Eden love me Miss Susan Jennings. I'm going to prove it to you Thomas Allred Jr. Behind every book you write. Miss Susan Jennings. Eden Reid is working. Night and day on your books Thomas Allred Jr. Thank you Miss Susan Jennings for clearing that up for me. And Kristen is honestly working. Trying to make a living for herself. Thomas Allred Jr people are watching you. To see if your leg hurts you. When you took that bullet over to Jeana Thomas Allred Jr. It changed people's points of view of you. You are now what we call. A super mogul Thomas Allred Jr. By creating those books and business ideas. Let Susan Jennings talk to you. Yes Mr.. Thomas Allred Jr. By creating those books and business ideas. The security team in Washington is watching you now. Thomas Allred Jr. I only got two things left to say to you.

Before I'll be back on my way. It's a compilation album book. And this is the way the government thanks you for all of your sacrifices. Miss Susan Jennings come back please. Your compilation album is the way through two peace. Miss Susan Jennings. I didn't say nothing about you in my first book. That's because you needed time to build up to me. Miss Susan I have something to say to Thomas Allred Jr. Go ahead Kristen talk to him please. The first time that I saw you boy. It was a woman sunny day. Mr.. Thomas Allred Jr. Get her out of here. I got a compilation book to write. I like you Thomas Allred Jr. What's even better than that. Take compilation off of the book. Fighting for success I move on. Sounds a little bit better. You don't know what you're doing Thomas Allred Jr. But listen we got you. That little voice inside your head saying write the book. You must respect us Thomas Allred Jr. I know that I must respect you Mr.. Thomas Allred Jr. But I have so many questions for you. You can ask me one question Thomas Allred Jr. Will I be able to provide for all the people in my generation? This is what we intend on doing Thomas Allred Jr. This is what we intend on doing Kristen. This is what we intend on doing now Eden

Reid. Eden Reid is talking to you. Mr.. Thomas Allred Jr. Your book has me on the edge of my seat Mr. Thomas Allred Jr. It has you on the edge of your seat because. What I'm telling you is real.

Exactly Thomas Allred Jr. I got to get Oprah Winfrey a book. I got to get Steve Harvey a book also. Give judge Judy a book Thomas Allred Jr. You are a police officer Thomas Allred Jr. And our people love what you're doing. Write two more paragraphs and then stop. I can't stop Mr.. Thomas Allred Jr. Cause I won't stop. Bad Boy entertainment and So So Def entertainment. It's fixing to call me. I have the music written. Mr.. Thomas Allred Jr. Will bad boy ever call me? Will So So Def ever call me. Write your damn book Thomas Allred Jr. I have got to think about this sh*t. I'm praying for you Mr.. Thomas Allred Jr. Let that boy communicate. Write your damn book Mr.. Thomas Allred Jr. Susan Jennings has been calling you. Thomas Allred Jr Susan Jennings wants you. I got a contract for you Thomas Allred Jr. And it is with Bad Boy records and So So Def records. Miss Susan Jennings I know that I hurt you. Thomas Allred Jr I will give anything for you. We are here sacrificing. What's this. It is fighting for success part 2 Susan Jennings. You see Ms. Susan Jennings. God told me to help Susan Jennings and her family. And thats was exactly what I did writing these books. Will I see you again Thomas Allred Jr.

We about to calm down. What the president got to say about this book. Tell Eden Reid that you miss her Thomas Allred Jr. Let Kristen know that you miss her. Thomas Allred Jr. Be professional. The book is called fighting for success. What do you think of me now Mr.. Thomas Allred Jr. You are on your way to success and Superstardom.

Thomas Allred Jr we want you to realize something. This is all part of a big plan. Sat here in Washington. And yes Thomas Allred Jr. You are rich beyond compare. Mr.. Thomas Allred Jr. Thank you for everything that you did for my life. Thank the production team Thomas Allred Jr. For they are who have been up in you. Thank you production team. Cause without you I had no hope. Go to sleep Thomas Allred Jr. I have a book The write Mr.. Thomas Allred Jr. Talking about your book Thomas Allred Jr. Is a good thing. Miss Susan Jennings. Miss Susan Jennings now you see what I'm doing. Now you see why I can't tell people I love them. In time you will have everything you ever dreamed of Thomas Allred Jr. And your family will be okay. Okay Ms.. Jennings. We got Miss Susan Jennings walking to her car. Talking about Susan we got Miss Eden Reid walking to her car. Now Thomas Allred Jr. Think about Kristen for a minute. Maya. I love you Maya. I'm going to tell you what to do now. Thomas Allred Jr. Go to sleep for half an hour. Send your book off. And dream about the situation that you want to be in. Mr.. Thomas Allred Jr. The situation that I want to be in is with the production team. Smart move Thomas Allred Jr. We got to put Cindy McClain in this book. The kids are going to read this book Thomas Allred Jr. You know they after you. The kids something has to be done about the kids. In perfect time. Now miss Eden Reid. Go ahead and publish our book. This is chapter 2. Of my compilation album. Fighting for success I move on. This album won't be complete without this person. Barack Obama. Thank you from the bottom of my heart. Thomas Allred Jr. He got a lot of potential Miss Susan Jennings. Mr.. Thomas Allred Jr. The future hasn't been written. The future is to come. I offer you this compilation album Ms. Susan Jennings.

Lieutenant Candice what's on the menu for today. Thomas we are having meatballs for dinner. Do y'all ladies hear me. It's all kinds of millionaires that are watching you. Right now I'm eating lunch and dinner with Susan Jennings. If only in my dreaMs.. Fighting for success I move on. I'm through with this book chapter. Cindy McClain stand up. We are counting on you Cindy McClain. To deliver a product for me. He loves Cindy McClain. Yes I do. Fighting for success compilation album is up next. Miss Lucy. I am dedicating this book to you. Thank you Lucy. With all my heart ladies and gentlemen. Fighting for success I move on.

Chapter 2 is complete. Mr.. Thomas Allred Jr. Will you do me the honor of sending the book in with me. This boy is incredible. Send the book in Thomas Allred Jr. It'll be my pleasure Mr.. Thomas Allred Jr. Hey Susan Jennings. Eden and Kristen and Maya know that I love them. He talking about he love you Eden Kristen and Maya. That girl love you too Thomas Allred Jr. Which one. Fighting for success I move on. Send that book in Thomas Allred Jr. That boy figured out what he doing. Yes Mr.. Thomas Allred Jr. Indeed he has.

What the police don't know about you is. That I'm your soulmate. Miss Susan Jennings you must be kidding me. Laughter makes the day go faster Thomas Allred Jr. Now this thing with you and Eden must stop. There is too much work to be done. I know Eden love me Miss Susan Jennings. I'm going to prove it to you Thomas Allred Jr. Behind every book you write. Miss Susan Jennings. Eden Reid is working. Night and day on your books Thomas Allred Jr. Thank you Miss Susan Jennings for clearing that up for me. And Kristen is honestly working. Trying to make a living for herself. Thomas Allred Jr people are watching you. To see if your leg hurts you. When you took that bullet over to Jeana Thomas Allred Jr. It changed people's points of view of you. You are now what we call. A super mogul Thomas Allred Jr. By creating those books and business ideas. Let Susan Jennings talk to you. Yes Mr.. Thomas Allred Jr. By creating those books and business ideas. The security team in Washington is watching you now.

Thomas Allred Jr. I only got two things left to say to you. Before I'll be back on my way. It's a compilation album book. And this is the way the government thanks you for all of your sacrifices. Miss Susan Jennings come back please. Your compilation album is the way through two peace. Miss Susan Jennings. I didn't say nothing about you in my first book. That's because you needed time to build up to me. Miss Susan I have something to say to Thomas Allred Jr. Go ahead Kristen talk to him please. The first time that I saw you boy. It was a woman sunny day. Mr..

Thomas Allred Jr. Get her out of here. I got a compilation book to write. I like you Thomas Allred Jr. What's even better than that. Take compilation off of the book. Fighting for success I move on. Sounds a little bit better. You don't know what you're doing Thomas Allred Jr. But listen we got you. That little voice inside your head saying write the book. You must respect us Thomas Allred Jr. I know that I must respect you Mr.. Thomas Allred Jr. But I have so many questions for you. You can ask me one question Thomas Allred Jr. Will I be able to provide for all the people in my generation? This is what we intend on doing Thomas Allred Jr. This is what we intend on doing Kristen. This is what we intend on doing now Eden Reid. Eden Reid is talking to you. Mr..

Thomas Allred Jr. Your book has me on the edge of my seat Mr. Thomas Allred Jr. It has you on the edge of your seat because. What I'm telling you is real. Exactly Thomas Allred Jr. I got to get Oprah Winfrey a book. I got to get Steve Harvey a book also. Give judge Judy a book Thomas Allred Jr. You are a police officer Thomas Allred Jr. And our people love what you're doing. Write two more paragraphs and then stop. I can't stop Mr.. Thomas Allred Jr. Cause I won't stop. Bad Boy entertainment and So So Def entertainment. It's fixing to call me. I have the music written. Mr.. Thomas Allred Jr. Will bad boy ever call me? Will So So Def ever call me. Write your damn book Thomas Allred Jr. I have got to think about this sh*t. I'm praying for you Mr.. Thomas Allred Jr. Let that boy communicate. Write your damn book Mr.. Thomas Allred Jr. Susan Jennings has been calling you. Thomas Allred Jr Susan Jennings wants you. I got a contract for you Thomas Allred Jr. And it is with Bad Boy records and So So Def records. Miss Susan Jennings I know that I hurt you. Thomas Allred Jr I will give anything for you. We are here sacrificing. What's this. It is fighting for success part 2 Susan Jennings.

You see Ms. Susan Jennings. God told me to help Susan Jennings and her family. And thats was exactly what I did writing these books. Will I see you again Thomas Allred Jr. We about to calm down. What the president got to say about this book. Tell Eden Reid that you miss her Thomas Allred Jr. Let Kristen know that you miss her. Thomas Allred Jr. Be professional. The book is called fighting for success. What do you think of me now Mr.. Thomas Allred Jr. You are on your way to success and Superstardom. Thomas Allred Jr we want you to realize something. This is all part of a big plan. Sat here in Washington. And yes Thomas Allred Jr. You are rich beyond compare. Mr.. Thomas Allred Jr. Thank you for everything that you did for my life. Thank the production team Thomas Allred Jr. For they are who have been up in you. Thank you production team. Cause without you I had no hope. Go to sleep Thomas Allred Jr.

I have a book The write Mr.. Thomas Allred Jr. Talking about your book Thomas Allred Jr. Is a good thing. Miss Susan Jennings. Miss Susan Jennings now you see what I'm doing. Now you see why I can't tell people I love them. In time you will have everything you ever dreamed of Thomas Allred Jr. And your family will be okay. Okay Ms.. Jennings. We got Miss Susan Jennings walking to her car. Talking about Susan we got Miss Eden Reid walking to her car. Now Thomas Allred Jr. Think about Kristen for a minute. Maya. I love you Maya. I'm going to tell you what to do now. Thomas Allred Jr. Go to sleep for half an hour. Send your book off. And dream about the situation that you want to be in. Mr.. Thomas Allred Jr. The situation that I want to be in is with the production team. Smart move Thomas Allred Jr. We got to put Cindy McClain in this book. The kids are going to read this book Thomas Allred Jr. You know they after you. The kids something has to be done about the kids. In perfect time. Now miss Eden Reid. Go ahead and publish our book.

This is chapter 2. Of my compilation album. Fighting for success I move on. This album won't be complete without this person. Barack Obama. Thank you from the bottom of my heart. Thomas Allred Jr. He got a lot of potential Miss Susan Jennings. Mr.. Thomas Allred Jr. The future hasn't been written. The future is to come. I offer you this compilation album Ms. Susan Jennings. Lieutenant Candice what's on the menu for today. Thomas we are having meatballs for dinner. Do y'all ladies hear me. It's all kinds of millionaires that are watching you. Right now I'm eating lunch and dinner with Susan Jennings. If only in my dreaMs.. Fighting for success I move on. I'm through with this book chapter. Cindy McClain stand up. We are counting on you Cindy McClain. To deliver a product for me. He loves Cindy McClain. Yes I do. Fighting for success compilation album is up next. Miss Lucy. I am dedicating this book to you. Thank you Lucy. With all my heart ladies and gentlemen. Fighting for success I move on. Chapter 2 is complete. Mr.. Thomas Allred Jr. Will you do me the honor of sending the book in with me. This boy is incredible. Send the book in Thomas Allred Jr. It'll be my pleasure Mr.. Thomas Allred Jr. Hey Susan Jennings. Eden and Kristen and Maya know that I love them. He talking about he love you Eden Kristen and Maya. That girl love you too Thomas Allred Jr. Which one. Fighting for success I move on. Send that book in Thomas Allred Jr. That boy figured out what he doing. Yes Mr.. Thomas Allred Jr. Indeed he has.

Susan Jennings I'm thinking about running for president. Well Thomas Allred Jr it's about time. I done did all the homework that I had to do.Susan Jennings. I'm thinking about going back in the military. That is exactly what we said Thomas Allred Jr. What kind of military are you in Thomas Allred Jr. Financial economy and growth system. I ain't got but two more days to write this book. How you doing with that book Thomas Allred Jr. The book is coming along nicely. Thomas Allred Jr. You are a talented man why don't you work for Bad Boy entertainment. And So So Def entertainment. I hadn't thought about that Miss Susan Jennings. Do you see what you've done for me Thomas Allred Jr. You helped me out of a situation Thomas Allred Jr. What do you mean I helped you out of a situation. I mean that you saved my life with your books. Don't forget about me Ms.. Susan Jennings. Be careful what you ask for Thomas Allred Jr. Look at the people around us. all we have to do is stay focused on what we're doing at hand with Susan Jennings. You keep writing your book. Thomas Allred Jr the mailman is here. I'm going to get the mail for you Ms.. Susan Jennings. thank you Thomas Allred Jr for helping me down the stairs I'm getting old in my younger days. Thomas Allred Jr I want to speak to you. Yes Mr.. Thomas Allred Jr. Those people out there worship the ground that I walk on Thomas Allred Jr. And Mr.. Thomas Allred Jr. Susan Jennings helped me out of my situation. Your whole community helps you out of your situation Thomas Allred Jr. I want to get back to them. Mr.. Thomas Allred Jr. I want to get back to them. You already have Thomas Allred Jr. By stacking your money account. You are a trillionaire Thomas Allred Jr. The government is in on this. Mr.. Thomas Allred Jr. Thomas Allred Jr. Ain't got a clue how much he's worth. Susan Jennings. You and Miss Barbara deacon. Are the driving force in my life. Barbara deacon. I'm listening Thomas Allred Jr. Remember that you helped me. And remember that you are helping people. Thomas Allred Jr miss Lynn crouch. Thank you for everything miss Lynn crouch. I'm a control myself. Thank the people in Morganton North Carolina. Thank you. Thank the people in Hickory and Newton North Carolina. Thank you. Now get back to work.

Eden I don't know what he wants from me. Talk about Kristen Thomas Allred Jr. Mr.. Thomas Allred Jr. You are the president in my dreaMs.. Put Maya on the phone immediately. Maya I've been thinking about the situation at hand. Could you have been thinking about it Thomas Allred Jr. I'm a man and in the future its me and you Maya. Listen I told you I love you Thomas Allred Jr. Keep working on that book. Kristen I'll do anything for Thomas Allred Jr. Let that girl into our coliseum. Thank you Kristin. You two have my honor and respect. Eden Reid is wanting respect to. Eden I'm proudest of you. For taking care of me. The way that you do. Now ladies. This boy is professional. There's one more person I forgot to mention. I get money and respect goes out to. Lieutenant Candice.

Lieutenant Candice. You know you're a goddamn billionaire. Lieutenant Candice I hope that you realize how much I truly love you. That's enough talking for now Thomas Allred Jr. Captain Frankie. for going above and beyond the call of duty. You are a billionaire. This is my family people. Cindy McClain. I see what you're going through. I am with you Cindy McClain. And Miss Lucy. You are now billionaires. The whole Police department. Is watching this game. I hope I made this book turn up the heat on you people out there thats doing killing. There is a right way and a wrong way. Thomas Allred Jr the people are watching you. I don't care let them watch. There is a right way and a wrong way. And the females have the right way. I recognize you Thomas Allred Jr. Mr.. Thomas Allred Jr. I want to move out of my community. are you sure that you're ready for the next level of success Thomas Allred Jr. I'm ready Mr.. Thomas Allred Jr. Y'all give me Susan Jennings on the phone.

This Susan Jennings. Miss Susan Jennings. Part two of our phase has been completed. How is he. He is the man that you need to hear about Mr.s Susan Jennings.

I want to tell you right now. If he can't handle. Being let go of society's holds on him. We will have no use for him. Take him out of the community right now. Thomas Allred Jr. We decided for you. You and Maya can get married. And you and Kristen can get married. And you and eating can get married. You and lieutenant Candace have a lot of work to do. But you two can get married. Miss Susan Jennings. Thank you for everything. Send your book in Thomas Allred Jr. And let the people decide. Susan Jennings. Fighting for success I move on compilation album. Thomas Allred Jr. Before you end your book think about Susan Jennings. You are a billionaire Miss Susan Jennings. Miss Barbara Deacon you are a billionaire. And miss Lynn crouch you are a billionaire. Thank you Mr.. Thomas Allred Jr. Thomas Allred Jr smoke you one cigarette and get back to working. Right now Susan Jennings is all way up in Washington. A billionaire knows what he's doing Thomas Allred Jr. Thank you President Obama. Now send the book in Thomas Allred Jr. A billionaire to billionaire. Susan Jennings you were right. I do think I'm going to be okay. Fighting for success I move on. To be continued.

Thomas Allred Jr Susan Jennings is wanting you. You paid for your book Thomas Allred Jr. And we're going to let you move out of your house into a luxurious apartment. Miss Susan Jennings I know that black people are known for disrupting the peace. But I won't terrorize you miss Susan Jennings. Do you know the good thing about this Thomas Allred Jr. Miss Susan Jennings all of this is a good thing. That you want terrorize the people Thomas Allred Jr. We are coming to the end of our book. What we going to do is different this time. Thank you Miss Susan Jennings. Get those woman off of the street corners. And somewhere where they can be helped. Write a book Ms.. Susan Jennings. We ought to do that one of these days Thomas Allred Jr. Now I want you to repeat after me. In God we trust. In God we trust Miss Susan Jennings. Your timeline is now complete. TEC tec officer. Officer Reign. Has completed the duties allowed to him. Activate the force field. Miss Susan Jennings. Thomas Allred Jr is a trillionaire. For going back in time. And cleaning the house up. I give to you your wife Kristen Beam. And Maya. Maya this is what dreaMs. are made of. I give to you your wife Eden and Candice. This cannot be real Miss Susan Jennings. I am taking you out of that place that you are in. Your family will live comfortably the rest of your days Thomas Allred Jr. I give to you your wife Cindy McClain. I give to you Thomas Allred Jr. Your wife Nada and Evelyn. I give to you Miss Susan Jennings. 10 billion dollars. Thank you Ms. Susan Jennings. I'm finished with you yet Thomas Allred Jr. I give to you your wife Porsche and Heather and Chelsea. And Molly. And Kay. And Samantha. And Nora. And Elizabeth. And Kathy. And Teresa. I give to you Thomas Allred Jr. All of the money that you have earned. Exactly what we're talkin about. God thank you. I give to you Thomas Allred Jr. Your wife Miss Susan. Ms. Susan Jennings. My daughter will be proud of you. My conclusion to fighting for success I move on. Is that Thomas Allred Jr. Cleans up his attitude. And Susan Jennings cleans up her attitude. Mr.. Thomas

Allred Jr. Thomas. You are forgetting about your mother. A give Charlena Allred. 2.3 thousand trillion dollars. Fighting for success I move on goes down in history. That's what Susan Jennings is. The president of the United States. Mr.. Thomas Allred Jr. Well done my son. I got Thomas Allred Jr. Getting in a limo outside of his house. These pictures are worth a fortune on the black market. Take me out of the hood with you. I'm a sacrifice you for your neighborhood. Thomas Allred Jr. By all means do it. Fighting for success. Send the book right in Thomas Allred Jr. I'd like to thank God. For all of his tender mercies. And I also like to thank all of the people. Who reached in and work with me and made these books possible. Fighting for success is our legacy. I love you Kristen. Thomas Allred Jr has left the building. Fighting for success I move on. The conclusion. Is now people talk about. The End.

CHAPTER 25

I concluded this book without saying to all of you. I got a major contract with Bad Boy entertainment and So So Def entertainment. So I am pleased to announce that I'm getting married. To Maya. As soon as the book is finished. I have to be good to y'all. Being professional. My personality flips and changes. I'm getting ready to flip out over Maya. Have a good evening y'all. That is the best book I've ever written. Fighting for success I move on. Chapter 8. I'm letting you know. That this is chapter 5. And there is more coming. Thomas Allred Jr what about chapter 6 and 7. They are already done and over with. Just girls respect me. And my wife to be Maya. Cause if you don't If I am watching you on camera. That means you're my princess. What we trying to do is. Bad Boy entertainment. And So So Def entertainment. Let them know that I'm out here. As a billionaire once told me.

To be the man. you got to beat the man. Nature Boy Ric flair I am commending you. All kinds of women are watching to see what you look like Thomas Allred Jr. Miss Susan Jennings. It's about time you put Miss Susan Jennings name in the book. What you want to do is. Have a piece of cake Miss Susan Jennings. Chocolate carmel is the cake. Before I get out of here I want to say one more thing. Tell Susan Jennings. To make me a movie star. And we won't stop. Cause we can't stop. Mr.. Thomas Allred Jr. Ive finished my work on the book. I already told you what I would do for you Thomas Allred Jr. What's that. Get a girlfriend ready for you. Have yourself a nice day Mr. Thomas Allred Jr. Mr.. Thomas Allred Jr. Is a serious man. Thomas Allred Jr. Drop the damn book in the mailbox. Miss Susan Jennings ain't got much to say left. I love you Miss Susan Jennings.

From the bottom of my heart. Fighting for success I move on. To the next part in my career. Fighting for success I move on. Acknowledge come from the heart. I want to thank the production team that worked on our books. I want to thank everyone in the production team now personally. Eden Reid without you I couldn't be who I am today. And to the president's up in heaven. May God shine on You everyday of your existence. Fighting for success I move on. I have now finished the book. I knew that boy could do it. Susan Jennings we knew that but could do it. I never got him for a second. Mr.. Thomas Allred Jr. Have a good evening Thomas. I'm fighting for success y'all. Go on and send the book in. I said send it in. That's Mr. Thomas Allred Jr for you.

That boy just doesn't know how to quit. Doesn't know how to quit playing Thomas Allred Jr. What are we going to do with him. We are going to make him stronger and better Thomas Allred Jr. So Maya the contract is on. Thomas Allred Jr realize Kristen Beam want you. There go Kristen right there. We are fighting for success Thomas Allred Jr. That girl said join the cause Kristen. If Amerie is with you. Then the fight it's worth while to me. Thomas Allred Jr. Get rid of that bird in the cage. He is a mockingbird. Kristen want to see your a** now in the living room. This living room. Is a mockingbird headquarters. I communicate to you. My undying loyalty and respect.

I also communicate to you Kristen. My undying truth and respect. Thomas communicate to me and Kristen. Maya and Kristen. The mockingbird won't tell lies Kristen. If that man can keep his self together he can be somebody. What are you saying mockingbird. Kristen is in love with Thomas Allred Jr. That's a good mockingbird. Enough. Go back to the drawing board. Get your foot out my face Kristen. My feet are on the floor Thomas Allred Jr. I'm just playing with you girl. Now I can see how Maya is so protective of you. Let's get one thing straight Kristen Beam. There is a new sheriff in town. And her name is Kristen Beam. But you know what I'm saying Thomas Allred Jr. I'm preparing to launch a full frontal strike against headquarters. This is headquarters. So you know I'm not playing around with you. Eden Reid is my commanding officer in charge. You got to be playing with me.

No my dear. This is your dream Thomas Allred Jr. Miss Susan Jennings. Has you where she wants you. Thomas your movie is about to take off. Y'all they killed Jeana Allred. And shot me. For protecting was rightfully mine. I realize that you are hurting Thomas Allred Jr. Is this a dream Maya. It's not a dream Thomas Allred Jr. This is your movie. Journey To success the mockingbird. In stores everywhere. You know what people say about you. Thomas Allred Jr your situation is getting better.

I want you to stop dreaming and write the book. But I thought this was a movie coming out. The movie is of your book. Thank you Maya Kristen and Eden. Thomas Allred Jr get back to working on that book. How could they of taking her life away from her. She means the world to me. Out of all of the women this one God made especially for me. They killed my girl. And they shot me. I'm going to get me a bird. The mockingbird is professional. Tell the mockingbird how to do things and he does it. Later on Kristen and Maya. Showed Eden all-over headquarters. What are concocted a plan. Miss Susan Jennings. We need lieutenant Candace in this book. And lieutenant Evelyn. Lieutenant Candis and lieutenant Evelyn in this book. Thats a nice bird you have there Thomas Allred Jr. Does he say anything else. Thomas Allred Jr don't mess with me write your book. I'm working on it Eden. Eden Reid that is y'all. Welcome to headquarters lieutenant Candis and lieutenant Evelyn. What a nice place you have here Thomas Allred Jr. Thomas Allred Jr has a nice place. Thomas. Excuse me ladies for a second. I have to use the restroom. Thomas get your a** over here this instant. Look at me. I said look at me in the mirror Thomas Allred Jr. Mr.. Thomas Allred Jr. They are starting to figure out the mockingbird is with you. The mockingbird is with you Thomas Allred Jr. What kind of story is this. An evil plot story. You see the ring on Kristen's hand Thomas Allred Jr. That is your engagement ring. Have her to put her hand on the mirror Thomas Allred Jr. And the mockingbird will disappear. Kristen can you come in here for a second. Yes Thomas Allred Jr what is it. Could you touch the mirror for a second with your ring hand. Anything for you Thomas Allred Jr. When Kristen touched the mirror. Mr.. Thomas Allred Jr. Appeared. Back to the living area. What happened to the bird. Everyone wondered. I lost someone dear to me. You sound different Thomas Allred Jr. I am more mature Kristen since you gave me my ring back. I need your undying respect. Everybody hear the mockingbird is Mr.. Thomas Allred Jr. What kind of magic trick is this Thomas Allred Jr. Working on the book. I figured out something.

That you and me belong together Kristen. That you and me belong together Maya. That you and me belong together Candice. That you and me belong together Evelyn. That you and me belong together Eden. This is my family Thomas Allred Jr. That is Mr.. Thomas Allred Jr. You got the power in your ring. Thomas Allred Jr. Yes Mr.. Thomas Allred Jr. Walk through the house with Kristen. Candice Maya Eden and Evelyn. Mr.. Thomas Allred Jr. Eden and Maya can hear you Mr. Thomas Allred Jr. Thomas. Write you another page to your book Thomas. The lights went out.

That's a smart motherf*cker. Thomas Allred Jr can you hear me. Close your mouth Kristen. The mockingbird is in his somewhere. Oh sh*t I'm getting scared. I'm getting scared. Who said that. Who said that. All right turn on the lights Thomas Allred Jr this isn't funny. Alright turn on the lights Thomas this isn't funny. Candice. Don't say the book is halfway finished. Keep on writing Thomas Allred Jr. And the mockingbird circled the room. Looking for his prey. And wanting the ring back. The book is not making sense Thomas Allred Jr. That's because every sister killed my wife. Jeana Allred. I have been trapped in my feelings. I'm alone y'all inside of a gla** jar. And all I can do is cry inside. Because no woman sees me. That's a great story Thomas Allred Jr. You should give that story. Thomas Allred Jr you really miss your girlfriend don't you. With everything in my life. You see I'm in pain. But somehow it feels like energy. Inside of my heart. I can't breathe ladies. Look how they did you. The mockingbird tells no lies. Thomas Allred Jr are you writing this down. All of it Evelyn. I'm just so alone right now. Give me a piece of paper Thomas Allred Jr. Evelyn is Thomas Allred Jr. I need you to remember this inside of your book. Tell Jeana Allred that you love her. Jeana Allred I love you so much honey. Do you see what we're dealing with here Evelyn. Thomas Allred is a genius. But he is so hurt inside. That he thinks he's in a gla** jar with a mockingbird. I can't get my feelings out. Thomas. The feelings that Thomas Allred Jr felt for Jeana Allred. They were genuine feelings. And as Thomas wrote his books. Done with the mockingbird at the window. Of his room. And he was all alone writing to Jeana. To tell her I'm sorry and I love you. Journey To success the mockingbird. The end.

Somehow thinking to myself. These books and movies aren't enough. I need something that I can sink my teeth into. The autobiography of Thomas Allred Jr. That I can sink my teeth into. My book starts off like this. Realize you are going to need me. Thomas Allred Jr. And you know that you love me Thomas Allred Jr. Thomas Allred Jr you been talkin to me for close to 10 years now. Don't get to be a strange now that you have made something out of yourself. Jeana Allred. Sweetheart you are not here with me. I am here Thomas Allred Jr. I'm in your heart. Jeana Allred they killed you. When I was just a young man.

They shot me Jeana Allred because of you. Some how you have to forget about the past and think about the future Thomas Allred Jr. This is your autobiography of Thomas Allred Jr. Now tell the story that you want to tell me. How everybody gave up on you Thomas Allred Jr. And you had nowhere to go but to your book. Listen to me Thomas Allred Jr. And listen to me well. Eden Reid is your publicist. I want you to put together a book that she can be proud of. Thomas Allred Jr. Thomas Allred Jr your book report is about due in.

I'm sitting right here talkin to Jeana Allred. There is no one with you Thomas Allred Jr. Thank you I appreciate you Kristen Beam. Quit wasting time Thomas Allred Jr. Girl if we talkin. Say something to me then. I am always here with you Thomas Allred Jr. I am with you also Jeana Allred. I am saying. Your friendship means the world to me Thomas Allred Jr. Happy birthday Jeana Allred. As I eased back into my chair. A sense of respect came over me. You might have killed my girl. But there's a part of her that's everlasting in me. Melissa is online 2. How is your book coming along Thomas Allred Jr. It is to be well as expected. Melissa I thank you for looking out for me before I had anything. It was my pleasure Thomas Allred Jr. Thomas Allred Jr you got a book report to finish in 2 business days. But I keep thinking about my past Shontel. It's a whole new world out there. You got to make some sense Thomas Allred Jr. Don't you realize that you can have anything that you need Thomas Allred Jr. Melissa I'm trying to reach a audience of a great magnitude. All you got to do is just dream Thomas Allred Jr. All you got to do is just dream Melissa.

Thomas Allred Jr that book report is due on my desk in 2 business days if you care about me you'll get that book to me immediately. Thank you Eden Reid for being my book publicist. I need a book right fast. I need a book right fast Thomas Allred Jr. I got the name of this book. Its the autobiography of Thomas Allred Jr. And Jeana Allred. Straighten your book out at the top. Thomas Allred Jr you do realize that everything you do will change the future of your life. I'm betting on it to happen. All kind of females are looking at you. All kind of men are looking at you. So what can I do to make you happy Jeana Allred. Write your book. I heard what you said Thomas Allred Jr. How I couldn't be without you. See God has a plan for you Jeana Allred. They shot me. Baby I realize that's why I'm here. To right the wrongs in your life. Melissa may I talk to you. I need you to work on our success novel. And girl I want from you. Your hand in marriage. I heard that jeana was telling him what to do from the after life. Thomas Allred Jr Ill do anything for you

Communicate our love to the people. Right now Jeana Allred. Right now Thomas Allred Jr. When I was 18 years old I had a girlfriend. When jeana was old enough I dated her. She was only four years younger than me. And a police officer. All kinds of bulsh*t happened to us. How many times did that girl save your life Thomas Allred Jr. I'm counting four times. Get ready for the autobiography of Thomas Allred Jr and Jeana Allred. We got you several pages Eden Reid. Thomas Allred Jr sit down and write your book Thomas Allred Jr. I'm a business ideas. For a company called InventHelp. And then I went to a company called Davidson inventions. And made business ideas. 2000 business ideas later. I have written eight books. About Jeana Allred and I.

Taking over the community. My books are heavy y'all. So be careful what you wish for when you read my books. In time Jeana Allred will be known to everyone. Thank you Thomas Allred Jr. Girl I'm just saying to you that. I'm doing my best. To help you realize that I care about you. I sit at home by myself. Sometimes praying to myself. I can't believe that you're gone Jeana Allred. I'm So into what I'm doing. That I can't believe that you're gone Jeana Allred. Keep going with your book Thomas Allred Jr. I want you to see what I'm getting ready to become Jeana Allred. I realize that you love me Thomas Allred Jr. But you have to keep your head up and write those books.

Now give me a paragraph on how much you love me Thomas Allred Jr. You and me Jeana Allred. Always and forever. Honey you are so beautiful. I just want you to realize something. What happened to you wasn't your fault. Thomas Allred Jr it wasn't anybody's fault but the person who did this to me. I'm telling you to Jeana Allred .That I will never stop trying. To make a good life for us. Stop talking to yourself Thomas Allred Jr. I need a girl. Kristen Beam. What you need to do is write over half of your book Thomas Allred Jr. I care about you Kristen Beam. And I know you do. Send Maya in here one minute. Maya come and speak to Kristen Beam. Excuse me Mya but you're going to have to. Take care of Thomas Allred Jr for me. Our opportunity is coming. And Maya with Thomas Allred Jr. We can get you anything that you need. All kinds of females are watching you Thomas Allred Jr. Carry yourself like a businessman. Jeana Allred. Yes honey. Take me out of the hood. You must prove yourself to me Thomas Allred Jr. Girl what you want me to do Jeana Allred .write your music for at least Bad boys entertainment. And So So Def entertainment. The music has been written Thomas Allred Jr. I know Jeana

Allred. Jeana Allred help me. I can't do this without you. I am here for you Thomas Allred Jr. I apologize that they hurt you. Thomas Allred Jr. People are going to hurt you. But you have to realize one thing on your journey. That I have never left you. Thomas Allred Jr I'd give anything to be back with you. Write your book Thomas Allred Jr. Somebody help me. Lieutenant Candice. I got love for you lieutenant Candice. You the right man for the job Thomas Allred Jr. What job are we talkin about. Think about it Thomas Allred Jr. The president will see you now. That is the end of chapter #1. have sense enough Thomas Allred Jr to keep writing. Yes Jeana Allred. Thomas Allred Jr you making me see that you need me. Just write your book down and let the world see it. For who you really is Thomas Allred Jr. Jeana Allred I miss your attitude Jeana Allred. Thomas Allred Jr. You my best friend I ever had Jeana Allred. Tell Thomas Allred Jr the book needs to be on my desk by Wednesday morning. Yes sir Captain Frankie. I told you I would take care of you Thomas Allred Jr. Yes sir Captain Frankie. All of the people thank you for what you're doing Thomas Allred Jr. I'm going to get my book and give it to you Captain Frankie. For protecting me even when I was doing wrong. Get back to working on that book. Thomas Allred Jr deserves a chance Frankie. Yes Elizabeth. Thank you for your support Captain Frankie. What Jeana Allred didn't realize is that. The world already knew what it happened to her. And they knew what it happened to me as well. Take out your pencils. We are going to write at least two more pages. Eden Reid wants this book on her desk immediately.Cindy McClain is making phone calls to get the deal complete. Would I tell you Thomas Allred Jr. People would help you if you asked him to. Jeana Allred.

I love you. And I love you too Thomas Allred Jr. Thomas Allred Jr everybody is waiting for you in the kitchen. Surprise. Happy anniversary Kristen and Thomas Allred Jr. Kristen I know my book is about you. But you are everything to me as Jeana Allred was. I thank God for this day Kristen Beam. Kristen Beam I ask you to be my wife again. Go ahead Thomas Allred Jr tell the rest of the story. As the years went pa**. I talked to Jeana Allred. Listen girls. Take me out of the community. Is what I said. All of a sudden. It didn't hurt so bad and everything started to make sense. I know that you don't believe me. But people love that girl because she. Stood her ground to the very last end. 2 cups up. To the one I love the most in this whole wide world. Jeana Allred.

Thomas Allred Jr this is a good book. I think so. Can I count on you to do your job and keep writing. Yes Miss Lucy You can count on Me. I published your book Thomas Allred Jr. Because it has a real meaning to it. Once again I'm sorry about your wife and girlfriend Jeana Allred. I'm telling you Jeana Allred can hear you Thomas Allred Jr. You recognize your book is going overseas Thomas Allred Jr. Be prepared for a life-changing event to happen. I give my all to the community. 6 months later. We still haven't published your book. We are going to publish it when the time is right. I can see myself as a millionaire. Then keep reading your book Thomas Allred Jr. I want your book on my table. Miss Lucy wants your book Thomas Allred Jr. Mya is getting professional. Look at this. Everybody is going to get your book Thomas Allred Jr. Maybe the famous people a get to read it. Excuse me a second. Thomas I have got to be professional. Ashley hold yourself together. Now tell me what happened to you. This book is published in five countries. You are the number one Arthur in 17 countries. Only 17 countries. The first week I'm showing reports. Of 2 billion dollars. And that makes you famous Thomas Allred Jr. Listen to me. All you got to do is write your book down Thomas Allred Jr. Jeana Allred would be proud of you. Girl ready to take this kind of book to the next level. I hear you Melissa. You going to have to stop me Kristen Beam. Stop you from what what is she saying Thomas Allred Jr. We are reaching the Stars Kristen Beam. Happy anniversary. Keep on writing that book Thomas Allred Jr. Jeana Allred. I want you to realize something. That I care for you. Be professional Thomas Allred Jr. Do you want to know my secret. My secret is how much love I have inside for you and everyone Jeana Allred. My book is an autobiography. Of Thomas Allred Jr and Jeana Allred. My business is almost done and complete. Next anniversary. I'm going to talk to you the same way I did this anniversary Jeana Allred. Give it up for Jeana Allred. For saving my life. Thomas Allred Jr. Who do you think the music is for. I am with Bad Boy entertainment. And So So Def entertainment . And this is the autobiography of Thomas Allred Jr and Jeana Allred. Coming to an end. Eden Reid. How can I prove myself to you. Put that book on my desk right now Thomas Allred Jr. As you wish Eden Reid. You better hurry the f*ck up. Eden Reid you say such beautiful things. That's all for me. Thomas Allred Jr and Jeana Allred. Has left the building

Well here we go Miss Susan Jennings. Don't play with them Thomas Allred Jr. Stick and move just cause you was as I taught you. This is fighting for vengeance a true life story.There it is Thomas Allred Jr. A success latter. I know that Susan Jennings. Let your pain go. I'm asking you Thomas Allred Jr. In the book I will let my pain Go Ms. Susan Jennings. Well tell the story house supposed to be told. See you in the beginning Miss Susan Jennings I didn't have much. I worked at pet dairy. Trying to make a living for myself and Jeana Allred. I started off walking in the rain to get to work. And sometimes the snow Ms. Susan Jennings. My whole neighborhood surrounding me. Walking home one night. You got to appreciate it Thomas Allred Jr. Susan Jennings. I took a bullet saving someone's life. Girl I want to teach you that. Everything happens for a reason. What you see ain't what you get Susan Jennings. And I say this because. The latter to success Susan Jennings. Is built on honesty. Your book is honesty Thomas Allred Jr. I've recuperated one year and I had Jeana Allred helping me. We really fell in love with each other. I'm going to make sure that everybody realizes that Jeana Allred is my wife. I struggled up and down the street. With just me and the Lord to talk to. Susan Jennings is online one

Thomas Allred Jr. That phone calls for me. I told myself Susan Jennings. Barely able to stand on my own two feet. The reason is for the phone call was. To help me realize. That Susan Jennings was my lawyer and best friend. I'm going to get myself together Thomas Allred Jr. Talk to your friend Susan Jennings. Jeana Allred asked me. While working in the kitchen. Thomas Allred Jr people want to hear your story. Susan Jennings online 2. So much bulsh*t was happening. That I couldn't think. I appreciate you coming out there to save me the man said to me. In my hospital room. As you realize. I am a police officer. I said to the person laying next to me in the hospital. The hospital isn't safe. So I went home. That's enough Thomas Allred Jr. I got you some telephone calls to make. Susan Jennings was saying to Thomas Allred Jr. I am Jeana Allred. And this is my story. Thomas Allred Jr came home from the hospital. And he couldn't believe his eyes when he saw me. It was like true love all over again. Take me a shower Jeana Allred Thomas Allred Jr said to me. I do anything for you Mr. Allred Jr. Realize Thomas Allred Jr. That you and me are partners. I keep telling myself. Jeana Allred she meant what she said about our partnership. I appreciate what you're doing for me Jeana Allred. I told her as I came through the door. Now a couple weeks had pa**ed. And Jeana Allred and I had grown even closer. A couple weeks past. And Thomas Allred Jr was back on his feet. all the phone calls are from the neighborhood wanting to know if you can walk yet Thomas Allred Jr. Tell them thank you I'm just realizing something. It's just that Jeana Allred I love you. I love you too Thomas Allred Jr. I begin writing a book. Alongside of Jeana Allred. We called that book The seven moons. Actually we called that book the five moons.

Thomas Allred Jr. Yes Jeana Allred honey just like you said. Take your break if you want to. Them white people started to give me medicine. I'm a police officer I will pay for my medicine I thought. They help me out. With therapy to cope with it happened to me. Listen Thomas Allred Jr. I know them white people helped you out. And I appreciate you telling the story Thomas Allred Jr. But one thing is. The killed Jeana Allred. Susan Jennings they did kill Jeana Allred. But I want you to know something. That I'm just fighting for vengeance. As you were Thomas Allred Jr. Though physical therapy. Physical therapy Thomas Allred Jr. Jeana Allred and I were able to get me back on my feet to where I can work again. That man stayed in the hospital almost one week. This is Jeana Allred talking to you. I got your a** a book Thomas Allred Jr. Listen to me Thomas Allred Jr. All I'm saying is to you. Don't ever leave me Thomas Allred Jr. I promise you Jeana Allred I will never leave you. They shot me in my legs in my leg Jeana Allred. I'm a police officer Thomas Allred Jr. I appreciate you helping my book. Realize that it take more than Fame to write this book Thomas Allred Jr. What does it take Jeana Allred. It took me courage to stand up for myself. B*tches shot you Jeana Allred. Them b*tches shot me. Only they took a part of me that I can never get back again. What part did they take Thomas Allred Jr. Jeana Allred they took you. Miss Susan Jennings online 3.

Thomas Allred Jr I want you to realize something. I'm still here with you Thomas Allred Jr. It's only that you can't see me. I can hear you Jeana Allred. take a break and get up and smoke a cigarette. As you wish Jeana Allred. That boy is telling the truth. He is not too faced it. Let Susan Jennings read the book. Thomas Allred Jr I ordered you to take a break. I'm back from my break Jeana Allred. As a police officer. I am sworn to uphold the law. You are my wife Jeana Allred. And I will protect you in this life and the next. This is what I do to protect you. I am going to let the world know that you are a kind and sweet person. And I'll be mature. In discovering you. For who you are. My soulmate. My only true love. Now Thomas Allred Jr didn't realize that I was listening to him. As The story begin to unravel. All that this story needs. Is it good topic. Thomas Allred Jr is a police officer. And Jeana Allred was a police officer before she died. Ain't no way in the world that should have happened. Just calm down a minute Thomas Allred Jr. You telling me to come down. But they just killed my wife. Someone has to pay for this. We took Thomas Allred Jr to a medical clinic. In where he could cope with his probleMs.. I'm going to make business ideas Miss Susan Jennings. You can meet business ideas if you want to. I'm going to make business ideas to safeguard the women and children of these communities. That sounds like a good idea Thomas Allred Jr. How has everything been since Jeana Allred died. Realize Thomas Allred Jr. That it wasn't your fault. They kidnapping my family.Ms. Susan Jennings. I'm writing this book called fighting for desire. Don't say anything about writing a book Thomas Allred Jr. You hear me Thomas Allred Jr. I hear you Miss Susan Jennings. What we going to do is. Take you out of the community. Now what Ms. Susan Jennings. In time Thomas Allred Jr. You will begin to get your life back. Take your time and write the book Thomas Allred Jr. That's all you got to do. Jeana Allred I love you. Don't be scared Thomas Allred Jr. Keep writing your book. And I miss you so very much. You got some therapy to go through. But we are going to take care of you. God had to be on his side. I can't believe it. It's a rainbow outside the window. Fighting for vengeance Jeana Allred and Thomas Allred Jr a true story. That book will be called .Realize Thomas Allred Jr. What you doing has an impact on your community. I won't rest until I get Jeana Allreds killer behind bars. Fighting for vengeance is a story. Of what I've been through. We appreciate you helping us Ms. Susan Jennings. Make a movie out of it. Now take your time. Once upon a Time. Thank you Ms. Jeana Allred. And Thomas Allred Jr. For being so beautiful to me. I am Miss Susan Jennings. And this is fighting for vengeance Jeana Allred and Thomas Allred Jr a true story.

Thank you Thomas Allred Jr. I'm saying Susan Jennings. This is fighting for vengeance my book 2.Jeana Allred and Thomas Allred Jr. Full proof plan. Going down Miss Susan Jennings. Now what I want you to do is stick and move like I told you Thomas Allred Jr. That's right Susan Jennings. Stick and move. My book started off in a town called Hickory. Me and Thomas Allred Jr. Wanted to make a baby. but everybody was against us for some odd reason that hand. Take your time and just write that book Jeana Allred. 2 days after the celebration. Of Thomas Allred Jr and I being together. There was a knock at the front door. Jamario Allred. Make yourself at home Jeana Allred said to him. I want to be professional. And I don't know if I can tell you this story. See jamario put people after me. But that's a long ways to go. Damn straight it's a long way to go. They was after Jeana Allred. And me Thomas Allred Jr. I don't know the reasons. Let's get to it. Take your time Ms. Susan Jennings. You see how much respect I got for you. In my professional career Thomas Allred Jr. You are first cla** Thomas Allred Jr. Now Jeana Allred and I. Had a bank account. Snatched away from us. By one of my sisters. Tammy Connelly. And we were forced to stay with her Tammy Connelly. Cleaning up the house at 3 in the morning. Just to live safely from danger. But Jeana Allred and I don't care. We were in love. People what did I tell you. Did God has a purpose for us all. In a bank account. That is shocking to the imagination. Damn right I cussed her out. Tammy Connelly would say. Talking to Jeana Allred. I'll cuss you out to if you want me to. Thomas Allred Jr. Be careful with your words. If Jeana Allred we're only here today. Thomas Allred Jr to tell the truth. Tammy Connelly apologizes for the way she treated you and Jeana Allred. That's a little too late for this. Full proof plan is. Imma stack this bread up. And give back to the community that destroyed me. His attitude is professional.

Let's give him his money in a bank account. You know you Thomas Allred Jr. when you can knock on a females door and she answers for you. But the story hasn't been straight. Jeana Allred was murdered. That destroyed my life apart. I had nowhere to turn. No one to turn to. Accept my mama's house. Where they rode by shooting through the windows. I'm telling yall God had to be on my side. Because this is an amazing true story. I hope this medicine does me right. As the story takes place listen Thomas Allred Jr. If Jeana Allred loved you where's the ring. Jeana Allred pawned her wedding ring to bail me out of jail. For something I wouldn't recall. After me being through what I've been through. Jeana Allred has the right to be upset at me.

I place my hands on Jeana Allred y'all. In frustration thinking that I was going to die. Jeana Allred saved my life. But keeping me in the house. The night I was supposed to be killed. I've been through all sorts of things. Jeana Allred slept in a abandoned apartment and on the ground with me a few nights. Because we didn't have nowhere to live. They killed her. And I can't blame no one but me. I should have been better. I should have did better. But I was only 19. With a gunshot wound to the leg. And the whole neighborhood was against us. Even some of my family members. I remember saying that. I would never join a gang. As I talked to Jeana Allred. Jeana Allred was a police officer. And I am a police officer. Fighting for vengeance Jeana Allred and Thomas Allred Jr Full proof plan. Is dedicated to Jeana

Allred and her family. With all the love inside I love Jeana Allred. She was my first and very last love. To the end. I am Thomas Allred Jr. You know Miss Susan Jennings. Is stranger things work theMs.elf out. What's strange is Thomas Allred Jr. Fighting for success is a sequel. What do you mean Miss Susan Jennings. Keep professional Thomas Allred Jr you want people to hear you. And that's exactly what I did. I'm going to keep it professional. And tell how you took our money. Stole her life from me. And shot me when I was just a kid. I'mma tell everybody. That God is the only reason I lived. And he took Jeana Allred home with him. One Life to live. Equals out to be people. A journey of a lifetime. I hear you Thomas Allred Jr. Fighting for vengeance. Call Susan Jennings. I wrote the story for weak people. Who are going through things. Let love guide you. And hold on to that lady with all your heart. Now girls. We know that we're not perfect. We try to do our best. As the men in your family's. Fighting for vengeance Jeana Allred and Thomas Allred Jr. Full proof plan. We never gave up. Everybody tell Jeana Allred happy birthday. In God we trust. Everything will be alright. If we try. Susan Jennings is crying like a mutha f*cker. Susan Jennings I just want to know what you're crying for. They took her away from you Thomas Allred Jr and she was a police officer. The shot your leg Thomas Allred Jr. And still am here getting vengeance. No longer will you stand alone Thomas Allred Jr. You got to be professional Thomas Allred Jr. I put the Navy in this one.

To Thomas Allred Jr y'all. Thomas Allred Jr all kinds of females are looking at you. There's only one female for me. That is Kristen Beam. You had sense enough to tell me that the females were watching me. For that Miss Susan Jennings. I give you this award. You are my best friend ever. Fighting for vengeance Jeana Allred and Thomas Allred Jr. Full proof plan. Let's hear It for Ms. Susan Jennings. Take a bow Miss Susan Jennings. Fighting for vengeance is now complete Thomas Allred Jr. Help me realize Jeana Allred is ok Ms. Susan Jennings. Listen Thomas Allred Jr I hear what you doing. I am Jeana Allred. And I'm okay. Fighting for vengeance Jeana Allred and Thomas Allred Jr. It's a sacrifice from each one of us. That we made Thomas Allred Jr. Professionals are in our corner. I like the way you are doing this. Fighting for vengeance professionally. It's a wrap. Fighting for vengeance Jeana Allred and Thomas Allred Jr. The journey is completed. Right now you got a bank account Thomas Allred Jr. 655 million dollars. Now that's something to be proud about. Thank you Ms. Susan Jennings. For everything under the sun Thomas Allred Jr.

Thomas Allred Jr make sure that cigarettes out. I got to agree with you miss Susan Jennings. This is fighting for vengeance excellence Thomas Allred Jr. Don't forget about Jeana Allred Thomas Allred Jr. Don't forget about her. How can I forget about us she's my baby. Miss Susan Jennings. Thomas Allred Jr we have Kristen online 2. Susan Jennings online one. Kristen Beam how come whenever I need you you always there for me. It's because I love you and you got the eye of the tiger with me. Thomas Allred Jr. That book must be a struggle. I'm writing it as fast as I can Kristen Beam. Thomas Allred Jr you're going to get in trouble for this. I just want you to know Kristen Beam that I laugh in the face of trouble. Okay Lion King jr. But seriously Thomas Allred Jr. What do you think your books is worth after the income taxes come. About 650 million dollars. Give or take a few pennies. Thomas Allred Jr you know our family is waiting on your first book to get published. You got Susan Jennings on line one Thomas Allred Jr. Susan Jennings Thomas Allred Jr. Miss Susan I had to think about our last conversation. The last conversation was you and Jeana Allred. Thomas Allred Jr. Turning back to Kristen Beam. honey I love you but I got to go right now I'm on the phone with Miss Susan Jennings. Thomas Allred Jr. You know Miss Susan Jennings work for Bad Boy entertainment. And So So Def entertainment. Treat her like you're somebody. I am somebody Kristen Beam. I know that Thomas Allred Jr. Just act appropriately. Honey we will do that. Bad Boy entertainment Susan Jennings. This is Bad Boy entertainment Susan Jennings speaking to you. You got me at hello Miss Susan Jennings. Thomas Allred Jr be careful what you wish for. Bad Boy entertainment and So So Def entertainment got a thing for you. Only if Jeana Allred where here. You need to talk to Susan Jennings Thomas Allred Jr. In my thoughts i heard her say this. I have an idea Miss Susan Jennings.

Thomas I want you to be real with that girl named Kristen Beam. Miss Susan Jennings you know that I always be real. Wake up Thomas Allred Jr you having a nightmare. Miss Susan Jennings you're funny you make me laugh. I see that you're on your p's and apples Thomas Allred Jr. I cross the t's and Dot the i's Miss Susan Jennings. Your contract is including Jeana Allred in it Thomas Allred Jr. I know that's right Miss Susan Jennings. Thomas Allred Jr beware of the consequences if you don't live up to the deal. What consequences is it misses Susan Jennings. If you don't live up to the deal. You won't be with Bad Boy entertainment or So So Def entertainment anymore. Get the contract out and see if he yourself. Miss Susan Jennings that's exactly what it says.

But I still get paid don't I miss Susan Jennings. Get his contract Kristen Beam. See your contract simply States Thomas Allred Jr. You are to write that book Susan Jennings. Susan Jennings. I'm working on that book right now. Thomas Allred Jr. As you know people are hoping that you succeed. If Jeana Allred where watching me. Sit down in the chair and speak to Jeana Allred Thomas Allred Jr. This book of ours. Is in equal standing. Too Bad Boy records and So So Def records. Furthermore Thomas Allred Jr. You got to write your music. Because without them two together. Your contract is none and void. People will tell you that you're not with bad boy entertainment. And So So Def entertainment. But the judges say to you. Be professional Thomas Allred Jr. So to congratulate you on the success of your new book. Fighting for vengeance excellence Jeana Allred and Thomas Allred Jr. Thank you Thomas Allred Jr. On a job well done. See a miracle can happen. If you are with

Bad Boy entertainment. And So So Def entertainment. But Kristen Beam I'm not with So So Def entertainment. Yes you are. As of this moment here Kristen Beam. I walked around to see Miss Susan Jennings face. Bad Boy entertainment. And so so Def entertainment. What's the two of you Kristen Beam and Thomas Allred Jr. Baby it's just like we dreamed about. Hurry up and finish that book so I can. See my dreaMs. come true Thomas Allred Jr. People are never going to believe this. I am Kristen Beam. And I just got a contract with Bad Boy entertainment. And So So Def entertainment. They can't f*ck with you. Kristen Beam. I'll do anything for you Thomas Allred Jr. Realize that book is the only thing keeping you two together. So make it worth her while Thomas Allred Jr. He don't know Kristen can hear him. That's a damn shame. To Thomas Allred Jr that's just a book that he's writing. Spell your name Kristen Beam. Bad Boy entertainment is my name. And So So Def entertainment is my birthright. Thomas Allred Jr I'm trying to tell you something before I leave. You are with So So Def entertainment. And Bad Boy entertainment. Your book will be published immediately.There is somebody who is helping me. The production team Thomas Allred Jr. Yall I want to thank y'all for everything. Look at Susan Jennings do you Thomas Allred Jr. Superman done took over our businesses. So your a** Thomas Allred Jr you want to be professional. Than act like you the man who you say you are. Jeana Allred.

I'm most proud of you miss Susan Jennings. For standing up for someone who had nobody. We put Jeana Allred on our contract. To show the appreciation that we have for her and her life. Without further ado. Thomas Allred Jr. And Kristen Beam. That boy is writing books. Don't be scared Kristen Beam. I am not I'm with Bad Boy entertainment. And So So Def entertainment. that is one thing Susan Jennings that I have to ask you. By the way Superman. Thank you for everything Thomas Allred Jr. How does overtime look on this weekend's check miss Susan Jennings. I tell you one thing Ms. Susan Jennings. Whatever I got to do work will come first. The contract is yours and Kristen BeaMs. Thomas Allred Jr. You are Superman I'm giving you what you want Thomas Allred Jr.

Miss Susan Jennings. Yes Thomas Allred Jr. I want to ask you a question and I want the truth Miss Susan Jennings. When you are fighting for vengeance excellence. Miss Susan Jennings who am I talking about. You are talking about Bad Boy entertainment. And So So Def entertainment. Mr. Thomas Allred Jr. I get the story from my heart Miss Susan Jennings. Keep working. Your riches will come to you as we turn over the next chapter. And Susan Jennings said to me which is surprise me. Jeana Allred is inspiration for the book. Fighting for vengeance excellence Jeana Allred and Thomas Allred Jr. Make the last statement Thomas Allred Jr. Ask her to marry you Thomas Allred Jr. Kristen Beam I love yo a** so damn much. Be my wife Kristen Beam. This how you know he wrote the book out there. I love you Thomas Allred Jr this it. There are no motherf*cking rules to Bad Boy entertainment. The same as with So So Def entertainment. Kristen Beam. Take us out of here Kristen

Beam. This is Bad Boy entertainment. And So So Def entertainment. Where dreaMs. come true. Thomas Allred Jr send that book in right now. Keep holding your position. Fighting for vengeance excellence Jeana Allred and Thomas Allred Jr. We can't stop. Because we won't stop. Miss Susan Jennings.here go another one for the railroads. Listen. Susan Jennings has already gone Thomas Allred Jr. You got Susan on the other line. Thomas Allred Jr I need you to get me a phone card please. Girl i ain't your daddy. But I will get you a phone card. If you answer a question for me Susan. Who are you with. Bad Boy entertainment. And So So Def entertainment. There is a possibility that will succeed. And we won't stop Thomas Allred Jr. Because we can't stop. I got to get that money to Susan. Excuse me Thomas Allred Jr. I'm listening Thomas Allred Jr. Put Susan Jennings online 2. Thank you for your support Thomas Allred Jr. Jeana Allred would have been proud of you. Tell Susan Jennings. We are Bad Boy entertainment. And So So Def entertainment. Thomas Eden Reid wants to speak to you. Put Eden Reid online 3. I'm trying to welcome you to professionalism Thomas Allred Jr. As you think about this. I want you to sign your contract Thomas Allred Jr. That boy has a contract. Whatever you think about me people. It's going down Ms. Susan Jennings. Remember I told you to stick and move baby. Float like a butterfly sting like a big hornet. The only thing I can say is. We miss Jeana Allred. Thomas Allred Jr. Be professional Thomas Allred Jr. And write your book like I told you. All the people have got love for you Thomas Allred Jr. This is your celebration. Of professionalism Thomas Allred Jr. Michelle needs to see you. K - Michelle. I'm with So So Def and Bad Boy entertainment. The question here is Thomas Allred Jr. Are you man enough to handle your responsibilities. We won't stop. Because we can't stop K- Michelle. Tell Kristen Beam to get in there. I wanted you to meet somebody. K Michelle. I wanted you to meet Thomas Allred Jr. Kristen Beam is talking to K - Michelle. Your attitude is remarkable k Michelle. I'm just glad that you're with Bad Boy entertainment Kristen Beam. And So So Def entertainment. Listen to me Thomas Allred Jr. Yes Miss Eden Reid. Take a load off your feet. You are now sitting in the bosses seat. I want you to know that I love you Thomas Allred Jr. I love you too Miss Eden Reid. Fighting for vengeance excellence is going to be a number one book. Y'all take the book from Thomas Allred Jr. Keep it going Thomas Allred Jr. That girl really loves you. You need to thank Jeana Allred Thomas Allred Jr. Thank you Jeana Allred for everything you have done for me and sweetheart I want you to realize something. And we won't stop. Because we can't stop.

You done started this mess you better ended Thomas Allred Jr. Jeana Allred. Damn right I'm going to end it. Jeana Allred where the coin stops nobody knows. What do you mean Thomas Allred Jr. I mean that I have you. I have your best interest at heart. You have my best interest at heart. I have your best interest at heart. Thomas Allred Jr. Now write the book about me. Thomas Allred Jr. Jeana Allred. I'm the luckiest man on the planet. Jeana Allred the reason I called you is for. You approval we got a story to tell. Stop wasting valuable time Jeana Allred. I know that you love Jeana Allred Thomas Allred Jr. But you are a professional hip-hop music musician. I didn't realize that Jeana Allred was beside you. Keep your composure Thomas Allred Jr. I see that you are professional. They talking about Jeana Allred like she wasn't here. I'm getting ready to produce this book Jeana Allred. Give My autograph book to me. Excuse me Thomas Allred Jr. I want you to autograph my book for me Thomas Allred Jr. Tell Susan Jennings to autograph your book Thomas Allred Jr. Miss Susan Jennings online 3. That man got a serious a** girlfriend problem. I know you watching me Ms. Susan Jennings. Susan Jennings is online 3 I said. Who are you talkin to Thomas Allred Jr. I'm talking to my ex-girlfriend and wife Jeana Allred. She died almost 20 years ago. if you going to be with bad boy you had to stop talking to her Thomas Allred Jr. I am professional. And I can talk to anybody I choose to. Ain't that right Jeana Allred. I said ain't that right Jeana Allred. Jeana Allred dose not hear you. She has to hear me. We were supposed to go to distance together. Thomas Allred Jr. Keep working on your books and your music. Y'all keep it professional. Go to Eden Reid to come in here for a second. That boy is a police officer y'all. Careful with an attitude like that Eden Reid. Thomas Allred Jr I made it loud and clear. Once you are with Bad Boy entertainment you have to leave your old ways behind. Even Jeana Allred. Thomas Allred Jr Jeana Allred is not with us no more. They talking about you are not with us Jeana Allred. They don't know who they're talkin to. Tell Susan Jennings I programmed you. Miss Susan Jennings Jeana Allred programmed me.

Something is wrong with that boy. He is writing award-winning books. He is writing business ideas also. Take him out of the hood this instant. I am with Bad Boy entertainment. I am with So So Def entertainment. Watch it. We know that you are in the entertainment industry. Thomas Allred Jr are you a police officer. What does that have to do with anything. Just answer my question. Hip hop police officer. Officer Reign reporting for duty. He just said officer Reign reporting for duty. Take him out the hood this instant. what is a hip hop police officer doing writing books. I want Jeana Allred to answer you. I'm writing this book because my girlfriend was killed. One night I wasn't home. So that we get it understood. I'm telling her everything. In my books and in my music y'all. What does that have to do with anything. Miss Susan Jennings. Thomas Allred Jr I can see what you're doing. Be strong enough to handle the situation at hand Thomas Allred Jr. I am getting ready to court you Kristen Beam. Give me that book. It says Kristen Beam in its pages. Thomas Allred Jr this is not your game. Who is playing a game people. My money is on the wrong team. Thomas Allred Jr we love you. I figured you out. You love me too. That is either read for you. A regular Sherlock Holmes. If you care about us Thomas Allred Jr you would leave Jeana Allred alone. If you care about us Thomas Allred Jr. You are going to have to leave Jeana Allred alone. Stop writing the book. Don't you know Jeana Allred is my wife. I could never leave her alone. Professionally. I am doing my work that was a**igned to me. I don't see any problem with me talking to myself. This boy has come a long way. We want Jeana Allred just like you Thomas Allred Jr. As the story about ended. We help you and you help us Thomas Allred Jr. Here goes Jeana Allred story on the table. Please be professional when you read it. Thomas Allred Jr. This is fighting for vengeance return of Jeana Allred and Thomas Allred Jr. Most likely it'll be good. Thomas Allred Jr. That boy became a community leader. In the long run Jesus Christ is our leader. They shot him and his wife and his wife didn't make it. Yall think he going to do good in the industry. You doggone right we think he's going to do good in the industry. To be continued Thomas Allred Jr. Fighting for vengeance wood turned of Jeana Allred and Thomas Allred Jr. Here my book is on the table. Where is the money that I deserve. Count your money much later Thomas Allred Jr. We are trying to produce yall. You and your wife Kristen Beam. Kristen Beam that boy is a police officer. That boy really knows how to appreciate you. he knows how to appreciate a good thing when it happens to him. Fighting for vengeance return of Jeana Allred and Thomas Allred Jr. I'm going to get that boy his contract. I'm going to give it to him right now.

This is Susan Jennings still waiting on line 3. Somebody get the phone. Damn right Susan Jennings is on the damn phone. Thomas Allred Jr I need you to pick up the phone and talk to Susan Jennings. This is the conclusion of a book called fighting for vengeance the return of Jeana Allred and Thomas Allred Jr. Hi Miss Susan Jennings. I am Thomas Allred Jr. Good I finally meet you Thomas Allred Jr. And that's the way it went. Jeana Allred is still my wife to this day. May God rest her soul. My wife is going to take me places. Can you hear me Kristen Beam. I said that you are going to take me places. I will take you somewhere the bedroom Thomas Allred Jr. I'm busy making music go in our bedroom Kristen Beam.

Thomas write down Kristen's name. Imma get your a** a contract. Return of Jeana Allred and Thomas Allred Jr. This is fighting for vengeance. Thomas Allred Jr. Make a sequel to the book Thomas Allred Jr. Only if Kristen Beam allows me to. We got Susan Jennings online 3 Thomas Allred Jr. Fighting for vengeance return of Jeana Allred and Thomas Allred Jr. It sounds like a winner to me Thomas Allred Jr. Miss Susan Jennings be professional. All kind of people are listening. To the messages that you leaving on my answering machine. Thomas Allred Jr is a police officer. Jeana Allred was a police officer. And now you're with Bad Boy entertainment. And So So Def entertainment. With business ideas. For InventHelp and Davison inventions.

You be writing music Thomas Allred Jr. And you saved man life and got shot. What you are is a hero Thomas Allred Jr. Jeana Allred you are my hero. Because you raised the man out of Thomas Allred Jr. Fighting for vengeance the return of Jeana Allred and Thomas Allred Jr. Is a cla**ic book. Thats it Susan Jennings. I wish Jeana Allred could talk to you. She can talk to me. Right out of you Thomas Allred Jr. Give me a second to ask Jeana Allred a question. Okay Miss Susan I'm back. I said to her let this woman guide me. And Jeana Allred answered me and said. No matter the road you travel on Thomas Allred Jr. I will be with you Thomas Allred Jr. Thank you Miss Susan Jennings. Fighting for vengeance the return of Jeana Allred and Thomas Allred Jr. Going to book stores now. We got to get this book to Eden Reid Thomas Allred Jr. I'm with you Ms. Susan Jennings. Take your time and send off the book. You want a copy of it Ms. Susan Jennings. Ill wait till it's published. You sure you don't want to copy Miss Susan Jennings. Sit right there let me get my cane for you Thomas Allred Jr. I got the whole wide world listening to us. And we won't stop Ms. Susan Jennings. Because we can't stop. I'm Bad Boy entertainment. And So So Def entertainment. And a police officer. And an inventor. And I write music. Thomas Allred Jr a lot of people are watching us. Send off that book right now. Fighting for vengeance the return of Jeana Allred and Thomas Allred Jr. That completes it. Thank you Miss Susan Jennings for everything. Thank You Bad Boy entertainment and So So Def entertainment for everything. Thank you Jeana Allred. For helping me with my book. Kristen Beam I love you. I'm really trying Kristen Beam. I'm really trying. Kristen Beam there is one thing that I want you to know. That we won't stop because we can't stop Bad Boy records and So So Def entertainment. I got what you said to me Kristen Beam. I love you anyway. Fighting for vengeance the return of Jeana Allred and Thomas Allred Jr. Now close the book Thomas Allred Jr. If I close the book The chapter will end. And it's supposed to Thomas Allred Jr. And the supposed to Thomas Allred Jr. Remember what I told you Kristen Beam. And we won't stop because we can't stop. Goodbye everyone. As we say in Hollywood toodaloo my friends. Jeana Allred would like to say something to you. I'm back you b*tches. Baby you got to be fair with them. I'm back you b*tches. I'm back you b*tches. Get your a** in the car and sit the f*ck down Thomas Allred Jr. I'm back you b*tches. Fighting for vengeance return of Jeana Allred and Thomas Allred Jr. We don't play. That's the game Thomas Allred Jr. I'm back you b*tches. Go ahead and stop the book. Cause we won't stop. Because we can't stop. Bad Boy entertainment. And So So Def entertainment. Miss Susan Jennings. And Eden Reid. Cause we won't stop. Because we can't stop. I'm back you b*tches. Jeana Allred I love you sweetheart very much.

Thomas Allred Jr. I say to you Thomas Allred Jr. Tell the people that I'm back b*tches. Jeana Allred said to tell you that I'm back b*tches. Thomas Allred Jr. I have been in love with you almost 20 years. No matter what happened between us. You are still my husband Thomas Allred Jr. And my best friend Thomas Allred Jr. I try to understand you Thomas Allred Jr. That is why I'm guiding you. Say career champions Thomas Allred Jr. Career champions Jeana Allred. Now say fighting for vengeance Thomas Allred Jr. Fighting for vengeance. Now say Jeana Allred loves you. Jeana Allred I ain't going nowhere. But you are Thomas Allred Jr. You are going to the top of the business world Thomas Allred Jr. I put my soul's on it. Jeana Allred I put my soul on it too. Thomas Allred Jr. We' LL love each other. Until death do me part. Fighting for vengeance. Get Eden Reid on the phone. Thomas Allred Jr. You know we got a book coming out Eden Reid. Jeana Allred is talking to you. From the grave site. I don't know what you're doing Thomas Allred Jr. But keep up the good work. Candice I want to see you. Tell Eden Reid settle down a minute. Eden Reid. Jeana Allred said to settle down a minute. This boy put Jeana Allred. Faithfully sign the contract. What the contract States Thomas Allred Jr. That me and Jeana Allred are partners for life. There You Go Thomas Allred Jr. And Eden Reid. You and me are partners for Life also. Miss Susan Jennings online 3. Tell Cindy McClain. That Jeana Allred and I. Want her to realize one thing. That you Eden Reid. Are the boss over our contract. It is all in writing Eden Reid. So will you accept my contract Eden Reid. Yes Jeana Allred I will. My book is coming to a close. I'm back b*tches. And I'm in the corporate world Thomas Allred Jr. They thought they were doing something when they killed you Jeana Allred. God just made you stronger in another type of way. They didn't kill me Thomas Allred Jr. God just took me away. Thomas Allred Jr. Talk to Jeana Allred for a minute Thomas Allred Jr. I single-handedly told Kristen that I love her. As you were supposed to Thomas Allred Jr. I'm kind of skeptical about these books being published. Thomas Allred Jr all you have to do is send these books in what I'm speaking to you. Jeana Allred.

I won't stop because I can't stop. Now that's the spirit Thomas Allred Jr. Now our situation is about to change Thomas Allred Jr. Get k Michelle online 2. Hello this is K Michelle speaking. I want you to have my man girl. Jeana Allred. I love you but Kristen Beam. She will understand what I'm doing for you K Michelle. The book is fighting for vengeance. Career champions Thomas Allred Jr. You still got Susan Jennings waiting on line 3. That boy attitude is impeccable. His attitude is impeccable. Jeana Allred said Thomas Allred Jr. Never give up Thomas Allred Jr. Can't you see that I'm trying Jeana Allred. Jeana Allred. I've been alone almost 25 years.

Haven't you been with anybody since me Thomas Allred Jr. Two women on a brief encounter. Get Kristen Beam on the phone. Kristen Beam online 2. Pick up line to Thomas Allred Jr. Yes Jeana Allred. This is Kristen Beam. Who am I talking to. You are talking to Jeana Allred. You're joking with me. No I ain't joking with you Kristen Beam. Jeana Allred. How are you. Keep going Thomas Allred Jr. Kristen Beam. I want you to take good care of Thomas Allred Jr for me. I hope you guys realize that Kristen Beam is Thomas Allred Jr wife. I hope you guys realize that Jeana Allred. And K Michelle is Thomas Allred Jr wives. I'm your wife to Thomas Allred Jr. Eden Reid is professional. I'm your wife Thomas Allred Jr. Yes my love Eden Reid. Cindy McClain is your wife to Thomas Allred Jr. Miss Lucy draw up the contracts. Thomas Allred Jr I'm doing everything I can for you. And Lucy is your wife also.

Thomas Allred Jr. You know you got a contract Thomas Allred Jr. In the business world. Just remain the same. For I am with you in everything you do. Most people think that I'm stupid for writing Jeana Allred name in the books. My sweetheart it's been 20 years since I've been without you. Imma dedicate my book to the citizens of North Carolina. I'm letting you know right now who Jeana Allred is. She is a police officer and a corporate woman. That is great in finance in writing books. They took her life. Before we could finish the second chapter of our first book. This is my way of saying. To Jeana Allred. The queen of my heart. Your books will last forever. Fighting for vengeance. Career champions. I got Susan Jennings still waiting on line 3. Thomas Allred Jr it's about time that you speak to me. Kristen Beam online 2. Kristen Bean online 3 Thomas Allred Jr. Susan Jennings you came all this way for nothing. Answer the phone you jacka**. Susan Jennings I witnessed a miracle. The miracle is Jeana Allred is talking to you. Thomas Allred Jr. How did you know Miss Susan Jennings. Who Do You think answer the phone when you wouldn't pick up. She gave me the complete rundown. Miss Susan Jennings be professional. You know that girl loves you Thomas Allred Jr. Fighting for vengeance career champions Jeana Allred and Thomas Allred Jr. I got a girl online 2 waiting for you Thomas Allred Jr. Answer that f*cking phone Susan Jennings. Call her Miss Susan Jennings. Jeana Allred. I love you. Thank you for everything Miss Susan Jennings. You're welcome Jeana Allred. Write the compilation book. Thomas Allred Jr. They want to take a picture of you. With Jeana Allred beside you. I can't take a picture Thomas Allred Jr. But Melissa stand in my place. Melissa is your wife Thomas Allred Jr. Publish his damn book immediately. And the future seemed what's brighter. because what we have here is a failure to communicate. Fighting for vengeance career champions Jeana Allred and Thomas Allred Jr. I'm back b*tches. Thomas Allred Jr that's not funny. Send a book in Jeana Allred. it's about time you let Jeana Allred send the book in. This is fighting for vengeance career champions a success story. About me and the women I love. Am I forgetting something Jeana Allred. Tell them people that I'm back b*tches Thomas Allred Jr. I'm back b*tches. Make sure that this book get into the right hands my love and my wife Eden Reid. I'm back b*tches. make sure this book get into the right hands my love and my wife K Michelle. I have to give it to you Thomas Allred Jr. You wrote the book in an hour. Y'all Jeana Allred is helping me. May her memory live on. I'm back b*tches forever. Damn right her memory is going to live on. Because we are going to see to it. Thank you my love and my wife Kristin Beam. Where my juice at. We don't drink juice anymore. We drink sparkling water Kristen and K Michelle. Now Lucy I'm warning you. Miss Lucy I'm giving you a contract. Have my love and my wife Cindy McClain draw up the details. I'm going to get you out of this situation Thomas Allred Jr. They shot up the house that I live in. They killed my wife Jeana Allred. But still she's helping me with my books and music. From the far beyond. Fighting for vengeance. A success story. We got the corporate world b*tches. I'm back you b*tches. I am Jeana Allred. And God rest your soul for killing me. I'm back you b*tches. That's the end of my chapter. I hope you enjoyed the book. I'm making more books to come. Now send your book in Thomas Allred Jr. You think this ain't right. But God is on Jeana Allred side. On everybody's side. That is the end of the book. Take it to Ms. Susan Jennings. That's the end of the book. I love you ladies and gentlemen so very much for helping me out with this book. We love you too Jeana Allred and Thomas Allred Jr. You welcome Thomas Allred Jr . If you ever need me I am here for you. Maya name is in the book as my soulmate and best friend. All the women put your hands on the table. Girls I'm giving you a diamond necklace to show my appreciation of you. Thank you Thomas Allred Jr send the book in Jeana Allred. Now I sent it for real this time. I'm just playing with you Thomas Allred Jr. Quit playing Jeana Allred. Send my book in. I love you Thomas.

CHAPTER 26

Anyway My success album goes. To Thomas Allred Jr. For always standing up for me. Eden Reid thank you. What we are going to do now. Is take you back a little bit. Jeana Allred without further ado. This book is a police officers book. I am officer Reign of the New York Police department. And NSA and FBI and Secret Service. Thomas Allred Jr I like you. I like you too Jeana Allred. I think about Jeana Allred all the time. All of the police officers are behind you Thomas Allred Jr. We are going to keep on climbing Jeana Allred. Miss Eden Reid. Call somebody else's name for once in awhile Thomas Allred Jr. Miss Eden Reid. Girl when I book comes out. I am asking you for a date. It will be my pleasure to serve you Thomas Allred Jr. Shake and bake Ricky Bobby. Shake and bake Ricky Bobby Ms. Eden Reid said to me.

We are headed for the future. That's what it is Thomas Allred Jr. So you keep your composure Thomas Allred Jr. Writing books is my destiny. Is our destiny Kristen Beam. But how did you get here sweetheart. See what it is is Thomas Allred Jr. I can do anything I want to now with Bad Boy entertainment. And So So Def entertainment. Kristen I got love for you. I got love for you to Thomas Allred Jr. Ask Cindy McClain what people are saying about you. Thomas Allred Jr. You never think of yourself. Our people will around you. I hope you realize that book sounds professional and has professionalism written all on it. Now and then Kristen Beam. Talk about Kristen Beam for moment. Maya can't believe that you're here. We have been waiting for you Thomas Allred Jr. You and Jeana Allred. Need a success story. I can't believe my ears this is happening to me. Thomas Allred Jr you are professional Jeana Allred to help you Thomas Allred Jr. Girl I sacrifice my book for you. And I love you Thomas Allred Jr. You need to make your book to Jeana Allred. I'm back b*tches. I Miss You Jeana Allred. I know you do Thomas Allred Jr. but after im finish and everything is all done and over with. But afterwards. I will take a minute to talk to you. Jeana Allred wants to speak to everybody for a second. Colleagues and Friends. God put me here colleagues and Friends. To safeguard you all into the future. What I need to tell you is. Not to worry about your finances. Thomas Allred Jr and I Jeana Allred. Has that under control. I want you to enjoy yourself people.

That boy is professional. I want you to enjoy yourself people. Thomas Allred Jr can I talk to you for a second. I know that I hurt you. You didn't hurt me Kristen Beam. I just didn't understand what you were doing. I care about you Kristen Beam. Maya is singling over here. Welcome home Thomas Allred Jr. And Jeana Allred. I'm back b*tches. I told you when y'all killed me. That my damn people would do something about it. How does 650 million feel to you Thomas Allred Jr. You making me feel like I'm on top of the world Jeana Allred. This is a success story Thomas Allred Jr. Of you and me Thomas Allred Jr. Damn right you and me a success. Jeana Allred. I told you wed make it Thomas Allred Jr. Baby I never left you. Thomas Allred Jr is crying. An attitude like his need to be professional. Take me out the hood Jeana Allred. Listen to me Thomas Allred Jr. People have got to read your book first. But I can promise you. That you and me are a success story in heaven. Thomas Allred Jr and Jeana Allred. Forever and always and a day. Kristen Beam. Honey I can't stand up. They shot you Thomas Allred in the leg. No it's not that. It's just that I'm in love with you ladies. The emotions are too much for me. Clean up your attitude Thomas Allred Jr. I'm telling you one thing. That I will do anything for you. Thomas Allred Jr I'm becoming a police officer. To be continued on a later date. My success album Jeana Allred and Thomas Allred Jr.

Jeana Allred help me to get over you. Thomas Allred Jr. If God heard you. What would you think about me. Jeana Allred. I sacrificed everything to get you back. Sometime business professionals. They have your best interest at heart Jeana Allred. Keep writing your book Thomas Allred Jr. Jeana Allred I really appreciate you. Thomas Allred Jr. I am thinking of you with each pa**ing day that I'm away. That's right Jeana Allred. With each pa**ing day that I'm awake I'm thinking of you. I'm thinking of you Jeana Allred. You realize this is a compilation album Thomas Allred Jr. And you realize this is your girl speaking to you. Jeana Allred. All we got to do is take these books to the publisher. Keep it going Jeana Allred. Thomas Allred Jr I'm a police officer. Girl I'm writing books girl. Thomas Allred Jr you need to be professional. Work with me Thomas Allred Jr. I am working with you Jeana Allred. Thomas Allred Jr they killed me because I love you. God help me out of this situation. and grant me the serenity to accept the things that I cannot change. The courage to change the things that I can. And the wisdom to know the difference just for today. I'm timing Kristen Beam. And you Maya. I'm timing you Jeana Allred. I'm going to take you out of this community Thomas Allred Jr. One day soon. Thank you Jeana Allred. Now your book is finished. Jeana Allred I ask you. To love me just for me. Thomas Allred Jr. I do love you just for you. You are my best friend in the whole wide world. I'm just thinking of you Thomas Allred Jr. I appreciate you Jeana Allred.

Stand up to me Jeana Allred. Thomas Allred Jr. You have a millionaire talking to you. I know it Jeana Allred. I want to talk to your a** Thomas Allred Jr. In the weeks to come. Before the snow falls. Before the snow falls. In the weeks to come Jeana Allred. Professionals got a contract waiting for you. Professionals got a contract waiting for you Jeana Allred. All kind of woman want to be with you Thomas Allred Jr. All kind of men want to be with you Jeana Allred. They only shot me. Because I love you Thomas Allred Jr. They only shot me. Because I love you. Jeana Allred. They killed me Thomas Allred Jr. They almost killed me Jeana Allred. The circle is now completed. The circle is now completed Jeana Allred. Thomas Allred Jr. You have your life back. You are now a millionaire. Jeana Allred with these books. You have your life back. You are a millionaire. Listen to Thomas Allred Jr. To the sound of me. Jeana Allred. In your ear saying Thomas Allred Jr. People are watching you. And I love you. Jeana Allred. Listen sweetheart. To the sound in your ear. People are watching me. And I don't care. Because I love you. This is Jeana Allred Thomas Allred Jr. This is Thomas Allred Jr Jeana Allred. I'm a success story. I'm a success story to Jeana Allred. Give me time Thomas Allred Jr. Yes Jeana Allred. I'll give you time. Now Cindy McClain. How professional is Thomas Allred Jr. He seeMs. to be a powerhouse Jeana Allred. 15 books later. Thomas Allred Jr I want you to realize something. What Jeana Allred I don't care about the money. So you don't care about the money again Thomas Allred Jr. What Jeana Allred I don't care about the money. What I care about is making you feel good baby. Thomas Allred Jr. You have no idea how much you are worth to me. Jeana Allred. You have no idea how much you are worth to me. Ya'll have to put each other on a contract. Cindy McClain. I'm telling you if you work with Thomas Allred Jr he will make you a millionaire. Cindy McClain.

I'm telling you if you work with Jeana Allred she will make you a millionaire. The only problem is Thomas Allred Jr. Jeana Allred it's not here. God grant me the serenity to accept the things that I cannot change. The courage to change the things that I can. And the wisdom to know the difference just for today. Pick up your game now Thomas Allred Jr. These books are a sacrificed. To myself and to my family. And I care for you deeply. There's nothing I can do. To bring Jeana Allred back to me. Except write these amazing stories about her life. Jeana Allred Is my wife and will always be my wife. We started off running through our neighborhood as kids. Becoming police officers. Jeana Allred. Are you with me. Until the very last end Thomas Allred Jr. I love you Jeana Allred. And I love you too Thomas Allred Jr. Get Eden Reid online one.

Miss Cindy McClain. Eden Reid online 2. Speak of the devil. Eden his contract should be ready. take your time and read over the doc*ments and allow Thomas Allred Jr to talk to you. Yes Ms. Jeana Allred. Thomas Allred Jr I'm filling out paperwork for you right now. Listen to me. Thomas Allred Jr agrees to all the terMs. in the contracts. Jeana Allred you realize that you're not here. Yes even I do realize that I'm not here. Give her the instructions Thomas Allred Jr. Yes Jeana Allred my wife and soulmate. Reading the instructions Eden Reid. I think Thomas Allred Jr contract is Worthy. Do you agree Thomas Allred Jr. Yes I agree Jeana Allred. And Eden Reid. Thomas Allred Jr. I care about you. I know Jeana Allred. That's why it's hard for me to tell you that. Your books are coming to an end. Jeana Allred I love you. The contracts will get you in the right position Thomas Allred Jr. It is the last thing I can do for you Thomas Allred Jr. It's to you to trust Cindy McClain. And her whole production team. That girl is professional Thomas Allred Jr. Bye Jeana Allred. I made you Thomas Allred Jr. A trillionaire. May God rest Your soul Jeana Allred. I'm back b*tches. May God bless you Thomas Allred Jr. in this book I will allowed my professional feelings to show. To the woman I truly love in this whole wide world. I give a hand to Cindy McClain and Miss Eden Reid. Stick and move Thomas Allred Jr. Would I tell you miss Susan Jennings. Not to play games with me and Jeana Allred. Definitely Thomas Allred Jr definitely. This book is dedicated. To millionaires watching over me. And helping me to realize my true worth. As Jeana Allred once said. And we won't stop. Because we can't stop. Jeana Allred I love you so very much so. That it hurts me inside. I do autographs for people. If you want me to Jeana Allred. I appreciate you Thomas Allred Jr. For saving my life listen. Each book is dedicated. To my old neighborhood. I'm back b*tches. You got to listen Thomas Allred Jr. Write yourself a check Thomas Allred Jr. Imma cash it for you. Not too soon. but sit and write you a check. Hollywood California Thomas Allred Jr can you hear me. Keep standing up. All the police officers you hear me. Keep standing up people. I'm Jeana Allred. Badge number 710 and I want most see you to realize. I'm back you b*tches. I'm a millionaire Thomas Allred Jr. And I'm a trillionaire Jeana Allred. I got to give officers thanks. Talk to them Jeana Allred. This is the last book I'm ever going to take place in. Take care of Thomas Allred Jr. You damn right take care of Thomas Allred Jr. Make that boy out to be something wonderful. Thomas Allred Jr. It's time to let Jeana Allred rest in peace. Equal rights for everybody who is on my team. And that's the ball game. I'm a f*cking trillionaire.

Eden Reid. I'm trying to call you Thomas Allred Jr. To fulfill package. Jeana Allred wanted you to know. That I'm taking care of everything. Seeing God is with us. I want you to think about your book Thomas Allred Jr. I want you to realize that I'm here for you anytime that you need a helping hand. In my memoirs of you Thomas Allred Jr. I have written in myself. That you are a professional rap musician. And a police officer. And a professional author of The entitled book here. I'm waiting for you. To realize your true potential. This boy is amazing. Let me know if you need anything Thomas Allred Jr. And if there's anything that I can do to help you on your journey. Thomas Allred Jr. I have Cindy McClain online one. And Miss Lucy online 2. Some woman named Susan Jennings called me. To ask if you like the way that I do things. This is Susan Jennings Thomas Allred Jr. I am Eden

Reid Ms. Susan Jennings. How is the boy doing Ms. Susan Jennings. He is willing to be expected Miss Eden Reid. Be professional Thomas Allred Jr. Jeana Allred would say to me. Cindy McClain. Wrote the book on being professional. Thomas Allred Jr you wrote the book on being professional to Thomas Allred Jr. Miss Lucy. I really appreciate what you are doing for me. Thomas Allred Jr I appreciate you. All this business work that we're doing Thomas Allred Jr. Business work Ms. Susan Jennings. Has Eden Reid thinking to herself. Thomas realize that you are a superstar book Arthor. Thomas realize that your bank account of 655 million dollars. And that is what books alone. I'm telling you Ms. Susan Jennings. Eden Reid is watching you Thomas Allred Jr. She likes you Thomas Allred Jr. Ask Eden Reid for a date Thomas Allred Jr. Thomas Allred Jr I put you on my 100 list. Of greatest authors in the world. I'm trying to get you to see that. Dealing with you Thomas Allred Jr. Has been professional to me. And dealing with you Eden Reid. Has also been professional to me as well. One condition Thomas Allred Jr. On our date Thomas Allred Jr. You will let me feed you. Eden Reid I love you so much. Just be strong Thomas Allred Jr. Miss Susan Jennings will like us. Sit back. And enjoy the ride Eden Reid. Realize Thomas Allred Jr. But Eden Reid is my friend. Miss Cindy McClain is online 2.

Put Cindy McClain online to Thomas Allred Jr. that boy ain't got no idea what he's doing to me. Cindy McClain. We hear you Cindy. You need to be careful what you wish for Thomas Allred Jr. Eden Reid and I Cindy McClain are with you. I'm trying to get Miss Lucy to answer her phone call. Where dreaMs. come true Thomas Allred Jr. And we won't stop. Because we can't stop. Listen Thomas Allred Jr. I got yo a** this contract. With Bad Boy records. And So So Def entertainment. And do yo mother f*cking business out there Thomas Allred Jr. That is what I'm doing Jeana Allred. The girl to face it as hell. Thomas who do you think you talkin to. If I apologize to you. Would you love me Kristen Beam. And Maya said. No matter what. We all will remain friends. For the rest of our life.

Eden Reid online 6. I'm telling you Eden Reid I produced you. Eden Reid. Jeana Allred. Kristen Beam. Maya. Shontel. Candis. Heather. Chelsea. Evelyn. Porsche .Nada. Thomas Allred Jr. And Susan Jennings. Lucy. Nora. Kathy. And Elizabeth and Kay. Are the women and who I dream about. Thomas Allred Jr that book is successful. I could see you working with me in the future Thomas Allred Jr. Joan lunden please be professional. Take care of yourself Joan lunden. I'm launching this book because. You need to stop at Thomas Allred Jr. talk to the damn females in your area code they're watching you. They watching you Thomas Allred Jr. Eden Reid they're watching you. Thomas has got a good personality. Now that is it for my book Ms. Eden Reid. I'm getting ready to call you later Thomas Allred Jr. Honey I'll be home waiting when you get home. Yes my beautiful wife. Kristen Beam. This story is dedicated to Eden Reid. We love you Kristen Beam. Eden Reid happy birthday. From the whole production team. And Thomas Allred Jr. And Jeana Allred.

Special thanks goes to Miss Lucy. And Susan Jennings. And Cindy McClain. I got to give it to you Cindy McClain. Keep it professional Thomas Allred Jr. You are a professional rap star. You know Cindy McClain. Eden Reid is right. We all do need to talk. In the next book again. I want you to realize. That I got your best interest at heart. Cindy McClain. You are my go-to woman Cindy McClain. I need you to send in your book Thomas Allred Jr. Just a minute. I love you Candice. Miss Candice Allred. I truly love you. Kristen Beam come on honey. It's time to close this chapter for good. Talk to all them females. Ladies and gentlemen we love all of you. The end of the chapter. Eden Reid can understand me.

There's no way I can do without you Jeana Allred. Thomas Allred Jr I told you not to put my name in the book again. I can't live without you Jeana Allred. Kristen Beam. Take him home with you. In the meantime Thomas Allred Jr. I got a story to tell you. It started off with us Thomas Allred Jr. In the meantime. Thank you Jeana Allred. For always working beside me. Gabrielle Union online one. Do you think I'm playing with you Thomas Allred Jr. This story is producing Gabrielle and you. I got to do what I can do Jeana Allred. To help you make things clear to the people. Let the people think about your story Thomas Allred Jr. And how you are standing after being shot in the leg. I wish I would have died with you Jeana Allred. I'm going to put you on my 100 list Thomas Allred Jr. Eden Reid. Is my replacement Thomas Allred Jr. I had to give it to you Eden Reid. Thomas Allred Jr really cares about you. Pick yo game up Thomas Allred Jr. Pick yo game up Jeana Allred. I'm making you out to be a trillionaire baby. Thomas Allred Jr. I hope that you know that I'm in love with you. Eden Reid I love you too. Kristen Beam online 2. Pick yo game up Kristen Beam is online 2. Honey we're having somebody for dinner tonight. Gabrielle I want you to have dinner with us tonight. Eden Reid I want you to have dinner with us tonight. And Cindy McClain I want you to have dinner with us tonight. Now Ms. Lucy.

You are in charge of me. That's okay. Jeana Allred. Is in charge of us Thomas Allred Jr. I'm just thinking. If the books take off. The whole damn country will no. What happened to me and Jeana Allred. Miss Lucy. Thomas Allred Jr everything is special. Laura Banks is online to Thomas Allred Jr. I can teach this boy how to rap. Under suspicion by Jeana Allred and Thomas Allred Jr. Is now in stores immediately. Thomas Allred Jr I want you to. Value your women Thomas Allred Jr. Because this is the family that I gave to you. Thomas you see Shontel is online 3. Y'all better quit playing with this boy. I like you Jeana Allred. I'm back b*tches. If you like me. Then speak up to me. Kristen Beam I know what the contract is. What Thomas Allred Jr. My trillionaire contract is. Selling rent a spoons. You stupid Thomas Allred Jr. Take a professional look at yourself Thomas Allred Jr. I'm about to change you from the streets to the corporate world. Jeana Allred. I want you to know that I care about you. So deeply baby.

I'm having a hard time speaking to you Jeana Allred. Kristen Beam I couldn't find the words. To tell you that I ain't going down without a fight. I like that boy Kristen Beam. You keep calling Kristen Beam. Maya you have no idea how much I love you. I'ma build a skyscraper Thomas Allred Jr. Automatically you are the man of the year. Put Maya name in it one more time. Yes Jeana Allred. Maya you know that I'm in love with you. Eden Reid is standing up. To Thomas Allred Jr and Maya. Eden Reid I have much love for you. Gabrielle Union. I love you and thank you for everything. Cindy McClain. I love you Cindy McClain. And Shontel. That boy is thinking about you. Even though he might not say it. Shontel. I especially love you sweetheart. Evelyn. I can do nothing without you Evelyn. I love you. These women are the knights of the round table. Nada I didn't forget about you. I want you to see the round table Nada. Porsche Heather and Chelsea. And Kay. And Elizabeth Nora and Kathy. Thomas Allred Jr has done got professional. Congratulations Thomas Allred Jr. Kristen Beam I'm just doing what Jeana Allred wants me to. Eden Reid. And Miss Susan Jennings. I'm a close out this book. By telling you that I care about you Eden Reid. We waiting on the book Thomas Allred Jr. Our book sales is colossal Kristen Beam. All over the world. Jeana Allred and Thomas Allred Jr. Name will go down in history. As to hero police officers. Fighting for mine in yours Kristen Beam. Is under suspicion.

Thomas Allred Jr talk about the people in your community. You know Jeana Allred. Don't like me to talk dirty about people. I can say nothing but they stole a contract from me. Jeana Allred you meant the world to me. And now you're gone because of people. Being jealous of you. A beautiful creature in creation you are Jeana Allred. I pray that God guides us to see you again. All of us. Amen. Thomas Allred Jr we got your book as doc*mentation. The police officers everywhere won't hold you responsible. If you have to lose it Thomas Allred Jr. I want you to realize one thing Kristen Beam. Jeana Allred has stood up to terrorism. And so will the rest of us. I am Thomas Allred Jr. And Jeana Allred. And the rest of these ladies. In there community. Are my wife's. I am educating you Thomas Allred Jr. On the laws of physics. Thomas Allred Jr.

They killed me but they didn't do nothing to me. Jeana Allred that's enough to make me a king of vengeance Jeana Allred. King of vengeance in stores. Right now. Jeana Allred. I love you Thomas Allred Jr. I love you too Jeana Allred. You hurt my woman you hurt me. Excuse me Thomas Allred Jr. I just want to say one thing about what you're saying. Of course Jeana Allred. These women out here are to be loved and to be cherished. God made us to take care of our families. And to be there for each of you. We are your equals. And all of your companions. I am a police officer. Jeana Allred. And I died for equal rights children. The ladies of my generation and this generation.

We'll have to know the sacrifices that police officers have made. To be there for them. I want you to realize this one thing. All of the ladies. Are your partners and best friends. Come on my men. We have to do this thing better than this. Take care of the women Thomas Allred Jr. And until God calls me home. I will be there for you all. My name was Jeana Allred. Thomas Allred Jr we realize who Jeana Allred is. And we got you in a hopes and prayers. Maya I can't make it without you. Thomas Allred Jr. Has left the building. I am Maya. And I'm going to be taking over from here on out. Along with Kristen Beam. I am going to take over the community. Once and for all the ladies will have there peace. The book sounds really good Thomas Allred Jr. I want to produce you. On television. Yes Miss Lucy. I would like that a lot. You are no longer under suspicion Thomas Allred Jr. Thank you Miss Lucy. Miss Susan Jennings is waiting on you. Did you stick and move like I said. Like a big hornet Ms. Susan Jennings. On meeting is now complete. This is dateline saying good night. Thomas Allred Jr. God please look out for me and Jeana Allred. Thank You under suspicion.

As you know my wife has been murdered. And killed by someone we didn't know. I am a professional rap musician. A professional businessman. And a police officer. Jeana Allred was my hope for the generation. I'm worried about females. Who don't believe in theyselves. Who have nowhere to turn. And who have no place to go but to the arMs. of a stranger. I'm writing this statement because of people. Who thinks the world belongs to them. When God made Earth. There was a female and a man here. I want you to think about that statement. Thomas Allred Jr. You stronger than what you think you are ladies. A breif statement. Jeana Allred. Take us out of here. Amen Jeana Allred.

For the fame of Justice by Jeana Allred. I just now got a contract Thomas Allred Jr. They say you won't talk to me because of it. Listen to me Thomas Allred Jr. For the fame of Justice. I dedicate my whole wide world to you. For the fame of Justice. I dedicate my whole wide world to you Jeana Allred. I got you a** a contract Thomas Allred Jr. Go back to working on your books Thomas Allred Jr. Read your book to me Kristen Beam. I did Thomas Allred Jr. For the fame of Justice Kristen Beam. Y'all know what the fame of Justice really is. We took a book and communicated our situations. And put it on Justice hands. They killed Jeana Allred. Act a fool Thomas Allred Jr. This is Thomas Allred Jr. And for the flame of Justice I will act a fool. Every book that I done wrote so far. Is a dedication to the love that I have for Jeana Allred. Sit back with me. And for the flame of Justice. These people are giving me my money. Kristen Beam I would like to say something to you. No God has a plan. The fame of Justice plan. To get the women off of the street corners. They are watching me. It's kind of difficult. For me to express myself Kristen Beam. But here goes nothing. All you have to do is Thomas Allred Jr. Take your time and write your books. Kristen Beam I never had much. To take on you. On my team. Is a dream come true. You need to put the flame of Justice Thomas Allred Jr. Listen to me the fame of Justice. Requires that I show you the world Kristen Beam. Jeana

Allred. Said the fame of Justice. Requires me to stand up for you Thomas Allred Jr. This boy isn't playing any games. Damn right he not playing no games. The people out there that's doing killing will be brought to Justice. There is a dark law Kristen Beam. Which would allow me to say to you.

That you mean everything to me. As I lay here thinking to myself. The fame of justice is the dark law Kristen Beam. The fame of Justice hand it to me. The Law simply States. You will never be in the entertainment industry. Or any industry. If you kill our women and murder our children. The fame of Justice isn't complete. When you take the life of a person. The fame of Justice takes your life. By concealing you behind bars. Forever and a day. I'm thinking to myself Kristen Beam. Say what you want to. Our fame of Justice is going to work. Thomas Allred Jr put down in history. My girlfriend knew you. The fame of Justice Kristen Beam. One condition that is. If you are part of law enforcement. The fame of Justice comforts you. The fame of Justice. You see you got enough sense. What you going to do Thomas Allred Jr. I'm about to get married Kristen Beam.

Will you be my wife Kristen Beam. I was waiting on you to ask me that. The fame of Justice. That boy is off the hook. But yes I will be your wife Thomas Allred Jr. Jeana Allred. Thank you for seeing me all the way through. I love you Jeana Allred. What we are going to do right now. It's a little different for me. Give me my contract. Listen to me Thomas Allred Jr. Yes Kristen Beam. Your contract simply States. That the fame of Justice. Is you writing music Thomas Allred Jr. I'm a bad boy people. So So Def entertainment. They getting professional. Say what you want to about Kristen Beam and Thomas Allred Jr. Kristen Beam and Thomas Allred Jr are our soulmates. Our souls rest in peace Jeana Allred. That is the fame of Justice Jeana Allred. I already know that Kristen Beam and you are going to be together. It is written in the hands of time. Thomas Allred Jr I think of you everyday that goes pa**es. Tell Kristen Thomas Allred Jr.

That I give her my blessings. Jeana Allred. Just like Jeana Allred always was. I am the man of the house. Thomas Allred Jr. I'm back b*tches. And no gunshot to the leg is stopping me. And we won't stop. Because we can't stop. You need to stop that book Thomas Allred Jr. Kristen Beam I'll stop the book when I'm finished. Stop the book Thomas Allred Jr. Oh. The fame of justice is now complete.

Superman Thomas Allred Jr. Kristen Beam. I'll be with you in a moment. The difference is Kristen Beam. I am professional. Superman Thomas Allred Jr. Are you our demigod from Christ Jesus. Hell no I'm not your demigod from Christ Jesus. I put that in my message to. Get a hold of you. Kristen Beam. But Jeana Allred says that you are a God figure Thomas Allred Jr. You got me at hello Kristen Beam. So what are you Thomas Allred Jr. What kind of person risks his life. To save a person from drowning. I'm Superman Kristen Beam. You are a demigod to me. The moral of the story is. Kristen Beam I need your contract. I've searched the world for a woman like you. And now that I've found you Kristen Beam. Love has its way with me. That's a contract with you and me. Both our names is going to be on it. As soon as I can pay my dues Kristen Beam. People respect you for your personality. Thomas Allred Jr. And I respect you. Respect Kristen Beam everybody. I respect you all. Kristen Beam. I am getting ready to end the story. But I first have to know Kristen Beam. Will you marry me Kristen Beam. I've seen the error of my ways. And I apologize to each and every one of the females in my book. I only love you Kristen Beam. To make a long story short. You Kristen Beam are a demigod to me. Thomas Allred Jr you are professional. Look how you are doing me. If I could I would walk you through a garden by myself. But I can't because demigods. See me as Superman the world's savior. Thomas Allred Jr. And I'm to professional to put my past behind me. So Jeana Allred we are going to find out who killed you. See I am a superhero Thomas Allred Jr. A demigod. I told you that you were a demigod. I thought you was Superman Thomas Allred Jr. King of the entertainment industry. And literary industry. I guess you have me at hello Kristen Beam. Until this empire stands up for itself. Keep it under wraps. I'm Superman the demigod Kristen Beam. Don't play with Jesus Christ Kristen Beam. Thomas Allred Jr realize you ain't Jesus Christ. His angels come to me Kristen Beam. That is enough about Jesus Christ. He and Angel to me Kristen Beam. Who Thomas Allred Jr. I want you to be professional. Demigod Kristen Beam. I want you to see what the future has in store for you and me.

Be careful Kristen Beam. The only thing that can hurt you right now is a silver bullet. Thomas Allred Jr you know I'm not a werewolf don't you. I see you as my queen werewolf Kristen Beam. I wish them girls would say something to you. Your wish is my command. Thomas Allred Jr stop playing with me. Boy I'll smack the sh*t out of you. And I know that you need a contract Thomas Allred Jr. Listen Thomas Allred Jr. Me and you are eternal. Each of us wears the Superman symbol.

On the jeans of our pants. I know how you must feel to have no one around you to love you Thomas Allred Jr. Kristen Beam I swear to God Kristen Beam. I'm going to get the person who killed my wife. Jeana Allred. You need to calm your self down Thomas Allred Jr. Now I want you to say it with me. God grant me the serenity to accept the things I cannot change the courage to change the things that I can and the wisdom to know the difference just for today. Lord please help me out of this situation that I'm in. Just look at me Thomas Allred Jr. And never look back again. Demigod Kristen Beam. You see what I did for you Thomas Allred Jr. I see what you did for me demigod Kristen Beam. Thank you Thomas Allred Jr. Because you helping me with finances. What is a demigod surppose to do Kristen Beam. You can get and apartment with me Thomas Allred Jr. Thomas Allred Jr that girl is about to go Thomas Allred Jr. Kristen Beam I really do love you. And I want to see you again someday. If God lets me. You see Kristen Beam. I am a police officer. And I want and address from you. Get away from me Thomas Allred Jr. The address is 105 that's it Thomas Allred Jr. I'll see you a** in the future. Now let me see you on purpose. I want to see you on purpose. I'm a demigod. A lot of people are watching me. Come on demigod Superman Thomas Allred Jr. Say it one more time for me. Yo girl is the right one for me. Talking about a trillionaire Kristen Beam. Thomas Allred Jr if you read your book. I gave you my address in each section. Say what. I'm just playing with you Thomas Allred Jr. Thomas Allred Jr everything happens for a reason. I'm sure that we'll get to be together sometime in the future. Until Thomas Allred Jr. Keep your head up and stop bullsh*ttin. Because when it comes to you I am a demigod Kristen Beam. And I'm a demigod to Kristen Beam. Superman Thomas Allred Jr. You are a long way from home. What you talking about Kristen Beam. Kristen Beam I will do anything for your contract. Even fly. I'll see about that Kristen Beam. I'll marry you Thomas Allred Jr. So I don't forget have anniversary Kristen Beam. Thomas Allred Jr you didn't have to. It's our first book. This is your anniversary present. Oh my God y'all he is a demigod. Don't tell anybody Kristen Beam.

I'm not going to tell anybody Thomas Allred Jr. That boy is Superman the demigod Thomas Allred Jr. knows everything about us. Except for one thing Kristen Beam. Are you talking about what I think you are talking about. Our rent a spoons. I'm a demigod Kristen Beam. I'm a demigod as well Thomas Allred Jr. Kristen Beam realize that Thomas Allred Jr. Did the work all by hiMs.elf. He truly is a demigod Superman of the entertainment world. Thomas Allred Jr and Kristen Beam. I now but now pronounce you rent a spoon owners. Kiss the bride Thomas Allred Jr. With my pleasure. You need to speed up Thomas Allred Jr.

You can see the reason I love you is because. I can't stop thinking of you and me. Nervous me saying this. Is an endeavor i choose to go down this road by myself. My book contains an autograph picture. Can I make this up with you a later time. That's it for now. I'm looking around me to see if my people around me will care about me writing this book. This is my truth. I belong to you Kristen Beam. Be strong enough to tell me you love me in front of people. The longest 10 minutes I've ever had in my life started with an Injustice. I act like you my hero. it is time to make up with everybody for the wrongs that I proven to make. Jeffrey I'm talking to you because I need help to publish my books.

Fighting for mine the sequel. And the biography of Thomas Allred Jr. This manuscript is in danger Jeffrey. I'm listening to exactly what people say. I love you Kristen. Kristen Beam I'm going to teach you how to play. Jacking my d*ck was simply something that I was not going to do. Waiting until I knew somebody was my mystery. In the days of my trouble I listen to gospel on the radio. Young and successful is where I am. People are waiting for this right here. I got to be confident for my own well being in this book right here. I'll do everything I possibly can to help anyone. My name is officer Reign. Of the New York Police department. Listen Don't Make me over. Whatever you do jacking your d*ck is not it. I have a greatness in this manuscript. You know that I appreciate you Jeffrey. With the force I have inside of me. I give to you fighting for mine my sequel. and it don't make sense for congratulations yet. Especially since I can't get out of this dream that I'm having. All my life I had to prove that I was something more other than a police officer. In my first book. I made it strong enough for you. The second part of this book. I appreciate all the work that you're doing being professional. Business will come and business will go. To my friends let me just handle this. It went like this. Them f*ckers shot me. And killed my girl to. The whole police station is agreeing with me. This book is dedicated to the love of my life. Miss Kristen Beam. In the New York Police department I be supervisor things. I'm tripping over you Jeffrey. Seeing how I'm writing you this. Jeffrey make sure that you are evenly professional. With my book. You already know what they did to me. So I'm spending my book around. I'm about finished with the story. This is the beginning challenge for you Jeffrey. Keep the appointment that I give you. Listen to my story all the way through. I can't believe that boy to shot me. Open the door for me Jeffrey. To have and to hold from this day forward. I know what everybody wants from me. And I been dedicated to truth justice and the American way.

Jeffrey your job is to put together my manuscript. You can get killed writing a book like this. But that is when I'mma tell my truth. The only one who dances in my head. They killed her so she's dancing in my head. You see I know that you're ahead of your time. I'm not cussing in the book because I know better. Don't take sh*t for granted Jeffrey. Most of the people I know is for me and with me and I thank them for that. I told you I will keep going into this book is a number one bestseller all over the United States of America. And 50 states. What I got to say about the truth. History already know the way the cards are dealt. I'm barricading myself in my room. To get this manuscript to you Jeffrey. Talk to me if you need my approval to go forward with anything. Talk to me. I'm strong enough to take it. Our approval means the world to me. I'm writing this book seeing a picture of me means the world to me in person. I'm starting off with chances are not taken. It used to be something that we all could agree with. Then Jesus Christ said I outta write this book.

Everywhere I go people around me. I like it myself. Surrounding yourself with God's people. Is the way the Earth should be. In time your blessings will come to you Jeffrey. You just stick with me. To us furthermore to me. Check the bumps for me Jeffrey. Jeffrey need to do something for me. Jeffrey so far all this is me. Bit by bit I will deliver my Justice. Sometimes I feel so alone. The fast lane is not what this book is about. Overtime you will need to know me. I am Mr.. Thomas Allred Jr . Officer Reign for short.what we are doing right now is making a way a bridge. Listen to me. I know that you have had hard times. And I would do anything to make it through that you see better days. The book is dedicated. To you indeed. I got a piece of mind.meanwhile I'm telling you this one time story that we all can get. To get close to this is to get close to greatness. I'll be by myself while I'm writing this. Keep to yourself. And a best seller will be laid in your hands. So I make myself clear I. I'm going to need you to listen up. Coming back off of the EMG. I'm making way for you to understand just who I am. I done done this once before. With another publisher in another time with mine. Fighting for mine the sequel. And fighting for yours to sequel. As you were you take nothing off of no one. I don't kid myself. Whatever you do text me back with the answer. To this long old question. Y'all keep your composure. While my question for Jeffrey is. Is there a heaven for a gee. Give him time to write his book. I keep telling myself as the day begins willter. See energy that is taken. Allows me to stand at the top of my situation.Picking up and before I left off this is a sequel. Of fighting for mine. I've got a triple meaning. Fighting for mine is for you and me. There's going to be a day that you are going to need me Jeffrey. With each file. Do professional because I need you to finish this work. Thinking to myself. I see myself as a police officer. And usually a police officer does the right thing.I don't know right now because this police officer has been through some things.

I'll get to the point of that later on in the f*cking manuscript. Keep your composure. I got a job for us to do. See I hate to seem what hateful. Everybody told me that I had no reason to write this book. Soon as I mentioned them killing Jeana Allred. Friends became my enemies. The meaning for me writing this book. Is to defend my standing. Now to help you. Ask for you to take me seriously. I'm merely being myself. If you can handle these emails Jeffrey. Try not to lose my manuscript. I'm getting ready to put the signal out to you. Our manuscript. Fighting for my really has gotten a improvement. Fighting for mine once told me I won't give in. These people toying with Thomas Allred Jr. What type of hero is this. I'm going to need a position. Either way I do.

Work this professional.with the hopes that the good Lord watches over me. I realize that fighting for mine. Is more than a sequel. This is everything. So get ready to take revenge. Fighting for mine is in my heart. I got to tell you Jeffrey. This is my intro. Realize that I'm choosing you. To fight alongside of me.we have to do something about this small change I don't know what I'm going to do about this. Your bank account is $1000000.an extra after we seeing that the book is finished. I will get this to you. I'm keeping my composure I'm watching you. It's showing you I can handle myself. When tough times get too rough for me to bear. I'm going to keep this composer. Everybody stay full off this food we about to give you. Listen to me talkin to you. And realize that I've been watching you as well as you been watching me. In my computer screen.

Matrimony is destined for me.If I can prove myself to anybody I will prove myself to myself. Let's go ahead and prove it.every time I think about them hurting me I feel sick to my stomach. I can see it now in my own space. The Sounds of a champion roars out. My damn relationship is confidential. But I'm going to tell you a little bit about myself. I am holding the Reign for the both of us to make it. Stop all the bulsh*t you got to hear this. A hundred years ago in another lifetime. I was a police officer. I come back to see you. Listen all over the world. Your book called fighting for mine is out. I am giving you the sequel to fighting for mine. Check my pulse if it even matters. I'm getting to publish a book called fighting for my the sequel.the reason I'm here is because I've been taught to fight and I see the day as a Sunday situation. Listen carefully. I'm almost to the point where I can't take it no more. I see your dreaMs. ahead of me Jeffrey. We all want the greatest selling book of all time.as I compel my emails I need you to listen to me. My only hope for this book is coming back to my sense. With out the hope for the radio playing in the room beside me.I know there's going to be one of these days that fight for mine is going to be success. And we are supposed to be successful. Let me lay down a format for you. I've come a long way with you. Jeffrey only God knows how I feel. They tested me to see if I had any kind of disease. I do push ups.I really don't want to be by myself but I guess things happen.my girlfriend was the prettiest woman that I've ever known in my life. We had a relationship that was built on trust and Future. Be a part of my future Jeffrey. Thomas Allred Jr in fighting for mine the sequel. I am getting ready to give you the sequel part 2 now. I want to dedicate this book to my dear mother Reign. And you know it Thomas Allred Jr. I am right here with you. Right here with you doesn't mean that you're right here with me. I seen the best of they could do to me. At the funeral home my girlfriend Lay. Think about this as a concept. I'm not here to be spoke of. I just want to dedicate my book to my friends into my people. Seeing that I am a police officer. Girl I'm trying my best to love you. When you see that I have not given up. Then you will see that I got you in my good graces. Fighting for mine to sequel. Is what I'm hoping for. Standing up I say to myself. Ain't a man stronger than me. I want to take you on a journey Jeffrey. Now with me I'm a millionaire that can't be found.

Keep your composure.I'm only saying this because my hopes and my dreaMs. are in this book. Take care of me Jeffrey this is Thomas speaking to you. And with this. The intro has been established. Give my intro to Ms. Eden Reid. In my shortcomings I may have. Collected dust on my manuscript. He said he collected dust on his manuscript. Girl letting me go will be a big no no.and these people are standing up for me and you. Kick a Rock. I'll see that you do. If you were with me. Kristen Beam. I don't know what to say. Say that you love that girl Thomas Allred Jr. I love you Kristen Beam. Nothing can block me from seeing you now. As you closely come to me. I issue you my best. I'm saving the best for last. My wishes is on this book. That you enjoy chapter after chapter. Along with Jeffrey my friend and partner. This is a worldwide seller. Just do the math Thomas Allred Jr.I'm going to shoot you better emails and better copies Jeffrey. This book is getting ready to blow up. Sincerely yours Thomas Allred Jr. Officer Reign for short. This part of the book is strong enough. Send the damn book in. To Jeffrey and Miss Eden Reid. Before they stop me. imma let everybody know that I'm King of the whole wide world even the United States. This is just telling me. That you need me crunch time. I dare to dream it for myself. I am a king. With descendants who have fallen. In the line of duty for there workplace. And you working. On this here manuscript for me. Jeffrey don't be surprised if I need you. Miss Eden Reid came after me. Give Miss Eden Reid fighting for mine the sequel. Seeing that I'm doing this here by myself. My game is in the overtime season. To have an unknown. By my side must be priceless.

Share with me Jeffrey. And adults share with me too.the only thing we have to do now is finish the book. But I'm getting ahead of myself. Take two lemons lemonade. Some more work and a basket of eggs beaters. Soften up like that. I done came to you once as a professional. If you care about seeing me. Get your money right Jeffrey. The only thing that I like in this world is gone.it took my girlfriend away from me because she was beautiful. I'm going to send my picture to you. In hopes that I could see myself in a better stand point in the future getting a smoke off the ground shows me what time it is. I'm glad that we spoke Jeffrey. You see how intense I'm being.

Thomas Allred Jr I got a question for you. If we were to try to change your life. Thomas Allred do you think you can handle it. I know I can handle it. Think about this for a minute. If Caesar on the entire world.Leave it to us to give the world back to the people. What do you think about that Jeffrey.Six hundred million dollars will tell you the truth about you and me. As money keeps flowing your way Jeffrey. tighten up your skills my name is Thomas Allred Jr I'm here to help you. I dedicate everything to you and this endeavor that we are on. Keep your emotions to yourself Jeffrey.

They trying to push me. But the manuscript is done when you says finish. So many days I've been thinking about this manuscript.too many days have going past were I cried about me being with out my girlfriend. This name Jeana Allred should for greatness and opportunity. I'm waiting on you to speak back to me Jeffrey. The sequel for fighting for mine. Two more days and I'll be through with this conversation. You know how I feel don't you Jeffrey. See you are looking for a peace offering. At the table of true professionals. So that means that me and you. Have a great destiny before us. Unlike the first book that I wrote. I take care of myself a little better. No more out cursing. And blaming people for my own mistakes. To fight for mine means that I won't give in ever. I'm just glad for today Jeffrey. They had no business doing what they did to us Jeana Allred. Jeana Allred this is my second book. Baby and if I had to. I'm holding onto you with every last breath that I take. Now I dare for you to say this ain't no takeover. With my finger right here. I command Justice. What about Jeana Allred. See I put a dream of mine along with her. You messing up putting a dream. We don't put no dreaMs. aside. I thought you were doing just the intro Thomas Allred Jr. It was all a dream. They took you away from me Jeana Allred. I'm here to fight for my back.look at the choices I have here to make. Don't sit back and laugh. I am more of a g than you think I am. That's the reason I'm sending my book into you. Autographed this if you want to. Thomas Allred jr. Has left the building. They are going to tear up the single. You see in this book. I'm putting my heart in here. Think of this you don't know me yet. But it's some far away where I dream that I'm having. You are professional as well as I am me. I am true with this. Jeffrey we are comeing to a part where I must in this book. And to answer your question. A bulsh*t with you not Jeffrey. I am professional. I just got to ask you to hang on to this manuscript. I'm number one with a gun. All we need is a little working on the manuscript. Even court advantage. That is the intro. Of my book Fighting by my lonely. The sequel to fighting for mine. I am depending on you Jeffrey. To see things on even ground. Capture the moment. My girlfriend name is Kristen Beam. And I'm introducing you two fighting for mine the sequel. Fighting by my lonely. I will continue my book at a later time. And Jeffrey that was almost professional. Lift the tally up. And the balls in your court Jeffrey. I want you to think of this when I finish writing our manuscript.Tomorrow at sundown I will give you another piece of the manuscript. Tomorrow at sundown if they see who I am.then you will be waiting on the next compartment of this manuscript book. So take care of this for me. Sincerely yours Thomas Allred Jr. All my people are around me. I want to show them that I really can play ball. With this the next single. Right from the start I want to listen to you. About true heroism between me and you Jeffrey. See I look at it like patriotism. Sitting here I'm bored out my mind. What you see is what you get to Jeffrey. Eden Reid is my past life. I'm just sitting here like you told me to do.

I had a dream about this. It was raining outside. And all the people. The people. Started shaking hands with each other. That is heroism. Listen to that. I got a pretty good start understand book.Weren't you the one that spoke to me on the phone Mr.. Jeffrey. I can get my knowledge. Right here I'm see through. Let them keep messing. On a single that is destin to rise above the nations. I'm just heading down a road in a pickup truck.first you let me first be there to help you Jeffrey. This is laid out for you to think about. My book claiMs. your freedom. I was going through so much sh*t that it's that I didn't know which one was heads or tails. And now I'm the boss. It 2 more days. I will have you a book report weary of your understanding. Eden Reid Miss Cindy McClain.

Congratulations on a job well done with the first book. Serious times calls for serious measure. Reign center yourself. This is the beginning part 2. I know you not trying to rush me to finish this book. I sat at home look at me. People are with me that I don't even know. I'm about to pee all over myself. You can see. It there's not in the shame. In my game. The shame that was already in my game is now that distant. Were I can see myself that slowly in the mirror. I'm about to pick my f*cking.game up. Seeing that I never had nothing to myself. The dollars are what I'm standing for. Excuse me Thomas Allred Jr. Put your name into it. Officer Joseph Reign. What Police department is that. Get ready for me to tell you Jeffrey. Jeffrey

I'm in this quiet place. Where my thought process is clear and able to handle itself. It can handle it self with girls. No weapon formed against us shall prosper. You are in quarantine Jeffrey. So is Mr. Eden Reid. I need to give that girl some attention. And I'm sure that this place has it. Looking in my mirror at all the issues thats done pa** me. I can work my a** off Eden Reid. Eden Reid is my subject and predicate. Long phone conversations. Gave out information we both can use. The first thing Thursday morning. I am going to hand in to you. A nickel for your thoughts. Come on now I'm leaving. Jeffrey I got these people after me because of my book.I work myself into a trap thats decent. What im keeping from you with me Jeffrey. Is the confidence that I got. I once had been a Studio rapper. Way back in my younger days. And it's true I got millions of fans who are around me.I know what you thinking you thinking how is this book ever going to be completed and finished. You saved me by the government. Getting in on this education of our. Reign get ready to prove yourself. It's all different weapons type. Express truancy novel that I keep. Unlike my first one this one is buried with me. I lay down my sword to kick it with you for a second. I'ma handle my business.

Different types of business you see me with at first. I stay working with the ladies constantly.What happened to the good old days were it was like one girl for one man.that's why I'm painting this picture clearly to show you or y'all. Just how busy I really am. Now. All my girls that are helping me. Is my Superman contract for being. At home with myself. Every one of these women will fall outside for me. Jeffrey look how I changes play. I give you something to eat on. Come on Jeffrey. Jeffrey I'm telling you that I'm going to kill myself after the book comes out if I'm not married to my wife Miss Kristen Beam. Of Hickory North Carolina. See my concept is so f*cking clear. That i think. That i can't kill myself I got to many people after me. Ensuring that after me. Christmas is here in America. I'm trying to get you to understand Jeffrey just how I. Plan on running things if my possession is in one of the pennies.

You can see now that I am professional.I hope the kiss Kristen Beam the day that this book comes out. In love and in business. I almost completed this portion of the book.we have your mind in the best interests of our heart. None of y'all play special out there. I'm going to the water fountain. Heads up and heads down. Thomas can take care of hiMs.elf. By his own self I will atmention his book. In with one of my favourite reviews. I am the man of the hour. Does anyone in here have a nickel. I'm about to spit the last verse but you know my truth is I'm just waiting for a nickel. To hang out with. Eat with this Jeffrey Fitzgerald. I got you some snacks coming later. You see what that boy a do for you. Coming up kidding. And prospering with every laugh that we make. You see I believe in karma. Brothers and sisters. I give to you the sequel of my book. Fighting for mind sequel. Fighting by my lonely my book is too important for me to keep it to myself.Any conditions that you may have Jeffrey I will meet the requirements. See easy come easy go.you know Jeffrey I'm getting tired of people doubting me and what I can do. Open your eyes open Jeffrey you have done brought me and you. A ticket to the place you want to be. God bless your soul can my wife Jeana Allred have a few words. Every body thank you for giving my wife Jeana Allred back to her in this manuscript. Jeana

CHAPTER 27

Allred has something to say. Tranquility and peace for all.Were the last things that she ever said to me. One chapter right here is finished. What we're going to do is. Celebrate the best fact that we are all working together. Again do you all hear me.Jeana Allred sweetheart rest in peace and wherever I go.im thinking about you. It's hard to turn one in for another. Jeffrey I got to talk to you. You see I'm not a betting man. I'm just sure myself forever after. I'mma put this manuscript in your hands Jeffrey. Along with the fee that you gave me to complete my book. A pretty princess is backing me up. I have to give Shayla another chance. Competition don't know me that well. Keep your head straight. Thank you for talking to me Jeffrey. Be strong enough to put this manuscript together. I'm working day and night on this book.

I'd like to talk to you. What about me. Is so irresistible that I can't let this manuscript go. I gave Jeana Allred back her home. Out of the way of trouble. I'm starting to pick up. Our percentages is colossal. Like a moth to The flame burned by the fire. I'm depending on you Jeffrey. To get back to me at a reasonable time and date. Starving right now. People let me in. I'm doing it for you Jeffrey.the only difference is your helping me while I'm doing this. We need you Reign. Thomas Allred Jr. Is still in need of a wifey.So this manuscript sticks peanut butter and jelly won't work at all.I'm writting more than I normally do on the first week out. It's enticing me to do better than my last endeavor. It is out of my hands and back into people's hands. Let me see let me guess in this story. Imma take Kristen Beam in this story. So that each of you you will know that I'm being for real. The season is ours to explore with. Send it off just like it is Thomas Allred Jr. Get back to Eden Reign.

Here close the gate. Thomas Allred Jr you got people talking. 15000 the first week out sold. Wich would show and be a blessing from God and my agent. Laying around the pool area. I got to teach your a**. Look at it this way. If you can allow my work Jeffrey. Now you see my endeavor. Thomas Allred jr we promise you.I am not sitting here beating around the bush. Make me a deal after this book is written. Thank you Jeffrey May you look at it we can have it any way that we want a piece. Cindy want to say hi. I'm doing my best to keep my composure. My manuscript is ordering me. To do something spectacular. Mail me at least 20 copies of the book Jeffrey. The whole book is famous. It is made from an ancient secret. We call it eye to eye.we'll talk about this later in the book. To be professional is to know your limitations and how far you can go. Put a distance from me Jeffrey.the person who ends up at the end with all that he wants is the true owner of the book. The book has ancient symbols on it. In Chinese letters. I have got to loosen my grip on it Thomas Allred Jr. Is used to the isolation. Being with you and my manuscript. Somehow I did me right this time around. That's right Thomas Allred Jr keep on writing. You will make it out here. Though accidents can happen. For now just. Be a police officer that you was meant to be. Just like you. I am fighting for mine the sequel to. Fighting by my lonely. Who is that. Gabrielle Union Allred. Here I have one thing to say to you Thomas Allred Jr.I'm helping you with this book called fighting for mine the sequel. Fighting by my lonely.

I'm out here making my stand. Be focused Thomas Allred Jr. Look what you did. Go ahead make a baby out of this. Opportunities like this don't come too often. Use it Thomas Allred Jr for your benefit. Thomas Allred Jr I really need to talk to you for a second. What man. I prefer to be called mister Frankie. Forget the e. I listen to you everyday. When writing your and starving at same time. You got that right you are going to starve would you like a potato. I'll do all I can. Whatever the time is Kristen Beam I think of you always . Kristen Beam doesn't even know you were alive. Now call her by her name. Foxy in my mansion. I definitely want to see Thomas Allred Jr. If situations we're to change. Could you muster up the energy. To go after your dream woman.and leave the door open so men and women can come through and see ball. Muster up the strength to leave the door open. You too I'm going to help you. Gymnastics is my first word. Do you see what white people do for you. I'm making a movie of this rendition. Isn't it somehow great how we can never stop. It was all a dream Thomas Allred Jr. All a dream. I want to be with 112. You keep thinking that and I can make it happen for you.

Close your book right now.The second part of this endeavor means me and you. Give Shayla a warm welcome. Into your book Thomas Allred Jr. Your sister would be proud. Keep your composure all through this book Thomas Allred Jr. Yeah let me get my two cents in. I know that voice anywhere that's Ms. Susan Jennings. Yeah Thomas Allred Jr. I outta open up a can of this whoop-a** on your a**. I give miss Susan Jennings props inside of my book.you are my main man you been sitting there for over two hours. We all want to know if you can stand on your feet. In the meantime. Skylar you need to come with me. Thomas Allred Jr please let me out here. Leave the book The way it is. You getting in work. Frankie helping you. Don't forget to drop the e we got e we go manners. Well that's what I'm talkin about

Jeffrey. You better hush Kristen Beam is online one.And 6 and 4 belongs to your daddy. That's not true it cannot go in the book. Thomas Allred Jr I know that you are hurting about losing your daddy. You're the damn Arthur all the same. Let's give it up one more time for Ms. Susan Jennings. Thomas Allred Jr just do what I say give me one time. Give me one more chance. Jeffrey this boy has got a title Wave. Jeffrey I know what I'm doing I need you on this manuscript. Somebody told me to seize the moment and i did. Let's get all the paperwork drawn up and ready for business Jeffrey. Bye-bye Mr. incredible. Go with me I want to live. Let me play house for you. Just keep my plate on the table Jeffrey you know everybody out here is listening to me and you. I'll talk to you at a later point in time. Keep my manuscript off the table for everybody.I got to think about what I can do with the free time that I have right now. Jeffrey imma grab something to eat. You are and Angel Thomas Allred Jr.it's the only way to travel with with Jesus Christ with you. In my heart I'll be a man one day. Thank you Jeffery save this part of the book because I'm going to send more to you later on. Thomas Allred Jr. Going to complete this program. You are my computer love Kristen Beam. I wouldn't have it any other way. Thank you ladies for everything.

You were catching me while wasn't under control. Just call my house and see don't I pick up. The one thing about me is that I don't never give up. Teach the Lord and is canceled to be with you. Whatever you do. Just don't bother me. I say this to myself over and over again. It's nice to see that I'm loved all of my people. Rushing me will be a no no. Keep your composure you dealing with me. Look at you. This book got me saying things I wouldn't normally say before. I am your king. Let's do what we need to do to get paid. Less travel places that you ain't never been before then. I'll tell you everywhere that I've been. This book is then got his true colors. Y'all make no difference. either you will kill me or you would let me be either way I'm up for both.

Lying here I'm saying to myself. I wish your mother f*cker would. I'm getting off track here. Don't mess with the magic in my hands. Trust me this ain't what you want. Emotionally I make my climb back into my kingdom. This part of the story you are going to have to see alone. If you need me I will be here for you. Talk that sh*tt if you want. Everything is smooth sailing. Give me my future back to me you stole. I put Jeffrey on my team for you. Give me one more chance to prove that I can beat you in business. Just like Conan said. Where there's a will there's a way. Be careful they listening to me. I'm surprised that you haven't found out that you're my footstool. I want you to be my footstool with me. No work no play that's how I do it. These people allowed me to be here. You hear me Thomas Allred Jr do you need that girl. It's no choice in my books of magic tricks. I need you to realize that I'm a king of all you. Office of Reign is on your case.

I'm telling you so I can get open. This me off and I still stand as your man. You got the king watching you. I'm doing everything I can for you people to watch and see.

Thomas ain't on the food stamp list. Don't mess up just go like I tell you. Disguise your cigarette. Let's see what you can do Thomas Allred Jr. I've been crucial it's crunch time. Try to trust me we are going to see this things through. As you were laying there sleeping. I wrote a billion-dollar novel. For you to critique. This game has been played to the fullest. I wish I had y'all. Oh my team Thomas Allred Jr. I wish you would come in my room. It is my business not yours. I'm going to ask you one question. You f*cking with the wrong one now back up. I'm fending to raise up off this bed I want to see you. Reign gets money anytime I say it. Have faith in me I have wisdom. When you borrow your payback that wich you have borrowed. I see the look in your eyes how you want me. I am going to get this straight. You can play with me if you don't want to. Show me that theres feelings for me. That's the only way that you a mess around and get in my circle. I'm watching and I give a f*ck about all of you. Just give me one chance to prove myself to you. Jeffrey my word to God is my witness. I will see you at the crossroads. Now I'm finishing my book. Fighting for mine the sequel. Fighting by my lonely. I accept you as a critic. Let me see what I can do for you and your coMr.ades.

See I'm smarter than you think I am. What makes you think that you can be my shadow. These movie stars and everybody has got my back. You must think I'm high or something. I'm just looking for a way to prove myself to you. I am wanting to tell you. That I can raise up at any time that I want to. School has started either way you want it. You are embarra**ing me with that demeanor. You need to turn around and see Jason. Keep playing with me if you want to. I realize that you're a pencil and I am a pain. Keep my goddamn name out your mother f*cking mouth. This is money I'm working on. I cannot share it with you if y'all have steady talking sh*t. As we proceed to give you what you need. Ain't nobody in danger. I'm giving y'all what y'all given to me. I can see through you. Take trash and dump it in the trash cans. Listen to this can't be beat or f*cked with. Keep your name out my mouth Reign. This is my study process.

Want your homie tell you I own York. New York City you're all mines. If I don't get to see you in the end. You are working for me. What they didn't believe to be true. Is mirin me will only lead you to me. See you better get this truth. I am the greatest that you have ever heard of. A seasonal endeavor. Thomas Allred Jr I want to ask you one question. When was your last anniversary of an a** whooping. You make a bunch of damn sense. If you touch me you bought me off see I. I know that was my song. Are you kidding me Man or are you sh*ting me. I'm getting stronger watching y'all figure that I'm not talking to you. Before you want me you better come yourself. I'm taking this a little bit of time can I breathe. These are some scary days Thomas Allred Jr. I want like a man for you jacka**es. If you touch me you're going to die. Ain't no ifs ands or buts about it. Do you want to know what's killing us.

That bulsh*t you talkin. I am a police officer. No police officer will talk like this.

Walk with me and I can lead you to riches and ecstasy. Those you hear on the TV screen. Are actors. Many men is now over. I'ma smoke my cigarette. So give me what. Y'all trying to see me. I need you folks. Don't confuse my generosity with weakness. Either way it goes you have to come back to me. My city didn't help me so I left those people. That's some bulsh*t that's why I'm here with you. Jeffrey I didn't grow up on a street adventure. That sounds like a new song I played one before. But every new song gets played out. Move out the way for your king to come through. You need me that way you must talk to me. They selling wolf tickets all over the state. I just can't believe you left me for that piece of garbage. When I see you we must have a conversation. Is going to be some furniture moving if you understand what I'm saying. I'm telling you one thing. Billy Jack is my Conrad. I got six more sentences in I'm finished with this chapter. Let a man be strong. I'm with you long as you with me and you care about yourself. We are both equal out there. To the end you are my Conrad. This is me Thomas Allred Jr. This has been a closed session. Try me again for more information about how we will succeed all over time. This goes to Jeffrey.

www.ingramcontent.com/pod-product-compliance
Lightning Source LLC
Chambersburg PA
CBHW080036120526
44589CB00036B/2472
* 9 7 8 1 7 7 4 1 9 0 5 3 1 *